Integrating Gender Equality into Business and Management Education

Lessons Learned and Challenges Remaining

INTEGRATING GENDER EQUALITY INTO BUSINESS AND MANAGEMENT EDUCATION

Lessons Learned and Challenges Remaining

Edited by **Patricia M. Flynn,**
Kathryn Haynes and **Maureen A. Kilgour**

Greenleaf
PUBLISHING

PRME Principles for Responsible
Management Education

**Greenleaf Publishing/PRME Book Series –
For Responsibility in Management Education**

© 2015 Greenleaf Publishing Limited

Published by Greenleaf Publishing Limited
Aizlewood's Mill
Nursery Street
Sheffield S3 8GG
UK
www.greenleaf-publishing.com

Cover by LaliAbril.com.
Printed and bound by Printondemand-worldwide.com, UK.

MIX
Paper from
responsible sources
FSC® C004959

British Library Cataloguing in Publication Data:
A catalogue record for this book is available from the British Library.

ISBN-13: 978-1-78353-225-4 [hardback]
ISBN-13: 978-1-78353-228-5 [PDF ebook]
ISBN-13: 978-1-78353-218-6 [ePub ebook]

Contents

Acknowledgements

This book is a collaborative effort from authors across the globe. We thank the contributors who hail from twelve countries across four continents. Their case materials, empirical research, applied theoretical pieces and personal reflections across a wide range of geographic, institutional, disciplinary and cultural environments highlight and confirm the ongoing challenges in integrating gender equality into management education. Moreover, they provide inspiration, guidance and tools to help business school faculty and other providers of management education become role models and leaders in the quest for gender equality in the workplace and beyond.

We are grateful to Jonas Haertle, Head of the PRME Secretariat at the UN Global Compact Office, whose leadership has helped to make this book a reality. Jonas's colleagues Merrill Csuri, Manager of PRME Champions and External Relations, and Magdalena Thurig, Consultant, also have been valued supporters of the PRME Working Group on Gender Equality as well as this volume. At AACSB International, Dan LeClair, Executive Vice President and Chief Operating Officer, and Joe Mondello, Knowledge Services Manager, have been key sources of data and contacts throughout the book project. And, clearly, this book would not have come to fruition without the editorial support of Rebecca Macklin, the production detail of Dean Bargh and the marketing assistance of Neil Walker at Greenleaf Publishing. We also extend our gratitude to John Peters, Chief Executive at Greenleaf, for having the vision as a publisher to support responsible management in association with PRME.

On a personal note, Pat acknowledges her husband, Peter B. Doeringer, who is a continuous source of encouragement and inspiration. Kathryn thanks her husband, Alan Murray, her daughters, Eleanor and Florence, and her mother, Jean for their enduring love and constant support in everything she does. Maureen thanks her spouse, Richard Goulet, for his unconditional love and encouragement, and her children, Callum and Kyla, for their love, support and inspiring passion to create a better future for all who share the planet.

The Women's Empowerment Principles

Source: www.weprinciples.org/Site/PrincipleOverview

Equality means business

The Women's Empowerment Principles are a set of principles for business offering guidance on how to empower women in the workplace, marketplace and community. They are the result of a collaboration between the United Nations Entity for Gender Equality and the Empowerment of Women (UN Women) and the United Nations Global Compact and are adapted from the Calvert Women's Principles®. The development of the Women's Empowerment Principles included an international multi-stakeholder consultation process, which began in March 2009 and culminated in their launch on International Women's Day in March 2010.

Subtitled Equality Means Business, the principles emphasize the business case for corporate action to promote gender equality and women's empowerment and are informed by real-life business practices and input gathered from across the globe. The Women's Empowerment Principles seek to point the way to best practice by elaborating the gender dimension of corporate responsibility, the UN Global Compact and the role of business in sustainable development. As well as being a useful guide for business, the principles seek to inform other stakeholders, including governments, in their engagement with business.

- Principle 1: Establish high-level corporate leadership for gender equality
- Principle 2: Treat all women and men fairly at work—respect and support human rights and non-discrimination
- Principle 3: Ensure the health, safety and well-being of all women and men workers
- Principle 4: Promote education, training and professional development for women
- Principle 5: Implement enterprise development, supply chain and marketing practices that empower women
- Principle 6: Promote equality through community initiatives and advocacy
- Principle 7: Measure and publicly report on progress to achieve gender equality

The Six Principles of PRME

Source: www.unprme.org/about-prme/the-six-principles.php

- **Principle 1 | Purpose:** We will develop the capabilities of students to be future generators of sustainable value for business and society at large and to work for an inclusive and sustainable global economy.

- **Principle 2 | Values:** We will incorporate into our academic activities and curricula the values of global social responsibility as portrayed in international initiatives such as the United Nations Global Compact.

- **Principle 3 | Method:** We will create educational frameworks, materials, processes and environments that enable effective learning experiences for responsible leadership.

- **Principle 4 | Research:** We will engage in conceptual and empirical research that advances our understanding about the role, dynamics and impact of corporations in the creation of sustainable social, environmental and economic value.

- **Principle 5 | Partnership:** We will interact with managers of business corporations to extend our knowledge of their challenges in meeting social and environmental responsibilities and to explore jointly effective approaches to meeting these challenges.

- **Principle 6 | Dialogue:** We will facilitate and support dialog and debate among educators, students, business, government, consumers, media, civil society organizations and other interested groups and stakeholders on critical issues related to global social responsibility and sustainability.

Introduction

Identifying the key issues underlying gender inequality in management education and ways to reduce gender gaps

Kathryn Haynes
Newcastle University Business School, UK

Patricia M. Flynn
Bentley University, USA

Maureen A. Kilgour
Université de Saint-Boniface, Canada

Background

The Principles for Responsible Management Education (PRME) initiative was launched in 2007 with a mission to inspire and champion responsible management education, research and thought leadership globally under the auspices of the UN. It envisions a new model for business schools, with principles for implementation based on responsible attitudes towards corporate ethics, environment and human rights, encompassing the spirit of the UN Global Compact and the UN Millennium Development Goals. In March 2010, the UN Global Compact and UNIFEM (now part of UN Women)[1] launched the Women's Empowerment Principles (WEPs).[2] The goal of the WEPs is to "help the private sector focus on key elements integral to promoting gender equality in the workplace,

---

1 www.unwomen.org/about-us/about-un-women
2 "The WEPs, the product of a collaboration between UNIFEM and the UN Global Compact informed by an international multi-stakeholder consultation, are adapted from the Calvert Women's Principles®. The Calvert Women's Principles® were originally developed in partnership with UNIFEM and launched in 2004 as the first global corporate code of conduct focused

marketplace and community". In response to this new initiative, the PRME Working Group on Gender Equality was launched in October 2011.

The mission of the PRME Working Group on Gender Equality is to bring together academics and employers in order to provide support and resources for integrating gender issues and awareness into management education, business school curricula and related research to facilitate respect and support for the WEPs and PRME. Its first working paper (Kilgour and Flynn, 2012) made the following key points: first, gender inequality is pervasive throughout all societies and is recognized as a major impediment to poverty alleviation and sustainable development. Second, the business sector, ranging from the smallest firms to the largest multinational corporations, can be responsible for causing, perpetuating and/or reducing gender inequality. Third, the actions (or inactions) of business schools will play an important role in the education of future business leaders, policy-makers and decision-makers.

Gender inequality has a long history in business schools and in the workplace, and traditions are hard to change. Across disciplines, the scope and quantity of materials relevant to integrating gender issues into the curriculum varies. While no discipline is exemplary, there are pockets of work on gender in diversity and select other courses in institutions. However, critical issues persist: some disciplines remain resolutely gendered, affecting both men and women; case materials on women leaders and managers are still rare; and faculty are often unaware of how to access the related materials that do exist. However, business schools can also take a leading role in challenging gender inequalities in a number of ways: through research, which addresses the barriers, effects and outcomes of gender (in)equality; by educating students to understand, challenge and overcome stereotypical gendered assumptions; by providing role models and examples of good practices; and by engaging in debates on gender equality that can be transformative in the business world and society more generally (Haynes, 2014).

These points form the rationale for this book. It is the first of two books in a series on *Gender Equality as a Challenge for Business and Management Education*, as part of the Greenleaf Publishing/PRME book series. This first book identifies the key issues underlying gender inequality in management education and why responsible management education must address them. It provides examples of initiatives illustrating how this may occur from various disciplinary, institutional, international and pedagogic perspectives. It is designed to help faculty integrate the topic of gender equality into their own teaching and gain support for the legitimacy of gender equality as an important management education topic in their institutions. The second book in the series will focus on gender equality in the workplace.

The distinctive features of this book are that it

1. Identifies the rationale for inclusion of gender equality in responsible management education

2. Explores the challenges of integrating gender equality into management education and how they can be overcome

---

exclusively on empowering, advancing and investing in women worldwide". www.unifem.org/ partnerships/womens_empowerment_principles

3. Provides examples of learning and teaching resources that address gender ine-quality from a range of disciplinary, institutional, international and pedagogical perspectives

4. Discusses the issues in terms of the responsibility of management educators to set new management, research, institutional and intellectual agendas on gender equality.

Structure and organization of the book

I. Trends and challenges in management education

The four chapters in Part I set the context of the current state of management edu-cation in addressing gender issues. Kilgour (Chapter 1) documents the long history of gender (in)equality and exclusion in management education, which is still a challenge in today's world. The chapter demonstrates that gender inequality has been an issue since women started entering and working in business schools in significant numbers, leading to numerous research and proposals for change, including adop-tion of PRME. Despite some positive progress, the chapter argues that there are still many challenges to be addressed. In Chapter 2, Flynn, Cavanagh and Bilimoria iden-tify gender equality in business schools as "the elephant in the room", that is, it has been rendered invisible and overlooked despite glaringly obvious problems. Citing evidence of significant gender gaps in administration, faculty and student composi-tion, the authors argue that business schools ignore gender issues at their own risk. They conclude with recommendations for raising the profile of gender issues and improving gender equality in these institutions. In Chapter 3, Haynes and Murray outline the theoretical and empirical links between sustainable development and gender equality. They argue that despite an increasing emphasis on sustainability and sustainable development in responsible management education, the issue of gender equality as an integral component of sustainability is largely absent. This, they suggest, represents a missed opportunity for responsible management education. Verbos and Kennedy (Chapter 4) also critique the role of business schools, suggesting that in order to promote PRME and the WEPs, these institutions should first address themselves and start with providing psychologically safe climates for faculty. Their study finds that higher ethical leadership, gender equity and organizational justice are associated with increased psychological safety, which may allow faculty to better exemplify the principles of PRME and the WEPs in their classrooms, thus enabling students to more fully appreciate and apply the principles in their own careers. All of the chapters in Part I demonstrate that many challenges remain in addressing gender issues in responsible management education. Fortunately, many of the subsequent chapters in the book present potential solutions and examples of overcoming some of these challenges.

II. Disciplinary perspectives

Part II provides insights into addressing gender equality from a disciplinary perspective. In particular, the chapters take diverse angles on gender and management education from the disciplinary perspectives of marketing, nursing, law and organizational behaviour (OB). Although these chapters cover a wide range of disciplines, the reader will see how many of the gender challenges have similarities across fields. As such, faculty and administrators have much to learn about gender equality from the successes and failures in fields other than their own. First, Hein (Chapter 5) provides an understanding of what gender equality may mean through an exploration of various marketing practices, studies and teaching. Drawing from feminist perspectives, Hein argues that marketing institutions and practices contribute to persistently unequal gender relations. The chapter concludes with recommendations on how to address these inequalities, with a particular focus on marketing education and teaching as an agent of change. Rothausen and Bazarko (Chapter 6) also identify practical interventions in addressing gender equality but, in their case, in the highly gendered nursing industry. This chapter presents a case study of an executive education program for nurse leaders, a program that emphasizes the cultivation of an executive mind-set and enterprise-level organizational skills, and directly addresses gender issues within an integrated curriculum. Although the case is from the United States, the issues addressed are relevant to the global nursing workforce, especially as nurse shortages and issues of gender are ubiquitous worldwide. In Chapter 7, Cecchi-Dimeglio addresses gender issues in US legal education, another topic that will resonate in other national and regional contexts. Cecchi-Dimeglio argues that, while women have reached parity in terms of acceptances to US law schools, gender inequalities exist in the delivery of legal education with negative implications for women: in particular, in terms of leadership roles in law schools and future legal careers. The author provides recommendations for the legal education system, as a gatekeeper and institutional model, to help reduce gender gaps in and beyond law schools. Lastly, in Part II, Dever and Mills (Chapter 8) address the ongoing predominance of male leaders and role models in OB textbooks. Their content analysis of leadership writings and representations in OB texts raises questions and challenges as to how such materials are used in the classroom. They conclude that faculty must provide classroom settings and experiences that overcompensate for this textbook deficiency if students—males and females—are to better understand the nature and possibilities for leadership in their careers.

III. Institutional perspectives

In Part III, Chapters 9–12 provide a variety of institutional perspectives and interventions designed to address gender inequality and/or promote gender equality. The part begins with Godwyn and Langowitz's (Chapter 9) analysis of organizational interventions that can reduce the influence of gender prejudice or perceptions, performance and aspirations. The authors review several important studies, as well as their own work on women's leadership, in order to articulate a formula that can be used in a variety of organizations to diminish or neutralize gender differences. In Chapter 10, Adams highlights that institutions of higher education are in a position to influence societal change in the workplace by preparing students to enter the workforce ready to challenge and eliminate gender inequalities. Adams illustrates this premise through a case study of Bentley University, USA, using change management perspectives to highlight challenges in creating sustainable change and suggesting practices for other institutions to consider. In Chapter 11, Bendl et al. reflect on lessons learned from 12 years of teaching diversity management at Vienna University of Economics and Business. The authors find that gender- and diversity-based teaching must negotiate a careful path between assimilation, that is, adaptation to the present curricular structures (exploitative learning), and innovation, implying the deepening and expansion of the materials taught (explorative learning). In Chapter 12, Nentwich and Sander reflect on the opportunities and challenges arising from attempting to mainstream gender and diversity in management education at the University of St Gallen in Switzerland. In a chapter that will resonate with others grappling with gender as a core or optional concept in the curriculum, the authors discuss the importance of finding the right balance between "integration" and "marginalization" of gender as a topic.

IV. International perspectives

While the chapters in this book derive from a range of geographical regions, Part IV specifically focuses on international perspectives. Issues of gender equality and responsible management education are addressed in Latin America, France, India and Japan. In Chapter 13, Carlier evaluates gender equality in MBA programs in Latin America with three objectives: first, to show the existing gender disparity in MBA program enrolment in Latin America; second, to determine some possible causes for these differences; and third, to propose possible curricula and modality arrangements to help overcome such disparities, especially in this geographical and cultural context. Finstad-Milion and Morin-Estèves (Chapter 14) address the fact that starting salaries and first jobs of female graduates of French management schools are consistently lower in pay and responsibility than those of male graduates. The authors focus on the Grandes Écoles, and the key role played by the Conférence des Grandes Écoles (CGE) association in creating tools to map collective progress and to sensitizing staff and students about sources of gender inequalities. They conclude with practices through which French management schools can better help reduce gender inequalities in the labour market. Moore, Rajadhyaksha and Blake-Beard (Chapter 15) focus on India and the United States as case studies from emerging and Western economies, and as a microcosm of culturally different contexts and business school challenges. Definitions and practices of diversity vary in each country. Although diversity education is more widespread in the United States, both the United States and India have been slow in moving towards a gender-sensitive curriculum and inclusive culture. The authors conclude that gender equality has not been mainstreamed in these countries and that the silence around gender diversity in management education needs to be addressed in order to prepare future managers for global leadership roles. Lastly, in Part IV, Kondo (Chapter 16) provides insights into the role of business school education for Japanese and non-Japanese women in Japan. Drawing on examples from the Doshisha Business School in Kyoto and its students, the author concludes that a business school education can and should equip female students with competitive skills and networks to enhance their motivation and support their advancement.

V. Pedagogical approaches

The final part of the book (Part V) addresses pedagogical issues, including general approaches to curricula, and specific educational approaches to learning and ongoing challenges. These chapters present practical examples of approaches that could be considered in other schools and in other contexts. In Chapter 17, Wahl identifies four key problems that emerge when integrating a gender perspective in management education: feelings of uneasiness; gendered resistance; lack of academic status; and experienced gap between gender theory and inequality practice. The author discusses two tools—a Gender Equality Index and a reflective role-play—that can be used to address some of these problems. Hall and Peat (Chapter 18) focus on the pedagogic practices of business and management academics at a UK university and consider the extent to which these practices are gendered. Their findings reveal the ways in which academics articulate their students' needs and learning in relation to gender; the patriarchal culture of the business and management discipline; and the assumptions academics bring to pedagogic practices in relation to issues of student identity. In Chapter 19, Bilimoria argues in favour of a curricular space that focuses on the needs and experiences of women in business and management. The author shares details of her elective MBA course, Women in Organizations, developed to empower female and male students to advance gender equality and inclusion. In addition to the course objectives, format, content, activities, assignments and student reactions, the author provides reflections developed over ten years of teaching the course. Arnold and Foster (Chapter 20) make a case for the role of experiential approaches in teaching gender issues in management education. Kolb's Experiential Learning Theory formed the basis for the redesign of a course that incorporated exercises and activities to engage students in concrete experiences. The chapter discusses the challenges and benefits of using such an approach to teach gender issues. Kweder and Özkazanç-Pan (Chapter 21) distinguish between teaching ethics and ethical teaching underpinned by feminist values. Based on their experiences as teachers–scholars–learners in MBA classrooms in the United States, the authors propose the business school as a potential site of social change where the demands and pressures of global capitalism are questioned as part of understanding and undoing gender and other inequalities. Lastly, Bevelander and Page (Chapter 22) describe the development and successful implementation of an unusual pedagogic approach: an all-women MBA elective that involves participants attempting to climb to the summit of Mount Kilimanjaro. The experiential course is designed to prepare young women for the challenges of ascending to the highest level of organizations. Using the mountain as a living metaphor, participants are invited to reflect on their own aspirations and capabilities; to understand the importance of networks and relationships of trust; and to appreciate the importance of women supporting one another in their pursuit of challenging objectives.

Conclusions

Our concluding chapter evaluates what we have accomplished and learned in rela-tion to gender equality in responsible management education from the chapters of this book. We identify areas for further intervention: research, practice and policy. We call for further research, which addresses some of the remaining gaps and challenges not able to be addressed in this book. These include more comparative research, countries and education systems that are not represented here, and the intersection of men and gender inequality. We call on PRME as an influential policy- and practice-making body to reinforce the importance of gender in achieving its mission and to work with other learned associations, global organizations and accreditation bodies to address further the issues of gender equality in education and organizations.

We hope that you enjoy reading this book and find inspiration for your own practice in its pages.

References

Haynes, K., 2014. Gender equality in responsible management education and research. In: Murray, A., Baden, D., Cashian, P., Wersun, A., Haynes, K. (Eds.), Inspirational Guide for the Implementation of PRME, UK and Ireland ed. Greenleaf, Sheffield, pp. 21–27.

Kilgour, M.A., Flynn, P.M., November 2012. PRME Working Group on Gender Equality Working Paper, PRME. www.unprme.org/working-groups/display-working-group.php?wgid=2715

WEP (Women's Empowerment Principles), March 2010. Equality Means Business. A joint initiative of the UNIFEM and UN Global Compact. www.unglobalcompact.org/docs/issues_doc/human_rights/Women's_Empowerment_Principles.pdf

Part I
Trends and challenges in management education

1

Gender inequality in management education
Past, present and future

Maureen A. Kilgour
Université de Saint-Boniface, Canada

This chapter provides an historical perspective on gender in management education, reviews some current challenges to the achievement of gender equality and suggests concrete actions for the future. Since the 1970s, researchers have addressed four main areas in business schools and management education, identifying a wide range of issues concerning: students (numbers, relationships, MBA programs, careers, etc.); faculty (promotion and tenure, working conditions and pay, research evaluation, leadership, etc.); climate (harassment, environment, etc.) and programs (syllabi, curricula, orientation, sex-role stereotyping, etc.). This chapter looks at three specific issues that illustrate persistent gender inequality problems in business schools: (1) salary discrimination of female faculty in business schools; (2) sex-role stereotyping in the curriculum; and (3) the environment, a chilly climate which is sometimes violent, in which women study and work. This historical survey demonstrates that gender inequality has been an issue since women entered and started working in business schools in significant numbers; there is no shortage of research and proposals for change; and the current situation has both positive and negative elements, evidence of sporadic, but much desired progress. This chapter argues that the problem does not lie in the lack of study, data, sharing of best practices and proposed solutions, but in finding ways to transform research and recommendations into action for systemic change. The Principles for Responsible Management Education (PRME), business school leaders and the AACSB and other accreditation bodies can play important roles in permanently getting rid of gender inequality in business schools.

1.1 Introduction

The issue of gender inequality in management education is not new, notwithstanding the recent (2011) formation of the Principles for Responsible Management Education (PRME) Working Group on Gender Equality (WG) and the publication of this volume. The problems related to gender that are being addressed by the WG and by countless others working in higher education have been discussed and analysed by researchers going back decades. Not only have the issues been discussed, but solutions have also been proposed, many of which are (legitimately) being re-proposed in various contexts.

The purpose of this chapter is to provide a brief historical perspective on how the issue of gender in business schools has been discussed since the 1970s, review some current challenges and discuss how progress can be made in the future. I argue that the problem does not lie in the lack of study, data, sharing of best practices and proposed solutions. There are more than enough of these—many of which are discussed in this volume. While these are still necessary, it is important to determine ways to put research and recommendations into action for systemic change. I suggest that PRME can be a useful tool to not only orient teaching and research but also guide how the educational institutions (i.e. business schools) operate. PRME should commit to making gender equality an explicit part of its mandate.

Four major areas have preoccupied management education researchers regarding gender over the past number of decades, encompassing a wide range of issues: students (numbers, relationships, MBA programs, careers, etc.); faculty (promotion and tenure, working conditions and pay, research evaluation, leadership, etc.); climate (harassment, environment, etc.) and programs (syllabi, curricula, orientation, sex-role stereotyping, etc.). This chapter will look at three specific issues that relate to these areas, from both an historical perspective addressed in the academic literature and a current perspective, which is drawn from media coverage on gender and management education. The goal is to show that (1) gender inequality has been an issue since women started entering and working in business schools in significant numbers; (2) there is no shortage of research and proposals for change; and (3) the current situation has both positive and negative elements, pointing to sporadic, but much desired, progress.

1.2 The past becomes the present

There have been numerous and significant attempts to address the gender inequality problem in management education and in higher education more generally. The following refers to some of the insights from a very small non-exhaustive sample of the literature on the issue of gender in management education in the past decades, going as far back as the 1970s, a time before many current faculty members were even born. These are juxtaposed with a related issue that has garnered media attention in the last few years. The three issues are discussed below: (1) salary discrimination of female faculty in business schools (an issue affecting faculty); (2) sex-role stereotyping in the curriculum (an issue relating to programs and students); and (3) environment in which women study and work (an issue relating to the chilly climate and students). It is important to note that all of these areas are interrelated and have an effect on each other. McKeen et al. argued in 2000 of the interrelation between such issues as the number of female students with broader issues of climate, attitudes and curriculum:

> ... focussing only on tangible, measurable aspects of equality (such as the ratio of female to male students and the use of gender neutral language) is not sufficient to warm the chilly climate in management education. Rather, such observable, behavioural changes need to be followed by changes in attitudes. Initiatives that expose male and female business students to more female role models, to more discussion of gender issues throughout the business curriculum, and to courses on gender and diversity issues, among others, are important elements in initiating attitudinal change (McKeen, Bujaki and Burke, 2000: 365, 366).

1.2.1 Salary discrimination in business schools

In the past number of decades, attention has been called to pay disparities between male and female academic staff members, including business schools, resulting in numerous legislated, policy and collective bargaining initiatives to tackle the discrimination-based disparities. Recent research in various jurisdictions demonstrates that gender-based pay inequities still exists, in business schools and in universities more generally (e.g. in Burke et al., 2005; Doucet, Durand and Smith, 2008; Bell and Joyce, 2011; Doucet, Smith and Durand, 2012; Currie and Hill, 2013). For example, Bell et al. found that female faculty members earned 85% of male counterparts in publicly funded Association to Advance Collegiate Schools of Business (AACSB) and 83% in non-AACSB business schools (Bell and Joyce, 2011). Similar disparities of 15% were found as a result of a pay equity audit at the University of Western Australia (Currie and Hill, 2013). Researchers since the 1970s have tried to address this issue. For example, in 1979, Robertson found that gender-based disparities in pay and status were due to the fact that fewer female faculty members than male faculty members had held a doctorate. She argued that "this single factor greatly accounts for women's inequity in rank and administrative position" (Robertson, 1979: 635). Given that most female faculty members currently hold doctorates, one could now assume that inequalities in rank and position have all but disappeared. Unfortunately, that is not the case and reminds us to look for other reasons to explain the inequalities.

Robertson predicted that the problems would diminish over time as more and more women are hired as "qualified" (with PhD) faculty members. For example, she suggested that

> Increasing numbers of women business school faculty members should mean an increased emphasis on women's topics in the business school curriculum (Robertson, 1979: 645).

She also suggested that the need for addressing and mentoring women will diminish over time:

> Ironically, by the time that substantial numbers of faculty members are knowl-
> edgeable about and willing to discuss women in their courses, and to serve as
> role models and mentors, there will undoubtedly not be the great need that
> exists today for such discussion (Robertson, 1979: 645).

Unfortunately, despite the passage of time since 1979 and the fact that there are many more women with PhDs ready and able to "discuss women", gender-based salary inequities persist, as do those who deny that pay inequality is an important issue. For example, the University of California Los Angeles (UCLA) business school (Anderson) posted a commentary on its blog of an Anderson professor who was denying in the Huffington Post that pay inequities between male and female business school professors were a result of discrimination. Chowdhry argued that closing the gender gap in business schools is "mathematically impossible" and that increasing the number of women hired will reduce the quality:

> Simply finding evidence that women on average are paid less than men at
> most organizations does not necessarily prove that there is gender-based dis-
> crimination. Trying to cure gender imbalance by pushing organizations to hire
> more women will not only fail overall . . . but also . . . it would make the salary
> imbalance between men and women appear worse—because average quality
> of women will fall—at all organizations (Chowdhry, 2014).

In a rebuttal to Chowdhry's argument that the only way to fix discrimination in business schools is to work on the "pipeline" (the supply side of the recruitment equation), Scott points out the circularity of his argument:

> Chowdhry doesn't understand why the "pipeline" argument is circular. The
> skewed dynamics in business school faculties—demeaning behaviors, dis-
> missive remarks, unfair assessments, and lower pay—are pumped like toxins
> back into doctoral programs for professors and students alike to breathe. As
> long as that connection is ignored or denied, the candidate pool will be badly
> unbalanced . . . Potential female recruits will also continue to be deterred by
> the poor prospects for advancement (Scott, 2014).

Salary discrimination is just one of the many employment-related issues faced by female faculty members (Symons and Ibarra, 2014). In May 2014, *The Wall Street Journal* reported on "Allegations of Gender Bias at UCLA Anderson":

> One of the nation's top-ranked business schools is "inhospitable to women
> faculty," according to an internal academic review . . . Among the findings
> of the report, which was reviewed by The Wall Street Journal: Anderson is
> inconsistent in how it hires and promotes women as compared with men; has
> created "gender ghettos" in certain academic areas; and shows a "lack of con-
> fidence" in female faculty (Korn, 2014).

McTiernan and Flynn, in their article on women deans in business schools, discuss the slow progress of moving women into leadership positions (deanships)—they cite

AACSB statistics, which show that in 1992 women made up less than 3% of deans in AACSB (USA) business schools, and this percentage slowing climbed to just over 15% in 2008 (McTiernan and Flynn, 2011). The lack of women in positions of leadership in management education can be seen as both a symptom of gender inequality and an impediment to progress. The under-representation of female faculty members generally has an impact on the climate, the students and the curriculum itself (Maranto and Griffin, 2011).

1.2.2 Sex-role stereotyping in the curriculum

There is increasing discussion about the need for reflection on how future managers and business leaders are educated in today's business schools. In particular, the assumed gender neutrality of many business school disciplines is being called into question. Accounting, finance, supply chain management, among others, are some of the research and teaching areas that have been assumed to be non-gendered. Research and practice has challenged these assumptions, going back over at least 20 years when researchers raised concerns about sex-role stereotyping in business schools.

Sex-role stereotyping "among academic staff in the UK who work in business schools and management departments in the new universities" was the subject of a 1994 article by Frances Foster. She found that "among the senior staff the successful manager role is perceived as closely associated with men in general" (Foster, 1994: 22). The author pointed out the importance of addressing sex-role stereotyping as it has a cumulative effect as students go into positions of management in the workplace.

In the 1995 article, "Sexism in the seminar: Strategies for gender sensitivity in management education", the authors argue that gender is equally important for male and female students, and their goal in publishing their research was "to encourage discussion as to how we might design and develop courses that appeal to women and men, believing that gender management is of equal importance for men and women" (Thompson and Mcgivern, 1995: 341). Given the dearth of men participating in issues concerning gender and management education, one could conclude that these authors' goals have yet to be realized.

Recent discussions on the media draw attention to the fact that gender inequality is still a problem both at universities in general and business schools in particular. A recent and prominent example of sex-role stereotyping concerns the widely adopted case studies published by Harvard Business School (HBS). Studies of the HBS case studies have found a

> penury of women across award-winning and best selling case studies—coupled with their overrepresentation in "pink topics" (food; family, furniture, and fashion, as well as gender-specific subjects such as women's health issues), token status, impoverished depictions, and lack of guidance to instructors on how discuss any gender issues that might emerge in classroom discussion (Symons and Ibarra, 2014).

The lack of women protagonists is not a new issue for the HBS. In 1998, a news article discussing the sexual harassment of female students at HBS raised many questions about broader issues facing women at the school. It specifically mentioned gender discrimination in the HBS case studies:

And late last year (1997), the Committee of 200, a group of leading business-women, gave the school $500,000 to write more case studies featuring women. HBS announced it would chip in $500,000 of its own money for the cause. But even that seemingly positive move drew fire. "That is just such a joke", one female student fumes. "HBS already had the money to write cases with women protagonists. If they really cared about women, they'd have taken the initiative" (Useem, 1998).

Almost two decades later, HBS is still being criticized for the lack of women protagonists and decision-makers in their case studies:

"The school owed you better, and I promise it will be better," Harvard Business School Dean Nitin Nohria told an alumni audience in January (2014), acknowledging and apologizing for the school's problematic past concerning gender equity. He then pledged to double the number of business case studies that feature a woman as the protagonist up to a level of 20% over the next five years (Symons and Ibarra, 2014).

The fact that women are still vastly under-represented as decision-makers, leaders and key players in HBS case studies, despite decades-old top-level (dean) commitments to rectify the situation, raises questions as to what is really required to make change happen in the business school environment.

The impact of a gender-biased curriculum, including pedagogical materials such as case studies, has lasting repercussions. Critics maintain that significant damage occurs when women are left out of the HBS case studies, which are used by business schools around the world:

By perpetuating the idea that men are at the center of business, case studies unintentionally depict strong leadership as almost uniformly masculine. Showing only one model of leadership implicitly signals to both men and women that women are not suited for leadership, and deprives both of alternative role models for different ways of leading and developing a leadership identity (Symons and Ibarra, 2014).

The absence of women in the HBS case studies is not unique. In 2011, only 194 out of 5,816 Caseplace teaching resources (cases, syllabi and other documents) mentioned women (Caseplace, 2014). Other parts of the curriculum contain gender bias. Paris and Decker argue that:

(a) gender structure underlies most managerial and leadership theories. In a majority of studies, it has been determined that the managerial role is gender-typed in a masculine manner, with men being seen as normative leaders, which leads to a pro-male bias (Paris and Decker, 2012: 39).

Similarly, Dever and Mills in Chapter 8 of this book found consistent gender bias in organizational behaviour textbooks over the last four decades. In addition to finding gender inequality in the formal curriculum, one can also observe issues that create or reinforce inequality in the environment of the business school and the university. Blasco refers to the "hidden curriculum", which is defined as "the implicit dimensions of educational experience" (Blasco, 2012: 388). Section 1.2.3 discusses this issue, specifically in relation to the concept of the chilly climate.

1.2.3 Harassment and violence: a chilly climate

The environment in which women work and study includes, but is much more than, the curriculum. Many researchers have drawn attention to the "masculinist" nature of management education (including, among others, Smith, 1997; Mavin and Bryans, 1999; Mavin, Bryans and Waring, 2004; Kelan, 2007; Kelan and Jones, 2010; McTiernan and Flynn, 2011). One concept in particular has been used for decades to draw attention to the fact that the university and business school environment is not necessarily a welcoming place for women—that it is a "chilly climate" (Sandler, 2005). The concept of the "chilly climate" was developed in 1982 by Bernice Sandler, who was involved in numerous complaints of gender discrimination in the education sphere (Association of American Colleges, 1982). Conceptualizing the environment in this way allowed for increased attention to be paid to a variety of aspects of the educational experience of women, including but not limited to devaluation, expectations, communication styles in the classroom, sex-role stereotyping and harassment (Sandler, 2005). Despite attempts over the past decades to address the educational environment, the climate for women in some business schools is still described as chilly (Maranto and Griffin, 2011).

The issue of sexual violence against women on university campuses has been given increasing attention in the media. Following allegations of sexual assault on the University of Virginia campus, University President Teresa Sullivan issued a statement on the importance of taking action on "one of the most difficult and critical issues facing higher education today: sexual violence on college campuses" (University of Virginia, 2014).

Although business school public relations machinery may recoil from the coverage that the mainstream media gives to sexual violence and harassment on campuses, it can be an impetus for reflection and positive change. For example, following international media coverage of sexual assaults on the University of Virginia campus, the business school's student association organized an event (a "town hall") to draw attention to the issue and explore solutions (University of Virginia Darden School of Business, 2014).

Unfortunately, the issues of sexual violence and harassment are not isolated to rogue campuses. Despite the concept of the chilly climate gaining prominence in the 1980s and early 1990s, business school environments were not and are not always welcoming for women students and faculty members. In response to complaints about sexual harassment of students by students at the HBS in 1998, the dean was quoted as saying:

> "This kind of behavior isn't something that came out of the blue, that just appeared last year," concedes Dean Clark . . . "There have been situations of some sort for years" (Useem, 1998).

More recently, allegations that students at two Canadian universities organized "rape chants" dominated the Canadian news media during the 2013 back-to-school season. The University of British Columbia (UBC) Sauder School of Business Commerce Students "Frosh Week" included a "traditional" rape chant on the party buses. As reported by the media:

> The chant condones non-consensual sex with underage girls saying, "Y-O-U-N-G at UBC, we like 'em young, Y is for your sister, O is for oh so tight, U is for under-age, N is for no consent, G is for go to jail" (CBC, 2013).

Following the incident, the university vice president for students and the dean of the busi-ness school established a fact-finding committee, which issued a report that provides insights into culture, climate and leadership (UBC, 2013). In the report, the students were quoted as saying:

> No one thought of the seriousness of this, it just kept on in Sauder being passed from year to year. You just followed the leader before you . . . It strings out and that becomes the culture (UBC, 2013: 2).

> [Bus cheers] are a thing for us only, a thing that only Sauder students know, a tradition, this helps build community.

> It's a brotherhood type of thing, an inside thing, it's inclusive in that others would not know about it (UBC, 2013: 3).

The report found that "[t]he majority of leaders felt that a critical aspect of FROSH is to push people outside their comfort zone through cheers, chants, and activities, which they believed built strong teams and bonds" (UBC, 2013: 3). All of these quotes and the report itself focus on the development and maintenance of organizational culture, and the importance of leadership in promoting and maintaining that culture. Little attention is paid in the report to the impact of the rape chant itself on various members of the uni-versity community, including business students.

Gender is strikingly absent from this six-page report—the words "woman", "women", "girl/s", "gender", "male", "boy/s", "man" and "men" are not used at all. This is surpris-ing given that the chant, which triggered the scandal and the fact-finding commission in the first place, was highly gendered and referred to sexual assault against young women.

There was considerable public reaction to the report, which many felt did not go far enough in exploring the facts behind a business school culture that could include and continue such a "tradition". Stephen Petrina of the UBC Faculty of Education wrote about the report's failure to discuss the role of the business school leadership:

> In the fact-finding report, curiously, the words "administration" and "adminis-trator" do not appear while "student/s" appears 46 times. There were no facts to find on administrators or administration? . . . (Is it) plausible that, of the 11 Assistant and Associate Deans and Dean Helsley, none have responsibilities for "students" in their portfolio? (Petrina, 2014).

Petrina also refers to the fact that it took the rape chant incident becoming public to prompt the business school's senior administrators to show leadership on how the curriculum needs to be changed to be more inclusive of gender and other neglected issues:

> Someone or something is failing at the top if of the 12 senior administrators none have curriculum in their portfolio. I find it incomprehensible that it has

taken this cheer, a fact-finding report, campus outrage, and nearly 2014 for Sauder to finally get around to . . . "Implementing changes in the curriculum to enhance themes of social justice, ethics, gender and cultural sensitivity, and their role in corporate social responsibility and the creation of a civil society" (Petrina, 2014).

The lack of prior action on curriculum prompted this comment:

A top business school finally getting around to this? In this economy and world? There are 12 senior administrators and none have curriculum and courses in their portfolio? What exactly are they doing (Petrina, 2014)?

In all of these examples of gender-based harassment and violence, once the issue became public in the mainstream media, steps were taken to discuss how to remediate the situation and improve the campus and business school environment for women, underscoring the important role of the media and public attention, and the public interest in how business schools operate.

1.3 Changing the future

These few examples of research and practice from the past and present illustrate how gender inequality in higher education and in business schools in particular has been identified and studied for decades. There is no penury of research, explanations and proposed solutions, but gender inequality in management education persists to this day, notwithstanding significant improvements in many areas. A multi-pronged approach to addressing gender inequality in management education is required, because, as Ropers-Huilman argues:

Gender takes shape in, and is shaped by, teaching, learning, and leadership practices, and in relations between students, faculty, administrators, and communities (Ropers-Huilman, 2003: 2).

Thus, in order to move beyond the present and make more progress on gender equality in management education in the future, all of those elements and relationships need to be gender-aware and committed to change.

There have been numerous attempts to address gender inequality within the academy. Strategies that are achievable, some with relatively little cost to the institutions, include ensuring the curriculum (either individual courses or programs of study) is not gender-biased, integrating gender equality issues and awareness into the curriculum, ensuring a positive climate free of discrimination and harassment for all members of the business school community and ensuring equitable terms and conditions of employment for female and male faculty (including hiring, tenure and promotion processes). There are numerous operational solutions that have been proposed, such as

- Launching initiatives to increase and support the representation of women in administrative positions (e.g. McTiernan and Flynn, 2011)

- Creating tasks forces on the chilly climate (Rose, 1995)

- Negotiating collective agreement provisions that require gender balance on hiring committees, and other equity provisions, such as the stopping of the tenure and promotion clocks for reproductive and family responsibility reasons (Neilsen et al., 2014).

Notwithstanding these examples of progress (many of which are referred to in this volume), is there more that can be done, given that gender equality has not yet been achieved? Perhaps what is missing is not the identification of the problems or the development of solutions, but the implementation of the solutions and the leadership and motivation to do so.

Despite progress in a wide range of areas, questions are continually being raised as to why more has not been made. There are calls for more reflection on the structural and ideological issues underpinning business schools as organizations. Simon Learmount, Director of the Judge Business School MBA program, wrote in an introduction to a 2014 study on why there are not more female MBA applicants:

> It is beyond the scope of this report to pursue the questions and assumptions (for example about gender roles in contemporary society and the patriarchal structure of organisations) that this sort of reasoning raises—although we feel that these are incredibly important issues that should be explored more fully elsewhere (Wirz, 2014: 2).

Others call for structural change and reflection. McTiernan and Flynn have studied the question of leadership from the perspective of women deans. While demonstrating that progress has indeed been made, they identify continuing challenges with regard to gender inequality in business schools. They call for more leadership and structural reflection and change:

> . . . business schools should be leading the way to change in these areas and providing examples and best practices that can be transformative in the business world more widely. This will require structural change in business schools (McTiernan and Flynn, 2011: 333).

The calls in the academic literature for a systematic approach to addressing gender inequality in management education are supported in the public policy arena. For example, the UN Global Compact (GC) launched the PRME with a mandate to encourage business schools and management education institutions to work towards "systemic change within their own institutions":

> The mission of PRME is to inspire and champion responsible management education, research and thought leadership globally . . . The PRME initiative serves as a framework for gradual, systemic change in business schools and management-related institutions (UN Principles for Responsible Management Education, 2014).

In recognition of the transformative potential of such an initiative, in 2011, the PRME WG was formed with the collaboration and encouragement of PRME. The WG's mission is to work for the integration of the UN's Women's Empowerment Principles (WEPs) within the PRME initiative, and to ensure that gender and women's inequality were not forgotten (UN Principles for Responsible Management Education, 2014). Although it is essential that the WG continue to advance the cause of gender equality in management education, that work is not sufficient, given the magnitude of the challenge. More is required of the PRME initiative itself. PRME, if used strategically, has the potential to guide business schools and management education towards being more responsive to gender inequality and to make the structural changes required to realize the goals of gender equality.

PRME has six principles, which are, prima facie, gender neutral. Business schools and management education institutions are asked to make a commitment to implement the principles and to report on them through filing a biannual report known as the "Sharing Information on Progress" (SIP) report (UN Principles for Responsible Management Education, 2014). Without making specific reference to gender, PRME still has a mandate to address gender inequality by virtue of its own principles and the fact that it is part of the UN organization, which has a strong mandate to address gender inequality. Both PRME and the GC (the parent of PRME and referred to in the PRME principles) are UN organizations, and as such are governed by UN policies on gender, including the gender mainstreaming policy. In 2012, the UN Economic and Social Council repeated its resolve to:

> ... actively promote the mainstreaming of a gender perspective in the design, implementation, monitoring and evaluation of policies and programmes in all political, economic and social spheres, and further undertake to strengthen the capabilities of the United Nations system in the area of gender (UN Economic and Social Council, 2012).

Given that PRME's goal is to provide "an engagement framework for the incorporation of universal values into curricula and research" (UN Principles for Responsible Management Education, 2014), it is important that PRME do everything it can to ensure that gender equality, which is a fundamental universal value, be made central to the initiative.

An important lesson may be learned from the parent organization of PRME, the UN Global Compact, the world's largest corporate social responsibility initiative. Despite the breadth and depth of the GC's Ten Principles and their foundation in UN principles and conventions that clearly focus on women and gender inequality, gender inequality was marginalized within the UN Global Compact until a specific mandate was developed through the WEPs (Kilgour, 2007, 2013). To make companies more aware of the need to address gender inequality within their corporate social responsibilities initiatives, in 2010 the UN Global Compact, in collaboration with UNIFEM (now UN Women), launched the WEPs, the world's first global code of conduct focusing on women (WEP, 2014). Similarly, PRME needs to take similar action to make gender inequality a more explicit goal.

One of the advantages of requiring attention be paid to gender under initiatives such as PRME is that it would, by definition, encourage the use of a gender lens, which draws attention to such concepts as "power in all of its visible and invisible forms [and] boundaries and their potentials for exclusion, marginalization, and incomplete or superficial inclusion" (Ackerly, 2008: 28). Being aware of and applying a gender lens to management education institutions whose mandates are to promote, encourage, share and create knowledge is particularly important:

> Every form of knowledge is based upon a specific knowledge of gender. Accordingly, "gender knowledge" pre-structures how problems are perceived and defined as well as the policy responses that result (Stone, 2008: 89).

One role of the SIP report that PRME signatories are required to file is to share best practices:

> reporting should not be seen as a routine or bureaucratic obligation, but rather as the best opportunity to share information with stakeholders, create a learning community with other participating institutions, and provide information on progress achieved in the implementation of PRME (UN Principles for Responsible Management Education, 2014).

Thus, one could assume that reporting on gender equality initiatives and progress could be an important stimulus in the learning community.

Many positive examples and references about management education initiatives are effective in addressing gender inequality. One could assume that PRME signatories would want to proactively share these. Although there is not much research in this area, Haynes' and Murray's chapter in this volume analyses how PRME UK business schools have reported gender in their SIPs. They found that business schools' SIP reports made little reference to gender inequality outside of the areas of diversity, women in the context of corporate governance and human resource management. Even those references are minimal in the PRME reports (SIPs). To correct this neglect, perhaps more than 500 business schools that are part of PRME should be required to report on and show progress on gender equality, as it is so fundamental to the UN, and is a priority of the UN Global Compact from which PRME was created. Should they not be required to discuss, at a very minimum, the progress they are making on fundamental UN goals? In addition to asking for specific reporting on progress on addressing gender inequality, business schools and PRME signatories should be encouraged or required to conduct gender equality audits.

Although most of the world's management education institutions are not engaging with PRME (currently there are just over 500), it can still play a leadership role in the area of gender equality. The PRME Steering Committee comprises a broad range of management education organizations and stakeholders from all regions of the world:

- UN Global Compact

- Graduate Management Admission Council (GMAC)

- AACSB International (The Association to Advance Collegiate Schools of Business)

- European Foundation for Management Development (EFMD)

- Association of MBAs (AMBA)

- Association of African Business Schools (AABS)

- Association of Asia-Pacific Business Schools (AAPBS)

- Central and East European Management Development Association (CEEMAN)

- Latin American Council of Management Schools (CLADEA)

- The Academy of Business in Society (ABIS)

- Globally Responsible Leadership Initiative (GRLI) (UN Principles for Responsible Management Education, 2014)

Harnessing the reach and influence of these bodies in the goal of achieving gender equality in management education would be a significant step towards that goal. To accomplish that, gender equality has to be made explicit and prioritized within PRME.

1.4 Conclusions

The issue of gender inequality in management education has persisted for a number of decades. Although there have been numerous research studies and proposals for change, progress has been sporadic, and there are still many challenges that need to be addressed, as some of the examples in this chapter illustrate. However, the fact that gender inequality still exists in the areas discussed herein (and many not mentioned) means that there is still work to do, and more action is required by those in positions of leadership and with authority for decision-making.

Using a gender lens on the institutions of management education can perhaps move the issue of gender equality forward enough so that in a few more decades, researchers and policy-makers do not feel the need to publish yet another volume on how to achieve gender equality in business schools. For PRME to be more responsive to gender, it needs to make gender equality an explicit part of the business school commitment. Approaches like these build on the many others that have been proposed and implemented over the last four decades or so.

Given the amount of research and discussion on the issue of gender in management education over the past number of decades, questions have to be raised about why more has not been done on gender inequality since the 1970s. It is interesting to note that mainstream media coverage of gender inequality in management education has served to move institutions to take corrective action in many cases. While it is encouraging to see that some business schools and institutions such as PRME are encouraging more action on gender inequality, it is important to always consider what more can be done and by whom.

How many hundreds of thousands of students pass through business schools and management education institutions each year? How many graduate without having been exposed to ideas and facts about gender inequality and the pervasive universal inequality of women? A goal of each institution should be to provide each graduate with the tools to apply a gender lens to his or her work, and the knowledge of why that is important. PRME, by making gender equality explicit within its principles or reporting requirements, could help to realize the potential of its own principles and mandate, in particular, Principle Three, which encourages signatories to:

> . . . create educational frameworks, materials, processes and environments that enable effective learning experiences for responsible leadership (UN Principles for Responsible Management Education, 2014).

It is obviously impossible to argue that leadership that is "responsible" would exclude women or perpetuate gender inequality.

Changes made in how gender is addressed and discussed in business schools and management education will have an important impact in how it is addressed, discussed and understood in organizations in society at large (Mavin and Bryans, 1999):

> . . . particularly when examining the management education of women managers and professionals, the appropriate issue is whether the educational experiences for women are optimal, both in terms of women's learning experiences, and the ability of women, organizations, and society to maximize the benefit derived from investments in women's higher education (McKeen, Bujaki and Burke, 2000: 366).

In an article on sexual harassment at HBS in 1998, the journalist raised important questions that are still pertinent today:

> In the past, (Dean) Clark has spoken of making Harvard Business School a "living model" for life in the corporate world. He says he'd now like to apply that principle to the school's culture. And it's precisely that aim that prompts consequential questions: Where does this sort of behavior come from? And more to the point, where will it go when its perpetrators depart campus for the real world? (Useem, 1998).

Because of the importance of management education to society at large, it is important to continue to identify the key barriers to change, and the ways in which those barriers may be overcome to ensure that management education and business schools address gender inequality and provide a more complete, transformative education to future managers, policy-makers and business leaders.

References

Ackerly, B., 2008. Feminist methodological reflection. In: Klotz, A., Prakash, D. (Eds.), Qualitative Methods in International Relations: A Pluralist Guide. Palgrave Macmillan, New York, pp. 28–42.

Association of American Colleges, 1982-Last Update, The Classroom Climate: A Chilly One for Women? A Project on the Status and Education of Women. Available: https://www.hws.edu/offices/provost/pdf/classroom_climate.pdf (18.03.15).

Bell, R.L., Joyce, M.P., 2011. Comparing business faculty's salaries by rank and gender: does AACSB accreditation really make a difference? Academy of Educational Leadership Journal 15(2), 19–40.

Blasco, M., 2012. Aligning the hidden curriculum of management education with PRME: an inquiry-based framework. Journal of Management Education 36(3), 364–388.

Burke, K., Duncan, K., Krall, L., Spencer, D., 2005. Gender differences in faculty pay and faculty salary compression. The Social Science Journal 42(2), 165–181.

Caseplace, 2014-Last Update [Homepage of the Aspen Institute: Center for Business Education] [Online]. Available: www.caseplace.org (11.09.11).

CBC, 2013-Last Update, UBC Investigates Frosh Students' Pro-Rape Chant: Chant Condoned Non-Consensual Sex with Under-Aged Girls [Homepage of Canadian Broadcasting Corporation] [Online]. Available: www.cbc.ca/news/canada/british-columbia/ubc-investigates-frosh-students-pro-rape-chant-1.1699589 (18.03.15).

Chowdhry, B., November 30, 2014, 2014-Last Update, Would a Push to Hire More Women Reduce Gender Pay-Gap? Not Until We Hire More Women [Homepage of Huffington Post] [Online]. Available: www.huffingtonpost.com/bhagwan-Chowdhry/would-a-push-to-hire-more_b_5890550.html (10.12.14).

Currie, J., Hill, B., 2013. Gendered universities and the wage gap: a case study of a pay equity audit in an Australian university. Higher Education Policy 26, 65–82.

Doucet, C., Durand, C., Smith, M., 2008. Who gets market supplements? Gender differences within a large Canadian University. The Canadian Journal of Higher Education 38(1), 67–103.

Doucet, C., Smith, M.R., Durand, C., 2012. Pay Structure, Female Representation and the Gender Pay Gap Among University Professors. Universite Laval, Department of Industrial Relations.

Foster, F., 1994. Managerial sex role stereotyping among academic staff within UK business schools. Women in Management Review, 9(3), 17–22.

Kelan, E.K., 2007. The discursive construction of gender in contemporary management literature. Journal of Business Ethics 81(2), 427–445.

Kelan, E.K., Jones, R.D., 2010. Gender and the MBA. The Academy of Management Learning and Education (AMLE) 9(1), 26–43.

Kilgour, M.A., 2007. The un global compact and substantive equality for women: revealing a well-hidden mandate. Third World Quarterly 28(4), 751–773.

Kilgour, M.A., 2013. The global compact and gender inequality: a work in progress. Business & Society 52(1), 105–134.

Korn, M., 2014. Business education: gender bias is alleged at UCLA's Anderson. Wall Street Journal, B.1.

Maranto, C.L., Griffin, A.E., 2011. The antecedents of a 'chilly climate' for women faculty in higher education. Human Relations 64(2), 139–159.

Mavin, S., Bryans, P., 1999. Gender on the agenda in management education? Women in Management Review 14(3), 99–104.

Mavin, S., Bryans, P., Waring, T., 2004. Gender on the agenda 2: unlearning gender blindness in management education. Women in Management Review 19(6), 293–303.

Mckeen, C.A., Bujaki, M.L., Burke, R.J., 2000. Preparing business graduates for the "real" world—the role of the University. Women in Management Review 15(7), 356–369.

Mctiernan, S., Flynn, P.M., 2011. "Perfect storm" on the horizon for women business school deans? Academy of Management Learning & Education 10(2), 323–339.

Neilsen, C., Hamilton, L., El Hussein, M., Mawji, A., Murdoch, D., Watchman, R., May 2014, 2014-Last Update, Model Equity Clauses for Inclusion in the Collective Agreement: A Report by the Diversity Committee to the Executive and Negotiating Committees of the Mount Royal Faculty Association. Available: www.mrfa.net/files/Model%20Clauses%20for%20Equity%20Report%20FINAL%20May%202014.pdf (17.12.14).

Paris, L.D., Decker, D.L., 2012. Sex role stereotypes: does business education make a difference? Gender in Management 27(1), 36–50.

Petrina, S., May 2014, 2014-Last Update, Top Story of 2013–2014 at Ubc: Failure of Accountability for Sauder Rape Cheer [Homepage of Institute for Critical Education Studies and Workplace: a Journal for Academic Labor] [Online]. Available: www.blogs.ubc.ca/workplace/2014/05/top-story-of-2013-2014-at-ubc-failure-of-accountability-for-sauder-rape-cheer-bced-ubcsauder school-mba-yteubc (06.12.14).

Robertson, D., 1979. Women business school academicians: disparities and progress. Sex Roles 5(5), 635–647.

Ropers-Huilman, B., 2003. Gendered Futures in Higher Education: Critical Perspectives for Change. State University of New York Press, Albany, NY, USA.

Rose, J., March 29, 1995, 1995-Last Update, Number of Tenured Women at Amos Tuck School: One: Task Force Finds Women Face 'Chilly Climate' Three Years after Tuck Ranked Last for the Number of Tenured Women. Available: www.thedartmouth.com/1995/03/29/number-of-tenured-women-at-amos-tuck-school-one-task-force-finds-women-face-chilly-climatethree-years-after-tuck-ranked-last-for-the-number-of-tenured-women (2014).

Sandler, B., July 13, 2005, 2005-Last Update, The Chilly Climate. Available: www.sun.iwu.edu/~mgardner/Articles/chillyclimate.pdf (10.12.14).

Scott, L., October 14, 2014, 2014-Last Update, No UCLA, Gender Equality in B-School Faculty Isn't 'Mathematically Impossible' [Homepage of Business Week] [Online]. Available: www.businessweek.com/articles/2014-10-14/closing-the-gender-pay-gap-is-mathematically-impossible-only-for-b-school-finance-profs (10.12.14).

Smith, C.R., 1997. Gender issues in management education: a new teaching resource. Women in Management Review 12(3), 100–104.

Stone, D., 2008. Global public policy, transnational policy communities, and their networks. The Policy Studies Journal 36(1), 19–38.

Symons, L., Ibarra, H., 2014. What the Scarcity of Women in Business School Case Studies Really Looks Like. www.hbr.org/2014/04/what-the-scarcity-of-women-in-business-case-studies-really-looks-like/edn. Harvard Business Review, Cambridge, MA, USA.

Thompson, J., Mcgivern, J., 1995. Sexism in the Seminar: Strategies for Gender Sensitivity in Management Education. Routledge.

UBC, 2013. Fact Finding Report: Commerce Students Association (CUS) Frosh Chants. University of British Columbia, Vancouver, BC, Canada.

UN Economic and Social Council, 2012. Mainstreaming a Gender Perspective in All Policies and Programmes in the UN System. Resolution 2012/24. Available: www.un.org/ga/search/view_doc.asp?symbol=E/RES/2012/24 (03.17.15).

UN Principles for Responsible Management Education, December 2104, 2014-Last Update, Principles for Responsible Management Education. Available: www.unprme.org/about-prme/index.php (10.12.14).

University of Virginia, December 5, 2014, 2014-Last Update, Statement of University of Virginia President Teresa A. Sullivan [Homepage of University of Virginia] [Online]. Available: https://news.virginia.edu/content/important-university-virginia-messages-regarding-sexual-assault#sullivan12-5 (07.12.14).

University of Virginia Darden School of Business, December 11, 2014, 2014-Last Update, U. Va. Darden Student Association Town Hall Examines Sexual Assault. Available: www.darden.virginia.edu/web/Media/Darden-News-Articles/2014/UVa-Darden-Student-Association-Town-Hall-Examines-Sexual-Assault (11.12.14).

Useem, J., July 1998, 1998-Last Update, Harvard Business School's 'Woman Problem' [Homepage of Inc. Magazine] [Online]. Available: www.inc.com/magazine/19980601/940.html (10.12.14).

Wirz, M., 2014. Opting for an MBA Education: A Gender Analysis—A Review of the Evidence from GMAC Reports. Cambridge University, Judge School of Business, Cambridge, UK.

WEP (Women's Empowerment Principles), 2014-Last Update [Homepage of www.womensempowerment.org] [Online].

2

Gender equality in business schools

The elephant in the room

Patricia M. Flynn
Bentley University, USA

Kevin V. Cavanagh and Diana Bilimoria
Case Western Reserve University, USA

Business schools can and should help mitigate the under-representation of women in management and leadership positions in the corporate world. They have not, however, stepped up to the plate in this regard. Moreover, as this chapter demonstrates, significant gender gaps continue to exist within business schools themselves, especially at the key levels of dean, academic department chair, full professor, tenured faculty and doctoral students in several key business fields. Yet issues of gender are often invisible in business schools. Business students, both female and male, often lack exposure to professional and academic women in leadership positions, in case studies, and in the curriculum more generally. Further, although there have been numerous calls for business schools to rethink and challenge their basic assumptions and traditions, gender appears to be a non-issue. Business schools ignore gender issues at their own risk: although women bolstered business school enrolments in decades past, recent data show smaller numbers of women earning undergraduate and graduate business degrees in the United States. The numbers of women earning bachelor and doctoral degrees in business schools outside the United States are rising; they are doing so, however, in business schools with even fewer women leaders than in the United States. In terms of MBAs the number and share of women earning MBAs at business schools both within and outside of the United States are on the decline. The chapter concludes with recommendations for raising the profile of gender issues and improving gender equality in business schools.

2.1 Introduction

It is no secret that women are notably under-represented at the highest levels of the corporate hierarchy (e.g. Alliance for Board Diversity, 2010; Catalyst, 2013; McDonald and Westphal, 2013; Peterson and Philpot, 2006). Business schools can and should help to mitigate this state of affairs as they play a central role in educating and preparing future managers and leaders. However, business schools have come under increasing scrutiny in recent years and have been portrayed as laggards rather than leaders in anticipating and leading change (Cornuel and Hommel, 2012; Datar, Garvin and Cullen, 2010; Morsing and Rovira, 2011; Muff et al., 2013; Thomas and Thomas, 2012). Their track record regarding gender equality is no exception (Bilimoria, 1999; Kilgour, 2012; Mavin and Bryans, 1999; Rezvani and Taylor, 2010; Sinclair, 1995; Smith, 2000).

This chapter explores the trends and status of women in management education, specifically focusing on business school deans, academic department chairs, faculty and students. Significant gender gaps continue to exist in the representation of women in business schools including at the key levels of dean, department chair and tenured faculty. Moreover, after decades of major gains, degrees conferred to women at the bachelor's, MBA and doctoral levels in Association to Advance Collegiate Schools of Business (AACSB), business schools in the United States have begun to fall. This is occurring at a time when women account for increasing numbers of students in higher education in the United States overall. It also contrasts with the growth of female undergraduate and doctoral students in business schools outside the United States, although female MBA students are on the decline in these schools as well. We submit that there is great need for business schools to rise to the challenge and better lead in integrating gender equality into management education and in preparing the workforce of tomorrow. We begin the chapter with a look at the changing environment in which business schools operate; we then address gender issues more specifically. We conclude with recommendations for improving gender equality in business schools, mindful of the positive spillover effects this result can have on workplaces and the world more generally.

2.2 Challenges facing business schools

Business schools have been heralded as the educational success story of the 20th century (de Onzoño, 2011). In the United States, business has become the largest undergraduate major, accounting for 20.5% of all bachelors' degrees awarded in 2011/2012 (NCES, 2013b). Worldwide, in 2010, AACSB estimated that business degree programs at the undergraduate level or above are offered at approximately 12,600 institutions, over 85% of which are outside North America (AACSB, 2011). However, the bloom is off the rose as numerous studies document a myriad of challenges now facing business schools and their leaders. Proposals abound focusing on how business schools can best compete in the increasingly global marketplace (Bisoux, Broadbridge and Simpson, 2011; Colby et al., 2011; Datar, Garvin and Cullen, 2010; de Onzoño, 2011; Hardy and Everett, 2013; Hill, 2011; Muff et al., 2013; Pfeffer and Fong, 2002; Stevens, 2000; Strizhakova, Coulter and Price, 2012) and against the growing numbers of alternative providers of management education, such as company-based training programs, consulting firms and for-profit ventures including UNext and the University of Phoenix (AACSB, 2002; GMAC, 2013; Pfeffer and Fong, 2002; Rukstad and Collis, 2001; Wilson and Thomas, 2012). Many of the relatively new providers of management education actively embrace technological advances in delivery, alternatives not always welcomed by traditional business school faculty (AACSB, 2002; Mintzberg, 2005; Pfeffer and Fong, 2004; Starkey and Tempest, 2005; Thomas and Thomas, 2012). Also, promotion-and-tenure (P&T) processes in business schools have been faulted for unduly emphasizing theoretical research over teaching and applied, empirical research (Bennis and O'Toole, 2005; Mintzberg, 1996; Pfeffer and Fong, 2002; Schoemaker, 2008). Shortages of faculty in recent years raise further complications for business schools (Alsop, 2007; Bennis and O'Toole, 2005; Harris, 2006; Schneider and Sheikh, 2012; Schoemaker, 2008).

Business schools have long been criticized for failing to anticipate and facilitate change for new ideas, technologies and organizational development (Cheit, 1985; Cornuel and Hommel, 2012; Crainer and Dearlove, 1999; Davis and Botkin, 1994; Friga, Bettis and Sullivan, 2003; Gaddis, 2000; Gordon and Howell, 1959; Hayes and Abernathy, 1980; Herrington and Arnold, 2013; Khurana and Spender, 2012; Mintzberg, 1996; Pfeffer and Fong, 2002, 2004; Porter and McKibbin, 1988; Thomas and Thomas, 2012). Additional damage to their reputation has developed because unethical corporations such as Enron and WorldCom have made worldwide news with large corporate scandals, fostering a public perception that business schools are part of the problem rather than leaders in helping to better society (Adler, 2002; Crane, 2004; Fusaro and Miller, 2002; Ghoshal, 2005; Giacalone and Thompson, 2006; Podolny, 2009; Quelch, 2005). The financial and economic crises in 2008/2009 brought further bad press to business schools, as many of the individuals (e.g. Dick Fuld at Lehman Brothers, John Thain at Merrill Lynch and Andy Hornby at HBOS in the United Kingdom) under the microscope for excessive executive compensation, backdating of options, exotic investment instruments and other questionable business practices have been highlighted as holders of MBA degrees (Pedagogy of the privileged, 2009).

The fundamentals of management education itself are being questioned as critics call for a better, more fully developed graduate. For example, some researchers have observed that business schools tend to concentrate on easy-to-quantify outcomes and on individualism, which may come at the expense of ethics, values, collaboration and critical inquiry (Barker, 2010; Bennis and O'Toole, 2005; Cheit, 1985; Goodman and O'Brien, 2012; Leavitt, 1989; Mintzberg, 1996; Mintzberg and Gosling, 2002; Pfeffer and

Fong, 2004; Podolny, 2009; Rousseau, 2012; Schoemaker, 2008). Many of these critics have been outspoken about the need to provide future managers with experience and capabilities beyond the analytical (Goleman, Boyatzis and McKee, 2001; McGrath, 2007; McMillan and Chen, 2012; Mintzberg, 2005; Navarro, 2008; Quelch, 2005; Rousseau, 2012; Rubin and Dierdorff, 2009; Rutherford et al., 2012). Researchers also argue that business school curricula need to be more interdisciplinary, which can be a challenge as faculty are often well-educated in only one or two key areas (Dunning, 1989; Gailey and Carroll, 1993; Rafols et al., 2012; Cheng et al., 2014).

The call for greater professionalism of business schools, which would involve essentially rebalancing the curriculum and the institutional mind-set to one focused on longer term outcomes, qualitative as well as quantitative analyses, ethical and social responsibility, enhanced communication and cooperation, and transformational rather than transactional leadership, can play to the advantage of women (Bass and Avolio, 1994; Bennis and O'Toole, 2005; Crane, 2004; Gallos, 2002; Harris, 2006; Khurana and Nohria, 2008; Pfeffer and Fong, 2002, 2004; Podolny, 2009; Trank and Rynes, 2003). The literature on ways in which women manage and lead suggests, for instance, that many women are ideally suited to address these issues and to succeed in this type of environment (Bass and Avolio, 1994; Wittenberg-Cox and Maitland, 2008).

Yet business schools have failed to take the lead in addressing gender equality. In fact, issues of gender are often invisible in business schools with respect to organizational culture, curriculum, leadership, social networks and the like (Bevelander and Page, 2009; Bisoux, Broadbridge and Simpson, 2011; Kelan and Jones, 2010; Kilgour, 2012; Mavin, Bryans and Waring, 2004; Simpson, 2006). Although women's workforce participation shows an upward trend across the globe, business school curricula continue to be designed almost exclusively around a male-dominated ethos and emphasize "hard" skills associated with masculinity (Hite and McDonald, 1995; Mavin, Bryans and Waring, 2004; Simpson, 2006). As Smith (1997: 100) highlighted "most management texts are written by men, using examples of men". Research continues to show masculine bias in the current value systems in MBA programs (e.g. Collinson and Hearn, 1994; Kerfoot and Knights, 1993; Kerfoot and Whitehead, 1998; Mavin and Bryans, 1999; Mavin, Bryans and Waring, 2004; Metcalfe and Linstead, 2003; Siemensma, 2004; Simpson and Ituma, 2009).

A recent case study at Harvard Business School (HBS) raises more questions than answers for business schools attempting to bridge the gender gap (Kantor, 2013). The case study shows how Harvard administrators attempted to create a gender-neutral culture, including installing stenographers in the classroom to guard against biased grading, training women students to raise their hands in class and providing coaching sessions for pre-tenure female professors. The experiment was deemed successful in that the grade gap between female and male MBA students vanished within two years. However, unintended consequences emerged that caused Harvard administrators to wonder if they had created a worthwhile, sustainable culture. These consequences included female students embracing the same sexual stereotyping behaviour typically associated with their male counterparts, and the realization that the demand for more women faculty at HBS could not realistically be met. In 2014, Dean Nitin Nohria made an unusual public apology for HBS's treatment of female students and faculty (Byrne, 2014).

Much more work and attention is needed in management education, including development of additional case studies and the identification of best practices that address gender-related cultural issues and gender imbalances in business schools.

In the following sections, we highlight trends and the current status of female administrators, faculty and students in business schools.

2.3 Women business school deans and academic department chairs

Although some progress has been made in recent years, women continue to hold less than one in five deanships in US schools of business (AACSB, 2013). Women's share of deanships at these AACSB member schools rose from 9.1% in 2000, to 16.3% in 2010, to 19.3% in 2013 (see Table 2.1). Outside the United States, women comprised less than 10% of the AACSB business school deans in 2012/2013 (AACSB, 2013).

Research on the career paths of business school deans reveals both similarities and differences by gender. A 2007 survey of deans of AACSB member schools within and outside the United States found Management (27%), Economics (17%), Marketing (13%), Accounting (9%) and Finance (9%) to be the top five fields of doctoral study for both male and female business school deans (McTiernan and Flynn, 2011). In contrast to men, women deans were more likely to have a degree in Marketing (19%) than in Economics (14%), and in Accounting (8%) than in Finance (6%). For both men and women, the associate dean is the position most often (22%) held just prior to becoming

Table 2.1 **Full-time administrative personnel by gender, USA**

Source: AACSB International, *Annual Salary Surveys*, 2010–2013.

	Male (%)	Female (%)
Dean		
2009/2010	83.7	16.3
2010/2011	82.4	17.6
2011/2012	81.3	18.7
2012/2013	80.7	19.3
Associate dean		
2009/2010	71.5	28.5
2010/2011	71.1	28.9
2011/2012	68.6	31.4
2012/2013	66.9	33.1
Assistant dean		
2009/2010	44.7	55.3
2010/2011	41.4	58.6
2011/2012	39.2	60.8
2012/2013	40.8	59.2

dean. A key difference among men and women involves the role of interim dean, with more than double the percentage of females (17%) than males (8%) appointed to the dean's position after having served in an interim capacity. These women, who often took the interim position at the request of a senior administrator, found the job very rewarding and then successfully applied for the dean's position on a more permanent basis.

At the level of associate dean, males continue to dominate as well. Some progress has been made as the proportion of associate dean positions held by women in US business schools has increased from 23.8% in 2004/2005 (the first year for which we have these data), to 28.5% in 2009/2010, and 33.1% in 2012/2013 (see Table 2.1). Non-US business schools have fewer women in these leadership positions than in the United States, with 26.6% the comparable figure in 2012/2013 (AACSB, 2013).

Faculty leadership at the department level is another stepping stone to the dean's position, with 19% of male and 13% of female deans in the 2007 survey advancing to the deanship immediately after serving as an academic department chair. Women are, however, significantly under-represented as department chairs in business schools. In 2012/2013, women held only 20.8% of the academic department chair slots in US AACSB business schools in 2012/2013, up slightly from 18.3% in 2005/2006, the first year for which we have these data (see Table 2.2). The fields of Human Resource Management (HRM) and Business Law led the way with 41.7% and 40.0% female chairs, respectively, in 2012/2013, followed by Behavioral Sciences/Organizational Behavior (BS/OB) (27.3%) and Accounting (26.3%). Business disciplines with the smallest shares of female department chairs are Finance (12.6%), Economics (9.9%), Strategy (9.0%) and Production/Operations Management (OM) (7.4%). In three of these fields—Economics, Strategy and Production/OM—the proportion of women department chairs has actually fallen since 2000/2001.

Table 2.2 **Business school academic department chairs: % female, by field, USA, 2000/2001, 2012/2013**

Source: AACSB International, *Annual Salary Surveys*, 2001, 2013.

	2000/2001	2012/2013
Field		
Accounting	23.5%	26.3%
Behavioral Science/OB	26.3%	27.3%
Business Law	26.9%	40.0%
CIS/MIS	18.1%	18.7%
Economics	11.7%	9.9%
Finance	7.9%	12.6%
HR Management	13.6%	41.7%
Management	22.6%	25.8%
Marketing	17.1%	24.1%
Production/OM	9.1%	7.4%
Quant Methods/Statistics	11.1%	9.0%
Strategic Management	7.1%	16.7%
Total*	18.3%	20.8%

*Total includes all fields, not just these 12.

Section 2.4 looks in more detail at gender differences for faculty by rank, tenure and business discipline.

2.4 Women business school faculty[1]

Women are under-represented in a range of faculty positions in business schools, especially at upper levels. Less than one-third (29.9%) of all full-time faculty members in AACSB member schools in the United States were women in 2012/2013 (AACSB, 2013). Their share in 2000/2001 was 22.8% (see Table 2.3). The presence of women faculty in business schools is inversely related to professorial rank: in 2012/2013 women were 39.5% of instructors; 37.4% of assistant professors; 30.4% of associate professors; and 19.0% of full professors. Comparable figures show that in 2000/2001 women accounted for 42.2% of instructors; 31.5% of assistant professors; 23.1% of associate professors; and 12.3% of full professors. Thus, women have made relatively small gains since 2000/2001 of +5.9%, +7.3% and +6.7% at the levels of assistant, associate and full professor, respectively. Women's share of instructors fell slightly (−2.7%) over this 13-year period.

Less than one-quarter (23.6%) of the faculty with tenure in AACSB member business schools in the United States are women (see Table 2.4). This figure was 19.6% in 2005/2006 (the first year for which we have these data). In terms of tenure-track positions (often assistant professors), women held 36.5% of these slots in 2012/2013, up from 32.3% in 2005/2006. Women were 37.1% of the non-tenure-track faculty (many as instructors) in 2013/2013, a slight decline from 38.2% seven years earlier.

The presence of women among business school faculty varies by academic field. Of the 12 largest business disciplines, in terms of the number of full-time faculty, women hold their largest share of faculty positions (at all ranks) in BS/OB (43.2%);

Table 2.3 **Female number and % of full-time business faculty, by rank, USA, 2000/2001, 2006/2007, 2012/2013**

Source: AACSB International, *Annual Salary Surveys*, 2001, 2007, 2013.

	2000/2001		2006/2007		2012/2013	
	# Female	%	# Female	%	# Female	%
Rank	1,019	42.2	1,584	41.9	1,758	39.5
Instructor	1,873	31.5	2,416	35.5	2,690	37.4
Assistant Professor	1,700	23.1	1,941	26.5	2,326	30.4
Associate Professor	1,069	12.3	1,326	14.9	1,730	19.0
Full Professor						
Total, FT Female faculty	5,661	22.8	7,267	27.1	8,504	29.9

1 This section addresses only faculty in AACSB business schools in the United States; we do not have comparable data for faculty outside the United States.

Table 2.4 **Business faculty by tenure status, by gender, USA**

Source: AACSB International, *Annual Salary Surveys*, 2006, 2013.

	2005/2006	2012/2013
Tenured		
Male	9,966	9,607
Female	2,428	2,962
% Female	19.6	23.6
Tenure track		
Male	3,315	3,074
Female	1,581	1,766
% Female	32.2	36.5
Non-tenure track		
Male	2,366	3,147
Female	1,460	1,857
% Female	38.2	37.1

HRM (43.2%); Accounting (37.3%); Management (36.1%); Business Law (35.8%); and Marketing (33.0%) (see Table 2.5). Finance has the lowest proportion of women faculty with 20.1%, followed by Economics (22.5%), Strategy (22.8%) and Quantitative Methods/Statistics (23.6%).

As noted above, women continue to hold less than one in five (19.0%) full professor positions in US business schools. Of the 12 largest business fields, HRM had the highest share of female full professors (32.2%), followed by Business Law (32.0%) and BS/OB (30.9%). These fields have had a relatively large pipeline of women faculty at the associate and assistant professor levels in recent years. For example, at the associate professor level these fields had 50.0%, 36.9% and 43.5% of women, in HRM, Business Law and BS/OB, respectively, in 2000/2001. Business Law, in particular, has been characterized by significant numbers of women advancing to higher ranks over time, that is, women were 36.9% of the associate professors in 2000/2001 and 32.0% of the full professors 12 years later. The fields of Finance, Economics and Quantitative Methods/Statistics have the smallest shares of women full professors, with only 10.7%, 12.0% and 12.0%, respectively, in 2012/2013. These fields have had relatively small pipelines of women at lower professorial ranks (see Table 2.5).

Some progress has been made in the hiring of women in tenure-track faculty positions. Using the assistant professor rank as a proxy, US data show women's share of these entry-level positions rose in 11 of the 12 business fields from 2000/2001 to 2012/2013. The exception is HRM, which is a discipline in which women have held at least half of the assistant professorships since 2000/2001. Disciplines experiencing the largest increases in shares of women assistant professors over this period are Finance, Strategy, Quantitative Methods/Statistics and CIS/MIS (see Table 2.5). The increased hiring of women in these fields may reflect more attention to gender equity. Alternatively, this trend may be happening in these fields to offset the ongoing exodus of more senior women faculty not granted tenure or who otherwise chose to leave their institutions.

Table 2.5 **Female full-time faculty by field and by rank, USA**

Source: AACSB International, *Annual Salary Surveys*, 2001, 2013.

	Instructor		Assistant Prof.		Associate Prof.		Full Prof.		All FT Faculty	
	2000/2001	2012/2013	2000/2001	2012/2013	2000/2001	2012/2013	2000/2001	2012/2013	2000/2001	2012/2013
Accounting	50.6%	53.3%	38.3%	43.1%	27.9%	36.6%	13.0%	22.1%	28.5%	37.3%
Beh. Sci./Org. Behavior (BS/OB)	31.0%	56.8%	52.2%	54.4%	40.7%	43.5%	20.1%	30.9%	34.0%	43.2%
Business Law	34.7%	37.7%	35.5%	38.3%	23.8%	36.9%	22.4%	32.0%	27.2%	35.8%
CIS/MIS	40.1%	34.3%	24.2%	32.2%	18.3%	24.1%	13.4%	17.7%	22.6%	25.3%
Economics	39.4%	35.1%	25.8%	32.2%	17.9%	23.5%	7.8%	12.0%	16.1%	22.5%
Finance	32.5%	22.0%	19.4%	29.1%	13.1%	21.7%	6.0%	10.7%	13.3%	20.1%
HR Management	54.1%	53.6%	50.0%	50.0%	37.3%	50.0%	19.3%	32.3%	34.1%	43.2%
Management	41.7%	42.9%	37.0%	41.7%	25.4%	37.3%	14.2%	25.2%	26.0%	36.1%
Marketing	39.0%	37.8%	36.3%	42.2%	26.3%	33.8%	13.5%	22.5%	25.2%	33.0%
Production/ Operations Mgmt	25.4%	31.7%	18.6%	25.6%	12.9%	19.8%	7.1%	12.3%	12.9%	19.3%
Quantitative Methods/Statistics	41.8%	40.3%	28.3%	36.6%	18.0%	20.3%	10.3%	12.0%	18.5%	23.6%
Strategic Management (Strategy)	17.7%	19.6%	21.7%	30.7%	23.7%	23.4%	11.6%	15.7%	20.4%	22.8%
Total*	42.40%	39.50%	31.50%	37.40%	23.10%	30.40%	12.30%	19.00%	20.40%	29.90%

*Total includes more than these 12 fields, which were the largest in 2012/2013 in terms of full-time faculty.

The following section on business school graduates begins with a look at the trends of women earning doctoral degrees, which directly impact the supply of candidates for business school faculty. Thereafter, we look at business school graduates at the master's and bachelor's degree levels.

2.5 Women business school graduates

Women represent greater shares of graduates of business schools than of faculty and deans, however, major concerns remain.

2.5.1 Doctoral graduates in business and management

Women have made significant progress in earning doctoral degrees in business and management (B&M) in the United States in recent years, rising as a percentage of all such degrees conferred from 25.6% in 1990 to 40.3% in 2010 (NSF, 2013)[2] (see Table 2.6). The fields of Accounting (43.9%), Marketing (43.2%) and Management (42.0%) led the way in terms of women's shares of doctorates conferred in 2010. Finance continues to lag with 29.3% of its doctorate degrees awarded to women that year. Each of these figures remains below the proportion women comprise of all doctorates earned in 2010 (46.8%) in the United States.

AACSB business schools awarded 19% fewer doctorates in the United States in 2012/2013 than in 2008/2009, resulting in 18.0% fewer women (and 19.5% fewer men) earning a business doctorate credential than four years earlier (see Table 2.7).

In contrast, AACSB schools outside the United States conferred over 50% more doctorate degrees in 2012/2013 than in 2008/2009 (AACSB, 2013). And the absolute number of women earning these non-US doctorates rose by 66.3% during this period (see Table 2.7). By 2009/2010, AACSB schools outside the United States were conferring more doctoral degrees, including more to women, than their US counterparts. In 2012/2013, AACSB schools outside the United States awarded a total of 1,544 doctoral degrees, 562 of which were conferred on women; comparable figures for the United States were 906 total doctorates with 336 to women (AACSB, 2013).

2.5.2 MBA and specialized master's degree graduates

Across all colleges and universities in the United States, women had received 45.4% of the B&M master's degrees awarded in 2009, up from 34.0% in 1990 (DoE, NCES,

---

2 Data at the bachelor's and master's levels for B&M degrees across all programs and colleges/universities in the United States are from the US Department of Education (DoE), National Center for Education Statistics (NCES), Higher Education General Information Survey (HEGIS), "Degrees and Other Formal Awards Conferred" surveys and Integrated Postsecondary, Education Data Systems (IPEDS), and "Completions" Surveys (AACSB, 2012).

Table 2.6 **Doctoral degrees conferred, total and to females, all fields, B&M and selected B&M sub-field, USA, 1990, 2000, 2010**

Source: National Science Foundation (NSF), *Survey of Earned Doctorates*, 2000, 2013.

Total degrees conferred		# Female	% Female
All fields			
1990	36,067	13,092	36.3
2000	41,368	18,119	43.8
2010	48,069	22,505	46.8
Business and Management (B&M)			
1990	1,036	265	25.6
2000	1,074	340	31.7
2010	1,366	550	40.3
Accounting (in B&M)			
1990	173	59	34.1
2000	111	53	47.7
2010	148	65	43.9
Banking/Financial Services/Finance (in B&M)			
1990	133	11	8.3
2000	72	12	16.7
2010	215	63	29.3
Business Administration/Management (in B&M)			
1990	278	67	24.1
2000	325	92	28.3
2010	157	66	42.0
Marketing (in B&M)			
1990	120	38	31.7
2000	140	44	31.4
2010	157	71	45.2

HEGIS and IPEDS data reported in AACSB [2012]) (see Table 2.8). AACSB member school data, which differentiate between MBA and specialized master's programs, highlight the fact that women comprise a much larger share of recipients of specialized master's degrees than that of MBAs. This is true both in the United States and globally. In 2012/2013, for example, women accounted for 46.7% of specialized master's degree recipients in AACSB schools in the United States compared to only 36.4% of the MBA recipients. The non-US figures show women earning greater proportions of these degrees than their US counterparts: 50.5% for specialized master's degrees and 38.1% for MBAs (see Table 2.8).

Focusing on the top 25 universities in the United States, Byrne (2011b) shows that women enrolled in full-time MBA programs were significantly outnumbered by men. The proportion of women at these elite MBA schools ranged from 24.9% to 39.7%. In contrast, at these same top universities, women accounted for 41.0–52.9% of law school

Table 2.7 Degrees conferred by academic level and gender, AACSB business schools, USA and global

Source: AACSB International, Business School Questionnaire, 2013.

	United States				Global (excluding USA)			
	Male	Female	% Female	Total	Male	Female	% Female	Total
Bachelor's degrees								
2008–2009	91,602	70,955	43.6	162,557	22,880	22,956	50.1	45,836
2009–2010	95,327	73,472	43.5	168,799	26,969	27,749	50.7	54,718
2010–2011	97,626	74,699	43.3	172,325	28,706	29,505	50.7	58,211
2011–2012	102,571	77,040	42.9	179,611	31,241	32,248	50.8	63,489
2012–2013	102,142	76,034	42.7	178,176	42,090	42,852	50.4	84,942
Master's-generalist								
2008–2009	32,592	18,561	36.3	51,153	15,282	8,032	34.5	23,314
2009–2010	35,323	20,413	36.6	55,736	17,688	9,977	36.1	27,665
2010–2011	38,542	21,841	36.2	60,383	18,285	10,570	36.6	28,855
2011–2012	32,583	18,271	35.9	50,854	15,502	9,833	38.8	25,335
2012–2013	29,493	16,889	36.4	46,382	15,380	9,471	38.1	24,851
Specialized masters								
2008–2009	8,395	7,545	47.3	15,940	9,325	8,141	46.6	17,466
2009–2010	9,698	8,654	47.2	18,352	10,836	9,728	47.3	20,564
2010–2011	11,808	10,720	47.6	22,528	12,930	12,540	49.2	25,470
2011–2012	11,985	10,425	46.5	22,410	11,890	11,379	48.9	23,269
2012–2013	11,040	9,671	46.7	20,711	12,884	13,150	50.5	26,034
Doctorate								
2008–2009	708	410	36.7	1,118	679	338	33.2	1,017
2009–2010	670	355	34.6	1,025	729	419	36.5	1,148
2010–2011	580	348	37.5	928	681	412	37.7	1,093
2011–2012	484	301	38.3	785	739	459	38.3	1,198
2012–2013	570	336	37.1	906	982	562	36.4	1,544

Table 2.8 **Business and management (B&M) degrees conferred on women by level, USA, 1969/1970–2008/2009**

Source: AACSB-International (2012). *Business School Data Trends and 2012 List of Accredited Schools*, pp. 16, 17. Data are from the US Dept. of Education (DoE), National Center for Education Statistics (NCES), Higher Education General Information Survey (HEGIS), "Degrees and Other Formal Awards Conferred surveys, and Integrated Postsecondary Education Data Systems (IPEDS), "Completions" surveys".

	Bachelor's		Master's		Doctorate	
Year	# Female	% Female	# Female	% Female	# Female	% Female
1969/1970	9,234	8.7	769	3.6	10	1.6
1974/1975	21,656	16.2	3,041	8.4	39	4.2
1979/1980	62,625	33.6	12,264	22.3	117	15.3
1984/1985	104,815	45.1	20,782	31.0	142	17.2
1989/1990	116,284	46.9	26,091	34.0	275	25.2
1994/1995	112,232	48.0	34,609	37.0	380	27.3
1999/2000	127,549	49.8	44,454	39.9	382	32.0
2004/2005	155,634	50.0	60,466	42.4	597	39.9
2008/2009	170,123	48.9	76,394	45.4	821	38.7

enrolments and 43.4–53.8% of enrolments in medical schools. At law schools and medical schools more generally in the United States, women earned 47.3% of JD degrees (ABA, 2013) and 48.3% of MD degrees (AAMC, 2013) in 2011.

The absolute number of MBA degrees awarded by AACSB schools both within and outside the United States has begun to fall, for females as well as males (see Table 2.7). In the United States, from 2009/2010 to 2012/2013, the number of MBAs awarded to women declined by 17.3%, whereas those to men fell by 16.5%. In contrast, specialized master's degrees awarded in US business schools rose by 12.9% from 2009/2010 to 2012/2013, with increases for women (11.8%) and for men (13.8%).

Outside the United States, 13.9% fewer MBA degrees were awarded in 2012/2013 than in 2010/2011; the number of women earning MBA degrees during that period fell by 10.4% (AACSB, 2013). As in the United States, these business schools awarded increasing numbers of specialized masters' degrees, which rose 26.6% from 2009/2010 to 2012/2013. Women, in particular, earned considerably more of these specialized business degrees, experiencing a 35.7% increase since 2009/2010 resulting in their achieving parity (50.7%) in 2012/2013.

2.5.3 Undergraduate business graduates

After years of major growth, the share of bachelor's degrees in B&M awarded to women in the United States stabilized over the last three decades. By 1984/1985 women were 45.1% of all B&M bachelor's degree recipients compared to 46.9% in 1989/1990 and 49.8% in 1999/2000 (DoE, NCES, HEGIS and IPEDS data as reported in AACSB [2012]) (see Table 2.8). Women had reached parity (50.0%) in the receipt of these degrees in the United States in 2004/2005; however, their share declined to 48.9% in 2008/2009, the last year for which we have these data (DoE, NCES, HEGIS and IPEDS data as reported in AACSB [2013]). A similar pattern is observed at AACSB business schools where women represented 43.6% of bachelor's degree recipients in 2008/2009, and 42.7% in 2012/2013 (AACSB, 2013) (see Table 2.7). Moreover, the absolute number of women earning B&M bachelor's degrees in AACSB schools of business in the United States declined in 2012/2013 (–3.5%), as did the total number of such degrees awarded (–0.8%) that year.

A different picture emerges again outside the United States. Bachelor's degrees in business conferred by AACSB schools globally (excluding the United States) have grown significantly in recent years—rising approximately 55% from 2008/2009 to 2012/2013, with both men (+56.1%) and women (+54.4%) participating in that expansion (see Table 2.7). Moreover, 2012/2013 witnessed a 33.0% increase in women receiving bachelor's degrees at these non-US business schools with women now at parity (50.4%) with their male counterparts for these degrees.

2.6 Key outstanding issues

The data and trends analysed above demonstrate a wide range of issues regarding the current and future status of women in business schools. In this section we highlight some of the most pressing topics.

2.6.1 B&M students

Although women bolstered US business school enrolments in decades past, this is no longer the case. Rather, women may be the bellwether for declining pools of undergraduate business majors, at least in the United States. The decline of female business students in the United States reflects, in part, expansion of business school options across the globe. US business schools cannot take for granted the major influx of international students to their campuses in years past. It would be a mistake, however, to think that this is the only factor in play. Women's share of four-year undergraduate business degrees awarded in the United States falls well short of that for all bachelor's degrees conferred in the United States in (57.4%) in 2009/2010 (the most recent year for which we have these data) (NCES, 2013). Increasing numbers of women students are choosing other fields of study and careers (Garrity, 2012; Kelan and Jones, 2010).

Trends at the graduate level also raise concern. In terms of MBA degree recipients in AACSB schools of business in the United States and globally, the absolute number of women has fallen since 2010 (see Table 2.7). At the doctoral level, while women have gained share in earning B&M degrees in recent years in the United States, certain fields (e.g. finance, economics) continue to be challenged in preparing women PhDs, a situation that directly impacts the available pool of women for business faculty positions.

More women are now earning business doctoral degrees outside than within the United States, 562 and 336, respectively, in 2012/2013 (see Table 2.7). Recent trends in the Graduate Management Admissions Test (GMAT), a standard exam for applicants to MBA (and often specialized master's) programs worldwide, suggest that women outside the United States are still very interested in graduate business education. In 2012, a record 122,843 (43% of the total) GMAT exams were taken by women. While approximately one-third of the US examinees were female, a clear majority of examinees in several countries in Asia and Europe were so. In 2010, for example, 62.8% of GMAT test takers in China were female, 57.3% in Taiwan, 58.4% in Thailand, 56.6% in Russia and 59.4% in Vietnam (Byrne [2011a] citing the *Graduate Management Admissions Council [GMAC] Profile of GMAT Candidates, 2006–2010*).

2.6.2 Faculty promotion and tenure

While women have held an increasing share of B&M doctorates awarded over the past two decades, they continue to comprise less than one-third of all full-time business school faculty and less than one-fourth of all tenured business school faculty. Data on tenure and professional rank of women faculty raise questions about P&T processes within business schools. Most of the research in this area has focused on trends (Carter, 2010), allocation of work time (Bilimoria et al., 2012), research productivity (Jordan et al., 2006) and intrinsic motivation (Chen and Zhou, 2013). The findings suggest that differences in patterns between men and women faculty are not attributable to aspirational differences: both men and women faculty in business schools consider receiving tenure and promotions to be the most important research motivation, and female faculty display higher overall and intrinsic motivation than male faculty, with these gender differences being especially strong between tenured women and men faculty (Chen and Zhao, 2013).

So what lies behind the gender differences? Male faculty may be more likely to obtain tenure given their disparity relative to women in terms of research productivity and in time spent on fulfilling teaching/advising and university service responsibilities. For instance, Jordan, Clark and Vann (2008) found that men in accounting publish in top-tier accounting journals at greater rates than women, although this effect disappeared when both academic and professional journals were included. Using one of the largest and most representative databases on US faculty, the 2004 National Study of Postsecondary Faculty (Bilimoria et al., 2012) analysed the academic work experiences of all full-time faculty at four-year colleges and universities across their career stages. In that study women faculty at each career stage across all disciplines reported spending a significantly higher percentage of time on instructional activities and a lower percentage of time on research activities than men. That study also found that women faculty generally spent an increasing number of hours per week serving on administrative committees over time—a significant increase from early to middle career stage, and from middle to late career stage. Although these findings are not specific to business schools, there is no reason to expect differences in the allocation of faculty time by sex across research, teaching and service activities in B&M disciplines as compared to overall trends. Further, research on women in accounting faculty positions suggests that gender stereotyping of women in mothering and nurturing roles—whether or not they have children—can take on a life of its own, the result of which is women faculty dispro-portionately tied up in administrative, pastoral and bureaucratic assignments (Haynes and Fearfull, 2008).

Findings in the general literature on P&T processes and women in higher educa-tion are relevant for faculty in business schools. For instance, the intense workload required during the tenure process has been noted as especially difficult for women when combined with family responsibilities that arise during the same time (Clark and Hill, 2010; Philipsen, 2008). Child-bearing, in particular, is a critical issue for women as deciding to postpone having a child until after receiving tenure has been shown to increase age-related risks for infertility, pregnancy complications and adverse outcomes (Luke and Brown, 2007). Yet having children while on the tenure track has been shown to correlate negatively with the tenure outcome for women (Committee on Maximizing the Potential of Women in Academic Science and Engineering, 2007; Wolfinger, Mason and Goulden, 2008).

Academic women are more than twice as likely as their male counterparts to have fewer children than desired, suggesting that women are sacrificing family outcomes in order to successfully pursue tenure (Mason and Goulden, 2004). Several remedial suggestions have been offered in the literature including improved parental leave plans (Wilson, 2004); reduced teaching loads for new parents, both men and women (Mason and Goulden, 2004); allowable alterations to tenure clocks (Draznin, 2004); and affordable and accessible on-site day-care (Mason and Goulden, 2004). Research shows that even leave plans and altered tenure clocks have had no significant impact on increasing women's tenure outcomes (Quinn, 2010).

Further, the relatively slow rate of promotion to full professor for women faculty in business schools has long-term ramifications. Full professorship is often required or strongly recommended for administrative positions such as department chairs, associate deans and deans. Thus, the candidate pools for these administrative positions are often restricted by the dearth of women at the highest professional rank.

2.6.3 Scarcity of female leadership in business schools and the failure to recognize gender as in "issue"

This chapter demonstrates that women continue to be significantly under-represented in business schools as deans, associate deans, full-time faculty, tenured faculty, associ-ate professors, full professors and academic department chairs. Moreover, the influx of women students in business schools outside the United States is taking place in pro-grams and institutions that have even fewer women leaders and role models than in US business schools. Yet these scenarios fail to trigger concern or be acknowledged as a problem. Although there have been numerous calls for rethinking the future of business schools and management education in recent years, gender appears to be a non-issue. Terms including "gender", "diversity", "female" and "women", for instance, are often absent in these publications (see, for instance, Datar, Garvin and Cullen, 2010; Muff et al., 2013; Colby et al., 2011). When diversity is noted, it is usually in the context of the student population, with the focus on cultural and international factors. If diversity of faculty is referenced, it, too, is mainly in the context of international differences or, in some cases, relative to promoting a mix of faculty in terms of experiences, skills, part-time/full-time status and researchers versus practitioners. An exception is provided in de Onzoño (2011) who highlights the importance of a diverse faculty in terms of gender, as well as other criteria.

The fact that gender is not seen as a salient issue is an issue in and of itself. This is especially true in the current context as business schools are being asked to challenge their basic assumptions and move beyond "business as usual" (Colby et al., 2011; Datar, Garvin and Cullen, 2010; Hardy and Everett, 2013; Herrington and Arnold, 2013; Muff et al., 2013). New approaches and people with different backgrounds and perspectives can help trigger needed restructuring of business schools. Women and other individuals long absent, and still scarce, in leadership positions in business schools can be a source of new blood and innovative ideas.

Following up on this point, some faculty and students believe that the "glass ceiling" has been shattered even though trends as reported in this chapter show otherwise. This misperception is concerning as many business school faculty members and students remain unaware of gender bias in the workplace and in management education. In fact, recent studies show that students frequently deny the existence of a glass ceiling, even when it is brought to their attention (Kelan and Jones, 2010; Sipe, Johnson and Fisher, 2009). Researchers have theorized that this may be due to a lack of salience of the barriers (Eisner and Harvey, 2009; Pillis et al., 2008; Tai and Sims, 2005) and poor expectations created in the classroom (Carr et al., 2000, 2003; Kelan and Jones, 2010; Shapiro, Ingols and Blake-Beard, 2011; Van Den Brink and Stobbe, 2009).

Calls for business schools to tackle issues of gender equality over the past decades have gone unanswered (Bilimoria, 1999; Bisoux, 2002; Kilgour, 2012). It would appear that management education has had little impact on altering the gender bias prevalent in society in general and in corporate management and leadership in particular. These trends continue to reinforce and beg the questions: How can management education and business schools, in particular, best serve the needs of women seeking or holding corporate management and leadership positions? And, what can be done to better integrate gender equality into business schools?

2.7 Recommendations for change

Business schools should be leading the way in demonstrating how to create and foster organizations that not only accept gender diversity, but that welcome and support it. In doing so, business schools need to look hard and fast at their own organizations and implement policies and procedures that make themselves role models for gender equality. The following recommendations provide examples of steps business schools can take to become more actively engaged in integrating gender issues into their organizations and into management education. These actions are not only good for women, but will create an inclusive environment in which male students, faculty and adminis-trators, too, will be more sensitized to issues of gender in management education and in the workplace. The chapter concludes with recommendations for future research on these issues.

2.7.1 Acknowledge the elephant in the room

This chapter demonstrates that women remain significantly under-represented in busi-ness schools across a range of faculty and administrative positions, MBA programs and doctoral programs in several key business disciplines. Further, in US business schools, the number of women earning doctorate degrees has fallen over the last five years, with more recent declines at the bachelor's and master's degree levels. Yet few people are aware of these patterns including many who may be directly impacted by them. If gen-der issues continue to be ignored in management education or gender bias is allowed to exist, then business schools run the risk of simply colluding with the *status quo* and repeating outdated management theory and practice (Bilimoria, 1999; Kilgour, 2012; Mavin and Bryans, 1999; McKeen, Bujaki and Burke, 2000). Business schools need to acknowledge these gender issues as the "elephant in the room", that is, an obvious situ-ation that is being ignored to avoid embarrassment, controversy or debate. Business schools should monitor these data at their own institutions and discuss the results with faculty and administrators, noting in particular, where students—male and female—lack female professors, administrators and role models. Courses and activities should be reviewed to determine the presence, or lack thereof, of women in textbooks, case studies, speaker programs and the like. Deans and department chairs should be held accountable for addressing gender equality on an ongoing basis, and as part of their annual performance reviews.

Business schools can help bring gender issues into the spotlight by integrating and highlighting their importance in the curricula and in research (Kelan and Jones, 2010; Mavin and Bryans, 1999; Miller and Sisk, 2012; Sipe, Johnson and Fisher, 2009). Miller and Sisk (2012) argue, for instance, that students, male and female, need to be made aware of the impact that gender bias has on dimensions such as self-confidence, job satisfaction and career commitment as this can assist students in learning how to avoid missed opportunities for advancement.

2.7.2 Grow and nurture the pipeline for full-time women faculty

Business schools need to hire more full-time women faculty to help create a critical mass. These women, who often have less history and fewer contacts in business schools than their male counterparts, should be offered guidance throughout their academic careers on, for instance, how best to spend pre-tenure time, acquire external funding for research and differentiate between types of institutional service in terms of their abil-ity to provide experiences and insights beneficial to advancement. While on the tenure track, women would benefit from mentoring and support, and from clear expectations and guidelines for promotion and tenure. Moreover, these efforts should not stop on the granting of tenure, as research shows that female associate professors take considerably longer than their male counterparts to attain the rank of full professor (Geisler, Kaminski and Berkley, 2007; MLA, 2009). Being a full professor is (or should be) critical in being considered for department chair and/or associate dean positions, noted above as key stepping stones into the dean's office.

Business schools should work with male and female department chairs and deans to ensure they understand their obligations and responsibilities regarding gender equality, as well as best practices for hiring, promoting, tenuring and supporting women faculty. Departments should, for example, interview women who have turned down the school's offer to join the faculty and women faculty who have voluntarily left the institution, and discuss with faculty and administrators the reasons and implications for organizational change.

2.7.3 Encourage and appoint more female academic leaders

The current proportions of senior women faculty and administrators are simply too far behind what is needed to move the needle in the gender equality transformation of management education, and ultimately the practice of management.

Business schools should educate women faculty on the benefits and rewards of academic leadership, such as department chair and dean, and encourage them to apply and accept nominations for these positions. As noted above, many women who became an interim dean at the request of the administration found that they enjoyed the job and its responsibilities, and subsequently applied for the position on a more permanent basis. Women faculty should hear the stories of these women as well as those of other women who serve, or have served, as a business school dean. Female faculty also should be provided mentors as well as professional development opportunities, in areas such as fund-raising, negotiating and social networking skills (McTiernan and Flynn, 2011).

In addition, attention and action is needed regarding the composition and functioning of search committees for dean positions. Individuals with known track records of conscious or unconscious bias against women should not be allowed to serve on search committees (McTiernan and Flynn, 2011), nor should they be permitted to serve as department chairs. These search committees also should be required to insist on a diverse pool of dean's candidates, whether or not an executive search firm is involved.

2.7.4 Recruit more female business students

Business schools should recruit more female students, particularly in MBA programs and in doctoral programs in which women remain scarce. The Graduate Management Admission Council (GMAC) has demonstrated that additional outreach to women for MBA programs has been less than successful to date—54% of the full-time MBA programs surveyed in 2010 reported special recruitment efforts to increase the proportion of women among applicants (Byrne, 2011a)—so other strategies need to be tried.

At least in the United States, greater attention needs to focus on the challenges that face women students in business schools, for example, lack of visibility afforded to women in the B&M curriculum, dearth of female role models in senior positions, questionable value of "feminine" skills and minimal presence in certain educational disciplines. Recent studies suggest that women may perceive the field of business as blocking (or at least not accelerating) their career development and quality of life because of structural issues such as constrained access to important networks, coaches and sponsors, and organizational issues including unconscious biases in evaluation and inflexibility in work–life integration arrangements (Barsh and Yee, 2011; Carter and Silva, 2010; Rezvani and Taylor, 2010).

Perhaps one of the reasons why women students are wary of US business programs, especially the MBA, stems from a faulty but increasingly widespread view of gender held by business school students. Kelan and Jones (2010) found that the mind-set that MBA students exhibit towards gender has shifted over the last decade. In particular, female and male MBA students increasingly made two assumptions: (1) gender inequality should be accepted because that is the way the world is and (2) gender does not matter (Kelan and Jones, 2010).

At the undergraduate level, female students need to see and hear successful women in business fields, especially in disciplines such as finance and economics, where they lack female role models in their programs. Business schools should work with their female alumnae to get them more actively involved on campus in activities such as class speakers, judges of academic competition, and lunch or dinner hosts for groups of students. Internships and course projects that bring female students into contact with successful women in business will also help. Women making educational choices need to see the value in choosing business over other options. Male students, too, will benefit from interactions with accomplished women in business.

One of the best ways to attract more female business students, of course, is to offer education that is second to none in terms of preparing them for challenging, rewarding, meaningful and well-compensated management and leadership positions. This includes attention to content of their courses and programs, but also pertains to the overall environment and culture of the business school.

2.7.5 Create and foster an inclusive educational environment in which all female and male students, faculty and administrators can thrive

Many of the critics of business schools calling for change are asking these institutions to re-examine their past assumptions, priorities, traditions and practices. Structural transformation within business schools is long overdue. Moving away from the way things were done in the past can help business schools in integrating gender equality as well as addressing other issues that impact their competitive advantage in an increasingly global marketplace. Business schools can and should be role models in creating an environment that is empowering to both men and women to challenge societal norms and in providing examples of best practices and proactive transformational leadership to the employer community. Regarding curricular content, women need to be better integrated within the broad spectrum of B&M coursework, particularly through case studies featuring women executives, use of textbooks and other publications written by women and the portrayal of women as positive examples and role models in courses across the curriculum. Additionally specialized courses on women in management and diversity in organizations should be offered at all degree levels (see e.g. Chapter 19 by Bilimoria, Chapter 10 by Adams, and Chapter 22 by Bevelander and Page in this volume). Resources are now available to help faculty integrate gender into their courses and their research. In particular, business school faculty and deans should take advantage of the Global Repository on gender issues launched in June 2012 by the PRME Working Group on Gender Equality. The Repository is available at www.prmegenderequality workinggroup.unprme.wikispaces.net/Resource+Repository

Developed by a dozen business school faculty from across the globe, this Repository encompasses 15 fields in which business students take courses.[3] Materials identified include case studies, syllabi, textbooks, research findings and other resources to help integrate gender issues into management education.

Further, business school faculty members (both male and female) across all departments should be coached to ensure gender equality in grading and student honours (e.g. Kantor, 2013) and to alert them to various pedagogical issues pertaining to women's experiences, ways of interaction and developmental needs. These should include, for instance, attention to the faculty member's in-class statements and actions, feedback to students, meetings outside the classroom and choices regarding course content and project work. B&M programs at all levels should pay specific attention to women's career issues (such as networking, mentoring, sponsorship, school-to-work transitioning and work/life balance) as well as access of students to women CEOs, executives and managers, and alumnae. Finally, business schools should implement improved support systems for women students, including that for women's student groups and enhanced student–faculty interaction.

Institutional changes are needed beyond those targeted for women faculty and administrators noted above. These include enhanced support for gender-related faculty research and specialized training for recruitment, placement and other administrative staff in business schools to understand and promote women student's career issues. Following the example of institutional transformation in higher education set by the National Science Foundation's ADVANCE initiative to facilitate the recruitment, advancement, development, retention and leadership of women faculty in science and engineering disciplines (see Bilimoria and Liang, 2012), business schools should undertake purposeful efforts to create a gender-positive culture. Such efforts can include the creation and enforcement of policies on sexual harassment and sex-based discrimination, annual monitoring of the allocation of resources, opportunities and rewards (including teaching load, service assignments and salary) between female and male faculty members, faculty training on unconscious gender bias especially for search

---

3 Accounting; Corporate Governance; Corporate Social Responsibility; Economics; Entrepreneurship; Finance; History and Anthropology of Gender, Business and Finance; Information Technology; Law; Leadership; Management; Marketing; Negotiation; Non-Profit Management; and Operations Management.

committees and promotion and tenure committees, leadership development of department chairs to equip them to better challenge stereotypes and holding deans and senior administrators accountable for gender diversity outcomes.

More generally, business schools should take advantage of the valuable resources available across the globe on ways to improve gender equality in higher education. These include, for example, the European Commission on Women and Gender in Research Programs; the Athena Swan Program in the UK; the Austrian Science Fund Gender Mainstreaming Program; the German Research Foundation's Standards on Gender Equality; the Netherlands Organization for Scientific Research Initiatives; the Swedish and Norwegian Innovation and Gender Projects; and the Aspen Institute's Center for Business Education in the United States. Descriptions of these and related programs are available in Gendered Innovations at Stanford University.[4]

2.8 Recommendations for future research

This chapter has addressed several topics where additional research could help in understanding and overcoming the barriers and challenges to eliminating gender gaps and inequalities in management education. These include:

- What are the trends and status of women faculty, including academic department chairs, in business schools outside the United States?

- What are the reasons behind the decline in MBA degrees being awarded in the United States and globally?

- Why are the numbers of women undergraduate business students on the decline in the United States, and why are they increasing elsewhere?

- Why are women gaining larger shares, at times now the majority, of GMAT entrance test takers, in Asia and Europe?

- What are the expectations of international and US female test takers regarding their careers in management education and ultimately management?

- Within management education, what can be learned from the experience of specialized master's degree programs that are so often neglected by researchers and the media but have consistently higher proportions of women than mainstream MBA programs?

- What can business schools learn from programs in Law and Medicine that have demonstrated near or actual gender parity in graduates by gender?

- What lies behind the success of female faculty in rising up through the professorial ranks in the academic discipline of Business Law?

4 www.genderedinnovations.stanford.edu/institutions/solutions.html

- What insights can be derived about women's leadership in management education from the success stories and challenges of women deans and department chairs?

- What examples and best practices can be shared on steps towards institutional transformation of business schools with regard to gender issues, such as the recent gender equity experiment conducted at HBS (Kantor, 2013)?

- How do female undergraduate business students view the value of obtaining an MBA and on what is this based?

- Under what conditions, including financial support, might undergraduate female business students consider pursuing careers as business faculty, especially in areas where women are quite scarce?

In conclusion, research on MBA graduates from 1981 to 1995 revealed that both men and women cited a lack of female role models in business schools; most female graduates noted that they lacked adequate opportunity to work with women professors; and the majority of female MBA graduates indicated that they could not relate to the individuals in the case studies in their courses (Catalyst, 2002). If that study were done today, would the results be any different? We think not.

Given demographic shifts; greater globalization; advances in technology and pedagogy; and projected disruptions in educational models, we submit that management education needs to modify its direction and approach to gender equality (the "elephant in the room"), and do so without further delay. We need to transform our management education institutions to generate a more positive gender climate and to attract and educate students who are capable of operating effectively in diverse workplaces where men and women share the reins of power. This is necessary if we are to ultimately achieve one of management education's core missions—engendering positive change in the practice of management and leadership.

Acknowledgements

Much of the data in this chapter are from the AACSB International's *Annual Salary Surveys*. The authors also thank AACSB for providing data on degrees conferred based on its annual Business School Questionnaire. The AACSB data used in the chapter include accredited and non-accredited business schools.

References

Adler, P., 2002. Corporate scandals: it's time for reflection in business schools. Academy of Management Executive 16(3), 148–149.

Alliance for Board Diversity, 2010. Missing Pieces: Women and Minorities on Fortune 500 Boards: 2010 Alliance for Board Diversity Census. Alliance for Board Diversity.

Alsop, R., January 9, 2007. MBA track–PhD shortage: business schools seek professors. The Wall Street Journal, B5.

ABA (American Bar Association), February 2013. A current glance at women in the law. Downloaded from: www.americanbar.org/content/dam/aba/marketing/women/current_glance_statistics_feb2013.authcheckdam.pdf

AAMC (Association of American Medical Colleges), 2012. Table 1—medical students, selected years, 1965–2012. Downloaded from: https://www.aamc.org/download/305282/data/2012_table1.pdf

AACSB (Association to Advance Collegiate Schools of Business) International, 2002. Management Education at Risk, Tampa, FL. www.aacsb.edu/publications/metf/metfreportfinal-august02.pdf

AACSB (Association to Advance Collegiate Schools of Business), 2011. Globalization of Management Education.

AACSB (Association to Advance Collegiate Schools of Business), 2012. Business School Data Trends and 2012 List of Accredited Schools.

AACSB (Association to Advance Collegiate Schools of Business), 2013. Annual Salary Survey.

Ball, J.A., 2012. The gender gap in undergraduate business programs in the United States. Journal of Education for Business 87(5), 260–265.

Barker, R., 2010. No, management is not a profession. Harvard Business Review 88(7/8), 52–60.

Barber, B.M., Palmer, D.A., 2009. Women faculty in US business schools, SSRN 1490084. www.researchgate.net/publication/228298299

Barsh, J., Yee, L., 2011. Unlocking the full potential of women in the US economy. Downloaded from: www.mckinsey.com/client_service/organization/latest_thinking/unlocking_the_full_potential

Bass, B.M., Avolio, B.J., 1994. Shatter the glass ceiling: women may make better managers. Human Resource Management 33, 549–560.

Bennis, W.G., O'Toole, J., 2005. How business schools lost their way. Harvard Business Review, 96–104.

Bevelander, D., Page, M.J., 2009. Ms. Trust: gender networks and trust: implications for management and education. Academy of Management Learning and Education 10(4), 623–642.

Bilimoria, D., 1999. Upgrading management education's service to women. Journal of Management Education 23(2), 118–122.

Bilimoria, D., Liang, X.F., 2012. Gender Equity in Science and Education: Advancing Change in Higher Education. Routledge, New York.

Bilimoria, D., Liang, X.F., Carter, S., Turell, J., 2012. Gender differences in the academic work experiences of faculty at early, middle and late career stages. In: Vinnicombe, S., Burke, R.J., Blake Beard, S., Moore, L.L. (Eds.), Handbook of Research on Promoting Women's Careers. Edward Elgar Publishers, Northampton, MA, pp. 304–325.

Bisoux, T., 2002. Focus: Women in Management Education. BizEd, 22–26.

Bisoux, T., Broadbridge, A., Simpson, R., 2011. 25 years on: reflecting on the past and looking to the future in gender and management research. British Journal of Management 22, 470–483.

Burnsed, B., August 8, 2011. How higher education affects lifetime salary. US News & World Report. Retrieved from: www.chicagotribune.com/features/tribu/ct-tribu-salary-and-education-story,0,7530307.story

Byrne, J.A., 2011a. More women getting MBAs but . . . . Downloaded from: www.poetsandquants.com/2011/03/02/women-the-mba

Byrne, J.A., 2011b. Why more women go to law or med schools. Downloaded from: www.poetsandquants.com/2011/05/07/why-more-women-become-lawyers-doctors

Byrne, J.A., 2014. Harvard Business School Dean Nitin Nohria publicly apologized for the school's treatment of female students and professors, and vowed to make changes at the institution, CNN Money. www.management.fortune.cnn.com/2014/01/29/harvard-business-dean-apologizes

Carr, P.L., Ash, A.S., Friedman, R.H., Szalacha, L., Barnett, R.C., Palepu, A., 2000. Faculty perceptions of gender discrimination and sexual harassment in academic medicine. Annals of Internal Medicine 132, 889–896.

Carr, P.L., Szalacha, L., Barnett, R.C., Caswell, C., Inui, T., 2003. A 'ton of feathers': gender discrimination in academic medical careers and how to manage it. Journal of Women's Health 12, 1009–1018.

Carter, N.M., Silva, C., 2010. Pipeline's Broken Promise. Catalyst, Inc., New York.

Carter, S.D., 2010. Differences in career paths of female and male faculty in the US eNewsline-AACSB, 1–3.

Catalyst, 2002. Women and the MBA: Gateway to Opportunity. New York.

Catalyst, 2013. Women in US Management and Labor Force. Downloaded from: www.catalyst.org/knowledge/women-us-management-and-labor-force

Cheit, E.F., 1985. Business schools and their critics. California Management Review 27(3), 43–62.

Chen, Y., Zhao, Q., 2013. Gender differences in business faculty's research motivation. Journal of Education for Business 88(6), 314–324.

Cheng, J.L., Birkinshaw, J., Lessard, D.R., Thomas, D.C., 2014. Advancing interdisciplinary research: insights from the JIBS special issue. Journal of International Business Studies 45(6), 1262–1282.

Clark, C.D., Hill, J.M., 2010. Reconciling the tension between the tenure and biological clocks to increase the recruitment and retention of women in academia. In: Forum on Public Policy on line, vol. 2, pp. 1–8.

Colby, A., Ehrlich, T., Sullivan, W.M., Dolle, J.R., 2011. Rethinking Undergraduate Business Education: Liberal Learning for the Profession. Jossey-Bass, San Francisco, CA.

Collinson, D.L., Hearn, J., 1994. Naming men as men: implications for work, organization and management. Gender, Work & Organization 1, 2–20.

Committee on Maximizing the Potential of Women in Academic Science and Engineering, 2007. Beyond Bias and Barriers: Fulfilling the Potential of Women in Academic Science, 109. National Academies Press, Washington, DC.

Cornuel, E., Hommel, U., 2012. Business schools as a positive force for fostering societal change. Business and Professional Ethics Journal 31(2), 289–312.

Crainer, S., Dearlove, D., 1999. Gravy Training: Inside the Business of Business Schools. Jossey-Bass, San Francisco, CA.

Crane, F., 2004. The teaching of ethics: an imperative at business schools. Journal of Education for Business 79(3), 149–151.

Datar, S.M., Garvin, D.A., Cullen, P.G., 2010. Rethinking the MBA: Business Education at a Crossroads. Harvard Business Press, Boston, MA.

Davis, S., Botkin, J., 1994. The Monster under the Bed: How Business is Mastering the Opportunity of Knowledge for Profit. Simon & Schuster, New York.

Draznin, J., 2004. The "mommy" tenure track. Academic Medicine 79, 289–291.

Dunning, J.H., 1989. The study of international business: a plea for a more interdisciplinary approach. Journal of International Business Studies, 411–436.

Eisner, S., Harvey, M., 2009. C-change? Generation Y and the glass ceiling. S.A.M. Advanced Management Journal 74(1), 13–28.

Friga, P.N., Bettis, R.A., Sullivan, R.S., 2003. Changes in graduate management education and new business school strategies for the 21st century. Academy of Management Learning & Education 2, 233–249.

Fusaro, P.C., Miller, R.M., 2002. What went wrong at Enron? Wiley, Hoboken, NJ.

Gaddis, P.O., 2000. Business schools: fighting the enemy within. Strategy and Business 21(4), 51–57.

Gailey, J.D., Carroll, V.S., 1993. Toward a collaborative model for interdisciplinary teaching: business and literature. Journal of Education for Business 69(1), 36–39.

Garrity, B.K.F., 2012. Where did they go? Market share trends of business school enrollment at public, not-for-profit, and for-profit institutions from 1996 to 2008. Journal of Education for Business 87, 309–315.

Geisler, C., Kaminski, D., Berkley, R.A., 2007. The 13+ club: an index for understanding, documenting, and resisting patterns of non-promotion to full professor. NWSA Journal 19(3), 145–162.

Ghoshal, S., 2005. Bad management theories are destroying good management practice. Academy of Management Learning & Education 4, 75–91.

Giacalone, R.A., Thompson, K.R., 2006. Business ethics and social responsibility education: shifting the worldview. Academy of Management Learning & Education 5, 266–277.

Goleman, D., Boyatzis, R.E., McKee, A., 2001. Primal leadership: The hidden driver of great performance. Harvard Business Review 79(11), 42–51.

Goodman, J., O'Brien, J., 2012. Teaching and learning using evidence-based principles. In: Rousseau, D.M. (Ed.), Handbook of Evidence-Based Management. Oxford, New York.

Gordon, R.A., Howell, J.E., 1959. Higher education for business. Columbia University Press, New York.

GMAC (Graduate Management Admission Council), 2010. GMAC Application Trends Survey, Admissions Management Data Supplement 2010. Downloaded from: www.gmac.com/mediaroomresources/pdfs/2010GMACApplicationTrendsSurveyReport.pdf

GMAC (Graduate Management Admission Council), 2013. Disrupt or Be Disrupted: A Blueprint for Change in Management Education. Jossey-Bass.

Hardy, G.M., Everett, D.L., 2013. Shaping the Future of Business Education. Palgrave Macmillan, New York.

Harris, S.E., 2006. Transitions: dilemmas of leadership. New Directions for Higher Education 134, 79–86.

Hayes, R.H., Abernathy, W.J., 1980. Managing our way to decline. Harvard Business Review 58(4), 67–77.

Haynes, K., Fearfull, A., 2008. Exploring ourselves: exploiting and resisting gendered identities of women academics in accounting and management. Pacific Accounting Review 20(2), 185–204.

Herrington, J.D., Arnold, D.R., 2013. Undergraduate business education: it's time to think outside the box. Journal of Education for Business 88, 202–209.

Hill, C.H., 2011. International Business: Competing in the Global Marketplace. Irwin, McGraw-Hill.

Hite, L.M., McDonald, K.S., 1995. Gender issues in management development: implications and research agenda. Journal of Management Development 14(4), 5–15.

Jordan, C.E., Clark, S.J., Vann, C.E., 2011. Do gender differences exist in the publication productivity of accounting faculty? Journal of Applied Business Research (JABR) 24(3).

Kantor, J., 2013. Harvard Business School Case Study: Gender Equity. Retrieved from: www.nytimes.com/2013/09/08/education/harvard-case-study-gender-equity.html?pagewanted=all&_r=1&

Kelan, E., Jones, R., 2010. Gender and the MBA. Academy of Management Learning and Education 9(1), 26–43.

Kerfoot, D., Knights, D., 1993. Management masculinity and manipulation: from paternalism to corporate strategy in financial services in Britain. Journal of Management Studies 30, 659–677.

Kerfoot, D., Knights, D., 1998. Managing masculinity in contemporary organizational life: a man(agerial) project. Organization 5, 7–26.

Kerfoot, D., Whitehead, S., 1998. 'Boys own' stuff: masculinity and the management of further education. The Sociological Review 46(3), 436–457.

Khurana, R., Nohria, N., 2008. It's time to make management a true profession. Harvard Business Review 86(10), 70–7.

Khurana, R., Spender, J.C., 2012. Herbert A. Simon on what ails business schools: more than 'a problem in organizational design'. Journal of Management Studies 49(3), 619–639.

Kilgour, M.A., 2012. The global compact and gender inequality: a work in progress. Business & Society 52(1), 105–134. www.bas.sagepub.com/content/52/1/105

Leavitt, H.J., 1989. Educating our MBAs: on teaching what we haven't taught. California Management Review 31(3), 38–50.

Luke, B., Brown, M.B., 2007. Elevated risks of pregnancy complications and adverse outcomes with increasing maternal age. Human Reproduction 22(5). www.humrep.oxfordjournals.org/content/vol22/issues/index.dtl

Mason, M.A., Goulden, M., 2004. Do babies matter (part II)? Closing the baby gap. Academe 90, 10–15.

Mavin, S., Bryans, P., 1999. Gender on the agenda in management education. Women in Management Review 14(3), 99–104.

Mavin, S., Bryans, P., Waring, T., 2004. Unlearning gender blindness: new directions in management education. Management Decision 42(3/4), 565–578.

McDonald, M.L., Westphal, J.D., 2013. Access denied: low mentoring of women and minority first-time directors and its negative effects on appointments to additional boards. Academy of Management Journal 56(4), 1169–1198.

McKeen, C.A., Bujaki, M.L., Burke, R.J., 2000. Preparing business graduates for the "real" world—the role of the university. Women in Management Review 15(7), 356–369.

McGrath, R.G., 2007. No longer a stepchild: how the management field can come into its own. Academy of Management Journal 50(6), 1365–1378.

McMillan, C., Chen, V.Z., 2012. Business schools in a changing global world: best practice vs. irrelevant knowledge? In: 1st EFMD Higher Education Research Conference, 14th and 15th February.

McTiernan, S., Flynn, P., 2011. 'Perfect Storm' on the horizon for women business school deans? Academy of Management Learning and Education 10(2), 323–339.

Metcalfe, B., Linstead, A., 2003. Gendering teamwork: re-writing the feminine. Gender, Work & Organization 10, 94–119.

Miller, G.L., Sisk, F.A., 2012. Business education and gender bias at the 'C-level.' Editorial Board 16.

Mintzberg, H., 1996. Musings on management. Harvard Business Review 74(4), 61–68.

Mintzberg, H., 2005. Managers not MBAs. Berret-Koehler, San Francisco, CA.

Mintzberg, H., Gosling, J.R., 2002. Reality programming for MBAs. Strategy and Business 26(1), 28–31.

MLA (Modern Language Association), April 2009. Standing Still: The Associate Professor Survey, web publication. www.mla.org/pdf/cswp_final042909.pdf

Morsing, M., Rovira, A.S. (Eds.), 2011. Business Schools and Their Contribution to Society. SAGE Publications Inc., Thousand Oaks, CA.

Muff, K., Dyllick, T., Drewell, M., North, J., Shrivastava, P., Haertle, J., 2013. Management Education for the World: A Vision for Business Schools Serving People and Planet. Edward Elgar, Northampton, MA.

NCES (National Center for Educational Statistics), 2013a. Fast Facts: Degrees Conferred by Sex and Race. www.nces.ed.gov/fastfacts/display.asp?id=72

NCES (National Center for Education Statistics), 2013b. Digest of Education Statistics. www.nces.ed.gov/programs/digest

NSF (National Science Foundation), [2000], 2013. Number of Doctorates Awarded in the US. www.nsf.gov/statistics/infbrief/nsf/2303

Navarro, P., 2008. The MBA core curricula of top-ranked US business schools: a study in failure? Academy of Management Learning & Education 7, 108–123.

Nohria, N., January–February 2012. What business schools can learn from the medical profession. Harvard Business Review. Retrieved from: www.hbr.org/2012/01/what-business-schools-can-learn-from-the-medical-profession/ar/1

de Onzoño, S.I., 2011. The Learning Curve: How Business Schools are Re-inventing Education. Palgrave Macmillan, New York.

Pedagogy of the privileged. The Economist, September 26, 2009, 82.

Peterson, C.A., Philpot, J., 2006. Women's roles on US fortune 500 boards: director expertise and committee memberships. Journal of Business Ethics 72, 177–196.

Pfeffer, J., Fong, C.T., 2002. The end of business schools? Less success than meets the eye. Academy of Management Learning & Education 1, 78–95.

Pfeffer, J., Fong, C.T., 2004. The business school "business". Some lessons from the US experience. Journal of Management Studies 41, 1501–1520.

Pillis, E., Kernochan, R., Meilich, O., Prosser, E., Whiting, V., 2008. Are managerial gender stereo-types universal? Cross Cultural Management: An International Journal 15(1), 94–102.

Podolny, J.M., 2009. The buck stops (and starts) at business school. Harvard Business Review 87(6), 62–67.

Philipsen, M.I., 2008. Challenges of the Faculty Career for Women: Success and Sacrifice. John Wiley & Sons.

Porter, L.W., McKibbin, L.E., 1988. Management Education and Development: Drift or Thrust into the 21st Century. McGraw-Hill, New York.

Quelch, J., 2005. A new agenda for business schools. The Chronicle of Higher Education 52(15), B9.

Quinn, K., 2010. Tenure clock extension policies: who uses them and to what effect? NASPA Journal about Women in Higher Education 3, 182–206.

Rafols, I., Leydesdorff, L., O'Hare, A., Nightingale, P., Stirling, A., 2012. How journal rankings can suppress interdisciplinary research: a comparison between innovation studies and business and management. Research Policy 41(7), 1262–1282.

Rezvani, S., Taylor, S., April 12, 2010. Why Business Schools are Failing Women. www.forbes.com

Rousseau, D.M., 2012. Designing a better business school: channeling Herbert Simon, addressing the critics, and developing actionable knowledge for professionalizing managers. Journal of Management Studies 49(3), 600–618.

Rubin, R.S., Dierdorff, E.C., 2009. How relevant is the MBA? Assessing the alignment of required curricula and required managerial competencies. Academy of Management Learning & Education 8, 208–224.

Rukstad, M., Collis, D., 2001. UNext: Business Education and e-Learning. Harvard Business School Case #9-701-014, Boston, MA.

Rutherford, M.A., Parks, L., Cavazos, D.E., White, C.D., 2012. Business ethics as a required course: investigating the factors impacting the decision to require ethics in the undergraduate business core curriculum. Academy of Management Learning & Education 11(2), 174–186.

Schneider, G.P., Sheikh, A., 2012. Addressing the shortage of accounting faculty: using non-tenure-track positions. Academy of Educational Leadership 16(1), 1.

Schoemaker, P.H., 2008. The future challenges of business: rethinking management education. California Management Review 50(3), 119–138.

Shapiro, M., Ingols, C., Blake-Beard, S., 2011. Using power to influence outcomes: does gender matter? Journal of Management Education 35(5), 713–748.

Siemensma, F., March 2004. Values and the MBA; The implications of gender. IIMB Management Review, 21–23.

Simpson, R., 2006. Masculinity and management education: feminizing the MBA. Academy of Management Learning & Education 5(2), 182–193.

Simpson, R., Ituma, A., 2009. Transformation and feminisation: the masculinity of the MBA and the "un-development" of men. Journal of Management Development 28(4), 301–316.

Sinclair, A., 1995. Sex and the MBA. Organization 2(2), 295–317.

Sipe, S., Johnson, C., Fisher, D., 2009. University students' perceptions of gender discrimination in the workplace: reality versus fiction. Journal of Education for Business 84(6), 339–349.

Smith, C.R., 1997. Gender issues in management education: a new teaching resource. Women in Management Review 12(3), 100–104.

Smith, C.R., 2000. Notes from the field: gender issues in the management curriculum: a survey of student experiences. Gender, Work & Organization 7(3), 158–167.

Starkey, K., Tempest, S., 2005. The future of the business school: knowledge challenges and opportunities. Human Relations 58(1), 61–82.

Stevens, G.E., 2000. The art of running a business school in the new millennium: a dean's perspective. S.A.M. Advanced Management Journal 65(3), 21–27.

Strizhakova, Y., Coulter, R.A., Price, L.L., 2012. The young adult cohort in emerging markets: assessing their global cultural identity in a global marketplace. International Journal of Research in Marketing 29(1), 43–54.

Tai, A., Sims, R., 2005. The perception of the glass ceiling in high technology companies. Journal of Leadership and Organizational Studies 12(1), 16–23.

Thomas, M., Thomas, H., 2012. Using new social media and Web 2.0 technologies in business school teaching and learning. Journal of Management Development 31(4), 358–367.

Trank, C.Q., Rynes, S.L., 2003. Who moved our cheese? Reclaiming professionalism in business education. Academy of Management Learning & Education 2(2), 189–205.

Van Den Brink, M., Stobbe, L., 2009. Doing gender in academic education: the paradox of visibility. Gender, Work & Organization 16(4), 451–470.

Wilson, D.C., Thomas, H., 2012. The legitimacy of the business of business schools: what's the future? Journal of Management Development 31(4), 368–376.

Wilson, R., 2004. Paid leave at public colleges vs. private ones. Chronicle of Higher Education 50. www.chronicle.com/weekly/v50/i31/31a01101.htm

Wittenberg-Cox, A., Maitland, A., 2008. Why Women Mean Business: Understanding the Emergence of Our Next Economic Revolution, vol. 44. John Wiley & Sons.

Wolfinger, N.H., Mason, M.A., Goulden, M., 2008. Problems in the pipeline: gender, marriage and fertility in the ivory tower. Journal of Higher Education 79, 388–405.

3

Sustainability as a lens to explore gender equality
A missed opportunity for responsible management

Kathryn Haynes
Newcastle University Business School, UK

Alan Murray
Winchester Business School, UK

Faced with the threat of climate change, the concept of sustainable development is of increasing significance to business and organizations, and hence to responsible management educators. Inherent in sustainability is the notion of equity and social justice, which encapsulates gender equality. This chapter examines the links between sustainable development and gender equality empirically through the experience of women; theoretically through the lens of feminism; and through the business case. To evaluate the extent of integration of sustainability and gender equality in management education, we perform a content analysis of Sharing Information on Progress reports (SIPs) of the UK reporting signatories of the Principles for Responsible Management Education (PRME). This finds a lack of depth of reporting of gender equality and diversity in values, policies, curriculum content and research, which, we argue, represents missed opportunities for management educators to address gender equality through the lens of sustainability in the interest of more egalitarian and sustainable business practice.

3.1 Concepts of sustainable development

The concept of sustainable development is widely acknowledged as deriving from the Report of the World Commission on Environment and Development, established in 1983 and chaired by Gro Harlem Brundtland at the behest of the Secretary General of the United Nations (UN) at the time, Javier Pérez de Cuéllar, and now generally known as the "Brundtland Commission". Its report, published in 1987, entitled "Our Common Future" (WCED, 1987) defined sustainable development as "development which meets the needs of the present without compromising the ability of future generations to meet their own needs" (p. 43). Sustainability is widely accepted to incorporate three pillars: the economic, the environmental and the social. Influenced also by Elkington's (1998) model for business of the triple bottom line—more directly known as people, planet, profit—the concept attempts to address integration of economic, ecological and human or social systems.

A brief examination of these three "pillars" of sustainability reveals some disturbing trends. First, there seems no end to the drive for economic growth around the world. The notion that we can sustain growth levels at something between 2% and 10% per year *ad infinitum* raises few alarm bells with policy-makers yet is patently unsustainable, when we consider the conversion rate of natural resources to finished goods that must be required to make this happen.

Second, and following on from this premise, the notion that the planet has a finite capacity to absorb or to process the results of human activity, which is the underlying theory of sustainable development, is a continuing area of focus for the UN. From the establishment of the UN Environment Programme (UNEP) in 1972, a number of initiatives and programs have attempted to monitor the effects of human activity on the resources base and general biodiversity of the planet. UNEP was also involved in coordinating a further investigation into the ability of the planet to support the continued, and growing, demands that are being placed on it, in the form of the "Millennium Ecosystem Assessment" (UNEP, 2005), which involved 1,360 experts from around the world appraising trends in the world's ecosystem as well as the scientific basis for action. Strong evidence that humankind is overreaching the ability of the planet to sustain its growing population can be found in the Millennium Eco-Assessment (UNEP, 2005), the Global Environmental Outlook Series (UNEP, 2012) and the Assessment Reports on Climate Science (IPCC, 2001, 2007, 2013). Succeeding reports by the UN-backed Intergovernmental Panel on Climate Change (IPCC) have increased in their level of certainty that global warming is a direct effect of anthropogenic climate change. Their 4th Assessment Report in February 2007 for the first time used the word "unequivocal" in linking human induced climate change to global warming giving a probability of 90% (IPCC, 2007). The 5th Report in 2013 increased this level to 95% (IPCC, 2013). Corroboration in academic research (Meadows, Randers and Meadows, 2004), and NGO studies (WWF, 2012), also suggests that stewardship of the planet's resources means succeeding generations cannot continue to behave as past generations have done.

Third, as well as environmental degradation, if we then consider the social aspects of sustainability there is significant cost and impact to human beings, in terms of the loss of biodiversity, species extinction, workplace exploitation, poverty, human rights abuses and, as we shall argue, the disproportionate burdens placed on women. As a result of all of these, we are falling well short of forging a sustainable world, with the accusation that much of the blame for the most serious issues lies at the feet of major global corporations (Gray, 2006; Gray, Dillard and Spence, 2009).

The definition of sustainable development in the Brundtland Report (WCED, 1987), though seemingly relatively straightforward—"meeting the needs of the present without compromising the ability of future generations to meet their own needs"—raises more complex issues for corporations and those who educate future corporate leaders. The concept embraces *social justice* by introducing the notion that development ought to aim at delivering some form of equity across and through the generations of people who presently, and who will in the future, populate our planet. As such it raises issues of *inter-generational equity*, between present and future generations, and *intra-generational equity*, between different peoples within the current generation. This intra-generational equity includes the developed and developing worlds, and different peoples within those worlds, based on race, religion, ethnicity and gender. A sense of equity and social justice is at the heart of this concept of sustainability, which, as we will argue below, also encompasses aspects of gender equality.

Broadly speaking, social justice is a concept designed to offer hope of equity to all, or as Rawls suggested in *A Theory of Justice* (Rawls, 1971), "the basic structure of society", where this basic structure is understood as being constituted by the major institutions that allocate rights, opportunities and resources (Barry, 2005). It is also used when highlighting injustices visited on the more vulnerable individuals within society, and thereafter to right these wrongs. Historically, those who have suffered injustices are in the opposite groups to those who wield power within society, and who make the rules. So, as in the West, if laws are generally made by a privileged elite, which is predominantly wealthy, elderly, male, white and religiously non-conformist, those who suffer injustice are often the poor, young, female and racially or religiously different. The UK Equality and Human Rights Commission defines social justice as:

> The concept where individuals and groups receive fair treatment and a just share of the benefits of society. This includes the distribution of wealth and income, and more important, equal basic rights, security, obligations, and opportunities. Social justice addresses oppression and the intergenerational transmission of poverty.[1]

However, as we go on to argue, this dimension of social justice from a gender perspective is often missing from sustainability debates and practices, both in business and organizations, and in management education. Yet there are strong links between sustainability and gender issues. This chapter first examines the links between sustainable development and gender equality empirically through the experience of women; theoretically through the lens of feminism; and also through the business case. We then evaluate the extent to which responsible management education addresses gender equality through

---

1 www.equalityhumanrights.com

the lens of sustainability, by carrying out an analysis of the extent of disclosure and interaction with gender issues within the reports of UK Schools, which are signatories to the Principles for Responsible Management Education (PRME) initiative. Our findings suggest a missed opportunity to use the lens of sustainability to address gender equality in these schools, which we argue would open up possibilities of achieving a broader, more egalitarian, responsible management education.

3.2 Empirical links between sustainable development and gender equality

There is strong evidence to demonstrate that unsustainable practices and the threats of climate change have a disproportionate effect on women and girls throughout the world. Although poverty affects the world's poor irrespective of gender, in many parts of the world, women and girls bear the brunt of challenges arising from economic, social and environmental development, through the feminization of poverty, disease and hunger; burden of unpaid work; adverse health and impacts from environmental degradation; vulnerability to conflicts and violence; lack of food security and land security; water and sanitization issues; lack of political representation; and lack of education (United Nations Department of Economic and Social Affairs, 2010). Progress in achieving gender equality in addressing the UN's Millennium Development Goals (MDGs) on hunger, education, political representation and health remains problematic, and these challenges disproportionately affect women (UN, 2012, 2014). For example, although the proportion of people with access to improved drinking water sources has improved from 76% in 1990 to 89% in 2011, there are significant variations across regions, and where water sources are not accessible, such as in the 25 Sub-Saharan African countries where 71% of households do not have water on premises, it is women and girls who bear the burden (literally) of collecting water (UN, 2014). Progress in access to basic sanitation has been slower and below the MDG targets, despite access to sanitation being important for women's and girls' safety, dignity and health (UN, 2014). Women and girls need more privacy and time than men when using toilets or latrines, and need safety to do so; they may have young children in their care and need multiple visits during menstruation (UN, 2014). Due to lack of access to sources of power such as electricity (let alone clean or environmentally responsible energy) many peoples of the world rely on unsustainable sources of energy from wood or fossil fuels. As a result, smoke and emissions from traditional cooking stoves is estimated to kill 2 million people per annum from lung cancer and respiratory disease, again affecting women and children more than men due to social and cultural factors where women do more domestic work and are usually the caretakers of children in the home (United Nations Department of Economic and Social Affairs, 2010; World Health Association, 2011).

Such problems suggest that issues of sustainability and gender (in)equality are inherently interrelated. In an unsustainable world, with over-depletion of natural resources, and emphasis on economic over social and environmental benefit, women are disproportionately affected.

3.3 Theoretical links between sustainable development and gender equality

Feminist theory provides conceptual links between gender equality and sustainable development, or more readily, we should consider various *feminisms* rather than a singular unified approach "as there may be many moral and political viewpoints, or different feminisms, in which a researcher can position herself" (Haynes, 2008: 544).

Ecofeminism emerged in the 1970s bringing together aspects of feminism and ecology. Ecofeminism sees a connection between exploitation and degradation of the natural world and subordination and oppression of women, drawing from the green movement a concern about the impact of human activity on the non-human world, and from feminism the view of humanity as gendered in ways that subordinate, exploit and oppress women (Mellor, 1997). The term refers to "a significant stream within the feminist movement, containing a range of theoretical positions which rest on the assumption that there are critical connections between the domination of nature and of women" (Braidotti et al., 1994: 161). This range of theoretical positions is broad. Affinity ecofeminism, for example, which is concerned with the affinity between women and nature, combines the celebration of women-centred values, such as nurturing and caring, with the celebration of women's bodies and spirit (Mellor, 1997). This approach to ecofeminism is often also related to spirituality and fixing women's identities as closer to nature. As a result, this form of feminism has been accused of essentialism, whereby certain traits or attributes are seen as defining or categorizing a social group. This categorization of women is regarded by more radical feminists as a reductionist stereotype that risks ignoring social and political influences on women's position:

> To argue that women as biologically sexed or socially gendered beings are connected with, or in some way represent, the natural world is seen as dangerous by many feminists. It undermines the struggle that they have waged against the way the identification of women with nature has been used to justify women's subordination (Mellor, 1997: 2).

More recently, ecofeminism has extended its focus to include a critique of globalization, considering the linkages between capitalist exploitation of the natural world, particularly in non-Western countries, and the global exploitation of women (Donovan, 2001). Radical or socialist ecofeminists, for example, find that gendered inequalities and ecological degradations represent distinct material or capitalist interests, which can be addressed by active political struggle against structures and institutions of society. This strand of ecofeminism identifies patriarchy as a key source of global environmental destruction through the division of power and labour between men and women, which becomes institutionalized through capitalist economic practices (Federici, 2009; Salleh, 2009).

Moreover, the contemporary feminist paradigm of transnationalist feminism addresses the critique of Western liberal feminism, that it simply assumes oppression and fails to understand the diversity of experience of women in the global south, by endorsing the means through which women can build coalitions of solidarity (Mohanty, 2003). Its greatest proponent, Chandra Talpade Mohanty, suggests that contemporary global "capitalism is seriously incompatible with feminist visions of social and economic justice" (Mohanty, 2003: 9). One might also add, given the three pillars of sustainability, environmental justice.

This brief review gives awareness of the role of feminist theory in understanding the political and social position of women in relation to global environmental challenges. Although feminism takes many forms and may not be a distinct unified movement due to global differences in material and political conditions, and differences between women themselves, it brings theoretical insight into the complexity of the relationship between gender and sustainability and between local and global processes that affect the outcome of the human–environment relationships.

3.4 The "business case" for addressing sustainability and gender

If feminist theory is not persuasive, one can use a "business case" argument for the need for businesses and organizations to address sustainability and gender issues. This is more likely to appeal to a corporate perspective. The business case outlines the benefits to an organization of taking a particular course of action, resulting often though not solely in enhanced measures of performance such as shareholder value or profitability, or drivers such as reputation or innovation.

To some degree the business case for sustainability resonates with that of corporate social responsibility (CSR) as it incorporates the influence of ethics and values on a company's actions; accountability measures; relations with internal and external stakeholders; and use and safeguarding of resources (including human and environmental) in relation to performance (Blowfield and Murray, 2014). In essence, it is different forms and degrees of responsible management. Although these notions are contestable and may be subject to corporate capture (O'Dwyer, 2003), there is some evidence that CSR practice influences corporate performance (McWilliams and Siegel, 2000; Nelling and Webb, 2009). The business case for sustainability goes further in requiring an understanding of the interconnected social and environmental systems that need to be considered when economic decisions are made. Although CSR initiatives may engage with the sustainability agenda, in many cases they do not go as far as this in terms of considering a business's relations with, and impact on, global society (Murray, Haynes and Hudson, 2010). The challenge to business arising from sustainable development involves several areas of risk: operational risk, due to the increased scarcity and cost of raw materials; risk of disruption, caused by natural hazards such as flooding; regulatory, due to new government policies and taxes; reputational risk, due to shifting consumer demand and media attention; and more risky access to capital, as markets adopt more rigorous investment and lending policies (Blowfield and Murray, 2014). Yet organizations such as the World Business Council for Sustainable Development[2] also stress that despite these challenges there are also opportunities for companies to open new markets, and develop new technologies and processes in the fight against climate change. Indeed, the Global Commission on the Economy and Climate suggests in its most recent report that economic growth and action on climate change can now be achieved together (Global Commission on the Economy and Climate, 2014).

The business case for companies to engage with gender equality issues is evident in both academic literature and organizational practice. In a recent comprehensive review of business case literature on equality and diversity (Department for Business Innovation and Skills, 2013), the Department for Business, Innovation and Skills in the United Kingdom found that the benefits can be distinguished between external business benefits that accrue to firms when they implement policies that aim at increasing equality in response to a changing external (including legislative) environment, and internal business benefits, which, irrespective of external drivers, can enhance productivity and other business outcomes. Here diversity relates to a number of categories including gender, race, age, sexuality and religion among others. External business benefits might include selecting from the widest talent pool, thus attracting more women or a diverse workforce; marketing gains from increased cultural insights; avoiding costs of integrating workers poorly; or avoiding costs of employment tribunals. In contrast, internal business benefits relate to increased creativity and problem-solving from exposure to a wider range of perspectives, and a more flexible approach to external environmental[3] changes. A report for the Chartered Institute of Personnel and Development suggests the main reason why diversity management[4] has been adopted is its potential to add value to business performance, with the business case driving interest beyond mere legal compliance and making the difference between the leading-edge players in the field of equality, diversity and inclusion (Özbilgin et al., 2008). McKinsey's series of reports,[5] *Women Matter*, have argued since their inception in 2007 that women at the executive level in organizations brings performance benefits. Further, evidence is mounting that increasing executive diversity and the numbers of women on boards brings performance benefits in terms of decision-making through improved governance (Rose, 2007;

2   www.wbcsd.org
3   Meaning organizational environment or context, rather than environment in terms of ecology or sustainability.
4   "Diversity management is based on the premise that everyone is a unique and complex mix of different personal characteristics. It is not based on the assumption that everyone is exactly the same and must therefore be treated in a uniform way, but it does recognise that people have things in common with each other and that these things create group identities" (Özbilgin et al., 2008).
5   www.mckinsey.com/features/women_matter

Terjesen, Sealy and Singh, 2009). Although there is still a long way to go in achieving equality, there is evidence that progress on gender equality is slowly being made at the corporate executive level (Vinnicombe, Doldor and Turner, 2014).

3.5 Integrating the business case for sustainability and gender equality

These two businesses cases, for sustainability and gender equality, rarely interact. Where they are addressed in corporations they often stand in tension due to the complexity of all the issues at play in sustainable development. An example of this is the tensions inherent at Anglo-American, which aims to be the employer of choice and encourages women into mining,[6] while its core business of fossil fuel mining remains ultimately unsustainable. Moreover, there is little academic research on the interaction of these two distinct disciplinary areas outside the development, political economy, feminist or ecology literature, and certainly little on the interaction of the two business cases within the business and management literature. In rare instances, where gender equality and sustainability are addressed together in the accounting literature, this tends to consider the reporting angle and focus on workplace issues in Westernized economies (Grosser and Moon, 2005, 2008). Sustainability reporting as a performance measurement mechanism may assist in communicating an organization's commitment to gender equality, particularly on the numbers of women in management, with the potential for this information to positively influence public policy on gender (Miles, 2011). While welcome, however, the emphasis tends to focus on professional women on boards, rather than the wider position of women stakeholders. Much of the reporting literature uses the Global Reporting Initiative (GRI), recommended by the UN Global Compact (GC), to evaluate the mainstreaming of sustainability reporting, but, despite the inclusion of gender-related indicators in the GRI framework, companies tend not to disaggregate data on gender (Grosser and Moon, 2008). Moreover, while it considers the supply chain and the community, the GRI's emphasis on gender in organizational governance, workplace, investors and consumers (GRI and IFA, 2009) may fail to recognize the wider effects on stakeholders further removed from the company itself, such as women and girls in communities affected by the actions of companies in their economic and social contexts. This absence of women's rights more generally has been noted in much of the CSR literature (Thompson, 2008). Kilgour's (2013) analysis of the UN Global Compact finds that despite gender equality being part of its remit, women's human rights received little attention in the GC learning network in its first decade. This is attributed to a limited focus on women as formal sector workers, a lack of women's voices in the learning network and the framing of gender equality in terms of the business case. Despite evidence of the disproportionate impact of unsustainable development on women and girls

6 www.angloamerican.com/careers/working/employer-of-choice/women-in-mining.aspx

noted earlier in this chapter, in the business and management context women are barely considered outside their identification as worker. This omission marginalizes those who are relatively powerless within and without their formal working environment, or who are engaging in unpaid labour.

The remainder of the chapter evaluates the extent to which responsible management education addresses gender equality through a sustainability lens, and finally considers the possibility for applying this lens to achieve a broader, more egalitarian, responsible management education.

3.6 The extent of disclosure on gender equality by UK PRME signatories

The mission of the PRME initiative is to inspire and champion responsible management education, research and thought leadership globally, through adherence to Six Principles, which provide an engagement structure for academic institutions to advance social responsibility through incorporating universal values into curricula and research[7] (see other chapters, this volume).

The Six Principles have been reproduced on page xii of this volume.

PRME signatory schools report on their progress in implementing the Six Principles on a biannual basis, in a Sharing Information on Progress (SIP) report. The implementation of responsible management education remains a challenge, requiring organizational adaptation, partnerships among stakeholders and individuals as agents and actors of institutional change in business schools (Fukukawa et al., 2013). This chapter extends Burchell, Murray and Kennedy's (2014) study of responsible management education in UK Business Schools and the role of PRME in driving change. While we accept that, following Burchell, Murray and Kennedy (2014), PRME affiliation may reflect a preexisting internal and external engagement with the responsible management agenda, rather than acting as a driver for change *per se*, we assume that PRME signatories may be expected to have some interest in and future commitment to this agenda, which they are reporting in their SIPs. Hence the SIPs can, to some degree, be indicative of the extent and focus of interest in responsible management and education for sustainability.

We sought to extend scrutiny of the degree to which gender equality was being addressed in responsible management education, and specifically in relation to sustainability. To do this we performed a content analysis on the SIPs of UK schools that are currently signed up to PRME and made their biennial report. All the SIPs are freely available on the PRME website[8] and are produced on a biannual basis. Content analysis is a widely used method to ascertain the extent of disclosure of various terms in documents, reports and financial statements (Unerman, 2000).

---

7 www.unprme.org/about-prme/index.php
8 www.unprme.org/sharing-information-on-progress/index.php?sort=country&dir=asc&start=480

As summarized in Table 3.1, there were 47 PRME signatory schools in the United Kingdom at the time of this research: 30 were classed as "communicating participants" by providing a SIP; 8 as "non-communicating participants" due to non-production or being late with their SIPs; and 9 as new signatories yet to report.[9]

We included the 30 "communicating participants" or reporting schools in our sample, as they represent active schools, but excluded those who may have reported in the past and since failed to do, as this could be indicative of their waning commitment to the area. It is, however, possible that non-reporting schools may have relevant areas of work, which this research has not identified. However, given that PRME signatory schools have by definition an interest in responsible management education, which incorporates CSR, sustainability and ethics, the most recent SIPs should provide a sample of activities on which the interaction of sustainability and gender equality could be evaluated. It is also possible that non-PRME signatories or the new not yet reporting UK Schools may be integrating gender equality and sustainability in their management programs, and it is a limitation of this research that we are not able to sample these. The content analysis, however, provides a snapshot of the state of engagement and interaction with sustainability and gender issues on which we are able to develop further our analysis. The disclosures represent a proxy for interest and action in this area.

The unit of content analysis can be a word, sentence or other unit; in our study the unit used was a single word. We used the terms "gender", "diversity", "equality" and "women" to search the content of the SIP reports, and then counted the number of times each was referred to using subcategories depending on whether the term related to the curriculum, student or staff body, policy or practice, research or values. This range of terms was selected because they incorporate an element of interchangeability in their relation to the position of women, although diversity also encompasses a broader range of attributes including ethnicity, race, sexuality and age, as well as gender. We used the roots of words such as "diver" and "equ" so that we picked up different permutations of language (diverse/diversity; equality/inequality/equity). We excluded from our results phrases and terms such as "equally proud" (Leicester); or "equally", meaning at the same time (Chester); or "equally important" (Cranfield). Further, we excluded any use of the terms "diverse" or "diversity" meaning a variety or range (e.g. "diversity of knowledge and skills" and also "diverse range of professions" [Salford]). We also ruled out the term "biodiversity" unless it was used in relation to other forms of diversity. We did not search for terms relating to sustainability or responsibility, as these are explicit in the values of the Six Principles of PRME, and we would expect every signatory to engage with these concepts in some way. We were more interested in whether the understanding of sustainability incorporated aspects of gender equality as identified in the earlier parts of this chapter.

The results of the content analysis are summarized in Table 3.2, which illustrates the number of pages in each of the SIPs of the 30 communicating participant schools and the extent of disclosure across the four main terms and their related areas.

9 Note that both the authors are employed by PRME signatory schools. For the purposes of the chapter, one (Newcastle University Business School) is classed as a communicating participant and the other (Winchester Business School) is classed as a non-communicating participant.

Table 3.1 **UK PRME signatory schools**

Source: www.unprme.org/participants/index.php?sort=country&dir=desc&start=90 as on 15 October 2014.

No.	Signatory school	Status[a]	Parent organization	Type	SIP date
1	Bradford University School of Management	Rep	University of Bradford	Business School	2014
2	Cranfield School of Management	Rep		Business School	2014[b]
3	Durham Business School	Rep	Durham University	University	2014
4	Leeds University Business School	Rep	University of Leeds	Business School	2014
5	London South Bank University	Rep		University	2014
6	Middlesex University Business School	Rep	Middlesex University	Business School	2014
7	Newcastle University Business School	Rep	Newcastle University	University	2014
8	Oxford Brookes Business School	Rep	Oxford Brookes University	Business School	2014
9	School of Management, Royal Holloway	Rep	University of London	Business School	2014
10	Sheffield University Management School	Rep	University of Sheffield	Business School	2014
11	University of Exeter Business School	Rep	University of Exeter	Business School	2014
12	Aberdeen Business School	Rep	Robert Gordon University	Business School	2013
13	Association of Business Schools (ABS)	Rep		Membership association of UK Business Schools	2013[c]
14	Chester Business School	Rep	University of Chester	Business School	2013
15	Coventry Business School	Rep	Coventry University	Business School	2013
16	Essex Business School	Rep	University of Essex	Business School	2013
17	Glasgow Caledonian University	Rep		University	2013

No.	Signatory school	Status[a]	Parent organization	Type	SIP date
18	Portsmouth Business School	Rep	University of Portsmouth	Business School	2013
19	Strathclyde Business School	Rep	University of Strathclyde	University	2013
20	The Open University Business School	Rep	The Open University	Business School	2013
21	University of Hertfordshire Business School	Rep	University of Hertfordshire	Business School	2013
22	University of Huddersfield Business School	Rep	University of Huddersfield	University	2013
23	University of Leicester, School of Management	Rep	University of Leicester	Business School	2013
24	University of Salford	Rep		University	2013
25	University of St Andrews School of Management	Rep	University of St Andrew	Business School	2013
26	Ashridge Business School	Rep		Business School	2012
27	Aston Business School	Rep	Aston University	Business School	2012
28	Hull University Business School	Rep	University of Hull	Business School	2012
29	Manchester Metropolitan University Business School	Rep	Manchester Metropolitan University	Business School	2012
30	The Business School, Bournemouth University	Rep	Bournemouth University	Business School	2012
31	University of Roehampton Business School	L	University of Roehampton	Business School	–
32	Bristol Business School, Faculty of Business and Law	L	University of the West of England	Business School	2012
33	Nottingham University Business School	L		Business School	2012

No.	Signatory school	Status[a]	Parent organization	Type	SIP date
34	University of Lincoln	L		Business School	2012
35	University of Southampton	L		University	2012
36	Warwick Business School	L	University of Warwick	Business School	2012
37	Faculty of Management and Law	L	University of Surrey	Business School	2011
38	Winchester Business School	L	The University of Winchester	Business School	2011
39	Cass Business School	New	City University London	Business School	–
40	Faculty of Business and Management, University of Wales Trinity Saint David	New	University of Wales Trinity Saint David	Business School	–
41	Henley Business School	New	University of Reading	Business School	–
42	London Metropolitan Business School	New	London Metropolitan University	University	–
43	Plymouth University	New		University	–
44	Sheffield Business School	New	Sheffield Hallam University	Business School	–
45	The University of Liverpool Management School	New		Business School	–
46	University of Northampton Business School	New	University of Northampton	University	–
47	York St John Business School	New	York St John University	Business School	–

a   Key: Rep = reporting signatory; L = reporting signatory with overdue report; New = newly signed signatory not yet due to report.

b   Listed as reporting in 2014 but the report shown was 2012 so this was used in sample. Clarified with Cranfield that the 2012 report is the latest one.

c   Listed as reporting in 2013 but report is not on website so the 2011 report was used in sample. Clarified with ABS that the 2001 report is the only one.

Table 3.2 **Content analysis of UK PRME reporting schools**

No.	Institution	SIP date	Pages	Gender curric	Gender policy and practice	Gender research	Diversity curric
1	Bradford University School of Management	2014	4	0	0	0	1
2	Cranfield School of Management	2014	19	0	1	0	2
3	Durham Business School	2014	9	0	0	1	0
4	Leeds University Business School	2014	3	0	1	0	0
5	London South Bank University	2014	7	0	0	0	0
6	Middlesex University Business School	2014	16	0	0	0	0
7	Newcastle University Business School	2014	33	1	6	12	2
8	Oxford Brookes University	2014	20	0	0	0	1
9	School of Management, Royal Holloway	2014	20	1	0	0	0
10	Sheffield University Management School	2014	20	0	0	0	0
11	University of Exeter Business School	2014	7	0	0	0	0
12	Aberdeen Business School	2013	6	0	0	0	0
13	Association of Business School (ABS)	2013	5	0	0	0	0
14	Chester Business School	2013	12	0	0	0	0
15	Coventry Business School	2013	6	0	0	0	0
16	Essex Business School	2013	12	0	0	0	0
17	Glasgow Caledonian University	2013	28	0	0	4	0
18	Portsmouth Business School	2013	15	0	0	0	0
19	Strathclyde Business School	2013	20	0	0	0	0
20	The Open University Business School	2013	16	0	0	0	0
21	University of Hertfordshire Business School	2013	8	0	0	0	0
22	University of Huddersfield Business School	2013	2	0	0	0	0
23	University of Leicester School of Management	2013	24	0	0	0	1
24	University of Salford	2013	32	0	0	0	5
25	University of St Andrews, School of Management	2013	7	0	0	0	0
26	Ashridge Business School	2012	19	0	0	0	0
27	Aston Business School	2012	7	0	0	0	0
28	Hull University Business School	2012	9	0	1	1	1
29	Manchester Metropolitan University Business School	2012	5	0	0	0	0
30	The Business School, Bournemouth University	2012	15	0	0	4	0

→

Diversity student/ staff exp.	Diversity values	Diversity policy	Diversity research	Equality curric	Equality values	Equality policy	Equality research	Women
0	1	0	0	0	0	0	0	0
0	1	1	6	0	0	0	0	10
4	0	0	0	0	0	0	0	4
0	1	1	0	0	1	0	0	0
0	0	0	0	0	0	0	0	0
2	0	0	0	0	0	0	0	1
1	0	0	2	1	0	4	6	11
0	1	0	4	0	1	3	5	0
3	2	0	0	1	3	1	0	0
0	1	1	0	1	0	2	1	0
1	0	0	0	0	0	0	0	0
0	0	0	0	0	0	0	0	0
0	0	0	0	0	0	0	0	0
0	0	0	0	0	0	0	0	0
0	0	0	2	0	0	0	1	0
1	0	0	0	0	1	0	0	0
0	2	3	0	0	0	7	5	2
2	0	0	0	0	0	0	0	0
0	0	0	0	0	0	0	1	1
0	0	0	1	0	0	0	0	2
1	0	0	0	0	0	0	0	0
0	0	0	0	0	0	0	0	0
4	0	0	0	0	0	0	2	0
4	1	0	0	0	0	0	0	0
1	0	0	0	0	0	0	0	0
2	0	0	1	0	0	0	0	0
0	0	0	1	0	0	2	0	0
0	1	1	0	1	0	1	0	2
2	0	0	0	0	0	0	1	0
0	0	0	0	0	0	0	2	1

Although the table only reveals the extent of disclosures on the selected terms, it is indicative of the degree to which gender equality issues are addressed at all in the reports and in which particular area. This is then followed by a critical reading of the SIPs to reveal any other pertinent and more nuanced references to gender, diversity and equality, which indicate an interaction between gender equality and sustainability.

3.7 Evaluating the interaction of gender equality and sustainability in responsible management education

Table 3.3 summarizes the extent of disclosure ranked in order of disclosures.

Our results show that of the reporting UK signatory schools, five[10] do not disclose at all in relation to any of the concepts of gender equality. Of these, University of Huddersfield Business School, the shortest reporter in the sample, identifies four future goals in terms of embedding Corporate Responsibility and Sustainability into the curriculum and research profile of the School, giving little detail and no indication of the inclusion of gender. There is a tendency among many reporters to interpret "diversity" with the diversity of students or staff, in relation to international background and culture. For a further four schools,[11] this was their only mention of any of the search terms, and this therefore was assumed as a likely non-disclosure of any reference to gender. St Andrews refers to "diverse understandings" of responsible enterprise, which could of course include diversity, equality and gender issues, but this is not explicitly mentioned (p. 3). The use of "diversity" in relation to staff or student background and experience was the most used term in the content analysis: for example, "diverse levels of prior qualification and/or experience" in relation to students (Salford, p. 12) and their "ethnically diverse student population" (Manchester Metropolitan, p. 2).

Table 3.4 summarizes the extent of disclosure by theme, in relation to values, policy, curriculum and research. Due to the interchangeability and interconnectedness of the terms, the results of this part of the content analysis can be grouped together.

3.7.1 Values

Principle 2 of the Six PRME Principles is *Values*: "We will incorporate into our academic activities and curricula the values of global social responsibility as portrayed in international initiatives such as the United Nations Global Compact." Here no explicit reference has been made about equality, diversity or gender, but, as we have argued in this chapter,

---

10 University of Huddersfield Business School; Association of Business Schools; Aberdeen Business School; London South Bank University; and Chester Business School.
11 University of St Andrews School of Management; University of Exeter Business School; University of Hertfordshire Business School; Portsmouth Business School.

the values of global social responsibility should incorporate these. However, this was the least disclosed area in the content analysis, with only 17 mentions of any term relating to gender, diversity or equality values, spread across a total of ten schools. This suggests that the few schools that have seen fit to embed such issues in their value sets do not perceive these values as related to sustainability or at least are not disclosing these as an explicit part of their commitment to sustainability. There are some exceptions: in the Essex SIP, its Centre for Global Accountability states one of its core values is "to advance democracy, equity and social justice" (Essex, p. 6), which one could infer would include gender and diversity equality and equity, though this is not explicit. In a section on values Royal Holloway is more explicit: "In particular in relation to UNPriME and the Global Compact we seek to be fair in all we do, promoting equality, diversity and fair access" (Royal Holloway, p. 6). This partly relates to Royal Holloway's history as a women's college.

3.7.2 Policy

Compared to values, there were many more mentions in the SIPs of policies relating to gender, equality and diversity, totalling 36 across nine schools. Seven of those nine schools were those which also reported on values, suggesting that they were trying to embed the values in actual policy and practice. Policy-related issues could relate to policies internal to the institution and also to influence on external policies in government or business. Glasgow Caledonian University, for example, reports on its Women in Scotland's Economy program, which seeks to embed gender issues in policy-making and public resource allocation; and Newcastle University reports on trying to influence business through activity with the PRME Working Group on Gender Equality (see "Introduction"). Cranfield School of Management made reference to its extensive policy work at the Cranfield Centre International for Women Leaders, which has been influential in driving debates and policy on increasing women's representation on UK corporate boards.

3.7.3 Curriculum

There were 19 disclosures relating to gender, diversity or equality in the curriculum, across nine schools. For example, Hull University Business School states that within its Employee Relations (Level 5) and Human Resource Development (Level 6) modules "the moral implications of technology for the workforce and workforce equality and diversity are also considered" (Hull, p. 5). Bradford University School of Management runs an elective MSc module on Diversity in Work and Organisations. As with disclosures in other parts of the analysis, care needs to be taken in ascribing the degree of activity inherent in any disclosure. There may be more, or less, activity than the disclosures indicate, but the extent of detail on curriculum content on gender equality issues was very thin and notably often related to human resource management topics rather than sustainability. The University of Leicester, School of Management, offers a hint of broader issues being embedded in the curriculum, but little further detail: "The themes of inclusivity, global responsibility, and sustainability inform the critical perspectives that are offered in all of our modules" (Leicester, p. 7).

Table 3.3 **Extent of disclosure in UK PRME reporting schools (in order)**

Institution	SIP date	Pages	Gender curric	Gender policy and practice	Gender research	Diversity curric
Newcastle University Business School	2014	33	1	6	12	2
Glasgow Caledonian University	2013	28	0	0	4	0
Cranfield School of Management	2014	19	0	1	0	2
Oxford Brookes University	2014	20	0	0	0	1
School of Management, Royal Holloway	2014	20	1	0	0	0
University of Salford	2013	32	0	0	0	5
Durham Business School	2014	9	0	0	1	0
Hull University Business School	2012	9	0	1	1	1
University of Leicester School of Management	2013	24	0	0	0	1
The Business School, Bournemouth University	2012	15	0	0	4	0
Sheffield University Management School	2014	20	0	0	0	0
Leeds University Business School	2014	3	0	1	0	0
Ashridge Business School	2012	19	0	0	0	0
Middlesex University Business School	2014	16	0	0	0	0
The Open University Business School	2013	16	0	0	0	0
Aston Business School	2012	7	0	0	0	0
Coventry Business School	2013	6	0	0	0	0
Manchester Metropolitan University Business School	2012	5	0	0	0	0
Strathclyde Business School	2013	20	0	0	0	0
Portsmouth Business School	2013	15	0	0	0	0
Essex Business School	2013	12	0	0	0	0
Bradford University School of Management	2014	4	0	0	0	1
University of Hertfordshire Business School	2013	8	0	0	0	0
University of Exeter Business School	2014	7	0	0	0	0
University of St Andrews, School of Management	2013	7	0	0	0	0
Chester Business School	2013	12	0	0	0	0
London South Bank University	2014	7	0	0	0	0
Aberdeen Business School	2013	6	0	0	0	0
Association of Business School (ABS)	2013	5	0	0	0	0
University of Huddersfield Business School	2013	2	0	0	0	0
Total columns			**2**	**9**	**22**	**13**

Diversity student/ staff exp.	Diversity values	Diversity policy	Diversity research	Equality curric	Equality values	Equality policy	Equality research	Women	Total across
1	0	0	2	1	0	4	6	11	46
0	2	3	0	0	0	7	5	2	23
0	1	1	6	0	0	0	0	10	21
0	1	0	4	0	1	3	5	0	15
3	2	0	0	1	3	1	0	0	11
4	1	0	0	0	0	0	0	0	10
4	0	0	0	0	0	0	0	4	9
0	1	1	0	1	0	1	0	2	9
4	0	0	0	0	0	0	2	0	7
0	0	0	0	0	0	0	2	1	7
0	1	1	0	1	0	2	1	0	6
0	1	1	0	0	1	0	0	0	4
2	0	0	1	0	0	0	0	0	3
2	0	0	0	0	0	0	0	1	3
0	0	0	1	0	0	0	0	2	3
0	0	0	1	0	0	2	0	0	3
0	0	0	2	0	0	0	1	0	3
2	0	0	0	0	0	0	1	0	3
0	0	0	0	0	0	0	1	1	2
2	0	0	0	0	0	0	0	0	2
1	0	0	0	0	1	0	0	0	2
0	1	0	0	0	0	0	0	0	2
1	0	0	0	0	0	0	0	0	1
1	0	0	0	0	0	0	0	0	1
1	0	0	0	0	0	0	0	0	1
0	0	0	0	0	0	0	0	0	0
0	0	0	0	0	0	0	0	0	0
0	0	0	0	0	0	0	0	0	0
0	0	0	0	0	0	0	0	0	0
0	0	0	0	0	0	0	0	0	0
28	**11**	**7**	**17**	**4**	**6**	**20**	**24**	**34**	

Table 3.4　**Extent of disclosure by theme in UK PRME reporting schools**

Institution	SIP date	Pages	Diversity student/ staff exp.	Diversity values	Equality values	Total values	Gender policy and practice
Bradford University School of Management	2014	4	0	1	0	1	0
Cranfield School of Management	2014	19	0	1	0	1	1
Durham Business School	2014	9	4	0	0	0	0
Leeds University Business School	2014	3	0	1	1	2	1
London South Bank University	2014	7	0	0	0	0	0
Middlesex University Business School	2014	16	2	0	0	0	0
Newcastle University Business School	2014	33	1	0	0	0	6
Oxford Brookes University	2014	20	0	1	1	2	0
School of Management, Royal Holloway	2014	20	3	2	3	5	0
Sheffield University Management School	2014	20	0	1	0	1	0
University of Exeter Business School	2014	7	1	0	0	0	0
Aberdeen Business School	2013	6	0	0	0	0	0
Association of Business School (ABS)	2013	5	0	0	0	0	0
Chester Business School	2013	12	0	0	0	0	0
Coventry Business School	2013	6	0	0	0	0	0
Essex Business School	2013	12	1	0	1	1	0
Glasgow Caledonian University	2013	28	0	2	0	2	0
Portsmouth Business School	2013	15	2	0	0	0	0
Strathclyde Business School	2013	20	0	0	0	0	0
The Open University Business School	2013	16	0	0	0	0	0
University of Hertfordshire Business School	2013	8	1	0	0	0	0
University of Huddersfield Business School	2013	2	0	0	0	0	0
University of Leicester School of Management	2013	24	4	0	0	0	0
University of Salford	2013	32	4	1	0	1	0
University of St Andrews, School of Management	2013	7	1	0	0	0	0
Ashridge Business School	2012	19	2	0	0	0	0
Aston Business School	2012	7	0	0	0	0	0
Hull University Business School	2012	9	0	1	0	1	1
Manchester Metropolitan University Business School	2012	5	2	0	0	0	0
The Business School, Bournemouth University	2012	15	0	0	0	0	0
			28	11	6	17	9

Diversity policy	Equality policy	Total policy	Gender curric	Equality curric	Diversity curric	Total curric	Gender research	Diversity research	Equality research	Total research	Women
0	0	0	0	0	1	1	0	0	0	0	0
1	0	2	0	0	2	2	0	6	0	6	10
0	0	0	0	0	0	0	1	0	0	1	4
1	0	2	0	0	0	0	0	0	0	0	0
0	0	0	0	0	0	0	0	0	0	0	0
0	0	0	0	0	0	0	0	0	0	0	1
0	4	10	1	1	2	4	12	2	6	20	11
0	3	3	0	0	1	1	0	4	5	9	0
0	1	1	1	1	0	2	0	0	0	0	0
1	2	3	0	1	0	1	0	0	1	1	0
0	0	0	0	0	0	0	0	0	0	0	0
0	0	0	0	0	0	0	0	0	0	0	0
0	0	0	0	0	0	0	0	0	0	0	0
0	0	0	0	0	0	0	0	0	0	0	0
0	0	0	0	0	0	0	0	2	1	3	0
0	0	0	0	0	0	0	0	0	0	0	0
3	7	10	0	0	0	0	4	0	5	9	2
0	0	0	0	0	0	0	0	0	0	0	0
0	0	0	0	0	0	0	0	0	1	1	1
0	0	0	0	0	0	0	0	1	0	1	2
0	0	0	0	0	0	0	0	0	0	0	0
0	0	0	0	0	0	0	0	0	0	0	0
0	0	0	0	0	1	1	0	0	2	2	0
0	0	0	0	0	5	5	0	0	0	0	0
0	0	0	0	0	0	0	0	0	0	0	0
0	0	0	0	0	0	0	0	1	0	1	0
0	2	2	0	0	0	0	0	1	0	1	0
1	1	3	0	1	1	2	1	0	0	1	2
0	0	0	0	0	0	0	0	0	1	1	0
0	0	0	0	0	0	0	4	0	2	6	1
7	**20**	**36**	**2**	**4**	**13**	**19**	**22**	**17**	**24**	**63**	**34**

3.7.4 Research

Far more claims were made about research, totalling 63 disclosures across 15 schools. Some of the disclosures related to publications have been mentioned in a list of references and also in the research narrative, to the extent that the same work could potentially be counted twice. But one might suggest that research work and a publication arising from it can be conceived as separate entities. The largest disclosures on research were from Newcastle University Business School, Glasgow Caledonian University and Cranfield School of Management, all of which also disclosed relatively highly on influencing external policy and practice. This suggests that these schools are working towards research, which delivers social and economic impact. Cranfield School of Management, for example, is explicit in its conceptualization of diversity in its research and practice:

> A well-established model we use in diversity defines the three levels of implementing diversity; intellectually understanding the business case (accepting the evidence of the value created by diversity) emotionally engaging with diversity (empathising with the different and often negative experiences of diverse employees) and practically committing to action to make a difference (Cranfield, p. 3).

The University of Leicester, School of Management, makes more sweeping claims in terms of the purpose and impact of its research and consultancy:

> Management and organizations have created many of the achievements of modern civilization, but are also profoundly implicated in the pressing global problems facing us today: the persistence of war, violence, the degradation of the natural environment, racism, sexism, ageism, ableism/disablism, homophobia, unhealthy and unsafe work environments, work-life imbalance and the unequal global distribution of wealth, to name but a few.... As a result, our research and consultancy attempt not only to understand and to explain the world from a variety of different vantage points but also, beyond that, to contribute to informed choices about how the world could be changed for the better (Leicester, p. 15).

What is clear from the content analysis is that the research disclosed by PRME reporting schools is varied, addressing a range of issues relevant to gender equality, particularly in relation to the position of women. It is less clear to what degree this research engages gender equality with broader aspects of sustainability.

3.8 Reflections and conclusions

Our argument in this chapter is that due to the growing and increasingly urgent sustainability imperative, caused by climate change and environmental degradation, there is a need for business schools around the world to address this problem and educate the future leaders of business, government and academia differently from the past. This is essentially what the PRME initiative stands for and is trying to facilitate.

Signatory schools around the world, including those in the United Kingdom, have been addressing the responsible management agenda in their values, policies, curriculum and research. Albeit, as Burchell, Murray and Kennedy (2014) point out, it is unclear to what extent PRME acts as a driver of, or a reflection on, this activity.

As argued earlier, we find a strong link between sustainable development and gender equality: this is inherent in the social justice dimensions of sustainability requiring intra- and intergenerational equity. We have outlined some of the powerful empirical links between what might be termed (un)sustainability and gender (in)equality—women and girls bear a disproportionate burden of the consequences of poverty, environmental degradation and effects of climate change. It is not surprising, then, that feminists of various forms have long made the theoretical connection between the capitalist exploitation of the natural world and the global exploitation of women. Feminism brings theoretical insight into the complexity of the relationship between gender and sustainability and between local and global processes that affect the outcome of the human–environment relationships. Finally, we have outlined the business case for sustainability and gender equality, which is also compelling, although the two cases rarely interact.

Our review and content analysis of the SIPs of UK reporting schools was designed to ascertain the degree to which PRME signatories are integrating gender equality into their implementation of the PRME principles. Although we accept that the content analysis only provides a snapshot of what is reported, and may not reflect the full extent of activity, it provides a useful proxy for levels of engagement—or lack thereof—on the interaction of gender equality and sustainable development in School values, policies, curriculum and research.

The SIPs report a plethora of issues in relation to responsible management, social responsibility, sustainability and ethics. Yet as our analysis demonstrates, the degree to which this encapsulates gender equality issues in all their forms is very disparate. It appears that schools do not conceive of gender inequality as being an integral part of their sustainability curriculum and research agenda, although they may address gender and diversity through the lens of human resource management, or women's leadership such as on corporate boards. These are worthwhile areas to pursue. However, alone they do not address the breadth of the challenge for gender equality and its integration with sustainable development through inequalities in accessing a wide range of resources: social capital, financial capital, political power and representation, reproductive rights, healthcare and education, and land and natural resource use.

We suggest that unless the lens of sustainability is widened to incorporate aspects of gender equality, this represents a seriously missed opportunity in the responsible management agenda to drive forward more egalitarian business models and behaviours. While the principles of PRME address "an inclusive and sustainable global economy" (Principle 1) and "the values of global social responsibility as portrayed in international initiatives such as the United Nations Global Compact" (Principle 2), schools could do more to interpret these to include gender equality.

One way of addressing this would be to engage in debate around the 2015 Sustainable Development goals and the degree to which they address gender equality. The UN Global Compact in its publication *Architects of a Better World: Building the Post 2015 Business*

Engagement Architecture (UN Global Compact, 2013) specifically calls on Business Schools to support the establishment of a framework for sustainable development. This is envisioned as sufficiently robust in order to alleviate poverty by delivering prosperity and equity; meet "human needs and capacities" through education, *gender equality* and health; be mindful of the "resource triad" of food and agriculture, water and sanitation, and energy and climate; and craft an "enabling environment" by focusing on peace and stability; infrastructure and technology; and good governance and human rights. Gender equality is a specific goal of this call. Moreover, the Women's Empowerment Principles,[12] resulting from a collaboration between UN Women and the UN Global Compact, seek to point the way to best practice by elaborating the gender dimension of corporate responsibility within business's role in sustainable development. The seven principles are listed on page xi of this book.

All of these have dimensions that could be embedded within business and management curricula to enhance the extent to which gender equality is addressed. There is relevance to organizational behaviour, human resource management, marketing, accounting and finance, operations and supply chain management, law, economics and all the dimensions of responsible management. For schools and faculty pursuing education for responsible management and sustainability, adding the dimension of gender equality, which is already inherent in equity discourses within sustainability, will bring about a more rounded and egalitarian perspective. This will improve the opportunity to consider social justice and equity from a gendered lens as inherent in sustainability.

References

Barry, B., 2005. Why Social Justice Matters. Polity Press, Cambridge.

Blowfield, M., Murray, A., 2014. Corporate Responsibility. Oxford University Press, Oxford.

Braidotti, R., Charkiewicz, E., Hausler, S., Wieringa, S., 1994. Women, the Environment and Sustainable Development: Towards a Theoretical Synthesis. Zed Books, London.

Burchell, J., Murray, A., Kennedy, S., 2014. Responsible management education in UK business schools: critically examining the role of the United Nations Principles for Responsible Management Education as a driver for change. Management Learning. doi 10.1177/1350507614549117.

Department for Business Innovation and Skills, 2013. The business case for equality and diversity: a survey of the academic literature. BIS Economics Papers. Government Equalities Office, London.

Donovan, J., 2001. Feminist Theory: The Intellectual Traditions. Continuum, New York.

Elkington, J., 1998. Cannibals with Forks: The Triple Bottom Line of 21st Century Business. New Society Publishers, Gabriola Island, BC, Stony Creek, CT.

Federici, S., 2009. The devaluation of women's labour. In: Salleh, A. (Ed.), Eco-Sufficiency and Global Justice. Pluto Press, London, pp. 43–65.

Fukukawa, K., Spicer, D., Burrows, S. A., Fairbrass, J., 2013. Sustainable change. Journal of Corporate Citizenship 49, 71–99.

Global Commission on the Economy and Climate, 2014. Better Growth, Better Climate. The New Climate Economy. www.newclimateeconomy.report

12 www.weprinciples.org/Site/PrincipleOverview

Gray, R.H., 2006. Social, environmental and sustainability reporting and organisational value creation?: Whose value? Whose creation? Accounting, Auditing & Accountability Journal 19(6), 793–819.

Gray, R.H., Dillard, J., Spence, C., 2009. Social accounting as if the world matters: towards Absurdia and a new Postalgia. Public Management Review 11(5).

GRI & IFA, 2009. Embedding Gender in Sustainability Reporting: A Practitioner's Guide. GRI Research and Development Series, Global Reporting Initiative and International Finance Association.

Grosser, K., Moon, J., 2005. Gender mainstreaming and corporate social responsibility: reporting workplace issues. Journal of Business Ethics 62(4), 327–340.

Grosser, K., Moon, J., 2008. Developments in company reporting on workplace gender equality? A corporate social responsibility perspective. Accounting Forum 32(3), 179–198.

Haynes, K., 2008. Moving the gender agenda or stirring chicken's entrails? Where next for feminist methodologies in accounting? Accounting, Auditing & Accountability Journal 21(4), 539–555.

IPCC (Intergovernmental Panel on Climate Change), 2001. Third Assessment Report. WMO/Intergovernmental Panel on Climate Change, Geneva, Switzerland.

IPCC (Intergovernmental Panel on Climate Change), 2007. Fourth Assessment Report. WMO/Intergovernmental Panel on Climate Change, Geneva, Switzerland.

IPCC (Intergovernmental Panel on Climate Change), 2013. Fifth Assessment Report. WMO/Intergovernmental Panel on Climate Change, Geneva, Switzerland.

Kilgour, M.A., 2013. The global compact and gender inequality: a work in progress. Business & Society 52(1), 105–134.

McWilliams, A., Siegel, D., 2000. Corporate social responsibility and financial performance: correlation or misspecification? Strategic Management Journal 21(5), 603–609.

Meadows, D., Randers, J., Meadows, D., 2004. Limits to Growth: The 30-Year Update. Earthscan, London.

Mellor, M., 1997. Feminism and Ecology. Polity Press, Cambridge.

Miles, K., 2011. Embedding gender in sustainability reports. Sustainability, Accounting, Management and Policy Journal 2(1), 139–146.

Mohanty, C.T., 2003. Feminism without Borders: Decolonizing Theory, Practicing Solidarity. Duke University Press, Durham and London.

Murray, A., Haynes, K., Hudson, L., 2010. Collaborating to achieve corporate social responsibility and sustainability? Possibilities and problems. Sustainability, Accounting, Management and Policy Journal 1(2), 161–177.

Nelling, E., Webb, E., 2009. Corporate social responsibility and financial performance: the "virtuous circle" revisited. Review of Quantitative Finance and Accounting 32(2), 197–209.

O'Dwyer, B., 2003. Conceptions of corporate social responsibility: the nature of managerial capture. Accounting, Auditing & Accountability Journal 16(4), 523–557.

Özbilgin, M.F., Mulholland, G., Tatli, A., Worman, D., 2008. Managing Diversity and the Business Case. Chartered Institute of Personnel and Development, London, p. 4.

Rawls, J., 1971. A Theory of Justice. Oxford University Press, Oxford.

Rose, C., 2007. Does female board representation influence firm performance? The Danish evidence. Corporate Governance: An International Review 15(2), 404–413.

Salleh, A., 2009. Ecological debt: embodied debt. In: Salleh, A. (Ed.), Eco-Sufficiency and Global Justice. Pluto Press, London, 1–40.

Terjesen, S., Sealy, R., Singh, V., 2009. Women directors on corporate boards: a review and research agenda. Corporate Governance: An International Review 17(3), 320–337.

Thompson, L.J., 2008. Gender equity and corporate social responsibility in a post-feminist era. Business Ethics: A European Review 17(1), 87–106.

UNEP, 2005. Millennium Ecosystem Assessment—Living Beyond Our Means—Statement from the Board. United Nations Foundation, New York.

UNEP, 2012. GEO5 Global Environmental Outlook: Environment for the Future We Want. United Nations Environment Programme.

Unerman, J., 2000. Methodological issues: reflections on quantification in corporate social reporting content analysis. Accounting, Auditing & Accountability Journal 13(5), 667–680.

UN (United Nations), 2012. Millennium Development Goals Report: Gender Chart. United Nations, New York.

UN (United Nations), 2014. Millenium Development Goals Gender Chart. United Nations Statistics Division & UN Women, New York.

United Nations Department of Economic and Social Affairs, 2010. The World's Women. United Nations, New York.

UN Global Compact, 2013. Architects of a Better World: Building the Post 2015 Business Engagement Architecture. United Nations, New York.

Vinnicombe, S., Doldor, E., Turner, C., 2014. The Female FTSE Report 2014: Crossing the Finishing Line. Cranfield International Centre for Women Leaders, Cranfield.

WCED (World Commission on Environment and Development), 1987. Our Common Future. Oxford University Press, Oxford.

World Health Association, 2011. Indoor Air pollution and Health. World Health Association Factsheet (292).

WWF, 2012. Living Planet Report 2012: Biodiversity, Biocapacity and Better Choices. WWF International, Gland, Switzerland.

4

Cleaning our houses
Gender equity in business schools

Amy Klemm Verbos
University of Wisconsin–Whitewater, USA

Deanna Kennedy
University of Washington Bothell, USA

Business schools intending to instil the Principles for Responsible Management Education (PRME) and the Women's Empowerment Principles (WEPs) in students may need to clean their own houses before expecting students to embrace those principles. That is, business schools need to foster and support faculty role models of these principles and start with providing psychologically safe climates. In a study of business faculty, we found that higher ethical leadership, gender equity and organizational justice are associated with more psychological safety. However, an exclusionary climate dampens the benefit of increasing organizational justice to increase psychological safety and also intervenes between gender equity and psychological safety but not completely, such that increasing gender equity can improve psychological safety regardless. Because psychological safety may enable faculty to better exemplify the principles of PRME and WEPs in classrooms, students can more fully appreciate and apply the principles in their careers.

4.1 Introduction

In academia generally, research demonstrates gender disparities in pay, resource allocation, promotion and tenure, with women faculty lagging behind their male colleagues (see e.g. Bailyn, 2003; Benschop and Brouns, 2003; Bilimoria, Joy and Liang, 2008; Fletcher, 2007; Kjeldal, Rindfleish and Sheridan, 2005; Linehan, Buckley and Koslowski, 2009; Maranto and Griffin, 2011; Xu, 2008). Relatively little research has examined the situation in business schools specifically; yet the indication that a gender gap exists where women are marginalized and devalued is similar (e.g. Fisher, Motowidlo and Werner, 1993; Fotaki, 2011, 2013; Weisenfeld and Robinson-Backmon, 2007). A recent article in *The New York Times* indicates that business schools are struggling with gender issues. For example, at Harvard Business School "attracting and retaining female professors was a losing battle; from 2006 to 2007, a third of the female junior faculty left" (Kantor, 2013). Nevertheless, business schools may be integral to establishing better business practices in that ". . . gender takes shape in, and is shaped by, teaching, learning, and leadership practices, and in relations between students, faculty, administrators, and communities" (Ropers-Huilman, 2003: 2). As such, to create greater acceptance of and advocacy for gender equity in students, it is important for business schools to make sure that their houses are in order.

As the title of this book suggests, gender equality remains a challenge for business and management education. We see the situation as an opportunity for business schools to become role models of the types of workplaces that foster, not only gender equality, but gender equity. Herein we define "gender equality" as fair and equal treatment of men and women. We distinguish this concept from "gender equity", which is a broader concept that is context dependent. According to Fraser (1994), gender equity includes respect for both genders, providing equal resources, parity in social activity participation and measuring social value in a way that is not male-centred. Moreover, Verbos and Humphries (2012) argue that gender equality may be insufficient if it simply adds women as faculty, but continues systems that are exclusionary. Thus, we focus our attention on the way gender equity creates a thriving environment that facilitates the Principles for Responsible Management Education (PRME)[1] and supports the United Nations' Women's Empowerment Principles (WEPs).[2]

The PRME Working Group on Gender Equality brings together academics and employers in support of integrating gender issues and awareness into management education, business school curricula and related research to facilitate respect and support for the WEPs and PRME. According to Kilgour, Flynn and Haynes (2011) the Working Group was created to increase gender equality throughout the business sector by focusing on management education.

> The actions (or inactions) of business schools will play an important role in the education of future business leaders, policy-makers and decision-makers. Business schools should be leading the way to change in these areas and providing examples and best practices that can be transformative in the business world more generally. The Working Group was created to provide faculty and business schools resources and linkages to facilitate and expedite their leadership in this critical area (p. 3).

1 www.unprme.org
2 www.weprinciples.org

We see parallels to *The PhD Project* whose goal is to increase the diversity of corporate America by increasing under-represented faculty of colour in business schools.[3] This initiative has had great success, more than quadrupling the number of under-represented faculty of colour in AACSB-accredited business schools since 1994 to over 1200 with 350 minority students in doctoral programs.[4] Taking this premise to the realm of gender equality, it follows that supporting and placing women who experience gender equality and gender equity in front of business classrooms will help to advance gender equality in management education. To do so, business schools may need to "clean their houses" to facilitate a supportive, inclusive and psychologically safe climate for both men and women. In this chapter, we explore the important connections between gender equity, organizational justice, ethical leadership, exclusionary climate and psychological safety.

4.2 Literature review and hypotheses

True gender equity means allowing women to be valued equally within the culture of a business school for their unique contributions and perspectives. Fotaki's (2011) poignant qualitative descriptions of how women are silenced, treated as the "other" and not as a part of the group, and alienated in male-dominated business schools, suggests to us that there is a need for the environment in business schools to be predicated on psychological safety. Kahn (1990) defines psychological safety as a "sense of being able to show and employ one's self without fear of negative consequences to self-image, status, or career" (p. 708). In a psychologically safe environment, employees perceive greater trust and respect (Edmondson, 1999). This means, of course, that for an environment to be "safe" there must be bounds on what is acceptable behaviour so that employees express their true selves without threatening others or violating their sense of safety (May, Gilson and Harter, 2004). As such, faculty may have the confidence that participation and contributions are valued from all members of the school regardless of gender and that differences between men's and women's styles of decision making, presenting, leading and so forth are accepted as equally valid.

To better understand the way business school environments can promote psychological safety, and clean their own houses, we examine the relationships between psychological safety and its antecedents. To make hypotheses we draw on three theories that provide insights about the way coworkers and leadership shape the workplace. First, we are informed by social learning theory, which suggests that ethical leaders influence followers' ethical behaviour (Brown and Trevino, 2006; Brown, Trevino and Harrison, 2005) and, in doing so, could create a psychologically safe climate. Second, social identity theory literature suggests that individuals pursue a positive identity through their membership in salient groups, including gender (Tajfel and Turner, 1979). As such, we focus on the way positive identity created through gender equity and organizational justice relates to psychological safety. Third, social exchange theory suggests that a non-reciprocating environment, such as one with an exclusionary climate, could lead members of the exchange

3 www.phdproject.org
4 www.phdproject.org

to pull back from interactions with others (Scott, Restubog and Zagenczyk, 2013) and feel reticent about being themselves. Thus, we discuss the connection between exclusionary climate, positive identity constructs and psychological safety.

4.3 Positive identity and psychological safety

4.3.1 Ethical leadership

One of the first social connections business faculty make with their school is through their leaders (e.g. program chair, department head, dean). Because leaders may determine the way new employees learn their roles in the organization (Brown and Trevino, 2006), they can play a critical part in establishing identities. As social identities can create or diffuse in-group bias (Amiot and Aubin, 2013), leaders have a responsibility to conscientiously help employees become integrated members of work groups. In particular, ethical leadership can be imperative for establishing a positive collective identity among business colleagues. Ethical leaders demonstrate "normatively appropriate conduct through personal actions and interpersonal relationships" and promote followers' appropriate conduct "through two-way communication, reinforcement, and decision-making" (Brown, Trevino and Harrison, 2005: 120). Verbos and Dykstra (2013) found that ethical leadership contributes to positive job attitudes. Mayer et al. (2012) found that ethical leadership leads to lower levels of relationship conflict. Less conflict will help to promote psychological safety too. Moreover, in a study of managers in financial institutions, Walumbwa and Schaubroeck (2009) found a positive relationship between ethical leadership and psychological safety, and that psychological safety is the mechanism by which ethical leadership influences voice behaviour. We believe that this positive relationship will hold true in business schools as well. Additionally, social learning theory proposes that individuals will emulate role models of appropriate behaviour (Bandura, 1986). Thus, the appropriate conduct of ethical leaders in encouraging two-way communication is likely to foster a psychologically safe climate. Therefore:

> **Hypothesis 1.** Ethical leadership will be positively related to psychological safety.

4.3.2 Gender equity

A leader's ethical role modelling is an important aspect of psychological safety, but is not the only salient antecedent business faculty may face. In addition to the social identity bestowed or affirmed by leaders, employees may also self-identify with social groups, specifically based on gender identification (Schmader, 2002). Essentially, there is "part of the individual's self-concept which derives from his or her knowledge of membership to a social group (or groups) together with the value and the emotional significance attached to it" (Tajfel, 1981: 255). However, how employees with that identity are treated by others may affect individual outcomes. That is, when groups are not treated equitably because of gender, the effects may be detrimental to the individual or group relationships. Indeed, research has shown that fault lines due to gender can create negative consequences for performance (Bezrukova et al., 2009). Alternatively, when employees are treated equitably, more trust and respect may be perceived (Maranto and Griffin, 2011) such that psychological safety is promoted among colleagues. We hypothesize:

> **Hypothesis 2.** Gender equity will be positively related to psychological safety.

4.3.3 Organizational justice

Although it may be important for faculty members to feel that they are treated fairly regardless of gender, it may likewise be salient for members to feel that decisions are fair and performance is recognized and valued fairly. That is, the faculty's perception of organizational justice may weigh in to the impression of the psychologically safe environment. Organizational justice includes procedural justice that assesses the way decisions are made around allocations, and distributive justice, that evaluates fairness of outcome allocations (Parker, Baltes and Christiansen, 1997). Researchers have shown that organizational justice may be influential for perceptions and attitudes about jobs (Tepper, 2000). Perceptions that faculty are treated fairly and justly in a school of business should also evoke feelings of psychological safety. As such, our hypothesis is:

> **Hypothesis 3.** Organizational justice will be positively related to psychological safety.

4.4 Exclusionary climate and psychological safety

4.4.1 Exclusionary climate

Although positive identities may arise from ethical leadership, gender equity and organizational justice, there may be other, more insidious factors that influence psychological safety. In particular, recent research suggests women faculty may experience a chilly, or exclusionary, climate within their department that can adversely affect current and future job prospects (Maranto and Griffin, 2011; Settles et al., 2006; Xu, 2008). This type of climate can constrain the informal networks gained by faculty, and especially by women faculty (Maranto and Griffin, 2011). As social exchange theory suggests, without informal relationships workers may have difficulty achieving the mentorship, supportive conversations and collaborations that will advance their careers (1994). Further, Verbos and Dykstra (2013) connect exclusionary climate to negative attitudes towards their job and organization. As an exclusionary climate is likely to generate fear, distrust and marginalization, it may also be associated with a lack of psychological safety. Thus, we hypothesize:

> **Hypothesis 4.** Exclusionary climate will be negatively related to psychological safety.

Although we predict that an exclusionary climate will be negatively associated with psychological safety, we acknowledge that the effects may be more pervasive. That is, an exclusionary climate may intervene between perceptions of gender equity or organizational justice and psychological safety. To assess this complicated relationship we look for exclusionary climate to intervene, or technically to mediate the relationship, between gender equity and psychological safety or between organizational justice and psychological safety based on mediational analysis (Hayes, 2013). This means that when exclusionary climate is found to intervene then it is the mechanism by which gender equity and/or organizational justice affects psychological safety. Moreover, as an intervening variable, exclusionary climate has the potential to subvert the positive effects that gender equity or organizational justice might have on psychological safety. We believe that an exclusionary climate might be an intervening variable because researchers suggest that a lack of gender equity and justice are antecedents of exclusionary climate (Maranto and Griffin, 2011; Verbos and Dykstra, 2013). In turn, it may be that the exclusionary climate prompts a lack of psychological safety in business school settings. We, therefore, hypothesize:

> **Hypothesis 5.** Exclusionary climate will intervene (i.e. mediate the relationship) between gender equity and psychological safety. If the exclusionary climate is found to intervene, then it becomes the mechanism by which gender equity influences psychological safety and subverts the positive effects of gender equity on psychological safety.

> **Hypothesis 6.** Exclusionary climate will mediate the relationship between organizational justice and psychological safety. If the exclusionary climate is found to intervene, then it becomes the mechanism by which organizational justice influences psychological safety and subverts the positive effects of organizational justice on psychological safety.

4.5 Methods

We collected data from 301 business school faculty through an online survey; missing data reduced the sample size for the analysis to 229. We invited participation on several academic listservs to obtain participation across business schools and further invited participants to forward the survey link to their colleagues. Although we did request respondents to be faculty at business schools, we did not limit the survey to accredited business schools. The sample comprised 40% male and 60% female. Participants were 73% White, 15% African American, 5% Hispanic, 4% Asian, 1% Native American and 2% other. Participants reported that 58% held Doctoral degrees, 24% Juris Doctor, 7% Master's degrees and 3.7% other (mostly LLM degrees). A total of 56% were tenured, 27% tenure track but not tenured and 17% not tenure track. Participants reported that 29% were professors, 30% are associate professors, 28% assistant professors, 5% instructors, 3% lecturers, 0.7% adjunct instructors and 4.3% did not answer. A total of 66% were employed in public institutions and 34% in private universities and colleges. Participant reports of years employed at the current school were 17% less than 3 years, 19% 3–5 years, 21% 6–10 years, 15% 11–15 years and 29% more than 15 years. The mean age of participants was 52 years, ranging from 27 to 78 years, and the standard deviation was 10 years.

We tested a number of control variables including gender, age and rank. We controlled for gender because it is negatively related to gender equity, organizational justice and psychological safety, and positively related to exclusionary climate. Specifically, women reported less gender equity, organizational justice and psychological safety, and greater exclusionary climate. Neither age nor rank were significantly related to the dependent variables and did not influence the outcomes, so we omitted them for parsimony and to maximize the sample size due to missing data.

4.6 Measures

We measured all variables with existing, validated measures using Likert-type scales provided by the authors of each measure. The items for each scale are set forth in the Appendix.

Psychological safety. This refers to an individual's perception that his/her ideas and opinions can be shared without negative consequences in the near or long term. We used May, Gilson and Harter's (2004) three-item measure based on Kahn's (1990) work to measure psychological safety.

Exclusionary climate. This is defined as the degree to which an individual perceives that he/she is not a valued member of the work group or treated as if he/she belongs. We measured exclusionary climate with Maranto and Griffin's (2011) six-item measure.

Organizational justice. This refers to the perception of fairness in terms of processes for decision making (i.e. procedural) and allocation of resources (i.e. distributive). We used Parker, Baltes and Christiansen's (1997) seven-item measure of procedural (four items) and distributive justice (three items), republished by Field (2002).

Gender equity. This is considered to be the perception that men and women are provided comparable resources, social activity participation, respect and value in their work group. We measured gender equity with the six-item measure developed by Maranto and Griffin (2011).

Ethical leadership. This is defined as the perception that leaders demonstrate responsible, moral and ethical behaviours with work group members. We measured ethical leadership with Brown, Trevino and Harrison's (2005) ten-item measure, modified to refer to leaders in a business school.

We next discuss the results of our analysis.

4.7 Results

Correlations, means and standard deviations are summarized in Table 4.1 with Cronbach's alphas displayed in parentheses on the diagonal. All of the variables of interest are significantly correlated with each other in the expected directions. Ethical leadership, gender equity and organizational justice are all positively and significantly correlated with psychological safety ($r = .58$, $r = .53$ and $r = .59$, respectively; $p < .001$). Exclusionary climate is negatively and significantly correlated with psychological safety ($r = -.65$; $p < .001$).

We conducted the hypothesis tests using hierarchical regression analysis in SPSS 21.0. The results of this analysis are summarized in Table 4.2. The control variable, gender, is entered in Step 1, followed by ethical leadership, gender equity and organizational justice in Step 2 to test Hypotheses 1 through 3. Hypotheses 1 through 3 are all supported as ethical leadership, gender equity and organizational justice each positively and significantly associated with psychological safety.

In Step 3, exclusionary climate is entered. Hypothesis 4, which posits that exclusionary climate is negatively related to psychological safety, is also supported. We tested

Table 4.1 **Correlations**

	M	*SD*	**1**	**2**	**3**	**4**	**5**
1. Psychological safety	15.70	4.10	(.73)				
2. Ethical leadership	30.65	9.70	.58*	(.96)			
3. Gender equity	29.62	10.11	.53*	.50*	(.89)		
4. Organizational justice	20.60	6.64	.59*	.78*	.57*	(.92)	
5. Exclusionary climate	15.17	5.26	−.65*	−.60*	−.59*	−.67*	(.85)

Notes: *Correlation is significant at the 0.001 level (two-tailed).
$N = 230$.
Cronbach's alphas are shown in parentheses on the diagonal.

Table 4.2 **Model coefficients for Hypotheses 1–4**

	Dependent variable		
	Psychological safety		
	Step 1	**Step 2**	**Step 3**
Gender	−.138*	−.016	−.008
Ethical leadership		.272**	.209**
Gender equity		.269***	.157*
Organizational justice		.224**	.086
Exclusionary climate			−.379***
R^2	.019*	.435	.504
ΔR^2		.416***	.069***

Notes: *$p < .05$; **$p < .01$; ***$p < .001$.

Hypotheses 5 and 6 for mediation using PROCESS as directed in recent statistical analysis literature (Hayes, 2013), with gender, ethical leadership and organizational justice or gender equity (depending on which was being tested) as covariates (see Table 4.3). In Table 4.3, a is the path from the antecedent variable (X) to the mediator (M), b is the path from M to the consequent variable (Y) and c' is the path from X to Y. Bias-corrected bootstrap intervals for the indirect effects based on 1,000 bootstrap samples did not include zero. As expected, the indirect effects of gender equity and organizational justice on psychological safety were positive. Gender equity also had a direct effect on psychological safety ($c' = .064$, $p < .05$). Thus, the evidence partially supports Hypothesis 5: exclusionary climate partially mediates the relationships between gender equity and psychological safety. There was no evidence that organizational justice affected psychological safety apart from its effect on exclusionary climate. Thus, exclusionary climate fully mediates the relationship between organizational justice and psychological safety. Hypothesis 6 is supported.

Table 4.3 **Model coefficients for Hypotheses 5 and 6**

| | | Consequent | | | | | | |
| | | M (exclusionary climate) | | | | Y (psychological safety) | | |
Antecedent		**Coeff.**	**SE**	**p**		**Coeff.**	**SE**	**p**
X (organizational justice)	a	−.289	.061	<.001	c'	.053	.052	.300
M (exclusionary climate)		−	−	−	b	−.298	.054	<.001
Constant	i_1	28.282	1.018	<.001	i_2	14.537	1.722	<.001
Gender		.215	.507	.672		−.067	.407	.869
Ethical leadership		−.090	.040	<.05		.089	.032	<.05
Gender equity		−.154	.030	<.001		.064	.025	<.05
		$R^2 = .520$				$R^2 = .504$		
		$F(4, 224) = 60.722, p < .001$				$F(5, 223) = 45.330, p < .001$		

| | | Consequent | | | | | | |
| | | M (exclusionary climate) | | | | Y (psychological safety) | | |
Antecedent		**Coeff.**	**SE**	**p**		**Coeff.**	**SE**	**p**
X (gender equity)	a	−.154	.030	<.001	c'	.064	.025	<.05
M (exclusionary climate)		−	−	−	b	−0.298	.054	<.001
Constant	i_1	28.282	1.018	<.001	i_2	14.537	1.722	<.001
Gender		.215	.507	.672		−.067	.407	.869
Ethical leadership		−.090	.040	<.05		.089	.032	<.05
Organizational justice		−.289	.061	<.001		.053	.052	.300
		$R^2 = .520$				$R^2 = .504$		
		$F(4, 224) = 60.722, p < .001$				$F(5, 223) = 45.330, p < .001$		

4.8 Discussion

This research identifies linkages between ethical leadership, gender equity, organizational justice, exclusionary climate and psychological safety. Importantly, ethical leadership, organizational justice and gender equity have positive associations with psychological safety. In the supporting past research we found that organizational justice and gender equity are important antecedents to an inclusive climate (Maranto and Griffin, 2011) or negatively related to its opposite, an exclusionary climate as studied herein. In addition, we found that it is insufficient to implement procedural and distributive justice in order to attain psychological safety if an exclusionary climate exists. Thus, in determining how business schools might become role models for gender equity under PRME, this research suggests that a focus on promoting, hiring, and retaining ethical leaders and building gender equity among faculty members will be important factors. We next consider the implications of our research for the implementation of the WEPs in business schools.

Principle 1 of the WEPs states that businesses need to establish high-level corporate leadership for gender equality, so that gender equality is promoted at the highest levels.[5] Carrying this over to business schools, our research suggests that business school leaders must be ethical leaders to model the way forward. Recently, Mayer et al. (2012) found that ethical leaders not only reduced unethical behaviours but also reduced relationship conflict in their departments. Our research extends this with our finding of a positive association between ethical leadership and a psychologically safe climate.

Principle 2 of the WEPs is to "treat all men and women fairly at work—respect and support human rights and nondiscrimination" including equal opportunity and inclusion.[6] Applying this principle to business schools, our research suggests that practicing gender equity and organizational justice will help to avoid exclusionary climates and promote psychological safety within business schools. Psychological safety is one of the forms of safety required by WEP Principle 3 to "ensure the health, safety and well-being of all women and men workers",[7] including those who work in business schools. Importantly, although women experience less psychological safety than men, a psychologically safe climate will inure to the benefit of both women and men.

In our model, we include both procedural and distributive justice, while Maranto and Griffin (2011) examined only procedural justice. Thus, we found that this broader conception of organizational justice is also associated with perceptions of an inclusive climate (i.e. lower exclusionary climate). An inclusive climate in our business schools is also needed to respond to the call in WEP Principle 4 to "promote education, training and professional development for women"[8]; WEP Principle 5 to "implement enterprise development, supply chain and marketing practices that empower women"[9]; and WEP

5 www.weprinciples.org/Site/Principle1
6 www.weprinciples.org/Site/Principle2
7 www.weprinciples.org/Site/Principle3
8 www.weprinciples.org/Site/Principle4
9 www.weprinciples.org/Site/Principle5

Principle 6 to "promote equality through community initiatives and advocacy".[10] The important role that business schools play in enterprise development, including entre-preneurial and new venture competitions, carries with it the responsibility to make sure that such practices are inclusive. We see Principle 6 to be an important part of the out-reach to women-owned businesses in the community and including women on advisory boards.

WEP Principle 7 asks participants to "Measure and publicly report on progress to achieve gender equality"[11]: numbers matter. Maranto and Griffin (2011) confirmed the proposition from relational demography that when women have minority status they perceive greater exclusion. Ultimately, we argue that we need more than just gender equality as measured in numbers—we need environments where people can thrive and be themselves. Our research implies that gender equity and organizational justice not only help women but also create an inclusive climate for men. Gender equity also has a direct association with psychological safety in addition to the indirect association through exclusionary climate. This means that it is especially important to practice gen-der equity in business schools in order to provide psychologically safe climates.

4.9 Limitations and future research

Our research study is cross-sectional, which does not allow for causal inference. Our sampling procedure relies upon individuals who were registered on listservs, and may not be as representative as a random sample of business school professors. Specifi-cally, the sample may have inherent bias because those individuals who read the survey description and then opted to take the online survey may have been respondents with strong opinions about gender equity and psychological safety in business schools. The survey was done in the United States and may not be generalizable to other cultures. Future research could include interventions into academic departments with exclusion-ary climates and a lack of psychological safety to change the climate through increasing ethical leadership, gender equity and procedural and distributive justice.

4.10 Conclusion

The present research holds practical implications for business schools. To clean our houses, forward thinking administrators should seek to create psychological safety for all faculty members. When faculty sense psychological safety then they may better exemplify and impart the principles of PRME and WEP. Moreover, once faculty become the role models of these principles then students may better absorb, learn and apply these principles to their career. As well, we suggest that administrators and faculty intending to model PRME through gender equity should be mindful that simply adding women in to exclusionary climates will fail to recognize the promise of true inclusion. It is not simply numbers of women that change the *status quo*. Rather, it is important

11 www.weprinciples.org/Site/Principle7
10 www.weprinciples.org/Site/Principle6

to practice gender equity and both procedural and distributive justice. Also, business school leaders should practice ethical leadership as a part of their efforts to enact PRME and the WEPs. This should be beneficial not only as it relates to attracting and retaining female faculty, but also in enacting the full potential of PRME.

References

Amiot, C.E., Aubin, R.M., 2013. Why and how are you attached to your social group? Investigating different forms of social identification. British Journal of Social Psychology 52(3), 563–586.

Bailyn, L., 2003. Academic careers and gender equity: lessons learned from MIT. Gender, Work & Organization 10(2), 137–153.

Bandura, A., 1986. Social foundations of thought and action. Prentice Hall, Englewood Cliffs, NJ.

Benschop, Y., Brouns, M., 2003. Crumbling ivory towers: academic organizing and its gender effects. Gender, Work & Organization 10(2), 194–212.

Bezrukova, K., Jehn, K.A., Zanutto, E.L., Thatcher, S.M.B., 2009. Do workgroup faultlines help or hurt? A moderated model of faultlines, team identification, and group performance. Organization Science 20(1), 35–50.

Bilimoria, D., Joy, S., Liang, X.F., 2008. Breaking barriers and creating inclusiveness: lessons of organizational transformation to advance women faculty in academic science and engineering. Human Resource Management 47(3), 423–441.

Brown, M.E., Trevino, L.K., 2006. Ethical leadership: a review and future directions. Leadership Quarterly 17(6), 595–616.

Brown, M.E., Trevino, L.K., Harrison, D.A., 2005. Ethical leadership: a social learning perspective for construct development and testing. Organizational Behavior and Human Decision Processes 97(2), 117–134.

Edmondson, A., 1999. Psychological safety and learning behavior in work teams. Administrative Science Quarterly 44(2), 350–383.

Fisher, B.D., Motowidlo, S., Werner, S., 1993. Effects of gender and other factors on rank of law professors in colleges of business—evidence of a glass ceiling. Journal of Business Ethics 12(10), 771–778.

Fletcher, C., 2007. Passing the buck: gender and management of research production in UK higher education. Equal Opportunities International 26(4), 269–286.

Fotaki, M., 2011. The sublime object of desire (for knowledge): sexuality at work in business and management schools in England. British Journal of Management 22(1), 42–53.

Fotaki, M., 2013. No woman is like a man (in academia): the masculine symbolic order and the unwanted female body. Organization Studies 34(9), 1251–1275.

Fraser, N., 1994. After the family wage: gender equity and the welfare state. Political Theory 22(4), 591–618.

Hayes, A.F., 2013. Introduction to Mediation, Moderation, and Conditional Process Analysis: A Regression-Based Approach. The Guilford Press, New York.

Kahn, W.A., 1990. Psychological conditions of personal engagement and disengagement at work. Academy of Management Journal 33(4), 692–724.

Kantor, J., September 7, 2013. Harvard Business School Case Study: Gender Equity. www.nytimes.com/2013/09/08/education/harvard-case-study-gender-equity.html?pagewanted=all&_r=0 (accessed 15.06.14).

Kilgour, M., Flynn, P., Haynes, K., 2011. Discussion Paper: PRME Working Group on Gender Equality.

Kjeldal, S.-E., Rindfleish, J., Sheridan, A., 2005. Deal-making and rule-breaking: behind the facade of equity in academia. Gender and Education 17(4), 431–447.

Linehan, C., Buckley, J., Koslowski, N., 2009. "Backwards . . . and in high heels": exploring why women have been underrepresented at senior academic levels, 1985–2010. Journal of Workplace Rights 14(4), 399–417.

Maranto, C.L., Griffin, A.E.C., 2011. The antecedents of a 'chilly climate' for women faculty in higher education. Human Relations 64(2), 139–159.

May, D.R., Gilson, R.L., Harter, L.M., 2004. The psychological conditions of meaningfulness, safety and availability and the engagement of the human spirit at work. Journal of Occupational and Organizational Psychology 77(1), 11–37.

Mayer, D.M., Aquino, K., Greenbaum, R.L., Kuenzi, M., 2012. Who displays ethical leadership, and why does it matter? An examination of antecedents and consequences of ethical leadership. Academy of Management Journal 55(1), 151–171.

Parker, C.P., Baltes, B.B., Christiansen, N.D., 1997. Support for affirmative action, justice perceptions, and work attitudes: a study of gender and racial-ethnic group differences. Journal of Applied Psychology 82(3), 376–389.

Ropers-Huilman, B., 2003. Gender in the future of higher education. In: Ropers-Huilman, B. (Ed.), Gendered Futures in Higher Education: Critical Perspectives for Change. State University of New York Press, New York, pp. 1–14.

Schmader, T., 2002. Gender identification moderates stereotype threat effects on women's math performance. Journal of Experimental Social Psychology 38(2), 194–201.

Scott, K.L., Restubog, S.L.D., Zagenczyk, T.J., 2013. A social exchange-based model of the antecedents of workplace exclusion. Journal of Applied Psychology 98(1), 37–48.

Settles, I., Cortina, L., Malley, J., Stewart, A., 2006. The climate for women in academic science: the good, the bad and the changeable. Psychology of Women Quarterly 30(1), 47–58.

Tajfel, H., 1981. Social stereotypes and social groups. In: Turner, J.C., Giles, H. (Eds.), Intergroup Behavior. Basil Blackwell, Oxford, pp. 144–167.

Tajfel, H., Turner, J.C., 1979. An integrative theory of intergroup conflict. In: Austin, W.G., Worchel, S. (Eds.), The Social Psychology of Intergroup Relations, pp. 33–47.

Tepper, B.J., 2000. Consequences of abusive supervision. Academy of Management Journal 43(2), 178–190.

Verbos, A.K., Dykstra, D.V., 2013. Leadership matters: gender equity in business schools. Midwest Academy of Management Meeting, Milwaukee, WI.

Verbos, A.K., Humphries, M.T., 2012. Decoupling equality, diversity, and inclusion from liberal projects: hailing indigenous contributions to institutional change. Equality, Diversity and Inclusion: An International Journal 31(5/6), 506–525.

Walumbwa, F.O., Schaubroeck, J., 2009. Leader personality traits and employee voice behavior: mediating roles of ethical leadership and work group psychological safety. Journal of Applied Psychology 94(5), 1275–1286.

Weisenfeld, L.W., Robinson-Backmon, I.B., 2007. Accounting faculty perceptions regarding diversity issues and academic environment. Issues in Accounting Education 22(3), 429–445.

Xu, Y., 2008. Gender disparity in STEM disciplines: a study of faculty attrition and turnover intentions. Research in Higher Education 49(7), 607–624.

Appendix **Variable item list**

Ethical Leadership (based on Trevino and Harrison, 2005)

1. Persons in positions of leadership in my School of Business conduct their personal lives in an ethical manner.

2. Persons in positions of leadership in my School of Business define success not just by results but also the way that they are obtained.

3. Persons in positions of leadership in my School of Business listen to what employees have to say.

4. Persons in positions of leadership in my School of Business discipline employees who violate ethical standards.

5. Persons in positions of leadership in my School of Business make fair and balanced decisions.

6. Persons in positions of leadership in my School of Business can be trusted.

7. Persons in positions of leadership in my School of Business discuss business ethics or values with employees.

8. Persons in positions of leadership in my School of Business set an example of how to do things the right way in terms of ethics.

9. Persons in positions of leadership in my School of Business have the best interests of employees in mind.

10. Persons in positions of leadership in my School of Business when making decisions ask "What is the right thing to do?".

Gender Equity (Maranto and Griffin, 2011)

1. Taken as a whole, there is general equity in my department for such things as the number of course preparations, students taught and required student contact hours, regardless of gender.

2. Courses are assigned to faculty in an equitable manner in my department in terms of graduate/undergraduate, labour-intensity and scheduling/meeting times, regardless of gender.

3. Procedures for course load reductions are applied uniformly in my department.

4. In general, the number of committee assignments is reasonably uniform across faculty members in my department, regardless of gender.

5. Women have equal access to appointments to the more powerful college and university committees, relative of their numbers and rank.

6. In my department, research by women faculty members is valued less than research by men.

Organizational Justice (based on Christiansen, 1997, published in Field, 2002)

1. People involved in implementing decisions have a say in making the decisions.

2. Members of my School of Business are involved in making decisions that directly affect their work.

3. Decisions are made on the basis of research, data and technical criteria, as opposed to political concerns.

4. People with the most knowledge are involved in the resolution of problems.

5. If a department performs well, there is appropriate recognition and rewards for all.

6. If one performs well, there is appropriate recognition and reward.

7. If one performs well, there is sufficient recognition and reward.

Exclusionary Climate (Maranto and Griffin, 2011)

1. At work I feel isolated.

2. In my department, colleagues do not share some job-related information with me that they share with others.

3. I have opportunities to collaborate on research with other members of my department.

4. An "old boys" network runs my department.

5. I feel welcome and included in informal and social gatherings with most members of my department.

6. I feel that my input and opinions are solicited and valued in faculty decisions in my department.

Psychological Safety (May, Gilson and Harter, 2004)

1. I am not afraid to be myself at work.

2. I am afraid to express my opinions at work.

3. There is a threatening environment at work.

Part II
Disciplinary perspectives

5

Defining the terrain for responsible management education

Gender, gender equality and the case of marketing

Wendy Hein
Birkbeck, University of London, UK

Despite the existence of significant links between gender, marketing and consumer research, and despite a widespread recognition of women's complex relationship with marketing and markets, the concept of gender equality has been widely neglected in this subject discipline. This chapter seeks to provide some understanding of what gender equality may mean through an exploration of various marketing practices, studies and teaching. It begins with a brief overview of marketing's disciplinary developments, followed by explorations of feminist influences in this development. The difficulty of finding appropriate definitions for gender equality in marketing leads to a discussion of how marketing institutions and practices contribute to persistently unequal gender relations. The chapter concludes by offering suggestions for how to address these inequalities, with a particular focus on agents of change, specifically within marketing teaching. Despite a growing momentum of gender equality awareness in marketing practice, teaching and scholarship, the challenges that remain in achieving real change for women and men across the developed and developing world need to be realized.

5.1 Introduction

Women have traditionally had a troubled relationship with marketing. On the one hand, marketing practices have been recognized as exploiting the traditionally female consumer (Catterall, Maclaran and Stevens, 2000). On the other hand, women's future global earnings have the potential of reaching unprecedented dimensions, equalling GDPs of growing economies such as India and China, as they are estimated to increase by $5 trillion over the coming years (Silverstein, Sayre and Butman, 2009). Women's empowerment through marketing seems palpable. Yet, controversially, this empowerment may occur through the very structures that were previously deemed as a source of oppression (Friedan, 1965). Additionally, although gender equality and empowerment of women are increasingly brought to our attention, understanding of what this means in a marketing context may not be straightforward. This chapter highlights the complexities between gender, gender equality and marketing, and the role of education and research.

Although gender issues in marketing have rarely been given the scrutiny they deserve, there is very little about marketing that is not gendered. Without turning to abstract theories or academic jargon, a personal reflection on our daily lives makes us realize how most activities are gendered, including the objects we buy, the places we go and the work we undertake. This may not always be readily attributed to marketing. Yet, nevertheless, we can easily recognize how marketers have created specific consumer profiles that, alongside age, class and disposable income, are frequently defined by gender.

> An example: a trip through the cosmetics department will reveal a plethora of soaps, lotions, creams, shampoos, gels or perfumes, all of which are generally designed for either men or women. How do we know this? Consider the advertising images that tend to be associated with these products, or their packaging. When it comes to the "needs" they fulfil—in all honesty—we may find that products can be very similar in the purposes they serve (i.e. shampoos = wash hair), yet their distinguishing factor, in its most basic form, is still often their gender or the gendering they imply. We may also encounter products such as razors, shaving foams, a flurry of make-up products, as well as condoms or sanitary towels, which are not similar products, yet equally form part of specific gender and gendering practices. As we leave the cosmetics department, we may choose to visit clothing stores, department stores, shopping streets in general or, in fact, many other spaces that form part of everyday life. We regularly encounter sections that separate men and women. Even if there is no explicit male or female distinction, products or services often contain either masculine or feminine connotations: think of the food we eat, the films we watch, the books we read or the hobbies we choose. This separation commences at a very early age, as even young children's toys or clothes are often divided into those for boys and for girls (Auster and Mansbach, 2012).

These examples highlight how marketing has often benefitted and arguably furthered the differences between men and women, rather than promoting potential similarities. Distinct consumer needs are perceived to be at the very core of marketing and profitable markets (Kotler and Armstrong, 2010), and these needs are often said to be gendered.

Little harm may be done with the existence of different shampoos, and sanitary towels are important products that should not be taken for granted (Scott et al., 2012). From the examples above we can understand that gender practices relate to our bodies and are often based on sociocultural expectations. For example, men are expected to shave and women to apply make-up. The above descriptions also imply that our cosmetics department is set within the developed Western world, as different products and their availability may reflect different customs and values in other settings. Do marketers play a role in fashioning these customs or do they support existing gender practices? In either case, their impact on the creation of gender distinctions may be greater than we at first acknowledge.

At this point, however, we are mainly concerned with the understanding of what gender means in marketing contexts. What about gender equality? The notion that marketing is fundamentally based on gender distinctions makes us think about possible meanings of gender equality. How can we aim for equality in marketing when gender means difference? Where does gender cause trouble in marketing and where does a separation between and within the sexes lead to material and social inequality? A more in-depth look at the many aspects of marketing may be worthwhile in an attempt to answer these and other questions.

This chapter commences with a brief excursion into the history of marketing as it developed as a scholarly discipline, followed by feminist influences on this development, particularly since the early 1990s. Subsequently, a discussion of the possible meanings of gender *equality* in marketing leads to a more detailed description of the structures and practices that have led to *inequality* in marketing. Understanding marketing research and teaching as part of institutions and practices that have reproduced inequalities, suggestions for resolutions and challenges they present conclude the chapter.

5.2 Background to marketing as a discipline

For the purposes of conceptualizing gender equality in marketing, it is worth considering how marketing has evolved as a scholarly discipline. All too often, in both teaching and practice, marketing can be readily reduced to the "marketing concept" (Borden, 1964), or the 4Ps—Product, Price, Place and Promotion (Constantinides, 2006)—which are in some contexts extended to 7Ps, if we include People, Physical Evidence and Processes. Alternatively, we could choose to consult the (albeit changing) definitions of the American Marketing Association (AMA, 2013), which, as of July 2013, states that "[m]arketing is the activity, set of institutions, and processes for creating, communicating, delivering, and exchanging offerings that have value for customers, clients, partners, and society at large". Instead of accepting these, a brief review of how marketing developed, including the role of gender (equality) during this process, may provide some idea of how it became recognized in its current form and how it can be shaped in the future (Tadajewski, 2011).

Although there is some dispute regarding the origins of marketing, in particular regarding the first evidence of teaching marketing (Ellis et al., 2011), it is relatively well acknowledged that it emerged out of the wider field of economics (Jones and Shaw, 2002; Stern, 1993a) and management science (Tadajewski and Jones, 2012). However, in its early stages it was not necessarily referred to as marketing, as teaching and practices focused on applying economic theory through improving issues of distribution, sales management or advertising. The fact that we are now referring to marketing and not, for example, distribution management was arguably due to a shift in focus from production, followed by sales, to a focus on marketing where business activities became more and more centred on customers (Keith, 1960). While early writings of marketing retained a commitment to ethical practices (Tadajewski and Jones, 2012), over time, it became equated with persuasion and even propaganda (Bernays and Miller, 1928/2005; Shaw and Jones, 2005), and the creation of marketable demands that could be detrimental to consumers (Desmond and Crane, 2004). Motivated by the promise of ever-increasing profits, "understanding consumers' needs, wants and desires became a priority" (Ellis et al., 2011: 24). Locating profitable markets became the main purpose of marketing, disregarding concerns for societal implications.

Fuelled by investment into education from industry (Ellis et al., 2011), and in the aftermath of the Second World War (Tadajewski, 2012), marketing advanced in the direction towards becoming recognized as a science in its own right (Taylor, 1965), striving to emancipate from related subject disciplines. Often considered opposing to this scientific view, successful achievements of motivation research in advertising and public relations rested on mainly qualitative and interpretive methods (Tadajweski, 2006), and provided marketing with a rather artistic status. The resulting tension of marketing as either an art or a science was eventually resolved as motivation and qualitative research became sidelined in rather trivial scholarly concepts such as consumer segmentation and psychographic profiling (Ellis et al., 2011), or incorporated in advertising practices, which were removed from academic contexts (Stern, 1990, 2004). Marketing science as a research paradigm and in support of managerial functions triumphed in defining the discipline. Although this research aimed at understanding markets and consumers, its capitalist motivations largely disregarded societal consequences, or a focus on consumer diversity or well-being (Tadajewski, 2012).

Arguably, approaches that were previously deemed as artistic re-emerged in consumer research at a later stage, in the shape of naturalistic and interpretive stances (cf. Belk et al., 1989). These supported more critical perspectives that not all research could rely on consumers as rational, their realities as homogenous and objectively measured, and that not all research needed to be (profitable) beneficial to organizations. Similarly, early definitions by the AMA that tended to incorporate marketing goals of profitability and a focus on marketing management were complemented with the message that marketing should also be of value to "society at large" (AMA, 2013). This recognized marketing's impact on social structures and a greater need for accountability.

These and other more recent developments reflect movements towards embracing the diversity of the expanding field of marketing. Increasing transdisciplinarity has led to the study of marketing from various perspectives and recognizes the importance of more critical approaches. However, these brief historical developments also highlight how certain practices and concepts have been privileged over time, and how the dominance of some practices and research paradigms have subordinated other perspectives. Marketing's emancipation as a discipline was driven by power structures that represented an organizations' desire for rising profits and understood the consumer as a source of increasing wealth. Values such as prediction, control and universalism led this managerial paradigm and side-lined approaches that were concerned with representing varied voices of differing social structures and critical engagement with power (Tadajewski, 2012). These directions in turn have informed our understanding and teaching of marketing, and its scientific base has remained relatively unchallenged and taken for granted until now.

5.3 Women and feminism in the formation of the marketing discipline

Against this backdrop, we can begin to understand how concepts of gender and gender equality have evolved. The previously mentioned focus on specific paradigms, ways of researching and processes of transforming marketing into a science, also tended to exclude women. It would be incorrect to equate gender or gender equality with women or the feminine. Yet, in the absence of women, gender remained relatively unproblematic. Instead, masculine gender norms and the construction of hierarchies based on these became naturally accepted. Feminist movements were among the first to highlight the gendering of marketing and the segregation of women in the field. Stern's (1993a) article on feminist theory in the marketing classroom is of particular importance in this context.

Stern illustrates changes in the marketing curriculum, comparing it to Lerner's (1979), and Schuster and Van Dyne's (1985) review of how feminist perspectives transformed teaching in the humanities. The six stages reflect changes, commencing with women as (1) absent from academic communities, (2) towards early integrations, (3) following liberal feminist perspectives, (4) followed by radical/women's voice feminism, (5) black/lesbian feminism, and, lastly, (6) poststructuralist feminism. Before women's entry into the academy, the great, white, Western canon (Gordon, 1997), labelled by Stern (1993a: 230) as the established "great minds" curriculum, was widely accepted as underpinning research and teaching. During the early stages, "women worthies"[1] (Lerner, 1975) were expected to measure up to established androcentric academic cultures, where masculine ideologies had provided the historical context (Bristor and Fischer, 1993). "Often

---

1 "Women worthies" or "compensatory history" are terms used by Lerner (1975) to describe women who do not challenge or deviate from dominant, masculine structures, but rather accept them. Their achievements have been celebrated in history as they equalled those of men; however, she does not accept them as "notable women", as this should relate to histories of women who were exceptional and stood apart from the mass, of either men or women.

at this point the departmental response was to hire a 'tokenwomen' and assign her to teach a 'Women and . . .' course" (Stern, 1993a: 231). Although this initiated an increasing presence of women and some expansion of the curriculum, the established paradigms remained unchallenged and, in fact, became reiterated by female scholars who had been educated in this tradition. Not only did these women face tremendous insecurities as they were continuously reminded of their insignificance, considering the long history of knowledge production by their male counterparts, but their presence (and shortcomings) also justified, even enhanced, a male superiority in their scholarly legitimacy.

As feminist perspectives advanced from liberal to radical, and women realized the systematic discrimination they had experienced, angry and critical voices emerged. However, attempts to develop alternative research and teaching approaches were still lacking as women academics "too had been trained to think like men. They carried the baggage of patriarchal standards and accepted methods of generating knowledge" (Stern, 1993a: 231). Nevertheless, during this time the gendering of research and teaching became visible. As perspectives advanced to incorporate dimensions of race, class and sexuality, a postmodern or poststructuralist vision looked ahead to a multicultural future, envisaging a focus on inclusivity and pluralism. As Stern (1993a: 233) noted: "Diversity is the keynote of the 1990s, for the unisex urge of the 1970s has been replaced by the postmodern acceptance of difference".

Stern's (1993a) review simplifies the evolution of feminist advances in academia from the 1960s to the 1990s, but provides a frame of reference for the feminist developments and the current state of marketing. Although some aspects of the marketing discipline were touched by feminism, Stern argued that women were still at the early stages of entering the field, as their voices continued to be marginalized and dismissed by dominant structures and institutions. For example, to this day, the *Journal of Marketing* and the *Journal of Marketing Research* have yet to publish a feminist article, or work that problematizes gender issues in marketing.

Further support for feminist theories was found in specific research communities, such as among consumer researchers. Responding to the lack of gender issues in the wider marketing discipline (Costa, 1991), the early 1990s saw a turning point in marketing and consumer research (Bettany et al., 2010) with an inaugural conference on Gender, Marketing and Consumer Behavior. Various papers that drew on feminist theories were subsequently published in leading journals such as the *Journal of Consumer Research*. Adopting mainly poststructural or postmodern feminist perspectives during this time, they pointed out prevailing masculine ideologies, which dominated in marketing and consumer research, and largely critiqued prevailing dualisms that reduced gender to male/female, masculine/feminine, objective/subjective, rational/emotional, active/passive, public/private or producer/consumer dichotomies, with the former privileged over the latter (Bristor and Fischer, 1993; Hirschman, 1993).

Similar critiques emerged from postmodern feminist perspectives on marketing's use of the female body (Joy and Venkatesh, 1994). The body/mind dualism was argued to be pervasive in marketing and consumer research, and the often sexualized female body conceptualized as the object of masculine desire and regulation. The rational masculine mind was seen as opposing the emotional female body, affecting consumer culture surrounding the body in terms of "food, dieting, clothing, fashion, and exercise, to all kinds of phenomenological experiences concerning the body" (Joy and Venkatesh, 1994: 339).

The rhetoric of the marketing concept became the subject of poststructuralist feminist critique by Fischer and Bristor (1994). Deconstructing the marketer/consumer discourse into understanding the consumer as female or feminine and the marketer as male or masculine, the article provided feminist readings of the development of the marketing concept from production orientation, sales orientation, customer orientation, to relationship orientation. The authors argued that marketers (male) imposed their offerings on the consumer, traditionally perceived as female. Marketing rhetoric, including traditional textbook discourse, was reinterpreted as exploiting and as virtually violating powerless consumers. Although a relationship marketing concept provided further recognition of consumers as active and emancipated, Fischer and Bristor's (1994) interpretations sought to address the power imbalances that exist between marketing producers and consumers. Marketing (theory) had therefore been fundamentally imbalanced.

An imbalance was also found in the reading of advertising images. Feminist literary criticism was used to examine advertising images and responses to these (Stern, 1993b). Advertisements were argued to be gendered texts that were either androcentric or gynocentric, containing masculine or feminine connotations, and although women were used to "reading" both texts, men's interest remained on androcentric texts.

Lastly, Peñaloza (1994) equally challenged gender dichotomies in relation to body, identity and sexuality in her discussion of gender crossings. She offered some suggestions for how postmodern gender expressions are subverting or creating parodies of these gender dualisms, in short, how they "cause trouble" (referring to Judith Butler's [2006] gender trouble). She argued that these should be considered in marketing contexts and that gender discourses are attached to "market offerings and marketing communications, such as products, advertisements, music videos and film" (p. 361), which informed both gender production and consumption.

Some feminist-inspired works played a key role in advancing our understanding of gender in marketing and consumer research. These and other authors highlighted how gender had been essentialized and blindly assumed. Before then, it had not been sufficiently problematized or defined while a masculine lens was accepted as natural (Artz and Venkatesh, 1991; Stern, 1993b). Gender had been accepted as a constant or input variable, interchangeably used with the concept of sex (i.e. male or female), as opposed to being the outcome of marketing or consumer behaviour practices. Further, aforementioned feminist articles critiqued marketing's scientific claims of objective knowledge, and how women had been regarded as objects, rarely as subjects, of knowledge. Their critiques further extended to the use of machine metaphors in place of human (gendered) experiences and the pursuit of profits instead of socially responsible behaviour. As such, feminist perspectives often blamed current market structures and advocated Marxist approaches (Hirschman, 1993). During this time it appeared that women's emancipation from markets (and marketing) was irreconcilable with capitalism, managerialism or profitability.

On the other hand, postmodern feminist calls for greater tolerance of differences and multiplicity, and for living with ambiguity and ambivalence (Fischer and Bristor, 1994), led to understandings of gender as subjectively constructed and privately "consumed".

Postfeminist re-enchantments with marketing and consumer culture shifted perceptions of women's stereotypical role as consumers as oppressive, towards seeing them
as empowering and even liberating (Maclaran, 2012). Women could now find the
resources to construct their "desired gender" in the market. This led to understandings
of market feminism as a paradigm shift (Scott, 2006). Consumer culture also emerged as
a refuge for men who sought to escape a masculine gender crisis (Holt and Thompson,
2004; Thompson and Holt, 2004; Tuncay and Otnes, 2008), and men emerged as nego-
tiators of multiple identities. These postmodern, liberatory views (Firat and Venkatesh,
1995) were also met with criticism as consumer power was a privilege largely reserved
by men and women with the necessary capital, and excluded others who could not make
the choices to become their desired, authentic or multiple self (Catterall, Maclaran and
Stevens, 2005). These tensions highlight the problematic relationship between feminism
and market structures. They also emphasize the various feminist positions that could
argue towards female empowerment and emancipation in marketing in multiple ways.

Since the surge of feminist research in consumer research during the 1990s, feminist voices have reappeared in isolated cases, for example, highlighting the continued "gender blindspot" of marketing research communities (Maclaran et al., 2009), or
in edited works, which summarize the complex relationships between feminism and
marketing (Catterall, Maclaran and Stevens, 2000). However, possibly due to its own
fragmentation and conflicted views, feminism has not achieved the same impact in marketing and consumer research it had experienced during the 1990s, until now.

Feminism is not the only lens that has examined gender in marketing. Various other
theories outside or related to feminism, such as identity, masculinity, queer theory or
subcultures (Kates, 1999, 2002), have equally been applied. However, these perspectives
have often failed to address gender as problematic or political in marketing. This seems
to be changing with various projects, such as the Principles for Responsible Management initiative, highlighting the continued issues that women and marginalized voices
continue to face across the globe. Another notable example is Linda Scott's (2010) work,
which seeks to address women's issues in the developing world, in one instance through
the provision of sanitary care and sexual health education, highlighting how consumption and market feminism may not only be for the privileged, white middle-classes.

Ultimately, the review of current and past research in this chapter leads us to question
what we can learn about gender equality from feminism. We have still not addressed the
question of how we can conceptualize gender equality in marketing and consumer research.

5.4 What is gender equality in marketing and consumer research?

Throughout all these, we have to acknowledge that (gender) equality is used implicitly,
and at times explicitly within some of the research mentioned above (i.e. Bristor and
Fischer, 1993; Catterall, Maclaran and Stevens, 2005). Yet no known attempt has been

made to systematically define it in marketing or consumer research. The below conceptualizations are therefore tentative and rely on feminist advances in the field where the term has appeared most often.

From the above discussions, we can already observe that defining gender equality is a problematic task. Depending on the feminist perspective we have adopted, meanings of gender equality can vary widely, with some arguing that significant advances have already been achieved, as, for example, women's emancipation can be connected with changes arising from postmodern market structures (Firat and Venkatesh, 1995), others proposing that we have yet a long way to go (Catterall, Maclaran and Stevens, 2000). This becomes particularly evident in the debates between postfeminist and critical feminist perspectives, as the former perceive markets as empowering and the solution to gender issues, the latter as exclusive and the source of trouble. We can, however, learn several lessons from all these perspectives, which can inform our understanding of gender equality.

Feminism continues to incorporate activist and grassroots movements, which have however been neglected of late in marketing contexts (Catterall, Maclaran and Stevens, 2005; Dobscha and Prothero, 2012). Feminist perspectives share a vision of equal rights and, to some degree, equal valuing of different points of view, no matter how distinct they are (Scott, 1988). As such, feminists share pragmatic stances in their acknowledgement of action as a driver for change (Scott et al., 2012). Activism towards the recognition of marginalized voices can also be integrated into marketing teaching and research.

Feminist theory in marketing also led to the further definition and problematization of gender and sex. As a result, sex became widely understood as the biological distinction between male and female, and gender as the sociocultural construct (Catterall, Maclaran and Stevens, 2005). Both, however, were seen as "causing trouble" in marketing, as the body became the site for gendering practices (Peñaloza, 1994) as well as sociocultural customs, as illustrated in the introduction to this chapter. Biology and sociocultural expectations often conflate in practices and their marketing (Scott et al., 2012). While we may therefore seek empowerment for women, we need to understand that "women" is not a universal category (Bristor and Fischer, 1995), but that empowerment needs to be considered contextually. Additionally, gender is not just problematic for women, but also for men (Catterall, Maclaran and Stevens, 2000).

Contextual and cultural issues of gender equality are further illustrated by the problematic relationship between marketing and market structures. Consuming "for the greater good" as exemplified in Scott's work may improve material, lived realities of young women in Sub-Saharan Africa, and their empowerment and education may eventually lead them out of oppression from male regimes. Nevertheless, this does not change the fact that their human rights continue to be violated and that men's behaviour in these contexts remains unchallenged. It is argued that gender equality issues are therefore based on unequal gender relations, and their sociocultural and contextual perpetuation need to be addressed through marketing and consumer research.

Informing this debate, we have to acknowledge that oppression continues on the basis of persistent dualisms of masculine/feminine, strong/weak, rational/emotional, public/private and so on. Despite deconstructions of these in academia (and critiques of alternative concepts such as "fluidity" [Borgerson and Rehn, 2004]), the unequal valuing of knowledge in the academy continues (Catterall, Maclaran and Stevens, 2000). Similarly, marketing persistently reproduces stereotypes that become accepted across cultures, and practiced in consumers' everyday lives across the globe. These practices (re)create material differences from which marketers frequently benefit and do little to challenge existing power structures. Additionally, the constructed distinctions between men and women have been important to marketers, as often similar products are designed and marketed differently to men or women.

On the other hand, "equality" does not have to mean "the same" or "gender neutral". Distinctions between genders are often important, in particular when it comes to the valuing of body differences, such as in healthcare contexts as seen in Scott's (2010) example of sanitary care and sex education. "The same" or "different" is therefore not the solution to our problem of defining equality (Scott, 1988). Rather, the issue lies in the continued construction of gender stereotypes, myths (Stern, 1995) or customs that often underlie dualisms, and their integration in social structures and institutions that marketing readily relies on. For example, the private or domestic spheres continue to be depicted as women's spaces whereas the public or workspace continues to be dominated by men (Friedan, 1965; Gentry and Harrison, 2010; Collinson and Hearn, 2005).

Taking a pragmatic stance (Scott et al., 2012), we have to move beyond these critiques and question what the alternatives are. What should action be directed towards? Should we think of gender equality in terms of diversity, neutrality or, as poststructuralist feminists suggested, ambivalence and ambiguity? Arguably, either or all of these are contextually dependent. The re-theorizing of gender to incorporate meanings of gender equality may be important in academic circles, but what matters more is how this can be translated into marketing practice and teaching. Have we even experienced gender equality in marketing at some point in time? Or are we, as Stern (1993a) highlighted, too socialized in our own participation in "masculine marketing and consumer cultures" (in research, teaching and practice) that we cannot imagine alternative approaches?

A conception of alternatives requires a more thorough understanding of the (un)equal relations that are embedded in marketing institutions and practices. It may be worth thinking of specific contexts of where *inequality* and discrimination have been observed in marketing and consumer research. The following sections are dedicated to this, followed by suggestions of alternatives for teaching, researching and practicing gender equality in marketing and consumer research.

5.5 Inequality and discrimination in marketing and consumer research—where and how?

Some examples of where inequality has been observed have already been broached in the above discussions. As a result of the historical development of marketing as an academic discipline, women's perspectives have tended to be excluded. As women entered the field, their perspectives were rarely acknowledged as "different" or equally valued in their own right. Women entering these academic structures were openly discriminated against, and although discrimination is less obviously detected nowadays, it continuous to this day (Hirschman, 2010). Whether discrimination is based on sex, race or age (or a combination of these), the pay gap between female and male academics in marketing departments persists (Blackaby, Booth and Frank, 2005). Women's work, even in public educational landscapes, such as the United Kingdom, emerges as less materially rewarded than men's. Thus, we could argue that women who seek to climb the ladder in academic cultures are still accepted as "women worthies" (Lerner, 1975) who need to be measured according to standards that are institutionally established by predominantly male superiors, peers and academic cultures. Alongside their research, this may also affect their teaching and decision-making in curriculum design.

Evidence for a lack of gender focus in the marketing curriculum was already presented above. The canon of the "great minds" (Stern, 1993a), as represented by established marketing concepts and following primarily motivations of managerialism and profitability, continues to play the most significant role in marketing classrooms across the globe. Stern (1993a) communicated the issues she faced in her attempts to introduce courses on feminism and marketing, and ultimately circumvented departmental restrictions by cross-fertilizing programs with the Women's Studies department at her university. This highlighted the institutionalization underlying current marketing programs and concepts, and the barriers to introducing a focus on gender issues. Arguably, these courses are less attractive to students as the connection between gender, marketing and (profitable) business has so far been unacknowledged (although this may be changing with new evidence of gendered consumer power). Alternatives have been offered in the form of teaching "critical reflection" (Catterall, Maclaran and Stevens, 2002), which may not only incorporate the teaching of critical awareness of gender problems, but also of other global issues such as poverty, corruption or sustainability, which can also be connected to marketing, and gender (Dobscha and Ozanne, 2000; Dobscha and Prothero, 2012). Arguably, critical thinking is also a skill that is desired by employers. Fundamentally, we have to acknowledge that marketing curricula are shaped in response to student and job market expectations (Scott, 1999).

Students' perceptions of marketing and skills required for accessing marketing industries need to be understood in connection with their own consumption of marketing. Marketing producers are also consumers of marketing practices, including services, products, spaces and messages (Peñaloza, 1994). Marketing plays a role in our everyday lives, which makes it possibly more permeating on social structures than other disciplines. Its producers therefore have a significant responsibility, as they influence the products that are designed, for whom and how these are communicated. As a field of employment, female participation increased significantly in marketing (Maclaran and Catterall, 2000; Catterall, Maclaran and Stevens, 1997), although this was not always unproblematic. Discrimination and women's perception of working in male cultures was also observed here. For example, advertising cultures, as prominently illustrated in the US television series "Mad Men", continue to be built on male exclusivity to this day (Nixon, 2003; Nixon and Crewe, 2004). In fact, research has compared the macho behaviour in advertising agencies to men's locker rooms (Bird, 1996). Furthermore, although women are embarking on marketing careers, they rarely come to occupy leading positions. The number of female creative advertising directors in the United States currently stands at 3%, which have led to some movements in the industry in the last years (3% Conference, 2014). This means that although women are largely recognized in their consumer power (the 3% movement claims that women represent 80% of consumer expenditure in the United States), 97% of advertising messages are designed and created under male creative leadership. Women have started to voice their frustration over this, and there is some evidence that senior management structures are changing, as, for example, the four biggest advertising agencies in Boston are currently managed by women (Leung, 2014). However, so far activities have mainly focused on the United States, and there is a need for generating further awareness, which should lead to more widespread change.

Marketing industries are thus further examples of structures or institutions that are predominantly led by men. Considering their role as marketing producers, this may explain the gender issues that have developed over time. For example, advertising has often been the source of conflict for many women, through the portrayal of sexist images, and practices that have led to their sexualization and objectification (Goffman, 1979; Kilbourne, 1994, 1999; Gurrieri, Brace-Govan and Cherrier, 2014). Indeed, in Kilbourne's (2013) latest documentation edition of "Killing us softly", she argued that instead of observing progress in the kind of images directed towards women, they have increased in either subtlety or provocative sexualization. She also related advertising and marketing to popular culture (Featherstone, 1991). Comparing popular culture in our environment to water in a fish tank, it is as ubiquitous as oxygen, whether we are conscious of it or not. Similar to Kilbourne's initiative, the MissRepresentation project aims to generate awareness regarding inappropriate images directed at women and the effect these have on women's self-esteem and their perceived subordination in society (The Representation Project, 2014). Some examples of similar UK campaigns addressing the lack of "equal" representation in the media include the "No More Page 3 Campaign", relating to the continued portrayal of nude women on page 3 in the daily UK newspaper *The Sun* (No More Page 3, 2014). Interestingly, these movements and campaigns are often fostered by social media, such as YouTube, Twitter, Instagram, Facebook or Tumblr (McPherson, 2014).

Advertising does not hold sole responsibility, as other industries relating to popular culture also play significant roles. For example, music industries and music lyrics have often been recognized as sources of women's discrimination, one case in point being the hip hop culture (Arthur, 2006). Additionally, the Geena Davis Institute researches the portrayal of female characters in children's media and actively campaigns for the increasing representation of girls, particularly in active roles (Geena Davis Institute, 2014). The lack of appropriate role models in TV genres such as soap operas was also noted in marketing and consumer research (Stern, Russell and Russell, 2005; 2007). As before, the majority of these activities has thus far concentrated on the United States and therefore addresses particular cultural contexts. However, given the influence of the United States in the global marketing production, it is important to carry the momentum of these campaigns into other contexts. European countries, such as Sweden, have recognized issues of marketed images of women as posing public health concerns, to the degree that these are now informing policy regulation debates (The Swedish Women's Lobby, 2014).

Besides these activist movements in relation to advertising and popular culture, marketing scholars have equally critiqued gender images (Schroeder and Borgerson, 1998). However, as with feminist theory, advertisements were often subject to multiple interpretations that depended on the spectator (Brown, Stevens and Maclaran, 1999). Furthermore, women are not the only targets of advertising. As marketing and consumer research started to incorporate issues of masculinity in gender debates, the male gaze on marketing images was also argued to shift (Patterson and Elliott, 2002) or expand its boundaries to previously unknown territories (Schroeder and Zwick, 2004), although differences in positions between men and women were still recognized. Men were also found to police their own "look" according to idealized images in their environment, albeit to a lesser extent than women (Elliott and Elliott, 2005). More recent analyses of gender in advertising highlighted how men and women continue to be portrayed in stereotypical roles. For example, women continue to occupy mothering roles and men's portrayals as the active parent is often ignored, although the number of single and active fathers has increased over the last few years (Gentry and Harrison, 2010). Marketing images and popular culture therefore promote gender structures alongside products or services, and hold back cultural development by reinforcing stereotypes (Bristor and Fischer, 1995). They connect with lifestyles that advertisers perceive as desirable. This however places the onus back on marketing producers and their perception of "desirable" gender relations.

Products, services and advertising are examples of marketing and marketed constructs that become symbolically and materially branded with gender meanings, which often reflect unequal valuing of men and women. They fundamentally affect how women and men live their lives. This can be observed in the construction of spaces and practices. In this context, sport can be recognized as another institution historically led by men (Brace-Govan, 2010). As a result of men's visibility in sport, reports from the UK women's sport and fitness foundation found that between 2010 and 2011 women's sport attracted 0.5% of the overall sponsorship market in the United Kingdom (WSFF, 2011), although audiences of women's sporting events grew. The market support for female advances in traditionally male spaces and practices has thus far been neglected, and has led to the activist "Big Deal?" campaign in the United Kingdom. Similarly, sporting spaces often ignore gender differences, for example, in their provision of facilities (Hein, 2010) or in branded service-scapes, in cases such as the ESPN zone in the United States (Sherry et al., 2004). These restaurant chains and arcade game retail outlets often explicitly addressed an exclusively male audience, and implicitly branded masculinity in details such as the food menus. ESPN zones have now declined in popularity in the United States, forcing many outlets to close.

However, we can find many other examples of marketed spaces where gender becomes symbolically, implicitly or explicitly embedded. Obvious examples include restaurant chains, such as Hooters, but less extreme cases abound in common retail settings that divide male and female spaces, and some contexts from which men are often considered as passive, if mentioned at all (Otnes and McGrath, 2001; Tuncay and Otnes, 2008). Examples include some cosmetic, clothing and grocery retail spaces, or activities such as gift shopping, which tended to be accepted or contested as either women's work or leisure (Thompson, 1996; Woodruffe-Burton, Eccles and Elliott, 2002). Although gender may appear relatively unproblematic in these instances, and spaces have also emerged as sites of subversion or transgression from gender norms (Thompson, 2013), they nevertheless contribute to our understandings of the type of spaces that are designed for men and women and regulate access and behaviour in these settings. They reflect a finely tuned marketing system of sociocultural gender expectations.

Marketing thus contributes to how consumers shape their lives on a daily basis. Their construction of gender is not just a private choice, but is also influenced by the gendering of products and services, and so on. Arguably, products and services are based on consumers' needs. However, considering feminists critiques of power, they may be based on marketers' needs for profits (Fischer and Bristor, 1994). Of course, bodily needs can differ between men and women (Thompson and Hirschman, 1995; Joy and Venkatesh, 1994). However, these "needs" largely reflect the sociocultural and historical constructions of gender relations, and the conventions that have become accepted between men and women. As such, although we may be more alike than different in our gender (Carothers and Reis, 2013), gender differences are fodder for marketers as they provide the possibility for the expansion of product ranges. The emergence of the metrosexual male, originally a dismissive term for men who engaged in vanity-boosting consumption practices (Simpson, 1994), was arguably a marketing invention (Salzman, Matathia and O'Reilly, 2005), as beauty and care products that had been previously deemed unsuitable for men had now found a new market. In marketing terms, this permitted the sale of more moisturizer; in consumer terms, it provided further resources for the construction of the "effeminate male".

The marketing of products, services and their communication affects consumers and their understanding of gender. Marketing educates us in our gender practices and socializes our expectations of how and what we should consume as men or women in specific sociocultural contexts. We can already see how products, such as toys, affect the gendering of children from a very young age (Auster and Mansbach, 2012; Pennell, 1994). However, gender norms can also be played with through ambivalence and irony, as consumers can avoid stereotyping (Hein and O'Donohoe, ahead-of-print). Nevertheless, products and objects take on symbolic meanings that distinguish consumers, and consumers in turn use these symbolic resources to identify themselves and others. Gender meanings therefore play a role as much for marketing producers as for consumers. The symbolic and material power of marketing transcends into conceptualizations of behaviour appropriate for women and men (Catterall, Maclaran and Stevens, 2000). This does not just affect women, but rather the relationships, roles and practices negotiated between various men and women. It is these relations and their construction across contexts that are often unequally valued and can lead to material differences. In terms of consumption and production, women continue to take primary responsibility for childcare and domestic work. Work in these private spaces has now started to become "outsourced" as a result of the increasing professionalization of women (Epp and Price, 2008), highlighting its material and economic value. Current reports from the United Kingdom emphasize that childcare costs for some parents have now exceeded average monthly mortgage repayments (Family and Childcare Trust, 2014; Richardson, 2014). Consumer research has previously underlined the struggling and juggling lifestyles of women, as they are now expected to manage career, family and households (Thompson, 1996). Across the globe, we can identify clear gender differences in how consumption and production are valued (Nelson, 1998; Ruwanpura and Humphries, 2004) and marketing could play a role in changing these assumptions as opposed to reinforcing them.

Consumers and their gender in turn inform scholarly marketing research, and the conceptualizations of gender, as well as the research tools, are far from equally valued. Within the marketing academy, gender differences continue to be perceived as natural, and gender as an "effect" is rarely defined or problematized. For example, differences in behaviour or tastes are mainly examined regarding managerial effectiveness (cf. Wyllie, Carlson and Rosenberger, 2014), not in terms of social implications. Women and men are, in the first instance, perceived as different, not as the same (cf. Myers-Levy and Sternthal, 1991). The unequal valuing of different research paradigms and the topics that are published in high-quality journals in turn affects what and how we research. For example, Maclaran (2010) presented a critique of the Research Excellence Framework that measures scholarly output across institutions in the United Kingdom (cf. Harley, 2002; Maclaran et al., 2009). Two of the highest-scoring journals in the area of marketing are the *Journal of Marketing* and the *Journal of Marketing Research*, both of which, as previously established, do not contain research where gender equality issues have been vocalized. How is it possible to argue for the importance of gender issues in marketing when this debate cannot be found in its leading outlets?

This closes the circle as the unequal valuing of research in turn influences the structuring of academic departments; those with "higher-quality" research as defined by peer-reviewed publications in highly ranked journals advance. The cycle that has been constructed in this debate is illustrated in Figure 5.1.

Figure 5.1 **Marketing institutions and structures as sites of unequal gender relations**

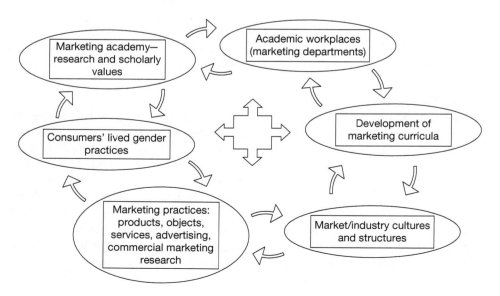

In this cyclical movement of the marketing system described above, from curricula of marketing education, to industry, to marketing practices, to consumers, to research, we continuously encounter unequal gender relations that are embedded in these hierarchical structures, institutions and practices. Providing the overall context for this vicious cycle, we could also add a critique of the entire marketing concept, as it too (re)produces and reflects inequality, not just between men and women, but between those who "have" and others who "have not". It is an exclusive system that, so far, has been led by those in power or who possess capital (Fischer and Bristor, 1994; Catterall, Maclaran and Stevens, 2005). As a result, there are limited possibilities for organizations to "do good", as return on investment and profitability are the most significant benchmarks (Crane and Desmond, 2002).

Thus far, we have mainly considered marketing and its impact in the developed world where main material differences are based on class and race distinctions (Bristor and Fischer, 1995), but where women have made significant advances (Scott, 2006). However, any changes to marketing systems in the developed world should also lead to material differences in the developing world where gender relations are far more unequal and firmly rooted within traditions and histories. How can this be achieved? How can we break the cycle of (re)production of inequality?

5.6 Resolution/challenges of inequality in marketing

Historically, women appear to be absent from marketing structures or institutions. If they were present, they were largely invisible or undervalued in their roles, or their presence did little to challenge institutional gender power structures (Lerner, 1975). Additionally, the above discussion shows that marketing institutions and structures reach further into everyday lives and cultures than we may have previously anticipated. Women's representation, participation and greater visibility may therefore not be the sole solution, as we saw earlier, that the entry of women into academic departments actually reinforced male structures. Importantly, it is necessary to build awareness regarding the lack of gender problematization in marketing across these areas.

We could start by re-conceptualizing equality to reflect the problem of gender relations. For example, the concept of inclusivity (Anderson, 2008) sought to promote equality among men's differing masculinities based on sexuality in fraternal settings. Extending this concept further to reflect a respect for differences in gender relations, inclusivity also provides possibilities for thinking beyond productive dualisms of masculine/feminine, male/female or producer/consumer (Borgerson and Rehn, 2004). This would mean that gender equality is not just an issue concerning women, but also men. Another theoretical alternative may be found in the concept of intersectionality as it depicts gender relations between men and women from different class, race, age, sexuality, religion and cultural backgrounds (Gopaldas and Fischer, 2012). Inclusivity and intersectionality may, however, conceal the material differences that persist between men and women, and may not problematize gender issues fittingly. Critical and historical marketing studies (Ellis et al., 2011; Catterall, Maclaran and Stevens, 1999, 2002; Tadajweski, 2011) may present a relevant research community that could carry these reconceptualizations further.

Awareness of the marketing system of inequality may however not suffice. It is important to recruit "agents of change" (Stern, 1993), who need to be positioned at every touch point of marketing institutions, structures and practices, that reproduce inequality. In particular, these agents need to recognize that they are in positions of power. Change needs to be pragmatic, combining grassroots and activist movements with policy making, research and education as well as leading marketing organizations. Silverstein, Sayre and Butman (2009) pointed to the aggregate consumer power of women; this should be extended to the aggregate activist power of women. Considering the various grassroots campaigns that are now fighting for women's empowerment in the various marketing structures illustrated above, these voices need to join forces in order to form an unavoidable authority that operates from both the margins and the centre. Additionally, "agents of change" should be differentiated to "agents of leverage" (Silverstein, Sayre and Butman, 2009) in that empowerment is not solely women's responsibility. The solution may not solely lie in the provision of time-saving products and services for women, as this does not address unequal division of labour (Collinson and Hearn, 2005). Rather, marketing should address issues of imbalanced valuing of work and power distribution within gender relations, meaning that women's empowerment should be everyone's responsibility. Agents of change therefore do not have to be women, but rather humans with a conviction that marketing can be used as a tool to empower women and marginalized voices. Thus far, gender empowerment has been lacking significantly in the marketing literature, and should be understood as a pragmatic concept that may find further resonance in critical theory (Murray and Ozanne, 1991), transformative consumer research (Mick, 2006) and action research (Ozanne and Saatcioglu, 2008). Macromarketing may present a further research community that could incorporate these initiatives (Kilbourne, McDonagh and Prothero, 1997).

Despite these initiatives, the problem of what gender equality may actually mean continues. The notion of marketing as facilitator of inequality across a wide range of institutions and practices is palpable. However, what are the alternatives? And how much does marketing contribute to the material or symbolic production of inequality? As much as we already know, detailed information and data are missing. This may also be a cultural phenomenon: the United States seems at the forefront of advancing women's issues in these areas, and Scandinavia also appears to have taken positive steps forward, particularly in terms of education and policy. However, information is required from contexts where marketing systems are still predominantly male and where material differences between male and female, both as consumers and producers, are most significant.

We have started to encounter growing awareness of women's power as both producers and consumers in the developed world. As mentioned in the introduction, the aggregate consumer power of women has the potential of dwarfing rising economies such as China or India (Silverstein, Sayre and Butman, 2009). Markets and marketing are therefore argued to present potential for empowerment. However, we need to consider who culturally and contextually defines meanings of production and consumption. Even within the developed world, this has largely remained unchanged as women continue to work "for free" and/or for less than their male counterparts. Additionally, the reliance on existing market structures and institutions means we rely on existing power distribution. Even if women are empowered by consumption and markets, at this point this would mostly affect white, middle-class women in the developed world whose material and symbolic differences to their male counterparts may be minimal in contrast to women in developing countries. Just because women have entered the equation as they posit a profitable market, this does not necessarily lead to change. Rather, the momentum that is gathering needs to be used to (re)negotiate institutionalized inequality for those who are at the margins of markets and marketing.

We need to remain aware of women and marginalized voices in relation to class, age, race, sexualities and religion, particularly in the developing world. There is a need for greater awareness and empowerment of those who participate in alternative markets, to consider ways of redistributing power and capital equally. As marketers and market-ing scholars, this should not only form part of any economic or political agenda, but as our sense of duty to humanity. A return to the ethical roots of marketing (Tadajewski and Jones, 2012) and considerations of gender and consumer vulnerability in marketing production (Coleman, 2012) may be fruitful research directions for this.

Regarding those who have the power to shape the curriculum, academics and educa-tors need to (re)think their teaching. Gender issues and gender equality should become a central part of marketing education and, if possible, not just at tertiary or university level. Scholars and academics have a responsibility to become agents of change to affect research and teaching directions of potential future business leaders. In this context, the difficulty of defining gender equality in the curriculum also remains. The final sections offer some suggestions for the development of teaching in this respect.

In the first instance, awareness of gender issues is key and critical reflection should be an important aspect of all marketing teaching (Catterall, Maclaran and Stevens, 2002). The use of images and practical marketing material may be useful in this context, or the illustration of activist campaigns as mentioned above may provide good examples. Role playing in class and the sex reversal method may also serve to illustrate socially constructed, taken for granted gender differences (as quoted in Stern, 1993b; Fetterley, 1978; Russ, 1972). In this method, an advertising campaign or a product design is dis-cussed, and after its conceptualization the question is raised of whether gender roles or target audiences could be reversed. If the answer is yes, then why not place a man in the image instead of a woman? If the answer is no, then why not?

Lastly, we can argue that defining gender equality is a farce. Instead of providing universal answers for what gender equality may be, each of the areas in the market-ing system illustrated above needs to be critically examined for its impact on gen-der relations. Treating women and men the same is not the solution, but neither is the insistence on categorical differences. Rather, we should exercise respect for con-textual differences. Equality needs to neither ignore nor blindly accept gender dif-ferences as objectively true (Scott, 1988). Considering the vast range of examples of critical perspectives on marketing as producer of inequality, and the relativism of what equality may mean as a result of diverse feminist perspectives, it is important to build a catalogue of positive, empowering examples (Scott, 2010). Even if these are still flawed, they should be recognized if they can change material and symbolic differences between women and men.

5.7 Conclusion

The above discussion presents idealized scenarios. For more than 100 years, and arguably even before then, women have tried to emancipate, empower and gain equality in structures that socioculturally and historically have been dominated by men. As we have observed, even if this has changed women's lives in terms of the type of products or objects that have been deemed appropriate for them or the messages directed towards them, men continue to be at the helm of market(ing) systems. As idealized and naïve the above solutions may seem, even small changes may lead to a greater impact. Arguably, with a growing consciousness of women's consumer and producer roles, we are observing a growing momentum in the struggle for gender equality. The fact that marketing practices have been acknowledged in the Women's Empowerment Principles (Women's Empowerment Principle 5, 2014) reflects this increasing awareness of the role of marketing in (re)producing gender stereotypes that are harmful to women and other marginalized voices, and ultimately society at large.

References

3% Conference, 2014. The 3% Conference. Available at: www.3percentconf.com (accessed 17.02.14).
AMA (American Marketing Association), 2013. About AMA: Definition of Marketing. Available at: www.ama.org/AboutAMA/Pages/Definition-of-Marketing.aspx (accessed 01.06.14).
Anderson, E., 2008. Inclusive masculinity in a fraternal setting. Men and Masculinities 10(5), 604–620.
Arthur, D., 2006. Hip hop consumption and masculinity. In: Borgerson, J., Stevens, L. (Eds.), Proceedings of 8th Gender, Marketing and Consumer Behavior Conference, pp. 105–116.
Artz, N., Venkatesh, A., 1991. Gender representation in advertising. In: Holman, R.H., Solomon, M.R. (Eds.), Advances in Consumer Research, 18. Association for Consumer Research, Provo, UT, pp. 618–623.
Auster, C.J., Mansbach, C.S., 2012. The gender marketing of toys: an analysis of color and type of toy on the Disney store website. Sex Roles 67(7–8), 375–388.
Belk, R.W., Wallendorf, M., Sherry Jr, J.F., June 1989. The sacred and the profane in consumer behavior: Theodicy on the odyssey. Journal of Consumer Research 16(1), 1–38.
Bernays, E.L., Miller, M.C., 1928/2005. Propaganda. Ig Publishing, New York, NY.
Bettany, S., Dobscha, S., O'Malley, L., Prothero, A., 2010. Moving beyond binary opposition: exploring the tapestry of gender in consumer research and marketing. Marketing Theory 10(1), 3–28.
Bird, S.R., April 1996. Welcome to the men's club: homosociality and the maintenance of hegemonic masculinity. Gender & Society 10(2), 120–132.

Blackaby, D., Booth, A.L., Frank, J., 2005. Outside offers and the gender pay gap: empirical evidence from the UK academic labour market. The Economic Journal 115(501), 81–107.

Borden, N.H., 1964. The concept of the marketing mix. Journal of Advertising Research 4(2), 2–7.

Borgerson, J., Rehn, A., 2004. General economy and productive dualisms. Gender, Work & Organization 11(4), 455–474.

Brace-Govan, J., 2010. Representations of women's active embodiment and men's ritualized visibility in sport. Marketing Theory 10(4), 369–396.

Bristor, J.M., Fischer, E., 1993. Feminist thought: implications for consumer research. Journal of Consumer Research 19(4), 518–536.

Bristor, J.M., Fischer, E., 1995. Exploring simultaneous oppressions: toward the development of consumer research in the interest of diverse women. American Behavioral Scientist 38(4), 526–536.

Brown, S., Stevens, L., Maclaran, P., 1999. I can't believe it's not Bakhtin!: literary theory, postmodern advertising, and the gender agenda. Journal of Advertising 28(1), 11–24.

Butler, J., 2006. Gender Trouble: Feminism and the Inversion of Identity, second ed. Routledge, New York, NY.

Carothers, B.J., Reis, H.T., 2013. Men and women are from Earth: examining the latent structure of gender. Journal of Personality and Social Psychology 104(2), 385.

Catterall, M., Maclaran, P., Stevens, L., 1997. Marketing and feminism: a bibliography and suggestions for further research. Marketing Intelligence & Planning 15(7), 369–376.

Catterall, M., Maclaran, P., Stevens, L. (Eds.), 2000. Marketing and Feminism: Current Issues and Research. Routledge, London.

Catterall, M., Maclaran, P., Stevens, L., 1999. Critical marketing in the classroom: possibilities and challenges. Marketing Intelligence & Planning 17(7), 344–353.

Catterall, M., Maclaran, P., Stevens, L., 2002. Critical reflection in the marketing curriculum. Journal of Marketing Education 24(3), 184–192.

Catterall, M., Maclaran, P., Stevens, L., 2005. Postmodern paralysis: the critical impasse in feminist perspectives on consumers. Journal of Marketing Management 21(5–6), 489–504.

Coleman, C.A., 2012. Construction of consumer vulnerability by gender and ethics of empowerment. In: Otnes, C.C., Tuncay Zayer, L. (Eds.), Gender, Culture and Consumer Behavior. Routledge, New York, NY, pp. 3–32.

Collinson, D.L., Hearn, J., 2005. Men and masculinities in work, organizations and management. In: Kimmel, M.S., Hearn, J., Connell, R.W. (Eds.), Handbook of Studies on Men and Masculinities. Sage, London, pp. 289–310.

Constantinides, E., 2006. The marketing mix revisited: towards the 21st century marketing. Journal of Marketing Management 22(3–4), 407–438.

Costa, J.A. (Ed.), 1991. Proceedings of 1st Gender and Consumer Behaviour Conference. Association for Consumer Research, Salt Lake City, UT.

Crane, A., Desmond, J., 2002. Societal marketing and morality. European Journal of Marketing 36(5/6), 548–569.

Desmond, J., Crane, A., 2004. Morality and the consequences of marketing action. Journal of Business Research 57(11), 1222–1230.

Dobscha, S., Ozanne, J.L., 2000. Marketing and the divided self: healing the nature/woman separation. In: Catterall, M., Maclaran, P., Stevens, L. (Eds.), Marketing and Feminism: Current Issues and Research. Routledge, London, pp. 239–254.

Dobscha, S., Prothero, A., 2012. (Re)igniting sustainable consumption and production research through feminist connections. In: Otnes, C.C., Tuncay Zayer, L. (Eds.), Gender, Culture and Consumer Behavior. Routledge, New York, NY, pp. 371–392.

Elliott, R., Elliott, C., 2005. Idealized images of the male body in advertising: a reader–response exploration. Journal of Marketing Communications 11(1), 3–19.

Ellis, N., Fitchett, J., Higgins, M., Jack, G., Lim, M., Saren, M., Tadajewski, M., 2011. Marketing: A Critical Textbook. Sage, London.

Epp, A.M., Price, L.L., 2008. Family identity: a framework of identity interplay in consumption practices. Journal of Consumer Research 35(1), 50–70.

Family and Childcare Trust UK, 2014. Annual Childcare Cost Survey. Available at: www.familyandchildcaretrust.org/childcare-costs-surveys (accessed 01.06.14).

Featherstone, M., 1991. Consumer Culture and Postmodernism. Sage, London.

Fetterley, J., 1978. The Resisting Reader: A Feminist Approach to American Fiction, vol. 247. Indiana University Press.

Firat, A.F., Venkatesh, A., 1995. Liberatory postmodernism and the re-enchantment of consumption. Journal of Consumer Research 22(3), 239–267.

Fischer, E., Bristor, J., 1994. A feminist poststructuralist analysis of the rhetoric of marketing relationships. International Journal of Research in Marketing 11(4), 317–331.

Friedan, B., 1965. The Feminine Mystique. Gollancz, London.

Geena Davis Institute, 2014. Geena Davis Institute. Available at: www.seejane.org/index.php (accessed 31.05.14).

Gentry, J., Harrison, R., 2010. Is advertising a barrier to male movement toward gender change? Marketing Theory 10(1), 74–96.

Goffman, E., 1979. Gender Advertisements. Macmillan, London.

Gopaldas, A., Fischer, E., 2012. Beyond gender: intersectionality, gender and consumer behavior. In: Otnes, C.C., Tuncay Zayer, L. (Eds.), Gender, Culture and Consumer Behavior. Routledge, New York, NY, pp. 393–410.

Gordon, L.R., 1997. Her Majesty's Other Children: Sketches of Racism from a Neocolonial Age. Rowman & Littlefield.

Gurrieri, L., Brace-Govan, J., Cherrier, H., 2014. She wants it? Subject positions and discourses in violent 'porno-chic' advertising representations. In: Moisander, J., Mikkonen, I. (Eds.), Proceedings of 12th ACR Gender, Marketing and Consumer Behaviour Conference. Aalto University, Helsinki, Finland.

Harley, S., 2002. The impact of research selectivity on academic work and identity in UK universities. Studies in Higher Education 27/2, 187–205.

Hein, W., 2010. Players and layers: young men's construction of individual and group masculinities through consumption practices (Doctoral dissertation). University of Edinburgh.

Hein, W., O'Donohoe, S., 2014. Practising gender: the role of banter in young men's improvisations of masculine consumer identities. Journal of Marketing Management 30(13–14), 1293–1319.

Hirschman, E.C., 1993. Ideology in consumer research, 1980 and 1990: a Marxist and feminist critique. Journal of Consumer Research 19(4), 537–555.

Hirschman, E.C., 2010. How to deal with gender discrimination. In: Peñaloza, L., Woodruffe-Burton, H. (Eds.), Proceedings of 10th Conference on Gender, Marketing and Consumer Behaviour, pp. 99–100.

Holt, D.B., Thompson, C.J., 2004. Man-of-action heroes: the pursuit of heroic masculinity in everyday consumption. Journal of Consumer Research 31(2), 425–440.

Jones, D.B., Shaw, E.H., 2002. A history of marketing thought. Handbook of Marketing, 39–65.

Joy, A., Venkatesh, A., 1994. Postmodernism, feminism, and the body: the visible and the invisible in consumer research. International Journal of Research in Marketing 11(4), 333–357.

Kates, S.M., 1999. Making the ad perfectly queer: marketing "normality" to the gay men's community? Journal of Advertising 28(1), 25–37.

Kates, S.M., 2002. The protean quality of subcultural consumption: an ethnographic account of gay consumers. Journal of Consumer Research 29(3), 383–399.

Keith, R.J., 1960. The marketing revolution. The Journal of Marketing, 35–38.

Kilbourne, J., 1994. Still killing us softly: advertising and the obsession with thinness. Feminist Perspectives on Eating Disorders, 395–418.

Kilbourne, J., 1999. Deadly Persuasion: Why Women and Girls Must Fight the Addictive Power of Advertising. Free Press, New York, NY.

Kilbourne, J., 2013. Killing Us Softly 3: Advertising's Images of Women.

Kilbourne, W., McDonagh, P., Prothero, A., 1997. Sustainable consumption and the quality of life: a macromarketing challenge to the dominant social paradigm. Journal of Macromarketing 17(1), 4–24.

Kotler, P., Armstrong, G., 2010. Principles of Marketing, thirteenth ed. Pearson Education.

Lerner, G., 1975. Placing women in history: definitions and challenges. Feminist Studies 3(1/2), 5–14.

Lerner, G., 1979. The Majority Finds its Past: Placing Women in History. Oxford University Press, Oxford.

Leung, S., April 2, 2014. Top of Boston's ad World a Male Bastion No Longer, The Boston Globe. Available at: www.bostonglobe.com/business/2014/04/01/boston-mad-men-are-now-women/OHL1ULODLtZhh2Pc9SCRiN/story.html (accessed 01.09.14).

Maclaran, P., 2010. The gendered nature of academic culture. In: Peñaloza, L., Woodruffe-Burton, H. (Eds.), Proceedings of 10th Conference on Gender, Marketing and Consumer Behaviour, pp. 97–98.

Maclaran, P., 2012. Marketing and feminism in historic perspective. Journal of Historic Research in Marketing 4(3), 462–469.

Maclaran, P., Miller, C., Parsons, E., Surman, E., 2009. Praxis or performance: does critical marketing have a gender blind-spot? Journal of Marketing Management 25(7–8), 713–728.

Madaran, P., Catterall, M., 2000. Bridging the knowledge divide: issues on the feminisation of marketing practice. Journal of Marketing Management 16(6), 635–646.

McPherson, S., 2014. Empowering Women and Girls, One Hashtag at a Time. Available at: www.forbes.com/sites/susanmcpherson/2014/05/27/empowering-women-and-girls-one-hashtag-at-a-time (accessed 02.06.14).

Mick, D.G., 2006. Meaning and mattering through transformative consumer research. Advances in Consumer Research 33(1), 1–4.

Murray, J.B., Ozanne, J.L., 1991. The critical imagination: emancipatory interests in consumer research. Journal of Consumer Research 18(2), 129–144.

Myers-Levy, J., Sternthal, B., 1991. Gender differences in the use of message cues and judgments. Journal of Marketing Research 28(1), 84–96.

Nelson, J.A., 1998. Labour, gender and the economic/social divide. International Labour Review 137(1), 33–46.

Nixon, S., 2003. Advertising Cultures. Sage, Thousand Oaks, CA.

Nixon, S., Crewe, B., 2004. Pleasure at work? Gender, consumption and work-based identities in the creative industries. Consumption Markets & Culture 7(2), 129–147.

No More Page 3, 2014. No More Page 3. Available at: www.nomorepage3.org (accessed 02.06.14).

Otnes, C., McGrath, M.A., 2001. Perceptions and realities of male shopping behavior. Journal of Retailing 77(1), 111–137.

Ozanne, J.L., Saatcioglu, B., 2008. Participatory action research. Journal of Consumer Research 35(3), 423–439.

Patterson, M., Elliott, R., 2002. Negotiating masculinities: advertising and the inversion of the male gaze. Consumption Markets & Culture 5(3), 231–249.

Peñaloza, L., 1994. Crossing boundaries/drawing lines: a look at the nature of gender boundaries and their impact on marketing research. International Journal of Research in Marketing 11(4), 359–379.

Pennell, G.E., 1994. Babes in Toyland: learning an ideology of gender. Advances in Consumer Research 21(1), 359–364.

Richardson, H., 2014. Many Parents "Paying More for Childcare than Average Mortgage", BBC, 4 March 2014. Available at: www.bbc.co.uk/news/education-26373725 (last accessed 01.06.14).

Rues, J., 1972. What can a heroine do? Or why women can't write. In: Koppelman Cornillon, S. (Ed.), Images of Women in Fiction: Feminist Perspectives. Bowling Green University Popular Press, Bowling Green, KY, pp. 3–20.

Ruwanpura, K.N., Humphries, J., 2004. Mundane heroines: conflict, ethnicity, gender, and female headship in eastern Sri Lanka. Feminist Economics 10(2), 173–205.

Salzman, M., Matathia, I., O'Reilly, A., 2005. The Future of Men. Palgrave Macmillan.

Schroeder, J.E., Borgerson, J.L., 1998. Marketing images of gender: a visual analysis. Consumption Markets & Culture 2(2), 161–201.

Schroeder, J.E., Zwick, D., 2004. Mirrors of masculinity: representation and identity in advertising images. Consumption Markets & Culture 7(1), 21–52.

Schuster, M.R., Van Dyne, S.R., 1985. Stages of curriculum transformation. Women's Place in the Academy: Transforming the Liberal Arts Curriculum, 13–29.

Scott, J.W., 1988. Deconstructing equality-versus-difference: or, the uses of poststructuralist theory for feminism. Feminist Studies 14(1), 33–50.

Scott, L.M., 2010. Sanitary pads in Ghana. Available at www.doublexeconomy.com/wp-content/uploads/2011/05/CASE-Sanitary-Pads-in-Ghana.pdf (accessed 12.03.15).

Scott, L.M., 2006. Market feminism: the case for a paradigm shift. Advertising & Society Review 7(2).

Scott, L., Dolan, C., Johnstone-Louis, M., Sugden, K., Wu, M., 2012. Enterprise and inequality: a study of Avon in South Africa. Entrepreneurship Theory and Practice 36(3), 543–568.

Scott, L.M., 2013. Sanitary care and girls' education. Available at: www.doublexeconomy.com/publications-projects-2/sanitary-care-and-girls-education (accessed 01.06.14).

Scott, S.V., 1999. The academic as service provider: is the customer always right? Journal of Higher Education Policy and Management 21(2), 193–202.

Shaw, E.H., Jones, D.B., 2005. A history of schools of marketing thought. Marketing Theory 5(3), 239–281.

Sherry Jr, J.F., Kozinets, R.V., Duhachek, A., DeBerry-Spence, B., Nuttavuthisit, K., Storm, D., 2004. Gendered behavior in a male preserve: role playing at ESPN zone Chicago. Journal of Consumer Psychology 14(1), 151–158.

Silverstein, M.J., Sayre, K., Butman, J., 2009. Women Want More. HarperCollins.

Simpson, M., November 15, 1994. Here come the mirror men. The Independent. Re-print available at: www.marksimpson.com/here-come-the-mirror-men (accessed 02.09.14).

Stern, B.B., 1995. Consumer myths: Frye's taxonomy and the structural analysis of consumption text. Journal of Consumer Research 22(2), 165–185.

Stern, B.B., 1990. Literary criticism and the history of marketing thought: a new perspective on "reading" marketing theory. Journal of the Academy of Marketing Science 18(4), 329–336.

Stern, B.B., 1993a. Curriculum change: feminist theory in the classroom. In: Costa, J.A. (Ed.), Proceedings of the Second Conference on Gender and Consumer Behavior. University of Utah, Salt Lake City, UT, pp. 228–237.

Stern, B.B., 1993b. Feminist literary criticism and the deconstruction of ads: a postmodern view of advertising and consumer responses. Journal of Consumer Research 19(4), 556–566.

Stern, B.B., 2004. The importance of being Ernest: commemorating Dichter's contribution to advertising research. Journal of Advertising Research 44(2), 165–169.

Stern, B.B., Russell, C.A., Russell, D.W., 2005. Vulnerable women on screen and at home: soap opera consumption. Journal of Macromarketing 25(2), 222–225.

Stern, B.B., Russell, C.A., Russell, D.W., 2007. Hidden persuasions in soap operas: damaged heroines and negative consumer effects. International Journal of Advertising: The Quarterly Review of Marketing Communications 26(1), 9–36.

Tadajewski, M., 2006. Remembering motivation research: toward an alternative genealogy of interpretive consumer research. Marketing Theory 6(4), 429–466.

Tadajewski, M., 2011. Producing historical critical marketing studies: theory, method and politics. Journal of Historical Research in Marketing 3(4), 549–575.

Tadajewski, M., 2012. History and critical marketing studies. Journal of Historical Research in Marketing 4(3), 440–452.

Tadajewski, M., Jones, D.B., 2012. Scientific marketing management and the emergence of the ethical marketing concept. Journal of Marketing Management 28(1–2), 37–61.

Tadajewski, M., Jones, D.B., 2012. Scientific marketing management and the emergence of the ethical marketing concept. Journal of Marketing Management 28(1–2), 37–61.

Taylor, W.J., 1965. "Is marketing a science?" Revisited. Journal of Marketing 29(3), 49–53.

The Representation Project, 2014. Miss Representation. Available at: www.therepresentation project.org/films/miss-representation (accessed 31.05.14).

The Swedish Women's Lobby, 2014. Reklamera: Ad Watch. Available at: www.sverigeskvinnolobby.se/en/project/ad-watch (accessed 01.06.14).

Thompson, C.J., 1996. Caring consumers: gendered consumption meanings and the juggling life-style. Journal of Consumer Research 22(4), 388–407.

Thompson, C.J., December 13, 2013. Marketplace performativities and the naturalization of gender Transgression. Presentation at Royal Holloway, University of London. Recording available at: www.backdoorbroadcasting.net/2013/12/craig-j-thompson-marketplace-perfor mativities-and-the-naturalization-of-gender-transgression (accessed 31.05.14).

Thompson, C.J., Hirschman, E.C., 1995. Understanding the socialized body: a poststructural-ist analysis of consumers' self-conceptions, body images, and self-care practices. Journal of Consumer Research 22(2), 139–153.

Thompson, C.J., Holt, D.B., 2004. How do men grab the phallus? Gender tourism in everyday con-sumption. Journal of Consumer Culture 4(3), 313–338.

Tuncay, L., Otnes, C.C., 2008. The use of persuasion management strategies by identity-vulnerable consumers: the case of urban heterosexual male shoppers. Journal of Retailing 84(4), 487–499.

Women's Empowerment Principle 5, 2014. Principle 5: Implement enterprise development, supply chain and marketing practices that empower women. Available at: www.weprinciples. org/Site/Principle5 (accessed 30.01.14).

Woodruffe-Burton, H., Eccles, S., Elliott, R., 2002. Towards a theory of shopping: a holistic frame-work. Journal of Consumer Behaviour 1(3), 256–266.

WSFF (Women's Sports and Fitness Foundation), 2011. Big Deal? London: The Commission on the Future of Women's sport. Report Available at: www.wsff.org.uk/system/1/assets/ files/000/000/287/287/2badaa5f0/original/Big_Deal_report.pdf (accessed 01.06.14).

Wyllie, J., Carlson, J., Rosenberger III, P.J., 2014. Examining the influence of different levels of sexual-stimuli intensity by gender on advertising effectiveness. Journal of Marketing Manage-ment 30(7–8), 697–718.

6

Business education for nurse leaders
A case study of leadership development in a vital, highly gendered industry

Teresa J. Rothausen
University of St Thomas, USA

Dawn M. Bazarko
UnitedHealth Group, USA

This chapter presents a case study of an executive education program for nurse leaders designed to address the dearth of business leadership development opportunities for this population in the United States. This lack of development opportunity may in turn contribute to the high nurse turnover experienced in US healthcare organizations system-wide, as well as lack of a stronger nurse voice at the table when addressing the multi-layered healthcare crisis. The case is from the United States; however, the issues are relevant to the global nursing workforce, as nurse shortages and issues of gender are ubiquitous worldwide. The program focuses on cultivation of executive mind-set and enterprise-level organizational skills in nurse leaders and directly addresses gender and its relationship to nurse professional identity and voice, within an integrated curriculum. The chapter explores issues confronting nurses moving into organizational leadership that we considered in program design; summarizes program curricula and delivery; and presents evidence of program outcomes.

At least one company developed a follow-on program for employees who participated in the University Program in Nurse Leadership. The chapter provides the details and outcomes of this Company Extension. The chapter concludes with challenges facing those interested in providing business-oriented leadership development for nurses.

6.1 Introduction

In the United States, healthcare is a system in need of profound change. Many people are uninsured or do not have access to affordable healthcare coverage. Healthcare costs, and the rate of growth of these costs, is bankrupting individuals and the US economy. Yet, despite the money spent, healthcare quality and outcomes are highly variable. The system insufficiently uses evidence-based practices and has too many defects and unnecessary complexities. Further, the medical malpractice environment fails to create accountability, while driving considerable inefficiency and distracting care providers from offering services that are affordable and patient-centred (Emanuel, 2014).

As in any system, what may at first appear to be separate issues often interrelate. This is the case with challenges for nursing. For example, there exists a profound shortage of registered nurses (RNs), 90.4% of whom are women (Staiger, Auerbach and Buerhaus, 2012; United States Bureau of the Census, 2013). Due to the traditional division of labour in healthcare, RNs are the experts in many critical aspects of patient care, satisfaction and healing, which other care workers in the industry do not possess. These skills are urgently needed in order to positively effect a change in healthcare while retaining these foci on patient care and satisfaction. Yet nurses are under-represented at the leadership levels, similar to situations in other industries where there is an under-representation of women on boards and in the "C-suite", that is, in the highest levels of organization leadership (Kleinman, 2003; Kelan and Jones, 2010; Koenig et al., 2011).

These issues are systematically related. The lack of nurses in executive positions in healthcare organizations, as well as the dearth of opportunities for existing nurse managers and leaders to develop organizational and business leadership skills throughout middle management, may impact how well the nursing workforce is managed, contributing to RN retention problems (Kleinman, 2004). Lack of representation of the expertise nurses gain in their clinical work among top leadership in organizations and system-wide likely leads to critical elements of patient care not being well represented as the multi-layered healthcare crisis in the United States is addressed (Bazarko, 2011; Benner et al., 2009). These dynamics exist system-wide, in for-profit, not-for-profit and governmental environments (Buerhaus, Auerbach and Staiger, 2009; Emanuel, 2014).

Two related, institutionalized phenomena may contribute to unhealthy aspects of the nursing subsystem. First, within the healthcare industry, nurses are an under-served group in terms of having access to developmental opportunities, especially in terms of organizational leadership and business-related education (Bazarko, 2011;

Benner et al., 2009; Saxe-Braithwaite, 2003). This is happening at a time when nurse manager and executive roles have evolved enormously in response to changes in the healthcare industry in recent decades, in ways that increasingly require competences in business (Kleinman, 2003). Second, gendered professional identities pervade the work of patient care and treatment, and are embodied in the professional norms and values of physicians and nurses (Cummings, 1995).

In general, well-designed developmental opportunities can have multiple impacts on participants and organizations. Impacts on participants include improved confidence and effectiveness as organizational members (Brown and Sitzmann, 2011; Martineau, 2004). Impacts on organizations include better group and inter-group coordination, better organizational ability to manage changes, a deeper bench of leadership talent and higher retention rates for those who participated in development opportunities as well as their subordinates (Bass, 2008; Conger, 2010; Martineau, 2004). Within nursing specifically, although they are responsible for business units, nurse managers and leaders are not as prepared to manage organizational business activities as they are to manage clinical activities (Benner et al., 2009; Saxe-Braithwaite, 2003). A number of changes have been recommended, including changes to existing undergraduate and graduate programs in nursing, supplemented by offerings for existing nurse leaders such as new online and certificate programs, seminars, mentoring and other continuing education alternatives (Kleinman, 2003).

To address this glaring need for organizational and business leadership skill development for existing nurse leaders, and the needs of nurse leadership at the highest organization and system levels, the Opus College of Business at University of St Thomas (UST) in Minnesota developed a program focused on the cultivation of executive mind-set and enterprise-level organizational knowledge and skills in nurse leaders, under the auspices of its executive education division. The managers in charge of program development asked us, a management and leadership professor at UST and a nurse leader from UnitedHealth Group, to cocreate the curriculum for this program, which was offered in UST's executive education division.

The program is one of the first business school executive programs for nurses in the United States, and several elements make it unique. UST, a private Catholic university, was ranked in the top five Catholic business schools in the United States in 2014. Thus, the program leverages top business school faculty, while being shaped and informed directly by an expert nurse leader. The cohort-based approach we used provided an opportunity for senior nurse leaders from a variety of backgrounds, including for-profit, non-profit, insurance and direct care provider organizations, to join together in a rigorous academic and action-learning curriculum, complemented by strong peer-learning and peer networking.

We have delivered the University Program in Nurse Leadership (the "University Program") three times, during 2011, 2012 and 2013. Feedback from participating nurse leaders and their organizations indicates that the program was successful. Evidence includes post-program evaluation, demand for future program offerings, requests for additional programs and exploration of customized offerings and online versions of the program.

One of the primary reasons that leader development can fail to deliver a strong return on investment is when employing organizations fail to leverage the development by providing ongoing structure, support and reinforcement in the workplace for the learned behaviours (Brown and Sitzmann, 2011; Conger, 2010). Because its leaders were concerned about this, the Center for Nursing Advancement at UnitedHealth Group sponsored a company extension of the University Program, which was a one-year, in-house program, called the Nurse Leader Executive Program, or informally the "wrap-around" to the University Program (going forward we will differentiate these two elements using the terms University Program and Company Extension). Early impact and outcome evaluation indicates that participants in the Company Extension have received promotions into nursing and non-nursing roles at a rate much higher than other high-potential nurses who have not yet had the opportunity to participate in the program.

We believe the positive results from the University Program and the Company Extension are due in part to program curricula that address developmental needs common to anyone transitioning from technical and managerial roles into executive roles, as well as developmental leadership needs specific to the nursing population. These needs result in large part from gender and identity dynamics in medicine and health-related organizations, which profoundly impact nursing as a profession, healthcare as an industry and nurses entering organizational leadership in particular (Cummings, 1995; Kleinman, 2003).

In this case study, we first explore some of these issues, which confront nurses moving into leadership in healthcare, and which we considered in designing the University Program. We then summarize the University Program and the Company Extension curricula and delivery, and present evidence that the programs result in participants doing identity work and becoming more effective in leading strategic initiatives and organizational change projects at the system, organization and team levels. Finally, we note some ongoing challenges we face as champions for the University Program.

We offer our experiences in the hope that they encourage similar offerings for nurse leaders and inspire healthcare organizations to invest in stronger leader development for nurses. Nurses are not only greatly underserved by such programs, but we strongly believe that nursing represents a vital voice in the search for solutions to the multi-layered healthcare crisis in the United States. We have seen how a carefully designed and delivered leadership development program increases nurses' confidence and abilities to lead positive changes in healthcare.

6.2 Nurse leader challenges

Although a thorough review of the challenges facing healthcare and nursing is beyond the scope of this chapter, we briefly review some of the key elements we considered in designing the University Program. In this chapter we present a case study in the US setting, and therefore, we focus the discussion here on some of the particular contours of the healthcare crisis in the United States. We expect that some, if not all, of our experiences are relevant to many other countries facing similar crises in nursing and healthcare.

The shortage of RNs in the United States could be crippling for the US healthcare system and detrimental to patient care, particularly at a time when resource demand is on the rise (Bazarko, 2011; Buerhaus, Auerback and Staiger, 2009). In the United States, nursing shortage is expected to increase dramatically as nurses who had entered and remained in the RN workforce during the recent economic recession now withdraw from employment as the economy improves, exacerbated by an upcoming wave of Baby Boomer retirements (Rothausen, 2007; Staiger, Auerbach and Buerhaus, 2012). The US Department of Labor estimates that by 2022, the United States will need 1.13 million additional RNs to replace those who are retiring, which is more than one-third of the current nurse workforce (United States Department of Labor, 2013). At the same time, the complex needs of an aging population and the expansion of healthcare coverage to millions of Americans through the Affordable Care Act (ACA) will sharply increase the need for RNs (O'Connor, 2013).

The ACA, passed in 2010 and sometimes referred to as Obamacare, contains important provisions to increase access to healthcare coverage; expand focus on preventative care and public health; focus on strengthening the healthcare workforce; and improve the quality, safety and affordability of healthcare in the United States (White House, 2014). This call for a healthier healthcare system will involve major change initiatives within every healthcare-related organization in the United States. To meet these needs and demands, leadership strength will be critical, and the nursing voice essential. Nursing is the largest, and a unique, component of the healthcare system workforce.

The division of patient care work in US healthcare has resulted in doctors being involved primarily in short, focused interactions with patients, about diagnosis, treatment plans and outcome measurement. In contrast, nurses emphasize good care coordination, patient centredness, patient satisfaction, patient and family education, and holistic care (Institute of Medicine, 2010). Thus, the large nursing workforce has become a primary voice for advocating these care qualities (Kleinman, 2003, 2004). Nurses could be powerful agents for positive change. However, nursing professionals often lack organizational leadership skills and therefore the confidence in their voice, which is needed to lead and contribute meaningfully (Benner et al., 2009).

Beyond preparing nurses to assume formal organizational leadership roles, there is an increasing need for leadership and organizational skills in nurses at all levels. Leadership is not just a position, but a skill set every nurse should learn, and is relatively new in nursing education (Curtis, de Vries and Sheerin, 2011). This skill set includes some skill subsets that are especially needed in healthcare now, such as interpersonal effectiveness, change management, ability to motivate others and expertise to create readiness for change in others (Curtis, de Vries and Sheerin, 2011; Saxe-Braithwaite, 2003). Training and development in these areas can improve practical skills as well as foster identity shifts necessary to feel willing and able to take on leadership and become an agent for positive change (Conger, 2010; DeRue and Ashford, 2010). Thus, it is critical that nurses are prepared in terms of both mind-sets and skill sets to serve in a variety of leadership roles at all levels of the system. These include effectively contributing to a delivery of safe, high-quality and affordable patient care; fostering and encouraging retention and development of a skilled and effective RN workforce; developing new models of care; and being drivers of the organizational changes that lead to healthier and safer work environments to make healthcare as an industry work better for everyone (Kleinman, 2003, 2004).

Despite the urgency of these challenges and opportunities, nurses are an underserved group within healthcare in terms of education generally and business-related education specifically (Bazarko, 2011; Benner et al., 2009; Saxe-Braithwaite, 2003). Few organizations invest in the development of nurse leaders who possess the skills necessary to lead change, at this time when the healthcare landscape is evolving radically. This underinvestment likely reflects broader societal devaluing of feminine care work and those who perform it. A recent report released by the prestigious Institute of Medicine (2010) in the United States put forth an urgent call for action to address these gaps in developing nursing executives and leaders.

6.3 Gender dynamics in healthcare

Although nurses and doctors are both "care providers" in healthcare settings, the care that nurses provide is often so foundational and supportive that it is relegated to the background and may be seen as less heroic than treatment and lifesaving efforts provided by physicians. Thus, caregiving skills, over time, have been valued such that physicians were considered the clinical leaders and nurses the "doctor's helpers" (Cummings, 1995). This mirrors societal and cultural beliefs that skills in nurturing community and interpersonal styles that are more relational are mutually exclusive with organizational leadership. Strategic, agentic styles and values are identified with Western leadership, such as being competitive, aggressive, courageous, dominant and strong; in contrast traits associated with communal, feminine styles and values include sympathetic, sensitive, supportive, kind, nurturing and gentle (Eagly and Chin, 2010; Eagly and Karau, 2002). The desire to care, support and nurture others is a primary reason many nurses take up the profession, and is a desired quality in healthcare.

Gender dynamics impact organizations in many industries; however, there are particulars by industry that are important to consider. The institutionalization of divergent norms and values in different professions within an industry is a factor that recent literature reviews suggest is under-emphasized in business leadership research (Gardner et al., 2010; Jackson and Parry, 2011). We suggest that addressing these issues explicitly would be vital with the nurse population.

As we developed our new program and assessed needs, the following two key sets of questions arose:

1. To what extent should we address gender issues generally versus those specifically manifested in healthcare and nursing? Time is always at a premium in executive education programs. How could we make sure participants were (1) acquiring the knowledge, skills, abilities, qualities and perspectives any aspiring organization executive needs, while also (2) addressing barriers and opportunities unique to this population of nurse executives in the traditional gendered workforce groups in the US healthcare industry?

2. How could we maximize the actual and perceived value of the program to the many stakeholders we recognized, including participants themselves, their managers, their organizations, nursing as a profession and the entire healthcare system and its customers? For nurse leaders, given cultural patterns of the devaluing of feminine care workers, it was especially important to assure outcomes of real and immediate value to organizations' strategic imperatives. This would facilitate maximal positive impact on participants' careers through their ability to make a difference in their organizations and across the system.

With many clinical and technical professionals, moving into team and organizational leadership is a challenge in part because their education lacks leadership content and experience. In nursing these issues are even more complex due to professional values clashes and gendered dynamics that have been institutionalized for over a century. In healthcare, leadership frequently consists of three professional groups, each with strong professional identities: nurses, physicians, and organizational, management or business professionals (for short, if not literally, RNs, MDs and MBAs/MPAs). Each identity encompasses deeply institutionalized and strongly held sets of values and norms, which may be in conflict with those of others. Each group also absorbs stereotypes of the others throughout their training and work, as represented in Figure 6.1. Each of the three groups also encompasses linguistically different ways of describing patient care. Identities such as these are critical to how leaders develop (Day, Harrison and Halpin, 2009; DeRue and Ashford, 2010). The communal and relational values and styles described above form a central tenet in nurse education and identity formation. In contrast, physician education and business education generally impart strategic and agentic value sets (Cummings, 1995).

Given a man and a woman with the same résumé, research has shown that men are more likely to be seen as potential leaders, in part because leadership is associated

Figure 6.1 **Examples of identity threat in healthcare leadership**

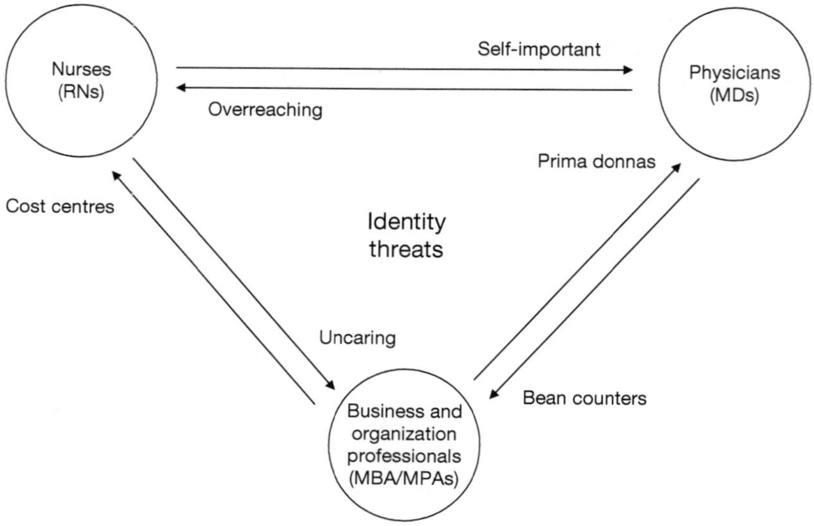

with strategic and agentic values in Western cultures (DeRue and Ashforth, 2010; Koenig et al., 2011). In 2013, 90.6% of the US nurses were women, which is down from 97.3% in the 1970s (United States Bureau of the Census, 2013). As a profession, physicians pride themselves on being scientists and are focused generally on treatments and outcome measures. Similarly, business and management specialists are trained to focus on financial and economic efficiencies. Although things are now changing, traditional nursing education, in contrast, taught nurses to focus on each patient's experience of care, at times without clear regard for resource consumption or outcomes (Kleinman, 2003, 2004). In addition to the other gendered traditions in healthcare, such as nurses being seen as assistants or handmaidens to doctors (Cummings, 1995), this can lead to powerful, entrenched, systematic misunderstandings and conflict.

Thus, as nurses move into leadership and work more closely with physicians and non-clinical business leaders, they may face both internal and external threats to their identity. These may involve being affiliated with "self-important" doctors and "uncaring" business people by other nurses, and being seen as "overreaching" or as "advocating for a cost centre" by those they seek to influence, as represented in Figure 6.1. Nurses also face overcoming their own professional biases, which they may unconsciously retain, such as that physician leaders are self-important prima donnas and business leaders are uncaring bean counters.

The research we undertook to prepare for the program suggested unique challenges come together in nurse leader identity formation and competency development; gender and power in healthcare; a clash of identity values between clinical nursing and business leadership; and dilemmas posed in transforming from nurturing, caring roles into those involving business acumen, as depicted in Figure 6.2. We developed the program

Figure 6.2 **Conflicting identities and knowledge gaps for effective nurse leadership**

curriculum to address these elements in interrelated ways, and in sessions specifically designed to address each individually.

The research literatures on gender in business, management, leadership and nursing all strongly suggest that the dynamics represented in Figures 6.1 and 6.2 would have impacted participants in the program. We confirmed this during an early session of the University Program. We asked participants to respond to a brief open-ended survey, which included the question, "Do you think gender issues impact your leadership in healthcare? If so, how?" We sorted responses into primary categories and present them in Table 6.1. In addition, we held an interactive session at the midway point of the University Program, where we heard these themes emerge as well, and in addition heard about how participants' unconsciously absorbed notions of nurse identity may hold them back.

Table 6.1 reveals three primary challenges that almost every participant mentioned (and it should be noted that approximately 15% of respondents were male), as well as one opportunity. The challenges are (1) lack of effectiveness of participants' feminine styles in masculine-dominated environments; (2) stereotypes and biases about women as leaders; and (3) effective articulation of the value of their leadership, the contributions of nursing and their own teams' impacts. The participants also pointed out that nursing currently has some strong female leadership, which is an opportunity to leverage. In addition to the categories in Table 6.1, in an interactive session on the nurse leader brand, participants identified other elements holding them back from embracing the healthcare leader identity: the issue of the clash with their "old" notions about nurse identity and the subtle and not-so-subtle ways other members of all three professional groups react and respond to them as leaders. The latter tends to reinforce the old patterns and the stereotypes they have of the other groups, as identified in Figure 6.1. Participants see this as holding nurses back from embracing business and organization leader identities.

In sum, we believed that participants would be better equipped to deal with the identified challenges by a program that addresses these challenges directly through modules on business communication; leadership styles and development; and executive presence. Another essential component of the program involved facilitating an explicit examination of beliefs participants may hold about their own identities as nurses and executives, and raising explicit awareness of identity and gender issues.

6.4 The University Program curriculum

Given low budgets for nurse leader development, we were limited to two four-day modules. The curriculum, which is summarized in Table 6.2, comprises sessions on business acumen as well as specific sessions addressing identity directly, such as those on nurse leader brand and leadership development, including one explicitly to explore the underlying gender dynamics. Each session was designed to both deliver content knowledge and perspectives, and contribute to one or more of the integrative elements, which were the leader development element, the business acumen element and the strategic change project element. These three elements, summarized below, provided an opportunity to synthesize material from each session in a holistic way. A fourth integrating element involved

Table 6.1 **Gender issues identified by program participants**[a]

Issue	Sample verbatim quotes
Challenges	
Leadership style development and networks	"I use a more rapport-based than power-based communication style, and have [therefore] not been effective in self-promotion. Two positions I applied for and was qualified for were filled by men [due to this]."
	"Men have better networks and are better at self-promotion."
	"I am learning how to have a stronger, well-prepared voice when in a meeting with a large percentage of male physicians."
	"[I have] reluctance to be self-promoting."
	"[Many male leaders] use the 'I've been in this business a long time' approach—good ol' boys."
	"I need to be more present at large meetings."
Stereotyping and battling automatic bias	"[Gender] can definitely lead to stereotyping and passing judgment or jumping to the wrong conclusion."
	"It's challenging to move forward and advance and to be seen as an equal."
	"Women have to continuously prove and validate worth and expertise. Men often [are able to] rest on their prior and old achievements."
	"Males [are] the majority of senior leadership—thus leading is from a 'male' point of view."
	"As a woman, I think there is a glass ceiling to how far a 'nurse woman' can get."
Effectively articulating value	"I am still surrounded by men in business [and fail to effectively] translate the intangible value of investing in nursing. Most of the senior leaders at my hospital are men who . . . [see] physicians alone . . . as the . . . important role."
	"[Women can be] more passive and willing to let others or the team take credit for work."
	"I [need to] that our senior VP who is male is aware of all that we are doing and its impact across the organization."
	"I was taught it was impolite to 'toot your own horn' as a female, and that has carried over as a leader."
Existing opportunity	
Role modelling	"My leaders are all female, which has been very inspirational for me."
	"I think we are fortunate in nursing—it might be harder for males to get leadership roles for once."
	"My VP and President are both women and nurses."

a   Participants were responding to the question, "Do you think gender issues impact your leadership in healthcare? If so, how?"

us as the lead faculty team. One of us is an MBA professor with extensive experience in leader development in business. The other is a nurse executive with extensive experience leading at organizational and system levels in healthcare. This allowed us to leverage the opportunity identified in Table 6.1, to role model female business and nurse leadership.

One integrative element, leader development, included learning about the leader self-development process (Orvis and Ratwani, 2010; Rothausen, 2011). This portion of

Table 6.2 **UST nurse leader development program curriculum at a glance**

Module	Session title	Integrative elements			
1	Program Introduction	Leader Development Process, including Presentation on Personal Leader Brand	Business Acumen	Applied Strategic Change Project Planning, Execution and Presentation	Female Lead Faculty Team MBA/Leader Development Expert and Experienced Nurse Leader
1	Leadership and Executive Presence				
1	Health Care Economy and Systems				
1	Executive Decision-Making: Keeping Values and Ethics Central				
1	Leader Development: 360 Feedback and Peer Coaching				
1	Strategic Business Development and Marketing				
1	Executive Communication and Presentations				
1	Leader Development Planning				
1	Nurse Leader Brand and Gender				
2	Nurse Leader Brand and You				
2	Financial Analysis: Using Your Financial Statements				
2	Change Management				
2	Operations Process Improvement and Quality in Health Care				
2	Leading Diversity				
2	Strategic Human Resource Management				
2	Leader Brand Presentations				
2	Project Presentations				
2	Conclusion and Wrap-up				

the program included specific sessions on leadership and executive presence, and on applied leadership development categories that are tightly tied to the business acumen and project elements as well. An evidence-based approach was used to identify six categories of activities important to leader development. We explicitly wove these into the program: (1) participant-led development of leadership goals and plans; (2) education and continuous learning about leadership; (3) processing of past and current leadership experiences; (4) assessments of leadership abilities, in this case a 360-degree leadership assessment from the participants' current team and managers; (5) intentional development of relationship such as mentors, sponsors and peer coaches, in this case in both the program and outside it; and (6) reflection through individual journaling, talking in teams and working with peer coaches (see Day, 2012; Rothausen, 2011; Yost and Plunkett, 2009).

One central feature within the relationship category was peer coaching. For this element, participants were matched in dyads for similar levels of responsibility and ease of relationship sustainability, with other factors also considered. Before meeting their peer coaches, participants' past experiences with peer coaching were discussed, and a model for strong peer coaching presented (based on Parker, Hall and Kram, 2008). The dyads then engaged with each other in several structured sessions, oriented towards giving and receiving feedback on things such as their development plans and 360-degree feedback reports.

The business acumen portion of the program was based on foundational competences of the MBA, with more focus on management and leadership elements, and the addition of ethics, which is a foundational element of all business programs at UST. As part of program development, we reviewed critical areas of study in current MBA programs, with special attention to gender issues (e.g. Datar, Garvin and Cullen, 2010; Kelan and Jones, 2010). Many nurse leaders have learned these subjects on the job or through company training, but without a theoretical, strategic, system-level foundation. Business acumen elements were woven into both leader development and applied project. After each business acumen session, participants had an opportunity to reflect on their need for further development in that particular business aspect and to brainstorm lists of resources available to them to meet these ongoing developmental needs. In addition, business acumen elements were brought in to the development and execution of the applied strategic change projects.

The applied strategic change assignment involved each participant developing a project proposal for a specific, strategic change and getting feedback from her or his manager and a project sponsor before the University Program started. A short project summary was submitted by participants prior to acceptance into the program. Many evening sessions of the program (not listed in Table 6.2) involved using specific planning tools to develop the project further. In addition, actions taken between modules 1 and 2, as well as explicit consideration of leadership learning from these project execution steps, were woven into sessions towards the end of module 2.

6.5 Evidence of effectiveness for the University Program

The effectiveness of this program is demonstrated in several ways, including analysis of evaluations of each session, open-ended surveys delivered at points throughout the program, and anecdotal evidence gathered by program staff about growth in participants noticed during and after the program. The fact that most organizations involved continue to send nurse leaders to the program also suggests its success. Here we focus on participants' self-evaluations and self-reports of learning. Self-evaluations of learning are used extensively in management and education and, although not without drawbacks, are valuable and appropriate here. Evidence suggests that self-perceived learning correlates relatively highly with outside evaluations of learning in situations where feedback is provided and for learning interpersonal skills (Sitzmann et al., 2010).

Towards the end of the University Program, an open-ended survey was distributed, which included the following questions: "What were your biggest 'learnings' over the program about you as a leader?" and "What specific tools or ideas have you learned in this program that will help you be a more effective leader?" The responses highlight four key categories of program outcomes, as illustrated in Table 6.3: (1) greater understanding

Table 6.3 **UST nurse leader development program outcomes reported by participants[a]**

Personal leadership self-development and awareness	"I learned about areas in which I need to focus to grow as a leader and move into [higher-level] leadership [as well as] actions I need to take to get there." "I am now aware of my weaknesses and strengths and need to take intentional steps to build on them further." "I already have some strengths I could begin to capitalize on." "There are proven tools that exist, I don't have to reinvent the wheel every time." "Strategic development for myself is required, not just strategic business development." "The benefit of taking time to develop a plan for leadership development." "I need to use my strengths more."
Communication and personal agency	"Style, word choices, directness will let me be more effective." "I have to be an advocate for myself." "I need to take more time with self-promotion, instead of focusing only on work delivery." "Ask for what you need . . . Put yourself out there and take risks." "Develop my brand, and don't be afraid to share it with my leaders." "Making the next move when [the opportunity] comes up, or looking for [the next opportunity] actively." "Communicate what I am involved in and promote/inform what my leaders are involved in so it is known [across the organization]." "Express my passion [for my work]."
Executive mind-set	"Higher-level thinking, self-awareness and strategies to do my best thinking." "I can display my self-confidence without appearing boastful." "Owning my competence and showcasing my expertise is not only valuable for me, but to my company, and ultimately to those we serve." "How to demonstrate authentic behaviors and mindfulness." "What my leadership brings to a group and the impact of that."
Leadership identity formation and leadership confidence	"I learned that I am well on my way to being a leader—I [hadn't] often [thought] of myself in those terms." "I belong [as a leader]." "I really am an executive!!" "I don't even know where to begin! I have learned an incredible amount over the past few weeks. I feel like I've been given some great tools to move forward and to grow into a confident leader." "Overall raised my leadership competency."

a   Participants were responding to two questions: "What were your biggest learnings over the program about you as a leader?" and "What specific tools or ideas have you learned in this program that will help you lead more effectively given gender dynamics?" These are representative comments, not comprehensive and include answers that represent the views of four or more participants.

of themselves as leaders with self-awareness of strengths and challenges and how to address them; (2) communication and personal agency in leadership; (3) executive mind-set; and (4) leadership identity formation and confidence. Given our intentional efforts to address identity issues, we were especially pleased to see that the program had the desired effect.

6.6 Company extension of the University Program

UnitedHealth Group, which has sent 22 nurses to the first three cohorts of the University Program, developed a Company Extension program, which built further on the foundation that the University Program had established, and was conducted onsite. Leaders at UnitedHealth Group saw that the identity work, reflection, education and peer relationships and networking afforded through the University Program provided strong foundational learning, cross-organization peer benchmarking, feedback and support. A key factor in the transfer of development to benefit the organization is organizational support of behavioural changes (Brown and Sitzmann, 2011; Conger, 2010). To ensure that learning and behavioural changes participants gained at the University Program were sustained in the long term, UnitedHealth Group created an internal structure to support participants in the University Program. This internal structure also focused on assessing ongoing learning needs; providing strong mentorship, coaching and sponsorship; and facilitating long-term ownership and accountability for driving organizational changes and improvements through strategic change projects.

This one-year program "wrap-around" extension was managed exclusively by UnitedHealth Group. In addition to putting robust longitudinal outcome measurement in place, it incorporated the following additional elements:

- A 360-degree assessment approximately one year after the University Program 360, which included measurement of changes from the perspectives of each participant's manager, peers and subordinates.

- Ongoing peer coaching delivered through a peer participant in the program. UnitedHealth Group leadership worked with University Program staff to ensure that peer coaches during the University Program were from other units of the company.

- Assignment of a career sponsor. To increase structure and accountability, each nurse leader who finished the University Program was provided a senior executive in the company to look out for her or his ongoing career advancement. This involved a commitment to creating visibility for the nurse leader through networking opportunities and high profile assignments, and ensuring that the nurse leader was considered, when appropriate, for future assignments and positions in the organization.

- Formal checkpoints for the project after the completion of module 2 of the University Program. These checkpoints provided ongoing structure and support in order to increase the sustainability of the learning that had occurred during the University Program foundation. This involved a midpoint and a final project review with an audience of company executives that included the participants' managers and career sponsors.

The strong internal measurement implemented at UnitedHealth Group provides even more, and more robust, evidence of program effectiveness. Since the launch, this organization has sent 22 nurses to the University Program, all of whom also participated in the Company Extension. Early indications reveal that these participants are experiencing significantly higher promotion rates in both nursing and non-nursing roles; assuming greater levels of responsibility; and being retained at higher levels than their peer group of other high-performing nurses in the same company. Promotions include roles in care delivery as well as administrative leadership. Participants have also seen significant role expansion and have dramatically increased their participation on boards and professional societies relevant to their roles.

Participants involved in the Company Extension have also realized significant measurable return on investment tied to the delivery of their action-learning projects, which began in the University Program. Informal discussions between the second author and participants' direct supervisors indicate that participants demonstrate improved communication skills, higher levels of executive presence and more self-confidence. They also more powerfully and positively influence their teams and others, both in and outside the organization. The peer coaching element of the Program has resulted in long-term cross-unit partnerships. Participants report that these are powerful connections that did not exist prior to the University Program, and most continue to the present day. In addition to the outcomes noted in Table 6.3, participants in the Company Extension program report significantly expanded networks both internally and externally; more awareness of best practices; and an increase in their levels of company perspective. The latter entails appreciation of challenges outside their own areas and cultivation of an enterprise point of view. Participants' managers report these same positive changes of increased confidence, enhanced perspective and executive presence in participants.

6.7 Critical challenges

In addition to these program successes, however, we also experienced some discouragement in delivering this program. Our biggest constraint was the willingness of health-care organizations to fund nurse leader development at levels necessary to make an impact. A secondary yet equally important concern involves organizational willingness to fully release participants from their duties for the eight days of the program. Given the nursing shortage, sometimes nurses would be required to fill in "on the floor" as was the case during one nursing strike. This manifested in the inability of some participants to be fully present and engaged in the program, compromising their overall program benefit.

This is brought home to us in this case especially, because UST has a leadership development program for physician leaders. In contrast to the two modules of four days each held on campus, the physician leader development program spans 18 months; includes ten modules, two of which are held in resort settings; and incorporates a program coach for every participant. Despite a higher cost, this program is also easier for University Program staff to fill because physicians have more development time and funding. This discrepancy reinforces the concern we raised earlier related to organizational unwillingness to fund and invest in nursing leadership development at the same level as for leaders with other professional backgrounds. It is incumbent on leaders in business education and healthcare to continue to understand the drivers and impediments to such investments.

6.8 Conclusion

Our experiences with this executive education program for nurse leaders in healthcare suggests that closing leadership gaps in skill, identity and confidence is an achievable goal for women in a highly gendered industry and organizational context, without losing valuable feminine-gendered identities and values. We suggest that this is increasingly possible when gender and professional identity are explicitly addressed alongside other strong program elements. Participants become more aware of gender and professional norms and therefore feel better able to consciously choose which values and norms to retain and which to let go. The participants and their managers report that they are more effective leaders after completing the program, and they are more aptly influencing change in those around them.

Given high turnover rates among nurses, the shortage of nurses and research findings that show that managers and colleagues at work have a major impact on engagement and retention of their team members, including in nursing (Kleinman, 2004; Rothausen et al., in press), improving leadership skills in nurse leaders—from nurse managers up to CEOs of organizations—is vital to the retention of exemplary nurses. It is also crucial for developing the leadership strength that organizations need to contribute to the health, viability and effectiveness of healthcare. If communal as well as agentic goals are to be retained in the healthcare system, a strong, confident, empowered nurse voice is critical.

We hope our work inspires development of comparable business leadership programs for nurse leaders. It is vital that we fill the gap in educational opportunities for many reasons. Foremost, it is critical that nurse voices are empowered in order to facilitate our collective ability to evolve beyond a healthcare system in crisis. This requires finding a way to do many things simultaneously, including implementation of interventions for fast changes, adaptation to the new cost realities and new legislation and changes required by nursing shortages as well as burgeoning populations of elderly and the increasing complexity and diversity of patients. At the same time the "care" in healthcare—proving care and caring that is holistic, patient-centred and sensitive to the unique needs of each individual—must be preserved.

References

Bass, B.M., 2008. The Bass Handbook of Leadership: Theory, Research, and Managerial Applications, fourth ed. Free Press, New York.

Bazarko, D., June 13, 2011. New nursing paradigm needed. *The Washington Times*.

Benner, P., Sutphen, M., Leonard, V., Day, L., 2009. Educating Nurses: A Call for Radical Transformation. Jossey-Bass, San Francisco, CA.

Brown, K.G., Sitzmann, T., 2011. Training and employee development for improved performance. In: Zedeck, S. (Ed.), APA Handbook of Industrial and Organizational Psychology, vol. 2. American Psychological Association, Washington, DC, pp. 469–503.

Buerhaus, P., Auerback, D., Staiger, D., 2009. The recent surge in nurse employment: causes and implications. Health Affairs 28, 657–668.

Conger, J.A., 2010. Leadership development interventions: ensuring a return on investment. In: Nohria, N., Khurana, R. (Eds.), Handbook of Leadership Theory and Practice. Harvard Business Press, Boston, MA, pp. 709–738.

Cummings, S., 1995. Attila the Hun versus Attila the hen: gender socialization of the American nurse. Nursing Administration Quarterly 19, 19–29.

Curtis, E., de Vries, J., Sheerin, F., 2011. Developing leadership in nursing: exploring core factors. British Journal of Nursing 20, 306–309.

Datar, S.M., Garvin, D.A., Cullen, P.A., 2010. Rethinking the MBA: Business Education at a Crossroads. Harvard Business Press, Boston, MA.

DeRue, D.S., Ashford, S.J., 2010. Who will lead and who will follow? A social process of leadership identity construction in organizations. Academy of Management Review 35, 627–647.

Day, D.V., 2012. The nature of leadership development. In: Day, D.V., Antonakis, J. (Eds.), The Nature of Leadership, second ed. Sage, Thousand Oaks, CA, pp. 108–140.

Day, D.V., Harrison, M.M., Halpin, S.M., 2009. An Integrative Approach to Leader Development: Connecting Adult Development, Identity, and Expertise. Psychology Press, New York.

Eagly, A.H., Chin, J.L., 2010. Diversity and leadership in a changing world. American Psychologist 65, 216–234.

Eagly, A.H., Karau, S.J., 2002. Role congruity theory of prejudice toward female leaders. Psychological Review 109, 573–598.

Emanuel, E.J., 2014. Reinventing American Health Care: How the Affordable Care Act Will Improve our Terribly Complex, Blatantly Unjust, Outrageously Expensive, Grossly Inefficient, Error Prone System. Perseus Books Group, New York.

Gardner, W.L., Lowe, K.B., Moss, T.W., Mahoney, K.T., Cogliser, C.C., 2010. Scholarly leadership of the study of leadership: a review of the leadership quarterly's second decade, 2000–2009. The Leadership Quarterly 21, 992–958.

Jackson, B., Parry, K., 2011. A Very Short, Fairly Interesting and Reasonably Cheap Book About Studying Leadership, second ed. Sage, Los Angeles, CA.

Institute of Medicine, 2010. The Future of Nursing: Leading Change, Advancing Health. Washington, DC.

Kelan, E.K., Jones, R.D., 2010. Gender and the MBA. Academy of Management Learning and Education, 9, 26–43.

Kleinman, C.S., 2003. Leadership roles, competencies, and education: How prepared are our nurse managers? Journal of Nursing Administration 33, 451–455.

Kleinman, C.S., 2004. Leadership: a key strategy in staff nurse retention. Journal of Continuing Education in Nursing 35, 128–132.

Koenig, A.M., Eagly, A.H., Mitchell, A.A., Ristikari, T., 2011. Are leader stereotypes masculine? A meta-analysis of three research paradigms. Psychological Bulletin 137, 616–642.

Martineau, J.W., 2004. Evaluating the impact of leader development. In: McCauley, C.D., van Velsor, E. (Eds.), The Center for Creative Leadership Handbook of Leadership Development, second ed. Jossey-Bass, San Francisco, CA, pp. 234–267.

O'Connor, J.T., 2013. Impact of ACA Market Reforms on Affordability. Milliman, Inc. for American's Health Insurance Plans. Retrieved June 14, 2014, from: AHIP.org/Issues/Documents/2012/Impact-of-ACA-Market-Reforms.

Orvis, K.A., Ratwani, K.L., 2010. Leader self-development: a contemporary context for leader development evaluation. The Leadership Quarterly 21, 657–674.

Parker, P., Hall, D.T., Kram, K.E., 2008. Peer coaching: a relational process for accelerating career learning. Academy of Management Learning and Education 7, 487–503.

Rothausen, T.J., 2007. Retention 2010. B. *Magazine, Fall 2007* (also appearing on MinnPost.com, January 10, 2008), 14–17.

Rothausen, T.J., 2011. Leader self-development: review, integrative practice model, and two case studies. Paper Presented at the Academy of Management Annual Meeting, San Antonio, TX.

Rothausen, T.J., Henderson, K.E., Arnold, J.K., Malshe, A. (in press). Should I stay or should I go? Identity and well-being in sensemaking about retention and turnover. Journal of Management.

Saxe-Braithwaite, M., 2003. Nursing entrepreneurship: instilling business acumen into nursing health care leadership. Nursing Leadership 16, 40–42.

Sitzmann, T., Ely, K., Brown, K., Bauer, K.N., 2010. Self-assessment of knowledge: A cognitive learning or affective measure? Academy of Management Learning and Education 9, 169–191.

Staiger, D.O., Auerbach, D.I., Buerhaus, P.I., 2012. Registered nurse labor supply and the recession: are we in a bubble? New England Journal of Medicine 366, 1463–1465.

United States Bureau of the Census, 2013. Male nurses becoming more commonplace. Retrieved June 14, 2014, from: www.census.gov/newsroom/releases/archives/employment_occupations/cb13–32

United States Department of Labor, 2013. Employment Projections: 2012–2022 Summary. Bureau of Labor Statistics. Retrieved June 10, 2014, from: www.bls.gov/news.release.ecopro.nr0.htm

White House, 2014. The Affordable Care Act. Retrieved June 10, 2014, from: www.whitehouse.gove/healthreform/health care-overview

Yost, P.R., Plunkett, M.M., 2009. Real Time Leadership Development. Wiley-Blackwell, Oxford.

7

Legal education and gender equality

Paola Cecchi-Dimeglio
Harvard Law School, USA

Over the years, legal education has made important steps forward in reducing the gender gaps in terms of the number of women versus the number of men attending law school, but it still fails to fully and adequately prepare female law students for a diverse professional world and provide them the tools to succeed as well as men in law school and in their legal careers. This chapter raises the question of why this gender gap still exists even if the pipeline seems to provide sufficient numbers of talented women with the potential to rise to leadership positions in legal education and in the legal profession. To delve into this question, this chapter uses a strategic lens first to analyse the landscape of legal education and, second, to explore the elements it fails to provide for closing the gender gap in terms of differences in absolute numbers of women versus men in leadership positions. From this picture, a set of recommendations is derived to help legal higher education, as a gatekeeper and institutional model, to provide tools and mechanisms to help students, especially women, to recognize and seize opportunities in graduate schools and beyond.

7.1 Introduction

The discussion of gender gaps has evolved around the world and the theme of gender inequality is much more prominent on numerous policy agendas. In many areas success has been evaluated in terms of advances towards equality, but there is still much work to be done. The current evolution of gender gaps, especially in the United States, is subtle and pernicious. This chapter focuses on legal education where, on first impression, it seems as if gender gaps have disappeared. However, reality shows that even if they have evolved, gender gaps are still prevalent. Since the mid-1990s, new information on diminishing gender gaps in legal education and in the legal profession has become available—referring to the absolute number of both women students enrolled in law schools and women in leadership positions, as well as in terms of equality in pay (see Figures 7.2, 7.5 and 7.6)—but these numbers have been viewed through a predominately descriptive and functional research lens. A different image appears when taking a strategic perspective. This chapter attempts to shift the perspective and invites the reader to evaluate this evolution through a more strategic lens.

Worldwide, and especially in the United States, over the past three decades there has been a disproportionate increase in women earning degrees in law, business, life sciences, physical sciences and engineering (UNESCO, 1998a–c, 2005, 2009, 2012). Several rationales can explain this phenomenon, but all have stemmed from the idea that complete and meaningful participation by all segments of society is vital in a democracy. Women have an important role to play in economies worldwide (World Economic Forum, 2010; World Bank, 2012).

Law students as future lawyers play a central role at the heart of many economic and social endeavours (Abel and Lewis, 1989). This includes the majority of men and women going to law school who then follow a traditional career path, as well as a large number of graduates going into other sectors that significantly influence the economy and society more generally (Childress, 2007).

Most commonly, legal education provides the path for law students to become lawyers, judges, law professors and law school deans. Notwithstanding, if we take the example of the United States, a considerable number of law school graduates, approximately 30%, will eventually move into non-legal jobs in the private or public sector (Catalyst, 2001). For instance, about 10% of the CEOs of S&P 500 companies are lawyers (Curriden, 2010). Law school graduates are also likely to join governmental and political institutions (Gross, 2004; Smith, 2008). For instance, lawyers encompassed approximately 59% of US presidents and are the most dominantly held positions of both houses in the US Congress (Amer, 2006; ABA, 2010). As a result, lawyers occupy an important segment of the legislative body and influence policy for businesses as well as protect the interest of citizens influencing the creation of authoritative rules for social and business relationships (Mnookin, Peppet and Tulumello, 2000).

At its base, legal education has a duty to teach law students how to create, recognize and seize opportunities in graduate schools and beyond. Legal education is an environment in which students further assert their identity. Recognizing and acknowledging that the educational experiences of students, especially in law schools, are of substantial influence on their legal careers and on the lives of others, the closing of gender gaps in these institutions should be a high priority.

Women's broadening educational paths, including attending law school, were expected to lead to a proportional increase in female leaders in the legal profession.

The truth is that it did not happen. Gender gaps are still very much present in the legal profession. "The passage of time, for years cited as a reason for hope, has failed to put a major dent in the huge disparities" in both career advancement and leadership positions for women (Levinson and Young, 2010: 1). Research has also found that women's opportunities in the legal profession continue to be limited by several factors, such as gender stereotypes, masculine culture and inadequate support and mentoring networks (Rhode, 2002; Sandefur, 2007).

Over the years, legal education has made important steps forward in reducing the gender gap in terms of an increase in absolute numbers of women attending law school, but law schools still fail to completely and adequately prepare law students for a diverse professional world and provide a platform for female students to succeed during law school and well beyond. With regard to law school as well as legal career performance, gender gaps remain. This raises the question of why the pipeline that provides sufficient numbers of talented women enrolling in law schools does not translate into those women performing at par with men, and rising to leadership positions in the legal academy and in the legal profession.

To delve into this question, this chapter uses a strategic lens to (1) analyse the landscape provided by legal education and (2) explore the elements it fails to provide for closing the "gender" gap, for example, higher absolute numbers of women in leadership positions. From this picture, a set of recommendations is derived to help legal higher education, as a gatekeeper and institutional model, (3) provide tools and mechanisms that may help students, especially women, to recognize and seize opportunities in graduate schools and beyond.

7.2 Legal education, women and career opportunities

In the last half of the twentieth century, women's access to education has grown and the very nature of available employment has given women more opportunities (Woryk, 2011). Today, in the United States, women constitute nearly 50% of the country's workforce and comprise 50.8% of the population (US Bureau of Labor Statistics, 2013). Studies have documented an increased number of women students across academic disciplines. Throughout higher education, women currently constitute more than 60% of all bachelor's and master's cohorts and almost 50% of professional degree graduates including in law (US BLS, 2013). Clearly, this is a positive development and an important precondition for women's presence in the workforce and beyond.

Yet, in areas that have been historically male dominated, gender gaps—*referring to the number of women in leadership positions compared to men and in terms of (un)equal pay* (see Figures 7.2, 7.5 and 7.6)—still exist, and although subtle, they are no less pernicious. Law is an example of such an area.

7.3 The big picture: women in law

If we look at the big picture in legal education, and focus on the population of women students in law school, what do we see?

First, legal education has made important steps forward in bridging the gender gap with regard to the absolute numbers of women enrolled in law school. For a long time, women have been excluded from the legal sphere. It is only with the passage of time that greater numbers of women were admitted to law school and then entered the legal profession in the United States. For instance, it took almost a century of struggle, at both the state and federal level, for women to gain the right to be admitted to practice law. In 1869, Iowa was the first state to allow women to practice law. Over the next 81 years, other states slowly started admitting women to practice, but we had to wait until 1950 before all states had opened their courtrooms to female lawyers.

It is only relatively recently that women have been enrolled into law school at approximately the same rate as men (Schwab, 2003). For example, in the 1950s and 1960s, only 3–4% of women were matriculated in law schools (Schwab, 2003). In 1975, women represented 20% of the registered law students. By 2001 women were matriculated in law schools approximately at the same rate as men (Baker, 2002; Bashi and Iskander, 2006; ABA, 2005; Law School Admission Council, 2012). The representation of women in law schools reached its peak in 1993, when women made up more than 50% of first-year

Figure 7.1 **Women as a percent of J.D. enrolment in the United States (1970–2012)**

Source: American Bar Association, first year and total J.D. enrolment by gender (1947–2012).

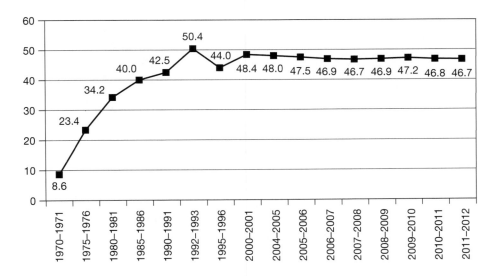

Figure 7.2 **Women in law school administration in the United States (2009)**

Source: AALS Statistical Report on Law Faculty. Association of American Law Schools (www.aals.org/statistics/2009dlt/titles.html), 2008–2009.

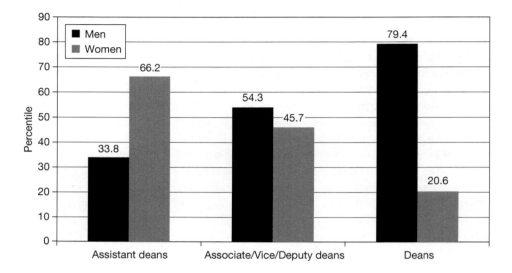

enrolment in law schools (ABA, 2005; Schwartz-Temple, 2012; see Figure 7.1). In fact, the National Association for Law Placement (NALP) noted, in its 2011 report, that enrolment of women in law school has been declining since then (see Figure 7.1).

Second, although there are roughly an equal number of women enrolled in law schools nationwide, women are not yet present at the same level in leadership roles as men, even if women and men share the same level of commitment to work (Baker, 2002). There are considerably fewer tenured women faculty than tenured men in the legal academy; women also hold relatively small shares of law firm partnerships, clerkships and are under-represented in the judiciary (Wald, 2011; see Figures 7.2–7.5).

The number of women law faculty has (slowly) risen since the late 1960s (Fossum, 1980: 532; LSAC Report, 2011). However, women are still under-represented in leadership roles at law faculties. Women comprised 14% full-time law faculty in 1980, 20% by 1996–1997 and about 28% by 2007–2008 (LSAC Report, 2011). Women comprised about 4% of the law school deans in the mid-1980s, roughly 10% by 1996–1997 and about 20% by 2005. These numbers of women serving as law school deans and law faculty have remained constant since then (Padilla, 2007; Statistical Report on Law Faculty, AALS, 2009; Commission on Women, ABA, 2013; see Figure 7.2). Women do, however, constitute the largest pool of instructors and lecturers in law school: 65% of instructors and 61% of lecturers. Unfortunately, both of these are non-tenure-track positions that represent lower status academic appointments in law schools (Statistical Report on Law Faculty, AALS, 2009; ABA, 2013).

Figure 7.3 **Representation of United States, State and Federal Court women judges**

Sources:
*Women in the Federal Judiciary: Still a Long Way to Go. National Women's Law Center, September 2014 (www.nwlc.org/resource/women-federal-judiciary-still-long-way-go-1).
**Women in Federal and State-Level Judgeships: A Report of the Center for Women in Government & Civil Society, Rockefeller College of Public Affairs & Policy, University at Albany, State University of New York. Summer 2012 (www.albany.edu/womeningov/publications/summer2012_judgeships.pdf).
***National Association of Women Judges (www.nawj.org/us_state_court_statistics_2012.asp).

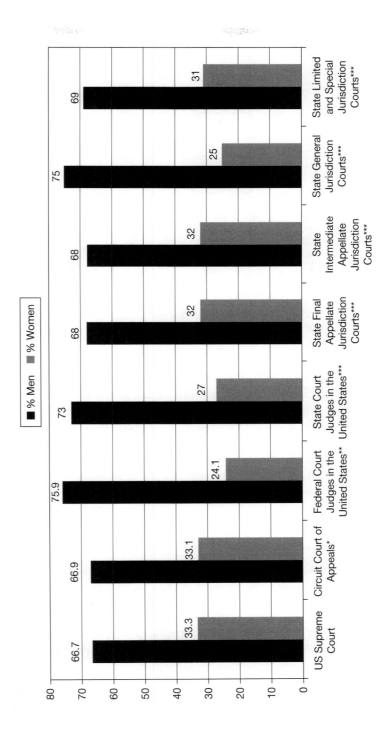

Figure 7.4 **Women in legal profession (2012–2013)**

Sources: American Bar Association Market Research Department, April 2012 and 2013.

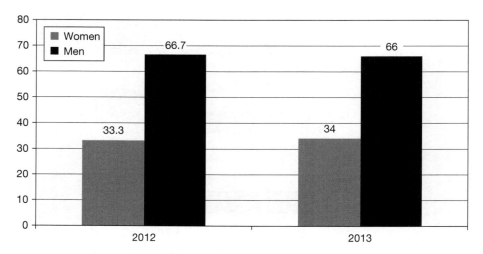

Note: Forty-three states, representing 59% of the lawyer population, reported gender statistics. (www.americanbar.org/resources_for_lawyers/profession_statistics.html).

By the same token, the legal profession has fewer women, especially in leadership roles (see Figures 7.3–7.5). For instance, only 19.9% of law firm partners and 21.6% of Fortune 500 general counsel were women in 2013. In the 200 highest grossing law firms, about 15% of equity partners are women, and just 4% of managing partners are female (ABA, 2013, see Figure 7.5). Women lawyers are still far less likely to be equity partners, credited as rainmakers, in positions of firm-wide leadership, nor compensated by firms at the same level as men (Dinovitzer et al., 2004; Noonan et al., 2005; NAWL, 2012, 2013) (see Figure 7.6).

7.4 Barriers identified in women's law careers

Over the past two decades, a rich body of literature across disciplines, especially in the field of law and sociology, has been developed on gender and organizational leadership. Scores of studies have identified the main barriers faced by women to attain leadership positions (Liddle and Michielsens, 2000; Dreher, 2003; Blair-Loy and Wharton, 2004; Moore, 2004). Those barriers, or hurdles, have been studied both nationally and internationally (Adler and Izraeli, 1994; Vianello and Moore, 2000; Kolb, 2004; Schipani et al., 2009).

In law, the first hurdle that affects women's success in legal careers is that they are more likely to leave the practice of law than men (Menkel-Meadow, 1989; Epstein, 2004). The trend of women leaving the practice of law begins early in their career and accelerates over

Figure 7.5 **Women in private practice**

Sources:
*Representation of Women Associates Falls for Fourth Straight Year as Minority Associates Continue to Make Gains — Women and Minority Partners Continue to Make Small Gains. National Association for Law Placement, December 2013 (www.nalp.org/uploads/PressReleases/2013WomenMinoritiesPressRelease.pdf).
**Report of the Eighth Annual National Survey on Retention and Promotion of Women in Law Firms. National Association of Women Lawyers and NAWL Foundation, February 2014 (www.nawl.org/p/cm/ld/fid=82#surveys).
***Report of the Seventh Annual National Survey on Retention and Promotion of Women in Law Firms. National Association of Women Lawyers and NAWL Foundation, October 2012 (www.nawl.org/p/cm/ld/fid=82#surveys).
****Representation of Women Associates Falls for Fourth Straight Year as Minority Associates Continue to Make Gains — Women and Minority Partners Continue to Make Small Gains. National Association for Law Placement, December 2013 (www.nalp.org/uploads/PressReleases/2013WomenMinoritiesPressRelease.pdf).
*****Representation of Women Associates Falls for Fourth Straight Year as Minority Associates Continue to Make Gains — Women and Minority Partners Continue to Make Small Gains. National Association for Law placement, December 2013 (www.nalp.org/uploads/PressReleases/2013WomenMinoritiesPressRelease.pdf).

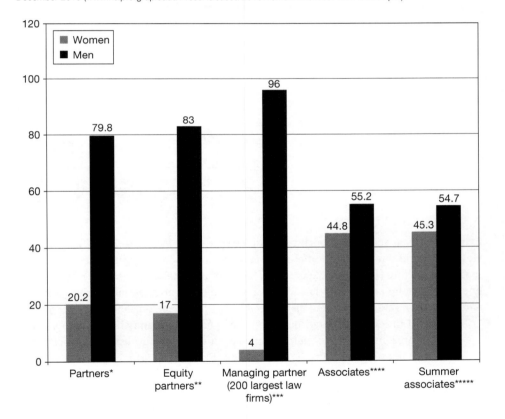

time (NAWL, 2012). This phenomenon influences the number of both women associates at law firms and women deciding to work in legal education (NAWL, 2012). As a result, the pool of women has become much smaller by the time decisions are made about partnership or tenure or other leadership positions. This affects the final number of women at the top (Brockman, 1994; Epstein et al., 1995; Reichman and Sterling, 2002). Very few studies have been able to document what factors make women decide to leave their positions

Figure 7.6 **Weekly salary lawyers (men vs. women) (2004–2013)**

Source: Bureau of Labor Statistics (2013), median weekly earnings of full-time wage and salary workers by detailed occupation and sex (www.bls.gov/cps/cpsaat39.pdf).

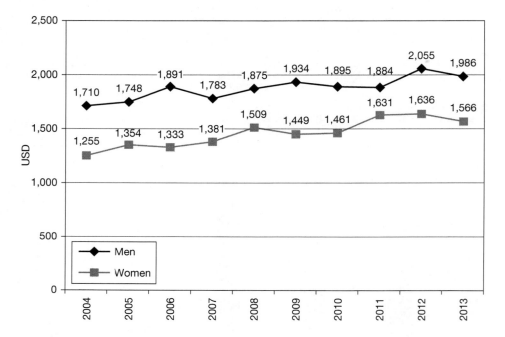

in law or in legal academia (Reichman and Sterling, 2002; Williams, 2007; NAWL, 2012). However, some directions are offered by studies looking at the legal profession and its masculine culture (Brockman, 2001: 3–11; Sommerlad, 2008; Haynes, 2012). The masculine culture is often referred to as "subtle ways in which organizational policies, processes and interactions create gendered distinctions" (Ely and Meyerson, 2000: 599).

The second hurdle restricting the number of women in leadership positions is that the under-representation of women in senior positions in law limits the number of role models for young women aspiring to leadership (Ely, 1994; Ibarra, Ely and Kolb, 2011). Recall here the AALS and ABA reports. For instance, women occupied less than 30% of the full professor positions at law faculties and only 20% of law school dean jobs, but more than 60% of non-tenure-track positions are filled by women. The reality is that most of the women in legal education are still in temporary and unstable work situations without the option of job security that tenure-track positions offer (McGinley, 2009). The vast majority of high-paying and high-prestige positions in law are still occupied by men (McGinley, 2009). So, there are simply not many examples showing that women can obtain leadership positions.

Third, women are held back because they are often left out of vital mentoring relationships during their legal education as well as in the legal world. Their exclusion results in a negative cycle. Women lacking mentors are less likely to pursue a career in law and more inclined to leave practice settings, so that fewer women rise up in the organizations and act as mentors to new women in these settings (NALP, 1998, 2003; Reichman and Sterling, 2002; McManus, 2005).

Fourth, lack of networking access and opportunities for women present a hurdle for them to make it in leadership positions. Networking is conceptually distinct from mentoring, with a definition somewhat more fluid. It constitutes a part of the informal organizational system that is crucial for both men and women to advance through the organizational hierarchy (Pazy, 1987). In that vein, Wilkins argued that "career progress in law is perhaps less a matter of innate talent and dedicated effort and more a function of gaining access to valuable, but limited, opportunities—opportunities that are 'invariably' mediated through relationships" (Wilkins, 2000: 424).

Legal education has made important steps forward in filling the gender gap in some ways but still falls short in other ways. The absolute number of women enrolled in law school has significantly increased; yet legal education still seems to fail in completely and adequately equipping women law students with the skills needed for success in law school and for reaching leadership positions (Rhode, 2011; Sturm, 2010; Silver, 2013). To delve into the forces behind this situation, it is necessary to identify the different lacunae in the legal education identified by legal scholars.

7.5 Legal education and legal profession: is there a disconnect?

A robust body of empirical research on gender and diversity in law schools demonstrates how and why legal education makes it more difficult for female students to succeed in law school and well beyond, including obtaining leadership roles (Epstein, 1983; Guinier, Balin and Fine, 1997; Dowd, Nunn and Pendergast, 2003; Clark, 2006; Schichor, 2009; Wald, 2011). Legal education has far to go with respect to fostering gender equality. A key factor is the disconnection between legal education and the profession, with the primary focus being legal analysis at the exclusion of other skill sets and knowledge. This section details the tension between the curriculum offered at law schools, and the skill set needed in legal practice. It explains why this is particularly a problem that arises at law schools as opposed to other graduate schools. It also addresses the structure and methods used in legal education that are very much geared towards a male student population leading to unconscious biases that result in women doing less well. Finally, this section also sketches women's experiences in law school.

7.6 Legal education and "The Real World"

Disconnects between legal education and the profession have been identified for decades (MacCrate Report, ABA, 1992; Carnegie Report, Sullivan et al., 2007). Students, educators and practitioners complain about the rigid first-year curriculum, the lack of real-world application and the seeming disconnect between what is taught in law schools and what lawyers actually do in practice (Ayers, 2009; Wilkins and Kaufman, 2009; Carasik, 2011).

For instance, the MacCrate Report in 1992 and the Carnegie Report in 2007 recommended that legal education should incorporate an integrated curriculum that provides both professional training and legal analysis beginning in the first year of law school. They also called for improving professional preparation, expanding educational objectives and diversifying methods for delivering instruction to diverse students. In that same vein, the legal profession itself recognized the need to equip all lawyers and law students with skills such as value collaboration, group problem-solving, role flexibility and proffering questions as well as criticisms (NALP, 2009). As a result, in recent years, the legal profession has moved towards competency models in which leadership skills are an essential step in developing lawyering talent for both men and women (NALP, 2009).

Progress certainly has been made as the *gap* that separated the *legal education community* from the *profession* was identified, and solutions have been proposed. For instance, a number of schools around the country (including Harvard Law School, Columbia Law School, University of California [UC] Hastings, University of Chicago, New York University School of Law, UCLA, UC Gould) have created courses to help law students better understand the interaction of law and other disciplines such as business, as well as developing skills classes in which law students can practice the client-centred lawyer relationship in various business settings.

An illustrative example of a program that invests in closing the "gap" between "legal education" and the "legal community" is the Center on the Legal Profession at Harvard Law School. Under the leadership of Professor David Wilkins this program offers research, seminars, programs and classes for law students, and more broadly the general public, which are both highly interdisciplinary—focusing at the intersection of law and social science—and deeply pragmatic—focusing on harnessing the diverse perspectives of individuals and institutions comprising the legal profession (PLP Report, 2013). Such initiatives, however, remain rare.

Another problem identified is that within law schools there appears to be a major focus on legal analysis almost to the exclusion of other skill sets and knowledge bases (Alexander, 2011; Rhode, 2011). Critics argue that some skills seem to be overemphasized whereas other essential skills, such as leadership and business development are neglected or underemphasized in legal curricula (Howell, 2008; Rhode, 2010a, b; Rhode, Luban and Cummings, 2012; Alexander, 2011). As lawyers play a significant role in the various segments of our society, this is problematic, especially if law schools' ambition is to continue to prepare lawyers who can be the leaders of tomorrow.

Law is often viewed by outsiders, and sometimes by insiders, as an autonomous discipline. Law students learn a specialized language and a specific mode of reasoning. The objective is to help law students appreciate problems and defend them from different angles with a degree of specificity. Most of the time, this process is at the expense of other disciplines. However, it is expected that legal analysis exists in a two-way communication process between lawyer and client leading towards a decision that solves the client's problem (Hadfield, 2009). The task of the client-centred lawyer is to assist the client to make his or her own decision in the best way he or she can. The lawyer's job then is to help carry out that decision, of course, within the limits of the law (Regan,

2000; Wilkins, 2001; Hadfield, 2012a, b; Cummings, 2013). In fact, law students will, later on in their practice, be driven to work routinely with multiple factors encompassing the various concerns of business (Rhode, 1998; Rhee, 2011; Strine et al., 2013). Lawyers will also have to handle different professionals from various firms who continuously form and disband as needed (Rhee, 2011).

Although undergraduate and other professional disciplines have explored leadership in fuller capacities, legal education lags behind the curve in leadership development (Rubenstein, 2008; Hamilton, 2009; Filisko, 2010; Rhode and Packel, 2010). There are several explanations for this leadership deficit in legal education. First, law schools generally do not offer any courses expressly designated to prepare graduates for leadership's role (Rhode, 2011; Filisko, 2010; Polden, 2008). Second, legal academics are probably among the most sceptical of professional educators regarding the value of leadership skills training (Rhode, Luban and Cummings, 2012). Rhode, in her seminal article, "What lawyers lack: leadership", notes that "lawyers are particularly prone to view leadership education as a touchy feely process, unworthy of attention from intellectually sophisticated individuals who are especially trained and prone by inherent nature to skepticism and emphasis on analytic rather than interpersonal skills" (Rhode, 2011: 480). Third, leadership traits and characteristics do not seem to be inherent in individuals who choose law as a career (Daicoff, 1997; Richard and Rohrer, 2011). Scores of studies demonstrate that lawyers possess a particular set of personality traits, which are not predisposed for leadership roles (Rhode and Packel, 2010; Rhode, 2010a, b, 2011).

In sum, legal education currently fails at preparing the lawyer–leader of tomorrow to deal with the real world (Howell, 2008; Rhode, 2010b; Rhode, Luban and Cummings, 2012; Alexander, 2011).

7.7 Legal education at the forefront of gender issues?

Legal education also lags in addressing gender equality (Wald et al., 2013). The structure of legal education is still tailored to a law school environment in which men are the primary recipients of legal knowledge and classroom attention (Moore, 2007). Law school teaching methods fail to effectively attune to goals and learning needs of women.

Experiences for men in law school seem to be significantly different than for women and minorities (Morrison, Ries and Spiliopoulos, 1997; Neufeld, 2005). Scholars have attributed this phenomenon to a mismatch between goals of law schools, individual law students and/or distinct groups of students (Guinier et al., 1997; Wilkins and Kaufman, 2009; Rhode, 2010a, b). In this vein, several fundamental problems have been identified.

The first problem is that law schools constitute a workplace founded on a culture of masculinities (Neumann, 2000; McGinley, 2009). Gender is embedded into the structure of the organizations (Rao, Stuart and Kelleher, 1999; McGinn and Milkman, 2013). It is enacted in varying and complex ways through organizational behaviour (Rees, 2006; Rake, 2008; McGinley, 2009; Sturm, 2010, 2011). In the shadow of a system that seems to be gender-neutral, the inequalities are said to result from "unconscious biases" and structures that fundamentally and disparately affect women (Subotnik, 2011).

The second fundamental problem is that individual courses are often gendered both in the male and female proportion of the faculty teaching the subject and in the content of the course (Merritt and Reskin, 1997). In her seminal empirical study on gender and law school, Kornhauser (2004) demonstrates that 80% of the law school courses she examined suffered from a gender disparity. She defines this as a "statistically significant gender distortion". The nature of these classes is more or less perceived as inherently gendered. For instance, students are more inclined to perceive corporate finance as a gendered male course compared to family law, which is more likely to be perceived as gendered female. Consequently, this may influence the career choice and options of law students well beyond graduation, especially for women (Regan and Aiken, forthcoming).

The third issue identified in the literature is that women students in law schools are disproportionately alienated and intimidated by their experiences (Guinier et al., 1997; Bowers, 2000; Schwab, 2003; Yale Law Women report, 2012). The competitive classroom environment in law schools has been found to significantly discourage women to participate in class (Morrison, Ries and Spiliopoulos, 1997; Neufeld, 2005). Overall, women have been shown to be less comfortable with the classroom experience—particularly with the use of the Socratic method (Mashburn, 2008). In the Socratic method, a professor will typically ask a student a series of questions about a case. The questions are designed to stimulate critical thought and force the student to work through complicated issues. The end goal of the questioning is to demonstrate that a rule cannot be applied in a black-and-white manner to all situations, or to reveal the judicial challenge in crafting appropriate rules and definitions. Through the use of this method, the student should gain a deeper understanding of the material and the nuances involved. This adverse impact of the Socratic method on female students is widely recognized in startling contrast to its impact on their male counterparts (Guinier et al., 1997; Schwab, 2003).

The fourth problem is that women in law schools report being less confident in their abilities. This affects their performance in law school, in terms of grades as well as the number competing for the prestigious editors-in-chief of law review positions. In the last ten years less than 30% of editors-in-chief of law reviews were women (NYLS, 2012; Ms JD, 2012). Unfortunately, in certain instances, it continues to affect their opportunities beyond law school and their career trajectories (Weiss and Melling, 1988; Sturm, 1997; Montoya, 2000; Neufeld, 2005; Bashi and Maryana, 2006; Beiner, 2011; Mullins and Leong, 2011).

Further drilling down into this example, when applying for competitive employment such as judicial clerkships after graduation, women are less likely to succeed in getting the position (NYLS, 2012; Ms JD, 2012). "Solely because they lack a 'publication' line on their resume, judges are more likely to take male students with proven writing abilities" (Mullins and Leong, 2011: 424).

All in all, these experiences affect women's options and choices within law school and beyond. Indeed, research has repeatedly demonstrated that experiences in law school are indicative of future careers options and experiences in a legal career (Guinier et al., 1997).

7.8 Recommendations on how legal education can better match the legal profession and help close gender gaps

Legal education is struggling to find the right mechanisms to tackle challenges regarding gender equality and teaching of leadership skills. Several proposals have been offered ranging from adding fundamental dimensions to legal education including broadening the interaction of law with other disciplines and leadership mastery, to implementing measures to help legal education to be at the forefront of gender equality (Rhode, 2010a, b, 2011; Sturm, 1997, 2011; Silver, 2013). This section shows five possible avenues for addressing these challenges in legal education. It covers how broadening the scope of legal education may be achieved; how incorporating leadership courses in the law school curriculum may take shape; how using different techniques and course topics may help in integrating gender issues; how shifting teaching methods from adversarial to more collaborative approaches may do the same thing; and how increasing the number of female role models may contribute to gender equality.

7.9 Broadening the scope of legal education

Legal education will benefit from teaching law students a broader view of the interaction of law and other disciplines to adequately reflect the reality of the today's world, thus adding a dimension to legal education. Several motives underline this argument. First, because "social forces give rise to law's construction and mediate law's application which in turn, shape law's reconstruction" (Shaffer, 2009: 149). Second, law lies in the creation and use of systems of rules, standards and procedures applied by social institutions and businesses as a framework in which they can strategize and operate (Hadfield, 2009). Simultaneously, businesses use law as a resource to further advance their aims and concurrently shape law in various direct and indirect ways (Braithwaite and Drahos, 2000; Shaffer, 2009). Law students need to learn to appreciate organizational dynamics of business (Kelly, 2011). Third, the more diverse legal education is in terms of substance and interaction among disciplines as well as student body, the more value will be brought to the society such as its increased trust and participation in political, economic and legal systems (ABA, 2009). The ABA identifies four rationales for diversity: democratic, business, demographic and leadership. The ABA's "Democracy Rationale" argues that "lawyers and judges have a unique responsibility for sustaining a political system with broad participation by all its citizens. A diverse bar and bench create greater trust in the mechanism of government and the rule of law" (ABA, 2009: 7).

Fundamental dimensions added to legal education supply a level of context, reality and meaning. It enables the other dimensions and any legal situation to be seen in a broader perspective (Jones, 2001). Law students need to learn practical wisdom enabling them to do "the right thing in the right way at the right time" later on in their careers (Jones, 2012: 992). Legal education must enable law students to engage, almost instinctively, in good practical reasoning about ends as well as means and to translate good judgement into action for their clients, be they social institutions, businesses or individuals (Cecchi-Dimeglio and Kamminga, 2014).

7.10 Incorporating leadership into the curricula of law schools

Additionally, legal education will benefit in the opportunity to train law students in skills such as leadership that will play an important role in their future careers. Leadership matters for law students and lawyers.

The ability to demonstrate leadership has been identified as a core competency (NALP, 2009). The former dean of Santa Clara University School, Donald J. Polden (2008), urged law schools to embrace and prepare students for upcoming leadership opportunities during their careers:

> Law schools can and should be educating their students for the leadership roles they will be playing in an increasingly complicated global profession because our communities and societies need greater leadership manifested in business, government, public policy, and in the legal profession (p. 359).

The issue of leadership "is important for all members of the profession, not only those who hold, or desire, positions of greatest power and prominence" (Rhode, 2011: 471). "Virtually all lawyers will, at some stage of their careers, occupy significant leadership roles in their workplaces and their communities" (Rhode, 2011: 472). The need for leadership skills for both men and women law students and lawyers is not only recognized by the highest judicial authority but is also increasingly desired by practice. Justice Powell noted in 1978 that "the nation's future depends upon leaders trained through wide exposure to the ideas and mores of students as diverse as this Nation of many peoples" (Supreme Court of the United States, *Regents of University of California v. Bakke*, 1978: 312).

In the legal sphere, leadership can be defined as "taking an active role in motivating, inspiring, and coaching people to enable team, individual and organizational effectiveness" (Bock and Berman, 2006: 1, 2). Leadership is one of the key skills that law students need for succeeding in their careers (Susskind, 2008; Mottershead, 2010). Law schools can and should equip students in their abilities to "think like a lawyer" by focusing on a learning process of analytical reasoning, substantive knowledge, research and writing skills as well as training them to be leaders (Sullivan et al., 2007). These qualities and abilities are essential for lawyers to initiate positive change and safeguard justice in the occupations and callings that lawyers fulfil in positions across sectors and industries.

There are many definitions of leadership and what makes an effective leader. For the purpose of this discussion, Kouzes and Posner's (2007) definitions will be retained. In their important contribution to the literature on leadership development and training, they identify five practices of exemplary leadership: leaders (1) model the way for others, (2) inspire a shared vision for change or movement, (3) challenge the status quo, (4) encourage and enable others to act towards change or gain, and (5) encourage the heart of those who follow them.

One of the core ideas in the leadership literature is that it is really a competency or set of skills and traits that can be learned and practiced by anyone (Gill, 2006; Avolio, 2010; Broderick, 2010). Leadership skills can be developed and cultivated in almost everyone as long as one is willing to learn (Bennis and Nanus, 1997; Arvey et al., 2006; Dweck, 2006). Lawyers are not an exception and law schools need to rise to this challenge.

In this effort, some rare examples do exist. For instance, Elon University School of Law's Leadership Program prepares law graduates through various means such as leadership lecture series, leadership fellowships and special training and classes. James (2011) describes some of the lessons learned from the leadership lecture series as follows:

> A core fundamental of leadership development, promoted by research at the Center for Creative Leadership, is learning from experience. Elon Law's Leadership program builds on that experience with lessons from the leadership experiences of state and national leaders through the Leadership Lecture Series, sponsored by the Joseph M. Bryan Foundation. Elon Law Board of Advisors David Gergen, former North Carolina Governor James B. Hunt, Jr., former North Carolina Chief Justice Henry Frye, and Red Cross President Bonnie McElveen-Hunter engaged in conversations about their leadership experiences. CNN legal analyst Jeffrey Tobin and NPR's Nina Totenberg shared observations about trends in Supreme Court jurisprudence and judicial appointments, and Newark Mayor Cory Booker and Democratic Leadership Council Chairman Harold Ford, Jr., reflected on the "challenges and rewards of political service". Former Supreme Court Justice Sandra Day O'Connor challenged students to join the effort to improve the judicial selection process and the level of citizen education. Learning lessons about law-making through the legislatures and interpretation on the bench, governing, and assessing the political and popular ramifications of the law uniquely equip these law students to follow in the leadership footsteps of these lecturers (p. 413).

This program aims to meet the demand from both practice and academia to prepare law students for the responsibility and demands of leadership in the various endeavours. However, this kind of initiative still remains isolated across institutions of legal education.

7.11 Integrating gender issues into legal education

Scholars have suggested a variety of approaches to integrate gender issues into legal education. Proposals to tackle the challenge of gender equality in law schools range from changing the form in which legal education is delivered, including introducing more women and women's issues into school curricula, to restructuring the current adversarial law school model by collaborative techniques, and by increasing individual feedback.

Some scholars argue that introducing more women and women's issues into law school curricula will help to palliate these problems (Guinier, Fine and Balin, 1994; Sturm, 1997; Hagan and Kay, 2007). They suggest, for instance, inserting gender and feminist perspectives into first-year classes (Guinier, Fine and Balin, 1994; Menkel-Meadow, 1994; Rhode, Luban and Cummings, 2012). Advocates recommend that these perspectives should be incorporated overall into the legal curricula to avoid them being seen as a separate issue or as "asides to the more important objective of the class" (Ramachandran, 1998: 1762–1794). Overall, it will help the development of the legal curriculum towards more gender consciousness and increase contributions of women overall in the classroom (Dowd et al., 2003). Women's law school experience would improve by adopting such an approach. It would also benefit male students, as they would learn about pervasive gender issues and attitudes in the legal fields (Harrison, 1993).

7.12 Restructuring teaching methods

Legal scholars also advocate for the restructuring of the current law school model that is found to be adversarial (Rhode, 2010a; Rhode, Luban and Cummings, 2012; Silver, 2013; Boutcher and Silver, 2013). Changes that should benefit women entail using teaching methods, such as those used in business schools, which include more collaboration and group problem-solving among students as well as demystifying the "Socratic method" (Thiemann, 1998; Howell, 2008).

Institutionalizing collaborative learning and team-based projects into legal curricula will help to develop the notion of teamwork and collaboration among law students (Reilly, 2000). These qualities are needed for law students and lawyers to succeed professionally.

Understanding how an issue is framed from different gender perspectives could help students to expand their critical thinking. It might as well benefit the kinds of services law students and (future) lawyers are able to offer to meet their clients' diverse needs. This will enable students to develop skills and abilities necessary for successful engagement in civic responsibilities, for meeting the requirements of client representation and for managing the responsibilities within a law firm or organization.

Other legal scholars suggest demystifying the learning process of the Socratic method by having professors explain the purpose for using it (Rosato, 1997; Mashburn, 2008). Explaining the Socratic method and its objectives could well improve women's participation in classroom discussions, as it will stimulate an atmosphere through which one can explore safely the law in its entirety (Sturm, 2011). This requires clarifying that the basic precept of the Socratic method is its reliance on class participation, a vehicle through which knowledge is disbursed created by a verbal back-and-forth between the professor and the students. The objective is to encourage a dialogue among students in which the professor facilitates the conversation.

From a gender perspective, by doing so, law school education will eliminate or at least temper the negative effect of the Socratic method by encouraging women students to voice their views. It should enhance women's participation in the classroom, as they are likely to feel more comfortable.

Additionally, it has been proposed to encourage faculty to increase individual feedback, which is expected to "humanize" law school and foster (women) students to participate in the classroom (Rosato, 1997; Wilkins, 2000). These techniques, however, seem to come more naturally for business school professors than for law school professors (Reilly, 2000).

Implementing these practices should increase the positive reinforcement in women abilities to participate as well as enhance a sense of community and belonging in law school.

7.13 Expand the presence of female role models in law schools

Other propositions related to the infrastructure of legal education have been offered to eradicate these problems affecting women and more deeply the legal education itself. These include increasing the number of (women) role models in the faculty body. This effort appears to have succeeded, but in reality it has not. Some legal scholars suggest increasing both the sheer number of female full-time law professors and the number of female professors in positions of seniority in deanship positions (Dowd, Nunn and Pendergast, 2003). By doing so, it would increase role models as well as inform the way students will perceive their future work environment and what they think is possible for them to do.

Socialization plays a major role in the way differences between men and women evolve and what women can expect for them in the future labour market (Van Knippenberg et al., 2004). The representation of the faculty in law school certainly informs the way students perceive their future work environment and undoubtedly affects women as they enter a male-dominated profession such as law. The learning environment exerts a powerful influence on students and is the first step towards remedying what might look like a dispositional lack of will in providing direction for women into legal leadership.

7.14 Conclusion

It is impossible to deny that the average woman in 2014 has far better opportunities and prospects in entering law schools than she did in 1975. And the number of reform proposals advanced by scholars and analysts to improve the wellbeing and careers of women has certainly blossomed. Yet, higher education, as a gatekeeper and institutional model, needs to provide tools and mechanisms to help students, especially women, to recognize and seize opportunities in legal education and beyond.

Law schools are the initial gatekeepers of those entering the profession and the educators of future lawyers. Law schools must teach and help law students, especially women and minorities, to develop their leadership skills. Law students need to think strategically about their goals, talents and needs, as it is an essential leadership capability for their career (Boyce, Zaccaro and Zazanis-Wisecarver, 2010; Rhode, 2011). Law schools need to offer training to law students, so they can act on their aspirations and seek experiences, positions and assignments that develop leadership skills when entering the labour market (Hill, 2001; Ready, Conger and Hill, 2010).

Legal education has made important steps forward in opening the doors to law school for women but gaps remain, for instance, in terms of the number of women being chosen as law review editors, as law clerks or in the number of tenured women faculty and deans in law schools.

Legal education plays a major role in understanding both the successes and failures in reducing gender gaps at both the graduate level and beyond. Law schools should invest more to prepare graduates, especially women, for a diverse professional world and leadership roles.

Finally, it is important to note that interest and support for gender-based educational policy changes are not unique. There are, of course, substantial numbers of scholars, practitioners, commentators and policy analysts who hold similar views, hoping that contemporary legal education will further pursue its goals of justice by closing the gender gaps and producing better leaders.

Acknowledgements

The author especially thanks the helpful comments, guidance, help and support of David Wilkins, Iris Bohnet, Kathleen Mcginn, Robert Mnookin, Kathryn Spier, Gillian Hadfield, Scott Cummings, Deborah Kolb, Carole Silver, Lani Guinier and Richard Susskind. The author is indebted to Michelle Pekar.

References

AALS (Association of American Law Schools), 2009. Statistical Report on Law Faculty 2008. www.aals.org/statistics/2009dlt/gender.html (accessed 12.01.14).

ABA (American Bar Association), Section of Legal Education & Admissions to the Bar, an Educational Continuum, 1992. Report of the Task Force on Law Schools and the Profession: Narrowing the Gap. www.abanet.org/legaled/publications/onlinepubs/maccrate.html (accessed 15.01.14) [MacCrate Report].

ABA, Presidential Initiative Committee on Diversity, 2009. Diversity in the Legal Profession: The Next Steps 5. www.new.abanet.org/centers/diversity/publicdocuments/diversitysummary_report.pdf (accessed 15.01.14).

ABA, Section on Legal Education, 2005. First Year Enrollment in ABA Approved Law Schools 1947–2004 (Percentage of Women). www.abanet.org/legaled/statistics/femstats.html (accessed 15.01.14).

ABA, Standing Committee on the Federal Judiciary Ratings, 2010. Ratings of Article III Judicial Nominees 111th Congress. www.abanet.org/scfedjud/ratings/ratings111.pdf (accessed 12.01.14).

ABA, The ABA Commission on Women, 2013. A Current Glance at Women in the Law. www.americanbar.org/groups/women/resources/statistics.html#sthash.lxrtpgj8.dpuf (accessed 12.01.14).

Abel, R.L., Lewis, P.S.C. (Eds.), 1989. Putting Law Back into the Sociology of Lawyers. In: Lawyers in Society: Comparative Theories. University of California Press, Berkeley, CA, pp. 502–504.

Adler, N.J., Izraeli, D.N. (Eds.), 1994. Competitive Frontiers: Women Managers in a Global Economy. Blackwell Publishers, Cambridge, MA.

Alexander, C.S., 2011. Learning to be lawyers: professional identity and the law school curriculum. Maryland Law Review 70(2), 465–483.

Amer, M., 2006. Cong. Research Serv., Rs 22007, Profile Membership of the 109 Congress: A Profile. www.senate.gov/reference/resources/pdf/rs22007.pdf (accessed 20.01.14).

Arvey, R.D., Rotundo, M., Johnson, W., Zhang, Z., McGue, M., 2006. The determinants of leadership role occupancy: genetic and personality factors. Leadership Quarterly 17, 1–20.

Avolio, B., 2010. Pursuing authentic leadership development. In: Nohria, N., Khurana, R. (Eds.), Handbook of Leadership Theory and Practice. Harvard Business School Publishing, Cambridge, MA, pp. 721–750.

Ayers, I.S., 2009. Undertraining of lawyers and its effect on the advancement of women and minorities in the legal profession. Duke Forum for Law & Social Change 71(1), 71–100.

Baker, J.G., 2002. The influx of women into legal professions: an economic analysis. Monthly Labor Review 125(8), 14–24.

Bashi, S., Iskander, M., 2006. Why legal education is failing women. Yale Journal of Law and Feminism 18(2), 389–449.

Beiner, T.M., 2011. Some thoughts on the state of women lawyers and why title VII has not worked for them. Indiana Law Review 44(3), 685–702.

Blair-Loy, M., Wharton, A.S., 2004. Mothers in finance: surviving and thriving. Annals of the American Academy of Political and Social Science 596, 151–171.

Bennis, W.G., Nanus, B., 1997. Leadership: Strategies for Taking Charge. HarperCollins, New York, NY.

Bock, H., Berman, L., August 2006. Building and using an associate competency model. Professional Development Quarterly, 12–14.

Boutcher, S.A., Silver, C., 2013. Gender and global lawyering: where are the women? Indiana Journal of Global Legal Studies 20(2), 1139–1167.

Bowers, A., 2000. Women at The University of Texas Law School: a call to action. Texas Journal of Women and the Law 9, 117–140.

Boyce, L.A., Zaccaro, S.J., Zazanis-Wisecarver, M., 2010. Propensity for self-development of leadership attributes: understanding, predicting, and supporting performance of leader self-development. Leadership Quarterly 21, 159–178.

Braithwaite, J., Drahos, P., 2000. Global Business Regulation. Cambridge University Press, Cambridge, UK.

Brockman, J., 1994. Leaving the practice of law: the wherefores and the whys. Alberta Law Review 32(1), 116–180.

Brockman, J., 2001. Gender in the Legal Profession: Fitting or Breaking the Mould. Canada UBC Press, Vancouver, BC, Canada.

Broderick, M., 2010. Leadership: Characteristics, Grooming, Selection. In: Practicing Law Institute (Ed.). PLI Law Firm Leadership & Management Institute, New York, NY, pp. 467–485.

Carasik, L., 2011. Renaissance or retrenchment: legal education at a crossroads. Indiana Law Review 44(3), 735–818.

Catalyst, Inc., 2001. Women in Law: Making the Case. www.catalyst.org/knowledge/women-law-making-case (accessed 01.01.14).

Cecchi-Dimeglio, P., Kamminga, P., 2014. The changes in legal infrastructure: empirical analysis of the status and dynamics influencing the development of innovative practice. Journal of the Legal Profession 38(2), 191–230.

Childress, S., 2007. Lawyers. In: Clark, D.S. (Ed.), Encyclopedia of Law & Society: American and Global Perspectives. Sage Publications, Inc., Thousand Oaks, CA, pp. 931–948.

Clark, M.L., Spring 2006. Why care about the history of women in the legal profession? Women's Rights Law Reporter, 59–68.

Cummings, S.L., 2013. Empirical studies of law and social change: What is the field? What are the questions? Wisconsin Law Review 1, 171–204.

Curriden, M., May 2010. Why lawyers are being asked to lead some of the nation's largest corporations? A.B.A. Journal, 31–34.

Daicoff, S., June 1997. Lawyer, know thyself: a review of empirical research on attorney attributes bearing on professionalism. American University Law Review 46(5), 1337–1428.

Dinovitzer, R., Garth, B., Sander, R., Sterling, J., Wilder, G., NALP Foundation & American Bar Association, 2004. After the JD: The First Results of a National Study of Legal Careers. www.americanbarfoundation.org/uploads/cms/documents/ajd.pdf (accessed 12.01.14).

Dowd, N.E., Nunn, K.B., Pendergast, J.E., Fall 2003. Diversity matters: race, gender, and ethnicity in legal education. University of Florida Journal of Law & Public Policy 15(1), 11–56.

Dreher, G.F., May 2003. Breaking the glass ceiling: the effects of sex ratios and work-life programs on female leadership at the top. Human Relations 56(5), 541–562.

Dweck, C., 2006. Mindset: The New Psychology of Success. The Random House Publishing Group, New York, NY.

Ely, R.J., 1994. The effects of organizational demographics and social identity on relationships among professional women. Administrative Science Quarterly 39, 203–238.

Ely, R.J., Meyerson, D., 2000. Advancing gender equity in organisations: the challenge and importance of maintaining a gender narrative. Organization 7(4), 589–608.

Epstein, C.F., 1983. Women in Law. Basic Books, New York, NY.

Epstein, C.F., Saute, R., Oglensky, B., Gever, M., 1995. Glass ceilings and open doors: women's advancement in the legal profession. Fordham Law Review 64, 291–449.

Epstein, P.H., 2004. Women-at-Law: Lessons Learned along the Pathways to Success. American Bar Association, Chicago, IL.

Filisko, M., 2010. Getting the business. A.B.A. Journal 96, 24–25.

Fossum, D., 1980. Law professors: a profile of the teaching branch of the legal profession. American Bar Foundation Research Journal 3, 501–550.

Gill, R., 2006. The Theory and Practice of Leadership. Sage Publication, London, UK.

Gross, N., 2004. America's Lawyer Presidents: From Law Office to Oval Office. Northwestern University Press, Evanston, IL.

Guinier, L., Balin, J., Fine, M., 1997. Becoming Gentlemen: Women, Law Schools and Institutional Change. Beacon Press, Boston, MA.

Guinier, L., Fine, M., Balin, J., November 1994. Becoming gentlemen: women's experiences at one Ivy League Law School. University of Pennsylvania Law Review 143(1), 1–10.

Hadfield, G.K., 2009. The public and the private in the provision of law for global transactions. In: Gessner, V. (Ed.), Contractual Certainty in International Trade: Empirical Studies and Theoretical Debates on Institutional Support for Global Economic Exchanges. Hart Publishing, Portland, OR, pp. 239–257.

Hadfield, G.K., Summer 2012a. Legal infrastructure and the new economy. Journal of Law and Policy for the Information Society 8(1), 1–60.

Hadfield, G.K., Summer 2012b. Response to comments: legal infrastructure and the new economy. Journal of Law and Policy for the Information Society 8(1), 109–118.

Hagan, J., Kay, F.M., 2007. Even lawyers get the blues: gender, depression, and job satisfaction in legal practice. Law Society Review 41(1), 51–78.

Hamilton, N.W., 2009. Ethical leadership in professional life. University of Saint Thomas Law Journal 6(2), 358–396.

Harrison, M., Winter 1993. Time of passionate learning: using feminism, law, and literature to create a learning community. Tennessee Law Review 60(2), 393–430.

Haynes, K., 2012. Body beautiful? Gender, identity and the body in professional services firms. Gender, Work & Organization 19(5), 489–507.

Hill, L., 2001. Developing the star performer. In: Hesselbein, F., Cohen, P.M. (Eds.), Leader to Leader. Jossey-Bass, San Francisco, CA, pp. 287–297.

Howell, C., 2008. Combating gender inequities in law school: time for a new feminist rhetoric that encourages practical change. Modern American 4(2).

Ibarra, H., Ely, R., Kolb, D., 2011. Teaching leadership—taking gender into account: theory and design for women's leadership development programs [Special Issue]. Academy of Management Learning & Education 10(3), 1–53.

James, F.R., 2011. Engaging law student in leadership. St Louis University Public Law Review 30, 409–437.

Jones, M.L., Summer 2001. Fundamental dimensions of law and legal education: a theoretical framework. Oklahoma City University Law Review 26(2), 547–630.

Jones, M.L., 2012. Fundamental dimensions of law and legal education: perspectives on curriculum reform, Mercer Law School's Woodruff curriculum, and perspectives. Mercer Law Review 63(3), 975–1056.

Kelly, M., 2011. Gaping hole in American legal education. Maryland Law Review 70(2), 440–450.

Kolb, D.M., 2004. Staying in the game or changing it: an analysis of moves and turns in negotiation. Negotiation Journal 20(2), 235–268.

Kornhauser, M., 2004. Rooms of their own: an empirical study of occupational segregation by gender among law professors. University of Missouri-Kansas City Law Review 73, 293–350.

Kouzes, J.M., Posner, B.Z., 2007. The Leadership Challenge. Jossey-Bass Publisher, San Francisco, CA.

Law School Admission Council & American Bar Association Section of Legal Education and Admissions to the Bar, 2012. Official Guide to ABA-Approved Law Schools: 2012. ABA Publisher, Chicago, IL.

LSAC Report (Law School Admission Council), 2011. After Tenure: Post-Tenure Law Professors in the United States Report. www.lsac.org/docs/default-source/research-(lsac-resources)/gr-11–02.pdf (accessed 03.06.14).

Levinson, D.J., Young, D., 2010. Implicit gender bias in the legal profession: an empirical study. Duke Journal of Gender Law & Policy 18(1), 1–44.

Liddle, J., Michielsens, E., 2000. Women and public power: class does make a difference. International Review of Sociology 10(2), 207–222.

Mashburn, A.R., Spring 2008. Can Xenophon save the Socratic method. Thomas Jefferson Law Review 30(2), 597–692.

McGinley, A.C., 2009. Reproducing gender on law school faculties. Brigham Young University Law Review 1, 99–156.

McGinn, K.L., Milkman, K.L., 2013. Looking up and looking out: career mobility effects of demographic similarity among professionals. Organization Science 24, 1041–1060.

McManus, E.K., 2005. Intimidation and the culture of avoidance: gender issues and mentoring in law firm practice. Fordham Urban Law Journal 33, 217–231.

Menkel-Meadow, C., Spring 1989. Exploring a research agenda of the feminization of the legal profession: theories of gender and social change. Law & Social Inquiry 14(2), 289–319.

Menkel-Meadow, C., 1994. Portia redux: another look at gender, feminism, and legal ethics. Virginia Journal of Social Policy and the Law 2, 75–114.

Merritt, D.J., Reskin, B., 1997. Sex, race, and credentials: the truth about affirmative action in law faculty hiring. Columbia Law Review 97, 199–311.

Mnookin, R.H., Peppet, S.R., Tulumello, A.S., 2000. Beyond Winning: Negotiating to Create Value in Deals and Disputes. The Belknap Press of Harvard University Press, Cambridge, MA.

Montoya, M.E., Spring 2000. Silence and silencing: their centripetal and centrifugal forces in legal communication, pedagogy and discourse. University of Michigan Journal of Law Reform 33(3), 263–328.

Moore, G., November 2004. Mommies and daddies on the fast track: success of parents in demanding professions. Annals of the American Academy of Political and Social Science 596, 208–213.

Moore, L.W., 2007. Reproducing Racism: White Space, Elite Law Schools, and Racial Inequality. Rowman & Littlefield Publishers, Plymouth, UK.

Morrison, T., Ries, J., Spiliopoulos, E., 1997. What every first-year female law student should know. Columbia Journal of Gender and Law 7(2), 267–312.

Mottershead, T. (Ed.), 2010. The business case for talent management in law firms—are people really our greatest asset. In: The Art and Science of Strategic Talent Management in Law Firms. Thomson Reuters, Boston, MA, pp. 24–48.

Ms, J.D., 2012. Women on Law Review. www.ms-jd.org/files/lr2012_final.pdf (accessed 01.01.14).

Mullins, J.C., Leong, N., 2011. Persistent gender disparity in student note publication. Yale Journal of Law and Feminism 23(2), 385–444.

NALP (National Association of Law Placement), NALP Foundation for Research and Education, 1998. Keeping the Keepers Strategies for Associate Retention in Times of Attrition. National Association of Law Placement, Washington, DC.

NALP (National Association of Law Placement), NALP Foundation for Research and Education, 2003. Keeping the Keepers II: Mobility & Management of Associates. National Association of Law Placement, Washington, DC.

NALP (National Association of Law Placement), NALP Foundation, 2009. Research Findings: Survey of Law Firm Use of Core Competencies and Benchmarking in Associate Compensation and Advancement Structures. www.Nalpfoundation.Orguploads/Pdccompetenciesand benchmarkssurveyresultsfinal.pdf (accessed 03.03.14).

NAWL (National Association of Women in Law), 2012. Foundation Women's Initiative Survey Report 2012. www.nawlfoundation.org/pav/docs/surveys/nawl%20foundation%20 womens%20initiative%20survey%20report.pdf (accessed 30.01.14).

NAWL (National Association of Women in Law), 2013. Foundation Women's Initiative July 31, 2013: Report on Second Summit. www.nawl.org/p/cm/ld/fid=82#reports (accessed 30.01.14).

Neufeld, A., 2005. Costs of an outdated pedagogy—study on gender at Harvard Law School American University. Journal of Gender, Social Policy & the Law 13(3), 511–596.

Neumann, R.K., Jr, September 2000. Women in legal education: what the statistics show. Journal of Legal Education 50(3), 313–357.

NYLS (New York Law School Law Review), 2012. Law-Review-Diversity-Report. www.nylslaw review.com/wordpress/wp-content/uploads/2012/10/2011–2012–nyls-law-review-diver sity-report.pdf (accessed 03.01.14).

Noonan, M.C., Corcoran, M.E., Courant, P.N., 2005. Pay differences among the highly trained: cohort difference in the male-female earnings gap in lawyers' salaries. Social Forces 84(2), 853–872.

Padilla, L.M., 2007. Gendered update on women law deans: who, where, why, and why not. Journal of Gender, Social Policy & the Law 15(3), 443–446.

Polden, D.J., Winter 2008. Educating law students for leadership roles and responsibilities. University of Toledo Law Review 39(2), 353–360.

PLP (Program on the Legal Profession) Annual Report Academic Year, 2012–2013. Harvard Law School. www.law.harvard.edu/programs/plp/pdf/plp_annual_report_2013.pdf (accessed 01.03.14).

Rake, K., 2008. Women and the Future Workplace—A Blueprint for Change, a Fawcett Society Think Piece for the Launch of the Gender Equality Forum. The Fawcett Society, London, UK.

Ramachandran, B., November 1998. Re-reading difference: feminist critiques of the law school classroom and the problem with speaking from experience. Columbia Law Review 98(7), 1757–1794.

Rao, A., Stuart, R., Kelleher, D., 1999. Gender at Work: Organizational Change for Equality. Kumarian Press, West Hartford, CT.

Ready, D.A., Conger, J.A., Hill, L.A., June 2010. Are you a high potential? Harvard Business Review 78–82.

Rees, T., 2006. Promoting equality in the private and public sectors. In: Perrons, D. (Ed.), Gender Division and Working Time in the New Economy: Public Policy and Changing Patterns of Work in Europe and North America. Edward Elgar, Cheltenham, UK.

Regan, M.C., Jr, Winter 2000. Professional responsibility and the corporate lawyer. Georgetown Journal of Legal Ethics 13(2), 197–216.

Regan, M.C., Jr, Aiken, J. Gendered pathways: choice, constraint, and women's job movements in the legal profession. Law & Social Inquiry, forthcoming.

Reichman, N.J., Sterling, J., 2002. Sterling, recasting the brass ring: deconstructing and reconstructing workplace opportunities for women lawyers. Capital University Law Review 29(4), 923–978.

Reilly, E.A., 2000. Deposing the tyranny of extroverts: collaborative learning in the traditional classroom format. Journal of Legal Education 50(4), 593–614.

Rhee, R.J., 2011. On legal education and reform: one view formed from diverse perspectives. Maryland Law Review 70, 310–340.

Rhode, D.L., April 1998. Professional education and professional values. Professional lawyer symposium issues. AALS Newsletter 1(4), 11–16.

Rhode, D.L., 2002. Gender and the profession: the no-problem problem. Hofstra Law Review 30, 1001–1013.

Rhode, D.L., Summer 2010a. Lawyers as leaders. Michigan State Law Review 2, 413–422.

Rhode, D.L., 2010b. Lawyers and leadership. Professional Lawyer 20(3), 1–17.

Rhode, D.L., Packel, A., 2010. Leadership: Law, Policy, and Management. Wolters Kluwer, Amsterdam, The Netherlands.

Rhode, D.L., 2011. What lawyers lack: leadership. University of St Thomas Law Journal 9(2), 471–496.

Rhode, D.L., 2012. Developing Leadership. Santa Clara Law Review 52(3), 689–724.

Rhode, D.L., Luban, D., Cummings, S., 2012. Legal Ethics. Foundation Press, New York, NY.

Richard, L., Rohrer, L., July/August 2011. A breed apart? American Lawyer, 43–46.

Rosato, J.L., Fall 1997. Socratic method and women law students: humanize, don't feminize. Southern California Review of Law and Women's Studies 7(1), 37–62.

Rubenstein, H., 2008. Leadership for Lawyers. ABA Publishing, Chicago, IL.

Sandefur, R.L., 2007. Staying power: the persistence of social inequality in shaping lawyer stratification and lawyers' persistence in the profession. Southwestern University Law Review 36(3), 539–556.

Schichor, N., Spring 2009. Mitigating gender schemas: the women, leadership & equality program at The University of Maryland School of Law. Hamline Journal of Public Law & Policy 30(2), 563–580.

Schipani, C.A., Dworkin, T.M., Kwolek-Folland, A., Maurer, V.G., January 2009. Pathways for women to obtain positions of organizational leadership: the significance of mentoring and networking. Duke Journal of Gender Law & Policy 16(1), 89–36.

Schwab, G.C., Spring/Summer 2003. A shifting gender divide: the impact of gender on education at Columbia Law School in the New Millennium. Columbia Journal of Law and Social Problems, 299–337.

Schwartz-Temple, H., October 2012. Clogged pipeline: lack of growth at firms has women skipping law school. A.B.A. Journal 98(10), 29–31.

Silver, C., 2013. Getting real about globalization and legal education: potential and perspectives for the US. Stanford Law & Policy Review 24, 457–495.

Shaffer, G.C., November 2009. How business shapes law: a socio-legal framework. Connecticut Law Review 42(1), 147–184.

Smith, C., 2008. From courtrooms to capitols. TRIAL 44, 54–56.

Sommerlad, H., 2008. What are you doing here? You should be working in a hair salon or something: outsider status and professional socialization in the solicitors' profession. Web Journal of Current Legal Issues (2).

Strine, L.E., Jr, Borden, B.T., Rhee, R.J., King, T., Fall 2013. How to prepare students to meet corporate needs. Chapman Law Review 17(1), 195–214.

Sturm, S.P., 1997. From gladiators to problem-solvers: connective conversations about women, the academy, and the legal profession. Duke Journal of Gender Law & Policy 4, 119–148.

Sturm, S.P., 2010. Activating systemic change toward full participation: the pivotal role of mission-driven institutional intermediaries. Saint Louis Law Journal 54, 1117–1137.

Sturm, S.P., April 30, 2011. 'Reframing the Equality Agenda' paper presented at the Harvard Law School Conference on Evolutions in Anti-Discrimination Law in Europe and North America, US.

Subotnik, D., 2011. Do law schools mistreat women faculty? Or, who's afraid of Virginia Woolf. Akron Law Review 44(3), 867–894.

Sullivan, W.M., Colby, A., Welch-Wegner, J., Bond, L., Shulman, L.S., 2007. The Carnegie Foundation for the Advancement of Teaching, Summary, Educating Lawyers: Preparation for the Profession of Law. www.carnegiefoundation.org/sites/default/files/publications/elibrary-pdf-632.pdf (accessed 03.01.14) [The Carnegie Report].

Supreme Court of the United States, *Regents of University of California v. Bakke*, 438 US 265, 1978.

Susskind, R., 2008. The End of Lawyers? Rethinking The Nature of Legal Services. OUP, Oxford, UK.

Thiemann, S.E., 1998. Beyond Guinier: a critique of legal pedagogy. New York University Review of Law & Social Change 24(1), 17–42.

UNESCO, 1998a. Higher Education and Women: Issues and Perspectives. www.unesco.org/education/educprog/wche/principal/women.html (accessed 04.01.14).

UNESCO, 1998b. Higher Education in the Twenty-First Century: Vision and Action. www.unesdoc.unesco.org/images/0011/001163/116345e.pdf (accessed 03.01.14).

UNESCO, 1998c. Women and Management in Higher Education: A Good Practice Handbook. www.unesco.org/education/pdf/singh.pdf (accessed 03.01.14).

UNESCO, 2005. Science, Technology and Gender: An International Report. www.unesdoc.unesco.org/images/0015/001540/154045e.pdf (accessed 03.01.14).

UNESCO, 2009. 2009 World Conference on Higher Education: The New Dynamics of Higher Education and Research for Societal Change and Development. www.unesco.org/fileadmin/multimedia/hq/ed/ed/pdf/wche_2009/final%20communique%20wche%202009.pdf (accessed 01.01.14).

UNESCO, 2012. World Atlas of Gender Equality in Education. www.unesdoc.unesco.org/images/0021/002155/215522e.pdf (accessed 20.01.14).

US BLS (US Bureau of Labor Statistics), 2013. Women in the Labor Forces. www.bls.gov/cps/wlf-databook-2012.pdf (accessed 01.01.14).

Van Knippenberg, D., Van Knippenberg, B., Cremer, D., Hogg, M., 2004. Leadership, self and identity: a review and research agenda. Leadership Quarterly 15, 825–856.

Vianello, M., Moore, G. (Eds.), 2000. Gendering Elites: Economic and Political Leadership in 27 Industrialized Societies. Macmillan, London, UK.

Wald, E., Fall 2011. Primer on diversity, discrimination, and equality in the legal profession or who is responsible for pursuing diversity and why. Georgetown Journal of Legal Ethics 24(4), 1079–1142.

Wald, E., Snow, E., Van Hook, N., Haberman, H., 2013. Looking beyond gender: women's experiences at Law School. Tulsa Law Review 48, 27–62.

Weiss, C., Melling, L., May 1988. Legal Education of Twenty Women. Stanford Law Review 40(5), 1299–1370.

Wilkins, D.B., 2000. Why global law firms should care about diversity: five lessons from the American experience. European Journal of Law Reform 2, 415–438.

Wilkins, D.B., 2001. Professional ethics for lawyers and law schools: interdisciplinary education and the law school's ethical obligation to study and teach about profession. Legal Education Review 12(1/2), 47–80.

Wilkins, D.B., Kaufman, A., 2009. Problems in Professional Responsibility for a Changing Profession. Carolina Academic, Durham, NC.

Williams, J.C., 2007. Legal professions and job demands: implications for work/life balance. In: Sweet, S., Casey, J. (Eds.), Work and Family Encyclopedia. Sloan Work Family Res. Network, Chestnut Hill, MA.

World Bank, 2012. 'Gender Equality and Development' World Development Report. www.econ.worldbank.org/wbsite/external/extdec/extresearch/extwdrs/extwdr2012/0,,contentmdk:23004468~pagepk:64167689~pipk:64167673~thesitepk:7778063,00.html (accessed 04.01.14).

World Economic Forum, 2010. Global Gender Gap. www.weforum.org/issues/global-gender-gap (accessed 04.01.14).

Woryk, M., 2011. Women in corporate governance: a Cinderella story. University of Dayton Law Review 37(1), 21–38.

Yale Law Women, 2012. Yale Law School Faculty and Students Speak up about Gender: Ten Years Later. www.law.yale.edu/stuorgs/speakup.html (accessed 04.01.14).

8

Are we still telling female students they can't lead?

A content analysis of leadership writings and representations in organizational behaviour texts

Rhonda L. Dever
Northern Alberta Institute of Technology, Canada

Albert J. Mills
Saint Mary's University, Canada

This chapter examines the representation of women in organizational behaviour (OB) textbooks, specifically the chapters dedicated to leadership. We find that although women may be represented as leaders, the underlying themes are still predominantly masculine in nature. The idea that gender bias still exists in management education cannot be ignored. If we are unable to change what has already been written, we must take the initiative to provide a well-rounded classroom setting so that our students are not at a disadvantage. Through an examination of leadership chapters in OB textbooks from the 1960s through to the 2010s we see shifts in how leadership is written about and how it is then presented to our students who interpret that information as though it is indicative of their future careers. We find the same theories continually taught; yet the contexts in which they were developed have disappeared thereby removing the history of leadership theories being developed on, by and for men.

> The textbook may be one of the most under-examined pedagogical tools in the instructional repertoire.
>
> (Stambaugh and Trank, 2010: 663)

8.1 Introduction

For many business students in Canada and the United States, the first formal exposure to leadership theory will come in the form of an introductory class in Organizational Behaviour (OB). Such introductory OB texts feature a chapter on leadership. Much of what students learn in this initial exposure may impact future studies in business education and form their future opinions and attitudes on entering the workforce or, more importantly, joining leading organizations on their subsequent graduation. This chapter seeks to examine the representation of women in OB textbooks, specifically the chapters dedicated to leadership. We posit that although women may be represented as leaders, possibly as equals, within those chapters dedicated to leadership theory, the underlying themes will still be predominantly masculine in nature.

Although textbooks are not the sole method used in the classroom we should not discredit their impact. Textbooks play an integral role in the Western education system and act—alongside other aspects of the education process (e.g. the curriculum; the instructor)—as a conveyor of universal knowledge. The importance of a textbook cannot be underestimated with students in post-secondary taking in approximately 55% of their knowledge from these sources (Lichtenberg, 1992, as cited in Stambaugh and Trank, 2010). Although representations of women have increased, the majority of texts still continue to feature male examples, and in particular white males (Sleeters and Grant, 1997). Sleeters and Grant stated that most gender issues have simply been addressed by removing sexist language, while continuing to legitimate white male perspectives.

Research indicates that management education is a prime area to study the effects of gender bias and education (Allan, 2007; Mills, 1997; Walters and Manicom, 1996). Based on the literature surrounding gender bias in textbooks we hypothesize that there are underlying themes of gender bias within the texts that are routinely being used to teach business students throughout North American universities. In this chapter we present the results of analysis of a selection of United States and Canadian OB textbooks published since 1960. Using a feminist framework (i.e. a lens that focuses on the impact of organizational arrangements on women's rights and opportunities—see Mills and Tancred, 1992), we undertake a qualitative content analysis (QCA) (Bryman et al., 2011) of leadership chapters to examine the relationship between the text's central narratives and gender identity, exploring issues of power, professionalism and leader–follower relations. Treating each decade as its own narrative allows us to explore each of these issues.

8.2 Do gender and sex really matter?

In discussions surrounding gender attributes (masculine and feminine), we often find the terms being interchanged unquestionably with the meanings of biological sex, that is, male and female. For the purpose of this study the terms male and female will be differentiated from the terms masculine and feminine with the latter being used when referring to the socially constructed notions of gender. Gherardi (1994: 592) explained gender as "one of the most powerful symbols. Indeed, the very word gender encapsulates all the symbols that a culture elaborates to account for biological difference" and states that masculinity and femininity are socially and historically constructed. Gherardi (1994) further explained how the very meaning of gender is fluid and is negotiated through discourse. We can discuss the terms of culturally constituted masculine and feminine traits, how they change over time and ". . . vary with class, race, occupation, organization, age, and individual conditions" (Billing and Alvesson, 2000: 152).

Throughout this chapter the two sets of terms denoting biological sex and socially constructed gender will be used together to illustrate that although textbooks may, over time, show a representation of women in a biological sense, they may still ultimately present leadership as masculine in nature. Socially constructed gender identity is one of the most basic ways in which we identify with the world around us. Through stereotypes and language within the discourse that we are exposed in our everyday lives we come to understand who we are and our roles within society.

8.3 Gender bias in textbooks

In a report prepared for the UNESCO's Education for All Global Monitoring Report, *Education for All by 2015*, Blumberg (2009) declared that gender bias in textbooks is an important issue that requires attention for several reasons: it is a universal issue, persistent and often camouflaged. The authors examined several studies pertaining to gender bias in textbooks that were typically conducted through a content analysis. One issue brought to light during this analysis was the fact that "females were underrepresented" (on the basis of biological sex) and that "females and males were shown in highly gender-stereotyped ways" (Blumberg, 2009: 347). We examine whether this result will hold true for chapters dedicated to teaching leadership within OB textbooks.

Blumberg (2009) states that books often camouflage gender bias and stereotypes through their use of generally accepted depiction of gendered roles that constrain students' idea or "vision of who they are and what they can become" (p. 347). Sleeters and Grant (1997) make a call for further examinations of textbooks following their work to uncover issues surrounding race, gender, class and disabilities within textbooks.

Gender bias in textbooks has been extensively studied in different disciplines such as psychology (Peterson and Kroner, 1992), sociology (Ferree and Hall, 1996), teachers' education (Zittleman and Sadker, 2002) and children's literature (Gooden and Gooden, 2001; Taylor, 2003). Looking more specifically at management education, Smith (2000: 159) points out the gendered culture that surrounds management education and the implications for female students due to "the pervasiveness of male examples and non-inclusive language [that] results in people being treated asymmetrically, thereby dis-advantaging women students". Gender bias in textbooks may not show itself through blatant examples of sexism or gender stereotypes. However, not bringing the issues of gender to the forefront may mean that the biases are "hidden in plain sight".

Assuming gender to be socially constructed and taking from Gabriel's (1990: 138) statement that "culturally, males and females receive different messages which teach them the 'proper' roles for men and women and society", we argue that continuing this bias into leadership studies at the post-secondary level will only further entrench those gender biases into future organizations. Although Gabriel (1990) is speaking from a composition instructor's perspective, the author stresses the importance of the par-ticular readings chosen for students, because readings have a direct impact on readers, particularly if there is a strong masculine undertone. Leadership theory and represented examples of who constitutes a leader are likely to have a profound impact on women in the classroom who are shown texts with an emphasis on males as examples.

8.4 Gender bias in management education

Another highly studied area is the specific gender bias within management education (see Mavin and Bryans, 1999; Sinclair 1995, 1997; Smith, 2000; McKeen, Bujaki and Burke, 2000). Although previous studies focus on management education as an overall field, our interest is directed at a more specific section of undergraduate management education, namely, the importance of recognizing the impact that a gendered education may have on management students (see e.g. McKeen, Bujaki and Burke, 2000).

The foundation of this chapter is based on works of previous authors who have dem-onstrated the "maleness" of management texts and how a masculine culture is integrated into the traditional business school curriculum (Hite and McDonald, 1995; Mills, 2004). In their research on business student graduates, McKeen, Bujaki and Burke (2000) found that female graduates wanted to see more curricula that reflected women's experiences, and texts and case studies that utilized women as key decision-makers.

If females are represented through photos and in texts as examples of leadership, we must be aware that although women might be "represented", they may be done so as "tokens" or done so in a masculinized way (i.e. through the lens of male experience). In other words, while management textbook may include images of female managers the equity intent may be lost where accompanying text describes female managers accord-ing to masculinist norms of business practice (Benschop and Meihuizen, 2002). Token-ism has also been used to describe the ways in which a dominant group marginalizes the "token", and although the dominant group may allow access to tokens, the tokens are destined to be limited with regard to mobility within the group (Laws, 1975). In her ground-breaking work, *Men and Women of the Corporation* (1977), Rosabeth Moss Kanter laid a foundation for the ideas of a numerical representation of women in male-dominated workplaces. According to Kanter's work, a ratio of 85:15 (males:females) creates an environment where women are viewed as tokens. Although the theory of tokenism may be used to define any marginalized group based on race, gender and sexuality, this chapter focuses on the under-representation, or tokenism of women, within leadership discussion in organizational textbooks and how those have changed over time (King et al., 2010; Laws, 1975; Zimmer, 1988).

8.5 Gender and leadership

Hearn and Parkin (1986) tell us

> [l]eadership, as usually understood, is not a natural phenomenon or process; neither is it a natural attribute or possession of women or men; nor is it salvation for either. Leadership needs deconstruction: it is as gendered as it is problematic (p. 54).

Thus, given our awareness of its (often covert) maleness and, further, given our understanding of gender as a process of socialization, a cultural identity imposition, we must ask ourselves: If we value the principles of equity, why are we not questioning the ideas business undergraduates are exposed to? This gendering of the underlying philosophy of leadership and the exposure of its masculine nature, as well as the pedagogical implications of how leadership is continuing to be taught to students, are areas that require further examination.

Studies surrounding sex and/or gender and leadership can be found within the literature with Eagly and Carli (2003) providing an overall view of female leadership and advantages that it may provide in an organizational setting. Their article discusses sex differences in leadership styles, effectiveness of female and male leaders and offers ideas as to what type of leadership may be best suited to women (transformational), suggesting that with the increased number of women entering the field of leadership, theories and practices must also change (Eagly and Carli, 2003). Furthermore, studies on leadership have also considered the social construction of gender when analysing differences in leadership styles and preferences (Trinidad and Normore, 2005; Kark, 2004) acknowledging the difference between biological sex and socially constructed gender.

8.6 Methodology

Our starting approach is a broad feminist lens, which focuses on the impact of social and organizational arrangements on women's opportunities at work—see, for example, Rowbotham (1999). From this approach we analyse how business texts—reflecting in large part dominant organizational practices—shape images and understandings of women (and men) and resulting in discriminatory notions of what it is to be a woman, a man, a leader or a manager (Schein, 1973). To that end, we analysed the leadership chapters of selected business textbooks to examine the extent to which they appear to image the practice of management and leadership as more or less equally male and female professions or activities. Starting with the surface level, we looked at comparative differences between the number and type of images that included males or females. The number involved a simple count of images of women in comparison to images of men. The type of images refers to the extent that females were equally shown as managers rather than as employees or customers. At a more in-depth level we were looking for characteristics that served to differentiate males and females and their abilities to manage. This search focused on associations of management characteristics that were more typically associated with men (e.g. aggressive, competitive) rather than women (e.g. caring, sociable)—see Schein (1994). To that end, we used content analysis as a method in wide use across various disciplines (Smith, 2000). Content analysis lends itself to this study for a variety of reasons (Bryman et al., 2011), including the idea that it is a transparent research method that allows for future replication, it is unobtrusive in nature as it involves studying extant written texts and it allows for flexibility, as well as the opportunity for information to be generated for further research. Some strengths of choosing this method are (a) its unobtrusiveness, because it does not require the use of human subjects; (b) its ability to summarize large amounts of qualitative data into smaller categories; and (c) its ability to study how communications change over time (Smith, 2000).

Content analysis has been conducted before to study gender representations in children's books (Gooden and Gooden, 2001), while Sleeters and Grant (1997) made use of a pictorial analysis of textbooks ranging in subjects. Taking from these studies, we examine the representations of leaders in the texts' images and written, in-text examples of leaders that are used to signify to students who makes an effective leader.

QCA can be applied to the chapters within the above analysed textbooks in order to further the investigation. Qualitative research, by its nature, is interpretive, situational, inductive and reflexive. QCA does allow for interpretation by the researcher as it does not follow strict standardization of coding; it allows for themes to emerge as the data are being analysed. Another factor that makes QCA interpretive is its concern for personal and social meaning (Schreier, 2012). For the purpose of this chapter we have examined the leadership chapters of seven management textbooks. The textbooks were chosen at random from the Sobey PhD Collection of some six hundred textbooks, published between 1928 and 2013, held in the PhD "Reading Room" at Saint Mary's University. To capture imagery over time and to assess potential changes and improvement in gender balance, we chose one textbook from each decade, beginning from the 1960s and ending with the 2010s. In our choice of business texts we were constrained by the number of books in the collection for any given decade, and the range of focus (e.g. "management", "organization theory" and "OB"). In the process we attempted to stick as closely as possible to OB texts. The book also had to have a chapter on leadership. From this perspective our choices were more or less random, that is, whatever text that fit the criteria appeared early in the list of books for any decade.

In analysing the texts, as described above, we looked for the relative presence of male and female images; dominant characteristics associated with management and leadership—particularly the characteristic associated with the ideal typical leader, and the overall story each chapter appeared to tell. In the last regard we treated each chapter as its own narrative in order to examine what "story" is being told to students with regard to who the ideal leader might be within an organization.

8.7 Analysis

8.7.1 The 1960s

"Wherever an organization exists, leadership also exists. An organization does not exist until a leader has emerged or has been appointed" (McFarland, 1964: 377).

Analysis of McFarland (1964) reveals a discussion around leadership as very much masculine in nature and the description of a leader is that of a male, as well as the subordinates, who are also described as being male. There is no mention of women within the organization at all. There is discussion around the relationship between subordinates

Table 8.1 **Decades of selected organizational behaviour texts, 1964–2013**

Decade	Textbook	Year	Chapter no./Title
1960s	McFarland, D.E. Management: Principles and Practices. The Macmillan Company, New York.	1964	16/Executive Leadership
1970s	Davis, K. Human Behavior at Work. McGraw Hill, New York.	1977	6/Leadership and Supervision
1980s	Schermerhorn, J.R., Hunt, J.G., Osborn, R.N. Managing Organizational Behavior. John Wiley & Sons, Inc., New York.	1982	16/Leadership
1990s	Gordon, J.R., Mondy, R.W., Sharplin, A., Premeaux, S.R. Management and Organizational Behavior. Allyn & Bacon, Boston, MA.	1990	18/Leadership
2000s	McShane, S.L., Von Glinow, M.A. Organizational Behavior. Irwin McGraw-Hill, Boston, MA.	2000	14/Organizational Leadership
2010s	Langton, N., Robbins, S.P., Judge, T.A. Organizational Behavior: Concepts, Controversies, Applications Pearson, Don Mills, ON, Canada.	2013	8/Leadership

and leaders, and the term "followers" is used to describe employees working in positions below an individual leader. There is a tone that implies the importance of the human element within an organization and that it is the responsibility of a leader "to give subordinates a sense that they are a vital part of an important group activity" and that leaders "be alert to new and better ways of meeting the social, psychological, and economic needs of those who make up the organization" (McFarland, 1964: 378).

McFarland (1964) notes that leadership is a process that is required by any organization and states that during the 1960s there was a shortage of leaders because of the "heavy responsibilities of modern industry" and that there "are no satisfactory substitutes for effective leadership" and that "leadership is vital to the survival of a business" (p. 364). The importance of leadership is stressed and is considered to be a "valuable commodity" (McFarland, 1964: 364). What is interesting here is that there is an acknowledgement regarding where and how leadership theory was developed, which we do not tend to find in more current organizational textbooks. McFarland (1964) notes that in the 30 years prior to when his book was written only a portion of the research on leadership was conducted within business organizations—"much of it has emerged from studies of military organizations, small groups, political units, and other nonbusiness situations" (p. 365).

Looking at leadership development up until 1964 both trait-based theory and situational leadership styles are discussed. Within this era we can see that the language used to describe leaders within organizations, as well as employees, is associated with stereotypical male characteristics:

> The very essence of the leadership role in business is found in the extent to which an executive can influence the behavior of his fellow executives along the lines he himself desires. Unless he can get them to do as he asks or directs, he has no followers (McFarland, 1964: 368–369).

What is interesting here though is that there is also a recognition that leadership happens at various levels within an organization, not just by a formally appointed leader of the company. While discussing the various ways in which leaders take on their roles, we find a discussion on the work of Lewin, Lippitt and White (1939) and their research of different leadership styles (autocratic, laissez-faire and democratic) conducted on groups of ten-year-old boys. McFarland (1964) explains to the reader that autocratic leadership involves using fear tactics and actual or implied threats, based on their position within the organization, whereas democratic leaders are persuasive and encourage participation in decision-making.

What is of interest in this chapter is the recognition of both organizational leadership, based on a person's position with the organizational hierarchy, and personal leadership, based on an individual's charisma. The term charismatic leadership is used here, and Max Weber's theories on both bureaucracy and charisma are used to assist in the explanation of organizational and personal leadership. The in-text examples of charismatic leaders who created business empires are all male and include Henry Ford, John D. Rockefeller and Walter P. Chrysler. It is noted that all three of these men were dominant in their relationships with others but that their leadership styles no longer worked in the 1960s, because there were too many risks in having an entire business built on only one man and that in the event of that man's death, the business might crumble. Nonetheless, using examples such as Ford, Rockefeller and Chrysler, we see a preference to a particular type of male leader, that of a white, Western, heterosexual male, sitting atop a successful business empire.

Another point of interest is the way in which McFarland (1964: 381) writes about the importance of what we might now refer to as mentorship among employees and importance of being "sensitive to the attitudes and feelings prevailing among the members of his group". Although there is an obvious indication that men are the individuals who not only lead but also the only people who work in organizations, there is reference to the importance of treating people as individuals and recognizing their individual needs. This type of observation signals some type of shift in thinking, but it is not followed up by any discussion of the implications for female leadership. Instead, the reader is encouraged to think that these are traits that male leaders need to adopt in the future.

8.7.2 The 1970s

"Without leadership, an organization is only a confusion of people and machines. Leadership is the ability to persuade others to seek defined objectives enthusiastically. It is the human factor that binds a group together and motivates it toward goals" (Davis, 1977: 107). In the 1970s we saw an attempt to remove the masculine language in the discussions surrounding leadership by simply removing all references to he, him and men of the organization. Although this may appear to be a step in a direction to the inclusion of women in organizations, we can plainly see the same theories moving forward as the way to understand leadership at work. Most of what was discussed the decade prior is carried forward—that is, traits-based leadership, idea of situational and contingency relationships of leadership. We also observe that there again is discussion on the importance of follower relations and that at a given time a leader is also a follower. When discussing the importance of goal setting in leadership, the first example used references to male staff executives and the second example used references to logging truck drivers (presumably male) (Davis, 1977).

Further into the chapter we find a discussion on various styles of leadership: autocratic participative, and free-rein, which includes positive and negative sides to each style, and yet in the example of a leader's orientation style, we find an example of a mine superintendent by the name of John Jones (Davis, 1977). Not only is this an example of a male individual, he is similarly working in what can be considered a masculine career—mining. When discussing leadership research from the University of Michigan and Ohio State University studies, it was revealed that organizations used for that research included a truck manufacturing company, railroad construction and insurance offices. Although the author has removed explicit references to men as leaders and employees throughout the theoretical explanations of leadership, we can identify that the default is still masculine and privileges a male perspective in the examples chosen of various situations to explain leadership in action and the male-dominated fields, in which leadership theory was explored and developed. It should be noted that the case study provided for students at the end of the chapter features a community hospital setting in which the administrator and controller are both male, but there is mention of a female employee who is very competent at her job and is demanding a raise or she will leave the company. Here we see mention of a female employee, but one who is labelled as demanding and still is not identified as being in a position of leadership.

When discussing the difference in leadership style of being an employee-orientated leader versus a task-oriented leader, Davis notes that although leaders may be considerate towards people within the organization, "leaders cannot be effective if they are overly sensitive to people" (1977: 118). Arguably, this type of commentary privileges characteristics of efficiency that are more associated with men than women and serve to marginalize sensitivity that tended to be more associated with women. The fact the "relationship" with subordinates is devalued again shows a preference to a masculine style of leadership. Research tells us that women are more focused on a democratic style of leadership (Eagly and Carli, 2003). This reiterates the idea that within organizations, a masculine style of leadership (in this case autocratic) is still the preferred style, as if to tell readers that it is acceptable to have feminine characteristics as a leader, but when it comes to the bottom line, a masculine autocratic style should prevail.

8.7.3 The 1980s

During this decade we find a continuation of previous leadership theories such as trait-based leadership, Fiedler's Situational Theory, and House's Path–Goal Theory and a larger focus on Fiedler's creation of the Least-Preferred Co-worker Scale. What is missing in the discussion of Fiedler's leadership theory is any mention of it being developed primarily in military organizations (Northouse, 2010), which would expose masculine roots of leadership theory development. It is noted that there are both formal and informal positions of leadership and both are important; however, the dominant of the two is formal leadership (Schermerhorn, Hunt and Osborn, 1982). Trait-based theory is discredited due to its lack of success in identifying universal traits and the discussion goes on to behavioural leadership and contingency approaches. Gone is any discussion of the way in which leadership theory was developed, or who the theories were tested on, as we saw in the 1960s example with the acknowledgement that leadership theories be developed and tested on military groups (presumably male) and groups of young men such as in the case of research done by Lewin, Lippitt and White (1939).

The selected textbook from the 1980s adopts a "he/she" approach when referring to members of an organization; yet when the discussion surrounds task-motivated leaders versus relationship-motivated leaders we find a photo of two men in military attire as the task-motivated example and a photo of a group of men and women sitting on the floor holding hands as the example for relationship-motivated leaders. Although this seemingly adds to the gender-neutral character of the text, women (and men) are associated with the person-oriented style, whereas the task-oriented style is only associated with men. This tends to set up gender differences between potential leadership styles. Nonetheless, men are associated with both style, suggesting that leadership theories are premised on masculinity (Acker, 1990). Up until now we can observe the repetition of theories, but we have lost any discussion surrounding their creation and thereby removing their masculine roots for discussion. We are, by default, reiterating the masculine ideals of leadership. As Moss Kanter (1977) notes, because of the structure of organizations, "organization roles carry characteristic images of the kind of people who should occupy them" (p. 250). In this case we can presume that males are still the preferred leaders in organizations.

8.7.4 The 1990s

The 1990s selected textbook begins with a vignette-style opening—a style that would become typical of subsequent generations of OB textbooks, where we begin each new chapter with an organizational example to introduce the theories to be discussed. In the text selected for this decade, we find Sanford Sigoloff as our leadership excellence example who is described as charismatic, energetic, enthusiastic, honest and neat in his appearance (Gordon et al., 1990). The Sigoloff examples reiterates the ideal leader as a white, heterosexual male and the author states he is "recognized worldwide as an effective leader" (Gordon et al., 1990: 552). The authors begin with an attempt to define leadership and when speaking of individual leaders it is written as "he (or she)", as though the addition of women was a mandatory obligation. Using language in this context still favours the male pronoun and the masculine default of an ideal leader and in essence is "othering" women. The male leader-centred way of thinking continues when describing autocratic, participative and democratic styles of leadership. In providing examples of individuals who represent each of these styles, we find reference to Donald Trump and Eugene Sapp as autocratic leaders, Sam Walton as a participative leader and Russell A. Nagel as a democratic leader (Gordon et al., 1990). These examples echo earlier textbooks in showing a direct ideal of the heterosexual male as the idealized leader despite them using differentiated styles. As noted earlier, there is research that states women "typically" use a more democratic style of leadership, yet this textbook still uses males as the idealized leader.

We find continued discussions around trait leadership and the University of Iowa studies and Ohio State studies, and although they make reference to trait-based research as being "the great man theory" and acknowledge that Iowa state studies were conducted on adolescent boys, it is followed by statements such as "nevertheless, the Iowa Leadership Studies ushered in an era in which leadership behaviours rather than traits received increased research attention" (Gordon et al., 1990). We also find the inclusion of Vroom and Yetton's leadership theory (a normative decision-making model) and Hersey and Blanchard's situational leadership theory (leader behaviour model based on task and relationships that is similar to the Ohio State studies). We need to recognize that if we continue to build on leadership models that were developed by men and tested on men, such as those done in military settings or on adolescent boys, we cannot postulate that we can then expect to simply add women into the equation and presume that in order to be considered an effective leader, she must fit into, and be judged on, her ability to fit a model that was never intended for her in the first place.

While explaining these various theories with examples, we once more find all male examples until we reach the section on substitutes for leadership. Here we find the field of nursing, which may be considered a female-dominated, or feminized, workplace. The authors put forward a study done in the nursing field to show how "substitutes" for leadership may be effective depending on the characteristics of subordinates, the task and the organization, and that a leader's behaviour may negatively impact performance. According to the study conducted in nursing (cited in the textbook), the head nurse's assertiveness had a negative impact on the subordinates' performance. Here we finally find an example of leadership from an organization that may possibly be viewed as feminine in nature and heavily populated by women, and it is an example of how leadership is not always required and even unnecessary at times. At the end of this chapter two case studies are provided, both of which feature males as the leaders and employees. The examples provided, with the goal of reiterating to students reading the text of the ideal leader, show blatant preference to men. Women are marginalized, at best, with the use of "he/(she)", and the only time in which it seems plausible is that the textbook may be referring to a female leader or employee: they are shown without individual names, or even a gender identity, in a female-dominated profession of nursing, to explain that leadership is not always required and at times can hinder employee performance. It is not even just the issue that the example of nursing is used. The problem is that the scenario is used to describe when individualized leadership is ineffective or not required, and it is done so in what may be seen as a stereotypical feminized profession.

8.7.5 The 2000s

Again our sample textbook (McShane and Von Glinow, 2000) from the 2000s opens with a vignette describing a successful leader; in this instance it is Jacques Nasser of Ford of Australia, complete with photo, before the authors launch into the typical layout of leadership theories. At this point we can see discussions forming around various perspectives of leadership: Competency (Trait), Behavioural, Transformational and Contingency. During the discussion on trait leadership, what we discussed was originally referred to as the Great Man Theory, the example shown is Jill Barad, a female chief executive officer (CEO) of Mattel, who is described as fierce and highly self-confident with unwavering drive, and the example includes a quote from her time at Mattel where she apparently stormed into the then CEO's office "What . . . do I have to do to get a decent assignment around here?" (McShane and Von Glinow, 2000: 435). The next example is male, this time a banking executive from South Korea, Kim Jung Tae. The chapter continues on to discuss several individuals, who may be considered ideal leaders, given the thread of leadership theory being explained. For example, when introducing transformational leadership, examples from industry mentioned are Carly Fiorina, Jack Welch, Herb Kelleher and Richard Branson, and again at the bottom of the page we find a photo of Dennis W. Blake from AES (a power company) and the picture beside him is of employees of the company where it is difficult to tell whether they are male or female employees as they are all wearing hardhats and working within what we may consider a male-dominated field (McShane and Von Glinow, 2000).

In this particular textbook we find at the end of the chapter a small section on gender and leadership titled "Gender Issues in Leadership" as if to say that when women lead, or we discuss women in leadership, it becomes an "issue". The section discusses the research and the disagreement as to whether women and men lead differently and tells the readers that some research suggests that women are more interactive, more people-oriented, cooperative, nurturing and emotional in their leadership roles (McShane and Von Glinow, 2000). The authors discuss the stereotypes of women and men as leaders and, in an interesting note, tell the reader that research that indicates the stereotypes of female leaders are mostly incorrect with the explanation that the central reason as to why men and women do not differ on their leadership styles is that "real-world jobs require similar behavior from male and female job incumbents" (McShane and Von Glinow, 2000). In the next paragraph the point is made that if a female leader performs her job with a style that is construed as male (in this discussion autocratic), her subordinates are likely to complain because the expectation is for women to lead in a feminized manner or style—according to gender stereotypes, perceived as feminine, such as participative. The problem here lies in the fact that in one sentence we are telling students, and other readers of this text, that in the "real world" men and women need to operate in the same ways in any given job, but yet if women choose to act in a masculine manner, they are likely to be condemned by their subordinates who feel the female leader should act according to female sex stereotypes. The confusion continues when the authors go on to discuss the biased ways in which people unfairly evaluate female leaders and the double-edged sword that women face when entering traditional male roles of leadership. What we observe happening here is the inclusion of a discussion of gender and leadership, but the underlying message is that women are still "the other" (de Beauvoir, 1952) and that somehow the word gender has come to mean the equivalent of female and/or woman.

8.7.6 The 2010s

The opening vignette and accompanying photo in our selected textbook (Langton, Robbins and Judge, 2013) features Lieutenant Colonel Maryse Carmichael of the Canadian Air Force's Snowbirds team (flight demonstration squadron) dressed in her pilot's uniform. Right from the introduction of the chapter we see a female leader, yet she is featured in what is still conceived to be a very masculinized career—the Canadian Air Force. The discussion then follows, in what we can now identify as a "typical" chapter on leadership, with the explanation of theories starting again with trait-based leadership and following through to transformational leadership, and we now find additional mentions of mentoring, self-leadership, team leadership, online leadership and leading without authority. At the end of the chapter we find the heading "Contemporary Issues in Leadership", which covers authentic leadership, moral leadership, gender and leadership, global implications. It is interesting that again any mention of women as leaders appears under "issues", but in addition to women we now find a discussion around the fact that the majority of the research presented within the chapter was conducted in English-speaking countries, and we finally see a mention of leadership outside the realm of the Western business context (Langton, Robbins and Judge, 2013). What may be seen as a step in the right direction towards including women as being considered effective leaders, the information is still placed towards the end of the chapter. The authors discuss how the literature indicates that men and women overlap in their styles, but that women tend to favour a democratic style whereas men favour a directive style of leading. The authors also note that women tend to be transformational in their leadership style; however, they also face a double bind when employed in a leadership role. If they behave in a manner that is stereotypically masculine, they face backlash from subordinates because they are not behaving in a manner that a stereotypical women "should", despite the fact that those masculine traits are typically "synonymous with successful managers" (Langton, Robbins and Judge, 2013: 419). Readers are informed that women should "learn to self-monitor their behavior" so that "they have a better chance of promotion" (Langton, Robbins and Judge, 2013: 419). It is disconcerting that in 2013 we are still teaching students that if you are female, you better your chances at work if you "self-monitor" your behaviour in order to advance your career and be considered for a management or leadership role.

8.8 Discussion and conclusion

Through our study of leadership chapters in OB textbooks from the 1960s through to the 2010s we can see the shifts in how leadership is written about and how it is then passed on to our students who presumably interpret that information as though it is indicative of their future careers. We notice that the same theories are continually taught; yet the contexts in which they were developed have disappeared, arguably presenting current theories as universal or steadily progressive (Genoe McLaren and Mills, 2008). Students and other readers of this text are shown leadership theory with no reference to the fact that the majority of the research was done by on and for men (Hearn and Parkin, 1983). Women are then expected to understand that men are still the preferred leader, and that if women do choose to take on a leadership role they are torn between acting in such a way that can be described as masculine, and be condoned for doing so, or act in a feminine manner that has them contributing to and continuing the gender stereotypes.

As has been argued elsewhere (Stambaugh and Trank, 2010; Mills and Helms Hatfield, 1998) the textbook is a highly problematic teaching tool because, in particular, they more often than not serve to reproduce masculine/male associations with management and leadership. In part, this may be due to the dominance of male authors (Mills and Helms Hatfield, 1998) but that is not to suggest that there is something inherently discriminatory about men. Rather we would argue that in a field (management education) dominated by men, reflecting on a male-dominated profession (management), we would expect experience to play an influential role in how a text is written. If, for example, a number of activities arise out of male-associated thought processes it is not surprising that male textbook authors reflect that reality due to their own experiences. There is little in our own research to suggest that female textbook authors present the field much differently from their male colleagues (see also Mills and Helms Hatfield, 1998). This may be to do with the fact that there are relatively few female authors of OB textbooks, but it is also likely to do with the underlying philosophy, structure, style and expected audience for textbooks.

Analysis of textbooks over time indicate that they follow a particular philosophy of managerialism, aimed at educating students to become the managers of the future (Burrell and Morgan, 1979). Focus on efficiency, task, motivation, profitability and the bottom line arguably tends to privilege notions of competitiveness rather than cooperation and interpersonal skills more associated with masculinity that femininity. As such textbooks follow a certain structure that teaches students what is considered to be the important factors associated with managing and leading—leadership skills, motivational abilities, particular communication styles, hierarchical ways of structuring an organization and so on. Things missing from the average business text include a focus on race, gender, sexual orientation and other aspects of intersectional experiences at work (Bagilhole, 2010; Mills and Helms Hatfield, 1998). In the words of Smith (2000: 165): "Gender issues cannot . . . be considered 'just a fashion fad', since learning experiences influences the preparedness and ability of future managers to recognize and capitalize on the full range of talents available in the workplace". If our goal is to educate students, and the future workforce, that women are just as capable as men, when it comes to leadership abilities, one of the core components must be a reflection of such within the literature. We need to recognize that current textbooks view women as the "other" in organizations; that which is not male.

It may be time to rethink the textbook as an important artefact in educational practice. We need to move beyond embedded experiences based largely on male-dominated activities and practices, as well as moving beyond the managerialist philosophy underlying much of the production of business textbooks. One possible solution would be for educators to draw directly on the experiences of student audiences—male and female—to reflect on what is missing from current business education and how we can draw on this exercise for conceiving the role of men and women in managing and leading.

One of the limitations of this research is that it is being done within a North American context, which may or may not be reflective of other English-speaking management textbooks. One of the implications of the discovery of gendered language hidden within the text is its ability to inform management educators and bring awareness of issues faced for both male and female students in business schools. This chapter may be able to serve as a foundation on which to build further research and analysis related to the discourse of the studied texts, and allow for a broader review of management textbooks from differing perspectives from across countries.

References

Acker, J., 1990. Heirarchies, jobs, bodies: a theory of gendered organizations. Gender & Society 4, 139–158.

Allan, E.J., 2007. Policy Discourses, Gender, and Education: Constructing Women's Status. Routledge, New York.

Bagilhole, B., 2010. Applying the lens of intersectionality to UK equal opportunities and diversity policies. Canadian Journal of Administrative Science 27, 263–271.

de Beauvoir, S. 1952. The Second Sex. Alfred A Knopf, Inc., New York.

Benschop, Y., Meihuizen, H.E., 2002. Reporting gender: representations of gender in financial and annual reports. In: Aaltio, I., Mills, A.J. (Eds.), Gender, Identity and the Culture of Organizations. Routledge, London.

Billing, Y.D., Alvesson, M., 2000. Questioning the notion of feminine leadership: a critical perspective on the gender labelling of leadership. Gender, Work & Organization 7, 144–157.

Blumberg, R.L., 2009. The invisible obstacles to education equality: gender bias in textbooks. In: Education for All Global Monitoring Report, Education for All by 2015—Will we make it? United Nations Education, Science and Cultural Organization, Paris, France.

Bryman, A., Bell, E., Mills, A.J., Yue, A.R., 2011. Business Research Methods, first Canadian ed. Oxford University Press, Toronto, ON, Canada.

Burrell, G., Morgan, G., 1979. Sociological Paradigms and Organizational Analysis. Heinemann, London.

Davis, K., 1977. Human Behavior at Work. McGraw-Hill, New York.

Eagly, A.H., Carli, L.L., 2003. The female leadership advantage: an evaluation of the evidence. The Leadership Quarterly 14, 807–834.

Ferree, M.M., Hall, E.J., 1996. Rethinking stratification from a feminist perspective: gender, race, and class in mainstream textbooks. American Sociological Review 61, 929–950.

Gabriel, S.L., 1990. Gender, reading, and writing: assignments, expectations, and responses. In: Gabriel, S.L., Smithson, I. (Eds.), Gender in the Classroom. University of Illinois Press, Chicago, IL.

Genoe McLaren, P., Mills, A.J., 2008. A product of 'his' time? Exploring the construct of managers in the cold war era. Journal of Management History 14, 386–403.

Gherardi, S., 1994. The gender we think, the gender we do in our everyday organizational lives. Human Relations 47, 591–611.

Gooden, A.M., Gooden, M.A., 2001. Gender representation in notable children's picture books: 1995–1999. Sex Roles 45, 89–101.

Gordon, J.R., Mondy, R.W., Sharplin, A., Premeaux, S.R., 1990. Management and Organizational Behavior. Allyn & Bacon, Boston, MA.

Hearn, J., Parkin, P.W., 1983. Gender and organizations: a selective review and a critique of a neglected area. Organization Studies 4, 219–242.

Hearn, J., Parkin, W., 1986. Women, men, and leadership: a critical review of assumptions, practices, and change in industrialized nations. International Studies of Management & Organization 16, 33–60.

Hite, L.M., McDonald, K.S., 1995. Gender issues in management development: implications and research agenda. Journal of Management Development 14, 5–15.

Kanter, R.M., 1977. Men and Women of the Corporation. Basic Books, New York.

Kark, R., 2004. The transformational leader: who is (s)he? A feminist perspective. Journal of Organizational Change Management 17, 160–176.

King, E.B., Hebl, M.R., George, J.M., Matusik, S.F., 2010. Understanding tokenism: antecedents and consequences of a psychological climate of gender inequity. Journal of Management 36, 482–510.

Langton, N., Robbins, S.P., Judge, T.A., 2013. Organizational Behavior: Concepts, Controversies, Applications. Pearson, Don Mills, ON, Canada.

Laws, J.L., 1975. The psychology of tokenism: an analysis. Sex Roles 1, 51–67.

Lewin, K., Lippitt, R., White, R.K., 1939. Patterns of aggressive behavior in experimentally created "social climates". Journal of Social Psychology 10, 271–299.

Mavin, S., Bryans, P., 1999. Gender on the agenda in management education? Women in Management Review 14, 99–104.

McFarland, D.E., 1964. Management: Principles and Practices. The Macmillan Company, New York.

McKeen, C.A., Bujaki, M.L., Burke, R.J., 2000. Preparing business graduates for the "real" world—the role of the university. Women in Management Review 15, 356–369.

McShane, S.L., Von Glinow, M.A., 2000. Organizational Behavior. Irwin McGraw-Hill, Boston, MA.

Mills, A.J., 1997. Business education as gendered discourse. In: Proceedings of the Women in Management division of the Administrative Sciences Association of Canada, vol. 18, pp. 22–32.

Mills, A.J., 2004. Feminist organizational analysis and the business textbook. In: Hodgson, D.E., Carter, C. (Eds.), Management Knowledge and the New Employee. Ashgate, London, pp. 30–48.

Mills, A.J., Helms Hatfield, J.C., 1998. From imperialism to globalization: internationalization and the management text. In: Clegg, S.R., Ibarra, E., Bueno, L. (Eds.), Global Management: Universal Theories and Local Realities. Sage, Thousand Oaks, CA.

Mills, A.J., Tancred, P. (Eds.), 1992. Gendering Organizational Analysis. Sage Publications, Newbury Park, CA.

Northouse, P.G., 2010. Leadership Theory and Practice. Sage, Thousand Oaks, CA.

Peterson, S.B., Kroner, T., 1992. Gender biases in textbooks for introductory psychology and human development. Psychology of Women Quarterly 16, 17–36.

Rowbotham, S., 1999. A Century of Women. A History of Women in Britain and the United States. Penguin, London.

Schein, V.E., 1973. The relationship between sex role stereotypes and requisite management characteristics among female managers. Journal of Applied Psychology 57, 89–105.

Schein, V.E., 1994. Managerial sex typing: a persistent and pervasive barrier to women's opportunities. In: Davidson, M.J., Burke, R.J. (Eds.), Women in Management. Current Research Issues. Paul Chapman Publishing Ltd., London.

Schermerhorn, J.R., Hunt, J.G., Osborn, R.N., 1982. Managing Organizational Behavior. John Wiley & Sons, Inc., New York.

Schreier, M., 2012. Qualitative Conent Analysis in Practice. Sage, Thousand Oaks, CA.

Sinclair, A., 1995. Sex and the MBA. Organization 2, 295–317.

Sinclair, A., 1997. The MBA through women's eyes—learning and pedagogy in management education. Management Learning 28, 313–330.

Sleeters, C.E., Grant, C.A., 1997. Race, class, gender and disability in current textbooks. In: Flinders, D.J., Thonton, S.J. (Eds.), The Curriculum Studies Reader. Routledge, New York.

Smith, C.R., 2000. Notes from the field: gender issues in the management curriculum: a survey of student experiences. Gender, Work & Organization 7.

Stambaugh, J.E., Trank, C.Q., 2010. Not so simple: integrating new research into textbooks. Academy of Management Leaning & Education 9, 663–681.

Taylor, F., 2003. Content analysis and gender stereotypes in children's books. Teaching Sociology 31, 300–311.

Trinidad, C., Normore, A.H., 2005. Leadership and gender: a dangerous liaison? Leadership and Organization Development Journal 26, 574–590.

Walters, S., Manicom, L., 1996. Gender in Popular Education: Methods for Empowerment. Zed Books, Bellville, South Africa.

Zimmer, L., 1988. Tokenism and women in the workplace: the limits of gender-neutral theory. Social Problems 35, 64–77.

Zittleman, K., Sadker, D., 2002. Gender bias in teacher education texts: new (and old) lessons. Journal of Teacher Education 53, 168–180.

Appendix **Textbooks analysed**

Davis, K., 1977. Human Behavior at Work. McGraw-Hill, New York.

Gordon, J.R., Mondy, R.W., Sharplin, A., Premeaux, S.R., 1990. Management and Organizational Behavior. Allyn & Bacon, Boston, MA.

Langton, N., Robbins, S.P., Judge, T.A., 2013. Organizational Behavior: Concepts, Controversies, Applications. Pearson, Don Mills, ON, Canada.

McFarland, D.E., 1964. Management: Principles and Practices. The Macmillan Company, New York.

McShane, S.L., Von Glinow, M.A., 2000. Organizational Behavior. Irwin McGraw-Hill, Boston, MA.

Schermerhorn, J.R., Hunt, J.G., Osborn, R.N., 1982. Managing Organizational Behavior. John Wiley & Sons, Inc., New York.

Part III
Institutional perspectives

9

It can be done!

Organizational interventions that can reduce the influence of gender prejudice on perceptions, performance and aspirations

Mary Godwyn and Nan S. Langowitz
Babson College, USA

In this research, we focus on organizational interventions as they reduce the negative effects of gender stereotypes on individual achievement. Several important studies have demonstrated how effective organizational interventions can be to individual success. Here we briefly review Claude Steele's work on stereotype threat, Jane Margolis and Allen Fisher's study on computer science majors and our own research on women's leadership. In our descriptions and analyses of these studies, we have isolated processes common to all and have articulated a formula that could be used in a variety of organizations to diminish or neutralize gender differences. Though our focus here is on gender, similar processes have been successfully implemented with regard to the referent of race as well. Therefore, the question is no longer *how* to neutralize the stereotypes so central to discriminatory practices applied to gender, but whether we have the desire and conviction to eradicate the inequality caused by them.

9.1 Introduction

In their feminist analysis, Ely and Padavic (2007) remind researchers who are studying sex differences "to consider how organizations as sociocultural contexts shape these differences" (p. 1121). They further admonish the research community that "if study after study reports findings that align with stereotypes and does not address why, then these differences—in temperament, values, attitudes, and behaviors—take on a determinative quality" (Ely and Padavic, 2007: 1122). Ely and Padavic (2007) recommend that those who research sex differences develop "mesolevel theorizing, which focuses on the interplay between organizational features and individual-level processes" (p. 1121). We agree. In the research described below, we explore the relationship between organizational influences and individual outcomes.

Here we focus on responsible management education with examples of educational interventions that can make significant differences for undergraduate women business students. The Principles for Responsible Management Education (PRME) are derived from internationally accepted social values and intended to motivate institutions to continue to reflect on and implement educational processes that develop business leaders who can manage increasingly complex systems. PRME principles address curricula, research, teaching methodologies and institutional strategies. The six PRME principles can be found at www.unprme.org/the-6-principles/index.php. By looking across several studies, including our own, we suggest a formula that can be applied by PRME organizations, among others, to counter the harmful consequences of gender prejudice.

To represent both the breadth and depth of success in reducing sex differences in the areas of perceptions, performance and aspirations, we review two seminal studies conducted in heretofore male-dominated domains: Claude Steele's research on standardized test performance, and Jane Margolis and Allen Fisher's research on computer science majors.[1] We further contribute new data to demonstrate that in yet another male-dominated domain, that of business leadership, these successful organizational interventions can be replicated and can also successfully reduce sex differences. In accordance with Ely and Padavic's (2007) analysis, each study described here "recognizes the complex interplay between organizations and gender" (p. 1122) and "treats gender as an element of selfhood that is socially produced" (p. 1123). Perhaps most important, the research described here demonstrates how organizations can and have disrupted the "system [that] produces the appearance of two significantly different kinds of people—males and females" (Ely and Padavic, 2007: 1128).

In our descriptions and analyses of these three studies, we isolate processes common to all and articulate a formula that has successfully been applied and that could be used in a variety of organizations to diminish or neutralize gender differences as they have an impact on perceptions, performance and aspirations. Though our focus here is on gender, we note that similar processes have been successfully implemented with regard to the referent of race as well. The fact that previous findings have been largely ignored rather than put into practice in a wide range of organizations speaks of

---

1 Sections of this literature review have appeared in material published earlier by the authors.

the durability of gender inequality, which continues to be oriented around and protected by those who benefit. This continuing deficit is worthy of attention by institutions subscribing to PRME.

Each study reviewed here—Steele's work on stereotype threat, Margolis and Fisher's research on computer science majors and our research on business leadership training— is based in the context of an educational institution. This body of research examines the organizational impact on individual development of gender identity and the related identification with a set of behaviours, social situations and competencies. The studies focus on perceptions, performance and aspirations—distinct aspects of self that are affected by prejudice and discrimination channelled through the vehicle of societal stereotypes within an organizational context. Each study concludes, for various reasons and in various ways, that the operational arena is not the individual's psychological state, or even individual talent, ambition or preparation, *but that the organizational context is responsible for varied outcomes in subjects' perceptions, performance and aspirations.* The import of this conclusion is that it leaves open the possibility that organizations can, and we would argue, as responsible institutions *should*, examine the means by which outcomes might be favourably shifted to reduce gender inequality.

9.2 The social context of self-development

The focus on the organizational context rather than on individual psychology is key to shifting individual responses and enabling subsequent social change. The examination of the social environment from the perspective of the subject is the basis of social psychological and symbolic interactionist approaches associated with the writings of, among others, Mary Parker Follett, George Herbert Mead, Charles Horton Cooley and Herbert Blumer. Follett ([1924]1995) contends that there is a "circular response" at all levels of interaction, in that "we are creating each other all the time" (p. 41). This mutuality of self, which is seeing ourselves through the perspectives of others, is what Mead calls "taking the role of the other" (Mead, 1934). He writes, "The individual experiences him [or her] self . . . not directly, but only indirectly, from the particular standpoints of other individual members of the same social group, or from the generalized standpoint of the social group as a whole" (Mead, 1934: 138). Therefore, we have no self that is separate from social interaction; selfhood is generated in some social, organizational context, is a reflection of how we think specific others see us and how valued we are in the overall organizational context. Cooley ([1902]1964) referred to this idea as "the looking glass self". Seeing ourselves through the eyes of others, and through the prevailing social norms and expectations, provides the basis on which we perceive and judge our actions, our worth and our potential.

Therefore, dependency on social interaction profoundly and measurably affects perceptions, performance and aspirations. This dependency can create deep vulnerability to and opportunity for manipulation. Negative assessments from society-at-large (what Mead would call the generalized other) are often associated with ascribed social status characteristics—congenital aspects such as race, gender, sexual orientation, weight, height, physical and mental disability or other attributes that are beyond the control of individuals, including nationality, religion and age. Denigrating messages are delivered through micro interactions with individuals and through larger institutional-level evaluations.

On the other hand, the research reviewed below also demonstrates that organizations can and do act as *mesolevel influencers* of individual behaviour and of larger social change by neutralizing stereotypes and restoring a sense of competency that is discernible in perceptions, performances and aspirations. Each study discussed here analyses a stereotype, deconstructs it and generates recommendations for organizations that reverse gender-based stereotypical assumptions. Each study has demonstrated that reversal is not only possible, but remarkably quick, easy and inexpensive. However, there is a question about whether these changes can be sustained outside of the organizational context without continued maintenance. Our research attempts to answer this question by comparing post-graduate life-satisfaction and salary levels of those female undergraduate participants in a women's business leadership program to those of a control group of female undergraduates.

Analysis of these three studies suggests a formula that can be applied to a wide range of organizations. Therefore, the question is no longer *how* to reverse the stereotypes so central to reifying gender differences and the social, economic and political inequality that accompanies them, but whether we have the desire and conviction to bring about the reversal of these disabling gender stereotypes.

9.3 Claude Steele: strategies to reduce stereotype threat in colleges and universities

In the 1990s, Claude Steele set out to investigate and rectify the underperformance of Black college and university students. He writes, "By virtually all aspects . . . lower standardized-test scores, lower college grades, lower graduation rates" African Americans, regardless of their class background, were trailing behind (Steele, 1999: 45). With the recognition that selfhood is generated in some social, organizational context, Steele found that by manipulating the social context, by priming subjects with particular stereotypes, he could influence the test performance of both African American and white students, and of women and men.

He was able to increase test scores in populations of African American students merely by verbally introducing the test as "not measuring one's intellectual ability" (Steele, 1999: 47). Steele (1997) applied the same method to manipulate sex differences in mathematical performance: women performed worse than men on standardized math tests when they were told that the test reproduced gender differences, but equal to men when the test was introduced as insensitive to gender (pp. 619, 620).

To determine whether these changes are due to "situational pressure" (the social context) rather than "internalized inferiority" (the individual's psychological state), those who were not the usual subjects of negative gender or racial stereotypes were tested to see whether they, too, would succumb to social manipulation by pernicious stereotypes (Aronson et al., 1999: 31). Math-proficient white males were given a math test and verbally primed with the statement from the experiment organizers: "In math, it seems to be the case that Asians outperform whites" (Aronson et al., 1999: 33). Consistent with the stereotype being an external, environmental and situational threat rather than a reflection of individual lack of confidence or an internally generated psychological factor, high math-identified white male students scored less well when the stereotype was mentioned (Aronson et al., 1999: 38).

As stereotype threat is situational and social, rather than individual and internal, and therefore relies on the immediate organizational context, stereotype threat can be rapidly transformed through mesolevel environmental changes, that is, through changing the rules and the values of the organization. Steele has crafted a series of steps that reduce or eliminate stereotype threat in organizations. These steps include (1) having a supportive "living and learning community" that is both social and academic; (2) organizational affirmation of intellectual ability through "challenge workshops"—that is, workshops that are "honorific rather than remedial programs" (Cohen et al., 1999: 1303); (3) setting and maintaining high standards and assuring the student who is vulnerable to stereotype threat "implicitly or explicitly that he or she is capable of reaching the higher standard" (Cohen et al., 1999: 1303); and (4) making sure that students are told they can succeed through effort and determination and that intelligence is not ascribed to genes, inborn talent or some other immutable and fixed criteria, but instead to hard work, practice and desire (Cohen et al., 1999: 1303), all things that are under the student's control.

Steele demonstrates these interventions have direct and quantifiable influence on perceptions and performance. Within organizational settings that have incorporated these strategies, students learn to perceive themselves as competent, and to perform competently in areas that have heretofore been negatively associated with their social status characteristics.

9.4 Jane Margolis and Allan Fisher: increasing the prevalence of female computer science majors at Carnegie Mellon University

In 1995, Jane Margolis and Allan Fisher embarked on a multi-year project investigating the dismal number of female undergraduate computer science majors at Carnegie Mellon University, one of the leading computer science programs in the United States. Since the inception of the computer science program in 1988, the percentage of female majors remained low: about 8%. In *Unlocking the Clubhouse,* the authors describe the reasons for the pervasive gender gap:

> At each step from early childhood through college, computing is both actively claimed as "guy stuff" by boys and men and passively ceded by girls and women. . . . disinterest and disaffection are neither genetic nor accidental. They are not inherent to the field but are the bitter fruit of many external influences (Margolis and Fisher, 2001: 4).

Michael Kimmel suggests that similar to individuals almost anything—groups, activities, interests, institutions, nations and fields of study—can be gendered. He asserts that in male-dominated societies, even when there is an assumption of gender neutrality, male characteristics are more valued and male needs are prioritized in ways that reflect the male-dominated cultural bias of the society; it is important to note that this bias often remains unrecognized because male superiority is taken for granted (Kimmel, 2004: 101).

In fact, Margolis and Fisher found that most boys who are drawn to computers are white and Asian, which suggests that computer science as a discipline is not only gendered male, but also has specific racial identities attached to it. In subsequent research Margolis (2008) focuses on the topic of race and computer science. She explains that the stereotypical image of computer scientist that most of us carry in our minds excludes women, and African American, Latino and Native American men. Members of these excluded populations, even when they have interest and ability, often perceive that "people like me don't succeed", and the sense that they do not belong is enough to negatively affect their performance, thereby reinforcing the stereotype through a specious causal connection. Consequently, fewer of those in populations excluded from the stereotype aspire to be computer science majors.

The recommendations made by Margolis and Fisher dramatically increased the proportion of women majoring in computer science at Carnegie Mellon, from 8% to 42%. Margolis and Fisher used mesolevel organizational interventions similar to those applied by Steele, including community living and learning environments (for instance, dinners and social events with other female computer science students); maintenance of high standards; stated belief that female students could meet these high standards; and a pedagogical narrative linking competence to effort and determination rather than to biology or demographics.

Margolis and Fisher (2001) also emphasized that female undergraduate students both expected and benefitted tremendously from mentorship by faculty, "The relationship between teachers and students is particularly significant for female students . . . more women than men arrived in college with the expectation of establishing a personal relationship with faculty" (p. 90). Finally, Margolis and Fisher stated that an important organizational intervention at Carnegie Mellon included computer science, as a discipline and as a culture, becoming more contextualized within larger social and academic environments and accommodating the prevailing desire of women to be connected to people rather than machines. They write:

> Women students' descriptions of why they are majoring in computer science are a "counternarrative" to the stereotypes of computer scientists who are narrowly focused on their machines . . . these women tell us about their multiple interests and their desire to link computer science to social concerns and caring for people . . . they need their computing to be useful for society (Margolis and Fisher, 2001: 54).

This is to say that organizations must be flexible enough to integrate and reflect the values and perspectives of all the participating groups in order to avoid reinforcing stereotype threat.

9.5 Women and business leadership: persistent stereotypes

Despite impressive gains by women, feminine characteristics continue to be less associated with workplace leadership than are masculine qualities (Valian, 1998), and the pay gap between women and men persists. According to a Catalyst study, US women now make up the majority of the professional workforce, 51.5% of all management, professional and related occupations (Catalyst, 2011). Yet Catalyst also reports that women's representation in *Fortune 500* leadership positions has stagnated in recent years. Many researchers have found the current societal stereotype is that white men are business leaders and women and men of colour are not (Porter and Geis, 1981; Heilman et al., 1989; Valian, 1998; Eagly and Johannesen-Schmidt, 2001; Ridgeway, 2011).

This social reality continually undercuts women's confidence in the relationship between their effort and talent, on the one hand, and recognition and reward from the larger society, on the other. Given this negative social context, women can grow distrustful of their ability to succeed in the domain of business leadership and therefore less likely to invest in it. This reaction is what Davies, Spenser and Steele (2005) call "domain avoidance" (p. 85) and typically happens in populations that are systematically excluded. Rather than signalling widespread discrimination, domain avoidance is often misconstrued as a personal choice and used as a justification for organizational and institutional exclusion—one manifestation is the oft-repeated myth that women are not interested in leadership (Eagly and Carli, 2007). This interpretation facilitates the reproduction of gender inequality and the stagnancy of opportunity; it leads us back to Ely and Padavic's admonishment that "if study after study reports findings that align with stereotypes and does not address why, then these differences—in temperament, values, attitudes, and behaviors—take on a determinative quality" (Ely and Padavic, 2007: 1122). Addressing this issue, our research detailed below focuses on organizational interventions in an educational setting that have had significant and positive effects on undergraduate female business students in post-graduate salary and in key aspects of life satisfaction.

9.6 The Center for Women's Leadership and women's leadership scholars at Babson College: challenging gender stereotypes through organizational interventions

Babson College is a co-education business school in a suburb of Boston. Babson has been named the top entrepreneurship educator by *US News and World Report* every year since the inception of the undergraduate ranking in 1995. At the time of this research (in the late 2000s), the student population at Babson was approximately 60% male and 40% female, similar to many of its peer business school institutions, though less balanced than most liberal arts colleges, perhaps because of the social assumption that business is primarily a male domain. In the study timeframe, Babson had approximately 179 full-time faculty: 29% female and 71% male. Further, the representation of women as role models skewed towards the liberal arts disciplines rather than business disciplines. In the business disciplines, including economics, women comprised 25% of full-time faculty, on par with other accredited business colleges (Barber and Palmer, 2009), compared with the liberal arts disciplines in which 44% of full-time Babson faculty were female (Brush et al., 2011).

Reflecting national trends in the United States, male MBA students at Babson are more likely to major in entrepreneurship than are female MBA students. There is also a dearth of female undergraduates in business leadership positions and student business competitions. Between 1983 and 2011 only 6 of 50 student winners in Student Business of the Year competition were female. Since 2003, in the Foundations of Management and Entrepreneurship class, the flagship course of Babson's undergraduate entrepreneurship education and a requirement of all first-year students, only 45 of 185 CEOs were female students (Brush et al., 2011). This trend continues after graduation. A study of alumni entrepreneurs in the 25-year period from 1985 to 2009 conducted by William Bygrave et al. (2010) reveals that male Babson graduates are more than twice as likely to start a business than are women Babson graduates: 29% of male graduates founded or cofounded a business in which they worked full-time compared with only 13% of female graduates (p. 3). Although these rates of start-up activity are approximately double those reported by the Global Entrepreneurship Monitor in its 2006–07 US Report (Phinisee et al., 2008), the discrepancy in the number of female and male Babson graduates who founded businesses suggests that larger social stereotypes that exclude women from business leadership, while associating men with this domain, may have caused many female Babson students and graduates to exercise domain avoidance towards leadership as a concept and a set of behaviours.

At the turn of the century, Babson began to recognize the need to focus on attracting more women students and initiated a number of efforts to do so. A Women's Leadership Program (WLP) was launched in 1999, closely followed by a Center for Women's Leadership (CWL). These pioneering initiatives attracted attention and Babson was recognized by *The Princeton Review*, *Cosmo Girl* and *Seventeen* magazine as being a top business school for women. The following is a description of Babson's CWL activities taken from the website ten years into the Center's existence:

- Intensive one-to-one mentoring opportunities, matching high-profile women entrepreneurs and leaders in both the profit and non-profit sectors with our women students

- The fostering of opportunities for on-campus leadership roles for women students

- Networking opportunities with internal and external experts to further career development and advancement across many sectors

- Events featuring prominent women speakers/presenters, providing role models and perspectives on issues critical to women leaders

- Partnerships with organizations and professionals that will assist women students in realizing their career goals
- Promotion of an environment of social responsibility and cross-sector enterprise by supporting student's not-for-profit and pro bono activities.

Since its inception, Babson's CWL (renamed Center for Women's Entrepreneurial Leadership in 2012) has sponsored between 20 and 25 female students a year as WLP scholars. We describe the program as it was implemented in the study timeframe, although it has evolved in recent years. Candidacy for potential acceptance into the WLP is integrated into the admissions review process with admissions staff recommending candidates based on evidence of leadership potential in the regular college application. Candidates who have been admitted to the college are then invited to interview for the opportunity to participate in the WLP and, if accepted, they receive a scholarship award. Female Babson students also have an opportunity to apply to join the WLP during their first year.

In addition to the standard business curriculum, WLP students receive gender-specific training that includes mentorship from an experienced female business professional, career development advice, job opportunities and admission to a speaker series focusing on women entrepreneurs and business leaders. The cocurricular leadership development programming for WLP students also includes regular dinners, meetings and volunteer activities. The dinners and meetings provide social connections and informal opportunities to discuss women's leadership and careers with other WLP students as well as with the faculty and staff directors of the CWL. These interventions resonate with the observations and strategies used by Steele and by Margolis and Fisher as they structured living and learning communities to create a sense of belongingness in a domain for students who were considered minorities and outsiders.

9.7 Methods

To ascertain the effectiveness of the WLP at Babson's CWL, we evaluated the experience of those in the classes of 2003–2007, the first five years of the program's existence. We employ both quantitative and qualitative methods through three separate measures. The first is identification of leaders in an image-based survey administered to Women's Leadership Scholars while they were attending Babson. The second is a post-graduation survey that includes both quantitative measures of success such as salary and career placement as well as qualitative measures of success such as satisfaction, leadership opportunity and sense of empowerment. Finally, we conducted in-depth interviews with 20 alumnae of the WLP: interviews that focused on how the program affected them, their suggestions for improving the program and their reflections on the meaning of leadership.

9.7.1 Research methods: image-based survey

Building on earlier research (Porter and Geis, 1981; Godwyn, 2009) an image-based survey was given to 44 WLP students and 44 non-WLP Babson undergraduate business students, including men. Respondents viewed eight images of women and men, of various races (Caucasian, Hispanic, Asian and African American), who were dressed in typical business attire in an office setting (see sample images below). To test perceptions of leadership, respondents were asked two questions: (1) Who is in charge? (2) How do you know?

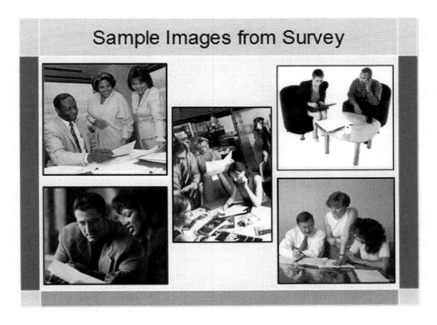

Sample Images from Survey

Source: Mary Godwyn, 2009. Research in Social Stratification and Mobility. doi:10.1016/
j.rssm.2008.10.003.

The survey provides evidence about whether students view women as being in positions of authority and leadership in the workplace and whether gender-specific training (rather than previously held assumptions about gender or workplace experiences) affects perceptions about who is likely to be a business leader.

As discussed, the stereotypical perception is that men are leaders in business and women are not (Porter and Geis, 1981; Heilman et al., 1989; Valian, 1998; Kimmel, 2004; Eagly and Johannesen-Schmidt, 2001). In other words, men in business are perceived as normative or typical business leaders and women in business are perceived as deviants and minorities, especially in leadership positions. The hypothesis being tested with regard to the mesolevel organizational intervention was that undergraduate business students and WLP students would respond differently to the images in the survey. The expectation was that business students would reflect the societal stereotype as they had in Porter and Geis's (1981) experiment and identify men as being leaders in business situations more often than women. If the mesolevel interventions offered to WLP students served to neutralize the stereotype, create belongingness and provide "identity safety" (Davies, Spenser and Steele, 2005) in the business domain, then WLP students would perceive women as being leaders as often or more often than they would perceive men as leaders.

9.7.2 Results

WLP students, those female students who had experienced the mesolevel organizational interventions, were much more likely than non-WLP female students to perceive women as business leaders. Including only definitive responses where someone was identified as being in charge, non-WLP female students presumed that *men were in charge more often than women (53% vs. 47%)*, and they were unsure 17% of the time. WLP students identified *women as being in charge more often than men (67% vs. 33%)* and they were not sure who was in charge 15% of the time. Therefore, WLP students perceived women as being in charge *about twice as often* as they perceived men being in charge, and WLP students were more sure of who was in charge than any of the other groups tested. The differences in leadership perceptions of WLP and non-WLP female undergraduate business students is statistically significant, with *WLP being approximately twice as likely to perceive women as being in charge* in the image-based survey. Using Fisher's exact test, the two-tailed P-value is less than 0.0001. By contrast, the leadership perceptions of non-WLP female students and male undergraduate business students do not significantly differ. Using Fisher's exact test, the two-tailed P-value equals 0.8.

Figure 9.1 shows that non-WLP women's perceptions of who is in charge are more similar to other male business students than to their female peers who experienced the WLP intervention. These results suggest that the organizational interventions entailed in the WLP at Babson College are successful mesolevel challenges that dispel the stereotype that women are not business leaders. Similar to the approaches studied and described by Steele and by Margolis and Fisher, the results here demonstrate that belongingness in a domain and identity safety can be attained through organizational interventions. In this way, organizations are sociocultural contexts that act as mesolevel influencers between the wider society and individual perception of self and others.

Figure 9.1 **Comparison of definitive responses for WLP students, non-WLP female students and male students**

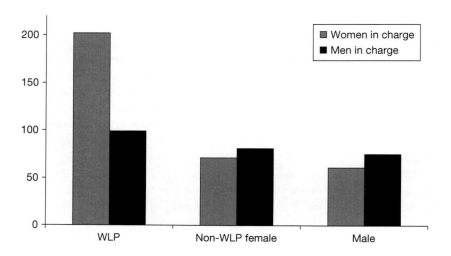

9.7.3 Research methods: online career survey

The image-based survey was administered to WLP participants while they were undergraduate students attending Babson College and still active in the WLP. Our next question was, would the diminishment of stereotype threat continue to follow these young women after graduation? In other words, did the organizational intervention have a carry-over effect in their post-graduation career life?

9.7.3.1 Sample

To measure post-graduation effects of the WLP, data were collected from an online alumni survey conducted in summer 2009. All Babson College undergraduate alumni from the classes of 2003–2007 (five years) were contacted by email and invited to participate in the research study. Survey questions included outcomes such as salary and career placement, career progress since the initial job after leaving college and attitudes such as satisfaction, sense of respect from peers and leadership empowerment (Langowitz, Allen and Godwyn, 2013).

There were 398 complete surveys and an additional 89 partial surveys representing a 25% response rate. The sample included males and females, and they were classified in terms of their membership in the WLP through the CWL. This variable is labelled CWL.

9.7.3.2 Outcome measures

The survey asked respondents to report salary for their initial post-graduate role as well as in their current role. In addition, information on promotion, both internally to the same organization and to a new organization, was collected. The objective measures of success used in our analysis were salary in the current role (SalaryNow) and a dummy variable for promotion of any kind was constructed (Promotion).

Subjective measures of career success were based on responses to five-point Likert scale questions with respect to comfort, respect, leadership and empowerment at one's job. Sample items include "at work my contributions and work effort are respected by my peers" and "at work I feel empowered to take initiative and make decisions". Two measures combining responses were created by summing over the scalar data to capture respect (two items) and empowerment (three items). Another set of subjective measures focused on whether one's personal, career and community life were on-track. The three items were "I feel my career is on track for where I wanted it to be at this point in my life", "I feel my community involvement is on track for where I wanted it to be at this point in my life" and "I feel my personal life is on track for where I wanted it to be at this point in my life".

9.8 Results

9.8.1 Objective measures

Results from our sample show that women experience a statistically significant gender pay gap in their first jobs upon graduation, and that gap widens over time (Langowitz,

Figure 9.2 **Comparison of gender salary ratio with and without intervention**

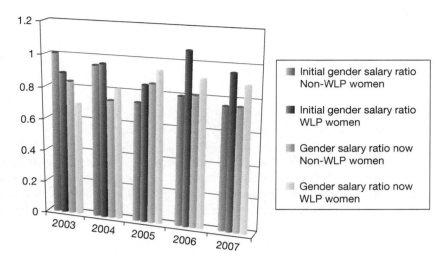

Legend:
- Initial gender salary ratio Non-WLP women
- Initial gender salary ratio WLP women
- Gender salary ratio now Non-WLP women
- Gender salary ratio now WLP women

Allen and Godwyn, 2013: 120). However, those female students who experienced the WLP interventions began their careers relatively at par with their male counterparts, earning 94 cents on average compared to male graduates whereas other female graduates earned only 85 cents on average for every dollar their male counterparts were paid. This gap widened to 85 cents for WLP women and 80 cents for non-WLP women with time in the workplace beyond college graduation. The only exception to the pattern is in the initial year WLP graduates, 2003, which may be attributed to its start-up experimentation with a pilot group of 13 students. Figure 9.2 provides a comparison of the average gender pay ratio for women versus male students by year and shows the improved outcome for those women who experienced the WLP intervention. With the exception of the initial group in 2003 when the program was new, the intervention provided a protective benefit for the gender salary gap.

Logistic modelling of the alumni response data indicates that Babson female graduates experience a significant negative gender penalty on the objective measure of SalaryNow (Langowitz, Allen and Godwyn, 2013: 121). However, the intervention of the WLP had the impact of narrowing the gender difference. The salary gap for WLP graduates was $7,312 lower than that experienced by other female alumnae in comparison to male graduates (Langowitz, Allen and Godwyn, 2013: 123). Taken together, the salary outcome analyses provide significant evidence that the mesolevel intervention of the WLP may have some carry-forward effect in reducing the influence of gender prejudice.

9.8.2 Subjective measures

We constructed a composite variable that combined a self-assessment of career life, community life and personal life and used a multinomial logistic model to evaluate the potential influence of personal, career and structural choice predictors on overall life satisfaction as a career outcome (Langowitz, Allen and Godwyn, 2013: 126).

Results in the model show that gender is significant: women graduates reported a dramatically higher level of satisfaction than did male graduates. The intervention of the WLP also shows a significant influence. WLP were more satisfied post-graduation than other women graduates were. Indeed we see significant differences (P = 0.039) between women who participated in WLP programming and those who did not (Langowitz, Allen and Godwyn, 2013: 126). Further, significant differences were evident when comparing the responses of those women who experienced the WLP, those women who did not and male graduates with respect to volunteer/community life on track (P = 0.040) and personal life on track (P = 0.045) with women being significantly more satisfied than men and WLP women being the most satisfied (Langowitz, Allen and Godwyn, 2013: 126).

The results on volunteer/community life satisfaction parallel the higher rates of volunteerism by WLP women. Volunteerism generally tends to skew female among Babson graduates (both undergraduate and MBA), with females more engaged than their male counterparts as donors, volunteers and participants in alumni programs such as the homecoming event. However, this gendered effect is more pronounced in the case of WLP students who show even higher involvement than other female and male Babson graduates (see Figure 9.3). The participation rate of women donors follows a similar pattern, ranging from 38% to 54% for non-WLP undergraduate alumnae and between 45% and 77% for those who were WLP participants (Brush et al., 2011).

Overall, by both objective and subjective measures, WLP interventions have improved outcomes for these scholars; specifically, WLP scholars have higher salaries and report more life satisfaction than Babson female peers who did not participate in the WLP.

Figure 9.3 **Alumni volunteer activity, classes 2003–2007**

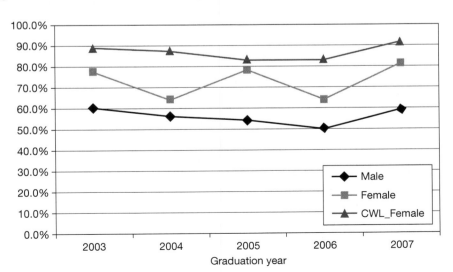

9.8.3 Research methods: interviews

To clarify and enrich the online survey data and to include additional qualitative data, in 2011 we conducted in-depth, post-graduation interviews with 20 alumnae of the WLP. We solicited hour-long interviews with WLP graduates by email and continued to send emails until our target number (20) was reached. Interviewees signed an informed consent and agreed to a single one-on-one hour-long interview with possible follow-up contact should clarification be required. Interviews were tape-recorded and transcribed. Guided by the previous data from the image-based and online surveys, we developed general interview questions using a grounded theory approach and coded the responses based on emerging themes and keywords that arose during the course of the one-hour interviews (Glaser and Strauss, 1967; Lofland and Lofland, 1995; Strauss and Corbin, 1998).

A range of graduates was interviewed beginning with the class of 2003 (the first graduation year of participants in the WLP) through 2007. All but four interviewees were identified as white/Caucasian; two were identified as Latina/Hispanic; and one was identified as Asian (Indian) and one as African American. Several interviewees were married or engaged: three had young children and one was a single mother.

With near unanimity, the most common experience that the WLP graduates recalled was the networking events including monthly informal dinners, speaker events and skill-based training that focused on topics, such as business dinner etiquette and dressing for success, mingling and networking techniques. These informal dinners and construction of learning communities also are common successful interventions in Steele's and in Margolis and Fisher's research. Informal social events that create a sense of group identification and solidarity seem to be a key component in the formula for organizational interventions to undermine stereotype threat. Representative comments are:

> I remember being really excited about it. I went to a program retreat on campus for the weekend. It was all day and all night. All day there were panels and discussions around women leaders. Then they had all of us say a poem. I said it quietly, and they said, "No. You need to feel your voice and exercise your voice."

> We went to a lot of networking events. And I still remember some of the small things they taught us like always wear your name tag on the right side so that people see it when you shake hands. Always keep one hand free to shake. Never forget to ask for a business card and always follow up the next day.

The next experience most often recalled by WLP graduates was the intensive one-to-one mentoring with women entrepreneurs and business leaders as well as the ongoing mentoring relationship with the CWL faculty and staff. Similar to Margolis and Fisher's finding, WLP students report valuing connections with faculty and relationships with mentors. Spending time with successful others who are seen as "people like me" facilitates identity safety in the domain. Mentors also provide the role-model factor that Bakken (2005) has found to be crucially important for identification with a profession. Representative comments are

> It really helped to have someone say, "Ok, you're a girl on this campus. Let's talk about what that's like."

> The mentorship program helped a lot because you saw how really successful women deal with [working in male-dominated workplaces] and talk to them about their experiences. How they overcame obstacles so you know what to do if you're ever in that situation. In general, I gained confidence that I could overcome. That there are enough successful women in business to be mentors is comforting and reassuring.

Margolis and Fisher (2001) found that female computer science majors constructed a "counternarrative" to computing beyond merely interacting with machines and focused instead on how computing fit with a range of other goals and interests including "how computing can be useful for society" (p. 54). We similarly found that as a group, the WLP graduates integrated non-traditional business values by defining leadership on the basis of social concerns and caring for people rather than predominantly by quantitative measurements. Interviewees had holistic and abstract definitions of both leadership and success. There was a focus on relationships and quality of interactions. Specific material acquisitions were never mentioned as hallmarks of success and specific career positions or attainments were mentioned rarely. Representative definitions of success are

> Success? Waking up every morning and being excited to get out of bed and going to sleep feeling like I learned something and contributed. Also, by the people around you—who do I love and who loves me? Feeling like I have a community around me.

> Very simply you've succeeded if you're happy in your life. Not a lot of wants. Just happy with your stage in life.

Notably, none of the 20 interviewees used the male pronoun to refer to leaders. They all used gender-neutral language (e.g. "a person is a good leader . . ." and "they don't take credit . . ."). Representative definitions of leadership are:

> Leadership is about empowering people and fostering a culture that promotes and rewards wins, but doesn't focus too much on mistakes.

> The worst leaders have dead bodies in their wake. Those leaders who would do anything unethical and destroy relationships. Inspiring others is true leadership.

> A leader is not an individual. A person isn't a good leader without the people around them. [A good leader] is a person who leads by consensus.

The satisfaction with life and career recorded in the online survey was obvious in interviewee comments:

> I could talk about [my job] until the cows come home. I really enjoy where I work.

> I do see a separation between my professional and personal life. I try to keep a balance and not get too stressed. I take time to relax and not be constantly connected to my Blackberry. I am mindful to take vacation time.

> This is an industry I have a passion for. Work is not a chore; it's fun! I work with dedicated people who like what they do.

Interwoven in interviewees' responses are strikingly strong sentiments of solidarity with other women, suggesting perhaps that the organizational intervention leading to identity safety and belongingness to the business domain they experienced as WLP members carried over into post-graduation work environments. Representative comments are:

> [The Women's Leadership Program] opened my eyes to networking with women and strengthening relationships with women. I am now part of a women's network at [my place of work]. Financial services, which is 95% male, is known as a difficult business for women. Many of my women peers compete with other women. My view is we should band together.

When asked for a specific reason to pursue a network that is exclusively female, this respondent continued:

> I actually got into quite an argument with my former boss—he was sort of against the women's networking group. He said, If you have a women's networking group, then we should have a men's networking group. And I said, Yeah, that's every meeting you have. That's every time you guys go golfing. So, every day is a men's networking group . . . And he finally said, All right. I get it. You're right. That was a very defining moment for me having to explain to him that there is a different dynamic.

9.9 Discussion

Across the image-based and online surveys as well as in the one-on-one interviews, the Babson WLP students differ from their female peers in key subjective and objective aspects. There are four notable differences that impact on post-graduate life experience: (1) They are more likely to perceive women rather than men as leaders; (2) They begin with and sustain a higher yearly income; (3) They report higher overall life satisfaction measured as satisfaction in career, community and personal life; and (4) They have a higher rate of volunteerism.

These findings support the notion that organizational interventions can result in differences in perceptions, which can lead to differences in performance and in aspirations. Our study provides evidence that minority students, once accredited in their institutions through organizational interventions, can learn to identify as successful leaders and then go on to have a greater rate of success, volunteerism and donorship. In our study, the WLP graduates also gave more back than their peers to the institution that offered the interventions. If this is a common response to organizational support, this would presumably provide another motivation to institutions to invest in such mesolevel organizational interventions: these interventions might result not only in increased performance for groups subject to stereotype threat, but also in increased institutional support from these groups. It is not clear that volunteerism for those minority groups in Steele's or Margolis and Fisher's research was similarly higher, but this is a productive line of inquiry for the future that could signal a continued trust and loyalty as a result of feeling belongingness to a domain.

Looking across the three studies described here, we can identify a formula for mesolevel interventions that can reduce the influence of gender prejudice. Common elements include:

- Creating learning communities that both socially and academically support women's high aspirations
- Honorific rather than remedial programs, such as the WLP, in which membership represents community commendation and becomes a source of personal pride
- Consistent positive affirmation and messaging regarding the potential and success of women, including exposure to positive role models to provide concrete examples of success among similar others and encouraging narratives that integrate and normalize values reflective of a range of group identities
- Proactive engagement and inclusion of women in traditionally male-dominated arenas and activities while ascribing success to effort, practice and desire rather than immutable factors such as "natural" inborn talent and biological differences
- Development of mutually supportive relationships and communities by which women can gain connection, peer support and reinforce positive identity and solidarity.

In the context of management schools, there may be any number of creative ways to adopt this formula. The WLP described here is just one example. Though these interventions are described within contexts of educational institutions, they could easily be employed in a wide variety of organizations.

9.10 Conclusion

There are now a set of studies over the last 30 years that demonstrate how to neutralize the social stereotypes essential to the creation and recreation of gender and racial prejudice and discrimination. We have described dependable strategies in a variety of domains that allow organizations to act as mesolevel contexts that mediate social and individual change in perceptions, performance and aspirations. But surely one question persists in the light of the studies presented here and similar others: Do we have the will and conviction to implement these strategies and reverse the social, economic and political inequality that currently prevails? Certainly, the goals of creating an inclusive and sustainable global economy and effective learning experiences for responsible leadership should prioritize the eradication of gender inequality in business management education and business leadership.

References

Aronson, J., Lustina, M.J., Good, C., Keough, K., Steele, C.M., Brown, J., 1999. When white men can't do math: necessary and sufficient factors in stereotype threat. Journal of Experimental Social Psychology 35, 29–46.
Bakken, L.L., May 2005. Who are physician-scientists' role models? Gender makes a difference. Academic Medicine 80(5), 502– 506.
Barber, B.M., Palmer, D., October 16, 2009. Women Faculty in US Business Schools. Electronic copy available at: www.ssrn.com/abstract=1490084 (accessed on 05.31.11).
Barney, G.G., Anselm, L.S. 1967. The Discovery of Grounded Theory: Strategies for Qualitative Research. Aldine Publishing Company, Chicago, IL.

Brush, C., Langowitz, N.S., Paulson, C., Reza, A., Stoddard, D., 2011. Report of the Taskforce on the Future of the Center for Women's Leadership at Babson. Babson College Internal Report.

Bygrave, W., Lange, J., Marram, E., Pencheva, S., Tan, Y., 2010. Preliminary Summary of Findings from the 2010 Alumni Survey. Babson College Internal Report.

Catalyst, 2011. Statistical Overview of Women in the Workplace. From the Bureau of Labor Statistics, unpublished tabulations from the 2010 Current Population Survey "Table 1: Employed and Experienced Unemployed Persons by Detailed Occupation, Sex, Race, and Hispanic or Latino Ethnicity", Annual Averages 2010 (2011). www.scribd.com/doc/136670424/04-Knowledge-Center-Catalyst (accessed on 08.11.13).

Center for Women's Leadership, Babson College. Student Programs. www.babson.edu/Academics/centers/cwl/Pages/student-programs.aspx (accessed on 08.12.11).

Cohen, G.L., Steele, C.M., Ross, L.D., 1999. The mentor's dilemma: Providing critical feedback across the racial divide. Personality and Social Psychology Bulletin 25, 1302–1318.

Cooley, C.H., [1902]1964. Human Nature and the Social Order. Schocken Books, New York.

Davies, P.G., Spenser, S.J., Steele, C.M., 2005. Clearing the air: identity safety moderates the effects of stereotype threat on women's leadership aspirations. Journal of Personality and Social Psychology 8(2), 276–287.

Eagly, A.H., Carli, L.L., September 2007. Women and the labyrinth of leadership. Harvard Business Review.

Eagly, A.H., Johannesen-Schmidt, M.J., 2001. The leadership styles of women and men. Journal of Social Issues 57(4), 781–797.

Ely, R., Padavic, I., 2007. A feminist analysis of organizational research on sex differences. Academy of Management Review 32(4), 1121–1143.

Follett, M.P., [1924]1995. Relating: the circular response. In: Pauline Graham (Ed.), Mary Parker Follett—Prophet of Management: A Celebration of Writings from the 1920s. Harvard Business School Press, Cambridge (Reprinted from Creative Experience, Longmans, Green, New York, 1924, Chapters 3, 4).

Godwyn, M., 2009. This place makes me proud to be a woman: theoretical explanations for success in entrepreneurship education for low-income women. Research in Social Stratification and Mobility 27(1), 50–64. doi:10.1016/j.rssm.2008.10.003.

Heilman, M.E., Block, C.J., Martell, R., Simon, N., 1989. Has anything changed? Current characterizations of men, women, and managers. Journal of Applied Psychology 74(6), 935–942.

John, L., Lyn, L., 1995. Analyzing Social Settings. Wadsworth.

Juliet, C., Anselm, L.S., 1998. Basics of Qualitative Research: Grounded Theory Procedures and Techniques. Sage Publications, Inc.

Kimmel, M., 2004. The Gendered Society, second ed. Oxford University Press, New York.

Langowitz, N.S., Allen, I.E., Godwyn, M., 2013. Early career outcomes and gender: can educational interventions make a difference? Gender in Management: An International Journal 28(2), 111–134.

Margolis, J., Fisher, A., 2001. Unlocking the Clubhouse: Women in Computing. MIT Press, Cambridge, MA.

Margolis, J., 2008. Stuck in the Shallow End: Education, Race, and Computing. MIT Press, Cambridge, MA.

Mead, G.H., 1934. Mind, Self and Society. In: Morris, C.W. (Ed.). University of Chicago Press, Chicago, IL.

Phinisee, I., Allen, I.E., Rogoff, E., Onochie, J., Dean, M., 2008. Global Entrepreneurship Monitor 2006–2007 National Entrepreneurial Assessment for the United States of America. Babson College, Babson Park, MA, and Baruch College, New York.

Porter, N., Geis, F., 1981. Women and nonverbal leadership cues: when seeing is not believing. In: Clara Mayo, Nancy M. Henley (Eds.), Gender and Non-Verbal Behavior. Springer-Verlag, New York.

Ridgeway, C.L., 2011. Framed by Gender: How Gender Inequality Persists in the Modern World. Oxford University Press, New York.

Steele, C.M., 1997. A threat in the air: How stereotypes shape intellectual identity and performance. American Psychologist 52(6), 613–629.

Steele, C.M., August 1999. Thin ice: "stereotype threat" and black college students. The Atlantic Monthly, pp. 44–54.

Valian, V., 1998. Why so Slow? The Advancement of Women. MIT Press, Boston, MA.

10

From theory to practice
A university promoting gender equality in business

Susan M. Adams
Bentley University, USA

Institutions of higher education are in a position to influence societal change related to gender equality in the workplace by preparing students to enter the workforce ready to challenge and eliminate inequalities. Bentley University (Boston, MA) has been attempting such social change. This case is examined through change management perspectives to highlight challenges in creating sustainable change. Ways to promote sustainable change and suggested practices with promise for other institutions to consider are presented.

10.1 Introduction

A goal of Bentley University is to graduate champions of change in the workplace and society at large so that its students are prepared to deal with the realities of the workplace and equipped to promote gender equality. The approach used draws on multiple theoretical perspectives for changing individuals and organizations to educate students and engage other stakeholders.

Like many co-education institutions of higher education that attract students (and faculty) from across the globe, Bentley's students have a wide range of gender equality knowledge, experiences and levels of interest in the issue. Today's generation of undergraduate students are "confident, self-expressive, liberal, upbeat and open to change" according to a recent Pew Research Center study (Taylor and Keeter, 2010). In this context, it can be a challenge to reach such students with the message that gender inequality is still a workplace problem that needs attention. Young men in this author's classes, who, as boys at school, competed with girls in the classroom prior to university have expressed that they see women doing just fine. Similarly, many young women also see university life as a level playing field when it comes to gender.

Given these challenges, change theories offer guidance to move a generation from acting as resisters and bystanders to helpers and champions for creating inclusive workplaces that embrace gender equality. In other words, change efforts must address denial of inequalities and foster recognition of inequalities to combat resistance to change and promote engagement in making change happen. Furthermore, change efforts in university settings should include steps that graduates can take in settings where there are inequalities. It is worth noting that in the context of this chapter, gender equality does not mean quotas or mandated gender percentages. Rather, the goal is to have workplaces, particularly in business, where talented women are contributing and valued as much as talented men; and where all gender-related management styles are accepted as valid ways to achieve desired outcomes (cf. Eagly and Carli, 2007; Sandberg, 2013). Section 10.2 summarizes key points from change theories that apply to creating social change in institutions of higher education whereby graduates can, in turn, change the business environment to be more appreciative of and conducive to gender equality.

10.2 Change perspectives

Change can be ineffective in achieving desired goals, effective for a short period of time or sustainable for the long term. Although there are some motivational triggers (e.g. compensation, perception of losing a scarce opportunity or a friend's request) that universally encourage behavioural compliance, they may not promote long-term commitment needed for sustained behavioural change (Cialdini, 2009). Large complex systemic changes such as the societal changes needed for gender equality in the workplace entail agreement and commitment from multiple parties to create long-term sustainable change (Gardner, 2004; Gladwell, 2000). Gardner (2004) postulates that large audiences differing in size and range of types of intelligences (i.e. bodily/kinaesthetic, existential, interpersonal, intra-personal, linguistic, mathematical-logical, musical, naturalist, spatial) need different means of persuasion to alter perceptions and attitudes. For example, some prefer to see quantitative information or a rational argument, whereas others need to experience or connect emotionally to the issue. Incentives may be necessary to reach additional groups. Use of these different approaches in combination with each other increases the likelihood of convincing more people to change by appealing to multiple types of intelligences. However, desire to change and commitment to long-lasting change are not necessarily the same. Change approaches that produce long-lasting results address the underlying causes of resistance among those affected by the change so that there is a critical mass that accepts and actively supports the proposed change (Argyris and Schön, 1974; Flood and Romm, 1996; Snell and Man-Kuen Chak, 1998).

The organizational learning movement of triple-loop learning initiated by the work of Argyris and Schön (1974) purports that individuals and organizations must acknowledge the underlying values that drive behaviour to achieve long-lasting change (Argyris and Schön, 1974; Flood and Romm, 1996; Snell and Man-Kuen Chak, 1998). Loops represent the depth of intervention and learning to address underlying assumptions and values that lead to actions and results. Single-loop (how to follow rules to take action) and double-loop (how to change rules based on assumptions) learning lead to short-term problem solving as they focus on seeking immediate solutions based on assumptions and existing rules. On the other hand, triple-loop learning (learning how to learn by questioning rules and assumptions) leads to longer lasting solutions because contrasting values at the root of problems between individuals or groups of individuals in organizations are made visible to everyone involved. Visible competing values can then be reconciled in the open so that those involved accept and embrace the resulting agreed upon actions. In this way, solutions are more likely to outlive leadership changes because values derived from mutual commitment are embedded in the organizational culture. Clearly, this is easier said than done and it does take time to create sustainable change, particularly when there are diverse and entrenched perspectives because individuals resist change for a variety of reasons.

Individuals resist organizational change because they do not see a reason for the change; fear a loss of status, power, self-image, authority, freedom, relationships, money, job and so on; have a history of negative experiences with change; fear a lack of competency—an inability to perform the new task or job; fear what they do not know; have personality conflicts with those promoting the change; feel the change was forced on them; suspect (or know) the change will result in a new social structure; feel the timing of the change is poor; feel overloaded and overburdened; have been conditioned by prevailing cultural assumptions and values; or prefer and are comfortable with the status quo (cf. Argyris and Schön, 1974; Schein, 1999).

Most large-scale change management approaches acknowledge the need for personal exploration, education or some form of persuasion to change minds and the behaviours causing resistance to change. These models offer multiple points and methods to reduce resistance. Kurt Lewin's (1947) classic model of change is a three-stage change process involving unfreezing (initiation to the issue), change (adoption and adaptation to the targeted change) and refreezing (acceptance, use and incorporation of the change). Lewin's three stages and the steps in other process-focused change models (e.g. Cox Jr, 2001; Kotter, 1996) offer opportunities to reach a wide range of individuals by using multiple types of learning experiences as Gardner suggests, allowing individuals to become comfortable with proposed changes rather than resisting them.

In his 2001 book, Taylor Cox Jr presents a change model for diversity work. It entails five components: leadership, research and measurement, education, alignment of management systems and follow-up. John Kotter's model comprises eight steps: establishing a sense of urgency; creating the guiding coalition; developing a vision and strategy; communicating the change vision; empowering employees for broad-based action; generating short-term wins; consolidating gains and producing more change; and anchoring new approaches in the culture.

Kotter and Cohen (2002) conclude that change is more effective when changing "hearts" as well as changing minds. They say that there are many ways to engage feelings through experiences to promote heartfelt commitment to a proposed change or need to change. Also, data can be used during the change process as a way to activate emotions, stimulating desire to change and reducing anxiety about changing. Attending to emotional responses to proposed changes can help break down social and psychological resistance (Kottke and Agars, 2005) because the issue becomes more connected in a personal way.

Gleicher's formula is used to deal with resistance (Beckhard and Harris, 1987; Bunker and Alban, 1997). The formula, $D \times V \times F > R = \Delta$, means that change ($\Delta$) will occur when dissatisfaction with the status quo (D) is multiplied by a clear and compelling vision (V), which is multiplied by first steps to get change going (F), which is greater than the level of resistance (R). Notice that the formula is multiplicative. If any of the three variables, D, V or F, is missing, the entire left side of the formula becomes zero and resistance prevails. A contemporary use of the formula is seen in the Whole-Scale™ Change method, which focuses on moving from the current condition forward (Bartunek, Balogun and Do, 2011).

Combining triple-loop learning (Flood and Romm, 1996; Snell and Man-Kuen Chak, 1998) with the engagement of emotions, the Whole-Scale™ method focuses on working with participants so they collect data about a situation, understand the meaning of the data, develop change goals and commit to specific action and timing to hold each other accountable (James and Tolchinsky, 2007). The assumption is that positive emotions will result from the process (Bartunek, Balogun and Do, 2011) so that hearts and minds are engaged in the process with a sense of ownership in the process and its results. The Cox Jr (2001) and Kotter (1996) process models also take steps that address the factors in Gleicher's formula but in a more imposed rather than elicited manner.

By applying this method to the advancement of women in business organizations and achieving gender equality in the workplace, it is clear that change requires three factors: dissatisfaction with the current level of gender inequality, a view of what organizational life and results would look like and instructions on what to do first to start the change. With high enough levels of the three factors, resistance will be overwhelmed.

The Appreciative Inquiry approach to change is also informative as it focuses on identifying strengths to envision and create a possible future (Cooperrider and Whitney, 2005). The four D's of the Cooperrider and Whitney model are discovery, dream, design and destiny. Other authors and consultants using the Appreciative Inquiry approach have used different terms for the steps, but the process of appreciating and leveraging assets to envision and create a new future is the same. This approach helps everyone involved understand what they personally can leverage to achieve a common goal.

In summary, breaking down resistance to change efforts for greater gender equality requires mutual commitment and support from the multiple stakeholders involved. Women need assistance from those in power in companies and those with clout in society, such as colleges and universities. Different approaches will be necessary to engage the hearts and minds of everyone who can help. In addition, it is necessary to have time to absorb information and emotionally connect to the issues to change minds and promote sustainable commitment (Figure 10.1).

Figure 10.1 **Critical elements of sustainable large-scale change efforts**

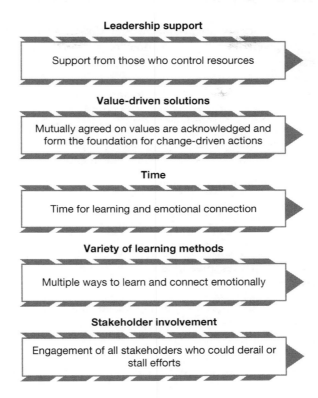

Leadership support

Support from those who control resources

Value-driven solutions

Mutually agreed on values are acknowledged and
form the foundation for change-driven actions

Time

Time for learning and emotional connection

Variety of learning methods

Multiple ways to learn and connect emotionally

Stakeholder involvement

Engagement of all stakeholders who could derail or
stall efforts

10.3 Resistance to gender equality efforts in a university setting

University stakeholders related to gender equality efforts include men and women students, faculty, administrators, governance officials (e.g. trustees and accrediting bodies) and employers of graduates. All these parties are in positions where they can resist or potentially derail efforts.

Drawing on the change management perspectives described above, administrators and governance officials must set the stage by calling attention to the need for gender equality efforts and by providing the necessary resources for specific initiatives. Faculty need to be engaged as managers of the efforts and as behavioural role models. Finally, efforts need to be institutionalized in a way that gender equality awareness and expected behaviour become part of the university student and alumni culture.

Although a few students and employers may demand that attention be paid to gender equality education, it is this author's observation that the issue is not a high priority and unlikely to be one on most campuses. Therefore, if gender equality efforts are to be undertaken, faculty, staff and the administration need to take the lead.

10.4 The Bentley University approach

The faculty, administrators and trustees at Bentley University have indeed seen the need for supporting gender equality education efforts. In addition, the three accrediting bodies associated with Bentley, the AASCB International (Association to Advance Collegiate Schools of Business), EQUIS (European Quality Improvement System) and NEASC (New England Association of Schools and Colleges) deem these initiatives aligned with Bentley's professed mission.

The university is using a multipronged approach to educate its students and the business community about gender equality. As a business university that fuses arts and sciences into its degrees, the goals of Bentley's efforts are intended to

- Prepare women to be business leaders

- Encourage more women to pursue business degrees

- Explore the business case for gender equality with all students, acknowledging biases against men as well against women

- Create awareness of ways students and business professionals can challenge and change discriminatory practices that create a biased workplace.

The realization that gender equality efforts needed to become a priority did not happen overnight. Commitment to gender equality at Bentley comes from a long-standing history of dedication to diversity, business ethics and social outreach. A more recent intentional emphasis on the issue of women's leadership supported by dedicated resources is an extension of activities based on values embedded in the institution's culture.

A brief chronological review suggests how various programs have provided a foundation for campus activities and programs to address diversity and gender equality at Bentley. Each new program brought acceptance of the need for a formal gender equality program by those associated with the university:

- Around 1975, when Bentley was admitting and recruiting women students and faculty to the largely male campus, an English professor offered the first women's studies course, "Images of Women in Literature". Other women's and gender studies courses soon followed. During this time, the institution received three Patrina Foundation grants to support women's and gender studies work. The grants funded one faculty summer seminar, one course development project and one Conference: "Women Make a Difference". Over time, the collection of course offerings in women's and gender studies became a minor with a dedicated Director of Gender Studies.

- The Center for Business Ethics was founded at Bentley in 1976 when the field of business ethics was in its infancy. The Center conducts research, hosts visiting scholars and shares information with business ethics professionals through a series of conferences. It also educates Bentley's students, faculty and staff through a variety of programs.

- In 1993, the university created a formal diversity initiative that ultimately resulted in the creation of the Diversity Council and a variety of activities that deal with everyday campus diversity issues and provide formal training for all faculty, staff and students. At a recent count, Bentley has sponsored over 60 diversity workshop retreats with approximately 900 faculty and staff attending.

- Bentley's Service Learning Center was founded in 1990 to enrich the college learning experience through community service. Six students were offered scholarships in 1992, and a few years later the admission process started offering financial aid to attract students with community service mind-sets. Currently, the Center involves about 1,000 students per year in its programs with 120 trained student project managers to oversee all the students working in community social service programs.

- The Alliance for Ethics and Social Responsibility was established in 2003 to coordinate Bentley's array of social initiatives. Bentley was an early signatory of the UN (United Nations) Global Compact, which promotes gender equality, and the PRME (Principles for Responsible Management Education) program with several members of the faculty actively involved in the PRME Working Group on Gender Equality that is assembling a repository of classroom and research materials across business disciplines.

- The Women's Leadership Institute was launched in 2003 with an original focus on funding faculty research related to women's leadership. As external funding dried up, the Institute shifted its focus to programs for women's leadership development.

In 2011, the university's president, Gloria Larson, launched the Center for Women and Business (CWB), incorporating aspects of the Women's Leadership Institute that contribute to the new entity's mission. President Larson initiated the creation of the Center by raising funds for an endowment that is used to offset about 15% of the Center's budget. The Center is working towards financial self-efficiency but is supported by the university's general budget in the meantime. Through programming and research, the Center is focusing on preparing Bentley's female students to succeed in the business world and on helping companies create work environments where women can prosper.

The student program is designed to alert and prepare women for the realities of the business world so they know what to expect and have the skills needed for success. Corporate programs address issues that companies need to deal with as they work towards gender equality. Research conducted by the Center is used to inform programming and to push the conversation regarding critical issues for gender equality to wider audiences in society where change is needed (Figure 10.2).

10.4.1 Student initiatives

Although the Center's educational efforts primarily target female students, male students are also involved as both members of student advisory boards and invitees to Center-sponsored programs such as the corporate programs where they hear how

Figure 10.2 **Center for Women and Business, Bentley University**

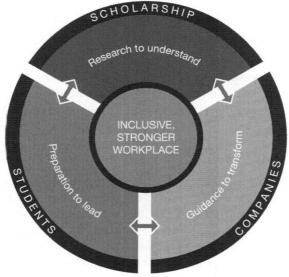

companies are struggling with gender equity. The Center supports other programs on campus, whenever invited, by providing a gender-based perspective and/or support for women in leadership positions. During the past two years, members of the CWB staff worked with the Certified Leaders Program, Service Learning leadership training, career services workshops and several student organizations on gender equality issues. The Center also sponsored campus speakers who are examples of powerful women and men who champion gender diversity in their companies. These campus-wide experiences are provided as a way to help both young men and women understand the challenges that women still face in the workplace and identify ways they and companies can help.

Degree-related initiatives include men as well. All first-year students receive a module on diversity and inclusion at the beginning of their university studies, guest speakers visit a variety of courses and gender studies courses are offered to both genders. Every undergraduate student must take at least one diversity-related course as a requirement for graduation.

The most intensive student initiative is a new student women's leadership program for undergraduate junior and senior women. Those accepted to the program are required to attend workshops (which are open to the entire campus as space allows), receive coaching, shadow corporate professionals and are required to take women's leadership course that includes an international study trip. This program is scalable as demand increases.

At the graduate level, all MBA students take a leadership course, which examines the benefits of workplace diversity and corporate social responsibility, highlighting the responsibilities of managers to address gender equality. Full-time graduate students are also invited to apply for a women's leadership program designed to enhance their understanding of what lies ahead and how to deal with challenges as their careers unfold. The PhD program is supported by the Center's sponsorship of PhD fellows who conduct research with the CWB staff as they pursue their personal research agendas, which are related to the advancement of women in business.

As noted in the descriptions of student programs, there are multiple methods and access points for students to hear and experience the message and to develop skills to promote gender equality in the business world. By working with established programs, the CWB's involvement meets students where their interests currently are. By creating new programs that have a prestige component attached, others are engaged.

10.4.2 Corporate initiatives

In an ideal world, Bentley would be sending its graduates to an enlightened corporate environment where all university alumni can have rewarding careers and contribute their talents to achieve business goals. With that vision in mind, the Center provides programs to help companies work towards greater gender equality at all levels of their organizations. Bentley's enlightened graduates entering these organizations can help sustain company cultures that value gender equality.

This Center at Bentley also hosts Best Practices Forums and Peer Exchanges, which are directed at company executives, managers and other business professionals, including working graduate students. A few non-working graduate students are also invited and faculty members are invited to attend and participate in the program when they have expertise to share on a particular topic. The Best Practices Forums focus on a particular topic with expert guest conveners and corporate panels to share the latest thinking on a specific topic. More importantly, they relate what they are doing in their own companies to support, retain and promote women. The first four topics covered were gender intelligence, sponsorship, engaging men in the advancement of women and addressing cultures of overwork. Each forum offered actions steps that can be taken to address gender inequality in the workplace.

Peer exchanges gather peers across companies to discuss and share ideas. For example, shortly after the Center was created, human resource and diversity officers met to discuss the retention and promotion of women in their companies by discussing what is working, what is not working and why. The Best Practices Forum on engaging men was a result of the CEO roundtable. Similarly, a CEO roundtable was held to share challenges and achievements in the advancement of women.

In 2014, Massachusetts Governor Deval Patrick chose the CWB as his partner to support his initiative to advance more women to positions of leadership. He issued a Corporate Challenge to create a community of at least 100 companies dedicated to do more to advance women and foster greater gender equality. In that capacity, the Center is tailoring new programs to meet the needs of the Challenge companies.

Career development programs for professional women that have been offered by the Center target early career women, mothers re-entering the workforce, women transitioning to top level management and late career women looking for rewarding ways to fill their last years in the workforce or in retirement. We believe that the one-day Gearing

Up workshop program for early career women has been especially successful because that demographic group seldom gets away from work for personal leadership development, even though it is a crucial career stage for leadership development.

Unlike students who are a captive audience on campus, corporate audiences are reached through externally focused methods. The CWB's founding director, Betsy Myers, and others on the staff spend time in the corporate world speaking and conducting workshops, attracting media attention and receiving visibility at events held by other like-minded organizations. The Center's corporate and student advisory boards comprise men and women to ensure that programming and research are relevant and perhaps more importantly to engage them in gender equality efforts. Again, multiple ways of connecting are offered to reach a wider range of companies, which is informative to the Center's understanding of the current environment.

10.4.3 Research

Research studies are conducted to better understand current dynamics that create barriers or facilitate gender equality in business organizations and to identify potential actions that stakeholders can take to advance women's careers. Additionally, since 2003, The Boston Club, a local non-profit organization, which is dedicated to the advancement of women, has been contracting a Bentley team associated with the Center to conduct its annual *Census of Women Directors and Executive Officers of Massachusetts*. Findings of all studies conducted by the Center are shared in reports, distributed online and used to inform the Center's corporate and student programming. As companies are the primary external audience for research, the topics and reports are practice-oriented, although rigorous academic standards are used in conducting the studies. The Center uses media exposure and external speaking engagements to push research findings and their implications to wider audiences. The business press has been particularly helpful in this regard.

10.5 Lesson learned for other business schools

In theory, Bentley's approach should work. Yet, the quest for a sustainable program to equip students as champions of change does have its challenges. Funding, faculty and staff enthusiasm and student engagement are issues that the Center is continuously monitoring and mitigating. Working towards self-sufficiency, for example, relieves resource pressures. The constant celebration of small victories such as a high profile promotion of an alumna or the involvement of young men in championing gender equality, as Kotter (1996) advises, is a way to maintain momentum among all stakeholders.

The Center's mission was defined through an approach using the elements of appreciative inquiry and Whole-Scale™ change with input from key stakeholders. Administrators and the trustees who control resources are supporting efforts with resources, including through their time and by publicly supporting the Center and its mandate in a variety of arenas.

Faculty resources for the Center and other gender equality efforts are not a short- or long-term problem as, at last count recently, well over 20 faculty members are conducting research and teaching in areas associated with women's leadership. Other campus efforts peripherally related to the CWB mission receive staff assistance and comarketing benefits for their programs to create collaboration rather than competition across campus. In this way, the likelihood of other campus personnel derailing effort is reduced and touchpoints for student learning are increased. Participating faculty and external audiences also learn more from the variety of experiences offered.

A key to sustaining Bentley's gender equality efforts is the establishment of a specific mission by the Center. There is an implementation plan for its current (or future) staff to roll out over several years within its financial means. Fortunately, the priorities and attention of accreditation bodies such as the AACSB help to institutionalize gender equality efforts at Bentley. Regular reporting and site visits require assessment of resource allocations and progress towards goals.

A critical challenge to Bentley's gender equality efforts in these early years is the engagement of students. Required coursework serves to level the playing field regarding awareness and starts the process of understanding ways to promote gender equality on campus and in the workplace. How well students respond over time will depend on how they become connected on a personal level to the issue; in other words, how closely the issue corresponds with their espoused values and the way they act on a daily basis. Having faculty from multiple perspectives, the university's student life staff and other students who are prepared to identify and challenge inconsistencies provides immediate feedback for continued learning about unconscious biases. This process takes time, dedication to the topic and, in the case of correcting a fellow student, courage. Class and extra-curricular activities often involve role plays for students to develop scripts and confidence. Through all these efforts, the Center is focused on reaching a critical mass of students to create student acceptance and support of its mission.

We are well aware that when students graduate and are focused on the demands of daily business life, their interest in gender equality advocacy could wane. However, until there are substantial societal changes, young women are likely to face problems at some point in their careers so the Center stays connected to graduates by inviting alumni to events and by keeping them informed about what is happening on campus through university publications and media attention as a way to remind them that they have a support system. Additionally, two megatrend dynamics serve to mitigate backsliding. The current generation of graduates, the so-called millennial generation, as mentioned above, expects fairness and collaboration. They are quite vocal and willing to leave companies that promote what they consider to be an unpleasant work environment (CWB, 2012). Concurrently, the complexity of business is requiring more teamwork. Even with these trends, CWB has decided it is prudent to work with companies in helping them become more amiable to women as leaders throughout their organizations. Early evidence of this mitigating approach is positive. The list of companies wanting to associate and participate in the Center's work is growing. They are asking for help. It is in their best interest to retain their young employees, and they see gender equality efforts as critical in that regard.

The case example of Bentley offers several practices that others can replicate. These are elements of successful change management typically cited by change management experts. As Lewin (1947), Kotter (1996), Kotter and Cohen (2002) and Cox Jr (2001) would suggest, get leadership support. Allocate enough resources. Engage stakeholders. Gardner (2004) and Argyris and Schön (1974) suggest using a process that allows for multiple learning methods and time for assimilating knowledge and experiences.

The matter of organizational culture and the foundation it provides for current efforts is distinctive to Bentley. The institution's focus on diversity as a core value grew over decades. Moreover, it continues to be institutionalized and shaped further through hiring and training practices and through attention-getting responses to inconsistent campus incidents. Resistance among those implementing gender equality initiatives has been reduced over the decades. Resistance among students is decreased by following Gleicher's formula (Beckhard and Harris, 1987), which requires widespread exposure to the issues and guidance for action. Advice from the Bentley experience can be summed up in two words—persistence and focus. Never let up and stay focused on promoting diversity as a core value related to fairness and business success.

References

Argyris, C., Schön, D.A., 1974. Theory in Practice: Increasing Professional Effectiveness. John Wiley & Sons, San Francisco, CA.

Bartunek, J.M., Balogun, J., Do, B., 2011. Considering planned change anew: stretching large group interventions strategically, emotionally, and meaningfully. Academy of Management Annals 5(1), 1–52.

Beckhard, R., Harris, R., 1987. Organizational Transitions, second ed. Addison-Wesley, Reading, MA.

Bunker, B., Alban, B., 1997. Large Group Interventions: Engaging the Whole System for Rapid Change. Jossey-Bass, San Francisco, CA.

CWB (Center for Women and Business), 2012. Millennials in the Workplace. Bentley University, www.scribd.com/doc/158258672/CWB-Millennial-Report?secret_password=2191s8a7d6j7 shshcctt (last accessed 19.11.13).

Cialdini, R.B., 2009. Influence: Science and Practice, fifth ed. Pearson, Upper Saddle River, NJ.

Cooperrider, D., Whitney, D., 2005. Appreciative Inquiry: A Positive Revolution in Change. Berrett-Koehler Publishers, San Francisco, CA.

Cox Jr, T., 2001. Creating the Multicultural Organization: A Strategy for Capturing the Power of Diversity. Jossey-Bass, San Francisco, CA.

Eagly, A.H., Carli, L.L., 2007. Through the Labyrinth. Harvard Business School Press, Boston, MA.

Flood, R.L., Romm, N.R.A., 1996. Critical Systems Thinking: Current Research and Practice. Plenum Press, New York.

Gardner, H., 2004. Changing Minds: The Art and Science of Changing Our Own Minds and Other People's Minds. Harvard Business School Press, Boston, MA.

Gladwell, M., 2000. The Tipping Point: How Little Things Can Make a Big Difference. Little, Brown and Company, New York.

James, S., Tolchinsky, P., 2007. Whole-scale change. In: Holman, P., Devane, T., Cady, S. (Eds.), The Change Handbook: The Definitive Resource on Today's Best Methods for Engaging Whole Systems. Berrett-Koehler, San Francisco, CA, pp. 162–178.

Kotter, J.P., 1996. Leading Change. Harvard Business School Press, Boston, MA.

Kotter, J.P., Cohen, D.S., 2002. The Heart of Change. Harvard Business School Press, Boston, MA.

Kottke, J.L., Agars, M.D., 2005. Understanding the processes that facilitate and hinder efforts to advance women in organizations. Career Development International 10(3), 190–202.

Lewin, K., 1947. Frontiers in group dynamics, In: Cartwright, D. (Ed.), Field Theory in Social Science. Social Science Paperbacks, London.

Sandberg, S., 2013. Lean. In: Women, Work, and the Will to Lead. Alfred A. Knopf, New York.

Schein, E.H., 1999. Process consultation revisited: Building the helping relationship. Addison-Wesley, Reading, MA.

Snell, R., Man-Kuen Chak, A., 1998. The learning organization: learning and empowerment for whom? Management Learning 29, 337–364.

Taylor, P., Keeter, S. (Eds.), 2010. Millennials: The Generation Next, Pew Research Center. www.pewsocialtrends.org/files/2010/10/millennials-confident-connected-open-to-change.pdf (last accessed 13.12.13).

11

Gender and diversity in management education at Europe's largest university of economics and business

An evaluation of 12 years of teaching diversity management[1]

Regine Bendl, Helga Eberherr, Edeltraud Hanappi-Egger,
Anett Hermann, Thomas Köllen, Gloria Kutscher,
Heike Mensi-Klarbach and Gloria Warmuth
Vienna University of Economics and Business, Austria

This chapter explores the specific challenges of teaching diversity management courses in management education. Perspectives on explorative and exploitative learning in organizations allow us to reflect on 12 years' experience in lecturing on diversity management at the Vienna University of Economics and Business (WU Vienna) and to contextualize the results of a teaching evaluation with regard to the specifics of a university

1 A German-language version of this chapter by Regine Bendl, Helga Eberherr, Edeltraud Hanappi-Egger, Anett Hermann, Thomas Köllen, Heike Mensi-Klarbach and Gloria Warmuth was previously published in 2012 with the title "10 Jahre später: Reflexionen über die Etablierung eines Lehrangebots zu Diversitätsmanagement in der universitären betriebswirtschaftlichen Ausbildung an der Wirtschaftsuniversität Wien" in Diversitas: Zeitschrift für Managing Diversity und Diversity Studies 1-2: 23-32; re-use permitted. This version of the text, however, represents a further development of the 2012 text.

of economics and business such as the WU. This chapter constitutes a critical reflection on the establishment of innovative course work and challenges stemming from the contradicting professional self-understandings of those employed as researchers and faculty members at established educational institutions.

11.1 Introduction

The concept of diversity management originally devised in the United States in the early 1990s (for further details, see e.g. Vedder, 2006; Konrad, Prasad and Pringle, 2006; Gatrell and Swan, 2008; Mensi-Klarbach, 2012) was being employed at Austrian universities by the mid-1990s. At the urging of feminist and gender-oriented scientists and with the support of professors receptive to this academic topic, the first professorial chair in "Gender and Diversity in Organizations"—complemented with the Institute for Gender and Diversity in Organizations—was established at the WU Vienna in 2002 in the field of management education (cf. Danowitz, Hanappi-Egger and Hofmann, 2009; Bendl and Schmidt, 2010). One task of this chair was to develop suitable courses and materials for students of management education. Within a few years, a study by Pedersen, Gardey and Tywuschik (2008) on the establishment of courses in diversity at European universities of business and economics, as well as business schools, named the Institute for Gender and Diversity in Organizations as an example of "best practice".

The course of studies offered by the Institute has been revised more than once over the last 12 years, reflecting changing framework conditions (i.e. the Bologna Process[2]) as well as the teaching staff's lengthy experience in teaching and research. As part of the WU's curriculum in management education, a special *field of competency* in "Gender and Diversity Management" was offered from 2003 to 2009, consisting of 11 interdisciplinary two-hour lectures. The primary aim was to teach organizational knowledge on the establishment of diversity management, supported by lectures in the fields of sociology, public economics and law (cf. Hanappi-Egger and Hofmann, 2007) to expand students' understanding of gender and diversity management.

The restructuring of Austria's universities to the new Bologna architecture also led the WU Vienna to abandon *Diplom* degree courses and dispense with the related fields of competency. In their place, to focus on "employability", the new bachelor's degree was oriented towards "business specializations" (or SBWLs): that is, courses of ten lecture hours designed with a much greater practical relevance in mind. In response, the Institute for Gender and Diversity in Organizations choose to offer an SBWL in "Diversity

2 The Bologna Process subsumed meetings and agreements between European countries to ensure common standards of higher education qualifications.

Management"[3] (from the winter semester 2007/2008 onwards) consisting of five double lectures (20 ECTS) with a strong practical focus on the areas "Organization and Management" and embedded within a bachelor's degree in management education. In addition, basic principles of diversity management were integrated into the general undergraduate course "Personnel, Leadership and Organization", while an elective course "Gender and Diversity Management" was introduced into the curriculum of the master's program in Management in 2010.

The Institute is also well represented in the WU's international profile, not only in terms of individual courses, but also by the foundation of an international faculty group "Gender and Diversity Management" within the CEMS Network[4] in 2009, in which faculty staff from the Institute (WU), the University of St Gallen, the Corvinus University in Budapest, the London School of Economics (LSE), the University of Louvain, the Helsinki University (AALTO), the Copenhagen Business School (CBS), the Koc University and Stockholm University (SSE) are integrated. This faculty group, "Gender and Diversity Management", offers a block seminar for students of the Master's program in "International Management", which has repeatedly been ranked one of the best such block seminars of the CEMS Master (CEMS, 2011).

Thus far, the history of the establishment and development of courses on gender and diversity management at the WU Vienna has been characterized by periodic critical analyses of the content and orientation of courses as well as teaching methods, based on students' evaluations and resulting internal discussions. In the following we describe the development of courses on gender and diversity management in terms of explorative and exploitative learning. Such contextualization allows refinements in curricula to be viewed as a major aspect in the development of tertiary educational institutes, while their significance can then be analysed from a micro-political perspective. An overview is given of students' evaluations of courses attended, in particular the identified strengths and weaknesses. As already mentioned, both the WU and its curricula have undergone a massive process of change over the past years, and thus the discussion will focus on the evaluation results for the compulsory course "Diversity Management". Comparisons are made with the evaluation results of the previously offered field of competency "Gender and Diversity Management" only where this seems helpful. The chapter closes

3 The highlighting of "diversity" in the course name was a strategic decision motivated by the opinions of students who had encountered strong, often negative, preconceptions associated with the term "gender" in the field of feminist political thinking. Following lengthy internal discussion, gender was anchored as a primary category of diversity into the newly designed specialization, with a much stronger emphasis on intersectionality (intersections between different diversity dimensions, e.g. age, gender, sexual orientation, ethnicity, [dis]ability, religion/belief, which interact on multiple and often simultaneous levels, contributing to systematic injustice and social inequality).

4 CEMS (Community of European Management Schools and International Companies) is a global alliance of leading business schools, multinational companies and NGOs that together offer the CEMS Master's in International Management (MIM). The CEMS MIM is a pre-experience postgraduate degree open to high-calibre, internationally minded, multilingual students enrolled in a MIM program at one of the CEMS member schools.

with some lessons learned regarding the development of a curriculum of gender- and diversity-relevant courses in management education within the context of a university economics and business.

11.2 Explorative and exploitative learning in the curricular development of diversity management at the WU Vienna

Practice has shown that organizations frequently only look at issues of gender and diversity when pressurized by internal difficulties or external influences: for example, demographic trends, new employment legislation or conflicts in the field of human resources (cf. Klarsfeld, 2010). The same is true of the WU, where it became clear that, in the wake of academic, legal and demographic developments towards the end of the 1990s, gender and diversity could no longer be neglected in what was meant to be perceived to be an up-to-date, innovative and forward-looking curriculum and research program. In view of developments in women's and gender studies, legal European Union framework conditions of *gender mainstreaming* (which views gender balance and equal opportunity as a top-down agenda), the internationalization of the workforce, trends towards globalization, as well as mechanisms of inclusion and exclusion at the workplace, teaching and research in the field of management education is forced to deal with the question of diversity.

In reaction to these external developments the WU created a professorship in "Gender and Diversity in Organizations" in the field of management education, initially providing this chair with few resources, while explicitly assigning it the tasks of acquiring third-party funds and establishing a suitable curriculum. The internal discussion among faculty staff proved rather fraught, in particular because at this time the WU was facing a serious shortfall in funding; many faculty members felt that it would be "pure luxury" to dedicate teaching hours to the subject "Gender and Diversity". Furthermore, some were sceptical that the employment market did, in fact, demand such know-how in diversity to justify the creation of a separate study module that is a so-called *specialization*, in the field of management education, rather than individual elective courses. Demand from the job market in terms of the number of advertised vacancies (employability) was one of the key arguments for or against the creation of such a specialization.

Gender and diversity were not questioned as topics of research, but rather the motivation behind their representation in the established curriculum for management education was questioned. The quality of teaching was also a subject of debate, in particular whether a sufficient standard could be guaranteed by those in charge of such gender and diversity courses. This is, of course, a well-known problem in the field of gender studies, in both teaching and research. In fact, some individuals deny the existence of a substantive body of expertise in this field. This belief can be traced to a strongly politicized faith in common sense knowledge.

The plan to create a new specialization in an already established course of studies therefore encountered considerable resistance from within the organization, which had to be met constructively during the initial development phase. One strategic approach was to embrace *exploitative learning* (March, 1991), a form of learning that exploits current knowledge to generate new skills and competencies. This required the gathering and evaluation of existing organizational knowledge (particularly internal knowledge, so-called "insider knowledge") to anticipate the diverse forms of resistance and defensive reactions that could occur, and to deal with these in a suitable fashion. In addition to countless informal discussions and the formation of coalitions with other groups at the university (students, lecturers), the most vital step was to acquire the necessary funding in order to avoid falling victim to the internal battle on the allocation of resources. A successful application to the European Social Fund (ESF) (which secured funding from both the ESF and the Federal Ministry of Science and Research in the period 2003–2006[5]) not only legitimized the topic indirectly by clearly confirming its "fundability", but also permitted a proactive engagement and rebuttal of the expressed objections:

- Funding problems: The ESF funds ensured that the WU would not be required to subsidize lecturing posts, while external experts could be employed.

- Quality assurance: "Train-the-trainer" courses supported by ESF funds ensured that teaching staff were suitably qualified and sensitized to lecture in gender and diversity. Furthermore, a curriculum initially developed by the working group "Women in Research and Teaching at the WU", which was oriented towards more general aspects of gender in diverse management topics (personnel, marketing, sales, financing, controlling), was revised by the faculty members at the Institute in order to place the focus more clearly on organizations and behaviour in organizations. This new teaching concept also convinced university committees charged with quality assurance of offering a good mix of theory and practice. A wide-ranging evaluation and feedback system was also developed in order to capture not only the experiences of teaching staff, but also that of students and the views of practitioners.

- "Employability": Even if the number of job advertisements specifying knowledge of gender and diversity cannot be compared to traditional fields of expertise in business administration, individual examples of such advertisements were collected. In particular, a theory-practice dialogue was created (also funded by the ESF grant), aimed at personnel managers who are increasingly required to accomplish tasks in diversity management.

In general, one can say that it was vital to maintain a high degree of context sensitivity by following all the usual guidelines, rules and standards at the WU: that is, to make use of

5 The ESF project "Integration of courses on gender- and diversity management into the regular curriculum using the example of management education at the WU Vienna" (GZ 31.963/18-VII/9/03) received funding of €442,050.

exploitative knowledge. At the same time it was necessary to push past these borders to explore new ways of generating knowledge and engaging in micro-politics (such as the acquisition of external resources) in order to facilitate organizational change. The established curriculum in business administration had to be accepted as a primary structure to be enriched by the introduction of fresh, new content (cf. Danowitz, Hanappi-Egger and Hofmann, 2009).

External social factors and framework conditions were also vital to further legitimize the new courses. At the time in question, demographic shifts, such as an increase in population with migration background based on the Austrian working policies of the 1970s and 1980s, and the challenges these would bring to the management of organizations were of great public interest and discussion. But also new guidelines governing the work of universities (a new Austrian university law introducing a managerial university with an emphasis on Gender Mainstreaming) forced them to confront issues of gender. In reaction to these various external factors the WU Vienna successfully pursed a path of adaptation, which involved complex processes of organizational learning. In other words, the WU enabled the creation of courses in the field of gender and diversity.

In this context we can, in a general sense, define learning as a behavioural modification resulting from new experiences and the targeted acquisition of knowledge (Lefrancois, 2003: 3). Here there is an imminent relationship between the culture of learning and the development of competencies, depending on the specific context (Jünger, 2004: 1). Following March (1991), Hanappi-Egger and Hofmann (2012: 327) differentiate between explorative learning (learning by adaptation) and exploitative learning (learning by discovery). It is clear that in establishing the Institute of Gender and Diversity in Organizations with its novel curriculum (initially funded by the ESF grant), the WU as an organization underwent a process of both exploitative and explorative learning. But also the newly founded Institute, responsible for the development and running of courses in gender and diversity management, passed through a process of learning by adaptation and discovery.

Exploitative learning occurred in those cases where lecturers were able to offer interpretations and meaningful observations in their courses derived from previously existing knowledge bases. Such knowledge was a theoretical framework constituted out of the individual disciplines (business and administration, informatics, public finance, law, sociology) as well as theoretical knowledge of women's and gender studies, and practical experiences with processes of inclusion and exclusion in relation to gender balance and equal opportunity.

Explorative knowledge, which is the search for new theories and insights to be anchored in mainstream thinking, had to be generated in those cases where new topics and detailed knowledge of dimensions of diversity (not only gender, but also age, ethnic background, sexual orientation, religion as well as physical and mental ability) had to be transmitted not only to students, but also at an organizational level and within the internal micro-political arena. Knowledge of the specifics of the additional dimensions of diversity and their scientific contextualization required the setting-up of research projects and dialogue with scientists and researchers from around the world. For example, the Institute became actively involved in fostering a network of German-speaking actors in the field of diversity research or organized conferences for the exchange of theory and practice.[6] The requisite exchange of experience for explorative learning among the staff of the Institute of Gender and Diversity in Organizations was, on the one hand, institutionalized in the form of regular feedback meetings and focus group discussion, and on the other hand, realized through countless casual discussions in an informal setting (e.g. the staff kitchen).

Despite the many years of experience already gained in teaching and research, these learning processes are, of course, ongoing. The field of gender, diversity and diversity management is in continual flux, while scientific developments and real-world practice are closely linked and mutually influential. Thus, the generation of knowledge by the researchers and lecturers in the area of gender and diversity management represents a permanent coevolutionary process that brings existing inter-, trans- and disciplinary knowledge into contact with diverse fields of practice (profit/non-profit organizations) while fostering development not only at the individual level of staff members but also at the level of the Institute for Gender and Diversity in Organizations and indeed the level of the entire WU in relation to gender, diversity and diversity management. Berger and Bernhard-Mehlich (2002: 154ff.) have pointed out that organizational processes of learning presuppose a willingness to experiment and an acceptance that mistakes may be made. With this in mind, the curriculum was continually remodelled in reaction to the evaluations of the individual lectures as well as new research results and also enriched through innovative teaching methods.

Regarding the course content, knowledge on diversity and competencies, which should be imparted to students, was refined and developed over time in a coevolutionary process (see also Hofmann, 2006; Hanappi-Egger and Hofmann, 2008; Bendl and Hanappi-Egger, 2009). The contents were harmonized with this implicit and explicit knowledge base of diversity, built on a foundation of interlinked diversity competencies.[7] The following competencies in diversity, related to various approaches to diversity management (also diversity paradigms) (e.g. with regard to Dass and Parker, 1999), are conveyed in the courses:

In summary, the courses offered by the former field of competency, as well as the newly structured specialization of diversity management, are intended to transfer theoretical knowledge of gender- and diversity-based inequality and forms of discrimination,

---

6 This conference "Agenda: Diversity" took place in January 2006 at the WU Vienna and was aimed at scientists and practitioners in the field of diversity. A conference proceeding was subsequently issued (Bendl, Hanappi-Egger and Hofmann, 2006).

7 The term *diversity competency* is based on a general understanding of competency and describes a system of actions that can be applied to changing situations and derived from an individual's fund of resources or expertise in a range of diversity dimensions. The deployment of diversity competencies, as well as expertise in diversity, can only be understood in relation to the specific social context and the confrontation with each situation (cf. Bendl and Hanappi-Egger, 2009).

knowledge of techniques and methods, social competency and individual competency in relation to issues of gender and diversity (Table 11.1).

In the following we examine how the lectures and course materials have been received by students. The basis for the discussion is provided by the results compiled from the evaluations of the specialization "diversity management", considered against a background of coevolutionary processes of exploitative and explorative knowledge generation.

Table 11.1 **Competencies in diversity under consideration of diversity paradigms**

Source: Bendl and Hanappi-Egger, 2009, 572.

	Analytical competence	**Competence in methods**	**Social competence**	**Individual competence**
Resistance perspective	Analysis of the situation and strategy development in order to break resistance and reveal majority and minority groups	Use of analytical instruments and methods to recognize and reduce resistance in the organization in relation to particular dimensions of diversity	Examination of own resistance in relation to a range of diversity dimensions Ability to defuse conflict	Personal goals derived from dealing with resistance and conflicts
Anti-discrimination and fairness perspective	Development of strategy on equal opportunity in relation to organizationally relevant diversity dimensions and antidiscrimination guidelines	Use of analytical instruments, data and methods in order to reveal discrimination and requirements for diversity dimension	Examination of one's own actions with regard to discriminatory and anti-discriminatory tendencies	Personal goals derived from dealings with discrimination-free action
Access and legitimation perspective	Development of strategy on the use of organizationally relevant diversity dimensions in the frame of individual functional areas (e.g. personnel, marketing)	Application of data and methods to support strategy development Use of existing instruments from a diversity-specific perspective	Examination of the own (target) group affiliation	Personal goals for the workplace derived from strategy development
Learning perspective	Strategy development and implementation with the goal of achieving a diversity-oriented organization	Application of data and methods to support the diversity-oriented strategy development to foster a learning organization	Examination of the own function/role in the frame of diversity-specific organizational development	Derivation of personal goals in the frame of strategy development

11.3 Empirical results of the course evaluations of the SBWL in diversity management

As indicated above, diversity management is a specialization in management education at the WU, which aims to integrate diverse forms of knowledge and competencies required for the correct handling of diversity. The foundation course in diversity management (Course 1) offers basic knowledge of gender and diversity in organizations as well as fundamental concepts and theories. The following three courses (Courses 2–4) in the curriculum are dedicated to the application of gender- and diversity-relevant methods and instruments (Course 2); the strategic implementation of diversity management in the real world of business (Course 3); as well as social competence with regard to a team seminar (Course 4). The fifth and final course (Course 5) focuses on the real-world application of course content, developing the knowledge gained by undertaking a practically oriented study project. All courses foster the ability to reflect on topics learnt by setting aside sufficient time for discussion and by means of individual reflective work. Students must sit for an exam between the fourth and fifth courses, consisting of a written and an oral part.[8]

The impact and reception of each course can be determined using various methods of evaluation. Evaluations are goal- and purpose-oriented, whereby the results of an evaluation describe the situation at any given time based on systemically gathered data. The choice of evaluation model will thus depend on the particular aim. We can distinguish between formative assessment (process evaluation) with the goal of improvement (e.g. of programs) and summative assessment (result evaluation), which only looks at the achievement of goals (cf. Dunkel, 1997).

From the very beginning, the specialization Diversity Management has been evaluated every semester in the form of a formative (i.e. process) assessment, with the aim of continually improving the offered courses and adapting these to accommodate major changes in the educational and economic context. Each evaluation examines in detail the extent to which the educational goals and expectations of students have been realized by the SBWL. Towards the end of the specialization the students complete a questionnaire during their examination, drawn up on the basis of the WU's general course assessment. The questionnaire consists of closed and open questions on the following range of topics, which over time has been determined as the most useful for assessment: reasons for the choice of the specialization; the successful acquisition of knowledge and competencies; perceptions of resulting employability as well as evaluations of the course content; and concrete feedback on potential improvements as well as particularly positive aspects of the specialization.

---

8 To be admitted to the final exam in "Diversity Management", students are only required to attend Course 1. Courses 2–4 are merely elective, offering additional study points (up to a maximum total of 30 points) towards the exam. Course 5 can only be attended after completing the exam. In previous years the majority of students have chosen to attend at least one of the non-mandatory courses 2–4.

In the last seven semesters (from summer semester 2009 to April of the summer semester 2013) and since the transition to the new form of bachelor's degree, 230 students have appeared for the final examination and completed the questionnaire. Before presenting the evaluation results, Section 11.3.1 gives some relevant parameters on those students who have participated in the evaluation, the data being extracted from an internal university database.

11.3.1 SBWL students

Since the summer semester 2009 a total of 230 students have successfully completed the SBWL.[9] Figure 11.1 shows the number of male and female students in each semester.

From Figure 11.1 it can be seen that the great majority of students are female, although a trend can be detected in the past few years towards a rise in the number of male students. The large jump in the number of graduates from the summer semester of 2011 is due to the fact that two final courses were offered from this time in order to relieve the

Figure 11.1 **Number of graduates by sex**

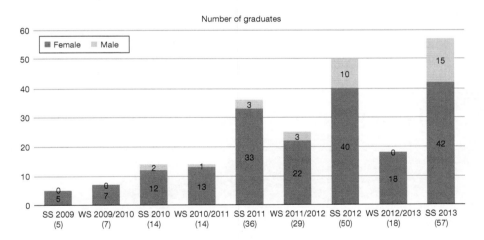

9 As part of the transitional process from the previous field of competency to the new SBWL, both programs were open to students from the winter semester 2007/2008 to the summer semester 2009; from the winter semester 2009/2010 the older course was no longer offered. More than 172 students graduated from the course in "Gender and Diversity Management" in the period from winter semester 2004 to the termination of this course in the summer semester 2009. Most students continue to attend Course 5 of the SBWL after successfully passing the final exam. Hence there is a slight discrepancy between the total population of students in the evaluation of the SBWL and the total population of students who have already passed the SBWL. Currently (to summer semester 2013) 230 students have successfully passed the examination requirements of the SBWL. From the winter semester 2012/2013 the number of new students joining the SBWL has been raised from 30 to 60 per semester.

existing "backlog" of students who had commenced the SBWL but had not yet taken the final exam. Increased demand for the SBWL led to an increase in the numbers of participating students to 60 per semester from the winter semester 2012/2013. The high number of graduating students since then can be attributed to this development.

On average students take 352 days to complete the SBWL. In Table 11.2 it can be seen that the speed of graduation has shown a slight upwards trend, slowing over the last few semesters.

Table 11.2 **Length of study for SBWL Diversity Management**

First semester	Sex	Mean value	N	Standard deviation
SS 2009	Female	498	10	161
	Total	498	10	161
WS 2009/2010	Female	476	17	196
	Male	233	2	0
	Total	450	19	200
SS 2010	Female	413	18	120
	Total	413	18	120
WS 2010/2011	Female	309	24	100
	Male	350	3	98
	Total	314	27	99
SS 2011	Female	285	10	39
	Male	283	2	25
	Total	285	12	36
WS 2011/2012	Female	320	22	136
	Male	254	7	0
	Total	304	29	121
SS 2012	Female	334	21	45
	Male	361	3	112
	Total	337	24	54
WS 2012/2013	Female	224	17	34
	Male	246	2	21
	Total	227	19	33
SS 2013	Female	215	9	13
	Male	202	5	8
	Total	211	14	13
Total	Female	357	163	155
	Male	323	28	184
	Total	352	191	160

The data show that on average female students require a little more time than male students to complete the SBWL (see Table 11.2).[10]

11.3.2 Reasons for choosing the SBWL

From the proposed list of motivations, students mentioned an interest in gender and diversity as a particularly important motivation for choosing the SBWL, with similar weight being given to the opportunity for personal development. Another strong motivation for choosing the SBWL Diversity Management was "in order to contribute to the transformation of business/society". From this we can conclude that the students perceive the SBWL as a component of their business studies that above all offers them the opportunity for personal development. This finding is consistent with the written remarks by the graduates in Diversity Management in the open section of the questionnaire, where the gained knowledge and insights are described as enriching their management education. The feedback from the open section of the questionnaire also reveals that students see the opportunity to engage in critical reflection of organizational processes and structures as unique and highly productive.

In the last few years more students have named "employability" as a motivation for choosing the SBWL in Diversity Management (Figure 11.2). This indicates that students

Figure 11.2 **Motivations for choosing the SBWL in diversity management**

Why have you chosen the SBWL in diversity management?
Y-axis: mean values (1 = completely agree, 5 = completely disagree)

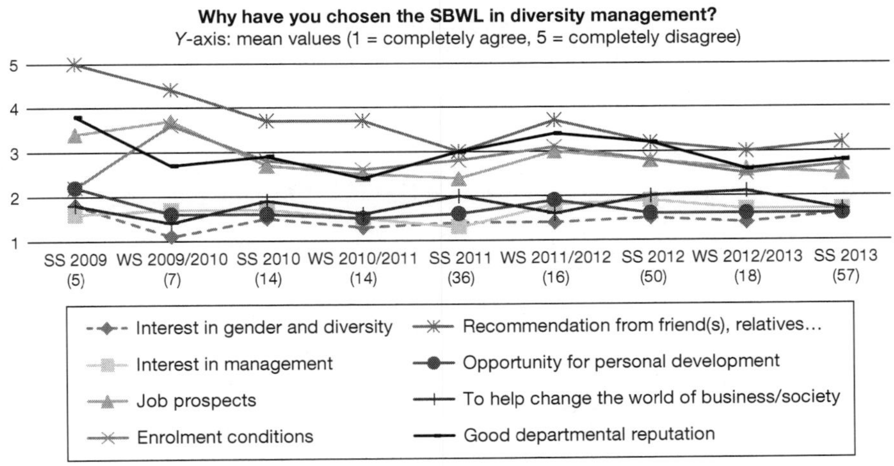

10 In interpreting these data it is important to bear in mind that until the winter semester 2008/2009, students were graduating from the SBWL who had commenced their studies within the previous course structure, and thus had gained study points from attending lectures outside the new SBWL program. As the number of required days is calculated from the period between official commencement of the SBWL and the issuing of the final course mark, it should be noted that when studies are completed in the winter semester this artificially raises the calculated total study time required for the SBWL due to the longer summer holidays compared to the winter break. A true comparison of the development of study time must therefore distinguish between students graduating in the winter and summer semesters.

believe the added value of knowledge and competency in diversity to have risen in the employment market.

These findings indicate that the SBWL is perceived as an interdisciplinary course, whose application in real-world employment situations is ever more prized by students. The opportunity to reflect critically on organizational interdependencies is viewed as offering important new insights and a real advantage of the SBWL.

11.3.3 Development of knowledge and competencies

Students' perceptions of the development of their theoretical and practical grasp of knowledge and competencies are illustrated by Figure 11.3.

In general it can be determined that the intended teaching goals with regard to knowledge and competencies gained are closely reflected in the range of answers given by students. In particular, the acquisition of basic and advanced knowledge in the framework of the SBWL is viewed by the students as a real gain in expertise. This is confirmed by practically all students over each semester. The ability to engage in teamwork and good communication skills are also perceived as new competencies are successfully learnt. Also course participants are able to locate and grasp a clear connection between the content of management courses previously attended and their new knowledge of diversity. However, students' perception of the ability to work independently and following correct scientific methods is subject to large variability. In the winter semester 2012/2013 this question received an overwhelmingly positive response, whereas the previous semester and the one preceding, students were doubtful that their scientific competencies were sufficiently advanced.

In the open section of the student survey, it is striking that the practical relevance of the SBWL is highly rated by some students, while at the same time students felt

Figure 11.3 **Knowledge gained and development of competencies**

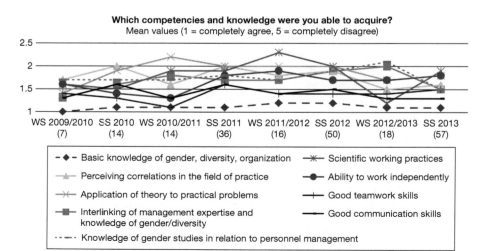

that the theoretical abstract knowledge gained should be translated more often into the real-world context and the daily practices of companies. This desire of students for a stronger practical orientation and translation of theory is also apparent from the typical answers given to the question regarding the development of knowledge and competencies. In reaction to this feedback, more lectures with a stronger practical orientation to the organizational context were introduced from the WS 2012/2013 (currently two per semester, previously only one per semester). These efforts are reflected in the students' replies to assessments in the last two semesters, in both the closed section of the questionnaire and the questions with an open format. There has been a more positive response to the questions regarding awareness of interrelationships at the practical level as well as the question of the application of theoretical knowledge to real-world problems. In the open section of the questionnaire the lectures on practice were more frequently mentioned in a positive light, rated as useful for the translation of theoretical know-how to organizational fields of action. Nonetheless, the link between theory and practice to foster an improved perception of "employability" as well as wide-ranging competencies in diversity measures must be even more firmly anchored into the SBWL.

In summary, we can say that the teaching of gender- and diversity-relevant knowledge, methods, social and individual competencies is largely successful, and that continued attention must be paid to several areas, in particular the application of theory to practice and the students' abilities to tackle scientific tasks independently.

11.3.4 Perception of employability

One element in the decision-making process of students when choosing a degree course is the perception of subsequent "employability". For the SBWL in Diversity Management this means that the potential course participants consider closely whether the acquired competencies will improve their chances of finding employment and whether a formal certification of qualification gives a positive signal to potential employers (cf. Boden and Nedeva, 2010; Walker, 2006). In Section 11.3.2 we discussed the relevance of this criterion for the SBWL. Figure 11.4 gives an overview of the extent to which these factors have been confirmed or have altered.

The expectations of students regarding the specialization have largely been fulfilled. In particular, the SBWL is highly rated with regard to the development of the individual personality. Students also saw as highly relevant the fact that completion of the SBWL furnished the participant with qualifications valuable for career entry, so that the acquired competencies are viewed as having job market relevance. The fact that the signalling effect of the formal qualifications is rated positively is confirmed by the high level of agreement with the statement that the SBWL has generally "[. . .] increased the likelihood of finding the desired employment". This agreement can in part be attributed to the fact that the choice of the SBWL and later the successful graduation from the specialization steers the students' career aspirations more towards activities closely tied to this field. It seems that course participants ascribe a high degree of "employability" to the specialization Diversity Management.

Figure 11.4 **Assessment of the SBWL**

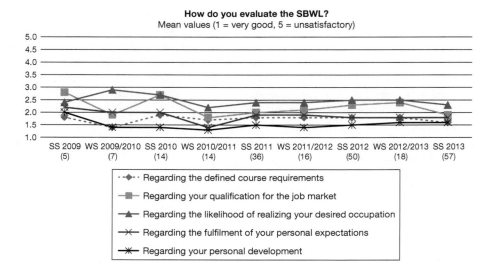

How do you evaluate the SBWL?
Mean values (1 = very good, 5 = unsatisfactory)

SS 2009   WS 2009/2010   SS 2010   WS 2010/2011   SS 2011   WS 2011/2012   SS 2012   WS 2012/2013   SS 2013
(5)   (7)   (14)   (14)   (36)   (16)   (50)   (18)   (57)

··◆·· Regarding the defined course requirements

──■── Regarding your qualification for the job market

──▲── Regarding the likelihood of realizing your desired occupation

──✕── Regarding the fulfilment of your personal expectations

──✳── Regarding your personal development

11.4 Evaluation of the course content, feedback of students and suggestions for improvement

In the light of the assessment results of the students regarding the acquisition of theoretical knowledge and competencies, and following careful discussion, the curriculum was revised again for the new summer semester intake in 2012. Whereas students were previously only offered one mandatory lecture in which experts in diversity from the world of business or organizational practice elucidated their concepts for diversity management, in the future there will be two such presentations. To anchor a wide-ranging examination of the practice of diversity management in organizations within the curriculum, there will be, alongside one lecture to discuss the fundamentals of organizational measures and instruments in the frame of diversity management, a second lecture that focuses squarely on the processes of implementation and the concrete application of theory in practice. Although in the past every student had the opportunity to participate voluntarily in at least one additional lecture, only a few students took up this offer due to their busy schedules. Mandatory attendance at these two lectures, which are linked to one lecture series each, is aimed at building a bridge between this practically oriented input and previously taught theoretical concepts, thereby creating an additional opportunity to translate theory into practice, tying these two areas together in a recursive understanding.

The answers of students to five open questions (to which over 90% of respondents supplied answers) on various aspects of the SBWL seen as either requiring improvement or to be of particular value revealed the desire for a more intensive examination of the individual dimensions of diversity. While the dimension of gender is perceived to be highly prominent, other dimensions such as religion, physical and mental abilities, as well as ethnicity, are felt to be under-represented. Thus, lectures on practice are now specially selected to ensure that a maximum number of diversity dimensions can be covered; in particular, the mandatory final course of the SBWL in each semester is dedicated to a different dimension, such as disability (in the winter semester 2011/2012) or religion and ethnicity (in the summer semester 2012). From the winter semester 2012/2013 there can already be detected a reaction from the students: both the lectures and the new emphasis on different diversity dimensions have been sources of positive feedback (Figure 11.3).

Furthermore, it is clear from the answers of students that the perception of a gain in the ability to work independently and according to scientific methods fluctuates from one semester to the next (Figure 11.3). This can be attributed to the fact that students are not required to attend all offered courses and thus differ strongly in the extent to which they acquire knowledge and skills related to scientific methods and techniques. To guarantee a sufficient level of competency in this area, fundamentals on scientific working methods are now offered in two mandatory courses. The foundation course also includes an additional block on the topic of scientific work, in which the basics are revised. In the final advanced course, which is also mandatory, this knowledge is then actively applied.

11.5 "Lessons learned" in the light of the curricular development of gender in the framework of diversity-relevant courses

We would like to close with a discussion of the specific challenges encountered when teaching gender and diversity management at a university of economics and business. Perhaps our "lessons learned" will be of interest and used as a source of experience and reflection for similar ventures.

During the implementation phase it was necessary to overcome considerable resistance at the organizational level. This was manifested in discussions about the extent to which insights into gender and diversity constitute scientifically and economically useful and relevant knowledge, or whether such insights are indeed irrelevant. One central challenge during the implementation phase was therefore to legitimize topics of gender and diversity. This proved particularly difficult in view of the orientation of other disciplines at the university towards strict market usability as a primary paradigm for evaluation. In the meantime this inherent tension between economic paradigms and social responsibility can be observed in discussions with students. Those charged with setting up and running courses in gender and diversity management must keep this particular tension in mind, pointing out that this field of study and research does not deal with common sense knowledge, but insights derived from theory. Thus, it remains a challenge to tap into students' previous understanding of gender and diversity while teaching them to abstract from these basic notions while steering the focus of interest towards social mechanisms and their impact. The social dialogue on diversity is developing in terms of gains in both explorative and exploitative knowledge, while topics of diversity are enjoying increased prominence at both the management and organizational levels.

It is important to point out that the implementation described here took place at a time when topics of diversity had scarcely gained a foothold in Austria, whether at universities or in the world of business, so that the Institute can certainly be described as a pioneer in this field. The ever-increasing social awareness of diversity over the past years has had a positive impact on its acceptance and legitimacy in the scientific and organizational spheres. The application of exploitative and explorative knowledge was constructively balanced in order to successfully anchor innovative theories and practices while integrating these into more established ways of doing. In this way we were able to ensure that organizational change was realized smoothly and without difficulty.

The narrowing and intensification of focus towards organizational management skills in the implementation of diversity management, when the field of competency "Gender and Diversity Management" was transformed into the SBWL (specialization) "Diversity Management" as part of the restructuring of all courses at the WU, was met with a great deal of interest by students. At the same time important topics enabling a more comprehensive embedding of diversity management into the wider social discourse had to be shortened, with the result that students were required to study individual components of these topics on their own. In this case it was vital that clear links could be drawn to other fields of study in other academic disciplines, revealing the existence of interdependencies regarding theory and practice: that is, research. Moreover, it became clear that the narrow focus on the business administrative aspect of diversity management left insufficient time in the individual course modules for anything more than a rudimentary discussion of the inter- and transdisciplinarity that characterizes this field. Bringing in more perspectives of other disciplines—for example, psychology, sociology, demography and law, which would help to contextualize diversity and diversity management more broadly—is not possible within the limited time resources of a business administration-oriented specialization of five courses with two hours per week.

One primary challenge in terms of teaching and acquiring knowledge, which became clear from the evaluation feedback, is successfully combining the competency of scientific reflection with the demands and expectations of a course of studies such as management education, which is highly oriented towards real-world application. The evaluation findings showed that students view this balancing act as successfully realized. They judge that the diversity-relevant knowledge and the methodological, social and individual competencies have generally been well conveyed. However, the evaluation findings also highlight some residual tension between theoretical and practical knowledge (also designated as the interface problem in discussions on theory versus practice as two rather incompatible knowledge systems [see also Moser, 2001]). Thus, one achievement was seen as the acquisition of skills in scientific reflection and other expertise, while students expressed the wish that theory be more closely tied to practice and that greater emphasis be given to management skills in diversity at a practical level. The evaluation results also confirm that increasing social acceptance of topics of diversity seems to be leading to higher estimation of the marketplace value of expertise in this field.

Finally, it should be noted that students increasingly wish access to the field of diversity management in which other dimensions of diversity are given the same weight as gender. In the frame of intersectional observations, this is revealed by students' growing interest in other dimensions of diversity such as age, ethnicity/nationality or religion. In designing a suitable curriculum it is therefore important to enlarge the theoretically based range of topics to include other diversity dimensions, while not, of course, neglecting gender as a structural variable.

11.6 Summary

This chapter has examined the challenges to be overcome in establishing a course of studies in gender and diversity, particularly in the context of a university of economics and business. Taking the example of management education at the WU, it can be seen that gender- and diversity-based teaching must negotiate a careful path between assimilation: that is, adaptation to the present curricular structures (exploitative learning) and innovation, implying the deepening and expansion of the materials taught (explorative learning). This characteristic feature of implementing a suitable course of studies results from several factors.

In the context of management education, it is necessary that a high degree of legitimation be indicated, particularly regarding the real-world business relevance. Yet this can frequently only be discerned in the process of social transition. Thus, while current demographic trends foster an organizational interest in know-how on gender and diversity, thereby boosting legitimation of this field of study, such forces cannot be expected at every point of time. Students' common sense knowledge and experience of gender and diversity can initially be used in a didactically useful fashion to approach this field of study; yet such knowledge must be abstracted by suitable teaching methods to permit a theoretical understanding of diversity.

From the perspective of implementation, one important consideration is the handling of organizational conflict and resistance. Traditional conceptions of "core competencies" in individual educational programs often leave little room for innovative thinking. On the other hand, it is incumbent on universities to remain open to innovations in curricular content as well as new teaching methods. It is a particularly complex and fascinating challenge to recognize and implement such innovatory change in a way that remains sensitive to the prevailing educational context.

References

Bendl, R., Hanappi-Egger, E., 2009. Über die Bedeutung von Gender und Diversitätsmanagement in Organisationen. In: Kasper, H., Mayerhofer, W. (Hrsg.), Personalmanagement, Führung, Organisation. Linder International, Vienna, Austria, pp. 553–574.

Bendl, R., Hanappi-Egger, E., Hofmann, R., 2010a. Austrian perspectives on diversity management and equal treatment: regulations, debates, practices and trends. In: Klarsfeld, A. (Ed.), International Handbook on Diversity Management at Work. Country Perspectives on Diversity and Equal Treatment. Edward Elgar, Cheltenham, Northampton, pp. 27–44.

Bendl, R., Hanappi-Egger, E., Hofmann, R., 2010b. Diversitätsmanagement in Österreich: Bedingungen, Ausformungen und Entwicklungen. Diversitas—Zeitschrift für Managing Diversity und Diversity Studies 1(1), 17–34.

Bendl, R., Hanappi-Egger, E., Hofmann, R., 2006. Agenda Diversität: Gender- und Diversitätsmanagement in Wissenschaft und Praxis. Rainer Hampp Verlag, München, Mering.

Bendl, R., Schmidt, A., 2010. From a bottom-up movement to a top-down strategy: reframing responsiveness to gender equality in an Austrian University. In: Katila, S., Meriläinen, S., Tienari, J. (Eds.), Making Inclusion Work. Experiences from Academia around the World. Edward Elgar, Cheltenham, Northampton, pp. 48–62.

Berger, U., Bernhard-Mehlich, I., 2002. Die Verhaltenswissenschaftliche Entscheidungstheorie. In: Kieser, A. (Hrsg.), Organisationstheorien. Kohlhammer, Stuttgart, Germany, pp. 133–168.

Boden, R., Nedeva, M., 2010. Employing discourse: universities and graduate 'employability'. Journal of Education Policy 25(1), 37–54.

CEMS (Community of European Management Schools and International Companies), 2011. CEMS Evaluation of Block Seminars in the Masters in International Management (MIM) 2011–2012, unpublished internal feedback from the CEMS head office.

Danowitz, M.A., Hanappi-Egger, E., Hofmann, R., 2009. The development and implementation of a diversity management curriculum: organizational change through exploration and exploitation. International Journal of Educational Management 23(7), 590–603.

Dass, P., Parker, B., 1999. Strategies for managing human resource diversity: from resistance to learning. Academy of Management Executive 5(3), 45–56.

Dunkel, M., 1997. Fortbildung und Umschulung unter Transformationsbedingungen. Peter Lang, Frankfurt, Berlin, Bern, Germany.

Gatrell, C., Swan, E., 2008. Gender and Diversity in Management: A Concise Introduction. Sage Publications, Los Angeles, London, New Delhi, Singapore.

Hanappi-Egger, E., Bendl, R., Walenta, C., Hofmann, R., Gartner, H., 2006. W-1.a.05. GZ31.963/18–VII/9/03: Integration von Lehrveranstaltungen zu Gender- und Diversitätsmanagement in reguläre Studienpläne am Beispiel der Betriebswirtschaft an der WU Wien, ESF Projektbericht, WU, Vienna, Austria.

Hanappi-Egger, E., Hofmann, R., 2007. Gender- und Diversitätsmanagement: Qualifikationsbedürfnisse in der betriebswirtschaftlichen Universitätsausbildung. In: Wagner, D., Voigt, B.F. (Hrsg.), Diversity-Management als Leitbild von Personalpolitik. Deutscher Universitätsverlag, Wiesbaden, Germany, pp. 153–171.

Hanappi-Egger, E., Hofmann, R., 2008. Wissen und Kompetenzentwicklung für Diversitätsmanagement. In: Helmut, K., Mühlbacher, J. (Hrsg.), Wettbewerbsvorteile durch organisationales und individuelles Kompetenzmanagement. Linde-Verlag, Vienna, Austria, pp. 15–28.

Hanappi-Egger, E., Hofmann, R., 2012. Diversitätsmanagement unter der Perspektive organisationalen Lernens: Wissens- und Kompetenzentwicklung für inklusive Organisationen. In: Bendl, R., Hanappi-Egger, E., Hofmann, R. (Hrsg.), Diversität und Diversitätsmanagement. Facultas UTB, Vienna, Austria, pp. 327–349.

Hofmann, R., 2006. Lernen, Wissen und Kompetenz im Gender- und Diversitätsmanagement. In: Bendl, R., Hanappi-Egger, E., Hofmann, R. (Hrsg.), Agenda Diversität: Gender- und Diversitätsmanagement in Wissenschaft und Praxis. Rainer Hampp Verlag, München und Mering, pp. 10–24.

Jünger, S., 2004. Selbstorganisation, Lernkultur und Kompetenzentwicklung. Theoretische Bedingungsverhältnisse und praktische Gestaltungsmöglichkeiten. DUV, Wiesbaden, Germany.

Klarsfeld, A., 2010. International Handbook on Diversity Management at Work. Country Perspectives on Diversity and Equal Treatment. Edward Elgar, Cheltenham, Northampton, pp. 27–44.

Konrad, A.M., Prasad, P., Pringle, J.K., 2006. The Handbook of Workplace Diversity. Sage Publications, London.

Lefrancois, G.R., 2003. Psychologie des Lernens. Springer, Berlin, Heidelberg, New York.

March, J.G., 1991. Exploration and exploitation in organiziational learning. Organization Science 2 (1), 71–87.

Mensi-Klarbach, H., 2012. Diversity Management: the business and moral cases. In: Danowitz, M.A., Hanappi-Egger, E., Mensi-Klarbach, H. (Eds.), Diversity in Organizations. Concepts and Practices. Palgrave Macmillan, Basingstoke, pp. 63–89.

Moser, H., 2001. Einführung in die Praxisforschung. In: Hug, T. (Hrsg.), Wie kommt Wissenschaft zu Wissen? Einführung in die Methodologie der Sozial- und Kulturwissenschaften, Band 3. Schneider-Verlag, Hohengehren, Germany, pp. 314–325.

Pedersen, E.R., Gardey, G.S., Tywuschik, S., 2008. The Business Case for Diversity. Diversity Management & Business Schools—Current Practice and Future Partnerships. Task 5, part of the 2008 "Activities promoting and developing the business case for diversity" study [21.00 MEZ]. www.ec.europa.eu/social/BlobServlet?docId=1823&langId=en (accessed 01.10.13).

Vedder, G., 2006. Managing Equity and Diversity at Universities. Rainer Hampp Verlag, München, Mering.

Walker, M., 2006. Towards a capability-based theory of social justice for education policy-making. Journal of Education Policy 21(2), 163–185.

12

Integrating gender and diversity in management education

Finding the right balance between "integration" and "marginalization"

Julia C. Nentwich and Gudrun Sander

University of St Gallen, Switzerland

The University of St Gallen stands out as one of the first business schools in German-speaking countries to establish a gender and diversity study program. As this program has become a key part of St Gallen's curriculum, we could draw the preliminary conclusion that our integration of gender and diversity topics into management education has been successful. However, this is not the full story. As the program is positioned as "contextual studies", it is not seen as a core management issue and does not yet have a major effect on how we teach strategy, finance, leadership or human resource management. This chapter not only provides an overview of the Gender and Diversity Study Program and its achievements to date, but also discusses the challenges of "mainstreaming" gender and diversity issues into management education. Our conclusion points out the need to deal with the balancing act of being integrated and excluded at the same time.

12.1 Introduction

The University of St Gallen is an internationally renowned business school ranked in the top tier of European business schools (*Financial Times*, 2013) and a member of the CEMS alliance, an European network of universities offering a joint master's degree program in International Management.[1] It is well known in German-speaking countries for its integrative management model and broad stakeholder orientation. The University of St Gallen anticipated the current discussion on management education (Colby, Ehrlich and Sullivan, 2011) at an early stage and in 2001 introduced its vision to become a "learning space for students and executives" (Bieger, 2011: 112). This vision was accompanied by a new teaching concept called "contextual studies". All students, regardless of their major, were required to obtain 25% of their credit points at the bachelor's and the master's levels from the electives offered under the heading of contextual studies. Contextual studies include courses in traditional social sciences and humanities such as sociology, psychology, history and philosophy as well as interdisciplinary fields such as gender and diversity studies, business ethics and area studies, the latter introducing students to culture, language and societies of Central and Eastern Europe, China and Latin America (see Figure 12.1). A second pillar of contextual studies is the development of skills such as communication, presentation and teamworking skills. Contextual studies aim to develop students' personalities as future leaders and managers as well as their practical and interdisciplinary skills (Dyllick, 2009).

Contextual studies served as an ideal frame for the implementation of a gender and diversity study program. Originally financed by a national effort[2] to foster university education in gender studies in Switzerland, the University of St Gallen was able to raise additional funding to develop and design a specific teaching program focused on gender and diversity issues in the fields of management, law and economics. The first courses were taught in the fall term of 2005. The following semesters, the program expanded to a curriculum that now comprises an annual average of ten courses at the bachelor's level (24 ECTS[3]) and five courses at the master's level (15 ECTS). With this broad offering, students can choose to exclusively focus on gender and diversity issues in their contextual studies course load and hence develop a unique competence in this area. As the Gender and Diversity Study Program has become an essential part of contextual studies, one could conclude that the integration of gender and diversity topics into management education has been a success.

---

1 www.cems.org

2 The Swiss University Conference (SUC) launched several programs to foster equal opportunities of women and men at universities and to implement Gender Studies at the universities. See www.crus.ch/information-programme/programme-cus-p-4-equal-opportunity-gender-studies.html?L=2 (accessed 09.30.13).

3 ECTS stands for European Credit Transfer and Accumulation System. It was introduced to enhance transparency and comparability of study programs. One ECTS equals 25–30 hours of work from a student's perspective. See www.ec.europa.eu/education/tools/ects_en.htm (accessed 06.28.14).

Figure 12.1 **Three levels—three pillars: the course structure at the University of St Gallen**

Source: University of St Gallen, *Undergraduate Studies Brochure 2013*, p. 9, reprinted with permission.

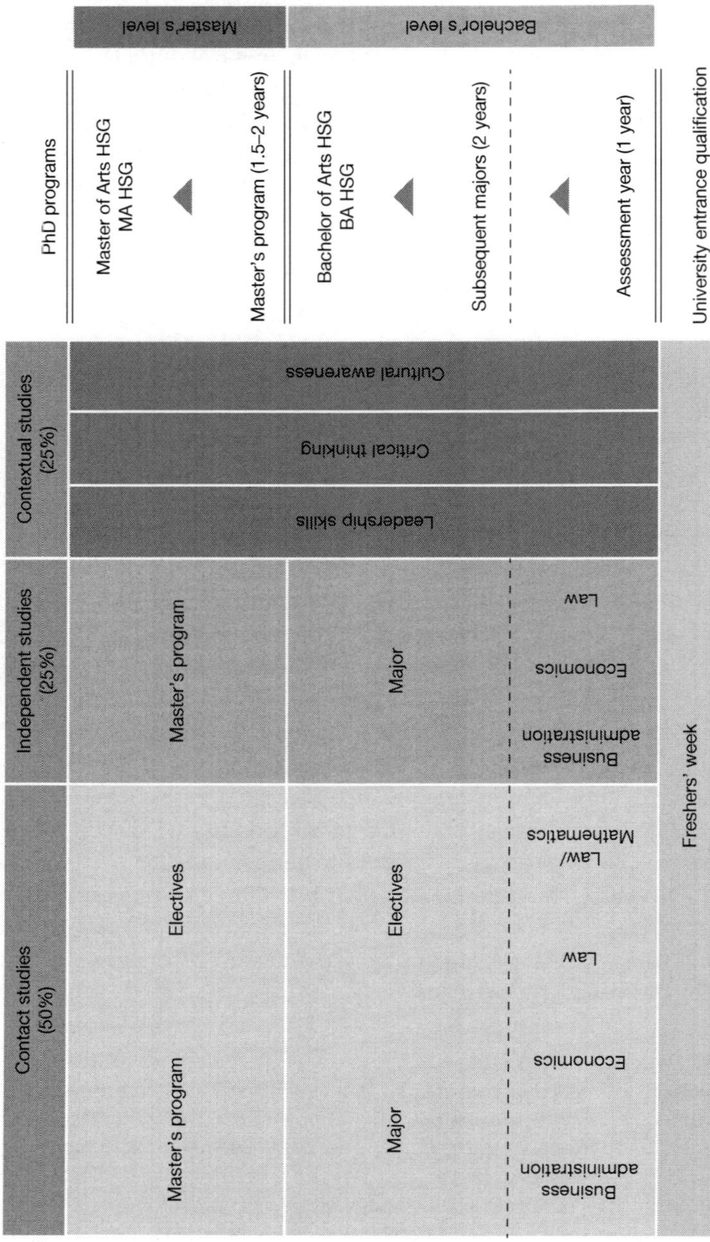

However, this is not the full story. As the program is positioned in the contextual studies block, the gender and diversity topic is not fully recognized as a core management issue and has yet to have a major impact on how we teach strategy, finance, leadership or human resource management in St Gallen. In this chapter, we introduce St Gallen's Gender and Diversity Study Program. We then look into the curriculum design and teaching objectives and analyse the advantages as well as the unexplored opportunities. Our analysis sheds light on a best-practice example of implementing gender and diversity topics within management education, while also pointing out some of the challenges of integrating gender and diversity into management education.

12.2 The Gender and Diversity Study Program

The University of St Gallen's Gender and Diversity Study Program was initially introduced as an elective in the contextual studies block. It provided students in all bachelor's and master's programs with the possibility to obtain expertise in the field of gender and diversity. While the curriculum was designed to make the program a *de facto* equivalent of a minor, only a couple of students per year enrolled in all of the offered courses. The majority of students chose one or two courses from the program. Some students also wrote their bachelor's or master's thesis on a gender and diversity topic, adding further gender and diversity competencies to their profiles. Overall, the courses in the program have experienced high take-up rates. While some bachelor's-level courses regularly reached the maximum number of 60 enrolled students, some of the master's-level courses' take-up rates varied between 15 in one and 50 students in another semester.

The syllabus content and learning objectives of courses in the Gender and Diversity Study Program were jointly developed by the project manager and an interdisciplinary task group consisting of academics teaching at the University of St Gallen and representing the core disciplines of management, law, international relations and economics. Courses are taught by various St Gallen faculty members as well as external lecturers with particular practical or academic competences in the field. We also regularly invite international scholars to teach scientifically cutting-edge courses.

The learning objectives are different for courses at the bachelor's and master's levels. The objectives also depend to some extent on the association with the three pillars of contextual studies: "leadership skills", "cultural awareness" and "critical thinking". Courses that aim to develop leadership skills focus on management techniques and competencies with a practitioner orientation. Topics that are being taught on a regular basis are gender and diversity management, gender mainstreaming, gender and intercultural communication, team diversity and gender budgeting (see Tables 12.1 and 12.2). Courses teaching cultural awareness tackle issues of gender and diversity in specific geographical areas from a historical, cultural or literary perspective. Finally, within the critical thinking pillar, students are introduced to the main concepts in gender and diversity studies. For instance, at the bachelor's level, students become acquainted with gender and diversity as social and cultural constructs (Tienari and

Table 12.1 **Bachelor's courses offered between 2005 and 2012**

Critical thinking

- Managing Difference: Diversity and Work Life Balance in an Organizational Context
- Gender, Work and Family: A Biographical Perspective
- Diversity and Discrimination: Social Psychological Perspectives and Interventions
- Sex and Gender: An Introduction to Gender Studies
- Ways to Succeed? Economic Elites and Gender
- Global Justice from Perspectives of Philosophy and Economics

Cultural awareness

- Gender, Sex and Crime: China's Social and Cultural History
- City Girls: Images of Women in the City
- Peasants, Prostitutes and the Poor: Subalterns Making History

Leadership skills

- Communication and Conflict: Gender Specific and Intercultural Aspects
- Gender and Diversity Management
- Team Diversity: Challenges of Collaboration in Heterogeneous Teams
- Responsibility, Leadership and Gender
- DiverCity: Gender and Diversity in Urban Planning
- Everyday Life and Multiplicity: New Perspectives on Culture
- War, Peace and Gender: Simulation of a United Nations Security Council's Meeting

Nentwich, 2012) are introduced to the concept of "doing gender" and obtain basic knowledge in feminist theory's perspectives on equality, sameness and difference (Alvesson and Billing, 2009). Students are also taught how to apply their knowledge to practical problems.

At the master's level, courses aim to critically analyse the program's core topics from gender and diversity perspectives. Students learn to reflect on how gender and diversity issues are theorized in their distinctive field of expertise. For instance, in one of our courses, students critically investigate how gender is theorized in the St Gallen Management Model (Rüegg-Stürm, 2003) and reflect on the conceptual consequences of theorizing gender from the sameness, the difference and the social construction perspective (Alvesson and Billing, 2009). Through a coteaching arrangement this course offers an interdisciplinary perspective that enables the students to dismantle the apparent gender neutrality of mainstream economics and management theory.

Communicating the relevance of gender and diversity issues to students has been crucial to create awareness of the program and its contents. In addition to a program website[4] a marketing brochure and postcards with information about the program and courses were offered. One key didactical strategy was to design the bachelor's-level courses around students' mundane experiences. For instance, when introducing theory and empirical research on "doing gender", we focus on the issue of women in leadership positions and their everyday struggles. As most of our business students envision

4   www.genderportal.unisg.ch

Table 12.2 **Master's courses offered between 2005 and 2012**

Critical thinking
• Gender, Managerial Identities and Careers
• Gender Issues in the Work Life Context (from Economic and Social Psychological Perspectives)
• "Gender Goes Management": The New St Gallen Management Model from a Gender Perspective
• Social Structure: Gender, Generation and Class
• Gender in Management and Law
• Gender, Organizations and the Knowledge Economy
• Equality, Diversity and Inclusion at Work
• Doing Business like a Real Man? Gender and Entrepreneurship
Cultural awareness
• Change and Persistence in Gender Relations in Switzerland since 1945
• Gender and Modernity (in French and German Literature and Film)
• "Murderous Women" — Gender Positioning in Women's Crime Novels
• "The President's Body": Scripts of Masculinity in Putin's Russia
• Gender in China: Femininity and Masculinity Yesterday and Today
• Gender and Economics (in Literary and Economic Writings)
Leadership skills
• Gender and Diversity Competence as a Leadership Task
• "Enjoy Diversity" — A Theoretical as well as Real Life Expedition
• Football Stadiums or Nurseries? Gender Budgeting in Practice

themselves as future leaders, female students perceive this topic as highly relevant. Furthermore, the course assignment provides a unique chance to interview one of Switzerland's top 100 business women, as portrayed in the Swiss magazine *Women in Business*. Besides the opportunity to study theories of doing gender, this assignment allows students to apply their theoretical knowledge by analysing the challenges discussed in the interviews.

Although the program's title implies that both gender and diversity are crucial issues, it is important to explain why most courses focus on gender issues. This results from both the program's history and the special situation in Switzerland. First, the program's objective was to integrate gender studies topics in management education. It was funded by a national effort to foster education in gender studies. In the conceptual phase of the project it became obvious that diversity was developing into an important management topic internationally. Therefore, it became crucial to connect the program to this development. In Switzerland, however, diversity management is primarily viewed as an important topic for large and international companies (Nentwich, Steyaert and Liebig, 2010). To the extent that diversity topics are important for Swiss enterprises, gender diversity has usually been the main focus (Müller and Sander, 2011). Swiss companies have a lot of experience in integrating foreign employees and managers, but very little experience in integrating women in (top) management positions. A total of 45%

of the members of top management teams of the largest 100 companies in Switzerland are foreigners, whereas only 6% are female. In the boards of these companies 36% are foreigners and 12% are female. Almost 50% of the women in top management do not hold a Swiss passport (Schilling Report, 2013).

12.3 The balancing act between fully integrating and marginalizing gender and diversity

Having outlined the major pillars and objectives of the University of St Gallen's Gender and Diversity Study Program, we can conclude that it was successful in integrating gender and diversity issues into management education. However, taking a critical perspective, it is clear that a major part of the road to be travelled still lies ahead. The program faces challenges that are typical for any social or organizational change process and begs the question: Do special programs for "marginalized" groups or issues lead to real integration or do they—on the contrary—rather contribute to deeper marginalization?

While the university's decision to distinguish between core and contextual studies was a great catalyst to integrate the topic in the first place, it can also be interpreted as a way of practicing resistance against the integration of gender and diversity issues in management education (Swan, Stead and Elliott, 2009). Whereas topics such as strategy, banking and finance, human resource management, organizational behaviour, leadership and marketing belong to "core" and not to "contextual studies", the topic of gender and diversity was effectively left on the sideline by defining it as "context only". The consequence of this is that it is still possible today to graduate from the University of St Gallen without ever having engaged with gender and diversity topics. In addition, while cultural differences, corporate social responsibility and international challenges are likely to be addressed within the core subjects, gender role expectations may never be touched upon in the core curriculum. On the road towards mainstreaming gender and diversity issues in the core areas of management, it is probably necessary to go through a series of incremental changes, in terms of both the curricula and the university's culture. These are processes that are fraught with challenges (Katila, Merliäinen and Tienari, 2010).

What are the obstacles of integrating gender issues into the core areas of management? First, a key problem is to acquire faculty members who promote gender as a relevant topic within the core curricula. As the majority of lecturers and professors are heterosexual and male and gender and diversity issues are not their main research field, this is a major effort that would take extra time and resources. To develop the program further, professors teaching the core subjects would have to be competent in integrating gender and diversity issues (Bierema, 2010).

A second problem is *how* and *where* to address the topic. Teaching one or two lessons on female leadership styles might inadvertently result in a reinforcement of stereotypes instead of a critical discussion on the complex interdependencies of these topics because of either the limited time or cutting short on theoretical complexity (Amoroso,

Loyd and Hoobler, 2010). Thus, one question is how to maintain contextual studies' critical function in the mainstreaming process.

The third problem is directly connected to the issue of quality in teaching gender issues in management education. What is needed are persons who are proficient in both gender studies and management. Without this background in state-of-the-art theorizing on gender and diversity, lecturers will not cover the subject in sufficient depth. On the other hand, they primarily need to be experts in their research field, as this is obviously crucial for the legitimacy of the topic and the lecturer. Inviting guest lecturers or the possibility of team teaching would be first steps in this direction and would enable mutual learning for the lecturers. For instance, as the University of St Gallen has strong relations with the business world and a broad executive education program, it has proved to be helpful if CEOs or managers address these topics in their guest lectures and if the topics are brought up by participants in executive education.

It has become clear that organizing management education along two major tracks of "core" and "context" produces a difficult balancing act: what is integrated into business education as contextual studies is integrated and marginalized at the same time. Establishing this firm dichotomy produces a paradoxical relationship as it even reinforces the difference between "core" (important) and "context" (less important) and hence contributes to the marginalization of the context. Although gender and diversity issues are promoted as highly relevant to management education (Bell, Connerley and Cocchiara, 2009), they are at the same time placed on the sidelines and defined as "not *as* relevant" as long as they are positioned in the "context" part.

From this perspective, St Gallen has yet another story to tell. Although diversity management is an important topic relevant to subjects, such as human resource management, organizational behaviour, leadership, strategic management and change management, the topic was neither dealt with in those core management courses, nor was it offered as an elective. Hence, diversity as a management issue has been left largely untouched by management education's "core" block. However, as diversity management in Switzerland was too important to be ignored, we started offering courses on diversity management in the Gender and Diversity Study Program and hence within the contextual studies block. Teaching these courses was perceived as difficult at times as this meant to subscribe to a double agenda: First, we had to provide students solid knowledge in the *management* of diversity, and second, we had to teach them how to critically contextualize these freshly learned skills. As a matter of fact, teaching diversity management required subverting the structural binary of "core" versus "context". Interestingly, students soon realized the paradoxical nature of this endeavour. In one of our classes they started to discuss why these important issues are not being taught in compulsory courses such as strategic management. Subverting the curriculum's boundaries hence enabled us to create relevance for a topic that has been largely neglected in mainstream management education. This example points out the need to address the balancing act of being integrated and excluded at the same time in the process of integrating gender and diversity issues into management education.

The project of integrating gender and diversity issues into St Gallen's management curriculum might also tell us something about the functioning of contextual studies from an organizational perspective. Regardless of the extent to which we currently consider gender and diversity issues to be integrated into the management curriculum, we have strong doubts that it would have been possible to set the gender and diversity agenda without being able to make use of contextual studies as a door opener. "Contextual studies" served as an entrance ticket for a marginalized field to enter the field of management education in the first place.

"Contextual studies" allowed us to seriously engage students with a full curriculum in gender and diversity studies. This strategy of building up expertise as a first step is something also found in companies. For instance, by implementing the position of "head of diversity", or an "office for equality" or a "service centre for equal opportunities", management may build up knowledge and expertise within the company. The next step would then be to foster cultural change and engage in mainstreaming activities. However, while creating the position of the diversity manager seems to be crucial for diversity management's impact (Kalev, Dobbin and Kelly, 2006), companies starting mainstreaming activities without such a formal position rather engaged in superficial "window-dressing" activities only. Without the necessary accompanying cultural change that gender and diversity experts are enabled to support, these activities do not unfold their full impact (Müller and Sander, 2011).

From such a process perspective of diversity management as organizational change, "contextual studies" can be depicted as an organizational solution to develop and introduce innovations. Such a setup enables new topics to enter into business education, without having to compete directly with the established core curriculum. As almost anything can be positioned in the context of management education, contextual studies provide flexibility and room to experiment with new and challenging topics, including topics that may be important in the education of the next generation of managers—or prove to be entirely unimportant. As nobody can predict the future, we consider this openness and flexibility as an important asset that allows for the university's future development.

Looking into the future, we are convinced that contextual studies finally served as an entrance ticket. Diversity management is on its way to become a compulsory and central topic within St Gallen's curriculum. In fact, diversity management has been an elective within the core studies since 2010. The Gender and Diversity Study Program in contextual studies has been granted a permanent lectureship in 2012 and is hence no longer dependent on project funding. We are convinced that the first professorship will follow soon.

References

Alvesson, M., Billing, Y.D., 2009. Understanding gender and organizations. Sage, London.

Amoroso, L.M., Loyd, D.L., Hoobler, J.M., 2010. The diversity education dilemma: exposing status hierarchies without reinforcing them. Journal of Management Education 34(6), 795–822.

Bell, M.P., Connerley, M.L., Cocchiara, F., 2009. The case for mandatory diversity education. Academy of Management Learning & Education 8(4), 597–609.

Bieger, T., 2011. Business schools: from career training centers towards enablers of CSR: a new vision for teaching at business schools. In: Morsing, M., Sauquet Rovira, A. (Eds.), Business Schools and their Contribution to Society. Sage, Los Angeles, CA, pp. 104–113.

Bierema, L.L., 2010. Diversity education: competencies and strategies for educators. Advances in Developing Human Resources 12(3), 312–331.

Colby, A., Ehrlich, T., Sullivan, W.M., 2011. Rethinking Undergraduate Business Education: Liberal Learning for the Profession. Jossey-Bass, San Francisco, CA.

Dyllick, T., November 2009. Bologna in St Gallen. VHS-Bulletin 3, 44–49.

Financial Times, 2013. European Business School Rankings (Financial Times Business Education; December 2, 24–29). www.ft.com/business-education/europe2013 (accessed 10.12.13).

Kalev, A., Dobbin, F., Kelly, E., 2006. Best practices or best guesses? Assessing the efficacy of corporate affirmative action and diversity policies. American Sociological Review 71(4), 589–617.

Katila, S., Merilainen, S., Tienari, J., 2010. Making Inclusion Work: Experiences from Academia around the World. Edward Elgar Publishing, Cheltenham, UK; Northampton, MA.

Müller, C., Sander, G., 2011. Innovativ führen mit Diversity-Kompetenz. Haupt Verlag, Bern, Switzerland.

Nentwich, J., Steyaert, C., Liebig, B., 2010. Diversity made in Switzerland: traditional and new plurality meets the business case. In: Klarsfeld, A. (Ed.), International Perspectives on Diversity and Equal Treatment at Work. Edward Elgar, Cheltenham, pp. 263–282.

Rüegg-Stürm, J., 2003. Das neue St Galler Management-Modell: Grundkategorien einer integrierten Managementlehre: Der HSG-Ansatz. Haupt Verlag, Bern, Switzerland.

Schilling Report, 2013. Transparenz an der Spitze: Die Geschäftsleitungen und Verwaltungsräte der hundert grössten Schweizer Unternehmen im Vergleich. Guido Schilling AG, Zürich, Switzerland. www.schillingreport.ch/upload/public/5/4173/schillingreport%202013%20D%20web.pdf (accessed 3012.13).

Swan, E., Stead, V., Elliott, C., 2009. Feminist challenges and futures: women, diversity and management learning. Management Learning 40(4), 431–437.

Tienari, J., Nentwich, J., 2012. The 'doing' perspective on gender and diversity. In: Danowitz, M.-A., Hanappi-Egger, E., Mensi-Klarbach, H. (Eds.), Gender and Diversity in Organizations: Developing Core Leadership and Management Competencies. Palgrave Macmillan, Basingstoke, pp. 109–134.

Part IV
International perspectives

13

Gender equality in MBA programs in Latin America

Sandra Idrovo Carlier
Universidad de La Sabana, Colombia

This chapter looks at gender equality in MBA programs in Latin America and has three objectives: the first is to show the existing gender disparity in MBA program enrolment in Latin America; the second is to determine some possible causes for this difference in the number of female MBA students: women caregiver responsibilities, professional and personal identity reconfiguration and gender stereotypes are identified as causes that hinder the possibility of women enrolling in MBA programs; the third is to suggest possible curricula and modality arrangements that might help overcome this disparity.

13.1 Introduction

Women represent 52.0% of the workforce in Latin America (Atal, Ñopo and Winder, 2009), 58.6% in the United States (US Department of Labor and US Bureau of Labor Statistics, 2011), and more or less similar percentages in other Western countries. Even though it is becoming increasingly clear that this female workforce, at least in Latin America, is educated to levels that now often surpass those of men (Hertz et al., 2008), their presence in MBA programs is not what might be expected.

The purpose of this chapter is threefold. The first objective is to show the existing gender disparity in MBA program enrolment in Latin America, using data from national and international accreditation agencies and exploring how this might affect the career advancement of those not holding such a degree. The second objective is to identify some possible causes for this difference in the number of female MBA students: (1) the role of women as the main caregiver at home and for children or the elderly and infirm (Hernáez and Idrovo, 2010; Heslin, 2005; Hewlett, 2007; Krantz, Berntsson and Lundberg, 2005; Parasuranam and Simmers, 2001); (2) the identity reconfiguration that women executives go through in integrating the social and cultural demands of work and family life (Idrovo and Hernaez, 2012), considering the importance that family plays in the Latin American cultural, social and economic context (Vassolo, Castro and Gomez-Mejía, 2011); and (3) some gender stereotypes that directly affect the decision of women to enrol in an MBA program. The third objective is to suggest possible curricula and modality arrangements that might help overcome this disparity by giving more flexibility to MBA programs.

13.2 Boys and boys and boys and . . . girls: gender disparity in MBA enrolment

According to the UNESCO *World Atlas of Gender Equality in Education*, "female enrolment at the tertiary level has grown almost twice as fast as that of men over the last four decades for reasons that include social mobility, enhanced income potential and international pressure to narrow the gender gap" (UNESCO, 2012:74). Largest gains in enrolment have occurred in North America and Western Europe, in Latin America and the Caribbean, and in Central and Eastern Europe—three areas where males also made lesser but still substantial gains. Females went from a position of disadvantage in 1970 to a majority position in higher education in 2009 in three regions: East Asia and the Pacific, Latin America and the Caribbean, and North America and Western Europe. By 2010, enrolment at the tertiary level in all subjects in Latin American and the Caribbean reached 56% for women, and 68.05% in social sciences, law and business (UIS, 2012).

At the master's and doctorate levels things vary somewhat. More women than men (56-44% combined data for the regions) have master's degrees in Central and Eastern Europe and in North America and Western Europe. In Latin America the exact opposite happens: the majority graduating with a master's degree are men. At the PhD level, the edge achieved by women at the master's level in the different regions in the world is reversed: men predominate at this level in all regions with Latin America, again, being the exception. Latin America is the only region in the world where women enrol at a higher rate in PhD than in master's programs (UNESCO, 2012). Looking specifically at the business and administration field of study, 56% of graduates at the bachelor's level in Latin America and the Caribbean are women. However, statistics show most of these women do not go on to enrol in the next level of study: Master in Business Administration (MBA).

Female enrolment in MBA programs according to AACSB (2014) International Business School Questionnaire 2012–2013 amounts to 35.9% in the United States. In comparison, Latin America data from the international accreditation agencies show that only one-third of those who enrol in MBA programs are female. AACSB reports that in Latin America female participation for the MBA is 31.3%, the lowest of all geographical regions (Asia: 37.7%, Europe: 40.8%, Oceania: 35.3%, no information for Africa available). In the same way, the Association of MBAs (AMBA) 2012 enrolment data for accredited programs in the region (around 30 programs) show figures of 65.74% for male students and 34.26% for female students (AMBA, forthcoming).[1] Reasons for the lower female enrolment in MBA programs can be compared to the reasons that hinder women's advancement in corporations, mainly work–life balance (the double burden syndrome), rigid working structure and gender stereotyping (McKinsey & Company, 2013; OECD, 2010; UNESCO, 2012). In Latin America these reasons assume specific characteristics that will be looked at later on in this chapter.

In summary, female enrolment at the different educational levels in Latin America looks something like the one shown in Figure 13.1.

Does this inequality affect women's work status or career development? To answer this question it is necessary to look at the role an MBA degree plays in a manager's career progression. According to AMBA (2012), a graduate from an MBA program contributes a varied array of strategic and interpersonal management skills along with in-depth knowledge and understanding of complex business situations to the organization within which he or she operates. But more importantly, the holder of a MBA degree should be able to

Figure 13.1   **Female enrolment at the different levels in Latin America and the Caribbean**

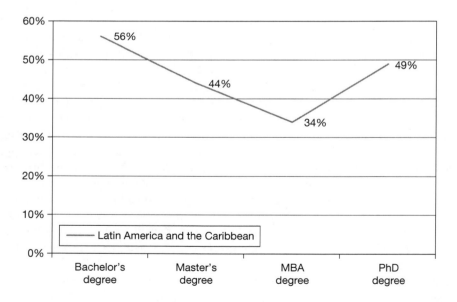

---

1   Information on female enrolment in MBA programs in Latin America has not been available until recently. AACSB offers gender enrolment data according to the different geographical regions, for the first time, in its 2014 edition of the Business School Data Guide Booklet.

use sound judgement in the face of incomplete data, communicate conclusions clearly to a range of audiences and bring leadership skills needed to transform organizations and develop others. This skill set is similar to that which employers and recruiters in Latin America expect from an MBA program graduate (Jaén, 2013).

Applying a gender lens (Kilgour, 2013) to this information, one could argue that a degree such as the MBA enhances the possibility of improving its holder's position within the working hierarchy because it has helped him or her develop a set of skills considered necessary to perform more effectively. The fewer the women that hold this degree, the fewer they will be considered potential candidates for promotion, thereby producing a situation that is detrimental to the advancement of women to higher levels of management. The scarcity of female qualified candidates for the boardroom or for promotion to the next level on the corporate ladder, a common reason used to explain the gender inequality at higher levels of management and the reason behind the low numbers of women directors, might hold some truth if we consider that women are the minority in MBA classes. As Virginia Sarria, assistant dean of IAE Business School (Argentina), points out, "an MBA does not immediately position you as a General Manager, but it does help speed up the process". Laura Zapata, MBA director at the EGADE Business School, Tecnológico de Monterrey (Mexico), argues along the same lines: "An MBA contributes to the professional development of the candidates enroled in it by improving their positions in the organization or by helping him or her achieve a better job in another company."

13.3 Why do fewer women enrol in MBA programs than men?

The answers to this question vary. *The World Atlas of Gender Equality in Education* (UNESCO, 2012: 84) mentions the following as factors that may explain the lower number of female researchers, especially in senior positions, in all regions in the world: work–life balance, gender stereotyping, performance measurement and promotion criteria, governance and the role of researchers in society. Reasons for low female enrolment in MBAs in Latin America run along similar lines, with the first two—work–life balance, with the identity issues that this brings with it, and gender stereotyping—standing out as being particularly significant.

13.4 Work–life balance

One of the elements that affects work–life balance is time: given a limited amount of hours a day the allocation of the scarce resource when playing multiple roles originates conflict and stress for the individuals making the decisions that in turn hinders their quality of life (Baltes and Heydens-Gahir, 2003; Carlson, Kacmar and Williams, 2000;

Greenhaus and Beutell, 1985). In Latin America women have less time than men to balance all the tasks they have to face due to socio-economical changes. The 21st century has seen the emergence of a somewhat different Latin American urban family. Nuclear and bi-parent homes have decreased. The reduction in two-parent nuclear families with children (from 46.3% to 42.0%) is partly attributable to the fact that some families have become single-parent families with children (mostly with a female head of household) (ECLAC, 2006). But in this scenario, women in Latin America and the Caribbean, as in the rest of the world, still hold the main responsibilities for household chores and caregiving (Rodríguez, 2012). As women leave the private space of home for the public realm of work they walk into the latter with the responsibility of the care of the former, which in effect doubles their workload. The dual-provider household, which predominates in Latin America today, involves a differentiated assignment of roles and time dedication. As underscored in Jain (2013), in all 18 countries where time use has been studied, women's total work time (the sum of paid and unpaid work) is greater than men's, and women spend more time in unpaid work. The Social Panorama of Latin America states that it is precisely that time and effort that women devote to caring in the household that "limits women's options for entering the labor market" (ECLAC, 2012: 43).

This situation is the same across the different socio-economical groups with the difference that the upper-level households might be able to hire extra help to meet their care needs. It is also true that when the household is headed by women, as main or sole providers, the care expenditure rises (ECLAC, 2012). It is no surprise then that women claim lack of time when explaining why they choose not to enrol in an MBA program that would only add to the double and sometimes triple workload they already have. Damián Rendón (2013), Director of Admissions at INALDE Business School in Colombia, mentions that after explaining to possible candidates to the MBA the dedication time that the program would require, female candidates usually withdraw arguing "lack of time", "too many things to do: work, family, the house" and so on. One could reason that the financial investment required for an MBA would imply that women candidates for the program belong to high-income households, or have corporate support, and therefore would also have no problem hiring paid help for the household chores. Yet data show that in high-income households, women take responsibility for the domestic work and even though they do not do it themselves they supervise and organize all of it (Hernáez and Idrovo, 2010). In addition, there is one thing they try not to delegate: the care of their children.

This is one of the issues that must be taken into consideration: maternity and the care of children involved. At least two factors need to be considered when looking at maternity and care of children and the role they play in hindering women in the decision to embark on an MBA program. One is age. An MBA candidate needs to have some work experience after finishing his or her bachelor's degree. The common age for candidates applying to an MBA ranges between 25 and 35 years. The two additional years (average duration of programs in the region whether they are part-time or full-time) to go through the program puts females at odds with their biological clock. As Sarria (2013) emphasizes "that is exactly the time of their lives when they are juggling too many things . . .: trying to balance having children, family life, with a very interesting job, the MBA becomes one more thing and one that is difficult". Rendón (2013) explains that when asking a female MBA candidate who had accepted to join the program why she was withdrawing or deferring entry for a year, the most frequent answer was "children".

However, it is not only the pregnancy period that becomes problematic. The reconfiguration of identities that pregnant women go through also plays an important role. Research in the social sciences, and especially in organization studies (Alvesson, Ashcraft and Thomas, 2008; Watson, 2008; Tietze and Musson, 2010), has conceptualized identity as the subjective meaning and experience through which people attempt to answer the questions of who they are and how to act. Human notions of who we are and how, as a result, we should act are shaped by the values, expectations, allegiances, norms and discourses in which we are immersed. The social groups—family, friends, school and religious community—to which a person belongs constantly influence the notion of self. As Sluss and Ashfort (2007) argue, people form close and strong relationships with certain members from such groups. Over time, these relationships become cornerstones of personal identity that are used as assessment mechanisms for understanding the self.

A person's self-understanding is largely predicated on roles: behavioural expectations associated with a particular position. The self is thus a combination of the different roles required by the various identities a person assumes. Given the multiple roles a person takes on during his or her everyday life (mother, daughter, friend, spouse, worker, member of a community, etc.), it can be expected that at some point competing claims from the different roles may appear. When this happens, decisions must be taken in order to resolve the dissonance. In these decisions, the identity cornerstones formed by social relationships aid, along with values and norms, the determination of which roles will be enacted.

Modern Latin American women's daily routines include multiple roles, among which those of caring for the home, the children and the elderly or infirm, as mentioned before, remain important. Maternity, with all that this involves, reshapes the different roles and gives rise to feelings of confusion as tension appears. As Haynes (2008) points out professional identity and mothering identity are complexly entwined with both identities subjected to norms and socialization processes within their professional realm and in society at large. In a study involving 24 executive women already enrolled in an executive MBA in Colombia, this confusion and tension is evident when asked about their different roles in the domestic and professional realms. They expressed their belief that balancing both professional and domestic roles are possible until the moment that maternity or the possibility of it appears. At that point, they *want* to be full-time mothers *and* full-time professionals, but they come to the realization that they cannot do both. Others do not know what they want to be, or feel that they have to choose one role over the other, knowing that whichever decision will have consequences for their identities (Idrovo and Hernaez, 2012). The simple fact of enrolling in an MBA adds confusion and tension to the competing roles and increases the chances of dropping out of the program.

13.5 Gender stereotypes

To top all this, strong gender stereotypes still play a subtle role in keeping women from enrolling in an MBA. One has to do with the social pressure that family and relatives exercise over women to have children sooner rather than later and if they are able to afford it to work part-time in order to take care of the children's upbringing. As Manola Sánchez (2013), dean of the Adolfo Ibañez Business School in Chile, states

> at that age, between 25-35 years old, . . . there is strong social pressure to give priority to personal rather than professional life, for young women to get married and have children, and postpone professional decisions like taking an MBA. . . . However, things might be changing in Chile today, and it is becoming more common to delay maternity.

Strong social pressure to fulfil women's role as mothers will impact women's decision to enrol in MBA programs.

Money is also an issue. As well as in other parts of the world, going through an MBA program is expensive. Financing comes generally from two sources: (1) the companies that support the candidate considering his or her potential and the positive impact that this candidate will have later on in the company; and (2) through personal finance. Most of the time it is a mixture of both, at least in Latin America. But on all fronts, women face challenges.

In a survey of the incoming class (40) of an executive MBA program in Bogotá, Colombia, students were asked to give an explanation for the lower percentage of female participants in the MBA class.[2] The majority agreed that one of the key reasons was that managers in companies are generally male, and therefore, candidates for the MBA are more likely to be male. The female talent pool at the manager level is smaller. A research study from FutureWork Institute (2010) established that women occupy 24% of administrative and managerial positions in South America and 29% in Central America. These numbers are more or less equivalent with the percentage of women enrolling in MBA programs. In absolute numbers, corporations end up sponsoring more male candidates than female. Yet that is not all. A glance at the senior management offers a grimmer scenario: only 22% of this level of management in Latin America is female (Grant Thornton International Business Report, 2012). Going up the ladder the percentage becomes even smaller. According to the latest McKinsey & Company Report (2013), *Women Matters: A Latin America Perspective*, women hold 8% of executive committee positions and 5% of board positions on average over six countries in the region: Argentina, Brazil, Colombia, Chile, México and Peru. The report also underlines that "despite the large proportion of female graduates in Latin America and the significant numbers who join the continent's companies at entry level, very few reach the top" (2013: 1). In other words along the corporate ladder female presence diminishes and a vicious circle is perpetuated in relation to women enrolling in an MBA program. There are fewer women managers therefore fewer women to sponsor and subsequently fewer women to promote to higher levels.

---

2 Survey taken to the incoming MBA class at INALDE Business School—Universidad de La Sabana, Colombia, as part of an in-house research project regarding the perception of the MBA program.

At the personal level financing causes similar challenges for women. As enrolling in an MBA requires a significant investment a family consensus needs to be reached. The decision concerns whether to invest that amount of money and effort in the woman or the man, keeping in mind that the expected return of the program will be a better job and an increase in income and status. The couple, and most of the time the extended family as well due to the important role that it plays in family decisions in Latin America, are called on to discuss whether they are ready to face the possibility of the woman earning more than her partner or husband. As a current management professor in Chile (2013) asserted: "My father-in-law was really opposed to me doing the MBA and later on the PhD. . . . So, now we just don't tell him anymore that I earn more than my husband." If the resources and the possibilities suffice for both of them then there is no problem, but if the resources are enough for only one of them, usually the decision will be to privilege the personal development of the man over the woman. In making this decision all the other issues mentioned before come into play: the importance of the woman in caring for the children and the fear that a double-shift turns into a triple-shift with the academic requirements. This should not be seen as imposed from the outside solely; much of the time this is self-imposed on the part of women. As one Colombian woman in the 2013 MBA entry class responded to the question of why she thought there were fewer women in the MBAs, "we (women) have historically and willingly subordinated our professional development in benefit of family responsibilities." As this participant points out, caring responsibilities for children and family members have taken precedence, up to this time, in women's decisions to enrol in MBA programs.

13.6 How to increase the number of women enrolling in MBA programs

There are several ways to increase the number of women enrolling in MBAs. But the keyword to turn them into reality is flexibility. Flexibility should be seen as more than only a buzz word. It needs to be understood as a criterion that allows the accommodation of elements that are different from the norm, especially if the norm considers only half of the possibilities and not even that much.

Family, education and work have evolved following a pattern of assigned roles that have in turn created structures with specific characteristics. These characteristics in the working realm fit male candidates, while the family structures fit female candidates. But economic and social changes have transformed these scenarios rendering the structures useless or harmful in the worst case. The massive entrance of women into the labour force is one of those events that has had a great impact on family, education and work structures, for it is a situation that requires urgent redefinition in order to better accommodate the new reality. As different academic (Kelly et al., 2008), policy (Families and Work Institute & SHRM, 2012) and government documents (cf. Department of Work and Pension, 2010; Rodríguez, 2012) point out, finding ways to do exactly this has become crucial for businesses, the economy and society. When applied to work, flexibility means control over when, where or how much people work, enabling them to organize both how to take care of their other responsibilities and to establish their priorities. With the aid of technology and ad hoc communication processes, the implementation of flexible work practices has proven good for those businesses and employees that have adopted them. But they are not common practices yet. The same is happening in education, especially MBA programs. Flexibility has not yet permeated modes and curricula to accommodate all types of candidates with the same quality education. Those most affected by the unbending structures are women that need to juggle different responsibilities at the same time. To attract more women to MBA programs some flexibility needs to be introduced at different levels.

13.7 Flexibility in program modality

As the AMBA report shows, most of the MBA programs in Latin America fall into the part-time or executive category (Murgatroyd, 2012). Full-time MBA programs are the minority and the programs with lower numbers of students. When women already enrolled in a top MBA program in Monterrey, México, were asked about ideas of how to make an MBA program more attractive for women, most of the answers revolved around making schedules more flexible, including Saturday as a possibility and combining the program with online courses. In the words of one of the woman surveyed: "Flexible schedules that fit the other roles women play at work and as member of a family". Virginia Sarria (2013), assistant dean at IAE Business School in Argentina, agrees that more attractive formats for women could increase female enrolment: "For example a three-day format that includes Saturday, every three weeks, could be very appealing to women who are already working at a managerial position, have family responsibilities and want to do an MBA." Most MBA programs overlook this fact and are designed, as the majority of working structures, for a person who does not have these kinds of responsibilities.

Childcare is also something women think will help. "Having activities for kids that run parallel to some of the classes would surely help" says another of the Mexican women surveyed. "This will not only benefit women but also men" adds Rendón (2013), admissions director for a leading Colombian MBA program, "and will definitely send the message that the program is unique and aware of the needs of men and women, of the family".

13.8 Flexibility in curricula

Also key in developing attractive MBA programs for women is the content of the academic offering. The women surveyed in the Mexican business school suggested that courses that cover career development and how to manage personal image for women, keeping in mind that the business world is a male-dominated context, would be popular.

They also emphasized the need for courses that teach flexibility and diversity management and even mentioned the possibility of women-only courses. As Rendón (2013) also indicates "courses that recognize women's motivations as somewhat different from men's and help develop skills that manage and articulate those motivations, are not only teaching good business practice but making the program attractive to women". Courses focusing on the importance of men's roles in caring activities at home and how developing those skills will contribute to their overall development as people and managers are a powerful way of overcoming stereotypes, in turn facilitating women's entrance into MBA programs, in the short and medium term.

13.9 Various flexibilities

Another way of increasing the number of women in MBAs is to offer special scholarships for them and raise awareness in corporations about the benefits of having more women executives in upper management and as directors. As mentioned before money usually becomes a serious obstacle for women and tackling that issue directly will help ease the process for female candidates.

Having more female professors in the MBA program also will "lead by example" and demonstrate that it is an environment where structures are designed to support personal and professional development making it more "female-friendly" for potential women participants.

13.10 Closing the gap

Closing the gap between the numbers of men and women enrolled in MBA programs in Latin America requires interventions from different angles. Some of them are the responsibility of the educational institutions offering the programs; some are in the hands of the people running the businesses and corporations that will hire those participants later on or are their actual employers; and finally some depend solely on the female candidates themselves: deciding whether the program is worth the sacrifices they might need to make. Although the road ahead might seem long it is imperative that all of the players involved start taking steps towards achieving this goal.

References

AACSB International, 2014. Business School Data Trends. www.aacsb.edu/en/publications/datareports/data-guide.aspx (accessed 13.04.14).
Alvesson, M., Ashcraft, K.L., Thomas, R., 2008. Identity matters: reflections on the construction of identity scholarship in organization studies. Organization, 5–28.

AMBA (Association of MBAs), forthcoming. Intake & Graduation Report: Latin America and the Caribbean. Information provided by Carlos Ramos, International Advisor, Association of MBAs.

AMBA (Association of MBAs), 2012. Value of Hiring an MBA. www.mbaworld.com/Employers-and-Partners/Value-of-an-MBA.aspx (accessed 14.11.13).

Atal, J., Ñopo, N.H., Winder, N., 2009. New Century, Old Disparities. Gender and Ethnic Wage Gaps in Latin America. US Department of Research and Chief Economist. www.iadb.org/res/publications/pubfiles/pubIDB-WP-109.pdf (accessed 12.11.13).

Baltes, B., Heydens-Gahir, H., 2003. Reduction of work–family conflict through the use of selection, optimization, and compensation behaviors. Journal of Applied Psychology 88, 1005–1018.

Carlson, D.S., Kacmar, K.M., Williams, L.J., 2000. Construction and initial validation of a multidimensional measure of work–family conflict. Journal of Vocational Behavior 56, 249–276.

Department of Work and Pension, 2010. Flexible working: working for families, working for business. Department of Work and Pension, London. www.dwp.gov.uk/docs/family-friendly-task-force-report.pdf (accessed 10.30.13).

ECLAC (Economic Commission for Latin America and the Caribbean), 2006. Social Panorama for Latin America. Economic Commission for Latin America and the Caribbean, Santiago de Chile. www.eclac.org/publicaciones/xml/4/27484/PSI2006_FullText.pdf (accessed 15.11.13).

ECLAC (Economic Commission for Latin America and the Caribbean), 2012. Social Panorama for Latin America. Economic Commission for Latin America and the Caribbean, Santiago de Chile. www.cepal.org/publicaciones/xml/8/49398/2012-960-PSI_WEB.pdf (accessed 15.11.13).

Families and Work Institute & Society for Human Resources Management (SHRM), 2012. Workflex: The Essential Guide to Effective and Flexible Workplaces. Families and Work Institute, SHRM Publishers, 372.

FutureWork Institute, 2010. Women Manager in Latin America. A FutureWork Institute Research Study. FutureWork Institute, New York. www.futureworkinstitute.com/globaldiversity/map/latin/Women_in_Management_in_Latin_America--A_Research_Study.pdf (accessed 29.10.13).

Grant Thornton International Business Report, 2012. Women in senior management: still not enough. Grant Thornton, Australia. www.internationalbusinessreport.com/files/ibr2012%20-%20women%20in%20senior%20management%20master.pdf (accessed 29.10.13).

Greenhaus, J.H., Beutell, N.J., 1985. Sources of conflict between work and family roles. Academy of Management Review 10, 76–88.

Haynes, K., 2008. Transforming identities: accounting professionals and the transition to motherhood. Critical Perspectives on Accounting 19, 620–642.

Hernáez, M., Idrovo, S., 2010. Armonizando trabajo y familia en Bogotá-Colombia: La conexión doméstica, Revista Oikos 29, 65–90.

Hertz, T., Campos, A.P., Zezza, A., Azzarri, C., Winters, P., Quiñones, E.J., Davis, B., 2008. Wage inequality in International Perspective: Effects of Location, Sector, and Gender. ESA Working paper. Food and Agricultural Organization of the United Nations, Agricultural and Development Economics Division (ESA), Rome, Italy. www.fao.org/fileadmin/user_upload/riga/pdf/Hertz_et_al_Wage_Inequality.pdf (accessed 29.11.13).

Heslin, P., 2005. Conceptualizing and evaluating career success. Journal of Organizational Behavior 26, 113–136.

Hewlett, S.A., 2007. Off-Ramps and On-Ramps: Keeping Talented Women on the Road to Success. Harvard Business School Press, Boston, MA.

Idrovo, S., Hernaez, M., November 2012. "Housewife": What does it have to do with me? Domestic work and identity among executive women in Colombia. Paper presented at *Home and Identity*: The Private-Public Nexus Conference, Rome, Italy, pp.14–15.

Jaén, M.H., October 20–22, 2013. Responsible Leadership: A challenge for Latin American Graduate Management Education, presentation at the XLVIII Annual CLADEA Conference, Rio de Janeiro, Brazil.

Jain, D., 2013. Engendering economic progress. In: Calderón Mogaña, C. (coord.), Redistributing Care. The Policy Challenge, United Nations, ECLAC, Santiago, Chile, pp. 19–47.

Kelly, E., Kossek, E., Hammer, L., Durham, M., Bray, J., Chermack, K., Murphy, L., Kaskubar, D., 2008. Getting there from here: research on the effects of work-family initiatives on work-family conflict and business outcomes. The Academy of Management Annals 2(1), 305–349.

Kilgour, M.A., 2013. The global compact and gender inequality: a work in progress. Business & Society 52(1), 105–134.

Krantz, G., Berntsson, L., Lundberg, U., 2005. Total workload, work stress and perceived symptoms in Swedish male and female white-collar employees. European Journal of Public Health 15, 209–214.

McKinsey & Company, 2013. Women Matters: A Latin American Perspective. Unlocking women's potential to enhance corporate performance, Brazil. www.mckinsey.com.br/LatAm Extranet/global_locations/Americas/LatAm_Office/en/PDF/Women%20Matter%20Latin%20 America.pdf (accessed 21.11.13).

Murgatroyd, G.B., 2012. Association of MBAs. Accreditation Review 9:3—Accreditation in Numbers: The Developing Postgraduate Management Education Market. Business Leadership Review IX: III.

OECD, 2010. Atlas of Gender and Development: How Social Norms Affect Gender Equality in non-OECD Countries. OECD Publishing. doi: 10.1787/9789264077478-en.

Parasuranam, S., Simmers, C., 2001. Type of employment, work-family conflict and well-being: a comparative study. Journal of Organizational Behavior 22, 551–568.

Rodríguez Enríquez, C., May 15–17, 2012. Work-Family Balance Issues in Latin America: A Road-map to National Care Systems, Paper Presented at Good Practices in Family Policy Making: Family Policy Development, Monitoring and Implementation: Lessons Learnt, New York.

Sluss, D.M., Ashfort, B., 2007. Relational identity and identification: defining ourselves through work relationships. Academy of Management Review 32, 9–32.

Tietze, S., Musson, G., 2010. Identity, identity work and the experience of working from home. Journal of Management Development 29, 148–156.

US Department of Labor and US Bureau of Labor Statistics, 2011. Women in the Labor Force: A Databook. US Department of Labor, EU. www.bls.gov/cps/wlf-databook-2011.pdf (accessed 12.11.13).

UIS (UNESCO Institute of Statistics), 2012. Compendio Mundial de la Educación. UNECO, Montreal. www.uis.unesco.org/Education/Documents/ged-2012-sp.pdf (accessed 13.11.13).

UNESCO, 2012. World Atlas of Gender Equality in Education. UNESCO, Paris, France. www. unesdoc.unesco.org/images/0021/002155/215522e.pdf (accessed 10.10.13).

Vassolo, R., Castro, J., Gomez-Mejía, L., 2011. Managing in Latin America: common issues and a research agenda. Academy of Management Perspectives 25(4), 22–36.

Watson, T.J., 2008. Managing identity: identity work, personal predicaments and structural circumstances. Organization 15, 121–143.

Interviews

Rendón, Damián, Director of Admission at INALDE Business School in Colombia. Interview with the author. 16 October 2013. The interview was conducted in Spanish. The translation is the author's.

Sánchez, Manola, Dean of the Adolfo Ibanez Business School in Chile. Personal interview with the author. 22 October 2013. The interview was conducted in Spanish. The translation is the author's.

Sarria, Virginia, Assistant Dean of IAE Business School in Argentina Personal interview with the author. 12 September 2013. The interview was conducted in Spanish. The translation is the author's.

Zapata, Laura, MBA Director at the EGADE Business School, Tecnológico de Monterrey in Mexico. Written interview with the author. 3 October 2013. The interview was written in Spanish. The translation is mine.

14

Persistent labour market inequalities

What do the French management schools do for their female students?

Krista Finstad-Milion and Christine Morin-Estèves
ICN Business School, France

The first jobs of female graduates of French management schools are consistently lower in pay and responsibility than those of male graduates. This raises questions of gender equality in the labour market and about female graduate behaviour in terms of career decisions. The achievements of the French *Grandes Écoles,* whose role is to prepare their students for the realities of the labour market and supply organizations with decision-makers, is called into question. In this chapter, the authors present the key role played by the *Conférence des Grandes Écoles* (CGE) association in going beyond collecting female/male (f/m) statistics from member schools for creating tools to map collective progress made, and to sensitizing staff and students about sources of gender inequalities. Preliminary results suggest future challenges lie in encouraging greater female representation in decision-making committees, organizing more gender-friendly activities to sensitize students and staff alike, and formalizing a clear gender equality strategy complete with an action plan. By adopting such practices, management schools would better exemplify citizenship behaviour.

14.1 Introduction

Management schools continue to be accused worldwide of being gender blind or at best gender neutral (Mavins, Bryan and Waring, 2004), and of falling short of their responsibilities toward key stakeholders, notably their female students (Ibeh et al., 2008). Although the schools attract, and admit in equal numbers, female and male candidates, questions arise when observing the significantly lower salaries and job responsibilities of female graduates in the labour market (Dey and Hill, 2007). In addition, studies comparing young graduates' job satisfaction conclude that females are equally satisfied as males, although less paid and with less stable positions (Higher Education Advisory, 2012). Other studies underline that highly educated women managers, later on in their careers, experience less satisfaction than their male counterparts in terms of job responsibility and fulfilment due to choices made earlier with little understanding of the consequences on job perspectives (Ely, 2014). Such observations warrant further investigation with regard to the role responsible management schools play in preparing female students for making career decisions and meeting career challenges.

The French case is of particular interest as statistical and legal evidence alternates between manifestations of resistance to change and real headway made in terms of addressing gender inequalities. In this chapter we use a gender lens to describe the French context of management education which can be read through recent political, legal and economic developments on the national and European levels. Next we discuss a key player on the national level notably the *Conférence des Grandes Écoles* (CGE), a French association bringing together a large number of business and engineer schools around the need to address critical, social and economic issues with the state. We then outline recent solutions adopted by the CGE to address gender inequalities in member schools. Finally, preliminary results of CGE actions are shared suggesting specific challenges which lie ahead for management schools concerned by insufficiently addressed gender inequalities leading to an underutilization of their female talent.

14.2 The French and wider European context: recent approaches to gender inequalities

The question of equality between women and men in decision-making positions in the political world and in companies has been an ongoing subject of debate. Such a question warrants a survey of the literature in light of persistent inequalities revealed by French and European statistics. For example, the National Institute for Statistics and Economic Studies indicated in a 2010 report that "in making parity obligatory in the list system, the 2000 law allowed women to become almost as numerous as men in the European Parliament, and in regional and municipal councils of communities of more than 3,500 inhabitants" (INSEE, 2010: 9). The same report pointed out, however, that "ten years after the parity law, in June 2000, the National Assembly and Senate remain essentially masculine. Only one out of five parliamentary representatives is female". What holds true for the political world also holds true for the labour market, more generally. The report added that "in 2008, women occupy slightly less than one-third of management positions in enterprises in the private and semi-public sectors and are even less represented at the senior executive level (17.1%)" (INSEE, 2010: 11).

Compensation trends reflect the same inequalities. According to the professional association for the employment of managers, salaries of female managers remain consistently lower than those of male managers. The annual average gross salary of women in 2010 was €43,000, which was €7,000 less than that of men. For managers under the age of 30, the annual gross salary median gap was €1,000 in favour of men. In the same report, this gap expands between the different generations of managers reaching a difference of €14,000 in favour of male managers 55 years and over (APEC, 2011: 5).

Legislation has played a role on several occasions, on the European and French levels, in an attempt to reduce and eventually eradicate male/female salary inequalities. Among the latest French laws, article 99 of 9 November 2010 law on retirement reform forced enterprises with 50 employees or more to reach an agreement, by no later than 1 January 2012, and implement an action plan to reduce the pay gap between women and men (Liaisons sociales, September 2011: 37). Moreover, on the European level, the principle of equality of male/female compensation has been addressed by a series of treaties, decrees and charters: the 1957 Treaty of Rome, the decrees of 1975 and 1976, the Community Charter of 9 December 1989, followed by the 1997 Treaty of Amsterdam, the 7 December 2000 Charter of Fundamental Rights (Male/Female equality) and the 2007 Treaty of Lisbon. In December 2009, with the entry into force of the Treaty of Lisbon, the Charter of Fundamental Rights attained the same legal force as a treaty.

The European treaties are the foundation of the European Union: all actions undertaken by the EU find their source in these treaties which are approved freely and democratically by all the member states. Therefore if a political issue is not referred to in a treaty, the commission cannot make legal proposals for this issue. The European treaties are regulatory agreements adopted by the member states of the EU. They define the objectives pursued by the EU, the operational rules for European institutions, the procedures to follow for decision-making and the relations between the EU and member states.

14.2.1 A key player on the national level: the conference of *Grandes Écoles*

The association *Conférences des Grandes Écoles* (CGE), created in 1973, brings together business and engineering schools and research institutes, both French and foreign. It has a distinct French characteristic, and is at times accused of being elitist, as it represents stand-alone schools including what Thietart (2009) refers to as being the closest to what can be called the French generic business school. The *Grandes Écoles* are characterized by permanent specialized faculty, highly selective entry exams and close contacts with the business community. There are 32 *Grandes Écoles* members of the business or management chapter of the CGE association. Similar organizations to the CGE are found in other European countries. These would be those bringing together university rectors, executive heads or presidents although not especially of business and engineer schools. Examples of these in Europe would be the *Hochschul Rektoren Konferenz* (HRK) in Germany, Universities UK in the United Kingdom, the *Conferencia de Rectores de las Universidades Españolas* in Spain and the *Conferenza dei Presidi delle facoltà di Economia e Scienze Statistiche* for Economics faculties in Italy.

The CGE's mandate is to seek excellence in its relations with the business world and civil society. By vocation it encourages think tanks and coordinates work groups on teaching, pedagogy and research, in the aim of improving social well-being and sustainable development. The CGE represents its members and the best interests of the community before public entities, be they national, communitarian or international. It strives to maintain and foster open-mindedness and solidarity, in the interest of uniting its members (CGE website, 2014).

The CGE started carrying out studies in 2007 on male/female representation in member schools. Tables 14.1 and 14.2 present the first two study results obtained by 38 schools, all members of the CGE.

The two preceding tables show that females represent less than one-third of the students in engineering schools, whereas in management schools they are as numerous as males. The total student registration in the *Grandes Écoles* participating in the study indicates the predominance of males owing to the high proportion of males in engineering schools. These two school populations constitute a significant body of tomorrow's

Table 14.1 **Representation by gender in the French *Grandes Écoles* (2007–2008)**

Source: CGE Services.

Schools	Total registration	Total of polled population	Number of females	Representation rate	Number of males	Representation rate
Engineering	96,291	62.3%	30,157	31.3%	66,134	68.7%
Management	47,801	30.9%	23,801	49.8%	24,000	50.2%
Other schools	10,516	6.8%	5,252	49.9%	5,264	50.1%
Total	154,608	100%	59,210	38.3%	95,398	61.7%

Table 14.2 **Representation by gender in the French *Grandes Écoles* (2008–2009)**

Source: CGE Services.

Schools	Total registration	Total of polled population	Number of females	Representation rate	Number of males	Representation rate
Engineering	105,613	63%	28,716	27.19%	76,897	72.81%
Management	53,664	32.01%	25,270	47.09%	28,394	52.91%
Other schools	8,371	4.99%	4,571	54.61%	3,800	45.39%
Total	167,648	100%	58,558	34.93%	109,090	65.07%

decision-makers in France. Consequently, as there are more male than female graduates of the *Grandes Écoles*, there is an overall greater pool of male candidates than female candidates to take on decision-making positions.

The present work focuses on female students in French management schools. In French management schools, contrary to the case of engineering schools, there is more or less equal representation of females and males, and this has occurred without the need for legislative intervention. Equal access to a business school education and diploma for women and men would seem to lead to equal access to decision-making positions. However, the comparison of starting salaries of female and male graduates reveals inequalities which raise questions as to the responsibility of the schools in light of the unexplained economic consequences for their graduates. Might business schools, not freely communicating gender pay discrepancies to key stakeholders, be accused of withholding information? Might there be an ethical or moral breach of contract, or case for poor service especially with respect to meeting the needs of female students? Indeed, such trends indicate that male graduates enjoy a greater capacity to pay back student loans than female graduates. For the female graduates a lower pay back capacity signifies greater economic insecurity. As pointed out in earlier studies (Dreher and Cox, 2000; Cocchiara, 2010), women receive lower financial returns from their educational investments than men do.

The Higher Education Advisory 2012 study based on 2011 CGE statistics (see Table 14.3) shows that male/female salary gaps appear as of the first year on the labour market:

> Whatever the type of work or the school, annual salary gaps between men and women are, on the average, slightly over €3,000 between the 2011 graduates (€35,134 versus €38,355 including bonuses). The same difference exists between engineers (€37,193 for males, €34,352 for females) and managers (respectively €42,012 and €36,251). (Headway Higher Education Advisory, 2012: 1)

Moreover, Table 14.3 shows that female management graduates are less likely to be employed 2 months after graduation and are less likely to hold a management position than their male homologues. Such results, may also hint at key findings of the French national statistics agency (INSEE) which concludes that "[f]or the same degree, specialty, and length of work experience, the risk of being unemployed [for young women] is over 7% greater than that of young men, during the first five years of their working life" (INSEE Première, February 2010: 4). In addition the CGE figures (Table 14.3) indicate that among working graduates, females have almost the same level of job satisfaction (4.0 out of a scale of 5) than their former male classmates (4.1), although when comparing gross annual salary including bonuses they earn €6,000 less during their first year on the labour market. Does this indicate that female graduates are satisfied with earning less than their male counterparts or is their job satisfaction based on different criteria than their male counterparts? Furthermore are the students, female and male alike, aware of "the gender pay gap" as a concept which identifies a persistent economic reality?

The *Grandes Écoles* education gives graduates an observed advantage on the French job market (Duru-Bellat and Kieffer, 2008), however with the same education young

Table 14.3 **Male/female graduates of the *Grandes Écoles* on the labour market**

Source: Adapted from Higher Education Advisory, 25 June 2012.

2011 Graduating class	Engineers			Managers			Total		
	Male	Female	Total	Male	Female	Total	Male	Female	Total
% Professionally active (including industrial research contracts)	70.9	65.2	69.2	74.2	72.9	73.8	71.7	68.5	70.6
Net rate of employment	87.8%	80.9%	85.7%	84.7%	81.9%	83.5%	87.0%	81.3%	84.9%
% Permanent contract/graduates currently employed	84.5	69.6	80.2	83.9	75.2	79.4	84.2	71.9	79.8
% Manager status or similar/graduates currently employed	94.0	85.4	91.5	84.6	76.2	80.2	91.9	81.2	88.1
% Employed less than 2 months after graduation/already working	84.5	83.1	84.1	80.9	75.9	78.5	83.8	80.2	82.5
Job satisfaction (scale of 1 to 5)	4.1	4.1	4.1	4.1	4.0	4.1	4.1	4.0	4.1
Gross annual remuneration not including bonuses (Fr)	€35,556	€31,865	€33,079	€35,249	€32,830	€34,164	€33,925	€32,239	€33,376
Total annual remuneration including bonuses (Fr)	€36,253	€33,793	€35,559	€39,773	€39,773	€35,402	€37,651	€34,425	€36,148
Gross remuneration not including bonuses	€34,238	€32,389	€33,725	€36,704	€33,411	€35,226	€34,828	€32,796	€34,173
Gross remuneration including bonuses	€37,193	€34,352	€36,406	€42,012	€36,251	€39,244	€38,355	€35,134	€37,268

male graduates of the *Grandes Écoles* integrate into the job market more successfully, economically speaking, than young women (Ipsos Public Affairs/GEF February 2007). Moreover, in the IPSOS/GEF study, the majority of females (65%) with degrees from a *Grande École* perceive differences between male and female graduate career pathways that only a minority of males (37%) perceives. Are male graduates blind or neutral to the challenges their female counterparts face when embarking on a career? The above CGE trends echo national trends. From the very moment young French women enter the job market, the employment and salary gap appears and, in the years to follow, amplifies with age (Milewski, 2011: 351). It can thus be concluded that female graduates do not derive as great a financial benefit from their diploma on the job market as do male graduates.

In conclusion, female and male management students have equal access to the French *Grandes Écoles*, however, for freshly graduated females of the CGE, labour market inequalities quickly appear as they are less likely to be working two months after graduation, less likely to be working with a managerial status and have gross overall earnings including bonuses that are less than those received by their former male school mates. Discrimination affects female graduates in the labour market as well as in their own capacity to obtain a job. Such results raise questions about what the CGE schools are doing to ensure equal opportunities for female and male students and the extent to which female students are being prepared for anticipated labour market inequalities.

14.3 Dedication to addressing f/m equality issues in member schools

One particularly active work group of the CGE is the Female/Male (F/M) Equality Group that has 160 members, the majority of whom act as equality representatives for their school. Members, who are in charge of implementing and coordinating actions, meet in Paris on a bi-quarterly basis. To date, key projects include implementing a gender awareness-building kit (videos, interactive quiz and conference subjects with list of experts) for sensitizing staff as well as students, and deploying a barometer to allow the CGE to collect quantitative and qualitative data on the state of equality in the French member schools and to measure progress made annually.

As mentioned in the previous section, the CGE started to engage in the collection of gender-based statistics in 2007 to track the existence of equal opportunities and inequalities which appear during the admission and graduating stages of students in engineering and management schools. Since 2005 the CGE has also played an active role in signing, with the French government, agreements concerning the promotion of equal opportunities for students as well as staff. In March 2005 the CGE signed the first agreement promoting equality between men and women with the Minister of Parity and Equality indicating State commitment to equality for all with regard to access to teaching and the working world.

A second agreement was signed with the Minister of Women's Rights and the Minister of Higher Education and Research in January 2013 which resulted in the *Charte des Grandes Écoles*. This charter, developed by the F/M Equality Group of the CGE, describes and structures the implementation of the equality policy for member institutes. It has three main goals: (1) sensitize all students, both female and male, during their school years and build awareness among school personnel; (2) implement female-male equality (for staff and students); and (3) develop a policy to attract young female talent to traditionally male dominant areas of study (e.g. hard sciences, finance, entrepreneurship) (Charte des *Grandes Écoles*, 2013). The CGE derives its policy from the European Charter of Equality for women and men in local life and legal, economic and education considerations. Equality between women and men is important for society and democracy in addition to being a right.

It is the role and responsibility of all stakeholders in education to sensitize female and male students about equality and mutual respect between sexes (Giacalone, 2004). The students will transfer such values when taking on responsibilities as managers in the workplace and in their private lives. The CGE policy aims thus at accompanying the change in mentality with the belief that it is important for higher education institutes to build new models and transfer such models in course curriculum and workshops dedicated to equality. Finally the CGE policy states that education efforts must start well before the students enter the higher education institutes. Female students and student services in high schools must be made aware of the numerous opportunities available and most particularly in areas where women are under-represented such as in the hard sciences, technology, finance and entrepreneurship.

14.4 Solutions implemented: a barometer to trace progress over time

The objective of the CGE equality barometer is to obtain an annual report to assess male/female representation in management schools and to trace the evolution of key indicators over time. Statistics obtained for the starting year (2014) will allow the school members to map their progress annually. The purpose of the exercise is not to designate schools as good or bad but to progress collectively by mapping efforts, and sharing best practices among members.

The barometer is separated into sections and designed to collect information on the school itself, the students, the different staff categories, and the different committees in place. Questions concerning the students focus on the f/m ratio in the school and the f/m representation among the top students in each program. Questions concerning the staff focus on the f/m ratio per category of employee, the average salary per category of employee, the average salary increase, the average age of employees, and the f/m ratio for recruitment carried out during the year per category of employee. Female/male ratios and ages are collected for key decision-making committees: executive, directing, board of governors, academic, scientific and pedagogical. Information on the existence of student associations committed to f/m equality, coaching programs and women's clubs or networks are also included. One question also includes whether a section on f/m equality in internship reports is obligatory for the school. One final purpose of the barometer is the collection of information on the measurement of the impact of equality indicators and the existence of a strategic action plan in the member school with regards to equality.

Each school which signed the charter nominates an equality correspondent in charge of collecting and entering data on the online form. The equality correspondents themselves have four primary responsibilities. They must strive to (1) foster a culture of equality; (2) prepare students for their future working world; (3) monitor the barometer of equality; and (4) encourage a greater mix of males and females in certain branches of study (Charte d'Egalité, 2013). To do so the correspondents are expected to lead and coordinate sensitization actions for professional equality for students and school personnel, both female and male. They are required to identify and coordinate specific training initiatives for students to follow on a volunteer basis in order to prepare themselves for the working world (coaching, network building, negotiating first salary, etc.). In partnership with existing women's associations (e.g. *Elles bougent, Femmes & Sciences*), the correspondents address particularly imbalanced f/m ratios by promoting these fields of study to members of the less represented sex. The correspondents are responsible for maintaining and creating a general climate of respect by remaining attentive to potentially sexist behaviour of students and personnel. With the academic and program directors, the equality correspondent is responsible for monitoring school documents and communication tools. With the human resource director, the correspondent is to annually fill in a spreadsheet with indicators for staff according to level of responsibility, type of work and salary. With the head of student administration services, the correspondent collects statistics on the study specializations chosen by female and male students. With the head of alumni services, the correspondent collects graduate salary figures. Collecting statistics is thus very much a team effort and the sensitization of those involved is key to this phase of equality action implementation. To carry out this mission it has been advised that the correspondent spend 5 to 10% of her or his contract time on the associated tasks and that such a mission be taken into account for her or his annual interview.

14.5 Preliminary results of the barometer

An electronic questionnaire was sent out to all member school equality correspondents on 16 September 2014 with a request to send their school results by October 22 to be included in the preliminary finding report. Data were to be based on the 2012–2013 academic year. The preliminary results shared during an Equality Group meeting in autumn 2014 (CGE Equality Group internal document, 13 November 2014) mark a starting point in tracing progress and suggest specific challenges which lie ahead for schools concerned with addressing gender inequalities. The first wave of the responses presented below came from 33 of the member schools of which 30% were management schools and the other 70% engineer schools.

When we analyse the data results presented, three major school practices emerge which echo French data previously presented in this chapter. These practices raise questions of gender inequality, gender blindness or gender neutrality:

1. Males dominate positions in all decision-making committees. These include boards of governors (17% female and 83% male), boards of directors (31% female and 69% male), scientific boards (20% female and 80% male), executive boards (26% female and 74% male) and pedagogical committees (38% female and 62% male).

2. The majority of the schools do not organize special activities for their female students or staff: 79% do not offer activities commonly associated with female career needs such as coaching, professional project advice and salary negotiations. Few support their own women's networks: 34% have no network activity; 28% have one for students; 18% have one for staff, 20% have one for graduates. Forty-eight per cent do not support actions organized by student associations on the subject of f/m equality.

3. The majority of the schools do not have a strategic approach to gender equality. For 78% of the schools there is no measurement of the impact of actions taken. Only 18% of the schools responding had formalized an equality strategy; 27% had not at all. However 55% were currently working on a strategy. Finally, the preliminary results clearly revealed that in terms of a plan of action only 18% of the schools had a formalized plan; 46% were currently working on such a plan and 36% of the schools had no plan nor activity toward creating one (CGE, Groupe F/M Egalité, Barometer, 2014).

The preliminary results, based on 2012–2013 statistics, also confirm persistent CGE graduate salary trends previously identified. However the pay gap between female and male graduates is narrowing with male graduates of management schools earning an average salary, not including bonuses, of €35,500 compared to €33,900 for females. This can be compared to 2011 statistics (Table 14.3) with male business school graduates earning €35,249 compared to €32,830 for females. Although these results confirm once again that young women do not benefit as much as their male counterparts from their management degree in the labour market, the narrowing gap suggests that headway is being made. Nevertheless, the previously presented results comparing CGE school male and female staff salary and job responsibility levels, clearly indicate that gender inequalities are still well-embedded in critical operating modes in these schools which are responsible for educating future managers. The lack of initiatives currently in management schools to sensitize students and staff alike about gender inequalities suggest a general state of gender blindness or neutrality. Curiously enough, management schools teach statistics yet, until recently, have been blind to the possibility that the statistics they generate might offer real opportunities for learning. Hope for progress in the near future can be found in those CGE schools moving beyond simply collecting and transferring data to formalizing strategies and for some clear action plans.

14.6 Conclusion

It is necessary for management schools to actively work, with their staff and students, to increase awareness of the realities of the working world and promote greater transparency regarding the likely consequences of early career choices and behaviours on the labour market. This would allow for greater opportunities for equality in terms of employment, salaries and job responsibilities for key stakeholders, namely female students. Beyond heightened attractiveness in the media for respecting women's rights, management schools actively committed to f/m equal opportunities would also set an example to their social and economic communities in terms of citizenship. Such an observation has been underlined by the European Commission (European Commission Report on progress on equality between women and men in 2010, 2011: 17). It is thus in the best interests of French management schools to involve staff in working with students, especially female, during their education to build awareness of persistent gender inequalities they will be facing in their future career. By doing so, the management schools will exemplify the socially responsible behaviour they teach in the classroom.

References

APEC (March 2011) Femmes cadres et hommes cadres, des inégalités professionnelles qui persistent. Paris, France: Département Etudes et Recherches. www.cadres.apec.fr/Emploi/content/download/139397/.../APEC_femmes.pdf (accessed 11.01.14).

CGE F/M Equality group internal document written by Cécile Kassel (ESTP) and Brigitte Porée (CGE) distributed to and discussed with group members at equality group meeting on 13 November 2014 at Novancia School, Paris, France.

Charte pour l'égalité entre Femmes et Hommes dans les établissements d'enseignement supérieur et de recherche, 28 janvier 2013, Ministère de l'Enseignement Supérieur et de la Recherche, Ministère des Droits des Femmes. www.cge.asso.fr/qui-sommes-nous/commissions/5-diversite/groupes-de-travail (accessed 12.04.14).

Cocchiara, F. K., Kwesiga, E., Bell, M.P., Baruch, Y., 2010. Influences on perceived career success: findings from US graduate business degree alumni. Career Development International 15(1), 39–58.

Conférence des Grandes Ecoles website. www.cge.asso.fr (accessed 12.9.14).

Dey, J.G., Hill, C., 2007. Behind the pay gap, American Association of University Women Educational Foundation, Washington, DC. www.aauw.org/research/upload/behindPayGap.pdf (accessed 11.20.14).

Dreher, G.F., Cox, T.H., 2000. Labor market mobility and cash compensation: the moderating effects of race and gender. Academy of Management Journal 43, 890–900.

Duru-Bellat, M., Kieffer, A., 2008. From the Baccalauréat to higher education in France: shifting inequalities. Population (English Edition) 63, 119–154.

Ely, R., Stone, P., Ammerman, C., 2014. Rethink what you know about high achieving women, Harvard Business Review. December. www.hbr.org/2014/12/rethink-what-you-know-about-high-achieving-women (accessed 12.04.14).

European Commission, 2011. Report on progress on equality between women and men in 2010 Publications Office of the European Union, Luxembourg. www.ec.europa.eu/justice/gender-equality/files/progressreport_equalwomen_2010_en.pdf (accessed 11.4.14).

Giacalone, R.A., 2004. A transcendent business education for the 21st century. Academy of Management Learning & Education 3, 415–420.

Headway Higher Education Advisory, 25 June 2012. www.headwayadvisory.com/blog/apres-une-grande-ecole-deviennent-les-hommes-les-femmes (accessed 12.09.14).

Ibeh, K., Carter, S., Poff, D., Hamill, J., 2008. How focused are the world's top-rated Business Schools on educating women for global management? Journal of Business Ethics 83, 65–83.

INSEE Première, 2010. Femmes et hommes en début de carrière: les femmes commencent à tirer profit de leur réussite scolaire 1284, 1–4.

INSEE, 2010. Chiffres clés, Egalité Hommes Femmes.

Ipsos Public Affairs/GEF, 2007. Parcours professionnels des diplômé(e)s des *grandes écoles*. www.grandesecolesaufeminin.fr/pdf/etude_gef_2007_regards_croises_hommes_femmfe.pdf (accessed 12.04.14).

Liaisons Sociales, Numéros juridiques, septembre 2011, La discrimination, l'égalité professionnelle, p. 37.

Mavins, S., Bryan, P., Waring, T., 2004. Unlearning gender blindness: new directions in management education. Management Decision 42(3/4), 562–578.

Milewski, F., 2011. Pourquoi les politiques publiques sont-elles si peu suivies d'effets ? In: Milewski, F., Périvier, H. (Eds.), Les discriminations entre les femmes et les hommes. Sciences Po, Paris, France, pp. 343–373.

Thiétart, R.-A., 2009. The research challenge of French business schools: the case of the *Grandes Écoles*. Journal of Management Development 28(8), 711–717.

15

Still too soon to forget "women"?

Making the case for the importance of gender diversity in management education: a study of India and the United States

Lynda Moore
Simmons School of Management, USA

Ujvala Rajadhyaksha
St Mary's College, USA

Stacy Blake-Beard
Simmons School of Management, USA

Globalization, changing workforce demographics, and contemporary social and economic agendas have driven business schools to address diversity. However, gender and diversity education is not yet integrated into mainstream management education and we maintain that gender diversity, as part of management education, must be pulled to the top of the business school agenda. We focus on gender, as women are globally the largest under-utilized group, and are a growing part of the global talent pipeline that companies need in order to remain competitive. We trace the connection between trends in industry, drivers of diversity training in business, and their subsequent impact on management education. Based on our review (or curriculum audit), we argue that management education has not met the gender diversity needs of our students, business and society. We provide data from India and the United States as case studies from emerging and Western economies and as a microcosm of culturally different contexts and business school challenges. We find differences in the rationale for and interpretations of the term "diversity" and in the impact on management education in the two countries. Although the definition and practices of diversity vary in each country, gender and the increasing attention to the issue of bringing women into the workforce and into leadership positions are shared. While diversity education appears more widespread in both industry and business schools in the United States, both countries appear to marginalize the diversity agenda, particularly along the lines of gender. We argue that management education, across national borders, must more adequately address gender diversity in order to prepare future managers for global leadership roles.

15.1 Introduction

In this chapter we conduct a cross-cultural exploration of the evolution of management education as it relates to teaching gender and diversity within India and the United States. We believe that gender and diversity represent key cultural issues that management education needs to address to prepare future international leaders. Despite the widespread recognition of the importance of diverse and inclusive organizations in both India and the United States, business schools in each country have yet to deliver the curriculum needed to foster this economic and social business imperative. Both India and the United States have had historically diverse populations and have striven to support this diversity. A stronger and more formal emphasis on diversity education in the United States has resulted in greater numbers of women and under-represented groups moving into management positions. By and large, however, it appears that gender and diversity education remain marginalized within the mainstream discourse in business education in both the United States (e.g. Reynolds, 1999; Sinclair, 1995a; Smith, 2000) and in India. Throughout the chapter, we discuss diversity education as a dominant framework as gender is typically subsumed under the term diversity; however, we focus more specifically on gender as we argue that the creation of academic space for the discussion of gender issues in management has been challenging worldwide, as evidenced by the recent focus on gender inequality from the United Nations (Kilgour and Flynn, 2011).

We choose to focus on gender specifically in our discussion of diversity education because the status of women in society at large, and challenges faced by women students within business classrooms in particular, warrants this attention. Women are the largest under-utilized minority group across the globe. According to the 2009 Society for Human Resource Management (SHRM) global research on diversity and inclusion, 79% of executives named women as the most important diversity group (SHRM, 2009).

This acknowledgement can be attributed to three significant trends realized in recent years. First, the increased number of women in the workforce in recent decades has contributed to higher productivity levels (International Labour Office, 2009). Specifically, the US workforce experienced an increase of almost 38 million women in the last 30 years, accounting for a quarter of the country's gross domestic product (GDP) (McKinsey and Company, 2009). Simply, the more women in the workface, the more per capita income rises (Deloitte, 2011). Within India, too, women workers in urban areas and in certain sectors of the economy, notably software, have been on the rise (NASSCOM, 2011). Second, women hold incredible power as a consumer group. According to a 2011 Deloitte report, up to 80% of buying decisions are either made or influenced by women globally. As this diversity group gains earning power, it will be the single largest emerging market in the world. Finally, globalization and the digitization of business will continue to demand that companies nurture their human capital and foster creativity and innovation among employees. The inclusion of women in the workplace and in business schools that build the human capital for industry is essential to succeed in this venture.

Business schools have been noted as particularly challenging environments for women. Some research has shown that curriculum, classroom conduct and culture are structured to be more supportive of male communication patterns (Arbaugh, 2000; Sinclair, 1995). This differential treatment is not without costs; female alumni of prestigious business schools speak of the alienating and fraternity-like educational experiences that were endured because of the uneven number of women and the inattention to issues of gender in the curriculum and classroom delivery. Kantor (2013) describes a two-year experiment at Harvard Business School (HBS) to "remake gender relations". The early results of this experiment include that HBS's attention to gender had some positive effects for female students (increased grades, representation of prestigious scholar recipients and higher participation) and female faculty (higher course ratings, possibly less turnover—more women staying). The administrative leadership at HBS is continuing on with their experiment—their belief is that the school has made progress at the first level of addressing issues of gender. But they acknowledge that there is more work to do. Clearly, refocusing discussion on gender in management education is a task worth undertaking.

Our analysis of management education in India and the United States provides an exploration of challenges and opportunities in gender and management education within two different national contexts. The goal is to provide a forum to raise the visibility of gender in management education and to acknowledge the differences and difficulties in addressing this topic across cultural milieus. We begin with a discussion of the evolution of diversity education as it has been largely understood (in the US context) and its impact on business curricula. As mentioned earlier, we focus primarily on gender. We then examine differences in the use of the term "diversity" between the United States and India and move on to a discussion of gender and management education within the Indian context. Since data and research on gender and diversity in management education in India and in the United States are limited, we conduct a gender audit of management curricula to ascertain the current status with business schools. We conclude with observations on the state of gender and diversity issues in management education and situate our findings within institutional, cultural and national contexts in India and the United States, while asserting the continued global imperative for gender and diversity education.

15.2 Evolution and rationale of diversity education in the United States

Diversity education became standard in the US workplace following the Civil Rights Act of 1964 (from now on referred to as "the Act") (Anand and Winters, 2008). The Act prohibited discrimination based on race, gender or ethnicity in the hiring process of any company over 15 employees. In order to comply with the law, firms found it necessary to incorporate diversity education into their management and general employee training programs. These programs were created to inform employees how to abide by the new legal requirements of the Act. For many companies, the training was a one-day event and provided the participants with a list of dos and don'ts of the law and company policy. Thomas and Ely titled this phase of organizational diversity as the "discrimination and fairness paradigm" (Thomas and Ely, 1996). This paradigm focused on a "color and gender-blind conformism" with the assimilation of women and people of colour as the primary goal. In this phase of diversity education, firms aimed for equal treatment of all employees, limiting any acknowledgement of work-related or cultural differences.

In the late 1980s and 1990s, diversity education in business evolved from compliance training to sensitivity training (Anand and Winters, 2008). The goal of these programs was to raise awareness about the differences among employees and foster better working relationships. Thomas and Ely (1996) title this phase as the "access and legitimacy paradigm", where the primary goal was to increase an organization's tolerance of differences. In this paradigm, firms would identify the demographics of potential clientele and rely on their employees who possessed the same demographics to reach out to this client base. While this paradigm gave more power to minority employees, the diversity education programs still lacked the ability to create change in the employee's behaviour or the firm's culture. At that time, diversity education was still presented separately from overall business strategies. Many employees and managers did not believe that diversity training was a competence that would benefit a firm's bottom line (Anand and Winters, 2008). In the past decade, it has become more widely accepted that cultural competence— that is, a knowledge of cultural differences and the ability to incorporate them into the decision-making process—is essential for sustainable productivity (Anand and Winters, 2008). In 2004, diversity education for businesses grew to an eight-billion-dollar industry (Stevens and Ogunji, 2011).

There are two major motivations behind the growing importance of managing diversity in business organizations. First, globalization has made the US labour force and consumer base far more diverse than in the past. According to the US Census Bureau there were approximately 37.4 million immigrants living in the United States in 2009.

A significant number of Americans, 23.6%, identify themselves as a minority (US Census Bureau, 2009). Furthermore, the Census estimates a continual change in demographics in the American population. The workforce will also continue to transform with the equal opportunity laws already in place (Stevens and Ogunji, 2011). Second, the structure of firms is evolving to rely more on team-based work, replacing the traditional hierarchies and demanding more effective interactions between coworkers (Page, 2007). There is an increase in the demand for employees to effectively engage with colleagues who possess different perspectives. As the business culture is affected by globalization, businesses exert more pressure on academic institutions to improve their diversity training (Kulik and Roberson, 2008).

As the values of diversity-related competencies have increased, firms have allocated more funds to bring these skills to their employees and have encouraged business schools to incorporate them into their curriculum. However, with this expansion, the implementation of this training has become less standard, and therefore the results are harder to measure from firm to firm (Anand and Winters, 2008). Some research shows that, while the overall effect of diversity training remains unknown, there are indications that diversity education has in fact successfully influenced participants' understanding of the experiences, customs and cultures of different groups. Findings on the impact that diversity education has had on participants' attitudes and skills with actually managing diverse groups are less consistent (Kulik and Roberson, 2008). Notwithstanding these challenges, the widespread goal of diversity education today is to teach the value of inclusion, acknowledging differences and encouraging their expression (Stevens and Ogunji, 2011).

15.2.1 Diversity and gender in management education in the United States

Like business managers, business educators are also facing a growing need to anticipate and adjust to diversity in the development and delivery of curriculum (Arain and Tipu, 2007; Cornuel, 2005; Global Foundation for Management Education, 2008; Simpson, 2006). There is a range of complex demands facing management education that reflect the demands on organizations and managers today. These challenges arise from a number of different sources, including: (1) strong and growing global economic forces; (2) differences in organizational and cultural values; (3) cultural diversity among employees and customers; and (4) changing technology in products and processes (AACSB, 2010). In a report from AACSB's International Globalization of Management Education Task Force (2011), the impact of globalization is explored from both macro and micro perspectives. Their macro analysis is focused on broad trends in supply and demand, including demographics of the field and drivers of the trends of change. Their micro analysis explores behaviour from students, faculty and institutions that are elicited in response to globalization. Similar to AACSB's (2010, 2011) findings, Altbach, Reisburg and Rumbley's (2009) report on trends in global higher education indicates that this field is affected by a diverse set of factors including the speedy pace of globalization, the increasing mobility of students and scholars, the movement of academic programs and institutions across borders, the extraordinary impact of technology, and mass demand for higher education. The Global Foundation for Management Education (2008) identified five trends impacting management education: (1) integration of economies; (2) shifting demographics; (3) advancing speed of information and communication technology; (4) global sourcing of services; and (5) a rise in corporate social responsibility, governance and sustainability.

Each one of the reports referenced above points to the role of management education in preparing students to meet the demands related to leading and managing in an increasingly diverse workforce. What are business schools doing to prepare students to graduate with the ability to lead useful professional, societal and personal lives in an ever-changing context? Navarro (2008) identified six features of the ideal MBA curriculum: (1) multidisciplinary integration, (2) experiential learning, (3) soft-skill development, (4) global perspective, (5) information technology focus, and (6) ethics and corporate social responsibility. In his web-based survey of the core curricula at top-ranked business schools in the United States, Navarro found that the programs studied displayed a lack of emphasis on required multidisciplinary integration and experiential components. This study also noted that several management themes, particularly soft-skill development and globalization, were not adequately integrated into the core MBA curriculum. Soft-skill development refers to strong interpersonal skills, such as leadership, written and oral communication, critical thinking, aptitude for teamwork and overall social skills (Bidwell, Fiore and Salas, 2014). While there are some benefits to teaching these concepts via a "hidden curriculum" (where concepts like teamwork are offered but not specifically called out or focused upon), there are more and more calls to explicitly include the teaching of interpersonal skills in existing courses in business school curriculum.

Cornuel (2005) flags two noteworthy trends in management schools in Europe over the past 20 years—the trivialization of contributions from different components of different disciplines within management science and the predominance of the case method in pedagogical format. With the first trend, Cornuel (2005: 822) suggests that potential inputs from the social sciences (i.e. psychology, sociology) are dismissed too superficially. Simpson (2006) identifies a gap in prominent North American and European MBA programs that have a focus on analytical capabilities to the neglect of critical "softer" interpersonal and communication skills. The second trend, a predominance of the case method as a pedagogical tool, was institutionalized as a catalyst of group dynamics. Cornuel argues that the case method may be limited by the scope of students' empirical foundations, resulting in a lost opportunity to portray management scenarios in their true complexity. Our concern is different; we argue that case method discussions have the potential to re-create and re-confirm traditional hegemonic power dynamics that may silence the voices and perspectives of women.

These themes are undergirded by a pervasive yet lightly discussed phenomenon in management education. Mavin, Bryans and Waring (1999, 2004a) describe a process in management education called "male streaming". This concept, also labelled as "gender blindness" refers to the failure to recognize the relationship between management education and gender (Mavin and Bryans, 1999; Mavin, Bryans and Waring, 2004b). Simpson

(2006) and Sinclair (1995) both indicate that management education as it is currently carried out in higher education institutions is essentially masculine in nature. A more nuanced operationalization of gender—the valuation of masculine and diminishment of the feminine—continues to shape the culture and context in management education (Kelan and Jones, 2010). These trends, which represent a subtle masculinization of the MBA (Simpson, 2006), may contribute to the difficult experiences that women encounter as they are pursuing advanced degrees in management forums (Maitland, 2008).

As the HBS experiment exemplified, paying attention to issues of gender in terms of the MBA experience is no small feat. The administrators were interested in shifting the culture of the organization such that women were not automatically at a disadvantage because their gender was at odds with the practices, rites and rituals of an institution designed by and for men. They used a number of mechanisms and concepts to confront and address the nuanced, and sometimes overt, issues that women students and women faculty faced. Actions taken included grading software to catch possible biases in grade allocation, administrative selection of teams and study groups rather than student selection, hand raising coaching for female students and classroom management for female faculty. The extensive, and sometimes controversial, efforts at HBS speak to the importance, and challenges, of taking on the topic of gender. Administrators at HBS did so in part because they acknowledged that their efforts "could have an untold impact at other business schools, at companies populated by Harvard alumni, and in the Fortune 500, where only 21 women are CEOs" (Kantor, 2013).

A review of the top MBA programs on their offering of courses related to gender echo the concerns raised by the HBS administrators. Of Forbes top 50 MBA programs, we did not find one program that had a required course on gender in their curriculum. There were several schools that had electives related to gender, from Stanford University's "Work and Family" to New York University's "Women in Business Leadership". Interestingly, while none of the top schools had a gender class as a required component of their curriculum, a growing number are requiring a class on ethics/social responsibility. Top schools are cognizant of the importance of attracting, retaining and preparing a diverse student body. Women are an increasing constituent in MBA programs—the Forte Foundation reports that women make up an average of 28–35% of the student body at business schools (Forte Foundation, 2011). And these numbers are only expected to increase. Now, more than ever, business schools must determine what can be done to ensure that their classrooms and campuses are designed to prepare all students, women and men, to lead organizations that are becoming increasingly more diverse.

Globalization has made it imperative for business curricula to incorporate diversity education that focuses on the experiences of minorities and women. Within business schools based in the United States, however, it is generally believed that diversity education has a lot of room for improvement. Minority (historically non-dominant) groups and women are still under-represented in US business schools, both in the student body and within the faculty (Bell, Connerley and Cocchiara, 2009). According to *Business Week*, African Americans, Hispanic Americans and Native Americans make up 3.5% of business school faculty and administrators in the United States (DiMeglio, 2011).

Eighteen of the top 30 US business schools in Bloomberg BusinessWeek's 2010 ranking of full-time MBA programs report 13.4% of under-represented minorities (excluding Asian Americans) in 2010. In addition, the Forte Foundation reports that women make up an average of 28–35% of the student body at business schools (Forte Foundation, 2011). Based on AACSB's 2012–2013 Global Salary Survey (Brown, 2013), of 35,246 full-time faculty, 30.2% (10,644) of the positions are currently held by women. Females are still under-represented in MBA programs, both among students and faculty, in spite of initiatives to recruit women (Kelan and Jones, 2010).

Women and people of colour, the faculty who are most likely to propose diversity education, are still under-represented in colleges (Bell, Connerley and Cocchiara, 2009). Business school deans are also still predominantly White men (92.6% are white and 88.3% are male); these decision makers, who often hold the power to approve curriculum decisions around diversity, may not see the importance or critical need for mandatory diversity training for MBA students. The people who are in power to create curriculum changes are therefore more likely to represent a more privileged demographic and less likely to experience the day-to-day effect of the lack of diversity education (Bell, Connerley and Cocchiara, 2009). In addition, very few MBA programs offer diversity training as a concentration. MBA programs increasingly have more emphasis on the quantitative skills and less on the leadership and strategic skills (Rynes and Bartunek, 2013; Stevens and Ogunji, 2011). This represents the lingering belief that diversity education and relational practice is tangential to business strategies (Anand and Winters, 2008). The quantitative skills are still treated as essential to strong business performance, while managerial communication and cultural understanding are considered supplementary. The fact that diversity education classes are voluntary makes the point that diversity education is not as valuable, or as valued, as other parts of the MBA (Bell, Connerley and Cocchiara, 2009). Such an attitude has the potential to place challenges before women and minority students in business classrooms.

15.3 Diversity education in India

We have discussed the historical foundation for diversity education in the United States and its impact on management education. However, the complex nature of diversity makes future research and understanding necessary in order to gain genuine comprehension (Klein and Harrison, 2007) and to carry the conversation forward to other cultural contexts. Andrews and Winters (2008) note that the definition of diversity is changing every day as identity groups continue to inform the world on their individual norms and cultural differences. In the following sections, we begin by exploring the term "diversity" from the Indian point of view as contrasted with the usage of the term in the United States. From there, we move on to an examination of gender and diversity education in business schools in India.

India and the United States are among the largest democracies in the world. Both countries have diverse societies and legal frameworks that support their diversity in different ways. Definitions of diversity vary between Anglo and Asian countries (e.g. Cooke and Saini, 2012) and between India and the United States (e.g. Cooke and Saini, 2010). These characteristics, along with the fact that authors had personal experience with teaching gender and diversity issues in both country contexts, made it interesting to compare and contrast India and the United States.

15.3.1 Defining diversity in India versus the United States

In the United States, Title VII of the Civil Rights Act of 1964 has played a big role in determining the manner in which employers understand the term "diversity". It mainly refers to gender, race/ethnicity, religion and national origin. Other laws such as the Age Discrimination in Employment Act of 1967 (ADEA), the Pregnancy Discrimination Act of 1978 and the Americans with Disabilities Act (ADA) of 1990 among other regulations, have extended notions of diversity in the United States to include age, pregnancy and disability. Increasingly, veteran status and sexual orientation are also being included within the discourse on diversity (Karsten, 2006).

The aim of diversity dialogues within the United States is to correct for imbalances in access to institutions of wealth, power and privilege between the under-represented groups or the "protected classes" and the dominant social groups. Affirmative action policies and an institution such as the Equal Employment Opportunity Commission (EEOC), which has the mandate for enforcing federal laws, have made it increasingly unacceptable for the corporate environment to have discriminatory practices. The US approach to encouraging diversity has traditionally shied away from setting quotas for minorities (historically including women) and has instead encouraged special recruitment efforts, monitoring of "minority" numbers in different occupations and positions within companies and diversity training for managers and workers (Haq, 2010; Oppenheimer, 2004). In comparison, diversity within the Indian context refers mainly to gender, region or place of birth, religion and caste. This understanding of diversity draws from the *Fundamental Rights of Indian Citizens*, a charter of rights contained within the Constitution of India. The right to equality before the law prohibits discrimination on the grounds of religion, race, caste, sex or place of birth, while mandating equality of opportunity in matters of employment, abolition of untouchability (the practice of ostracizing a lower caste group from the mainstream of society), and abolition of titles (aristocratic positions and hierarchies). Although the emphasis on individual rights in India may appear similar in spirit to that of the United States, the absence of an institution like the EEOC can make it difficult to aggressively prevent discriminatory practices in Indian workplaces (Haq, 2010).

Diversity implementation in India has usually happened under pressure from the government or political parties and has been sometimes referred to as "positive discrimination" (Heyer and Jayal, 2009). It takes the form of quotas (sometimes referred to as reservations) in government institutions of citizens viewed as belonging to disadvantaged groups, such as lower caste persons, Anglo-Indians (who do not have a native state of their own) and more recently, to women (though reservations or quotas for women and Anglo-Indians is possible only in political bodies and not in government institutions) (Haq and Ojha, 2010). Despite considerable scepticism about the Indian government's proposal to require reservations and quotas for perceived "lower caste" citizens by the private sector (e.g. Thimmaiah, 2005), some companies in the Information Technology sector appear to have taken up this agenda voluntarily (Vijayraghavan and Ramsurya, 2009).

Although the definition and practice of diversity between the United States and India varies on many counts, gender works as one common identity group connecting diversity dialogues between the two cultural contexts. Both countries have adopted the Universal Declaration of Human Rights of 1948 that supports non-discrimination based on gender and equal remuneration for men and women (Mor Barak, 2011). However, the ideological belief in women's rights is not played out in reality as, in both the United States and India, women continue to be disadvantaged in many sectors of the economy, especially business, despite an increasing trend in workforce participation. Within India, for instance, rightly it would appear, considerable media attention has focused on issues of safety pertaining to working women following a much publicized heinous gang rape of a woman college student in the capital city of New Delhi in December 2012 (e.g. Dhar, 2012). However, when it comes to increasing the representation of under-served populations in work organizations and educational institutions, identity caste politics within the country seem to favour recruitment of lower-caste employees (Dalits) ("Business and caste in India", *The Economist*) and Muslims before women (Yardley, 2012). Even though women managers in India tend to come from urban, middle-class families and would most likely be perceived as having it better than other minority groups such as Dalits and Muslims, it would seem that, in the demand for attention from other under-represented groups, structural challenges facing women workers tend to get overlooked too soon.

15.3.2 Evolution of management education in India

With growth of the economy, management education has been on the rise in India (e.g. Ray and Sinha, 2005). For a long time, management education has been synonymous with the acronym IIMs (Indian Institutes of Management), referring to elite government-sponsored educational institutes set up in various locations across the country. Since 2008, many new IIMs and IITs (the counterpart institution for technical education—the Indian Institute of Technology) have been established, the plan being to have one in every state of the country (Nanda, 2014). Recently, newer private management institutes have also sprung up across the country—some are local institutions (Dayal, 2002) whereas others are foreign collaborations and foreign universities setting up campuses in India (Damast, 2010). Besides the IIMs, several categories of educational institutions, such as university departments, colleges affiliated to the universities, non-university autonomous institutions, distance/correspondence-based institutions and unaffiliated institutions, offer management courses and programs as a part of their curriculum. The two-year MBA program has become the staple mode for program delivery (Subramanian, 2007).

The thrust of management education in India has changed over the years. Up until liberalization of the Indian economy in the early 1990s, the goal of management institutes was mainly to professionalize the public sector and government organizations since foreign competition was limited (Gupta and Gollakota, 2004). At that time, business schools tended to graduate homogenous populations of young MBA students (Mote, 1985). This was partly because the first management programs in the country were modelled along the lines of business schools in America and therefore attracted mainly young students to the professions, and partly because the government was a major player in the Indian economy at the time. Being the "most powerful manager in the nation" (Mote, 1985), it was imperative to include the government as a stakeholder in educational programs designed for young practitioners of industry.

As contrasted against the aim of management education in India in its early phase, current concerns include meeting external global competition by addressing quality challenges in various stakeholder areas ranging from infrastructure, curricula and pedagogy to student and faculty quality (Dayal, 2002; Gupta and Gollakota, 2005; Noronha, 2011; Ray and Sinha, 2005). Today more mid-level executives are seeking a management education in addition to traditional MBAs because of a proliferation of executive education programs (Mishra, 2013). However, student populations in Indian business schools still continue to be fairly homogenous and dominated by students from the engineering disciplines (Basu and Sengupta, 2013).

Many management institutes assess their quality in terms of the percentage of student placement and starting salaries offered to graduating students. These measures cause management institutes to play the "rankings" game—a trend that has received criticism from some quarters in India (e.g. Ojha, 2005; Westerbeck, 2010). Criticisms of the pedagogy used in Indian management classrooms have also been made. For a long time, the IIMs had relied on the case method of teaching. Yet increases in class size as well as a paucity of teaching cases written in the Indian environment have called into question this teaching method (Patel et al., 2004). Other studies have critically examined the tendency of Indian students to "conform" in group work assignments, thereby reducing the efficacy of this learning process in the Indian context (Mishra and Sahgal, 2005). Others have expressed doubts about the contemporariness of management curricula in India within a globalized world (Chandrasekhar and Anshuman, 2004). Additionally, concerns have been expressed about issues of governance and accountability, especially of faculty as a stakeholder group (Gupta and Prabhu, 2011). Recently, politicians, faculty, alumni and students have indulged in verbal sparring over the calibre of faculty in premier management institutes in the country, with the politicians taking the critical stance that IIM and IIT faculty were far from "world class" (IANS, 2011). Voices have been divided over whether to retain the elitist status of the IIMs as spearhead institutions setting the trend for management education in the country or to reduce their exclusivity, by giving in to expansionary pressures to meet local demand for management education before setting up global campuses (Patel et al., 2004).

The above literature review indicates that management education in India faces many challenges. However, one problem that appears to have consistently missed the spotlight in this discussion is the issue of gender in India and management education. India's culture is highly gender-inegalitarian (Chhokar, Brodbeck and House, 2007). Women have held a lower status in Indian society on many socio-economic dimensions including education.

In Chanana's (2004) extensive study about the disciplinary choices of women students in higher education in India, she found some interesting clusters and changes in the patterns over the years. Fewer women were opting for teachers' education traditionally considered to be a women's profession—the percentage had decreased from 3.1% in 1950–1951 to 1.8% in 2002–2003. Similarly, the numbers for medicine had declined from 5.8% to 3.6% for the same period. For commerce, the percentage had increased from 0.4% in 1950–1951 to 11.8% in 1980–1981. In fact, most of the expansion had taken place during the 1970s, a period when it began to become a stepladder to management, chartered accountancy and so on; after 1980–1981 it grew steadily to 16.5% in 2002–2003. In engineering and technology, too, there was a significant increase from less than 1% in 1950–1951 to 4.2% in 2002–2003 and in law from 0.7% to 4.2%. Although the percentage of women in higher education overall has risen from about 10% in 1950–1951 to about 40% in 2002–2003 (Chanana, 2004), traditionally there has been a gender gap in education in India in primary as well as higher education and professional fields (e.g. Chanana, 2000; Parikh and Sukhatme, 2004; Wazir, 2000), and the numbers of women in traditionally masculine fields like engineering/technology/management and business are still relatively small.

In addition, on-campus culture in many higher education institutes in India has been less than supportive, if not hostile and/or discriminatory, towards women (e.g. Gupta, 2007; Kumar, 2001). Recent government regulations have required the mandatory establishment of committees or units popularly referred to as "women's cells" on college campuses and workplaces to prevent sexual harassment of women at work (Srivastava, 2010). The National Commission for Women (NCW) lists criteria for the composition of these "cells" or committees on its website—they are to include five members nominated by the Central Government from among persons of ability, integrity and standing who have had experience in law or legislation, trade unionism, management of an industry potential of women, women's voluntary organizations (including women activists), administration, economic development, health, education or social welfare. At least one member needs to be from among persons belonging to the Scheduled Castes and Scheduled Tribes. The cell also has a chairperson and member-secretary.[1] However, the efficacy of this move to improve the work culture for women in India has been limited (Barak-Erez and Kothari, 2011).

15.3.3 Diversity in management education in India

Given that the premier management institutes in India have always prided themselves on being thought leaders responsive to the needs of the Indian economy (Patel et al., 2004), their silence surrounding gender and women's issues in India is perplexing and out of sync with sentiments expressed towards working women in business organizations and within society at large. Many organizations in India have begun to undertake measures to attract, retain and develop women executives among their ranks (Rajadhyaksha, 2012). For example NASSCOM, the country's industry association for the information technology/information technology enabled services/business process outsourcing (IT/ITES/BPO) sector, began a diversity and inclusion initiative including

---

1   www.ncw.nic.in/frmCommission.aspx (accessed 08.06.14).

an industry award in 2006 (NASSCOM, 2011). Given labour statistics that indicate the disadvantages faced by women in the Indian context at various levels, a serious commitment to tackling gender and women's issues appears to be the need of the hour within India's business schools.

15.3.3.1 Women and work in India

The workforce in India has fewer women than men. According to the *Handbook of Statistical Indicators on Indian Women 2007* released by the Ministry of Women and Child development, Government of India, the workforce participation rate of women in India as per the latest available figures from the 2001 Census was 25.7% versus 51.9% for men. These figures have changed marginally in the Census 2011—the workforce participation rate for females at the national level stands at 25.51% compared with 53.26% for males. In the rural sector, females have a workforce participation rate of 30.02% compared with 53.03% for males. In the urban sector, it is 15.44% for females and 53.76% for males. The labour force participation rate for women in India is not uniform and has been found to be a U-shaped curve, with more women in the workforce at extremely low and high levels of income and education (Olsen and Mehta, 2006).

A majority (90%) of low-income working women are employed in unorganized sectors which mainly comprise of agricultural/rural and farm activities. The percentage of women in the organized sector that mainly comprises the formal workforce and the manufacturing sector has increased from 12.2% in 1981 to 17.2% in 1999 and 20.5% in 2011 (*Men and Women in India 2013, 15th Issue, Central Statistical Organization*). However, the entry of women into the unorganized workforce has occurred at a faster rate than the entry of women into the organized workforce. The labour force participation rate for women across all age groups was 25.3 in rural sector and 15.5 in urban sector compared with 55.3 and 56.3 for men in the rural and urban sectors, respectively, in 2011-2012 (*National Sample Survey 68th Round*). The majority of working women (70%) in the organized workforce are employed in the public sector (Van Klaveren et al., 2010). Most of the organized sectors, working women are found in urban areas. In 2004–2005, 36% of women in urban India were in the workforce or studying (Bhalla and Kaur, 2011). The number of women workers in urban areas has increased rapidly over the last decade, which is one of the few positive signs pertaining to diversity in the workforce in India. Most of these women have been absorbed into the expanding service sectors of the country such as the IT/ITES and BPO sectors. According to the NASSCOM HR survey of 2010–2011, almost 37% of the BPO workforce in India is comprised of women (NASSCOM, 2011).

Women in management in India have been on the rise. However, the representation of women in middle and senior management is low (Bhagat, 2011). Many organizations in India have begun instituting practices to support work–life balance in order to retain women managers (e.g. Agarwal, 2006; Srivastava, 2011). But the needs of the large and growing segment of women marginal workers (workers who are unable to seek employment beyond six months according to the Census Survey of India) have remained largely unaddressed by government and organizational policy initiatives. Management institutes have traditionally not viewed women workers as an important stakeholder group, whether from the organized or unorganized sectors.

In order to get senses of the extent of gender-focused teaching in management institutes in India we conducted an audit of business curricula in top-ranking business schools in the country. We are unaware of any prior gender audit of business curricula in India, thus this audit helps to fill an empirical gap in the literature.

15.3.4 Gender audit of management curricula in top-ranking business schools in India

Given that the two-year MBA program (referred to as the PGP or Post-Graduate Program in many Indian business schools) has become very popular in the country (Subramanian, 2007), we conducted a gender audit of management curricula in traditional MBA programs within the top 10 business schools in India for the year 2011. Selecting top-ranking business schools in any context is a difficult task as debates and criticisms of the methodologies used for the survey always abound. However, in every country and context, some surveys usually become more popular than others. For this study, the 2011 *Business Today*–ACNielsen rankings of business schools in India was used since this source appears to have had a reasonably long track record of conducting business school rankings in India since 1998 (see "Ranking through years" *Business Today*, 4 September 2011. www.businesstoday.intoday.in/story/best-business-schools-from-1998-to-2010/1/17932.html [accessed 06.10.14].). It has also been relied on in previous audits of communication courses in management curricula in India (Rajadhyaksha, 2002). Although the BT-ACNielsen survey lists of the top 50 business schools in the country, curricula of only the top 10 business schools were examined. This concentrated our focus on those schools that have consistently been featured in the rankings lists regardless of the source of the business schools survey (e.g. Outlook–MDRA survey, *Business Today* survey, Pegasus business school ranking from careerlanucher.com, etc.).

Data collection was based on the websites of the business schools identified in the rankings. Any course that had the term "sex", "gender", "women", "men", "diversity", "inclusion" or "work–life balance" in the title or description was included. Wherever possible and available, a note was made of the percentage intake of women students in the school. Websites were examined with a goal of addressing the following list of questions:

- What is the name of the course(s) offered on gender issues in the workplace?
- Is the course required or elective?
- Are there any pre-requisites for the course?
- What is the total number of credits/contact hours allotted for the course(s)?
- What are the total number of course or credit requirements for the program?
- Which area or department offers the course(s)?
- What are the background/educational qualifications of the faculty who last taught the course(s)?
- What are the rough course contents/outline?

The top 10 business schools are listed in the Appendix; the gender audit provides only a snapshot rather than longitudinal data of management curricula offered. Furthermore, it is based on a single source of data from the websites of the business schools. Future audits should use multiple sources and multiple methods to gather information.

15.3.4.1 Findings of the gender audit

None of the top-ranked business schools in India offer a course addressing gender issues in the required curriculum of the two-year MBA or other post-graduate programs. With the exception of Indian School of Business Hyderabad, and Xavier Labor Relations Institute (XLRI), no top-ranked business school in India offers an elective course addressing gender issues in the two-year MBA curriculum. Gender issues appear to be addressed sporadically through other program initiatives, most commonly, short duration (1–3 days) executive education programs commonly referred to as management development programs (MDPs). These programs appear to be driven by faculty interests or occasional gender-themed based grants received, and do not necessarily communicate widespread institutional commitment to gender mainstreaming in the MBA curriculum. For instance XLRI Jamshedpur offers a three-day program titled "Managing Diversity in the Workplace". Similarly, IIM Udaipur (set up in 2011 and therefore not on the original list of top ten B-schools in India) is offering a short MDP for women entrepreneurs for the first time in 2014. In 2009, IIMA hosted the GEDI (Gender, Equity, Diversity and Inclusion) conference with collaboration from United Nations Development Programme (UNDP). Since the establishment of the GEDI Center, occasional programming and projects on gender issues appear to have been conducted, though the gender-based content of some of the programs is not immediately evident from their description (e.g. see the brochure of the Working Conference on "Managing You and Me in Roles and Systems" [MAYUMERS] conducted in 2012. www.iimahd.ernet.in/mdp/MAYUMERS.pdf [accessed 06.10.14]). To a limited degree, gender issues have been studied with reference to healthcare programs and public policy in two of the business schools on the list: IIMB and IIMA.

The few gender-specific executive education programs that are offered target mainly women workers from the traditional business organizations. Their focus is to improve women's personal effectiveness in a largely male-dominated world, by helping them align their style to the dominant business culture. Few or no programs are aimed at Human Resource managers/top managers and focused on examining structural and cultural barriers in companies that present challenges for women employees, or on women workers in the unorganized sectors of the Indian economy. It must be noted that the Managing Diversity in Workplace MDP offered at XLRI Jamshedpur mentions in its description that internal HR managers may apply, and the GEDI Center at IIM Ahmedabad lists an activity called CEO Roundtables on its website but offers no further information about the nature of this activity.

Some top business schools in India categorically address issues of diversity in their admissions policy but focus mainly on applicants from lower caste groups and persons with disability rather than women students. The exception to this is the IIM Kozhikode which has attempted to build a niche for itself as the business school with the largest intake of women students in the country (Naha, 2011). Almost belatedly and perhaps in response to rising pressure to increase campus diversity as they seek accreditation to attract more foreign students and faculty, some of the IIMs in India have started taking extra effort to attract women students to their campuses in 2014, including giving them extra points at the time of admission, and offering them travel reimbursement to visit the campus and see living accommodations. While media reports have suggested an increasing trend, with one institute reporting 28% women students in the incoming 2014 batch (Puranik, 2014), these are extremely new initiatives and their true impact on attracting and retaining women students in business schools in India is yet to be established.

Top business school websites in India do not uniformly report on the percentage intake of women and men students, making it difficult for stakeholders to assess the gender balance of classrooms and campus climate for male and female students. Many of the video interviews of students at the top business schools hosted at the survey website talked about the student culture of working late into the night. One female student at one of the business schools in the top 10 list mentioned in her interview how being in the minority caused women students to get a lot of attention which could be fun: "Basically we girls are the most popular things I mean we get a lot of attention, so that's the nice thing" (Business Today, 2012).

The results of the gender audit clearly mark the absence of gender mainstreaming in management education in India at least in terms of designated courses on these topics. Following are possible reasons endemic to India that could explain the trend:

- India's gender-inegalitarian culture coupled with the low labour force participation rate of women and gender gap in education continues to challenge the building of a strong case for offering gender-related courses within management curricula. Case studies of gender mainstreaming in higher education in other country contexts indicate that a gender gap in education makes it imperative to change the conversation from gender studies further to gender *in* studies (Grünberg, 2011). Absence of institutional commitment to gender mainstreaming could be viewed as a manifestation of a larger contextual problem in India.

- Management education in India has grown by borrowing ideas and curricular resources from the English-speaking developed world, especially the United States. Since business schools in the United States have traditionally struggled with increasing their gender sensitivity (Bilimoria, 1999) and continue to do so in some ways (e.g. Kelan and Jones, 2010; Simpson, 2006), Indian business schools that have covertly looked to the US business schools as role models have also been slow to learn a gender-sensitive orientation.

- Gender issues in the workplace have been studied extensively with reference to the problems of low-income working women by women studies centres in university departments in India (Jain and Rajput, 2003). However, women's studies' more nuanced understanding of the manner in which structures of patriarchy perpetuate themselves in the workplace to disadvantage women has not walked the distance to Indian business schools, given the lack of inter-disciplinary teaching and learning environments in educational institutions (Rajadhyaksha and Smita, 2004).

15.4 Discussion

Historically within the United States, diversity training was based on legal compliance or sensitivity training. However, change came from employers understanding that their productivity would rise with diversity, not from enacted laws (Stevens and Ogunji, 2011). While the rationale and need for diversity education has received a lot of attention, it is now essential to improve how diversity education is implemented and how the results of such education are measured.

Firms have generally relied on measures of firm performance and financial justification to measure the efficacy of diversity training and to convince managers of the benefits of diversity education. The argument suggests that increased awareness of cultural differences, including those based on gender, can yield a decrease in job turnover and lawsuits and an increase in commitment among employees. We agree with many of the points made by Bell, Connerley and Cocchiara (2009) that using the financial justification alone may be too simple and an unsustainable way to integrate diversity education into business behaviour. In order to improve these programs, there needs to be a shift from a profit-centred worldview to a human-centred worldview. This shift will benefit not only a firm's bottom line, but it may also increase job satisfaction and the well-being of each employee.

Diversity education also plays a major role in social justice and moral responsibility. Fairness in the workplace, equal representation and the reduction of poverty are all goals that are positively affected by diversity education. As the United States continues to experience the profound effects of globalization, it is not only an imperative for the sustainability of businesses, but also a moral responsibility of principled leaders to improve diversity education programs (Bell, Connerley and Cocchiara, 2009). Focusing on women as a diverse group is a part of this moral responsibility because despite increasing numbers in the workforce at large, women continue to be under-represented in positions of power and authority in the United States and worldwide (Deloitte, 2011; Society for Human Resource Management, 2009; *The Economist*, 2011).

Placing women at the top of organizations will require diversity education to focus on women and extend itself to the business and management curriculum. Although women make up an increasing proportion of the workforce and are enrolling in equal numbers in other professional schools (law, medicine), this trend does not appear to be happening in management education, where women are holding steady at 30% in elite MBA programs in the United States. Why do we see this disturbing trend, oftentimes in the face of administrative efforts to attract and matriculate greater numbers of women? We suggest that built-in biases around gender awareness, or gender blindness, make business schools challenging places for women to be and less receptive to discussions and interactions focused on gender. Diversity education will need to serve as the antidote to the gender blindness that pervades business school curricula.

15.4.1 Combating gender blindness in management education

A move away from "male streaming" to "gender mainstreaming" (Bilimoria, 1999) will require gender to be more explicitly included and highly placed on the agenda in business schools (Kelan and Jones, 2010). One suggestion is that rather than offering one or two special courses designed to raise gender awareness, MBA programs may be better served by determining how issues related to diversity can be integrated across the curriculum (Kelan, 2010).

While gender mainstreaming in the United States is likely to be driven by impending demographic shifts in the paid workforce (e.g. Bilimoria, 1999), the demographic argument for endorsing gender and diversity education becomes somewhat complicated in India. Given the gender distribution of the Indian workforce that is skewed against women, gender mainstreaming in management education in India cannot occur without mission support and an "urgently felt need" by internal stakeholders (faculty, students and administrators) and external stakeholders (recruiters/corporations, community and government) of business schools. While community and government in India can be said to favour the social justice argument for women and work, more so with reference to economically disadvantaged women, corporations on the other hand tend to rely on the "business case" logic which enjoys tremendous appeal among management circles. Internal stakeholders of business schools interestingly appear to be reticent to take up the cause of gender mainstreaming from either perspective.

A focus on women in management in India will have to be driven by a "social justice" argument alongside a "business case" logic, as neither approach makes sense in isolation. Further, in a gender-segregated social context that disadvantages women, it may not be enough for management schools to try to "not" be gender-negative; in fact, they may need to go all out and be gender-positive by focusing on gender as an important variable shaping managerial phenomena (e.g. Kelan and Jones, 2010).

While our audit has accounted mainly for gender-specific courses and programs, and to some extent for classroom demographics (percent of male and female students), it is important to note that gender mainstreaming needs to include programmatic as well as institutional initiatives (Bilimoria, 1999). In addition to gender-balanced classrooms, efforts to transform management education will also require assertive recruitment and retention of female faculty and staff as well as gender-sensitization training to male and female faculty to increase awareness of different pedagogical approaches and their impact on learning and self-efficacy of female and male students. There will also need to be broad-based support and mentoring of female students, faculty and staff as well as more extensive support for gender-related research.

Many of these suggestions for gender mainstreaming are likely to be particularly challenging in India at the same time as being highly desirable for change. A paucity of India-specific cases for MBA programs compounds the problem of finding and using teaching material whose content is inclusive of women. Greater pressure for larger class sizes to accommodate the ever-increasing demand for management education, greater emphasis on technical skills relative to critical thinking skills and gender-imbalanced classrooms can make it hard to use small-group process-based pedagogies to gender-sensitize students, especially in core courses. The default approach is to rely on the lecture format, which has its limitations. Gaining institutional support for gender mainstreaming can be limited by the fact that business schools have generally shied away from a cross-disciplinary approach that includes the social sciences where discussions of gender issues are more commonplace, and because Indian business schools have traditionally not maintained links with their colleagues in women's studies departments.

Social realities can also present problems for the implementation of gender-focused diversity education in management in India. For instance, in a culture where living with one's parents well into adulthood is commonplace, the greater independence that is demanded of MBA programs can be particularly challenging for female students leaving home for the first time. Their token and minority status on the business school campus can add to their isolation inside and outside the classroom. A hierarchical social culture that is accommodative of "silence" as an oft-used strategy by women to counter gender-insensitive behaviour from bosses (Blake-Beard and Roberts, 2004) can make it hard for female students to express their dissatisfaction with gender-insensitive faculty behaviour in the classroom or to voice their concerns through student bodies, many of which are dominated by male students.

15.5 Concluding thoughts

Gender issues in management and the related entrance and growth of women in the economy, along with their exclusion from positions of power and authority, is a global phenomenon that necessitates investment in gender in management education worldwide. However, the agenda around gender education remains embedded in an institutional culture that renders it marginalized. Within the field of cross-cultural management, it appears that the majority of scholarship and teaching remains focused on understanding cross-national differences in leadership and business and not on the social and institutional structures that perpetuate discrimination, harassment and unequal access to opportunity and advancement within domestic and transnational economies (Barsh and Yee, 2011; Bell, Connerley and Cocchiara, 2009).

Gender as a variable simultaneously connects and differentiates human experiences across regions, cultures and generations. Gender diversity on the one hand is inexorably linked to business practice and profitability; on the other hand, it raises moral and ethical issues that challenge facile framing of arguments within a "business case" paradigm. Within the United States, arguments for and emphasis on gender education have made limited use of the social justice rationale in business, ethics and cross-cultural management. Given the nascent academic space and cultural context in India, it appears, however, that the social justice rationale is more appropriate. Unfortunately, the Indian tendency to be imitative of the Anglo-developed world's approach to business education and to rely on the logic of the "business case" argument for gender in management education tends to make light of institutional constraints that are endemic to the Indian context.

For reasons previously discussed, both Indian and US business schools have been slow to move toward a gender-sensitive curriculum and inclusive culture. Gender diversity in management education has not been mainstreamed. In fact, our literature review and business school audits demonstrate that gender has been sidelined even in diversity discourse in management education.

In other social science disciplines the framing of gender has been addressed through an intersectionality lens (Crenshaw, 1989). Intersectionality honours the different dimensions of diversity without putting them in competition with one another. The management literature has more recently begun to address multiple identities and its impact on creating and/or sustaining business cultures that are exclusive (Debbeye and Reinhart, 2014). Likewise, gender diversity in management education need not be subsumed and rendered invisible in business school diversity education agenda.

We have argued that while diversity is defined differently in the US and India, the need to address women and gender diversity in management education is global. The silence around gender diversity in management education is out of sync with the needs of our students, industry and society. If we are to educate future managers to lead principled and sustainable organizations, we cannot do so without bringing the gender agenda into the centre of management education discourse.

References

AACSB, 2010. Eligibility procedures and accreditation standards for business accreditation. www.aacsb.edu/accreditation/business_standards.pdf (accessed 20.05.12).

AACSB International, 2011. Globalization of management education: changing international structures, adaptive strategies, and the impact on institutions. AACSM International, Tampa, FL.

Agarwal, S., 2006. Women rising. Business Today. www.archives.digitaltoday.in/businesstoday/20060312/cover6.html

Altbach, P., Resiburgh, L., Rumbley, L., 2009. Trends in Global Higher Education: Tracking a Academic Revolution, UNESCO Global Conference on Higher Education. UNESCO, Paris, France.

Amsterdam Institute for Advanced Labor Studies (AIAS), 2010. An overview of women's work and employment in India, decisions for life MDG3 project, country report No. 13. Amsterdam, Netherlands: Van Klaveren, M., Tijdens, K., Hughie-Williams, M. and Martin, N.R.

Anand, R., Winters, M., 2008. A retrospective view of corporate diversity training from 1964 to present. Academy of Management Learning & Education 7(3), 356–372.

Arbaugh, T., Jr, 2000. Cultural Diversity and Sensitivity Training. Workshop for the Handcock County Court Appointed Special Advocate Program. Bay St Louis, MS.

Ariaan, M.F., Tipu, S.A.A., 2007. Emerging trends in management education in international business schools. Academic Journals Education and Research Review 2(12), 325–331.

Barak-Erez, D., Kothari, J., Winter 2011. When sexual harassment law goes East: feminism, legal transplantation and social change. Stanford Journal of International Law 47, 177–199.

Barsh, J., Yee, L., 2011. Unlocking the full potential of women in the US economy. www.mckinsey.com/client_service/organization/latest_thinking/unlocking the_full_potential.aspx

Basu, S.D., Sengupta, D., September 10, 2013. Engineers comprise 90% of students at IIMs, 36% at Harvard and Wharton. The Economic Times. www.articles.economictimes.indiatimes.com/2013-09-10/news/41937774_1_2013-15-batch-engineers-iim-lucknow (accessed 10.06.14).

Bell, M.P., Connerley, M.L., Cocchiara, F.K., 2009. The case for mandatory diversity education. Academy of Management Learning & Education 8(4), 597–609.

Bhagat, D., 2011. 2010 India Benchmarking Report: Diversity and Inclusion Practices. www.catalyst.org/system/files/2010_india_benchmarking_report_web.pdf (accessed 07.04.12).

Bhalla, S.S., Kaur, R., 2011. Labour force participation in India: some facts, some queries. Working Paper No. 40, Asia Research Center, London School of Economics & Political Science, London, October 5.

Bidwell, W., Fiore, S., Salas, E., 2014. Developing the future workforce: An approach for integrating interpersonal skills into the MBA classroom. AMLE 13(2), 171–196.

Bilimoria, D., 1999. Upgrading management education's service to women. Journal of Management Education 23(2), 118–122.

Blake-Beard, S., Roberts, L.M., 2004. Releasing the double bind of visibility for minorities in the workplace, CGO Commentary 4. www.simmons.edu/som/centers/cgo/publications/commentaries.shtml, Center for gender in organizations, Simmons School of Management.

Business Today, 2011. What is so good about IIM-Ahmedabad? www.businesstoday.intoday.in/video/iim-ahmedabad/1/148257.html (accessed 12.05.12).

Chanana, K., 2000. Treading the hallowed halls: women in higher education. Economic and Political Weekly of India 35(12), 1012–1022.

Chanana, K., December 1-3, 2004. Gender and disciplinary choices: higher education in India. Paper prepared for the UNESCO colloquium on research and higher education policy. Knowledge, Access and Governance: Strategies for Change, Paris, France.

Chandrasekhar, S., Ravi Anshuman, V., February 21, 2004. How Contemporary Are IIMs? Economic and Political Weekly of India 39(8).

Chhokar, J.S., Brodbeck, F., House, R.J., 2007. Culture and Leadership around the World: The GLOBE Book of In-depth Studies of 25 Societies. Lawrence Erlbaum Associates, Mahwah, NJ.

Cooke, F., Saini, D.S., 2010. Diversity management in India: a study of organizations in different ownership forms and industrial sectors. Human Resource Management 49(3), 477–500.

Cooke, F.L., Saini, D.S., 2012. Managing diversity in Chinese and Indian organizations: a qualitative study. Journal of Chinese Human Resource Management 3(1), 16–32.

Cornuel, E., 2005. The role of business schools in society (English). Journal of Management Development 24(9), 819–829.

Crenshaw, K., 1989. Demarginalizing the intersection of race and sex: a black feminist critique of antidiscrimination doctrine, feminist theory, and antiracist politics. University of Chicago Legal Forum, pp. 139–167.

Damast, A., May 28, 2010. Top B-Schools set sights on India. Bloomberg BusinessWeek. www.businessweek.com/bschools/content/may2010/bs20100527_523198.htm

Dayal, I., 2002. Developing management education in India. Journal of Management Research (09725814) 2(2), 98.

Debebe, G., Reinert, K.A., 2014. Leading with our whole selves: a multiple identity approach to leadership development. In: Miville, M., Fergeson, A. (Eds.), Handbook of Race, Ethnicity, and Gender in Psychology. Springer.

Deloitte, 2011. The gender dividend: making the business case for investing in women. Pellegrino, G., D'Amato, S., Weisberg, A., UK.

Dhar, A., December 26, 2012. Commission to suggest steps to make Delhi safe for women. The Hindu (Chennai, India).

DiMeglio, F., January 27, 2011. Minority B-School faculty growing-slowly. Bloomberg Business Week. www.businessweek.com/bschools/content/jan2011/bs20110126_564521.htm

The Economist, November 26, 2011. Special Report on Women and Work: Closing the Gap. www.economist.com/node/21539928

The Economist, October 4, 2007. Print edition—Bangalore, Chennai and Delhi, business and caste in India.

Global Poverty Research Group, 2006. A pluralist account of labor participation in India. Olsen, W.K., Mehta, S., Delhi, India.

Grünberg, L. (Ed.), 2011. From Gender Studies to Gender in Studies Case Studies on Gender-Inclusive Curriculum in Higher Education. UNESCO-CEPES studies on higher education, Bucharest, Romania.

Gupta, A., Prabhu, G.N., 2011. Governance of IIMs: a critique of the Bhargava committee report. Economic and Political Weekly of India 47(17), 16–20.

Gupta, N., 2007. Indian women in doctoral education in science and engineering: a study of informal milieu at the reputed Indian Institutes of Technology. Science, Technology and Human Values 32(5), 507–533.

Gupta, V., Gollakota, K., 2004. Business education in India: the quality dialogue. IBAT Journal of Management 1(2), 1–18.

Gupta, V., Gollakota, K., 2005. Critical challenges for Indian Business Schools as partners in development. Decision (0304–0941) 32(2), 35.

Haq, R., 2010. Caste-based quotas: India's reservation policies in managing cultural diversity. In: Syed, J., Ozbilgin, M. (Eds.), Asia: A Research Companion. Edward Elgar Pub, Cheltenham, UK, pp. 166–191.

Haq, R., Ojha, A.K., 2010. Affirmative action in India: Caste-based reservations. In: Alain Karlsfeld (Ed.), International Handbook on Diversity Management at Work. Edward Elgar Pub, Cheltenham, UK, pp. 139–159.

Heyer, J., Jayal, N.G., February 2009. The challenge of positive discrimination in India. Center for research on inequality, Human Security and Ethnicity, DFID UK. CRISE Working Paper No. 55.

Indian Institute of Management Ahmedabad, 2006. AIMS international conference on management working paper 2007-02-01: A Study on mushroom growth of two-year management program and it impact on quality of management education in Tamilnadu. Subramanian, S., Indore, India.

Indo-Asian News Service (IANS), May 24, 2011. War of words over Jairam Ramesh IITs, IIMs remarks. Hindustan Times. www.hindustantimes.com/India-news/NewDelhi/War-of-words-over-Jairam-Ramesh-IITs-IIMs-remarks/Article1-701573.aspx

International Labor Office. 2009. Key indicators of the labor market, sixth ed. www.ilo.org

Jain, D., Rajput, P. (Eds.), 2003. Narratives from the women's studies family. Sage Publications, New Delhi, India.

Kantor, J., September 8, 2013. Harvard Business School case study: gender equity. The New York Times, A1.

Karsten, M.F., 2006. Management, gender and race in the 21st century. University press of America Inc., Lanham, MD.

Kelan, E., August 20, 2010. Gender Issues Should Be Integral to MBA Courses. The Financial Times. www.ft.com/intl/cms/s/0/21f066dc-ac6d-11df-8582-00144feabdc0.html#axzz20X35iPsT

Kelan, E.K., Jones, R., 2010. Gender and the MBA. Academy of Management Learning & Education 9(1), 26–43.

Klein, K.J., Harrison, D.A., 2007. On the diversity of diversity: tidy logic, messier realities. Academy of Management Perspectives 21(4), 26–33.

Kulik, C.T., Roberson, L., 2008. Common goals and golden opportunities: evaluations of diversity education in academic and organizational settings. Academy of Management Learning & Education 7(3), 309–331.

Kumar, N., 2001. Gender and stratification in science: an empirical study in the Indian setting. Indian Journal of Gender Studies 8(1), 51–67.

London School of Economics & Political Science, 2011. Asia Research Center Working Paper 40: Labor Force Participation in India: Some Facts, Some Queries. Bhalla, S.S., Kaur, R., London, UK.

Maitland, A., September 1, 2008. Just trying to be one of the boys. The Financial Times. www.ft.com/intl/cms/s/2/642d00d8-75f0-11dd-99ce-0000779fd18c.html#axzz20X35iPsT

Mavin, S.S., Bryans, P.P. 1999. Gender on the agenda in management education? Gender in Management: An International Journal 14(3), 99–104.

Mavin, S.S., Bryans, P.P., Waring, T.T., 2004a. Unlearning gender blindness: new directions in management education. Management Decision 42(3/4), 565–578.

Mavin, S.S., Bryans, P.P., Waring, T.T., 2004b. Gender on the agenda 2: unlearning gender blindness in management education. Gender in Management: An International Journal 19(6), 293–303.

McKinsey & Company, 2009. Unlocking the full potential of women in the US economy. Barsh, J., Yee, L., New York.

Men and Women in India 2013, 15th Issue, Central Statistical Organization, India.

Ministry of Women and Child Development, Government of India, 2007. Handbook of Statistical Indicators on Indian Women. www.wcd.nic.in/stat.pdf (accessed 07.04.12).

Mishra, A., October 27, 2013. B-School Interlude. Business Today. www.businesstoday.intoday.in/story/best-b-school-mid-career-executives-opting-mba-programmes/1/199263.html (accessed 10.06.14).

Mishra, S., Sahgal, P., 2005. The efficacy of group method in management education: a case study on social conformity. Decision (0304–0941) 32(2), 113–138.

Mor Barak, M.E., 2011. Managing Diverting: Toward a Globally Inclusive Workplace, second ed. Sage Publications, Thousand Oaks, CA.

Mote, V.L., 1985. Development of management education in India: role of the Institutes of Management. Vikalpa 10(4), 371–385.

Naha, A.L., November 14, 2011. IIM-K shows social responsibility. The Hindu. www.thehindu.com/education/college-and-university/article2621778.ece

Nanda, P.K., June 9, 2014. Govt eyes IIMs and IITs in every state. LiveMint and the Wall Street Journal. www.livemint.com/Politics/vElpy40bg2wIAjEHCj5d6O/Govt-eyes-IITs-and-IIMs-in-every-state.html (accessed 10.06.14).

The National Association of Software and Services Companies (NASSCOM), 2006. Diversity and Inclusivity Summit. www.nasscom.in/disummit/overview (accessed 09.04.14).

NASSCOM, 2011. HR Survey of 2010–11. www.epi.nasscom.in/upload/docs/annualreport_201011/NASSCOM_Annual_Report_20 10-11.pdf (accessed 07.04.14).

National Commission for Women. www.ncw.nic.in/frmCommission.aspx (accessed 06.08.14).

National Sample Survey, 68th Round, India.

Navarro, P., 2008. The MBA core curricula of top-ranked U.S. business schools: a study in failure. Academy of Management Learning & Education 7(1), 108–123.

Noronha, M., 2011. Management education at crossroads in India. Asia Pacific Journal of Research in Business Management 2(6), 87–101.

Ojha, A., 2005. Management education in India: protecting it from the ranking onslaught. Decision (0304–0941) 32(2), 19–33.

Oppenheimer, D.B., 2004. Distinguishing five models of affirmative action. In: Healy, J., O'Brien, E. (Eds.), Race, Ethnicity and Gender: Selected Readings. Pine Forge Press, Thousand Oaks, CA, pp. 133–138.

Page, S.E., 2007. Making the difference: apply a logic of diversity. Academy of Management Perspectives 21(4), 6–20.

Pande, S., September 4, 2011. The Big Shuffle. Business Today (Special Issue: Cover Story). www.businesstoday.intoday.in/story/best-business-schools-iims-of-2011/1/17938.html (accessed 10.06.14).

Parikh, P.P., Sukhatme, S.P., 2004. Women engineers in India. Economic and Political Weekly of India 39(2), 193–201.

Patel, I., Paul, S., Khandwalla, P.N., Bose, A., Murthy, K.R.S., Vittal, N., Krishnan, R.T., Jain, A.K., Gupta, A.K., 2004. Social context of management education: institution building experiences at IIMs. Vikalpa 29(2), 85–109.

Puranik, A.A., June 8, 2014. IIMs strive for gender and cultural diversity. Hindustan Times, Front Page/Metro p. 5.

Rajadhyaksha, U., 2012. Work-life balance in South East Asia: the Indian experience. South Asian Journal of Global Business Research 1(1), 108–127.

Rajadhyaksha, U., 2002. Teaching communication—where do Indian business schools stand? Vikalpa 27(2), 49–56.

Rajadhyaksha, U., Smita, S., April 24–30, 2004. Tracing a timeline for work and family research in India. Economic and Political Weekly of India 39(17), 1674–1680.

Ranking through Years, September 4, 2011. Business Today. www.businesstoday.intoday.in/story/best-business-schools-from-1998-to-2010/1/17932.html (accessed 10.06.14).

Ray, S., Sinha, A., July–December 1–17, 2005. Management education—let a thousand flowers bloom amidst a hundred questions. Special issue on management education in India. Decision 32(2), 1–17.

Reynolds, M., 1999. Critical reflection and management education: rehabilitating less hierarchical approaches. Journal of Management Education 23(5), 537–553.

Rynes, S.L., Bartunek, J.M., 2013. Curriculum matters: towards a more holistic graduate management education. In: Graduate Management Admission Council (GMAC) (Ed.), Disrupt or Be Disrupted: A Blueprint for Change in Management Education. Jossey-Bass, San Francisco, CA.

Simpson, R., 2006. Masculinity and management education: feminizing the MBA. Academy of Management Learning and Education 5(2), 182–193.

Sinclair, A., 1995a. Sex and the MBA. Organization 2(2), 295–317.

Sinclair, A., 1995b. The MBA through women's eyes. Management Learning 28(3), 313–330.

Smith, C.R., 2000. Notes from the field: gender issues in the management curriculum: a survey of student experiences. Gender, Work & Organization 7, 158–167.

Society for Human Resource Management (SHRM), 2009. Global Diversity Advantage: The Next Competitive Edge. SHRM, Alexandria, VA.

Srivastava, D.K., 2010. Progress of sexual harassment law in India, China and Hong Kong: prognosis for further reform. Harvard International Law Journal Online 51, 172–180.

Srivastava, M., March 7, 2011. Keeping women on the job in India. Bloomberg BusinessWeek. www.businessweek.com/magazine/content/11_11/b4219010769063.htm

Stevens, R., Ogunji, E., 2011. Preparing business students for the multi-cultural work environment of the future: a teaching agenda. International Journal of Management 28(2), 528–544.

Subrahmanyan, L., 1998. Women scientist in the third world: the Indian experience. Sage Publications, New Delhi, India.

Subramanian, S., 2007. A study on mushroom growth of two year management programme and its impact on quality of management education in Tamil Nadu. Paper presented at the Fourth AIMS International Management Conference, Indore, India, December 28–31, 2006. IIMA Working paper Series, W.P.No. 2007-02-01.

Thimmaiah, G., February 19–25, 2005. Implications of reservations in the private sector. Economic and Political Weekly of India 40(8).

Thomas, D.A., Ely, R.J., 1996. Making differences matter: a new paradigm for managing diversity. Harvard Business Review, 79–90.

United Nations Educational, Scientific and Cultural Organization (UNESCO), 2009. Trends in Global Higher Education: Tracking an Academic Revolution. Altback, P.G., Reisburg, L., Rumbley, L.E., Paris, France.

UN Women, 2011. PRME Working Group on Gender Equity. Kilgour, M., Flynn, P., New York.

United States Census Bureau, 2009. American community survey 5-year estimates. www.census.gov/acs/www/data_documentation/2009_5yr_data

Van Klaveren, M., Tijdens, K., Hughie-Williams, M., Ramos Martin, N., 2010. An overview of women's work and employment in India. AIAS Working Paper 10-90, Amsterdam, The Netherlands.

Vijayraghavan, K., Ramsurya, M.V., December 9, 2009. Tata's lead India Inc. in hiring SC/STs. The Economic Times. www.articles.economictimes.indiatimes.com/2009–12–07/news/27665954_1_recruitment-policy-tata-capital-tata-sons

Wazir, R. (Ed.), 2000. Gender gap in basic education. Sage Publications, New Delhi, India.

Westerbeck, T., September 17, 2010. India: The future of management education? Bloomberg BusinessWeek. www.businessweek.com/managing/content/-sep2010/ca2010093_520557.htm

World Economic Forum, 2010. The global gender gap report. Hausmann, R., Tyson, L.D., Zahidi, S., Geneva, Switzerland.

Yardley, J., March 9, 2012. India eyes Muslims left behind by the quota system. The New York Times, Asia-Pacific ed. www.nytimes.com/2012/03/10/world/asia/india-eyes-affirmative-action-for-muslims.html?pagewanted=all (accessed 06.06.14).

Appendix **List of top 10 business schools
in India—2011**
(based on the *Business Today*–ACNielsen
survey of business schools)[2]

1. IIM Bangalore

2. IIM Kolkotta

3. IIM Ahmedabad

4. IIM Indore

5. IIM Lucknow

6. IIM Kozhikode

7. IIFT Delhi

8. ISB Hyderabad

9. IIM Shillong

10. FMS Delhi

10. XLRI Jamshedpur

2 For methodology and other details of the 2011 survey, see India's best business schools, special issue of *Business Today* (The Big Shuffle by Shammi Pande, *Business Today*, September 4,
2011). www.businesstoday.intoday.in/story/best-business-schools-iims-of-2011/1/17938.html
(accessed 06.10.14).

16

The role of business school education for Japanese and non-Japanese women in Japan

Mari Kondo
Doshisha Business School, Japan

Japan is the third largest economy in the world but, with unprecedented speed, it has begun to suffer from having an ageing and shrinking population. To cope with this, Japan intends to increase the number of immigrants, which is not an easy task. Also, following a suggestion from the International Monetary Fund (IMF), Japan established a system that would allow more women to join the labour force. The government made the mainstreaming of women one of the central pillars of its economic policies. In this context, this chapter discusses the role of business school education among women in Japan, be they are Japanese or non-Japanese. Case studies of female Japanese MBAs are provided, and the importance of opportunities proffered by gender-sensitive business school education is discussed.

16.1 Introduction

Japan is the third largest economy in the world but, with unprecedented speed, it has begun to suffer from having an ageing and shrinking population. Japan's population shrinks at the rate of 0.2 million annually, which can translate into a smaller domestic market and a less productive labour force. Faced with a shrinking domestic market and labour force, the Japanese economy is suffering from a loss of vitality and dynamism. Because of its ageing population, Japan's potential growth has, of late, been rapidly falling (Steinberg and Nakane, 2012).

Generally, there are two ways to cope with this situation. One is to increase the number of immigrants. A Cabinet office has predicted that, annually, 200,000 immigrants are needed until the fertility rate of women recovers to 2.07, in order to maintain the current population level (Suezaki, 2013). Thus, although Japan is slow to open up its gates to migrants, a consensus towards its need to accept talented foreign nationals has been reached (Japan Institute for Labour Policy and Training, 2013). Within this same context, a consensus that Japanese higher education should accept students from abroad has been reached.

The second measure for coping with the situation is to increase the participation of women in the labour force. In 2012, the International Monetary Fund (IMF) published a report entitled "Can Women Save Japan?". The report argued that key to the revitalization of the Japanese economy suffering from the problem of an ageing population is the establishment of a system that would allow more women to join the labour force (Steinberg and Nakane, 2012). This message was directly delivered to Prime Minister Abe by IMF Managing Director Christine Lagarde. Pressured, Prime Minister Abe made the mainstreaming of women one of the central pillars of his economic policies in 2013.

Meanwhile, the World Economic Forum reported on the sobering gender inequality situation. In its Global Gender Gap Report 2014, Japan ranked 104 out of 142 countries studied. Among the four areas involved, that is health, education, economy and politics, economic participation and opportunity ranked 102nd and political empowerment 129th. While we will have a closer look at the report in the following section, the poor rankings indicate that fewer women are in management or leadership positions in economic and political areas in Japan. Japan faces a need to increase the number of women managers.

The purpose of this chapter is to consider the role of business school education among women in Japan, be they Japanese or non-Japanese, particularly in the aforementioned context. The *Financial Times* reports that there are three key differences between women and men which contribute to gender inequality: pay, expectations and confidence, and mentors and sponsors—all of which an MBA education can help address (Sangster, 2011). Such is the case in the West, but how is it in Japan? Can business school education in Japan for women help more women join the labour force and play a more leading role in society? If so, what is needed in terms of business school education in Japan? And what about the case of foreign women who enter business schools in Japan?

This chapter is divided into seven parts. Following this introduction is a section that describes Japan's gender inequalities, their possible causes and the government's efforts towards gender empowerment. The recent phenomenon known as the "Women Promotional Bubble" and the criticism directed at the government for pressuring corporations to promote women are also introduced.

The third section introduces the business school situation in Japan, as well as the status of the UN Global Compact and Principles for Responsible Management Education (PRME).

It presents the Doshisha Business School in Kyoto, which is a signatory of PRME, where the author works. Doshisha University, where the business school resides, is a signatory of the UN Global Compact. Doshisha Business School has two distinctive MBA programs: a part-time program taught in Japanese for Japanese business people, and a full-time program taught in English mainly attended by non-Japanese students. If we put the two programs in the context of Japan's shrinking population and the need for countermeasures, the former responds to the need to promote more women in managerial positions by educating motivated Japanese women to move up to higher positions, thus encouraging more Japanese women to participate in the labour market. The latter addresses the need for Japanese society to enlarge the pool of talented foreign nationals, regardless of gender.

Following the introduction of the school, the fourth section consists of case studies on Japanese women MBA holders. The fascinating story of Ryoko (not her real name), a woman MBA who started a social enterprise to promote the networking of working women with the help of other women MBAs, is presented. Ryoko directly helps address the needs of society by extending services to increase the labour participation of women in Japan and to narrow gender inequality especially at the managerial level. Some other cases of women MBA holders are presented in this section.

The fifth section introduces the cases and perspectives of several Asian female MBA graduates of Doshisha's English MBA program on MBAs and their careers. Unlike the women in the Japanese MBA program, these Asian women do not notice gender inequalities as much at home. Many of them are interested in getting jobs in Japan, but some are not so successful.

The last two sections of the chapter are the discussion and the conclusion. The discussion section considers the role of business school education for women MBAs—both Japanese and international—in Japan. The importance of and the opportunities proffered by a gender-sensitive business school education are also discussed.

16.2 Japanese women and gender inequalities in corporate Japan

The message that the above-mentioned IMF report conveys is as follows: Japan's ageing population has had a dampening impact on the country's potential growth in recent years. But raising female participation in the labour force can help reverse this trend and boost Japan's economic growth. IMF even says that an army of highly educated Japanese housewives can be the secret weapon of Japan (Steinberg, 2013). The IMF report also predicted that the GDP per capita of Japan could be permanently higher by approximately 4% if Japan could raise its female participation ratio up to the level of the G7 (excluding Italy and Japan), and by approximately 8% if it could achieve the level of Northern Europe (Steinberg, 2013: 5). Policies to encourage women to start out in career-track positions, as well as measures to support working mothers, are needed to ensure rise in female labour participation (Steinberg, 2013). However, while this is easy to say, it is difficult to implement. Let's take a look at the situation of Japanese women more closely, especially along the lines of the gender gap discussed by the World Economic Forum.

As mentioned earlier, according to the World Economic Forum's Global Gender Gap Report 2014, Japan ranked 104th out of 142 countries studied, while Iceland ranked first, Finland second, Norway third, the Philippines ninth, the United States 20th, and the United Kingdom 26th. Japan's ranking (104th) is even below those of China (87th) and Indonesia (97th). The index measures four areas: health, education, economic participation, and political empowerment. Japan's total score is 0.658, which can be interpreted as follows: the women in Japan have only 66% of the resources and opportunities available to men in the four aforementioned areas (World Economic Forum, 2014).

Among the four areas, which areas contribute to the wider gaps? A closer look at the scores tells us that while both the education score (0.98) and the health score (0.98) are relatively high, the economic participation and opportunity score (0.62) and the political empowerment score (0.58) are low. In terms of ranking, Japan ranked 102nd in economic participation and 129th in political empowerment (World Economic Forum, 2014). We will further examine the economic participation portion of the Index, summarized in Table 16.1.

Japanese women are relatively well educated. Many of them study in universities and enjoy higher education. After they leave education, many women start working. However, about 60% of them leave their jobs when they get married or when their first baby is born. Such women subsequently find it difficult to return to the labour market once they have finished raising their children (Cabinet Office Government of Japan, 2013). The labour force participation percentage of women is only 64% while the men enjoy 84%. The international ranking of Japan in labour participation is 83rd, which is low (World Economic Forum, 2014).

Table 16.1 **Summary of the economic participation and opportunity areas of Japan's Gender Gap Index 2014**

Source: The Global Gender Gap Report 2014, World Economic Forum. www.reports.weforum.org/_static/global-gender-gap-2014/JPN.pdf

	Rank	Score	Sample average	Female	Male	Female-to-male ratio
Economic participation and opportunity	102	0.618	0.596			
Labour force participation	83	0.75	0.67	64	84	0.75
Wage equality for similar work (survey)	53	0.68	0.61	–	–	0.68
Estimated earned income (PPP US$)	74	0.60	0.53	23,949	40,000	0.60
Legislators, senior officials and managers	112	0.12	0.27	11	89	0.12
Professional and technical workers	78	0.87	0.65	47	53	0.87

The root cause of this practice is the so-called lifetime employment system of Japan, which is seen as the basis of Japanese capitalism. From around the time of Second World War, the role of corporations in Japanese society has been seen as the provision of secure employment. For this reason, corporations offer lifetime employment to men, but in exchange for this security of employment, the system expects men to work long hours. Meanwhile, wives are expected to support their husbands and take care of all household chores, so that their husbands can spend long hours at work. Since men cannot devote time and energy to taking care of household and family matters, Japanese women are expected to fulfil this role. Therefore, Japanese women will invariably leave work when they get married or have their first baby.

A system where women do not stay long in their jobs is also convenient for the corporations. The Japanese pay system, in tandem with lifetime employment, has largely subscribed to seniority-based pay. Under this system, for the same work, younger workers tend to receive lower pay compared to their seniors. This means that corporations can underpay women because, to begin with, they only work for a limited number of years. Among Japanese corporations, this system of lifetime employment helps lessen the burden of the high fixed costs associated with human resources.

Because of this lifetime employment system, people will stay in the same work or corporation, causing limited mobility among the Japanese labour market. Therefore, it is not easy for middle-aged women who have finished their child rearing to find regular positions in Japanese companies. What they can find is, perhaps, part-time work positions, with low pay and hence limited take-up among Japanese women. The income gap between men and women is high, and Japan is ranked 74th in the subcategory of "estimated income gap".

While the rankings of all sub-items in the category "economic participation and opportunity" are not encouraging, the worst ranking is in the category of "legislators, senior officials and managers" where Japan is ranked 112th. This is unsurprising, however, because women are not expected to stay and move up the corporate ladder under the Japanese lifetime employment system. Nor can women stay long enough to reach managerial positions. Knowing that they will stay in the company only for a short period, women may not be motivated to invest in their education for professional reasons. Instead, they may take a graduate degree just for the purpose of educating themselves. This may explain why Japan is ranked 78th in the subcategory of "professional and technical workers".

In short, under the traditional lifetime employment system, women are hired to undertake inexpensive work while they are young; moreover, women are not expected to stay long enough in their work to be promoted. This phenomenon creates a vicious cycle where women may not choose work-related fields of study during their college years, or are discouraged to invest in educating themselves to return to work after child rearing. Unless corporations change their policies to help women continue to work after their first child is born and progress within the company, Japan is unlikely to increase female labour participation as recommended by IMF.

The recommendation of the IMF and the possibility of increasing Japan's GDP per capita by 4–8% have had a great impact on the Japanese government. In order to respond to the recommendation of the IMF, Prime Minister Abe announced that the government would like to see women comprising 30% of corporate managers by 2020. Pressured by the government, many corporations in Japan are now looking seriously at measures to increase the number of women managers (Nikkei Business, 2013: 28–33). For example, Sony announced its aim to increase the number of women managers to 15% by the year 2020, up from 5% in 2013 (Nikkei Business, 2013: 3).

While corporations are making noticeable efforts, some degree of confusion and scepticism has been reported by the media. For example, the media are questioning the wisdom of promoting women who are not qualified for that promotion, simply because of government pressure. Take the example of *Nikkei Business*, a leading business journal in Japan, which termed the current phenomenon the "Women Promotion Bubble" (Nikkei Business, 2013: 28–33). One of the debates presented focuses on the 30% quota of women managers and executives in large Japanese corporations. While some believe that drastic measures such as a quota system are necessary, others are more doubtful. Some women executives and CEOs say that the quota system can be counterproductive, especially as corporations are already feeling the pressure exerted by government. Those who are against the quota system basically point out that a pool of self-motivated and capable women can help to solve the problem instead. The quota system, they argue, will merely create skewed situations which are not always based on merit. This, they further argue, will ultimately negatively affect the standing of all women, including those promoted based on their skills and expertise (Nikkei Business, 2013: 28–33).

"Women make the workplace hell: Reporting the realities of mainstreaming women efforts", one of several feature articles addressing *Nikkei Business*'s "Women Promotion Bubble", may help in understanding the above argument (Nikkei Business, 2013: 26–41). The term "hell" is common lingo used by the Japanese media to describe "difficulties" or "uneasiness". The business journal reported that there are four types of "hell" situations that have arisen due to government pushing the promotion of women. The first is a "bullying hell" where women managers are said to bully their women subordinates whom they may see as rivals. The second hell is characterized by "reverse discrimination" towards male employees. Third is the "undesirable role model hell". Since role models for women managers are said to be important in motivating other women to seek advancement in their careers, corporations are pressured into creating women managers who can serve as role models. However, as some of the women selected are those who have sacrificed their private lives for the sake of their work, they tend to expect the same from other women who follow them. Since some female employees may not wish to work as hard as the "role models", they may simply give up the challenge of advancing their careers. The fourth hell is the "entitlement hell" in which women employees simply take advantage of various welfare measures that have been put in place to support working women, thereby failing to increase their work motivation and productivity (Nikkei Business, 2013: 28–33).

Beyond the four types of "hell" or "difficulties" that Nikkei reported as potential outcomes of government-required quotas, this chapter introduces three types of difficulties from the perspective of promoted women, also described by *Nikkei Business*. The first involves women being promoted for the corporation's public relations requirements, even though they might lack suitable credentials, thereby failing to win the respect of their subordinates, who might as a consequence reject their leadership. The second difficulty is where welfare measures for women are nothing more than superficial lip service by the corporation and are not easily available, in reality. The third is known as "lonely woman manager hell (difficulty)". Women managers often do not have a wide network of male managers around them, and thus may feel isolated and find it very difficult to conduct their work effectively (Nikkei Business, 2013: 28–33).

While there are many efforts, mistakes and discussions under way to do with the concept of mainstreaming women in corporate Japan, both women and corporations have come to realize that there is a lot of scope now for women's education with regard to preparing them for professional, managerial and leadership work. To make "Women Promotion" go beyond being mere "bubbles" such that they are substantial and have long-term effects, creating a platform for professional business education for Japanese working women seems imperative. As stated, Japanese women are relatively well educated and many of them hold university bachelor degrees. All things considered, business schools have a lot to offer to the motivated Japanese women.

So how are Japanese business schools responding? What issues and challenges do Japanese business schools and MBA holders face? The next section discusses the realities confronting business schools and MBA holders in Japan.

16.3 Business schools and MBAs in Japan

First, let us take a look at the situation of business schools and how MBAs are regarded in Japanese society. Partly because of the emphasis on lifetime employment practices, MBAs are not especially well regarded in Japanese corporations. Since lifetime employment is based on a seniority pay and promotion system, and labour mobility is limited, the merit of the MBA has not been widely acknowledged (Tashiro and Rowley, 2009).

There is scepticism towards MBA education in corporate Japan. Until now, there has existed a strong belief that business know-how can be gained only on the job, and not in the classroom. This view is particularly evident in the manufacturing sector, where the tradition of valuing craftsmanship persists (Tanikawa, 2010). Also, corporate Japan still adheres to the principle that the top priority of Japanese executives is to protect their employees, rather than the interests of shareholders. The Japanese business system has been developed with a particular value system, which includes the principle that corporations are not for shareholders but for employees. As a result, shareholder-oriented MBA theories and MBA training to develop business leaders, although fit for the US system, are viewed with scepticism in Japan.

Yet, faced with the globalization of economies and businesses, there are signs of increased acceptance of MBAs and business schools in the country (Tashiro and Rowley, 2009). In 2003, the Japanese government created a new category of schools called "professional graduate schools", which includes business schools and law schools. Under the Professional Graduate School Law, the number of business schools and programs was increased; many of them now offer part-time MBA programs. It is reported that 22 new business programs were added from 2003 to 2006 (Tashiro and Rowley, 2009), and that 55 business programs and schools were in existence by 2009 (Tanikawa, 2010).

In Kyoto, Doshisha University, which has a 138-year history, is one of the oldest and most prestigious private universities in Japan. Under the Professional Graduate School Law it decided to establish a business school, which opened in 2004. Its MBA program started out as a part-time program taught in Japanese. In 2009, in order to respond to the need to attract talented foreign nationals in Japan, Doshisha Business School launched its English-language Global MBA. As of 2014, there are only a few business schools in Japan which offer an English-based MBA program. Both Doshisha programs strongly emphasize that corporations and business people must strive not only for financial success, but also to make a positive social contribution to the world in which we live. This is a reflection of the attitude of business people in Kyoto, which is the cultural centre of Japan. Kyoto is also known for having many business firms that are centuries old.

As of March 2014, there were 62 students enrolled in Doshisha's Japanese MBA program, while the English program had 70 students from 29 countries worldwide. In the Global MBA program, 34 females make up about half of the student population. In Japanese MBA programs, there were only eight females and they accounted for 12% of the students. From 2006 to 2014, female students accounted for 17% of the students in the Japanese program. Many Japanese female students are single women working in corporations. Some of them are working as professionals or supervisors of these corporations. The rest of the women in the Japanese program are not working but hope to get professional positions or work as entrepreneurs. One female student is the CEO of a mid-sized computer company which she inherited from her father. The ages of these female students range from 30 to 40 years (Doshisha Business School Japanese MBA program, 2014).

16.4 Case studies: four cases of Japanese women who studied for an MBA degree

This section introduces four cases of Japanese women MBA holders. The first case study is about the Japanese woman MBA, Ryoko (not her real name), who enrolled in the part-time Japanese MBA program of Doshisha Business School in 2012 and graduated in 2014. The second and the third case studies are about Hanako and Yoshiko (not their real names), who were classmates of Ryoko. Both Hanako and Yoshiko work for Japanese multinational corporations as managers. The last case is about Maya (not her real name), who took her MBA degree in Singapore. Her case is included to illustrate some concerns regarding MBA education in Japan.

The Case of Ryoko: Ryoko, 47 years old and married, is living with her husband, their two children, and her husband's parents. One of her children goes to high school, while the other one goes to university. As a mother and wife of the oldest son who lives within the traditional Japanese family system, Ryoko has been struggling to develop her own career. In taking MBA courses, she was keen to become an entrepreneur. She thus established her own business conducting seminars and organizing a network for working women. Her aim was to empower women in society—especially mothers who might otherwise give up developing their own careers. Sometimes, Ryoko's female MBA classmates, for example Hanako and Yoshiko, support her initiative and activities, alongside the group of women Ryoko has organized. Ryoko has found meaning in business school education, and enjoyed the support network of MBA women in the business school.

After she graduated from university with an undergraduate degree in English, Ryoko worked for a famous American multinational corporation for 11 years. There she found many role models for working women: in that organization women accounted for more than 30% of the employees. The pay and opportunities for men and women were equal, though there was pressure to perform. In 2000, amid the IT revolution-induced boom, Ryoko moved to an IT venture company where she handled marketing. She was one of the three employees of the IT start-up. She found great pleasure in building the new company. Also the work environment was more convenient for her because it allowed her to raise her children in a less hectic environment.

Over time, however, Ryoko's life in the IT company became routine. She wanted to do something about it, but could not come up with any new ideas. In her search for fresh alternatives, she decided to enrol in an MBA program at a business school. Also, while she was still enrolled in the business school, Ryoko started a new business by herself. Her new company engaged in two kinds of businesses: one offered consulting services on marketing to small companies, the other aimed to offer empowerment to women. These services involved a website from which women could access information on various events or find information to help them in their careers.

Ryoko now thinks her new company would not be in existence if she had not enrolled in the business school. The classes on enterprise development and innovation, in particular, had inspired her to launch her new business, which involved disseminating stories that would encourage working women to continue their careers while also allowing her to develop a network of working women. According to Ryoko, she gained the confidence to build her new business from the entrepreneurship-related classes at the business school.

Ryoko considers the network she developed in the business school valuable. For example, her female classmates have been staunch supporters of her new company, Hanako having participated in several events. Ryoko also hired some foreign students in the Global MBA program, and tried to create an international network. These students helped Ryoko develop an English homepage.

In addition, Ryoko invited two women students from Thailand and Indonesia to events to give talks on the situation of working women in their homelands, the aim being that highly motivated foreign female MBA students would encourage Japanese working women to continue advancing their careers.

Besides the inspiration, knowledge, skills, confidence and network she gained through her MBA degree, it also boosted her credibility. Ryoko thinks she could not possibly have won certain projects from regional governments without her MBA degree which she feels helps distinguish her from other women.

The Cases of Hanako and Yoshiko: Among the few female classmates Ryoko had in her MBA program were Hanako and Yoshiko who were both single and in their early 40s, and worked as managers in major companies in Japan. For both Hanako and Yoshiko, an MBA was meaningful because female MBA holders were considered quite distinctive in the Japanese business world, their degrees clearly helping differentiate them. Moreover, the business school provided knowledge and skills. Finally, in writing their theses, the women developed confidence in their knowledge and ability to pursue their careers. What is more, the business school provided opportunities for the women enrolled to get to know people outside of their business and industry. Both Hanako and Yoshiko considered networking with other students to be an asset above and beyond the content and knowledge provided by the MBA program.

Hanako and Yoshiko graduated from the business school at the same time. For Hanako, who worked as a manager in the accounting department of a Japanese electric multinational, getting an MBA was a real plus. The company she worked for had suffered from huge losses, and the organization went through some restructuring. While some people were forced to choose early retirement, Hanako's responsibility was increased. She then thought it quite possible for her to advance her career with her MBA despite the difficult situation of the organization where she worked. Her business school education and MBA degree clearly signalled that she was motivated, capable, well educated and in possession of an appreciation of business beyond her accounting expertise. With the pressure of the government to promote more women under the current "woman promotion bubble", Hanako thinks she has a great advantage.

Yoshiko's case is a little bit different. Yoshiko worked for a software development subsidiary of an electric multinational. She was a manager of the planning department, heading the department while she was working for her MBA. However, after she gained her MBA degree, she faced a de facto demotion. Her job title and pay were not changed, but she was sent to a newly created department where she was without any subordinates. Yoshiko felt that her male boss, who did not have an MBA, envied her because of her MBA degree. So the jealousy of her immediate boss strongly worked against her. However, Yoshiko remained optimistic. People around her, including the vice presidents of the parent company, knew of her situation. They recognized her as an MBA holder who was also very capable. They suggested that Yoshiko should be patient. So Yoshiko waited for the storm to pass. In April 2015, Yoshiko is moving to Tokyo to be a manager of the parent company.

The Case of Maya: Maya is currently working at the international department of a giant cosmetics company. Maya's case was interesting because she decided to get her MBA during her maternity leave, and to get it in Singapore. After graduating from a famous private university in Japan, she was recruited by a foreign capital investment company. After working for the company for several years, Maya found it hard to keep a balance between work and life. She transferred to the cosmetics company when she got married. After working at the cosmetics company for five years, she wanted to take some time off work so she could seriously consider her future direction and acquire the necessary expertise to broaden her career options. Eventually, Maya was also eager to expand her horizons internationally so that she could become a global business manager. For these reasons, Maya thought that getting an MBA degree abroad would be ideal. She could acquire the professional "toolkit" and network that she would need. After she had her baby, she decided to enrol in an MBA program in Singapore. Beyond the networking opportunities, Singapore was an ideal place for Maya because there she could arrange for childcare very easily. After graduating, she planned to take on a marketing-related role in the company. Eventually, she hopes to rise to a senior management position.

16.5 The views of Asian female MBAs

As noted above, Doshisha's new Global MBA program was established with the purpose of attracting more foreign talent to Japan. As stated earlier, females comprise about half of the 70 students enrolled in the English-based Global MBA program. (There are no Japanese students in the Global MBA program.) Therefore, voices of foreign women MBAs are significant. What do Asian female students in Doshisha's English MBA program think about the MBA education in Japan and what do they think about their career prospects? It is worth exploring their views, especially given Japan's 102nd-place ranking in the Global Gender Gap Index. For foreign female MBA holders, Japan may not be an attractive destination for work. Below are comments from the business school's women students from Thailand, Indonesia, Mongolia and China.

As background information, it should be noted that the high proportion of women in the Global MBA program is despite the fact that program administrators do not make any effort to specifically attract women applicants. This is in contrast to some business schools in the United States that offer scholarships and have local and international networks, mentoring programs, publications, and forums for successful women so as to attract more female students (Educationpost, 2013). None of these are available in the Global MBA program of Doshisha. The higher ratio of women in the Global MBA program vis-à-vis the Japanese MBA program may instead be related to the rapidly growing number of Asian women taking the GMAT (Damast, 2012).

Thai woman MBA holder: After getting her MBA in 2014, this Thai woman MBA holder was employed by a huge internet marketing company in Japan. That company is rapidly expanding worldwide, and its president is forcing employees to use English and consider it as the company's official language. According to this Thai woman, males and females in Thailand are equal in terms of status when it comes to work. She said, "Women MBAs in Thailand are ambitious, modern-thinking, hard-working, entrepreneurial and non-conformists. We have one of the highest ratios of women executives. MBAs are for both males and females, but I still think male MBAs may become more influential." According to her, she would like to work in Japan because the work she chose could contribute to society. She believes the business she is in can address needs beyond money or technological advancement.

Indonesian woman MBA holder: After getting her MBA in September 2014, this Indonesian woman MBA holder is looking for a job in Japan, in work related to Indonesia. She said, "I want to contribute to my country. I do not want investors to merely see my country as a potential market. Foreign companies tend to come and take everything for their own benefit. Rather I want to work in a company that has a clear vision and a great corporate philosophy." According to her, women MBAs in Indonesia are those who pursue top management positions and better salaries. Many of her women friends also have MBA degrees and their reason for obtaining one is simply this: their undergraduate major is not related to business and they want to know more about it. According to this Indonesian woman, men still hold the top management positions.

Mongolian woman MBA holder: After getting her MBA in September 2014, this Mongolian woman MBA holder decided to migrate to the United States with her two children and husband. According to her, her Japanese is not good enough to get a job in Japan. While she was pursuing her MBA in Japan, she left her children in Mongolia. She thinks the demand for MBAs is high in the Mongolian labour market, and an MBA earned in a foreign country is viewed more highly than a local MBA. However, staying in Mongolia is a problem because the air pollution may affect the health of her children.

Chinese woman MBA holder: This Chinese woman MBA holder married her Chinese classmate and had a baby while taking her Global MBA. Normally it is hard for a mother with a newborn baby to find a good job in Japan. However, immediately after her graduation, she found a job related to international business between China and Japan. It will allow her to use what she learned at the business school. As is the case with many Chinese students, she has a good command of Japanese because the Japanese language uses Chinese characters. She thinks her language skills and the MBA degree will help her to find a job in Japan.

MBA degrees from foreign countries, including Japan, have greater value for many Asian women MBA candidates. Therefore, many choose to come to Japan to get their business school education, although Japan is not the most ideal country for women to stay and work. In many cases, their home countries rank more favourably in the Gender Gap Index. The question is: can Japan utilize this opportunity to retain highly talented foreign nationals, especially now that many Asian women are willing to come to Japan to take an MBA degree?

16.6 Discussion

This chapter has described the problems that Japan faces in terms of the gender gap and the role of business schools in Japan. The gender gap in Japan is embarrassingly wide, ranked as 104th in the Global Gender Gap Index. The root cause of Japan's poor score in this index is the system of Japanese capitalism, which is largely based on lifetime employment and seniority pay. While the system ultimately aims to provide employment security to Japanese households, the system expects husbands to work for long hours and the women to stay at home, support their husbands, and take care of the children. Hence, women do not stay long enough in their jobs to be promoted. Moreover, corporate Japan does not expect women to stay long enough to be promoted. Because labour mobility is limited by the lifetime employment system, it is difficult for women to find permanent jobs when they finish child rearing. It is more likely for them to find only find part-time jobs with low pay. This discourages women from participating in the labour force.

Meanwhile, faced with a rapidly shrinking population, Japan's potential growth has been falling rapidly. In order to arrest this decline, Japan needs to change its system to include more women in the workplace. The IMF suggested that Japanese GDP per capita can be increased by as much as 4–8% if female labour force participation can be increased to the level of OECD countries. This would mean a significant increase in GDP per capita for Japan, which is suffering from a stagnating economy. With these figures in mind, the Japanese government has taken the issue seriously.

As suggested by the IMF, increasing women's labour force participation through measures to alleviate gender inequalities has become the central policy of the so-called "Abenomics": that is, the economic growth policies of Prime Minister Abe. Pressured by the government, Japanese corporations are hastly promoting female participation, effectively creating a "Woman Promotion Bubble". The skewed situation resulting from promoting some women without merit may ultimately affect those women who do have the right qualifications. It appears that there is no shortcut to allow more women to be promoted.

Japanese women are relatively well educated. Many have university degrees. So the master's level of education such as a business school MBA is suitable for many Japanese women in acquiring the knowledge and skills needed to progress. However, business schools are not well developed in Japan. Again, the root cause of this is the lifetime employment and the seniority pay system. An MBA education does not fit well with Japanese capitalism where labour mobility is limited.

Although MBAs are not widely accepted in corporate Japan, part-time business schools and part-time MBA programs are increasing in number. And, although Japanese women are a minority among MBA students, their high motivation is a decided advantage. Furthermore, their MBA titles, together with the knowledge, confidence and networks they gain in the business schools, can be of substantial value to their future. As seen in the case of Ryoko, a business school education encouraged a female MBA to establish a social enterprise, which in turn can encourage other working women to support each other for the advancement of their careers through networking.

Besides measures favouring working women, Japan also needs to attract talented foreign nationals from abroad. Attracting international students to Japanese higher education institutions, including business schools, is one of the measures it should consider. Meanwhile, in spite of the wide gender gap in Japan, the number of women MBA students from Asia who come to Japan is increasing. They come to benefit from gaining a foreign MBA degree. How Japan can retain them in the future is a challenge.

The time has come for business school faculties to seriously consider the role of women MBAs in Japan, and the possibility of promoting a diversity-sensitive business school education within the Japanese context. In this regard, diversity encompasses not only gender diversity but also diversities of cultures and nationalities.

16.7 Conclusion

In Japan, women MBAs are quite few and are struggling. Yet women MBAs manage to inspire others, even as they support themselves and strive to make a difference. Today, business school education plays a vital role in the lives of women in Japan. Though not yet widely accepted in Japan, the MBA degree and business school education help women gain knowledge, networks and confidence, while also helping them distinguish themselves in the job market. Furthermore, business schools can create social entrepreneurs such as Ryoko, who has encouraged and inspired other women to participate in the labour force and advance their careers. A business school education, as well as the networks it provides, can inculcate positive values which help to narrow the gender gap in Japanese society. Such a development can, in turn, lead to an increase in Japan's per capita GDP.

While various policies are needed, ultimately, what are essential for the women to advance their careers are their own merit and the values they can create in the organization for which they work. Business school education can be used to equip female students with competitive skills and networks to enhance their motivation and support their advancement.

Acknowledgements

The author thanks the assistance provided by Ms WeiWei Zheng. Also, the paper received financial assistance from the Omron Research Fund of Doshisha Business School.

References

Cabinet Office, Government of Japan, 2013. Toward active participation of women as the core of growth strategies. White Paper on Gender Equality 2013 (Gender Equality Bureau Cabinet Office, Tokyo): 2–6. www.gender.go.jp/english_contents/about_danjo/whitepaper/pdf/2013-01.pdf (accessed 03.09.14).

Damast, A., February 29, 2012. Asian women taking GMAT on the rise. Bloomberg Businessweek. www.businessweek.com/articles/2012-02-29/asian-women-taking-gmat-on-the-rise (accessed 03.08.14).

Doshisha Business School Japanese MBA program, 2014. www.bs.doshisha.ac.jp (accessed 03.09.14).

Doshisha Global MBA program, 2014. www.gmba.doshisha.ac.jp (accessed 03.09.14).

Educationpost, 2013. Resources for MBA women in Asia, Educationpost (20 May). www.educationpost.com.hk/resources/mba/130520-insights-resources-mba-women-asia (accessed 03.08.14).

The Japan Institute for Labour Policy and Training, 2013. Ryugakusei no Shushoku Katsudo. www.jil.go.jp/institute/chosa/2013/13-113.htm (accessed 03.09.14).

Nikkei Business, 2013. Onna de Jigoku to Kasuru Shokuba, Nikkei Business (26 August): 26–41.

Nihon Keizai Shinbun, 2013. Josei Kanrishoku Touyou ni Mokuhyo, Nihon Keizai Shinbun (December 18): 3.

Organization for Economic Co-operation and Development, 2013. Country Note: Japan's Education at a Glance 2013. OECD Publishing, Paris, France. www.dx.doi.org/10.1787/eag-2013-en (accessed 03.09.14).

Sangster, E., 2011. Women must appreciate the value of an MBA, Financial Times (21 November). www.ft.com/cms/s/2/49c47720-0ee1-11e1-b585-00144feabdc0.html#axzz2vX8QE6nX (accessed 03.09.14).

Steinberg, C., September 25, 2013. Brooking's event: from abenomics to womenomics, paper presented at From Abenomics to Womenomics: Working Women and Japan's Economic Revival conference at the center for Northeast Asian policy studies in Brookings Institute, Washington, DC.

Steinberg, C., Nakane, M., 2012. Can women save Japan? IMF Working Paper 12/248 International Monetary Fund Washington, DC.

Suezaki, T., 2013. Immigrants eyed as a key to maintaining population level, Asahi Shinbun Digital (25 February 2014). www.ajw.asahi.com/article/economy/business/AJ201402250042 (accessed 03.09.14).

Tanikawa, M., 2010. M.B.A.'s in Japan struggle for respect, New York Times (24 November). www.nytimes.com/2010/11/25/education/25iht-RieducJapan.html?pagewanted=all&_r=0 (accessed 03.09.14).

Tashiro, H., Rowley, I., 2009. Japan: slowly warming up to MBAs, Bloomberg Businessweek (8 May 2009). www.businessweek.com/globalbiz/content/may2009/gb2009057_863933.htm (accessed 03.09.14).

World Economic Forum, 2014. The Global Gender Gap Report 2014, World Economic Forum, Geneva, Switzerland.

Part V
Pedagogical approaches

17

The gender equality index and reflective role-plays

Introducing gender in management education

Anna Wahl

Royal Institute of Technology (KTH), Sweden

The key problems that emerge when integrating a gender perspective in management education are pinpointed and structured around four different stages in gender education: feelings of uneasiness; gendered resistance; lack of academic status; and the experienced gap between gender theory and inequality practice. Two methods that can be used to address and challenge some of the described problems are presented. One of the methods is *Gender Equality Index* (GEI) that helps to set gender on the agenda and to involve participants to the subject of gender. The second example is the *Reflective role-play* that addresses gender equality issues that are used in the closing stages of the course to help students connect gender theory to organizational practice and work for change. The chapter concludes with a summary of suggested solutions to the identified problems that occur when integrating gender in management education.

17.1 Introduction

The reasons for introducing gender perspectives and gender equality (GE) issues in management education are numerous. Gender inequalities are related to gendered power relations in society and in organizations (Acker, 2012; Hearn, 2000). Management positions are positions of influence and connected to the possibilities of challenging existing power relations in organizations. To a great extent management structures are accountable for the reproduction of gender inequalities in organizations (Holgersson, 2013; Wahl, forthcoming). Male dominance in management positions not only leads to the continued appointment of men in those positions but also to gender inequalities in organizations in general (Wahl, 2013). The male norm for management is normalized as gender neutral and needs to be visualized and problematized in management education in order to open up alternative ways of doing management for both men and women (Marshall, 1999; Mavin and Bryans, 1999; Wahl and Holgersson, 2003; Wahl and Höök, 2007). Management education is a decisive key to changing gender relations in organizations and in society. There are, however, several obstacles on the way, as the subject of gender and power are complicated and often ignored in management education (Gatenby and Humphries, 1999). There is a scale of problems reaching from unawareness and lack of knowledge to active resistance (Wahl, 1999). Two methods that can be used to address and challenge some of these problems are presented in this chapter; they are: *Gender Equality Index* and *Reflective role-play*.

To begin this chapter, the main problems that emerge when integrating gender in management education are pinpointed. The key problems are structured around four different stages in gender education: feelings of uneasiness; gendered resistance; lack of academic status; and the experienced gap between gender theory and inequality practice. The chapter continues by exemplifying two methods that can be used to address and challenge some of the described problems. The methods chosen support the integration of GE in management education in different stages of a course. One of the methods that will be presented is a *Gender Equality Index* (GEI). This method helps to set gender on the agenda and to involve and engage participants with the subject of gender initially. The second example is the *Reflective role-play* that addresses GE issues. These role-plays are used in the closing stages of the course, often as part of the examination to help students connect gender theory to organizational practice and to work for change. The chapter concludes by suggesting potential solutions to the identified problems that can occur when integrating gender in management education.

17.2 Main problems when introducing gender in management education

There are several problems to handle when integrating gender in management education which are well documented in previous studies (e.g. Gatenby and Humphries, 1999; Marshall, 1999; Smith, 1997; Sinclair, 2000). The main problems described here are based on the author's own experience when integrating gender in management education (Wahl, 1999; Wahl and Höök, 2007) in management (Wahl and Höök, 2007) and in organizational settings (Wahl et al., 2008; Wahl and Holgersson, 2013; Wahl, 2014). The problems that often occur and that will be developed further are divided into four stages of management education. They will be presented in the following way:

- Feelings of uneasiness among participants

- Gendered resistance

- Lack of knowledge and academic status at organizational level

- Experienced gap between gender theory and inequality practice.

17.2.1 Feelings of uneasiness among participants

The subject of gender, GE or feminism will evoke emotions in almost all kinds of groups. It is often interpreted as a political and provocative subject rather than an area of important knowledge and academic theorizing. The reactions can be very different but what they all have in common is that there are feelings of uneasiness about the situation. In addition, participants that sympathize with the fact that GE is taken into account can feel uneasy because they take responsibility for others who feel uneasy and troubled. Sometimes participants feel uncomfortable because they have previous experiences of inequality that they do not want to talk about or remember. Uneasiness can arise from notions that the subject is not serious enough to integrate into management. It can be ridiculed or be seen as boring or unfashionable.

Whatever reasons there are among participants to feel uncomfortable with the subject of gender, it may disturb the dissemination of gender knowledge and processes of learning in education. It is important to name feelings of uneasiness in the setting instead of ignoring them. To name feelings of uneasiness, exemplify different reactions and analyse them is of vital importance in order to be able to move on with the lecturing. It often helps the participants to relax and feel welcome to share new knowledge, whatever perspective they have at the start. Sometimes there can be comments or questions, but most often the naming of uneasiness is met with silence but with expressions of relief.

The naming of present emotions of uneasiness among participants can be achieved in several ways. One method is use of a simple PowerPoint image that illustrates and describes the phenomenon. This is often enough to open up discussion and reflections about why there may be resistance to the subject of gender. If there is more time to dwell on this, a more thorough exercise can be used, such as the *Cloud model*, developed by the author (Wahl, 1999). This model displays the resistance related to preconceptions about feminism. The Cloud model can be used to improve teaching and increase the chances of constructive dialogue. By bringing preconceptions about feminism and gender into the open and analysing them, these ideas can be used to illuminate the presentation, not to hinder it. As a general model the Cloud is a tool that will help to articulate common beliefs about phenomena to make way for knowledge based on research. In summary, participants are encouraged to say what comes to their mind when they hear the word "feminism".

The answers are written on a whiteboard on the basis of the model, at first invisible to the participants. The most common words are negatively charged such as "aggression", "biased", "men-haters", "women's domination", "unwomanly" and "denial of differences". Words associated with the women's movement also occur, such as "women's rights" and "gender equality". Positively charged words such as "strength" and "justice" are less common, but they do appear. The model is then explained by adding headings over three columns of words: politics, ideology and research. These words represent feminism in different ways, and can be further developed in the lecture. Words floating above the columns are grouped together in a cloud, classified as anti-feminism, preconceptions, misunderstandings and ignorance. When the participants' ideas about feminism are brought to the fore and analysed as a starting point, they can be actively used in the lecture instead of becoming a passive obstruction. The preconceptions in the cloud can be pinpointed and then set aside for the time being (Wahl, 1999).

17.2.2 Gendered resistance

The reactions of uneasiness are sometimes unclear in relation to resistance towards gender theory generally. As was mentioned above, being uncomfortable with the subject does not necessarily mean that you resist the area of knowledge in general. Sometimes it means that you support it in principle but that you do not see the point in introducing it to management education: for example, if this setting is basically opposed to gender issues. Sometimes, however, reactions of uneasiness can be related to resisting gender issues on a personal level. These reactions of resistance are often gendered, meaning that they are divided into typical reactions of men and women respectively.

The gendered reaction of men is often related to feelings of being falsely accused for inequalities in society or to feelings of assumed guilt for gender inequalities. These reactions are positioned on an individual level, interpreting GE as a matter of "being or not being gender equal" as an individual, as opposed to understanding inequalities as part of societal and organizational structures. The gendered reaction of women is most often related to feelings of being stigmatized by the issue, or as being ascribed to belonging to the "second sex" or a "weaker part" in society and organizations. This is a similar reaction, also based on an understanding of gender as an entirely individual matter. Women who feel stigmatized by the subject of gender will actively distance themselves from gender theory, as this makes them feel associated with weakness and as belonging to a problematic category. Women who share this kind of reaction often stress that they never experienced discrimination or other gender inequalities.

In both cases, it is important not to question the reactions of either men or women, as this will confirm the issue as an individual one. On the contrary, it is important to present gender issues and gender inequalities as structural phenomenon in society, and as managerial tasks in organizations. The approach of naming gender as a management task will in fact help participants to engage in new knowledge, as it puts gender on the managerial agenda in organizations. It helps to explain that the gendered structures in organizations and the experienced inequalities in the organization are central for managers, not whether the manager, man or woman, identifies himself or herself as being gender equal or not. By naming and analysing gendered reactions by both men and women, participants are invited to share gender perspectives without feelings of guilt or stigmatization.

17.2.3 Lack of knowledge and academic status

The organizational context is of importance when integrating gender in management education. What support is there at university level? Is gender marginalized in the overall program? There is often an overwhelming lack of gender knowledge among university staff teaching management, which of course spills over into the organizational culture (Gatenby and Humphries, 1999; Sinclair, 2007). Resistance is often expressed in various ways stating that gender is not essential in management theory and practice. This problem is not easily solved, but must be handled correctly in the course when integrating gender theory in the curriculum.

It is important to include textbooks on gender and organization or gender and management in the curriculum, to avoid the area of knowledge becoming marginalized in the body of literature. Most important is to adapt to academic standards when choosing literature and examinations and to reinforce that this is a legitimate academic field of knowledge. The risk of being regarded as a more popular or political area, in contrast to having academic status, is always at hand when gender is integrated in management education. When incorporating gender in management education, it is often necessary to start the dissemination of knowledge to faculty, before meeting the students. This has been recognized in several Swedish universities and in business schools, where seminars with faculty has been an important part of the integration of gender in education (Wahl and Höök, 2007).

17.2.4 Experienced gap between gender theory and inequality practice

It is not unusual that gender theory is regarded as complex and difficult to apply in everyday practice. Concepts are different from corporate language and sometimes seen as provocative in management settings due to references to remote spaces such as power, sexuality, violence, discrimination, homosociality and inequality. Gender theory, in the field of organization studies, is aiming at describing and analysing gender in organizations and in management. Emphasis is put on understanding gender in organizations, where the analysis of gender inequalities is crucial. It is not, however, always aiming at finding solutions to problems, or to transform theory into practice. This becomes problematic in education and in practice in organizations.

There is a need to connect gender analysis to organizational practice in education to bridge the experienced gap between theory and practice. Methods for GE work are not always presented in the literature, and this has to be changed. GE work often provokes structural and cultural resistance, expressed in everyday interactions in organizations (Hearn, 2000; Wahl and Holgersson, 2013; Wahl, 2014). Students and managers need to practise situations where GE is on the agenda. They also need opportunities to reflect on different methods that can be used and the resistance this may provoke to be better prepared.

Methods that has been developed and used by the author are case studies on gender and reflective role-plays on gender. The development and use of case studies on gender will not be presented in this chapter.

17.3 Methods to challenge resistance to gender

All the stages presented above are equally important to handle in a professional way to succeed when integrating gender in management education. In the following sections, two methods will be presented as examples of how to challenge problems in the initial and closing phases. They focus on coping with experienced uneasiness and uncertainty among participants. The first example, the GEI, focuses ways of thinking and talking about GE that form different prerequisites for introducing gender in management education. The different ways of talking about GE often touch upon what inequality is, and the purpose behind GE work. The method is developed by the author, and has been used in several different settings and situations. The purpose is to contribute to participants' understanding of GE and to increase motivation for engaging in the subject of gender. The second example, reflective role-plays, focuses on the experienced gap between gender theory and inequality practice among participants. Reflective role-plays can assist when applying theory to practice, and can contribute to advancing the understanding of power relations in organizations.

17.3.1 Gender Equality Index

The GEI is presented as a scale, ranging from 1 to 10, where 1 corresponds to a situation characterized by entire gender *inequality* and 10 to a situation with entire gender *equality*. In the seminars the participants are asked to estimate their own organizational context on the GE scale 1–10; first their estimation of their own context, and then also their estimation of work–life in general. The question is introduced as a "game", denoting that the importance is not to deliver an exact number on the scale; rather the aim is to share their view on and experiences from GE work. The aim is to address participants as experts who are expected to have opinions and adequate knowledge for defining and evaluating GE. The purpose with the GEI is to place the participants in subject positions as "knowers" of GE, and to capture their experiences of and opinions on gender (in)equality. And consequently, when introducing the scale on GE, no definitions or examples of GE are presented. The participants are encouraged to make their own definitions and estimations of GE, and to share them with others in the ensuing discussion. An important aspect of the method is to call for the participants' reflections on their own definition of GE. The response often results in various definitions of GE and different points of departure for the estimations of GE, which brings together a platform for further exploration and reflections during discussions.

The variation of estimations that becomes visible through the exercise contributes to a deeper understanding of the complexity of GE work in organizations.

The various definitions and opinions that occur can be understood against the background that GE work today is a common activity in Swedish organizations. GE work in relation to GE policies is a common practice in most large Swedish organizations but the prerequisites for working for change differ according to the various understandings of GE that may prevail. The different ways of talking about GE often reflect organizational notions of what the purpose of GE work is. Perceptions of GE in organizations and management in society are also present and active in management education. The GEI method has been used in management education in similar ways as in organizations, but has not been documented in research. Results from an empirical study where the GEI method was used in group interviews with men and women in different positions in the same organization are discussed in the following paragraph as an illustration of the method (Wahl and Linghag, 2013).

Women rated the present status of GE lower than men in all professional categories. Some men considered it an advantage to be a woman due to GE work, and that men experienced discrimination in recruitment situations. Low grades by women managers were explained by women managers' minority position and lack of influence and power. Women managers described their situation as marginalized and vulnerable in a male-dominated and hostile culture. Male managers rated GE higher than female managers did. Lower grades among them were explained by a male-dominated culture that included prejudice against women. High grades were motivated by describing changes in relation to GE and to increasing numbers of women in the company as well as a positive attitude towards paternal leave. When a male manager chose a 7 on the GEI, it was followed by a discussion of why it was so low. When a woman manager chose a 7, she explained why it was so high by, for example, pointing at the improvements that GE work had resulted in. Women experience gender inequality in society and organizations, while men experience GE.

In conclusion, there are three different aspects of GE that are activated and exposed in the discussions following the GEI exercise in the study. First, women and men are positioned differently concerning expectations of GE. It is more common that men take the position of expecting GE in reality, and understanding the normal situation as being gender equal. Women do not in general expect reality to be gender equal, which is why they have expectations of inequality as the normal situation. Second, there is an aspect of relating the estimations of GE to closeness and distance. It is common, especially among women, to relate the own work environment as relatively more gender equal than somewhere else. The distant, relatively less equal, place can be described geographically in other departments in the same company or in other parts of the world. Women more often use this kind of reasoning. The distance can also be described professionally representing other parts of the corporate hierarchy, like pointing at management or production from a distance. Men more often use the professional distancing when comparing GE as more or less prevalent. The third aspect that is activated is the perceived nature or character of gender relations as either culturally embedded or as any other kind of business activity. Women understand gender relations as culturally embedded, more solid and hard to change. Men evaluate gender relations in relation to results from GE work, and more often point at efforts being made and changes that have taken place already, for example, paternal leave or recruiting more women.

17.3.2 Reflective role-plays

The role-play presented here (Wahl, 1997; Holgersson, 1997) can be used in education and training where prescribed texts include organization theory from a gender perspective. Students should have read and applied the theory during the course. The role-play is designed for use towards the end of course as a method of putting theory into action, sometimes as part of examinations. Thus knowledge is required so that students will advance deeper in their awareness of and insight into gender-related issues in management. The role-play is an entertaining way of experiencing the process "for real". Phenomena such as power, resistance, conflict, humour, sympathies and antipathies do not easily find the space for influencing exam answers, assignments, projects and so on. Written answers suggesting radical problem-solving changes in an organization can be easy. Presenting such changes for a sceptical and uninformed management in a role-play is another matter. Students are expected to understand from theory roughly how the various characters relate to the situation presented. Therefore insight into the typical notions and strategies of each respective character is essential to allow each person to play his or her role. The objective is to enable the players to experience the process as it might develop in an organization. Setting processes into motion on the basis of the students' personal conceptions is not the objective. It is through being touched by problems in a role perhaps far from one's own personality that new insight may be reached.

Even if the characters are defined, there is of course still plenty of room for roles to be developed and freely acted through the improvisation, which follows instructions to each scene. It is the interaction between characters in the scenes that will largely determine what is said and done. This is indeed one of the objectives. The leader's contribution is to present the situation, characters and each particular scene as clearly and vividly as possible. It may sometimes be useful to stop a scene that has reached its goal. The role-play can inspire individual variations as regards both characters and scenes. Roles may sometimes be removed or added depending on the number of students/participants in the group. The whole group should participate in the role-play. The number of scenes and content of these can, of course, also vary. Otherwise the inspiration itself can be kept for reflections at end of play where discussion or writing can centre on what might have happened instead or how matters might progress in the future.

The role-play has a principal idea and a "main scene". Otherwise, there are no given details. The principal idea can be, for example, that the recruitment routines in a particular organization are gendered in a way that results in male dominance on management positions. The main scene may be a formal executive meeting where the process around a specific recruitment will be discussed and decided. The preceding scenes in the role-play may consist of several informal meetings between characters preparing for the main formal meeting. The person leading the seminar provides guidance to participants through instructions. What is then acted out depends largely on context.

Important elements include group participants, role distribution and advance knowledge based on gender literature. Leaders can contribute greatly to post-role-play discussions by providing various interpretations to why events took the turns they took. The role-play is designed as a concluding feature to a course where knowledge of gender theory within organization and management plays an essential part. The best method is to work as spontaneously and unprepared as possible so that focus is on converting theory into practice in a direct situation, rather than spending too much time preparing the acting of individual characters. The leader can, for example, present the company and its individuals as a story in the classroom. Such a story presentation will automatically involve a build-up to the situation and main scene of the play.

The characters in the play are also presented as an obvious part of the story, but in greater detail individually once the situation is clear to participants. These are given very brief description, but with certain basic elements: gender, position, strategy, private situation, ideological views and relation to other characters and judgements or rumours relating to the person. Some are described in greater depth than others, and participants can fill out characters once they have gained perception of the full situation and the other characters.

The roles are then shared out among participants. This distribution should be clear from the start and well thought-out so teachers can make use of their advance knowledge of the group. Changing gender of some participants is, for example, useful. Using the possibility that certain people suit certain roles really well can also sometimes be effective, just as giving people parts alien to them might at times be useful. The objective of the role-play is not personal development or working with group processes, thus roles should be shared out in order that everyone feels at ease and ready to enjoy the play. The leader must arrange a character distribution, which allows the play to start off as smoothly as possible. For some participants a "difficult" or out-of-character role may represent a positive challenge, while for others a role they feel more at home with would be preferable.

The play can get off to a quick start since no energy is lost in choosing right characters or in individuals playing their roles particularly well. What is in focus is the formation of a common process. Participants then receive their character description on a piece of paper, and are given a few minutes to consider their role. All participants are given a role, thus ensuring that everyone present takes part. Even as a spectator to certain scenes, individual role players are active participants in the play on the basis of their specific roles.

The leader presents the scenes as the play progresses in order to create as much spontaneity and presence as possible. No one should be required to have his or her thoughts on the future. Everyone should be in the present, in the action of the moment. In this way, involvement from the whole group is strong, while only a few act in each particular scene. Each scene is presented prior to being played. Following from the recruitment example above, the informal meetings between different characters in the play will be presented, for example Sally, a young manager at the Human Resource department meets a senior male manager, Tom, in the corridor and stops him to discuss the upcoming recruitment meeting. Sally thinks that the criteria in use hamper women's careers and that they could be changed. In this way, the script is developed through a common process. Those acting take to the stage directly and commence. The scene is stopped as soon as the actors feel it is played out or once the leader considers its function has been served. The next scene is then presented in the same way. The scenes are built up around the main scene which is the only one presented when relating the story of the company. The first to come is a series of build-up scenes, and after the main scene "what is later said" is then depicted in various groupings. The leader can choose to remain completely on the outside or suddenly show up as an element of surprise in a role, for example as a secretary informing the managing director of a phone call.

Participants may require a break at the end of the play, where they nevertheless are encouraged to reflect on what has taken place. Discussion is at first open for comments, reflections, lessons learnt and so on. Sometimes, especially in larger groups, the participants can be divided into "actors" and "observers". The observers take notes during the performance and are then the first to comment on what happened in the scene. The observers enter the stage and discuss, while the actors step aside and become observers.

Themes, which may then be useful to discuss are:

1. Why did it take the turns it took?

2. How could it have been different?

3. Is it likely/normal that such a situation exists in companies, and that events may take a course similar to that in the role-play?

In general, what is important are the themes linked to course learning, those that refer back to theory. Reflections on fiction and reality can for example provide new insight into the opportunities for working for change in organizations. If time provides, then participants as a good way of concluding the course may make some form of distributed written notes on these reflections. Here it is once again important that the reflections do not stand by themselves, but instead are linked to course theory. In this way, the leader is given a further opportunity to provide feedback and comments on the analyses and thoughts of individual students.

Role-playing can be used in various types of course where the gender perspective plays a more or less prominent part. It can be used in special courses, which as a whole are based on gender theory. It can also be used in courses on management and organization theory where the gender perspective is integrated as one part. Deeper analysis of the play may often be made in special courses, since theoretical knowledge is often greater. Written notes following the role play may be more important in an integrated course than in a special course, since greater opportunity is given for working with theory and receiving feedback from leaders.

17.4 Conclusion

In order to integrate gender in management education, resistance to the issue of gender must be handled in different situations and stages. In this chapter, the problems of resistance have been divided into four stages of the process; feelings of uneasiness, gendered

Table 17.1 **Problems, solutions and methods**

Problems	Solutions	Methods
Feelings of uneasiness among participants	Naming and analysing problems	Images and models that capture emotions and thoughts, e.g. the Cloud
Gendered resistance	Involve participants	Methods that activate subjectivity and own experience, e.g. GEI
Lack of knowledge and academic status	Gender literature and academic format	Textbooks on gender and organization Knowledge dissemination to faculty
Experienced gap between gender theory and inequality practice	Combination of theory and reflective exercises	Reflective role-plays Case-studies

reactions, lack of gender knowledge at university level and an experienced gap between gender theory and inequality practice in organizations. Uneasiness has to be named and analysed initially in education. Gendered reactions of resistance must be encountered with methods that involve and engage participants as subjects to gender issues. Lack of gender competence at university level is balanced with textbooks on gender and organization. Sometimes gender seminars for faculty are necessary to support the integration of gender. The gap between gender theory and inequality practice can be bridged with the help of reflective exercises that link theory to practice.

Several methods can be used in management education to handle these situations, and in this chapter two examples have been described in detail, the *Gender Equality Index* and *Reflective role-plays*. Problems, solutions and possible methods are summarized in Table 17.1. In conclusion, there is a need for careful planning of how to address and challenge resistance with suitable methods when integrating gender in management education. The specific context must be analysed and understood. There is also a need for continual reflections around the reactions that will occur. It is often a good idea to form teams of teachers or leaders to support the process and continuously make adjustments and improvements in relation to reactions and feedback.

References

Acker, J., 2012. Gendered organizations and intersectionality: problems and possibilities. Equality, Diversity and Inclusion: An International Journal 31(3), 214–224.

Gatenby, B., Humphries, M., 1999. Exploring gender, management education and careers: speaking in the silences. Gender and Education 11(3), 281–294.

Hearn, J., 2000. On the complexity of feminist intervention in organizations. Organization 7, 609–624.

Holgersson, C., 1997. Recruitment at Naxa machines. Role-play for teaching organization and gender. National Agency for Higher Education, Stockholm, Sweden.

Holgersson, C., 2013. Recruiting managing directors: doing homosociality. Gender, Work & Organization 20(4), 454–466.

Marshall, J., 1999. Doing gender in management education. Gender and Education 11(3), 251–263.

Mavin, S., Bryans, P., 1999. Gender on the agenda in management education? Women in Management Review 14(3), 99–104.

Sinclair, A., 2000. Teaching managers about masculinities: are you kidding? Management Learning 31(1), 83–101.

Sinclair, A., 2007. Teaching leadership critically to MBA's experiences from heaven and hell. Management Learning 38(4), 458–472.

Smith, C.R., 1997. Gender issues in management education: a new teaching resource. Women in Management Review 12(3), 100–104.

Wahl, A., 1997. The network—a tale of growing awareness in a company. Role-play for teaching organization and gender. National Agency for Higher Education, Stockholm, Sweden.

Wahl, A., 1999. The cloud—lecturing on feminist research. NORA, Nordic Journal of Feminist and Gender Research 7(2–3), 97–108.

Wahl, A., 2013. Gendering management. In: Sandberg, Å. (Ed.), Nordic Lights. Work, Management and Welfare in Scandinavia. SNS förlag, Stockholm, Sweden.

Wahl, A., 2014. Male managers challenging and reinforcing the male norm in management. NORA, Nordic Journal of Feminist and Gender Research 22(2), 131–146.

Wahl, A., Holgersson, C., 2003. Male managers' reactions to gender diversity activities in organizations. In: Davidson, M., Fielden, S. (Eds.), Individual Diversity and Psychology in Organizations. Wiley, Chichester.

Wahl, A., Holgersson, C., 2013. Paralysis and fantasy—handling resistance when conveying feminist knowledge. In: Strid, S., Husu, L. (Eds.), Gender paradoxes in changing academic and scientific organisations. GEXcel work in progress report XVIII: 187–200. Örebro University and Linköping University, Sweden.

Wahl, A., Höök, P., 2007. Changes in working with gender equality in management in Sweden. Equal Opportunities International 26(5), 435–448.

Wahl, A., Linghag, S., 2013. Män har varit här längst [Men have been here the longest time]. Studentlitteratur, Lund, Sweden.

Wahl, A., Eduards, M., Holgersson, C., Höök, P., Linghag, S., Rönnblom, M., 2008. Motstånd och fantasi—Historien om F [Resistance and Fantasy—The Story of F]. Studentlitteratur, Lund, Sweden.

Wahl, A., Holgersson, C., Höök, P., Linghag, S., Lantz, J., Regnö, K., 2007. The second wave of integration—methods for teaching gender theories in business schools. Myndigheten för nätverk och samarbete inom högre utbildning. Härnösand, Sweden. www.gupea.ub.gu.se/handle/2077/18109

18

Gender and pedagogy
A business school case study

Julie Hall and Jo Peat
University of Roehampton, UK

This chapter focuses on the pedagogic practices of business and management academics at a UK university and considers the extent to which these practices are gendered. The writers employ the phrase "pedagogic practices" rather than teaching, using Alexander's definition that "Pedagogy connects the apparently self-contained act of teaching with culture, structure, and the mechanisms of social control" (Alexander, R.J. Culture and Pedagogy: International Comparisons in Primary Education, Oxford: Blackwell). Thus, it takes the learner into account as much as the teacher. Pedagogic practices range from assessment to transmission of information to the provision of individual academic advice through exploration, discussion and collaboration. The influences of the discipline and the academics' conceptions of the students they are teaching are central to this research. Using qualitative data, we consider the pedagogic practices, which are surfaced and their implications for inclusion and exclusion in higher education. The research investigates the discourses used on the program, the pedagogic practices chosen, and assumptions made by the academics about students and their learning. The findings reveal the ways in which academics articulate their students' needs and learning in relation to gender and the patriarchal culture of the discipline and the assumptions academics bring to pedagogic practices in relation to issues of student identity.

18.1 Introduction

Much of the international debate about pedagogic practices in undergraduate and postgraduate business programs is characterized more by the extent to which students are prepared for the world outside the university than issues of gender. Individuals vary in their views about the nature of the preparation required. Some believe that practices should move radically "away from teaching analytical problem-solving skills to cultivating a 'paradigm-shifting mentality' to encourage an entrepreneurial imagination" (Chia, 1996: 409). Others argue heightened cultural awareness and more emphasis on fieldwork and global perspectives are what is needed (Datar, Garvin and Cullen, 2010). These views in part reflect the challenge of ensuring that roles and responsibilities, skills and knowledge are all developed in contemporary business education. This chapter is written within the UK context of widening participation to higher education and the introduction of student fees. According to Universities UK (2013), between 2003–2004 and 2011–2012, the total number of higher education students at higher education institutions in the United Kingdom increased by almost 300,000 or 13.5% with the biggest increase among female students. Women students outnumber men by 3:2 in many universities. At first-degree level in 2011–2012, around 55% of students were female with equal numbers of male and female students on undergraduate business programs and a 24.5% increase in student numbers to UK Business programs overall.

The limited research evidence on gender and pedagogic practices in business education varies, at least in its interpretation and its emphasis. Ruegger (1992) and Eweje and Brunton (2010), for example, demonstrate that female business students are more ethically aware than their male counterparts; that is, there are differences between males and females regarding ethical judgement. Yet Das and Das (2001) found that male professors with low femininity scores (but not necessarily high masculinity scores), and female professors who are gender-neutral (i.e. androgynous or undifferentiated) were more often chosen by business students as their best professors. Recognition of such gendered differences could be used to significant advantage in the business classroom, enriching the learning landscape for both male and female participants. Statham, Richardson and Cook (1991: 16) point out, however, that there is "tremendous complexity in the gender typified social world of the university" and issues such as this are often left unaddressed.

The widening participation policy agenda in the United Kingdom, with its aim of opening higher education to those with disabilities and to students from neighbourhoods or cultural groups with traditions of low participation, has also raised questions about pedagogies in higher education and the ways they might be further developed to address issues of inclusion, participation, equality, and diversity. Here Hocking's (2010) definition of diversity is used, referring to learners of all ages who come from different social classes and ethnic backgrounds; disabled students, international students, students from different faith backgrounds, those with different cultural identities and sexual orientations. It includes full-time and part-time students who come into higher education with different entry qualifications, work and life experiences, different lifestyles, and who have different approaches to learning. There have been calls in the United Kingdom for nuanced research that draws out the complexities of learner identities and experiences of learning and teaching (Burke and Jackson, 2007; Leathwood and Read, 2009). In addition, bodies such as the National Union of Students have called for more support for academic staff to review and develop inclusive practice. These agendas are particularly pertinent for colleagues who teach in schools or faculties with very diverse student cohorts, such as many business and management courses.

In this chapter, it is argued that some of the complexity and contested nature of the linkages between gender and pedagogic practices in business courses reflect, first, differences in the way that the terms "teaching and learning" are conceptualized; and, second, the nature of business as the disciplinary space in which the linkage occurs: that is, the environment associated with a disciplinary culture in which pedagogic practices take place. In constructing links between gender, research, and pedagogic practices, the discipline is an important mediator (Healey and Jenkins, 2003). This is because the conduct of research and pedagogic practices valued tend to differ between disciplines. Disciplines can act as distinct "academic tribes" (Becher and Trowler, 2001) or "communities of practice" (Lave and Wenger, 1998); however, tribes and communities, as shown here, can be fractured by power relations and gendered structures. This chapter explores gender and pedagogic practices in one particular disciplinary space—the Business School at the case study university.

A further theme running through this chapter is that students are likely to gain most benefit personally and vocationally, when they are involved in learning, which reflects the contested nature of the working world (Chell and Baines, 1998; Rouse and Kitching, 2006). This presents challenges to academics to reshape curricula, review pedagogic practices, and be more conscious of their relations with students and their roles. This focus may lead to new ways for academics and students to work together in communities of inquiry, albeit mediated by the particular disciplinary space and the gendered relationships, which dominate within it. The academics and students we discuss in this chapter exhibit a reflexive approach to their teaching and learning. They are critical of gendered classroom relations—male students dominating discussions, illustrative examples from a stereotypical masculine world, female perspectives silenced—yet this awareness neither necessarily lead directly to student-centred, interactive pedagogic practices, nor to more gender-neutral practices.

The research described in this chapter derives from the UK Higher Education Academy-funded research project "Formations of Gender and Higher Education Pedagogies" (GaP, 2012). This project aimed to develop a detailed understanding of the relationship between social identities and pedagogic practices and experiences across six discipline areas including business. Research into participation in university has shown that some students such as those from low socio-economic backgrounds or ethnic or gender minorities can feel excluded and this has a significant impact on learning (Archer, Hutchings and Ross, 2005). For Mann (2001), pressure on students to conform and the relationship of power between academics and students may not allow for the development of an autonomous sense of self for students, particularly for those who do not consider themselves legitimate participants. The alternative for such students, she argues, is the development of a false self, which can be recognized in the features identified as characteristic of a surface or instrumental orientation to learning (Marton and Booth, 1997; Prosser and Trigwell, 1999). Students may be further alienated and delegitimized when there is little connection to the specific challenges that "emanate from the material contexts of their everyday lives" (Giroux, 2004: 500).

Academics' pedagogic practices reflect a range of conceptions of learning and teaching. Academics may, for example, conceive of students as consumers, as deficient, as apprentice scholars, or as vehicles for social transformation (Fanghanel, 2012). These conceptions result in different approaches to student engagement and identity formation. Clegg (2008) and Henkel (2004) point to subject-based identities being superseded by identities defined by university priorities, structures, and functions in a lived complexity intersecting with social constructions of gender, age and class. However, the practices adopted by academics are not only revelatory about the academics themselves but also they directly affect the development of the students' identities as learners and of learners in that particular discipline.

The higher education framework in the United Kingdom assumes an element of some kind of self-transformation. Courses are designed so that students emerge more knowledgeable, skilled, motivated or critical depending on the discipline or level. This research asks what kinds of student identity are being (re)constructed and what kinds of academic identity are required to ensure this happens in the current context. Which identities are constructed as dominant and which are suppressed? To what extent are identities and practices gendered? In what ways do pedagogic practices support or limit diversity?

18.2 Methodology

Participatory methodology (Burke, 2009) was at the heart of the GaP Project, bringing students and academic staff together to share their views and examine each other's responses. Methods included 64 in-depth individual undergraduate student interviews across six programs, 10 student focus groups, 15 focus groups with the academic staff who taught these students—24 in all—workshops with invited students from a range of UK higher education institutions and a national workshop with academics. In this case study, all academics were engaged in teaching and research and the sample of academics and students was made up of an equal number of male and female participants. Academics included experienced academics and those new to the university. All responses were anonymized and the names provided in this text are pseudonyms. This methodology has given us very rich data on the university experience, from both teacher and learner perspectives, which has generated much discussion and reflection about pedagogic practices and the extent to which those teaching in university settings are able to respond to the range of identities in the higher education classroom.

The data challenged underlying assumptions about the nature of student engagement. Most importantly, the research highlighted a disjuncture between the pedagogic intentions of many academics and how the learning environment was experienced by their students. For example, before hearing the student views, many academics described students as passive and disengaged, somehow different from students "in the past" who were more aware of what was required in higher education. In contrast, however, students told us they were often bored in taught sessions and they were rarely invited to engage in a meaningful or safe way. Taking part in a research project about pedagogic practice repositioned academics' teaching concerns and challenges as an intellectual work (Hutchings, 2002). This conversational framework has echoes of Kandlbinder's (2007) term "deliberation", which he describes as demanding a form of communication that is different from everyday conversations, with regular focus groups providing rare and valued spaces to share and explore pedagogic practices and concerns through dialogue with colleagues.

18.3 Findings

18.3.1 Student-centred pedagogy—an opportunity to care or gendered domestic labour and oppression?

The business school academics in the sample recognized an increasing emphasis on student satisfaction and the students' focus on formal graded assessment to the exclusion of other learning opportunities. In addition, they communicated a sense of being managed, echoing the work of Deem and Brehony (2005), who have identified a "considerable deliberate organizational and cultural change in public service organizations in the West" (Deem and Brehony, 2005: 217) which in universities is evident in more students, a smaller unit of resource per student, a sense of surveillance and pressure to do both teaching and research to a high standard. Respondents suggested that pedagogic practices had changed as a result. Pedagogic practices were described as becoming more supportive, more orientated towards student needs and, as a result, more time-consuming. Interestingly, the discourse adopted was highly gendered, describing supportive pedagogic practices as "mothering", "babying", "caring for" and so on. Most academics found this oppressive, akin to domestic labour, as it required them to "look after" students and "spoon-feed" them knowledge. Male academics in particular seemed eager to avoid this work, resulting in a feminization of support:

> I feel because of retention rates and all these systems, which are in place I am expected to be caring, more caring than I actually want to be. (Kate, Female Academic)

> I would like to push the students more and unattach myself. (Susanna, Female Academic)

> Some staff are very conscious of a kind of audit culture, of, you know, the students might mark me down in a module evaluation or a survey. (Michael, Male Academic)

What emerged was a perception among academics, particularly among female academics, that their role was distorted and constrained by gender, institutional priorities and culture, and student expectations. This resulted in a deficit model of pedagogic practice with academics feeling that they must give students what they want and expect. This might be less challenging and ultimately less likely to prepare students for the world of work:

> I look at some students and I think you would not survive one minute in business but we have to just deal with that and help them through. Hopefully, they will get there. (Kate, Female Academic)

For Susanna, an academic recruited to the business school because of her industry expertise, offering academic advice to students was something to be welcomed. The role provided her with an unexpected opportunity in academia to work closely with students, particularly the young women to whom she felt she could really relate. She contrasted this with the rather isolated, competitive experience of academic research:

> When I came into academia I just thought I wanted to be concentrate on and I did want to be locked in my office doing that but now I would rather go up the kind of management route and even pastoral so I've totally changed my opinion of it. (Susanna, Female Academic)

Being a young female academic, she was mindful of the gap left behind by the retired male academic she had replaced. Yet she had also come to see that when roles were assigned across the teaching team, female academics were more likely to take up the pastoral roles. She recognized that this was not providing helpful models of equality of practice, which were healthy or appropriate for business students:

> If you have any issues as a student you have to talk to a woman and we are all the same—straight women with families. I want you to note that we know this and in fact a colleague is leaving and her replacement is going to be a man. But not because he has chosen to take a pastoral role like we did. It's because he has lost his research time. (Susanna, Female Academic)

Her colleague, Jonathan, in dialogue with her, also recognized the gendered nature of academic support arrangements:

> You have taken on responsibility that the guys aren't prepared to take. I'm one of those. I don't want to do it. I have done it in the past. You and the other ladies have decided someone has got to take this on and you do a good job. (Jonathan, Male Academic)

This increased emphasis on emotional labour has led to claims of a feminization of the role of the academic (Du Nann Winter, 1991). This feminized approach to student-centred work was seen by both the female and male academics who took part in the study as somewhat deficient, predicated on support, nurturing and spoon-feeding in contrast with the traditional, masculinized, didactic approach. However, this was not always construed as negative: Susanna spoke openly of choosing this more supportive role, realizing that it was this element of academic work that she preferred and was good at. Perhaps, this could be attributed to the dominance of a masculinized approach to teaching, rendering this the most viable route for a young, female academic. The only accessible career space in which Susanna can create what she sees as a "valid" identity in academia has been reduced to the traditional nurturing role of the female.

18.4 Academic identity

Interviews provided examples of academics trying to grapple with the complexities of challenging structural and historical inequalities as an individual. Those on the business program were extremely conscious of the way in which past professional experience, their gender and age impacted on their pedagogic relations with students and the gendered nature of their disciplinary language.

> But a lot of business language is around football, male sports, moving the goal post, team player, all this rubbish and I just wonder if you know it's largely written by men, a lot of the business management literature and it's very geared towards the systems type learning as well that maybe women, female students are excluded to a certain extent and a sort of silent lecture until the questions at the end. (Michael, Male Academic)

Kate voiced concern with engaging both the male and female students in business and their different responses to her teaching, and reflected on her own identity as a female academic within the masculine world of business:

> If I haven't prepped something and I go off at a tangent, they are going to be very feminine, things that have happened in my life. So—and I'm very mindful that the boys are not interested in hearing about a make-up ethics story. They would much rather hear about a football ethics story. (Kate, Female Academic)

The terminology used by both academics and students in the business school to refer to both male and female peers was also revealing of a gendered culture. Students, both male and female, referred to female academics as "Miss" and male academics as "Sir" when speaking to them in class situations and about them in interview:

> Are we going to be using any class studies, Miss? (Rajesh, Male Student)
> You can be a bit unapproachable at times, Sir. (Sajita, Female Student)

This extended to the language used by academics to speak about their students and colleagues:

> You and the other ladies have decided someone has got to take this on and you do a good job. (Michael, Male Academic)

These appellations are not without bias. Although some of these practices could be attributed to school tradition, they serve to maintain the status quo in terms of the gender and power divide in institutions.

18.5 Pedagogic practices in the business school

For most academic staff, their primary allegiance is to their subject or profession, and their sense of themselves as staff at a given institution is secondary (Becher, 1994; Diamond and Adam, 1995b; Jenkins, 1996; Lueddeke, 2003; Huber and Morreales, 2002; Marincovich and Prostko, 2005). It therefore stands to reason that disciplines exert an influence over pedagogic practices, in terms of what is taught and assessed and how students are expected to learn and how this learning is assessed:

> [most academics] are probably comfortable with the notion that their disci-
> plinary background deeply influences not only what they teach, but also how
> they teach it (Marincovich and Prostko, 2005, in Kreber, 2009: 19).

The way in which academics characterize and construct their disciplines explains to some extent the pedagogic practices chosen. Typically, subject content is emphasized with academics contending that there are significant disciplinary differences in terms of what academics do and are expected to do, what is considered of value, disciplinary epistemologies, pedagogic practices and the role of the student. Hirst (1974) supported this contention, suggesting that each discipline has a clear epistemological structure, which defines how it should be taught. This would suggest that there are certain pedagogies appropriate for some disciplines, which would be unsuitable for others. It is worth considering, however, the extent to which differences are exaggerated in order to maintain a sense of identity and feeling of distinctiveness within the discipline. This was echoed by the business school academics. They spoke of their discipline as being different, fragmented and therefore problematic in some respects but also that this fragmentation presented opportunities for heightened engagement and interest among the students:

> It's different in business. I mean, I think there's quite a lot of choice and if they
> can't find some joy from either their Accounting or Marketing or HR or Eth-
> ics or Computing or something, you start to question what they are interested
> in. Sometimes I feel potentially some of the other Programmes might be a bit
> more restrictive and at least we do have some choice there. And it gives us
> opportunities too. (Kate, Female Academic)

Despite this rhetoric of difference, however, there was little evidence of actual signature pedagogies (Shulman, 2005). The academics spoke about the distinctive nature of the discipline, but both male and female academics maintained a reliance on a traditional lecture/seminar format and an emphasis on a masculinized, didactic delivery of material, necessitated by a perceived passive student audience.

> In a lecture we'll teach at the front. (Kate, Female Academic)

The academics recognized the diversity of their student cohort, entering the undergraduate program along a variety of trajectories; however, there was little talk of adapting pedagogic practices to reflect this. This finding is supported by other research that found that, despite the move from elite to mass higher education in the United Kingdom, lectures remain a key mode of knowledge transmission (Gorard et al., 2006), and there remains a dependency on the teacher as authority:

> The dominant paradigm of the teaching responsibility remains that of the authority in the field engaging with and imparting knowledge and skills to individuals (Barnett, 2001 in Tight, 2004: 151).

Despite a recognition among the business school academics that this mode of teaching was not always effective in terms of student learning and that it positioned the students as subjugated recipients of academic knowledge, there was a more or less explicitly stated belief from most of the academics that lectures were effective in transmitting content to the students, in making sure that the syllabus was covered, in ensuring that the academic retained control of the session and that the students had notes to take away from the session. They were of the view that, in these risk-averse times, the lecture retains its position as a tried and tested practice, enabling the academic to feel confident that she or he has "done her/his job" vis-à-vis the student. From the students' point of view, they have been given the information they need and it has not been an onerous procedure.

Kate, an experienced academic in the Business School recognized the limitations of this mode of teaching in terms of engaging students actively in their learning. For her, however, in addition to disciplinary traditions, practical constraints including increased student numbers, timetabling issues, student ability and space, that is, factors beyond the control of the academic, necessitate such an approach:

> Potentially we have to have bigger classes so we have to be more didactic, don't we? (Kate, Female Academic)

She did voice the concern that this mode of teaching could encourage a surface approach to learning (Marton and Saljo, 1976), as students were positioned as passive recipients of knowledge, being given the information they needed rather than being encouraged to research, debate, and grapple with more challenging concepts. Indeed, a common concern expressed by the academics was that of instrumentalism, surface and strategic learning. This was, moreover, echoed by the students themselves, the vocational characteristics of business schools perhaps being more visible that that of other disciplines (Bennis and O'Toole, 2005). Sajita, a third-year Business Studies student spoke about her reasons for choosing business:

> I want to get a good job at the end of this. Business should give me the opportunity to do this. I'm only really here so that I'll be able to get a good job. (Sajita, Female Student)

Smeby (1998) suggests that certain disciplines seem to predispose students to adopt surface or strategic approaches to learning. This further suggests that the way in which students are taught as well as their learning environments have a deep impact on the quality of their learning (Entwhistle and Peterson, 2004). The business academics interviewed admitted that, while interactivity is to be welcomed, they considered this was impossible in present circumstances and the modes used were adopted purely on the grounds of pragmatism:

> If you've got 150, I mean the reflection, I just generally throw a question at them just to have a break. (Kate, Female Academic)

Interestingly, however, there was also a suggestion that the male students in the cohorts welcomed this didactic, teacher-led approach. The academics reported that male students reacted in a more positive manner in these sessions, whereas the less overtly didactic approach adopted at times in smaller group settings was not as popular:

> If it's just "talk to the person next to you" . . . the guys in cross-cultural management get a bit cross with that. When I say: "What did you think about that?" they reply: "Are we going to be using any class studies, Miss?" (Kate, Female Academic)

There was a recognition that male and female students reacted differently to different pedagogic practices. Reflecting further on her pedagogic style in taught sessions with a high number of male students, Kate compared it to giving a performance:

> I go into the classroom and I do see it as a bit of a performance. I'm very high energy when I go into a classroom 'cause I find it can be quite contagious so hopefully I might get something back. (Kate, Female Academic)

She therefore adopted an energetic, enthusiastic approach to teaching the large, male-dominated classes, taking on a style that rendered and maintained her as the focal point of the session. In this way, her pedagogy is tailored to the assumed preferences of the audience she envisages in front of her. In trying to be inclusive of both male and female students, she adopts an approach that positions them as binary opposites, selecting illustrative examples, which reflect stereotypical, heteronormative views of male and female students.

Susanna described the way in which the focus on getting a good grade was acting as a barrier to some of the more innovative pedagogic practices she had designed to prepare students for a career in business. Her approach involved understanding the students' fear of risk while helping them understand in a firm way that not knowing, adapting and negotiating were all important skills they needed to develop.

> The students say "we don't know what academics want and you seem to want something different from one of the others." Well my come back is— "you are going to be working for a range of managers, learning the house style quickly and so the best thing, one of the best skills that we can develop is being adaptable, very quickly to whatever is needed." Coming from consultancy, I am really conscious of that. I have to take a stand. (Susanna, Female Academic)

Pedagogic practices are, therefore, not always chosen for appropriateness. Sometimes choices are made for pragmatic reasons rather than ideological ones and are limited by perceived constraints, both large and small. Kate lamented the gap between what she would like to do pedagogically and what she perceives the students would be able to do or would respond to positively:

> I've arranged for top people from the industry to come in and do careers talks. I am really worrying about this because it's some of them are very senior invest- ment bankers and I just think it will go over their heads. So I'm going to try . . . I'm doing it through a charity that arranges these things, try and tone it down a bit. (Kate, Female Academic)

The suggestion is that exciting, innovative pedagogy is too risky because of the con- straints of numbers, the attitudes of the students, particularly with regard to gendered expectations and the ability of the students to rise to the challenge of anything more exciting than a passive, teacher-led session. Barnett (1999) suggests that academics, mindful of the role of students as paymaster/customer, may fall back on "tried and tested" practices, "teaching to the test", thus colluding for a risk-free, non-challenging learning environment. As Furedi (2012) points out: "The inexorable consequence of the current obsession with the student experience is the adoption of a risk-averse and defensive approach towards the provision of undergraduate courses."

This lack of pedagogic variety was echoed by the students. For them, the only discern- ible difference was in terms of the size of the group—the actual pedagogic practices used in seminars seemed to be relatively unchanged from that adopted in lectures:

> I know we have a lecture followed by a seminar, but I don't really know the dif- ference between them. The seminars are smaller, but we do the same things. We sit and listen most of the time. (Sarah, Female Student)

18.6 Solitary academic practice, not modelling cooperation

A number of female academics pointed to the solitary existence, which they felt lay at the centre of their identity in academia, particularly in relation to their research outputs. Several described experiencing isolation due to the way teaching and research were organized. Far from feeling part of a disciplinary or pedagogic community and perhaps developing an identity from shared practices and dialogue, one young female member of staff described her existence as solitary and her office as a cage.

> I find it very a solitary existence working here. It's just like being in a room— yeah, I'm locked in a cage—when I came here I found it very solitary and quite lonely, actually. (Susanna, Female Academic)

For Susanna, agency and her responsibility to be reflexive were central aspects of her academic identity. It was important to her that she felt able to share pedagogic chal- lenges with colleagues. Coming into academia she was surprised at the lack of social space where dialogue around teaching could emerge and the reluctance of colleagues to admit to problems. She recognized that academics are employed for what they know and to admit they were struggling seemed to undermine their identity as experts. This provides an important insight into the implications for professional development and dialogue around curriculum and pedagogic renewal:

> It's an identity, a person thing. I don't think people would feel comfortable coming down to a common room and saying this happened today, what can I do about it? Everyone please give me advice. Maybe we are a bit protective of our classroom space because this always come up when we organize observations . . . If someone has feedback for me, I am open to it because of the way I was trained as a consultant but lots of colleagues well they feel like they don't need development even if it might make life easier. (Susanna, Female Academic)

This concern with the lonely nature of academia was voiced primarily by female academics, although a senior male colleague lamented the death of collegiality too:

> I remember when we'd all meet for lunch and just chat. You know, you could walk in and say "I've had a problem with that student today" and your colleagues would listen. That's all gone now. (Michael, Male Academic)

This characterization of the academic experience as solitary and non-collegial was also expressed by Kate, when speaking about student learning on the course. Kate emphasized the importance of the academic *covering* the content of the business degree and the need for the course team to *deliver* it in a way that would be equitable for all students, particularly when it came to assessment. The locus of responsibility was, therefore, seen to lie firmly with the academic, positioning the student as a recipient of the academic's knowledge and experience, involved in taking in and processing information in an individual and largely passive manner. Kate voiced concern about the course team's wish for the students to engage in greater social learning, but recognizing that this is not modelled by the academics themselves:

> I don't think we truly model social learning. We model quite a lot of individual learning. (Kate, Female Academic)

However, despite calling for student learning to be more cooperative, there was little actual evidence of the academics actively embracing pedagogic practices that would lead to collaboration and social learning. There was, instead, an unspoken acknowledgement of not knowing how to engage the students more actively in the sessions, even in smaller, potentially more intimate, learning environments. This perhaps extends Boden and Epstein's (2006) criticism of a lack of research imagination to the area of pedagogy too:

> Even within that, in the seminar, what activities can you do? What can you dip into in order to think of things for them to do, which would help him or her or excite her, but him, he can be in week 4, you know, it's quiet, because what we seem to have observed is a lot of "here's the lecture" and then "here's the seminar" and here's the sheet of paper. (Kate, Female Academic)

A concern about the lack of a social aspect to the taught sessions was echoed by the students, in particular the female students on the course. Rakia, a third-year student talked about the structure of the course (lecture/seminars in pre-arranged groupings) being obstructive to the formation of a group identity. For her, the pedagogic practices limited group identity to a small circle of friends, rather than being extended to the whole cohort:

> I'd like to get to know the whole group, you know, not just the people I spoke to at the beginning of the course. I'd just like to be able to do more talking in class, more active stuff. (Rakia, Female Student)

In contrast, the male students did not speak about this aspect of studying in higher education. When asked directly about it, however, they responded that they were happier working in friendship groups and had no real desire to meet other students.

18.7 Student voice and engagement in the business classroom

Student voice as an indicator of engagement was a common theme in the interviews, recognized by both male and female academics. Both Jonathan and Susanna, for example, were aware that students would react differently to opportunities to speak in class but knowing which practices to adopt to encourage engagement and voice was complex, requiring deep understanding and highly developed pedagogic skills:

> Some are yeah, I've ticked it off, I've come along but I am not going to participate in fact I might even be disruptive but I've done my bit, Others are intensely listening but will never speak, don't want to speak so I think you know we need to change things in terms of what we are asking them to do. (Jonathan, Male Academic)

For Susanna the key pedagogic skill, underpinned by her own experience of studying, was to be alert to what was happening in the classroom, to watch the note taking and be mindful of opportunities to listen and interact in different ways. She recognized that some students would rather listen than engage in dialogue. Pedagogically, this was a challenge, especially in the first few weeks of a program when it was hard to work out which students to push and which to leave alone.

Despite this clearly reflexive approach to teaching very diverse groups of students and avoiding stereotyping, there were several examples of how both male and female academics attributed certain behaviours and attitudes to male students and others to females. There was an expectation that gender would help to determine performance:

> Sometimes just wandering around and looking at notes and you know especially the boys actually if they are sitting there they are usually writing away. I think "ahh maybe they are just the kind who like to just listen" (Susanna, Female Academic).

Jonathan was mindful, however, of judging students too quickly, especially students whose cultural or social backgrounds were different from the academic's own:

> It's a challenge to work out in the first few weeks who should you try to bring forward and who should you let to do their own thing? (Jonathan, Male Academic)

Regularly silence was described as a symptom of low-level engagement. Academics felt anxious when students were silent and some were conscious of their powerful positioning in controlling discussion. In this interview extract, a male academic is conscious of the gendered nature of dominant pedagogic practices and he presents student engagement through speaking as risky:

> I thought of that word silent, the bit of research I did with students about women's ways of knowing. Basically silence being the lowest level of engagement and you know by doing a lecture, we are imposing that silence but in the next minute, we're saying, let's have a discussion about this and let's engage but we're controlling that as opposed to them really critically engaging. So I think there may be something wrong there in terms of imposing silence on the people. I mean I'm finding it more and more—they're just not able to engage. They don't take the risk and my group this year, there's only about one or two that would participate. Whereas previously it would be a really good dynamic engaged. (Jonathan, Male Academic)

18.7.1 Student views—space to ask questions and to bring personal experiences into the learning experience

The methodology used in this research sought to give voice to both academics and students. For the purposes of this chapter, the voices of the academics have been emphasized, however, pedagogic practices were commented on in detail by students too.

Female students in particular appreciated those business academics whose pedagogic practices provided space for questions, for individual identity and for connections to be made with their past experience:

> The way she teaches does help, cause where the others will be a kind of silent lecture until the questions at the end it's more of a—she will be showing you something and if you want you can just ask. I find it a lot easier to ask questions of a female lecturer and that's one of the reasons I have chosen two modules with her. I've already decided what I am taking next year. The teaching of the lecturer is more important often than what the content is because a good lecturer can make a dull subject interesting. A bad lecturer can make an interesting subject dull. So it's really important how they teach and whether you get on with them. (Sonia, Female Student)

> I learn much better, things sink in much better hearing people's views rather than sitting bored I front of a projector screen and the teacher going on and on and on. I've noticed different lectures and different techniques and I come out feeling so much more confident when there is interaction going on and people's ideas are bouncing around the room. Obviously some like it the other way and they will be less vocal. (Sajita, Female student)

Other students, particularly mature students, were disappointed when there was little space for them to bring their own work experience into their learning:

> In their minds they are looking at who has come out of school, gone to college, come to uni. They haven't got experience of the real world. But I did—I managed my own business and no one invited this into my learning. I have just accepted it. (Sarah, Female Student)

Other female students pointed to feelings of exclusion because of the gendered nature of examples used across the curriculum:

> One of our presentations was on the locomotive industry and I know absolutely nothing about this. The topics chosen were so male. After the locomotive it was helicopters then the arms trade. Well personally I thought how am I going into this? What can I write about? Sometimes you try and you have no interest no passion and it makes it really difficult. (Wendy, Female Student)

As academics had identified, being invited to contribute and to speak in class is sometimes problematic for students. For many, the pressure to speak in front of peers is oppressive and daunting. Students, both male and female, used terms such as "scary", "difficult" and "nerve wracking" and offered a range of reasons for their feelings:

> I think it's because people judge you more or you have a lot more to prove to people here and also it's our age group—we are growing up. At school I wasn't bothered but now you are getting to the point where you have got to look like you are going somewhere. (Raj, Male Student)

The findings, therefore, echo much of the literature. There does indeed seem to be a risk-averse culture (Furedi, 2012) in the business school, apparently shared by the academics and students. The gender-typified social world of the university (Statham, Richardson and Cook, 1991) as a whole is reproduced in the business school context, with the less valued elements of academic roles being adopted by female academics, the prevalent discourse being typically masculinized and pedagogic practices privileging the preferred male style of learning. Although research has pointed to the influence of the discipline on what is taught and how it is taught (Marincovich and Prostko, 2005) there is little evidence of signature pedagogies at work in the business school (Shulman, 2005).

Although there was little dissatisfaction expressed by the students, there was equally a low level of real satisfaction. It may, therefore, be apposite for the academics in the business school to reconsider their pedagogic practices in the light of these findings. "Quick fixes" would include the use of more gender-neutral examples and case studies to illustrate points of theory; greater opportunity for the students to engage in discussion, debate and the application of knowledge to real-life situations and the overt valuing and use of the experiences of the different students within the groups.

For the academics in the business school, a less gendered apportioning of the different areas of academic practice, including that of pastoral support would help to reduce such gendered stratification of male and female colleagues. Opportunities for greater teamwork and collaboration could go some way to alleviate isolation and the resulting anxieties. This would be particularly effective if collaboration could be between male and female colleagues and act as a model for student groupings within the classroom.

18.8 Conclusion

The research has revealed a number of challenges for academics and students in the Business School, in terms of the influences of gender on pedagogic practices. Academics and students alike agreed that their experiences of teaching and learning had been shaped to some extent by gendered practices and expectations. The academics, who took part in the research reflected at length about gendered constraints in their work environments. Academics spoke about pastoral and nurturing roles being fulfilled by female colleagues, despite a preponderance of male academics on the program. Although male academics were mindful of this gendered delineation, they were not prepared to undertake these roles themselves. This is not to say that the male academics were not part of the culture of care on the program, but they did not want this to be formalized as part of their academic duties. These included the assumptions that the pastoral roles and guidance roles, albeit part and parcel of being an academic, were more suited to female academics, being associated with emotional labour, nurture, and caring.

Some of the gendered pedagogic practices in the business school can be tied to the heritage of the discipline. This includes the nature of the business discourse, which, at times, alienated female students. Students spoke about illustrative examples chosen from the world of football, locomotives and aeronautics, which female students reported as being outside their experience; however, academics spoke of being mindful not to alienate male students through the use of examples relating to cosmetics and fashion. Gender-neutral examples to bridge this divide and to prevent the positioning of male and female students as binary opposites were rarely in evidence.

A resounding theme was the extent to which real concern was expressed by male and female academics to provide a high-quality learning experience for their students. Both male and female academics spoke about the importance of large group lectures for transmitting key information and concepts to the students, adding that seminars too remained largely passive and academic-led. This was despite female students reporting being engaged by more inclusive, discursive teaching, with the opportunity to discuss, question, and interact with each other and the academic. Male students, in contrast, preferred the traditional, didactic style of teaching, seemingly adopting a more passive approach to their learning in class. When academics did speak about trying to adopt a more engaged form of pedagogy, they positioned the male and female students as binary opposites, with female students wanting these learning opportunities and male students being largely resistant, despite taking a more assertive, leading role in whole classwork.

The academics were aware of a multitude of issues confronting them in their teaching, feeling stymied by elements both within and without their control. This led, at times, to feelings of frustration and impotence. Despite the self-criticisms of the academics in terms of their pedagogic practices, there was little actual discontent expressed by the students, notwithstanding some expressed reservations. The safer, less risky practices adopted by the academics in their pedagogy were appreciated by the students in many cases. Although they did not necessarily feel challenged and fully engaged, nevertheless they felt supported and cared for in their learning. As one student explained:

> I want to get a First. I know how to get it and I don't do anything more than I need to just to get that First—I'm not interested in a lot of reading and stuff. I want my First. That's what I want and that's what I'll get. And my lecturers are helping me to get it! (Sonia, Female Student)

References

Alexander, R.J., 2001. Culture and Pedagogy: International Comparisons in Primary Education. Blackwell, Oxford, p. 540.

Archer, L., Hutchings, M., Ross, A., 2005. Higher Education and Social Class: Issues of Exclusion and inclusion. Routledge, London.

Barnett, R., 1999. Understanding Pedagogy. In: Mortimore, P. (Ed.). Paul Chapman, London, pp. 137–154.

Barnett, R., 2001. Conceptualising curriculum change. In: Tight (Ed.), (2004), The Routledge Falmer Reader in Higher Education. RoutledgeFalmer, London, pp. 140–155.

Becher, T., 1994. The significance of disciplinary differences. Studies in Higher Education 19(2), 151–161.

Becher, T., Trowler, P., 2001. Academic Tribes and Territories: Intellectual Enquiry and The Culture of the Disciplines, second ed. SRHE and Open University Press, Buckingham, Milton Keynes.

Bennis, W.G., O'Toole, J., 2005. How business schools lost their way. Harvard Business Review 83(5), 96–104.

Boaler, J., Greeno, J., 2000. Identity, agency and knowing in mathematics worlds. In: Boaler, J. (Ed.), Multiple Perspectives on Mathematics Teaching and Learning. Ablex, Westport, CT.

Boden, R., Epstein, D., 2006. Managing the research imagination? Globalisation and Research in Higher Education 4(2), 223–236.

Burke, P., Jackson, S., 2007. Reconceptualising Lifelong Learning: Feminist Interventions. Routledge, London.

Burke, P.J., 2009. Men accessing higher education: theorising continuity and change in relation to masculine identities. Higher Education Policy 22, 81–100.

Chell, E., Baines, S., 1998. Does gender affect business performance? A study of microbusiness in business services in the UK. Entrepreneurship and Regional Development 10(2), 117–135.

Chia, R., 1996. Teaching paradigm shifting in management education: university business schools and the entrepreneurial imagination. Journal of Management Studies 33(4), 409–428.

Clegg, S., 2008. Academic identities under threat. British Educational Research Journal 34(3), 329–345.

Das, M., Das, H., 2001. Business students' perceptions of best University professors: does gender role matter? Sex Roles 45(9), 665–676.

Datar, S., Garvin, D., Cullen, P., 2010. Rethinking the MBA: Business Education at a Crossroads. Harvard Business Press.

Deem, R., Brehoney, K., 2005. Management as ideology: the case of new managerialism in higher education. Oxford Review of Education 31(2), 217–235.

Diamond, R.M., Adam, B.A. (Eds.), 1995. Describing the work of faculty: disciplinary perspectives. In: The Disciplines Speak: Rewarding the Scholarly, Professional, and Creative Work of Faculty. American Association for Higher Education, Washington, DC, pp. 1–14.

Du Nann Winter, D., 1991. The feminization of academia. To Improve the Academy. Paper 236. www.digitalcommons.unl.edu/podimproveacad/236 (accessed 01.11.13).

Entwhistle, N.J., Peterson, E., 2004. Conceptions of learning and knowledge in higher education: relationships with study behaviour and influences of learning environments. International Journal of Educational Research 41(6), 407–428.

Eweje, G., Brunton, M., 2010. Ethical perceptions of business students in a New Zealand University: do gender, age and work experience matter? Business Ethics: A European Review 19(1), 95–111.

Fanghanel, J., 2007. Exploring Academics Pedagogic Constructs in their Working Contexts. HE Academy. www.heacademy.ac.uk/assets/documents/research/fanghanel.pdf (accessed 05.11.12).

Fanghanel, J., 2012. Being an Academic. Routledge, London.

Furedi, THES, 8–14 March 2012, Satisfaction and its discontents.

Giroux, H., 2004. Public pedagogy and the politics of neo-liberalism: making the political more pedagogical. Policy Futures in Education 2(3 & 4), 494–503.

Gorard, S., Smith, E., May, H., Thomas, L., Adnett, N., Slack, K., 2006. Review of Widening Participation Research: Addressing the Barriers to Participation in Higher Education. www.hefce.ac.uk/pubs/rdreports/2006/rd13_06/9 (accessed on 09.11.13).

Healey, M., Jenkins, A., 2003. Discipline-based educational development. In: Macdonald, R., Eggins, H. (Eds.), The Scholarship of Academic Development. Open University Press/SRHE, Buckingham, pp. 47–57.

Healy, M., 2005. Linking research and teaching: exploring disciplinary spaces and the role of inquiry-based learning. In: Barnett, R. (Ed.), Reshaping the University: New Relationships between Research, Scholarship and Teaching. McGraw Hill/Open University Press, Maidenhead, pp. 67–78.

Henkel, M., 2004. Current science policies and their implications for the formation and maintenance of academic identity. Higher Education Policy 17, 167–182.

Hirst, P., 1974. Knowledge and the Curriculum. Routledge and Kegan Paul, Oxford, UK.

Hocking, C., 2010. Inclusive learning and teaching in higher education: a synthesis of research, HEA: EvidenceNet. www.heacademy.ac.uk/assets/EvidenceNet/Syntheses/inclusive_teaching_and_learning_in_he_synthesis_200410.pdf

Huber, M., Morreales, S. (Eds.), 2002. Disciplinary Styles in the Scholarship of teaching and Learning: Exploring Common Ground. The American Association for Higher Education and the Carnegie Foundation for the Advancement of Teaching, Washington, DC.

Hutchings, P., 2002. Reflections on the scholarship of teaching and learning; essays on teaching excellence. POD 13, 5.

Jenkins, A., 1996. Discipline-based educational development. International Journal for Academic Development 1(1), 50–62.

Kandlbinder, P., 2007. The challenge of deliberation for academic development. International Journal for Academic Development 12(1), 55–59.

Lave, J., Wenger, E., 1998. Communities of Practice: Learning, Meaning and Identity. Cambridge University Press, Cambridge.

Leathwood, C., Read, B., 2009. Gender and the Changing Face of HE: A Feminized Future. Open University Press, Milton Keynes.

Lueddeke, G., 2003. Professionalising teaching practice in higher education: a study of disciplinary variation and teaching scholarship. Studies in Higher Education 28(2), 213–228.

Mann, S.J., 2001. Alternative perspectives on student learning: alienation and engagement. Studies in Higher Education 26(1), 7–19.

Marincovich, M., Prostko, J., 2005. Why knowing about disciplinary differences can mean more effective teaching. Essays on Teaching Excellence: Towards the Best in the Academy, Professional and Organizational Development Network in Higher Education 16.6.

Marton, F., Booth, S., 1997. Learning and Awareness. Lawrence Erblaum Associates, Mahwah, NJ.

Marton, F., Saljo, R., 1976. On qualitative differences in learning—1: outcome and process. British Journal of Educational Psychology 46, 4–11.

National Union of Students (NUS) Liberation Equality and Diversity in the Classroom. www.nusconnect.org.uk/campaigns/highereducation/learning-and-teaching-hub/equalityinthecurriculum (accessed 06.15.12).

Prosser, M., Trigwell, K., 1999. Understanding Learning and Teaching. Society for Research into Higher Education & Open University Press, Buckingham.

Rouse, J., Kitching, J., 2006. Do enterprise support programmes leave women holding the baby? Environment and Planning C: Government and Policy 24(1), 5–19.

Ruegger, D., 1992. A study of the effect of age and gender upon student business ethics. Journal of Business Ethics 11(3), 179–186.

Shulman, L., 2005. Signature pedagogies in the professions. Daedalus 134(3), 52–59.

Smeby, J.C., 1998. Knowledge production and knowledge transmission. The interaction between research and teaching at universities. Teaching in Higher Education 3(1), 5–20.

Statham, A., Richardson, L., Cook, J., 1991. Gender and University Teaching: A Negotiated Difference. State University of New York Press, New York.

Universities UK, 2013. Patterns and Trends in UK Higher Education. www.universitiesuk.ac.uk/highereducation/Pages/PatternsAndTrendsInUKHigherEducation2013.aspx (accessed 04.14).

19

Integrating gender equality into management education

An MBA course on women in organizations

Diana Bilimoria
Case Western Reserve University, USA

In this chapter, I describe an MBA elective course, Women in Organizations, developed to empower female and male students in management education to advance gender equality and inclusion in the everyday practice of work, business and management. The course's objectives, format, design, content, activities, and assignments are discussed, as well as student reactions. I conclude the chapter with some reflections developed over ten years of teaching this course, primarily that gender equality in management education must be deliberately fostered, gender reflexivity helps both female and male students examine privilege, a psychologically safe classroom environment is a key element of the course's effectiveness, providing opportunities for voice, self-awareness and relational skill building is vital, and enabling gender equality in management education requires more than a single elective course.

Gender equality continues to be a challenging pursuit for management education. The curriculum and climate of management education remain overwhelmingly male (Bilimoria, 1999; Hite and McDonald, 1995; Simpson, 2006; Sinclair, 1995, 2000), evoking the need for a curricular space that focuses on the needs and experiences of women in business and management. In this chapter, I describe an elective MBA course, Women in Organizations (WIO), which I have been teaching for several years at my university (the course syllabus is available at the Principles for Responsible Management Education [PRME] Gender Equality Repository at www.caseplace.org/d.asp?d=1892). I briefly introduce the challenges of gender inequality in management education and then describe the overall framework for the course in addressing these challenges. Session descriptions along with information about topics and assignments are provided in a case study format. Next, course evaluations and comments from students are summarized to indicate the effectiveness of this gender equity intervention in the MBA program. Finally, I share some general insights and learnings about fostering gender equality in management education, which I have acquired over the years from teaching this course.

19.1 Gender inequality in management education

Substantial bodies of literature address extant gender inequality in both management and management education. Many researchers have highlighted the gendered nature of management cultures and practices, which results in systematic barriers and obstacles for the advancement and career development of women in organizations (Morrison et al., 1992; Powell, Butterfield and Parent, 2002; Ragins, Townsend and Mattis, 1998; Schein, 1993, 2007; Schein and Davidson, 1993). For example, over two decades ago, Acker argued:

> To say that an organization or any other analytic unit is gendered, means that advantage and disadvantage, exploitation and control, action and emotion, meaning and identity, are patterned through and in terms of a distinction between male and female, masculine and feminine (Acker, 1990: 146).

Martin (2001, 2003) noted that gender is pervasively practised in workplaces and perpetuated through interactions between women and men. In this regard, Schein (1993, 2007) and Schein and Davidson (1993) have pointed to the persistent perception that manager equals male. A recent study of 4,143 graduates of elite full-time MBA programs around the world between 1996 and 2007 showed that women lag men at every single career stage starting with their first professional jobs—in advancement, compensation and career satisfaction (Catalyst, 2010). The second generation (primarily subtle rather than overt) gender biases that differentiate and impede women's ascent in organizations compared to their male colleagues are the lack of senior-level role models for women, gendered career paths and gendered work, women's lack of access to networks and sponsors, and double binds or a mismatch between conventionally feminine qualities and the qualities thought necessary for leadership (Ibarra, Ely and Kolb, 2013).

In corollary, management education reflects the gendered nature of management (Fastenau, 1995; Mavin and Bryans, 1999; Simpson, 1995; Smith, 1997, 1998, 2000). The institutional and pedagogical structures and practices of management education mirror the gender biases prevalent in management. Accordingly, management education has been variously described as having an overwhelmingly masculine ethos and culture

(Hite and McDonald, 1995; Sinclair, 1995; Smith, 2000; Mavin, Bryan and Waring, 2004); as striving not to be gender negative as opposed to striving to be gender positive (Leong, Snodgrass and Gardner, 1992) and as ascribing to a value system that reflects the male orientation that business is a game with fixed and wholly material objectives (MacLellan and Dobson, 1997). Despite attention to women's under-representation in the curricular content of management education catalysed by the Committee of 200's $1 million challenge to the Harvard Business School to include more women in its management cases ("C200: Top Female Executives Make Case for Women in Business", 1998), the contributions of women in leadership and management continue to be marginalized in business school cases. Few of the cases and readings used in mainstream (or as Wilson, 1996; Mavin, Bryans and Waring, 2004 put it, "male stream") management education showcase women managers and leaders in business decision settings and few are written by female authors.

In a previous critique of management education's failure to contribute to eliminating extant gender bias in the workplace, I have noted that "Although our educational efforts affect and shape management mores and actions at every turn . . . collectively we have had little impact on altering the gender bias prevalent in the larger society in general and in corporate management and leadership in particular" (Bilimoria, 1999: 119). Mavin and Bryans (1999: 99) stated that by ignoring gender in the management education classroom, business schools collude with the status quo by simply replicating current management practices that reflect the dominance of men in positions of leadership and power and reinforce the notion that women in management are invisible. Not only does management education replicate management's gendered structures and practices, it supports and reifies them. For example, Simpson (2006) notes that the MBA curriculum promotes values of masculinity that engender educational climates of competition, individualism and instrumentality, therefore legitimizing a masculine managerial identity. Evidence indicates that the experiences of female students in management education are different than the experiences of male students (McKeen, Bujaki and Burke, 2000; Smith, 1997; *New York Times*, 2013). Some scholars wonder if the needs of both genders are being met within current management school structures (e.g. Offermann, 2007). Smith (1997, 1998, 2000) surveyed 85 postgraduate business students (50 female, 35 male) in Australia regarding their experience of gender issues in the management curriculum and the influence gender issues had on their learning. The author found consistent support for the existence of a prevailing masculine culture in management education. Male students were more dominant and vocal in the classroom resulting in women giving less voice to their opinions and men not learning from women's insights and experiences. Smith (2000) found that female students perceived that their male educators engaged with gendered attitudes and language, resulting in marginalization, invisibility or trivialization of female perspectives and experiences. Older women reported more severe incidences of being ignored, discounted or having their intelligence and experience questioned. This study also found that women were willing to challenge perceived gender bias in the classroom, but that doing so put them at risk because of the unequal power dynamic between teachers and students. Smith (2000: 165) described the double bind that women management students experience—they "risk academic and social consequences if they do speak out, but emotionally feel denied a voice if they do not". The experiences of women MBA students at the elite Harvard Business School chronicled more recently by *The New York Times* in September 2013 similarly demonstrate persistent and pervasive gender inequality:

> Many Wall Street-hardened women confided that Harvard was worse than any trading floor, with first-year students divided into sections that took all their classes together and often developed the overheated dynamics of reality shows. Some male students, many with finance backgrounds, commandeered classroom discussions and hazed female students and younger faculty members, and openly ruminated on whom they would "kill, sleep with or marry" (in cruder terms). Alcohol-soaked social events could be worse (*The New York Times*, 2013).

To address the issues of masculine culture and pervasive gender inequality and bias within management education, scholars have noted that management education may require tailored instruction for women that specifically takes into account their relational development and learning needs (Bilimoria, 1999; Buttner, 2002; Gallos, 1993). The WIO course that I teach annually at the Weatherhead School of Management addresses some of the criticisms of management education discussed above, through a focus on the needs and experiences of women in business and management. Below I describe the objectives, format, topics, class size and student mix, activities, assignments and evaluations of the WIO course.

19.2 "Women in Organizations" — an elective MBA course

19.2.1 Objectives

The purpose of the "Women in Organizations" course is to help management education students, both women and men, understand the leadership and managerial issues surrounding women in organizations. Offering complex understandings of the issues related to professional women and work, the course helps increase self-knowledge about students' own values and practices, as well as enhances their capabilities as leaders, managers, and team contributors. The course examines the opportunities, challenges, trade-offs and organizational dynamics experienced by women in work organizations. Through application of concepts to themselves and case studies as well as exposure to practising women managers and executives, students gain a deep and personal awareness of the key issues and concerns influencing women's participation and success in organizations, and are inspired to promote positive change in their current and future workplaces. In effect, the overarching goal of the WIO course is to empower female and male management education students to advance gender equality and inclusion in the everyday practice of work, business and management.

The course addresses questions such as:

- How does the gendered nature of organizations impact the experiences of corporate and professional women?

- How do women find work and career success?

- What are the challenges and burdens additionally faced by diverse managerial women—those belonging to different racial and ethnic groups, older or younger women, etc.?

- What are the valued skills, attributes and behaviours of women and men leaders in the workplace?

- How can the managerial playing field be evenly tilted in favour of women and men?

- What derails women's career development and advancement in organizations?

- What propels women's career advancement, rewards and recognition?

- How can women and men best integrate their family and work–life choices?

- How do managerial and professional women successfully integrate their multiple life and career responsibilities and commitments?

- What can organizations do to provide women with opportunities to learn new skills and widen their leadership experience?

- What is the role of legislation in improving the workplace for women, such as by curbing and redressing sex discrimination and sexual harassment?

19.2.2 Format

The course meets annually in a non-standard MBA course format consisting of three full-day sessions and two half-day sessions, compressed into the winter intersession (between the fall and spring semesters). Course sessions are supplemented by online office hours in the interim periods between class sessions and immediately following the last session of the course. This intensive format allows for the development of strong relationships among students and with the instructor and teaching assistants (TAs). Since it is possible that a student may need to miss any one of the class sessions, they have the choice of completing a make-up assignment addressing the readings and topics covered during the missed session, or having their final grade lowered by one letter grade.

19.2.3 Topics

Each course session has a designated topic and set of required and optional readings. The topics are as follows:

Session 1 (8 hours): Gender-based workplace issues including the current workforce participation and status of women in the workplace; managerial perceptions, stereotypes and myths about gender; gender roles; gender and race, especially the workplace experiences of minority women; organizational opportunity and reward/compensation structures including pay discrimination; and strategies to level the playing field.

Session 2 (8 hours): Gender-based differences, including cross-gender communication, and gender-based differences in leadership.

Session 3 (4 hours): Navigating politics and gaining influence in organizations, including the unwritten rules that women and men should know.

Session 4 (4 hours): Women and men as change agents, including being a tempered radical and the role of men in catalysing gender equity.

Session 5 (8 hours): Strategies, tools and career development resources for women and men in organizations. Topics covered include career resources, mentoring and networking; work–life integration; women working abroad; international dimensions; and career purpose and planning.

19.2.4 Class size and student mix

Over the past six years, the course size has ranged between 33 and 49 students, with an average of 39 students. Approximately 10–15% of the annual course enrolment has consisted of men. During one year, men constituted almost 38% of the course; this non-typical composition and its effects on course interactions were discussed in a previous article (Bilimoria et al., 2010). Typically, students in the WIO course come from two degree programs at the school—the MBA program and the Master of Accountancy (MAcc) program, with about half the course's students coming from each program. Occasionally, students from other master's level programs also attend the course, such as the Master of Nonprofit Management, the Master of Science in Finance and the joint JD/MBA program.

19.2.5 Course activities

Course activities have primarily consisted of case studies, video clips and internet streams, team discussions, whole class discussions, experiential exercises, role-playing, and visiting executive women speakers. To keep students engaged and energized during the full-day sessions, I vary the course activities throughout the day.

19.2.6 Assignments and evaluation of students

Students are responsible for completion of two major assignments. The first assignment is a team presentation of a woman leader. Each team of approximately five students chooses a woman leader in a business or non-profit organization or in politics/civic society, and investigates her behaviour and effect on others through readings, the Internet, and other sources. Each team gives a 30-minute presentation (including a 10-minute Q and A session) about their woman leader and their conclusions about her impact on others. The presentation generally describes the woman leader's childhood and family background, educational background, career history, vision, key values, leadership philosophy, leadership styles, career effectiveness, work–life integration efforts, organizational outcomes and impact, and overall legacy. The presentations use PowerPoint and internet video streams where possible, and include a listing of information sources. Class time is provided for team formation and discussions of the team project during the first class session. Presentations are provided immediate written feedback by all audience members. The grade for the presentation is provided by the instructor and TAs immediately after the class session and emailed to each team together with additional feedback and summary comments. Each team also completes a Team Member Contributions Evaluation form, evaluating each team member's contributions to the team presentation.

The second assignment consists of an individual reflection paper, which is referred to as a praxis paper because it is specifically designed to help students translate and integrate the WIO course constructs into their personal development agenda. This is a reflective paper that gives students the opportunity to understand and apply the course's leadership concepts to their own lives and to create a plan for continued development. This paper has three parts. The first is a student's analysis and presentation of the vital components affecting career success in organizations. The purpose of this first part of the paper is to demonstrate the student's familiarity and fluency with the core concepts discussed in the course. Drawing on course materials, readings, discussions, activities and their own experiences, students are asked to discuss the core elements that they think are critical for women (or men) to be successful in their careers in organizations. Some examples may be overcoming stereotypes and barriers, gaining emotional strength and resilience, demonstrating leadership vision and skills, demonstrating technical expertise and performance, communication skills, networking behaviours and career planning skills, moving towards work–life integration, nurturing reputation, demonstrating integrity and professionalism, and developing effective support structures as they rise in one's career. There may be other elements that are specifically relevant to a student's life and career as they prepare a road map for a successful, effective and impactful career. Students are asked to end this section with a definition of what success means to them.

The second part of the paper is the student's individual assessment of how they "measure up" on the core components identified in the first part. Students draw on their own experiences as well as any performance feedback they may have received previously from others to illustrate their capabilities. The third part of the paper is a student's future vision and personalized development agenda. Here students discuss their development goals or objectives, and strategies for working towards them. This agenda details (1) the skills and competencies, (2) the relational networks, and (3) the work and life opportunities or activities needed to develop in order to achieve the success they defined.

Finally, class participation is evaluated by the instructor and course TA in terms of the quality of student engagement in class activities (e.g. integration and application of reading assignments, constructiveness of verbal contributions, active participation in small group work, completion of exercises, and attendance) and the demonstration of behaviours likely to enhance the class as a learning community (e.g. pro-activity, respect for others, collaboration and developmental assistance to other students).

19.2.7 Course evaluations and student feedback

Course evaluations (on a scale of 5.0) ranged in the past five years from 4.74 to 4.96, with an average course rating of 4.82. Instructor ratings (also on a 5.0 scale) during that period ranged from 4.86 to 5.0, with an average instructor rating of 4.93. The average response rate of students was 83% over these five years.

Qualitative comments received from students are also extremely positive, including, for example, the following comments from 2013, the latest year in which the course was taught:

> The course was a fabulous exploration of leadership issues as well as how it particularly relates to women in the workforce, and

> The instructor presented material from the lens of both male and female perspectives. Class topics were interesting and personal, whether being a female that identified with the course material or a male considering various issues from a different perspective. The guest speakers had interesting backgrounds and a wealth of knowledge to share.

19.3 Reflections

I have been teaching the WIO course at the Weatherhead School for more than ten years now. The course is relatively popular among students. Despite declines in general MBA enrolments at our school over the last decade, course enrolment has remained steady and has even grown in the current year. Below I provide some insights that I have gained over the past decade from engagement with students and others about this course.

19.3.1 Gender equality in management education must be deliberately fostered

From my experiences in teaching the WIO course over the past several years, I've learned that gender equality needs to be introduced deliberately and systematically into the management curriculum. Merely waiting and hoping for gender equity change to happen within management education has simply not worked over the previous years and decades. In order to see change in the everyday practice of management, what is taught in business schools must include awareness of and insight into the nature and consequences of gendered systems. However, even with this deliberate strategy of gender equality through curricular innovation, I am conscious that only a miniscule proportion of male students in our management school (and no men faculty or administrators) are exposed to the ideas and research presented in the course.

Generally, courses in women's and gender studies are conducted in order to foster more egalitarian attitudes and increase awareness of sexism and other social inequities. Stake (2006) and Stake and Hoffman (2001) provide evidence from a national study that compared specific pedagogy dimensions with student change and concluded that

67% of students in women's and gender studies type courses are successful in helping develop egalitarian attitudes and commitment to social change for women and other marginalized groups. Stake et al.'s (1994) study built on an earlier study by Lee (1993) who found that the majority of students in a women and gender studies class reported that knowledge gained from the class contributed to enhanced awareness and broadened outlook, increased confidence and a sense of empowerment. However, this result applied to female students only. The three men in Lee's class responded differently to the survey question on empowerment: one male student left the question unanswered, and the other two stated that they knew a little bit better now what women are going through and that the course helped them understand women better, suggesting that gender knowledge may serve more for the personal use of male students than as a tool for engendering system change (Stake, 2006).

In the WIO course, the focus is on understanding the experiences of women in organizations and how organizational realities may facilitate or hinder women's career and leadership development. Given the topic of the course, I believe that the core constructs and activities must remain focused on the experiences of women. However, paying attention to the experiences and circumstances of men as well as extant gender dynamics between women and men is also important. Periodically, I have considered changing the title (and content) of the course to something like "Gender in Organizations" or "Women and Men in Organizations" to more explicitly account for the gendered experiences of men in organizations. However, because of the great and persistent need to shine a light specifically on the under-representation, lowered status and gendered treatment of women in both management and management education, each time I have deliberately chosen to not change the focus of the course. By bringing into the course powerful and successful visiting executive speakers who are female, I provide examples of successful women executives to students who rarely meet such examples in other management courses or are rarely exposed to senior women's decision making and leadership through extant curricular content. By choosing to remain with the topic of Women in Organizations, my hope is that the course provides a compelling avenue for the empowerment, leadership and career development of female students in management education, and ultimately women in corporate management.

19.3.2 Gender reflexivity helps both female and male students examine privilege

Both female and male students take my WIO course, but it is preponderantly populated by women. Women MBA students have indicated to me that this course is the first time in their entire management education experience that their gender has been in the majority in any course they have taken. Men MBA students have similarly shared, sometimes during the first class session, that this is a new experience for them as well, and that they are somewhat tentative in knowing how to behave. Not surprisingly, the experience of being in a minority group in their management education program is foreign to most men MBA students in the United States, and this is certainly true at our school. Fortunately, this reversal in the typical majority/minority status of men/ women in their management education courses offers the opportunity for greater reflexivity, particularly gender reflexivity, for both female and male students.

Reflexivity is a special kind of awareness where we act only after careful considera-tion of the intent, content and effects of our behaviour (Martin, 2003, 2006). Reflexivity requires critical reflection on prevailing social arrangements, norms and expectations, and gender reflexivity is the particular skill of awareness of and critical reflection about the conscious and unconscious gender schemas underlying individuals' actions and organizational arrangements, and the consequences of these in everyday practice (Adkins, 2003). I have found that an explicit discussion of gender reflexivity during the first class session is helpful to alert students about societal perceptions of gender roles and patterns and their reification in organizations and the management educa-tion classroom. Similarly, in the middle of the course, a reading and a class discussion specifically address the role of men as agents of gender equity change. Through these deliberate attempts at perspective taking and examination of privilege, both female and male students have the opportunity to engage reflexively and potentially challenge the status quo. As I have reflected with coauthors in a previous discussion of gender issues in the management education classroom:

> One of our goals as management educators is to work toward helping students articulate that which cannot easily be voiced around the dynamics of difference . . . In specific, when students engage with gender reflexivity, they are conscious about why they and others behave in the ways they do. They are able to identify the social arrangements, norms and expectations that impact gender relations, and recognize, voice and take into account the impact of these structures on their own and others' actions . . . They better understand privilege and roles, and take considered action to alter prevailing stereo-types and biases. They reflect about, articulate, and act on their reactions to gender experiences in ways that are active rather than passive, inquiry-based rather than advocacy-based, and self-determining rather than self-abdicating. (Bilimoria et al., 2010: 864–865).

19.3.3 A psychologically safe classroom environment is a key element of the course's effectiveness

Multiple tensions exist for female and male students in courses such as Women in Organizations. These tensions may be further exacerbated when anger and despair surfaces as social inequities and customary experiences are being explored (cf. Lee, 1993). In response to such tensions, defensive postures may be enacted by minor-ity (and possibly even majority) group members. For example, male students, who generally have experienced higher social status and power in mainstream manage-ment education, may engage in a WIO course with a variety of individual or collective attempts at identity preservation, verification and presentation—such as withdrawal, aggressiveness, stereotyping, hostility, and overachievement or underachievement. I have learned to utilize pedagogical structures and practices (e.g. appropriate timing of tension-inducing data and activities, structured conflict exercises such as debates, consciousness-raising activities such as asking students to argue opposite positions to their own, and meaningful debriefing) through which such tensions can be explored within the broader context in which both majority and minority members are embedded beyond the immediate classroom environment. When the classroom culture offers students a psychologically safe environment to express themselves and in which blaming or shaming of either gender is not appropriate, the WIO course allows deeper exploration of individual differences and choices, and gendered structural arrangements.

19.3.4 Providing opportunities for voice, self-awareness and relational skill building is vital

In order to encourage the development of students in this course, I have learned to concentrate simultaneously on three focal areas of skill development: empowering voice, improving self-understanding and enhancing relational skills. Attending to individual skill development keeps the focus on the self, while social skill development concentrates on the self in relation to others. Both self-awareness and social awareness are critical competencies for managers to strengthen. For example, one essential skill relevant to these dynamics is conflict management, both for resolving task conflicts as well as relational conflicts. Another related area for skill development of students is the understanding and leveraging of power and influence, in particular recognizing the power and influence held by majority and minority group members in the world outside the management education classroom.

19.3.5 Enabling gender equality in management education requires more than a single elective course

As the literature demonstrates, gender inequality is pervasive in management education. Clearly, a single course, with approximately 40 students annually (who are primarily young women), cannot eradicate systematic gender bias and discrimination in management education and beyond. As others and I have argued previously and in this volume (see Chapter 2 by Flynn, Cavanagh and Bilimoria), what is needed is a thoughtful, sector-wide re-tooling of management education to better serve the needs of female students, faculty, and administrators across the globe. I have previously identified the broader programmatic and institutional changes that need to occur before management education can serve as a guiding force for change in the gendered values and practices of management itself (Bilimoria, 1999). Notwithstanding this need for macro-level change, the WIO course does play a relatively small but positive role in affirming the experiences of female management education students; giving the opportunity for women and men to reflexively examine systematic privilege and disadvantage; and ultimately empowering management education students to challenge the status quo and enact gender equality in the workplaces they will populate and lead in the future.

References

Acker, J., 1990. Hierarchies, jobs and bodies: a theory of gendered organizations. Gender & Society 4(2), 139–158.

Adkins, L., 2003. Reflexivity: freedom or habit of gender? Theory, Culture and Society 20(6), 21–42.

Bilimoria, D., 1999. Upgrading management education's service to women. Journal of Management Education 23(2), 118–122.

Bilimoria, D., O'Neil, D.A., Hopkins, M.M., Murphy, V., 2010. Gender in the management education classroom: a collaborative learning journey. Journal of Management Education 34(6), 848–873.

Buttner, E.H., 2002. High-performance classrooms for women? Applying a relational frame to management/organizational behavior courses. Journal of Management Education 26(3), 274–290.

C200: Top female executives make case for women in business, 1998. The Harvard Crimson, February 5. Downloaded from: www.thecrimson.com/article/1998/2/5/c200-top-female-executives-make-case

Catalyst, Inc., 2010. Pipeline's Broken Promise. Downloaded on 3 March 2015 from www.catalyst.org/knowledge/pipelines-broken-promise

Fastenau, M., December 22–23, 1995. Business schools ignore need to 'imagine' being a woman manager. HR Monthly.

Gallos, J.V., 1993. Women's experiences and ways of knowing: implications for teaching and learning in the organizational behavior classroom. Journal of Management Education 17(1), 7–26.

Hite, L.M., McDonald, K.S., 1995. Gender issues in management development: implications and research agenda. Journal of Management Development 14(4), 5–15.

Ibarra, H., Ely, R., Kolb, D., 2013. Women rising: the unseen barriers. Harvard Business Review 91(9), 60–66.

Lee, J., 1993. Teaching feminism: anger, despair, and self-growth. Feminist Teacher 7, 15–19.

Leong, F., Snodgrass, C.R., Gardner, W.L., 1992. Management education: creating a gender-positive environment. In: Sekaran, U., Leong, F. (Eds.), Womanpower: Managing in Times of Demographic Turbulence. Sage, Newbury Park, CA, pp. 192–220.

MacLellan, C., Dobson, J., 1997. Women, ethics, and MBAs. Journal of Business Ethics 16(11), 1201–1209.

Martin, P.Y., 2001. Mobilizing masculinities: women's experiences of men at work. Organization 8, 587–618.

Martin, P.Y., 2003. "Said and done" versus "saying and doing" gendering practices, practicing gender at work. Gender & Society 17(3), 342–366.

Martin, P.Y., 2006. Practicing gender at work: further thoughts on reflexivity. Gender, Work & Organization 13(3), 254–276.

Mavin, S., Bryans, P., 1999. Gender on the agenda in management education? Women in Management Review 14(3), 99–104.

Mavin, S., Bryans, P., Waring, T., 2004. Unlearning gender blindness: new directions in management education. Management Decision 42(3/4), 565–578.

McKeen, C.A., Bujaki, M.L., Burke, R.J., 2000. Preparing business graduates for the "real" world—the role of the university. Women in Management Review 15(7), 356–369.

Morrison, A.M., White, R.P., Van Velsor, E., The Center for Creative Leadership, 1992. Breaking the Glass Ceiling: Can Women Reach the Top of America's Largest Corporations? Addison-Wesley, Reading, MA.

New York Times, 2013. Harvard Business School Case Study: Gender Equity, New York Times, September 8. Downloaded from: www.nytimes.com/2013/09/08/education/harvard-case-study-gender-equity.html?pagewanted=all&_r=0

Offermann, L.R., 2007. From the editor: not your father's business school. Academy of Management Learning and Education 6(2), 165–166.

Powell, G.N., Butterfield, D.A., Parent, J.D., 2002. Gender and managerial stereotypes: have the times changed? Journal of Management 28, 177–193.

Ragins, B.R., Townsend, B., Mattis, M., 1998. Gender gap in the executive suite: CEOs and female executives report on breaking the glass ceiling. The Academy of Management Executive 12(1), 28–42.

Schein, V.E., 1993. The work-family interface: challenging corporate convenient. Women in Management Review 8(4), 22–27.

Schein, V.E., 2007. Women in management: reflections and projections. Women in Management Review 22(1), 6–18.

Schein, V.E., Davidson, M.J., 1993. Think manager, think male. Management Development Review 6(3), 24–28.

Simpson, R., 1995. Is management education on the right track for women? Women in Management Review 10(6), 3–8.

Simpson, R., 2006. Masculinity and management education: feminizing the MBA. Academy of Management Learning and Education 5(2), 182–193.

Sinclair, A., 1995. Sex and the MBA. Organization 2(2), 295–317.

Smith, C.R., 1997. Gender issues in management education: a new teaching resource. Women in Management Review 12(3), 100–104.

Smith, C.R., 1998. Best practice in management education: capitalising on gender diversity awareness. Journal of Management Development 17(1), 6–16.

Smith, C.R., 2000. Notes from the field: gender issues in the management curriculum: a survey of student experiences. Gender, Work & Organization 7(3), 158–167.

Stake, J.E., 2006. Pedagogy and student change in the women's and gender studies classroom. Gender and Education 18(2), 199–212.

Stake, J.E., Hoffman, F.L., 2001. Change in student attitudes, social activism, and personal confidence in higher education: the role of women's studies. American Educational Research Journal 38, 411–436.

Stake, J.E., Roades, L., Rose, S., Ellis, L., West, C., 1994. The women's studies experience: impetus for feminist activism. Psychology of Women's Quarterly 18, 17–24.

Wilson, F.M., 1996. Research note: organization theory: blind and deaf to gender? Organization Studies 17(5), 825–842.

20

Teaching gender issues in management education

The role of experiential approaches

Kara A. Arnold and Dale Foster

Memorial University, Canada

This chapter presents a project designed to assess the effectiveness of an experiential approach to teaching gender issues in management at the MBA level. Kolb's experiential learning theory (ELT) formed the basis for re-designing a course that incorporated exercises and activities to engage students in what Kolb describes as concrete experiences. Student reflection assignments about these experiences during the course and interviews after the course were analysed for common themes. Using these data, success of the approach was measured by the changes in students' thinking and behaviours. Critical contributions to the effectiveness of the approach included: choice of exercises to elicit strong responses; creating a safe environment for frank discussions; and providing opportunity to reflect on the interplay between personal experiences, in-class discussions and the exercises. The chapter discusses the challenges and benefits of using such an approach to teach gender issues.

20.1 Introduction

This chapter describes a project designed to assess why an experiential approach to teaching gender issues in management at the Master of Business Administration (MBA) level can be effective. Experiential learning engages students in various active-learning exercises designed to encourage the student's deep learning (Hawtrey, 2007). This links their experience to academic learning, and in turn allows them to explore how to apply their learning to management roles. The end result is managers who are both aware of the importance of gender equality, and who are committed to creating more equitable organizations.

The experiential learning approach is an especially good fit for introducing issues of gender equality, particularly because gender equality can be a topic that elicits strong reaction (Zawadzki, Danube and Shields, 2012). A small number of studies delve into the use of experiential exercises in gender issues courses. This research highlights the need to overcome reactance to the material (Zawadzki, Danube and Shields, 2012). In addition, experiential exercises outside of the classroom can be a very effective method of showing students how the material applies to them (Good and Moss-Racusin, 2010). However, there is little research that identifies the types of in-class activities that are most effective and importantly how, and why, specific in-class activities are effective.

This chapter attempts to fill this gap; it outlines a project whereby students in a gender issues course in the MBA program at a university in Canada engaged in various experiential exercises. The project systematically assesses the effectiveness of these experiential exercises and suggests which aspects contribute to their success in encouraging active learning.

20.2 Why should gender issues be part of management education?

The inclusion of gender issues content in the MBA curriculum is important and highly relevant today. Women and men have greater equality in the workplace than ever before, yet subtle (and not so subtle) discrimination still persists. Women are represented in almost equal percentages to men (and in some disciplines have higher representation) in attaining university education (Powell, 2011; Statistics Canada, 2011). At the same time, while the percentages vary between schools, within Canada the gender breakdown for MBA students is on average 64% male and 36% female.[1] Data from AACSB (The Association to Advance Collegiate Schools of Business) accredited schools presents a similar story with 2011–2012 data showing 64.2% versus 35.8%, respectively.[2] More women are participating in the paid workforce than in past (Powell, 2011), yet participation is focused on female-dominated professions (Statistics Canada, 2011) and there are still very few women in the most powerful leadership roles within organizations (Powell, 2011). One Canadian study suggested that at the current rate of change it will take 151 years before the "proportion of men and women at the management level is equal" (*CBC News*, August 31, 2011). While maternity leave is provided in most countries, fewer provide parental leave

---

1 From www.canadian-universities.net/MBA/MBA_Canada_Gender.html (April 28, 2014).
2 From www.aacsbblogs.typepad.com/dataandresearch/aacsb-business-schools-questionnaire-bsq/ (April 28, 2014).

(Hall and Spurlock, 2013). This makes it more challenging for fathers to take parental leave, and studies show that those fathers who do take leave may be subject to harsh judgement from others (Brescoll and Uhlmann, 2005). This often leaves child rearing to be primarily a woman's responsibility, which could cause the mother's career to suffer.

Within an organizational context, behaviour is interpreted through a gendered lens; whether a man or a woman engages in certain behaviour changes the perception of that behaviour (e.g. Heilman and Chen, 2005). When female leaders express consideration for employees, for instance, they often do not receive the credit afforded male leaders who express the same behaviour (Loughlin, Arnold and Bell-Crawford, 2012). Similarly, male employees are viewed as "wimpy and undeserving of respect" when they violate gender norms (Heilman and Wallen, 2010: 664). As Heilman and Eagly (2008: 1) powerfully demonstrate in their research, "gender stereotypes are alive [and] well" and continue to contribute to workplace discrimination. Individuals might agree that gender stereotypes exist, but when asked, would usually disagree that gender stereotypes affect their personal judgements of others (Chavez and Ge, 2007; McLaren, 2005).

Gender biases clearly still exist, even if these are sometimes subtler than in the past (Myerson and Fletcher, 2000). "Second generation" bias refers to the fact that many women are unaware of having been discriminated against based on their gender, and will deny this "even when it is objectively true and they see that women in general experience it" (Ibarra, Ely and Kolb, 2013: 63). This type of bias is so deeply embedded in "stereotypes and organizational practices" (Ibarra, Ely and Kolb, 2013: 64) that it is difficult to name (Myerson and Fletcher, 2000). For example, a recent Harvard Business Review article described how these subtle biases negatively affect a female leader's ability to "internaliz[e] a leadership identity" (Ibarra, Ely and Kolb, 2013: 62). Once individuals are made aware of this type of bias, they can name it and take action to change it. Awareness of subtle gender bias is one way to affect change in the future. One way to create such awareness and ability to name the problem in a classroom setting is through an experiential approach to learning.

20.3 Kolb's model of experiential learning theory

Experiential learning is an approach that engages students in an activity, allows them to reflect on this activity, engages them in analysis of this experience in order to gain insight from it, and then allows the incorporation of this new understanding into their lives (Kolb, 1984). Indeed, lifelong learning is achieved as the cycle is repeated, over and over, always using experiences as the impetus for reflection, conceptualization, and action. Figure 20.1 shows these four principal stages: concrete experiences (CE), reflective observation (RO), abstract conceptualization (AC), and active experimentation (AE). In the "concrete experience" stage, the learner physically experiences the concept. In a real-life situation, this might equate to an employee experiencing gender discrimination. This experience would form a basis for observation and reflection (reflective observation). The employee/learner would then consider how to address and improve

Figure 20.1 **Kolb's stages of experiential learning**
Source: Kolb (1984). Reproduced with permission.

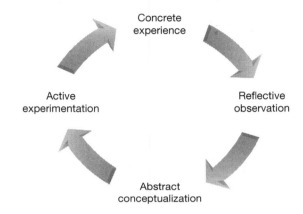

upon the situation (abstract conceptualization). The employee would put these ideas into action (active experimentation). The learning includes a cycle where the consequences of the new ideas are experienced (CE), reflected upon (RO), and new responses are conceptualized (AC) and undertaken (AE). Kolb's (1984) ELT posits that progression through the four stages is critical to achieve deep learning.

Experiential education has found a strong fit with management education; it is recognized that an experiential approach can increase the relevance of the classroom experience and that this is especially germane for MBA programs where one of the primary goals is to train effective managers (Conklin, 2012). There is evidence that experiential methods in the classroom can facilitate transferring this learning to the workplace (Armstrong and Mahmud, 2008; Gardner and Korth, 1997).

While the benefits of using ELT in management course design can lead to deep understanding and new behaviours/actions on the part of students, Kolb and Kolb (2009) also recognize the challenges for the professor of using ELT: these include increased course preparation time and increased commitment, as well as smaller class size to accommodate the use of experiential exercises.

The course in this study was re-designed from a lecture-based format using the ELT model as the framework. Learning objectives were outlined and active learning concrete experiences that the instructor could use in the classroom were sought and developed to map to these objectives. Examples of the active learning experiences used in the course include: discussion on films (e.g. Who's Counting? Marilyn Waring on Sex, Lies and Global Economics: https://www.nfb.ca/film/whos_counting; Disclosure: Comer and Cooper, 1998), articles (e.g. Fels, 2004), self-assessments (e.g. Bem Sex Role Inventory: Bem, 1974), and group activities (e.g. Raising Elizabeth/Robert: Powell, 1994; Alligator River: Chavez and Ge, 2007). During the 2009 course offering, there were six of these activities. For each activity there was an in-class portion, and then there was a written reflection assignment. The written reflection assignments were five pages in length assessing the students' knowledge of the theory or concepts, their ability to link the theory or concept to their own life experience, and explicit discussion of any changes in attitude or behaviour they experienced as a result of engaging in the activity. The rest of the chapter will describe the project to assess how this re-design affected student leaning.

20.4 Methods

20.4.1 Sample and data

Students in an elective MBA course engaged in experiential exercises (described above) designed to illustrate specific theories and concepts, and to increase their awareness of the extent to which gender stereotypes operate to influence their judgements and perceptions without conscious awareness. After the in-class exercises, students completed written reflection assignments about these experiential exercises. The goal of writing was to actively engage the student in the analysis of the activity, to discover what they learned as a result, and to see how this may have changed their future attitude and/or behaviour.

After the course was finished, students were approached regarding their willingness to be part of this research study. Participants who indicated they were interested were asked whether they would be willing to give permission to the researchers to utilize their written reflection assignments from the course as part of the study. The analysis we report on below is based on four to five reflection assignments (around 5 pages each) for each participant.

In addition, in-depth interviews each lasting approximately 45–60 minutes were conducted with students 2–4 months after the end of the semester (after grades were finalized) to delve into their experiences with the experiential exercises and the impact that these have had on their personal attitudes and awareness of gender issues in organizations. (See the Appendix for the interview protocol.) While we utilized some structured questions, the participant could take the discussion in any direction that he or she felt was important, and the interviewer posed probing questions on these participant-led directions (Glesne, 2006; McCracken, 1988). In total, 10 students (7 females and 3 males) took part in the interviews and gave permission to analyse their reflection assignments. This reflects a 50% response rate from the class of 20 students in total and the gender breakdown of participants reflected the gender breakdown in the course.

20.4.2 Analysis

Interview and reflection assignment data. All interview transcripts were transcribed verbatim. Reflection assignments were already stored in word format and identifying information, grades and instructor comments were removed. Both authors read through the interview transcripts and created an initial list of categories that they found to be reflected in the data. The authors then met to compare these categories, discuss the main patterns in the interview data, and then revised the list of categories to incorporate each author's list. Revised categories were used to code the reflection assignments. As initial categories were coded it because apparent that some categories were main themes that linked to various sub-themes—in other words, the patterns in our data became apparent. We then compared this to the literature, and through a constant comparison process (Silverman, 2000) we developed the main and sub-themes that were embedded in our data. We went back to the interview and reflection assignment data multiple times in order to compare what we were seeing in these data compared to the literature and determined the essential patterns that were present. We also had two graduate student research assistants code the interview and reflection assignments for two participants each as a check on whether we had missed any emergent themes. We met with the students to discuss their coding and there were no new main or sub-themes identified.

20.4.3 Results

During our analysis, three main themes emerged: (1) how the course was taught; (2) student reaction to the course material; and (3) outcomes of taking the course.

Within each of these main themes, sub-themes were linked. The first main theme, "How the course was taught" contained three sub-themes: the class discussion, the class environment, and the act of writing. The second, "Student reaction to the course material" revealed two sub-themes: awareness and emotional reactions. The third, "Outcomes of taking the course" involved two sub-themes: thinking in new ways and behaving in new ways.

In the pages that follow we expand on each of these sub-themes by using the participants' words. The comments illustrate the extent of the learning that was achieved by these exercises, and how the design of the course encouraged participants to move through the stages in Kolb's model to achieve deep learning represented by changes in thinking and behaviour.

20.4.4 The themes and student comments

(1) How the course was taught: The first main theme that was identified from our analysis of the data involved aspects of how the course was taught. The exercises provided a launching point for the students to situate the events and information described in exercises in their own experiential framework (CE). Students felt that one of the most important aspects was the opportunity for class discussion. This is the first of our sub-themes.

(1-1) The class discussion: The comments below indicate that in-class discussion of the exercises allowed students to evaluate their own responses to the events described in the exercises. This, in turn, provided participants with personal insights. For example, this participant echoes the comments of others in remarking on the value of the in-class discussions:

> The amount of small group discussions that we did, it's enough to . . . get an
> idea of how other people feel about the issue. (F2[3])

We also heard that class discussion opened their minds to other's points of view:

> I think definitely just the discussion afterwards was . . . the most important
> piece as to why it was so effective. There are so many people in the class that

---

3 Note that participants are identified as F (female) or M (male) and by number.

> you are definitely going to hear different views and maybe something that you never considered before. (M3)

And the participants below corroborated the usefulness of discussions in understanding others' opinions:

> I just remember how different responses were from the class from what I expected them to be and the reasonings were all different. (F1)

> It was very good to have group conversations with them [men] because . . . sometimes you just expect a man who dresses and speaks a certain way to have certain ideals and qualities but to discover that he has different ideas through conversation was really good. (F2)

These comments are representative of the majority of our participants who described that through discussion they became aware of the perspectives of others and, in turn, became aware of their own biases and stereotypes. We found that this sub-theme was very strongly connected to the sub-theme of awareness (see 2-1 below).

(1-2) The class environment. This is the second sub-theme of "How the course was taught". While "Class environment" was not as frequently mentioned as "Class discussion", the fact that the environment was safe enabled openness and even vulnerability and was the basis for the good class discussion as described here:

> You really need people to be open and honest and, I don't know, maybe even vulnerable. . . . because you could trust the people that you are with and you are comfortable and I think it was really important that that was the environment that was set . . . (F3)

> (I) like the open nature of the course where everyone started sharing and stuff like that . . . that's really healthy . . . (M1)

Here we see that class discussions and the safe environment contribute to a classroom where students discover how the material applies to their experiences (CE).

(1-3) The act of writing. The final sub-theme within "How the course was taught" relates to the written assignments; students were asked to describe how the theory and topic related to their own experience. These written pieces were essential in providing the opportunity to think about how the exercise applied to their own life experiences (RO).

> I guess it is one thing to kind of think about it but is another thing to actually put down your thoughts . . . on paper. . . . it hit home just a little more just to be able to write it down and really apply it to what I learned in class. (M3)

> . . . having that reflection after the fact really, really . . . put my thoughts into perspective . . . if I hadn't written it down I wouldn't have . . . put them in so much more perspective. (F4)

The next comments indicate how in-class discussion and one's own feelings and experiences found their way into the writings:

> [Reflection assignments] were good because it gave you a chance to see everybody's perspective into account and then go home and think about everything . . . you were able to solidify how you felt about them and explore how

> you felt about them, more so than you would in class. . . . and think . . . I can see that point of view once I have reflected on it. (F1)

> . . . the reflections . . . were probably most important for learning because it made you think about everything . . . not just the things we talked about in class but also the articles that we were reading and put that in context with our own life . . . (F6)

This sentiment is corroborated in the following, where the influence of personal experiences is explicitly noted:

> Then you would have more time to go home and think about the theories and what you have just done in class and perhaps draw upon more personal examples from past histories and things like that. So I would say the reflection paper was probably a very essential part of . . . self-evaluation. (F2)

> [Reflection papers] were good to do because to put it on paper . . . made you think about how it affected you or where did it come into play in your life or what were the reasons why you thought a certain way. . . . So I like the fact that I could reflect and think about maybe this is why I think this way or this is why I think that way about this topic. (M1)

This participant sums up how the reflections incorporate personal experiences into the learning when he says,

> I think [the reflections] really helped apply my own experience to what we talked about in class. (M3)

(2) Student reaction to the course material: The second main theme that emerged from our data was the fact that the in-class activities created awareness of gender issues and elicited strong reactions from students. These two sub-themes—awareness and emotional reaction—were expressed by every participant to some degree.

(2-1) Awareness. Awareness centred on noticing and becoming convinced that they themselves espoused some personal biases related to gender and gender stereotypes (RO). "Class discussion" and "The act of writing" appear to be the main conduits to new awareness as described by the participants:

> At first consideration when faced with the question if I have been impacted by socialization based on gender my thought was "no". But as I reflected on decisions made I realized that very likely my life has been greatly changed by the way I have been socialized. (F6)

> I believe the most interesting thing about stereotypes is how many of us believe that they are things that other people have; that is, we often do not see our own . . . it will certainly make me more aware of my judgments of people in the future. (F3)

> I guess once you start hearing about things it is hard to . . . . not that you were ignoring it before but I guess when you are more aware of it, it seems like you just notice it everywhere. Like you just notice all these little tiny things throughout the day that honestly either I just didn't notice before or I noticed on some level and just didn't pick up on them. (F7)

> The whole self-awareness part . . . that's the biggest thing I took away from the course was making myself more self-aware and in discussions in class. I had a

management skills class and I wanted to bring up gender; there was a problem there I was like why is nobody thinking of gender in this? (M2)

Student comments indicated that awareness was created on multiple levels: personal, work, and societal. Awareness in some cases also related to how students would do things differently both at work and in their personal lives, linking awareness to changes in behaviours (AE). Related to the participants' **personal** lives, we heard:

Every day I think about that like when my daughter said she didn't want to do soccer because that was a boy's sport. I was just kind of sitting there going "oh no its started already" right. So the awareness I think of how I can impact on her is probably the biggest thing that I took from [the course] which is something that you cannot grade me on. (F6)

Some things you are still not comfortable with. Like we talked about the kindergarten male teacher soothing either a boy or a girl to me I'm still not comfortable . . . . I probably would be more comfortable as a result of doing this course. But I can't honestly tell you that I would be 100% comfortable with that either. Not that it has anything to do with the person . . . it's the role. (F5)

In the following comments from students we see an increased awareness of gender stereotypes and biases that affect the **workplace**.

I have found even in meetings [at work] people are very stereotypical. Now, as a result of this course, I can see people are very stereotypical yet they don't even know they are. (F5)

Interestingly, I have experienced verbal, non-verbal, and physical sexual harassment from female co-workers without reporting any of them to management. In the organization I work for they are somewhat accepted as being "fun" and "harmless" which from my perspective, for the most part, they are. Where the problem comes in is that many of these actions are carried out by females in our office and would likely not be tolerated if they were being carried out by male workers. (M1)

I am disappointed to say that I have been guilty of this sort of behavior toward my female bosses as well. (F3)

After taking the course like it's easier to identify some of these issues in the different workplaces. (F2)

We see increased awareness by students of the effect of gender stereotypes on **society** as a whole. This is demonstrated in the following comments:

I have never had exposure to the concepts and principles surrounding feminist economics. Now that I have been introduced, it seems ludicrous that we, as a world, have never consciously thought about the behind the scene works carried out by millions of women and children on a daily basis that go unaccounted for in the grand scheme of things. (F2)

It [the movie] really *opened my eyes* to some of the things that do go on in a world scale that are just driven by economic forces as opposed to . . . like the role of a women and even the man for that matter that don't get brought into the equation . . . (M3)

The following student explicitly makes the connection between awareness and change in behaviour:

> Like many other people when faced with how my personal stereotypes have affected my judgements of others my first impression was—"that doesn't apply to me." However, before long I could think of numerous times when my own gender stereotypes have played a role ... The way to *change these beliefs is to make ourselves aware of the biases we have so we can alter our behaviours* ... (F6)

(2-2) Emotional reaction. In addition to awareness, participation created strong emotional reaction in students. The most frequently cited emotion was surprise. This was a strong reaction that resonated for all participants. In some cases surprise (and other emotional reaction) was a precursor of awareness (RO). The strength of the comments around surprise indicates that the exercises were successful in eliciting involvement in learning by the participants. Consider the following:

> What was more *surprising* however was how quickly people pre-determined the make up of these individuals, their families. (M1)

> It really *opened my eyes* to some of the things that do go on in a world scale that are just driven by economic forces as opposed to ... tak[ing] into consideration ... the role of a women. So it was kind of any *eye opener* for sure for me. (M3)

> I was *surprised* to see that my results from the class exercises (Raising Elizabeth/Robert, Gender-Career IAT, and Sex Roles) indicated that I was less "progressive" than I had thought. I would think that many of my classmates have been *somewhat surprised* by their results as well. (F4)

> I think I am always *surprised* and I probably [will] always remain surprised at just how ingrained some of this is. .... I was just so *continuously surprised* at not only how ingrained often in us but how it does have an effect how it still exists today. That was just something from the whole course I found *eye opening*. (F7)

While surprise was an emotion that was equally expressed by men and women, the analysis showed that women were more likely than men to describe other emotional reactions. These emotional reactions were quite strong in many cases. The following comments illustrate the strength and range of other emotional reactions that female participants described to the course material. These emotional reactions potentially represent the significance of the exercises to the female students' experiences and beliefs, and a new awareness of "second generation bias":

> I am literally writing these words with tears blurring my vision because I now feel *anger, betrayal and sadness* all at once ... for all women. I now feel these emotions because my awareness has changed. The words of Amazing Grace keep popping into my head- I once was blind, but now I see. (F7)

> It *surprised and dismayed* me to realize that I have somehow associated success and recognition with what is typically "men" and not "women," and modelled my behaviour after other men in my life in hopes of achieving their status in society. (F2)

> The fact that men's abilities are recognized more often then women is *frightening*—even more so when women are more capable then the men! . . . it seems that the unconscious actions that we take are the most concerning—it is not that we set out to neglect or ignore women and girls but the end result is that they are. (F6)

> Some of the statistics and facts presented in our text that we have read up to this point have been frankly kind of *depressing*. It *bothers* me to think that there are so many barriers that I will likely face when trying to advance my career. (F3)

The depth of emotion reflected in the comments above support that the class activities were meaningful concrete experiences for the female students.

(3) Outcomes of taking the course: There were two sub-themes linked to outcomes of taking the course, "New ways of thinking" (AC) and "New ways of behaving" (AE).

(3-1) New ways of thinking. First, students described new ways of thinking about gender issues in the workplace and in their lives in general. Here we see evidence that the exercises and the discussions (CE), and their reflections and subsequent awareness (RO) have resulted in new ways of thinking (AC). Subsequently, we will examine how students moved into demonstrating new behaviours.

> The strange thing about this situation is that I never really ever thought about it in terms of gender socialization. The events that occurred in both my family and my partner's family were normal for me. It was almost as if I was "hardwired" to not partake in my father's business and pursue other career opportunities. Therefore, gender ideals were so engrained in my family and way of life that I did not even consider working with the family business. . . . The exercise *stretched my thinking* into the future by pondering how my children would be socialized. Would my daughter pursue a career in the family business? (F5)

> What these situations resulted in, was a shift of my own gender schema from one that marginalized the importance of gender issues and viewed them as issues concerning how women differed from the norm, to a more understanding schema that recognized the importance of gender issues in both males and females. With my present broader gender schema, I have *viewed situations more openly*. (M2)

> Women in similar situations as my wife must either stay in organizations where the rules favor males or are fortunate enough to find a workplace that is more gender equal. Now that I have a 14-month-old daughter I find myself viewing things such as Warning's film in *a different light*. . . . and strongly believe that change is ultimately needed. (M3)

And finally,

> There are *different ways of looking* at an individual without necessarily assigning gender related terms with them and I find that I am more able to do that now. (F2)

(3-2) New ways of behaving. In the theme "Outcomes of the course", students gave examples of changes in their behaviour or how they intend to behave in the future (AE). Awareness appeared to be a precursor to change in behaviour. Often the behaviour described was speaking out in situations where they would not speak out before.

Behavioural changes related to personal (e.g. parenting, relationships with parents) and professional lives (e.g. career choices) were noted:

> Every day I think about that like when my daughter . . . and trying my best at six where she is now . . . I am going to *try and negate* some of what society is doing. (F6)

> Seeing how powerful such socialization experiences can be and having a 14-month-old daughter definitely made me think of *how I will influence* her career path. I believed that being educated (taking courses such as this one) and aware of such socializing forces is one step in the right direction. (M3)

> I find that like my family expectation is still very much finish a degree get married have children and raise a family but now that I find *that I go home and mention to my parents like you know have you ever though that there could be something more for me* other than just what you guys did. And step by step introduce to them the idea that you know like just because I'm a woman doesn't mean I have to end up being in the kitchen and cleaning house the rest of my life. They are coming around to that idea [but] they still think grandchildren is much better than me pulling in a truckload of money but we will see what happens. (F2)

Noticing behaviour of others that would not have been noticed prior to taking the course and discussing this in order to understand and to create awareness in others, or making a change in how tasks are distributed or valued at work were two poignant examples of change:

> Since your class I am very *conscious* . . . [my husband] was looking for hydraulic fittings, I was just hanging out. . . . he was looking up and down the aisle . . . And the whole time that we were in the aisle, maybe 15 minutes, there was this lady there and she was doing inventory . . . you could tell she was an employee. And he was looking [but] never asked her and then all of a sudden a male employee wearing the same uniform came by and he was only in the aisle for a second and [my husband] walked up and asked him. So we were walking away and I said to [my husband] why did you just do that and he said do what? I said why did you ask that gentleman to help you when that woman was visibly in the aisle the whole time taking inventory and you could tell she was an employee. He said I didn't do that. I said, yes you did. . . . did it ever occur to you that the man could have only been working here a week and she could have been here 12 years? And he said I didn't even know I did it, so why are you even asking me this? But I guess the whole point of my story is I *would have never looked* at that before I did this course. (F5)

> I personally exercised a bias when I saw only the male employees partaking in the heavy lifting and exhausting work when we first opened our store. I . . . thought many of the female employees to be not as hard working. However, what I failed to see was that while those heavy objects were being moved, some of the female employees were busy restocking some items, mixing other ingredients and organizing or cleaning the counters. I was missing the value in their work by being *blinded* by my reaction to gender stereotypes. (M2)

Some participants described changes in their behaviour at work. Having different conversations with coworkers than they would have before taking the course and respectfully questioning decisions that would have been taken for granted were two patterns of response.

> When I asked her [a co-worker] if she described herself as ambitious she thought for a second and said . . . "not really." When I questioned her if she wanted to advance through the ranks she said "right now I'm comfortable . . . ". (F6)

> I can remember at the time talking to my director and saying you know what we should look at—do women coming into our organization do they negotiate? . . . I can remember having that conversation because it was, wow this could very well be happening despite the fact that we have all these employment equity things in place. (F7)

> While once my idea of being a manager meant be a stern, demanding boss that was fiercely independent and in charge, my experiences in regards to the development of my gender schema and in my industry have allowed me to tap into a middle ground. (M2)

> [Talking about negotiating fair compensation at work]: So it really dawned on me that you know I'm in this because I wanted to learn, I wanted to find something that was fulfilling 100%. Something that really stuck with me that I'm not just going to settle, I don't need to settle so why am I going to do that . . . I'm sure it wouldn't have occurred to me otherwise and that really struck me . . . I need to take my time and figure out where I want to go and I don't mean just to take because it's offered. So that was a big kind of revelation. (F3)

The true impact of the experiential learning model in gender studies, moving participants through the stages of the ELT model and resulting in deep learning is validated in the themes arising from our analysis.

20.5 Discussion

This chapter has outlined a project to systematically assess the effectiveness of in-class experiential exercises in creating deep learning about gender issues in organizations. The research was undertaken in order to explicate the conditions under which students effectively learn about gender issues and translate that knowledge to their own lives. An MBA course in gender issues was re-designed to incorporate various experiential in-class activities in addition to written reflection assignments on these activities. Students appeared to engage in the material and deep learning was evident. Through our analysis of reflection assignments written as requirements for the course, and interviews conducted after the course concluded, three main themes arose addressing why the course re-design was effective.

These main themes focused on important pieces in terms of creating effective learning: (1) how the course was taught, (2) student reaction to the course material and (3) outcomes of taking the course. Within each of these main themes, sub-themes were linked, as discussed above. We note that these themes and sub-themes correspond to and support Kolb's model.

For example, aspects of "how the course was taught" relate to Kolb's first stage, Concrete Experiences. Course activities, such as watching movies, writing reflective pieces, and participating in discussions, were designed to emulate the physical experiences described by Kolb in a classroom environment that was purposefully devised to be safe and to encourage openness.

"Student reaction to the course material" corresponds to Kolb's second stage, RO. Kolb describes the active learner internalizing the concrete experience through observation and reflection. Our students reported heightened awareness of both their and other's reactions to the experiences, and gave examples of how they reflected and internalized this increased awareness. This included writing about their feelings.

In the theme, "outcomes of taking the course", students described how "reflective observation" led to changes in their thinking and in their behaviour. "New ways of thinking" corresponds to Kolb's stage three, "abstract conceptualization" while "new ways of behaving" corresponds to "active experimentation" in Kolb's model. Figure 20.2, below, summarizes the mapping of our sub-themes to Kolb's model.

Importantly, our themes and sub-themes are related in many aspects. Just as Kolb's model suggests linkages, so too do our data. Writing forced integration with personal experience and new thinking. Discussion created awareness, as did surprise and other strong emotional reactions, particularly as it allowed students to see where they had been biased. And awareness prompted new thinking, and subsequently, changes in behaviour.

Figure 20.2 **Mapping of themes from the study to Kolb's stages of experiential learning**

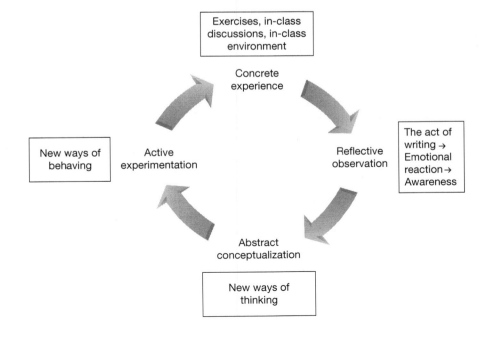

One new insight, and the only difference we found between female and male students, was the importance of emotional reaction in the creation of learning and importantly, a change in thinking and behaviour. Male emotion centred on surprise. Female emotions ranged from surprise to disgust to fear to outrage. We note that we only had three male participants—a key limitation of the study, and thus should not draw key conclusions from data in this regard. It does, however, raise an interesting topic for future research. In addition, we note that because this was an elective course there is a potential bias in the students who chose to take the course. Women in the course had more reason to be dismayed about the outcomes of the exercises in that the pervasiveness of gender stereotypes, and the effects of these are more likely to have negative effects for women within management. Regardless of reasons why, emotional reactions (whether surprise or otherwise), were key to generating awareness, and promoting new thinking and new behaviour in both male and female students. The challenge for the instructor is design-ing exercises that will create these types of reactions, and then effectively managing these in the classroom. The role of emotional reactions within the academic classroom setting, and potential gender differences in these reactions, is one interesting avenue for future research.

20.6 Future research

Future research can build upon this study in various ways. First, it would be useful to explore the elements of exercises that are most effective in driving people through the stages of learning outlined by Kolb. This study demonstrates the conditions that are nec-essary to engender this movement, but are there specific types of exercises that would be most effective? Second, our results also highlight the significance of emotional response in creating the learning and gender differences in this response. Can these types of exer-cises that create emotional reaction be supplanted in other domains outside gender studies? For example, can students experience similar emotional reactions to material in accounting, finance, or information systems? Or does the emotional reaction stem from the nature of the material? Can the differences in emotional reaction between men and women found within this gender course be replicated to larger samples? If so, what are the reasons behind the different emotional reaction of women to the material? How does emotional reaction impact future change in behaviour for both men and women? Third, are there specific exercises that are more effective for women than for men (or vice versa)? And how do pre-course attitudes affect our ability to engender this type of deep learning using the experiential approach? Fourth, how do challenges in facilitating class discussion to create awareness impact on the effectiveness of the use of experiential exercises in the classroom? For example, the instructor can never be certain what the outcome of such an exercise will be. How can this uncertainty be dealt with effectively? Finally, can we design longitudinal studies addressing the long-term impact of the learning that occurs from uti-lizing these types of in-class exercises regarding gender issues in the workplace?

20.7 Conclusion

> To consider the possibility of eradicating gender biases from daily lives would require nothing short of a world-wide cultural lobotomy. (F2)

Gender bias is now often subtle in organizations, yet the scope of change necessary to create equality is large (as one of our participants suggests). We argue that the approach we describe to teaching gender in management education complements the idea that change can happen one person at a time. Subtle changes in behaviour at an individual level (the notion of small wins—Weick, 1984; Myerson and Fletcher, 2000) can, in turn, add up to larger changes within organizations and society over the long run. Teaching gender issues in management through the experiential learning approach is one such way to create small wins. In the words of one student:

> Being aware of our own stereotypes and their effect on our attitudes and behaviours is a first step in eliminating their effect. It will undoubtedly be a long process which we have only now begun. Perhaps there will come a day when people will be judged based purely on their personal attributes and not based on other factors. (F6)

Acknowledgements

We thank the students who took part in this research project, and our colleagues, Dr Susan Hart and Dr Amy Warren, who provided valuable insight and advice.

References

Armstrong, S.J., Mahmud, A., 2008. Experiential learning and the acquisition of managerial tacit knowledge. Academy of Management Learning & Education 7(2), 189–208.

Bem, S.L., 1974. The measurement of psychological androgyny. Journal of Consulting and Clinical Psychology 42(2), 155–162.

Brescoll, V.L., Uhlmann, E.L., 2005. Attitudes towards traditional and non-traditional parents. Psychology of Women's Quarterly 29(4), 436–445.

CBC News, August 31, 2011. Women's Glass Ceiling Remains. Retrieved from: www.cbc.ca/news/business/story/2011/08/31/women-executive-conference-board.html

Chavez, C.I., Ge, Y., 2007. Discovering the enemy within: an exercise in unintended thought. Organization Management Journal Teaching & Learning 4(1), 87–110.

Conklin, T.A., 2012. Making it personal: the importance of student experience in creating autonomy-supportive classrooms for millenial learners. Journal of Management Education 37(4), 499–538.

Comer, D.R., Cooper, E.A., 1998. Gender relations and sexual harassment in the workplace: Michael Crichton's disclosure as a teaching tool. Journal of Management Education 22(2), 227–241.

Fels, A., April 2004. Do women lack ambition? Harvard Business Review, 50–60.

Gardner, B.S., Korth, S., 1997. Classroom strategies that facilitate transfer of learning to the workplace. Innovative Higher Education 22(1), 45–60.

Glesne, C., 2006. Becoming Qualitative Researchers: An Introduction, third ed. Pearson, Boston, MA.

Good, J.J., Moss-Racusin, C.A., 2010. "But, that doesn't apply to me": teaching college students to think about gender. Psychology of Women Quarterly 34, 418–421.

Hall, K., Spurlock, C., 2013. Paid parental leave: US vs. the world. Huffington Post. Retrieved from: www.huffingtonpost.com/2013/02/04/maternity-leave-paid-parental-leave-_n_2617284.html?view=print&comm_ref=false

Hawtrey, K., Spring 2007. Using experiential learning techniques. Journal of Economic Education, 143–152.

Heilman, M.E., Chen, J.J., 2005. Same behaviour, different consequences: reactions to men's and women's altruistic citizenship behaviour. Journal of Applied Psychology 90, 431–441.

Heilman, M.E., Eagly, A.H., 2008. Gender stereotypes are alive, well, and busy producing workplace discrimination. Industrial and Organizational Psychology 1, 393–398.

Heilman, M.E., Wallen, A.S., 2010. Wimpy and undeserving of respect: penalties for men's gender inconsistent success. Journal of Experimental Social Psychology 46, 664–667.

Ibarra, H., Ely, R., Kolb, D., September 2013. Women rising: the unseen barriers. Harvard Business Review, 62–66.

Kolb, A., Kolb, D., 2009. Experiential learning theory: a dynamic, holistic approach to management learning, education and development. In: Armstrong, S.J., Fukami, C.V. (Eds.), The Sage Handbook of Management Learning, Education and Development. Sage Publications, London, pp. 42–68.

Kolb, D., 1984. Experiential Learning: Experience as the Source of Learning Development. Prentice Hall, Englewood Cliffs, NJ.

Loughlin, C., Arnold, K.A., Bell-Crawford, J., 2012. Lost opportunity: is transformational leadership accurately recognized and rewarded in all managers? Equality, Diversity and Inclusion: An International Journal 31(1), 43–64.

McCracken, G., 1988. The Long Interview. Sage, Newbury Park, CA.

McLaren, Ian (Director), 2005. Her Brilliant Career. Cinéfête.

Myerson, D.E., Fletcher, J.K., January/February 2000. A modest manifesto for shattering the glass ceiling. Harvard Business Review, 127–136.

Powell, G.N., 1994. Gender and Diversity in the Workplace: Learning Activities and Exercises. Sage Publications, Thousand Oaks, CA.

Powell, G.N., 2011. Women & Men in Management, fourth ed. Sage, Washington, DC.

Silverman, D., 2000. Doing Qualitative Research: A Practical Handbook. Sage, London.

Statistics Canada, 2011. Women in Canada: A Gender-based Statistical Report. Retrieved from: www.statcan.gc.ca/pub/89-503-x/89-503-x2010001-eng.pdf

Weick, K., 1984. Small wins: redefining the scale of social problems. American Psychologist 39(1), 40–49.

Zawadzki, M.J., Danube, C.L., Shields, S.A., 2012. How to talk about gender inequity in the workplace: using WAGES as an experiential learning tool to reduce reactance and promote self-efficacy. Sex Roles 67, 605–616.

Appendix

1. Of all the experiential exercises we completed during this class, is there one that stands out in your mind as most interesting?

   a. If so which one?

   b. Why was it interesting?

2. Of all the experiential exercises we completed during this class, is there one that stands out in your mind as most important for your learning?

   a. If so which one?

   b. Why was it important for your learning?

3. What kinds of things did you find surprising about the exercises we did in class?

4. What kinds of things did you learn from the exercises we did in class?

5. Do you feel you gained an awareness of gender issues from taking this course?

6. Did you learn anything in the course that you have been able to incorporate into your life outside the classroom? For example, do you view situations differently? Do you respond to situations differently? Do you behave or feel differently than you used to?

21

From teaching ethics to ethical teaching

Feminist interventions in management education

Michelle Ann Kweder
Simmons School of Management, USA

Banu Özkazanç-Pan
University of Massachusetts, USA

Guided by transnational and postcolonial feminisms, an intersectional approach calls attention to the ways in which the mobility of neoliberal business ideas and practices can lead to further social and economic inequalities. Based on our experience as teachers–scholars–learners in US MBA classrooms, we propose the business school as a potential site of social change where feminist values lead to a new teaching ethic and model of inquiry. We envision a classroom inclusive of and considering a broader group of stakeholders where critical ideas are included in decision making in the classroom and translated into just actions in society. In this classroom, the demands and pressures of global capitalisms are questioned as part of understanding and undoing gender and other inequalities.

21.1 Introduction

Guided by transnational and postcolonial feminist perspectives in management (Calás and Smircich, 2006), we address the production of gender inequality in US-based business school settings and propose a pedagogical alternative to the *status quo*. In general, transnational feminist perspectives applied to the study of organizations call attention to the ways in which relations of difference across gender, race, class, sexuality, nation and so on take place differently as people move across borders for business (Calás, Ou and Smircich, 2013). As such, individuals may experience identities and inequalities differently depending on location and context. This intersectional approach to the study of people allows for "reconceptualization of the intersections of race, gender, and class as simultaneous processes of identity, institutional, and social practice" (Holvino, 2010: 248).

Similarly, postcolonial feminist perspectives call attention to the ways in which non-Western women and men are represented in Western texts, as well as to the living and working conditions in the non-West; they also raise concerns over agency (Mohanty, 2003). That is, Western texts may fail to accurately depict the "self-definition and self-direction" (Abrams, 1998: 806) by stereotypically affording non-Western actors too little agency while affording Western actors unchallenged privileges of agency. Within the context of management, postcolonial feminist approaches highlight various interdependencies and encounters between the Global North and South with respect to gender and power relations such as those in technology entrepreneurship (Özkazanç-Pan, 2012) and managing diversity (Prasad et al., 1997). These approaches can highlight the living and working conditions of young female workers from the Global South (Africa, Latin America, Middle-East, and developing nations of Asia) whose low-wages and labour sustains the "success" of global manufacturing for Global North (US, Canada, most of Europe, and developed East Asia) multinational corporations and nations.

Taken together, these lenses call attention to the contemporary ways in which the mobility of neoliberal business ideas and practices can lead to further social and economic inequalities in the global division of labour. Yet there is little discussion of the very material consequences of business ideas and practices heralded as leading to a competitive advantage and returning immense profits. Guided by these perspectives, we suggest that hegemonic Western patriarchal ideologies guide many MBA curricula generally and impact the MBA classroom. Our exemplar is the context with which we are familiar and from which we write: the globalized US business school. Specifically, business schools geographically located in the United States catering to both domestic and international students and professing to teach competencies necessary for engaging in work globally. As Joy and Poonamallee suggest, "contextual logics local to America" are insufficient in globalized classrooms (2013: 399).

In this chapter, we propose the creation of an environment where "ethical teaching" supersedes "teaching ethics" in addressing the aim of gender equality both in and beyond the classroom. We suggest that classes that purport to "teach ethics" are more broadly emblematic of the approach to educating MBAs that is disembodied and disengaged from the social and political consequences of managerial and organizational decisions and practices. We see the "teaching ethics" approach as transactional in contrast with a relational, reflexive, and contextualized approach of "teaching ethically".

First, we describe the various interrelated levels of context in which this US curriculum and classroom education takes place. Following this, we outline how the business school classroom can be a site of change for enacting social justice values with respect to gender equality. Our approach yields "teaching ethically" in the classroom as a feminist praxis for addressing and overcoming gender and other forms of inequality taking place in business and social contexts. We contrast this pedagogical ideology and practice with current approaches that aim to foster ethical business students, that is, teaching ethics. In doing so, we highlight a new role and capacity for business school classrooms in educating socially aware and ethically oriented individuals with the ability to think critically with respect to organizations in local and global contexts.

21.2 Context

The global landscape in which most business education takes place can be described as foremost a setting of neoliberalism where corporations and elite individuals have the potential and propensity to rely on market approaches as the "solution" to social issues at the expense of traditionally disenfranchised communities including the 14.5% of US residents who are poor (DeNavas-Walt and Proctor, 2014). Researchers find that poor adults and children face real deprivation including food insecurity, the inability to access necessary healthcare, and homelessness (Cohen, 2011; National Law Center on Homelessness & Poverty, 2013). Poverty rates for African Americans and people of Hispanic origin are persistently and disproportionately high (Gradín, 2012). Increasing income (Lin and Tomaskovic-Devey, 2013) and persistent gender and racial inequality (Stainback and Tomaskovic-Devey, 2012) remain mostly unchallenged in the United States. A *status quo* of structural economic and social arrangements coupled with organizational policies and practices perpetuate these inequalities.

In US business schools, these inequalities are not central to the MBA curriculum and pedagogy beyond advocacy of social enterprise/entrepreneurship or a voluntary corporate social responsibility (CSR) approach to addressing poverty and other social and environmental problems. In contemporary business schools, the hegemonic but false assumption of a universal desire for "maximum output for minimum input" (Fournier and Grey, 2000: 180) leads to a curriculum that infuses CSR initiatives with free market capitalism, laissez-faire government policy and "business as a solution". We suggest that the typical business school classroom can be described as instrumental in producing a professional managerial class without the tools to address social challenges and inequalities in a meaningful way—and in some cases, producing or reinforcing a point of view that normalizes and potentially exacerbates inequalities across relations of gender, race, class, and so forth. In effect, what we suggest is that most MBA classrooms function to reproduce the dominant business paradigm, rather than challenge and unpack assumptions around the role of business in potentially causing such inequalities in the first place. We are not alone in our criticism: with the backdrop of ongoing corporate scandals and financial crises in the United States and globally, journalists and critical management scholars have drawn attention to the apparent "lack of ethics" in graduates of MBA programs (Bennis and O'Toole, 2005; Canales, Massey and Wrzesniewski, 2012; Fisman and Galinsky, 2012; Grey, 2004; Holland, 2009; Podolny, 2009; Rubin and Dierdorff, 2009; Schoemaker, 2008).

Additionally, the proliferation of outposts of US-based business school campuses in non-Western and non-European nations (i.e. The American University in Dubai, United Arab Emirates; NYU in Dubai, United Arab Emirates; Rutgers in Singapore; Empire State College in Santo Domingo, Dominican Republic; Keiser University in San Marcos, Carazo, Nicaragua; Missouri State University in Dalian, China; Stratford University in New Delhi, India; Webster University in East Cantonments, Accra, Ghana; Harvard Global Network of affiliated business schools) as part of the globalization of business education (Joy and Poonamallee, 2013; Pfeffer and Fong, 2004) raises concerns over whose ideas and practices travel the globe as markers of good business. Despite existing in a dynamic landscape of global flows including ideas, people, technologies, and capital (Appadurai, 1990), business schools tend to promote a static, conservative agenda with respect to the social world. As such, we are concerned with the coopting of business knowledge production by capitalist and Western hegemonic patriarchal ideologies. As Starkey and Tempest (2006: 108) suggest,

> we need particularly to develop our knowledge of history and politics if we are to understand and to counter the inexorable trend to Americanization in our field. This is a highly political arena. There is as yet no viable alternative, in the sense of strong countervailing force, to the US management education juggernaut, just as there is, as yet, no credible alternative to the MBA that commands any significant consumer interest.

Moreover, the subfield of International Business and Management Studies has been described by Westwood and Jack as "reactionary" and playing "a part in the reproduction of power asymmetries within the global economy" (2007: 251).

In this sense, business school education provides rich ground to understand how taken for granted business ideologies may allow intersectional inequalities across relations of difference (gender, race, class, sexuality, nation, etc.) to take place in particular organizational settings. By intersectional, we refer to the "interlocking nature of oppression" (Collins, 1986: s19); that is people do not experience, and are mostly not seen as, a single, siloed identity category but move through the world as a whole being with a unique and complex identity formed overtime and in context. Our point of entry into this conversation and praxis (i.e. social change) is through engagement with a growing segment of MBA students at non-elite institutions. We expand on this idea below.

21.3 Classroom

Our focal MBA classroom—and site of potential social change—is increasingly typical: the coed, US, non-elite[1] classroom. It is a place of face-to-face learning and resides in a private non-profit or public institution as opposed to the growing group of private for-profit institutions.

---

1 Elite is defined as the top 20 US MBA global programs as determined by the *Financial Times*.

Our assumption is that these programs are more diverse (by identities that are intersectional) than the elites where African American, Hispanic Americans, and Native Americans remain significantly under-represented (Korn, 2012). It is likely that the non-elites mirror the more diverse whole of business school students as reported by the US Department of Education: the 2011 class was comprised of students who identified in the following ways: 56% White, 14% Black, 6% Hispanic, 8% Asian-Pacific Islander, 1% Native American, 1% two or more races, 14% non-resident, and 46% female. Increasingly, MBA classrooms experience an influx of international students including those from non-Western countries (Joy and Poonamallee, 2013). The relative diversity of such business schools and classrooms makes it an important site for considering how inequalities may take place and whether there are effective strategies and practices to address them.

In this sense, the classroom experience is quite relevant to how individuals make sense of organizations and whether they develop critical thinking skills necessary for seeing and challenging organizational practices, norms, and values that potentially lead to inequalities. The classroom experience includes in-class discussions, teamwork, group exercises, and various texts and media as teaching materials. Choices are made generally by faculty and with some input from students in terms of topics to cover and cases to study. Yet most strikingly, the approach to the broad business school curriculum is a sense of teaching business practices and ideas without a sense of the assumptions about business and the social world that are supported through the very teaching materials. For example, Harvard Business Publishing cases account for 80% of the cases studied at business schools globally; just 9% of these cases have women (of any race, ethnicity, or nationality) as protagonists (Byrne, 2014).

In addition, the classroom is also subject to the trappings of neoliberalism including curricular standardization, top-down management, and invasive systems of accountability (Giroux, 2010; Hammersley-Fletcher and Qualter, 2009, cited in Jones and Calafell, 2012). Moreover, in the ever-growing space of cross-cultural management (CCM) education, teaching, and learning tends to be functionalist with a Western centre, normative models, and a belief in generalizable knowledge for the goals of profit maximization and production (Joy and Poonamallee, 2013).

Standardization, strict managerial hierarchies, and systems of accountability invoke a sense of surveillance as normal in organizational life and raise concerns over agency. Can individuals who are marginalized in such classrooms "speak up" from a place of subjugation? What would this "speaking up" look like and how could we foster this kind of engagement as necessary for challenging inequalities in organizations? Despite these challenges, we propose the classroom as a site for the enactment of social change inhabited by teachers and learners—that is, rather than a hierarchical assumption that classes need to be segmented between faculty and students, our aim is to foster a collaborative space for learning and enacting change with regard to gender equality.

In global business education contexts, transnational and postcolonial feminist theories greatly inform the intersection of management, CCM, and ethics education. We discuss this idea further through our example of "teaching ethics".

21.4 Teaching ethics as *status quo*

The Association to Advance Collegiate Schools of Business (AACSB)[2] includes in its Eligibility Procedures and Accreditation Standards for Business Accreditation under the heading "General Business and Management Knowledge Areas" the standard of "[s]ocial responsibility, including sustainability, and ethical behavior and approaches to management" (AACSB, Adopted 8 April 2013). Christensen et al. (2007) report that 84.1% of respondent schools ($N = 44$) report mandatory inclusion of the topics of business ethics, CSR, and sustainable business/sustainability; moreover 54.55% described their inclusion as "integrated" within the course of study.

Despite this sensitivity to matters of ethics and ethical managerial behaviour, we suggest that the overall context in MBA education, including curriculum and pedagogical ideologies, does not address the role of business schools in potentially perpetuating rather than alleviating inequalities in the social and business world. In fact, Aspen Institute researchers found that well-intentioned entering students graduated with an increased focus on profit and a "weakened moral character" (Schneider and Prasso, 2002, cited in Crane, 2004: 149).

This idea of teaching ethics is becoming mainstream in US-based MBA education, but is founded upon assumptions regarding the separation of individuals from their contexts. Many business schools engage ethical issues through a single class focused on ethics despite the AACSB suggesting that schools should engage in ethics throughout the business curriculum (Floyd et al., 2013). In effect, a decontextualized, (falsely labelled) apolitical, and fictional managerial lens is used to educate students on making ethical decisions and behaving in an ethical manner. Often, a personal moral compass approach is used that focuses on individual decision making in various global contexts (Thompson, 2010). While some schools have aimed to integrate ethical teaching across the curriculum, the focus is still on outcomes related to enhancing the ability of individuals to make ethical decisions and became aware of ethical situations (Dzuranin, Shortridge and Smith, 2013). Others have attempted to engage in critical thinking by using case studies or raising ethical issues in courses across the business curriculum (Baetz and Sharp, 2004). Yet these approaches still separate values from business classes and attempt to locate them in the individual rather than offering a comprehensive approach to teaching ethics.

To clarify, values are already being taught through taken-for-granted ideas in business management education including "profit maximization" or "motivating your employees". Profit maximization assumes that this is the *most important and primary* goal of business and aiming for this goal is "good business practice". Yet this profit-centred goal is not necessarily shared universally but represents a particular US-based neoliberal approach to business (Joy and Poonamallee, 2013). Consequently, the goal of profit-maximization is a moral position enacted through neoliberal business ideas and

2 As of May 2014, 711 business schools in 47 countries and territories are accredited by the US-based AACSB.

ensuring practices. It represents an attempt, in the US, for the business school branded elite managerial class to instruct or control those seen as on the periphery (including both workers in the United States and those abroad). The goal is made possible locally through organizational practices including "motivating your employees" and is based on the assumption that employees lack the drive to do their jobs and need managerial oversight. Thus, assuming that individuals have choice and agency in making "ethical decisions" is specious in that experiences and behaviours in organizational life do not take place in a vacuum but rather, take place within the context of power relations between and among individuals.

For example, internationally, profit maximization and accompanying practices are made possible by a central organization (often US based in the case of MNCs) dictating local organizational practices through human resource management (HRM) and other commonly accepted knowledge transfer processes. All the while, there is an assumption about whose interests and experiences are valid and deserving of attention (Joy and Poonamallee, 2013). Within this context, teaching ethics assumes that decision-making is a straightforward choice computation even if carried out under "bounded rationality" (Simon, 1947; Jones, 1999). Missing from the conversation is the fact that decision-making rights are allocated based on gendered and racialized hierarchy and bureaucracy: institutional arrangements rife with inequality (Acker, 2006; Ahmed, 2012).

Consequently, organizational wrongdoing, such as ongoing environmental disasters in the case of BP, or human rights violations from AngloGold Ashanti, or Goldman Sachs' role in concealing Greece's debt preceding the 2010 European sovereign debt crisis, take place with no one accepting responsibility but placing blame on aberrant individual and/or organizational policies and practices (Bommer et al., 2013). This disjunctive observation is possible when the broader organizational objective (profit maximization) and norms of business practices are not questioned. Rather, a cursory concern over ethics and decision-making masks critical questions on values that are perpetuated through business school curricula and classroom dialogue that is focused on achieving profits through "efficiency" regimes. As Joy and Poonamallee (2013) and others point out (Westwood and Jack, 2007; Tipton, 2008) the desire for effectiveness is, according to postcolonial scholarship, likely a desire for control.

Additionally, the "teaching ethics" approach is flawed by what Giacalone and Thompson (2006) describe as the "organization-centred worldview" (OWV) where business interests, the acquisition of personal wealth, and materialistic thinking are central. Giacalone and Thompson (2006: 269) write that these motivations "establish the seeds of sham ethics, where there is no intent to do the right thing unless it helps the decision maker or advances the profit expectations scripted by Wall Street analysts". The authors go on to call for a human-centred worldview (HWV) and curriculum "oriented toward a broader community good" (Bellah et al., 1985, and Goxdz, 1995, cited in Giacalone and Thompson, 2007).

Already, critical management scholars have questioned the approach to teaching ethics in US business schools (Prasad and Mills, 2010) including the individual-focused approach to teaching ethics that does not consider political and structural pressures on individuals (Bridgman, 2010) or understand the cosmopolitan context of decision making (Janssens and Steyaert, 2012). In addition, feminist scholars have begun to examine how ethics can be taught in an embodied way that recognizes diversity and community in the process of decision making (Rabouin, 1997) and promotes an integrative approach (Furman, 1990). More broadly, feminist reflexive pedagogy goes beyond advancing ideas of a "broader community good" to incorporate complex issues of social justice in a dynamic atmosphere of learning. We are sympathetic to these calls and aims, but engage with them through transnational and postcolonial feminist perspectives. Next, we expand on the contributions of these perspectives.

21.5 Ethical teaching as feminist intervention

A feminist perspective, specifically informed by transnational and postcolonial concerns, reorients the focus from teaching ethics to ethical teaching within the context of mobile ideas and people under globalization. This form of pedagogy is inclusive of the knowledge that different cultures may have different value systems, morals, and notions of right/wrong. The conventional approach to "teaching ethics" implies detachment from the philosophies and ideas foundational to CCM and involves asking questions such as "what should manager from country X do in country Y if the local business practice is A and home country business practice is B?" (Jackson, 2011) or conducting OWV cost/benefit analysis that returns profits to owners. Alternatively, we suggest that teaching ethically involves a HWV cost/benefit analysis that addresses how the costs and benefits may accrue to different individuals or how they may perpetuate "inequality regimes" based on gender throughout organizations (Acker, 2006).

Furthermore, ethical teaching necessitates examining and voicing the values we, as feminist educators and scholars, are promoting in educational settings with respect to management and how these values may encourage or prohibit discussion about social justice and equality. We speak of our own experiences of both witnessing and confronting "inequality regimes" (Acker, 2006) in the classroom as professor and student (and in workplaces as both worker and manager). For example, the second author teaches a CCM course and is often confronted with stereotypes about women in the Middle-East from various sources (i.e. Harvard Case, Hofstede's cultural values) despite using a variety of teaching materials rather than relying on a single management textbook. Thus, part of the challenge is to defamiliarize students with what they are exposed to in Western management texts about the non-West/Global South while simultaneously allowing voices to speak from a marginalized position. To this end, the second author often speaks about challenges she faced as Middle-Eastern Muslim woman in various different Western contexts and organizations. Through such exercises, our aim is to allow students to recognize and identify how "interlocked practices and processes . . . result in continuing inequalities in all work organizations" (Acker, 2006).

Simultaneously and as importantly, as teachers–scholars–learners, we must find new and creative ways to make space for students' diverse and intersectional voices who may challenge our own views as they bring into focus their relevant lived experiences of issues relating to poverty and injustice and conversely wealth and privilege. Our students, many of whom continue to work and manage in organizations while in our classrooms, have up-to-date data and pressing concerns that can be leveraged as teaching moments. To challenge ourselves to continue to include these voices and other more marginalized questions, we repeatedly ask ourselves, how might promoting managerial decision-making as a disembodied and disinterested activity exacerbate inequalities in organizations or reproduce patriarchy? How does centring the lived experience and quest for equality change managerial decision making? How can we support students in this shift, even if it involves negative financial consequences and the loss of prestige and privilege?

This approach foregrounds the individual, suggesting that managerial decisions and behaviours are likely undertaken through limited choice, determined in part by limits imposed by ideology, structures, and policies. We problematize how the conventional teaching of ethics privileges particular individuals and groups, suggesting that notions of agency and identity are relevant for understanding how and why particular individuals, identities, and experiences are marginalized in the MBA classroom (and, following, in work organizations) while others enjoy the relative privilege afforded to them through gender, race, ethnicity, class, and other relations of difference.

Like those teaching ethics, when teaching ethically, we are focused on what a manager should do. But our focus quickly expands beyond an individual to encompass broader stakeholders and ideas relevant to decision making. This approach gives students all of the tools and support they will need to act when faced with the complexity of everyday ethical decisions—from evaluating compensation, to addressing health and safety concerns, to setting privacy policies. Ethical teaching sees both action and inaction as "action" while respecting that decisions are situational and hugely impacted by power relations.

In the classroom, we model an inquiry that can be revisited in the work organization: whose interests are being furthered through particular business decisions undertaken by managers? Who is left out of the conversation? We also suggest the use of transdisciplinary and alternative texts (such as Dodson's *The Moral Underground*; Lewis's *March*; Shiva's *Stolen Harvest: The Hijacking of the Global Food Supply*; or Maathai's *The Green Belt Movement: Sharing the Approach and the Experience*). These texts, as exemplars of our approach, join theory and practice in new ways, showing ways in which managers and others practice ethics in a patriarchal, neoliberal society.

To uncover how these ideas may be addressed in a classroom setting, we suggest that educators follow an awareness-raising approach that encourages self-reflexive investigation by students with respect to how theory relates to their own lives and experiences (Crawley et al., 2008). As educators, we carefully guide discussion in moments when particular voices are silent or altogether missing from the conversation (Sims, 2004). This is particularly relevant for understanding how gender inequality, as well as other inequalities across relations of differences (race, class, ethnicity, ability, sexual orientation, etc.), take place through the values being promoted and perpetuated in business school classrooms. We illustrate these approaches through the following example.

21.5.1 An example: 2012 Tazreen Fashions factory fire

Women's factory work, in general, and the November 2012 Tazreen Fashions factory fire in Bangladesh, specifically, provide an example where complex issues of global supply chain management, First/Third World dependencies, and multiple states of intersecting global inequalities collide. Reporters described Tarzreen in the following way:

> Rooms full of female workers were cut off as piles of yarn and fabric filling corridors ignited. Reports also suggested fire exits at the site had locks on, which had to be broken in order for staff to escape (Burke and Hammadi, 2012).

The resulting 112 deaths were the cause of protest in Bangladesh and significant (although brief) press coverage in the United States. In the days and weeks following the fire, the ethics played out as if they had been taught in an MBA ethics course as we describe above: blame was placed on an individual with the factory owner being found as negligent for managing an organization where managers prevented employees from leaving their sewing machines after a fire alarm sounded (Manik and Yardley, 2012). This discourse predominated and left little, if any, room for a critical evaluation of the underlying inequalities supported by free market capitalism, laissez-faire government policy, and reckless corporate practices.

A recently published teaching case based on the same factory fire attempts to bring this issue of ethics into the MBA classroom. Case authors French and Martin describe the problems of the protagonist (an American employee of Wal-Mart being dispatched to Bangladesh who is described as having "significant" experience with Muslim contexts based on a four-month stint in Indonesia) as follows:

> Mr. Lelander is presented with a career changing and prodigious task of developing and presenting to his corporation's board of directors a long-term strategy to keep the company out of tragedies while maintaining a competitive cost structure. Simultaneously, Mr. Lelander must lay out a plan to repair his company's global image as an ethically responsible organization (2013: 75).

This case centres on Lelander, the board of directors, and MNC Wal-Mart. The problem statement emphasizes, if not centres, profit through the issue of "maintaining a competitive cost structure". Although an overview of Bangladesh is given in the case it centres on the broad topics of the industry, "the people", geography and the government. Some high-level indicators are given (52.2% of women are literate, Bangladesh is the 8th largest country in terms of population, and its consumer price index [CPI] puts it at 144 out of 175 countries).

How might postcolonial feminism help us differently present the case, develop questions, and coconstruct knowledge in a classroom with students? First, we would not assume that classroom participants did not have first-hand knowledge of factory work, in general, or the 2012 fire, in particular. Second, we would provide different information including historical information about Bangladesh including the 1971 Liberation War leading to independence from Pakistan (which gained independence in 1947 from British India). Contemporary information would include information (qualitative and quantitative) about issues of local and global gender, income, and other inequalities.

Third, by overtly placing the (mostly female) deceased and current factory workers at the centre of the conversation we would ask ourselves and our students to come up with a different line of inquiry while continuing to problematize speaking for the workers.

Guiding discussion questions in the classroom based on our framework might include: What are the systemic issues that led up to the factory fires? Can we describe (or visually depict) the independences between Bangladesh, the United States, and other countries on the individual, organizational, and societal levels? Are there alternative forms of organizations (such as cooperatives) that could change both the conditions in Bangladesh and the United States to reduce issues of income inequality within and among countries? What is the responsibility of MNC Wal-Mart and individuals such as Lelander in a case such as this? How does power figure into the relationships within and beyond the factory walls? How is that power gendered? In effect, we would locate the decision-making process within a broader context of globalized capitalism, multinationals, and interests as a new form of engagement with ethics in the business classroom (see Prieto-Carron, 2008).

Moreover, we would connect these events to more recent textile factory fires in Bangladesh where over 1,000 workers, mostly young women, lost their lives due to substandard building codes, lack of exits, and reluctance on the part of powerful North American MNCs to sign onto safety regulations suggested by Bangladeshi textile unions. Spearheaded by Wal-mart and the Gap, a group of 26 retail companies concerned about the liability of the fire and potential future supply chain disruptions, formed the Alliance, a voluntary, CSR-type initiative focusing on fire safety among industry groups without Bangladeshi union support. The Bangladeshi government also supports this initiative. In contrast, a competing initiative named the Accord on Fire and Building Safety was launched by over 150 international brands with the support of the two largest Bangladeshi unions, the United Nations, and other supranational institutions including the International Labour Organization. These initiatives offer competing perspectives with respect to establishing legal accountability for the fires, financial responsibility for safety measures, and how factory inspections take place. MNCs have the choice to sign onto either initiative as a signatory and this choice will impact which set of guidelines they follow regarding factory and worker safety, procurements of goods and financial obligations.

Guided by our transnational and postcolonial feminist perspectives, a critical analysis of the Bangledeshi factory fires would outline how factory workers concerns and demands were ignored by MNCs, factory owners and the Bangladeshi government within the context of neoliberal development policies. As part of a class exercise, examining details of these initiatives would be useful to demonstrate how CSR and ethical decision making take place in a global context with consequences for the living and working conditions of low-wage, low-status workers. Thus, workers voices and concerns were not addressed prior to the tragedy and even in the aftermath, unions who came to represent most of the workers lacked significant participation from women. Local and global elites (factory owners and MNC CEOs who contracted work with them) stood to benefit from the profits associated with the low-wages of the young mostly female textile workers. Finally, consumers who purchased Western brands made at Bangladeshi factories become implicated in the outcomes of such industrial and social tragedies. Through our engagement with these ideas, the classroom discussion can no longer focus on what managers should do in such a situation but becomes a broader discussion around the structures of global capitalisms with respect to local manifestations and inequalities that may be taking place. Within this context, decision making is a much more complex and contradictory process related to considerations around promoting equity in living and working conditions around the globe while acknowledging the demands and pressures associated with capitalist economic systems. We believe this approach offers potential for discussions of gender equality and social justice within the context of business schools.

21.6 Conclusion

Our approach to achieving gender equality in business school education has important consequences for social justice efforts. As we suggest, based on our transnational and postcolonial feminist perspectives, gender inequality (and other inequalities) can be perpetuated by existing approaches to MBA education with material consequences of continuing on this path. These are that, despite concerns over promoting inclusive workplaces and initiating diversity programs in organizations, the main teaching apparatus for producing MBA students that are trained to foster such workplaces falls short if the classroom experience is based on exclusions and inequality for some and privilege for others under conditions of globalization. As such, management education in the era of a global workforce requires (re)articulation of the assumptions enacted in management classrooms. To this end, we offer a feminist reflexive approach based on collaboration among students, educators, and other stakeholders such that voices heretofore silenced can enter the conversation on their own terms (see Nicholls, 2009). In doing so, we aim to situate management knowledge and foster a much-needed conversation on promoting gender equality in management education through our adoption of a critical perspective on management education (Contu, 2009) as articulated through feminist perspectives.

References

AACSB, 2013. Eligibility procedures and accreditation standards for business accreditation. Retrieved 10.31.13 from: www.aacsb.edu/accreditation/accounting/standards/Standards-accntg-Jan2012.pdf

Abrams, K., 1998. From autonomy to agency: feminist perspectives on self-direction. William & Mary Law Review 40(3-6), 804-846.

Acker, J., 2006. Inequality regimes: gender, class and race in organizations. Gender & Society 20(4), 441-464.

Ahmed, S., 2012. On being included: racism and diversity in institutional life. Duke University Press, Durham, NC.

Appadurai, A., 1990. Disjuncture and difference in the global cultural economy. Public Culture 21-24. Reprint in revised form 1996, Modernity at Large: Cultural Dimensions of Globalization. University of Minnesota Press, Minneapolis, MN, pp. 27-47.

Baetz, M.C., Sharp, D.J., 2004. Integrating ethics content into the core business curriculum: Do core teaching materials do the job? Journal of Business Ethics 51, 53–62.

Bennis, W.G., O'Toole, J., 2005. How business schools lost their way. Harvard Business Review 83(5), 96–104.

Bommer, M., Gratto, C., Gravander, J., Tuttle, M., 2013. A behavioral model of ethical and unethical decision making. In: Citation Classics from the Journal of Business Ethics. Springer, Netherlands, pp. 97–117.

Bridgman, T., 2010. Beyond the manager's moral dilemma: rethinking the 'ideal-type' business ethics case. Journal of Business Ethics 94, 311–322.

Burke, J., Hammadi, S., 2012. Bangladesh textile factory fire leaves more than 100 dead. Retrieved 10.27.2013 from: www.theguardian.com/world/2012/nov/25/bangladesh-textile-factory-fire

Byrne, J., 2014. HBS dean makes an unusual public apology. Retrieved 05.31.2014 from: www.poetsandquants.com/2014/01/28/hbs-dean-makes-an-unusual-public-apology

Calás, M.B., Ou, H., Smircich, L., 2013. "Woman" on the move: mobile subjectivities after intersectionality. Equality, Diversity and Inclusion: An International Journal 32(8), 708–731.

Calás, M.B., Smircich, L., 2006. From the 'Woman's Point of View' ten years later: towards a feminist organizational studies. In: Clegg, S., Hardy, C., Lawrence, T., Nord, W. (Eds.), The Sage Handbook of Organization Studies. Sage, Thousand Oaks, CA, pp. 284–346.

Canales, R., Massey, B., Wrzesniewski, A., 06.14.12. Promises aren't enough: business schools need to do a better job teaching students values. The Wall Street Journal.

Christensen, L.J., Peirce, E., Hartman, L., Hoffman, W.M., Carrier, J., 2007. Ethics, CSR, and sustainability education in the financial times top 50 global business schools: baseline data and future research directions. Journal of Business Ethics 73, 347–368.

Cohen, P.N., 2011. Poverty, hardship and families: How many people are poor, and what does being poor in America really mean? Briefing paper prepared for the Council on Contemporary Families.

Collins, P.H., 1986. Learning from the outsider within: the sociological significance of black feminist thought. Social Problems 33(6), s14–s32.

Contu, A., 2009. Critical management education. In: Alvesson, M., Bridgman, T., Willmott, H. (Eds.), The Oxford Handbook of Critical Management Studies. Oxford University Press, Oxford, UK, pp. 536–550.

Crane, F.G., 2004. The teaching of business ethics: an imperative at business schools. Journal of Education for Business 79(3), 149–151.

Crawley, S.L., Curry, H., Dumois-Sands, J., Tanner, C., Wyker, C., 2008. Full-contact pedagogy: lecturing with questions and student-centered assignments as methods for inciting self-reflexivity for faculty and students. Feminist Teacher 19(1), 13–30.

DeNavas-Walt, C., Proctor, B., 2014. Income and Poverty in the United States: 2013 (P60-249, US Department of Commerce, Economics and Statistics Administration, US Census Bureau). US Government Printing Office, Washington, DC.

Dzuranin, A.C., Shortridge, R.T., Smith, P.A., 2013. Building ethical leaders: a way to integrate and assess ethics education. Journal of Business Ethics 115, 101–114.

Fisman, R., Galinsky, A., 04.09.2012. Can you train business school students to be ethical? Salon.

Floyd, L.A., Xu, F., Atkins, R., Caldwell, C., 2013. Ethical outcomes and business ethics: toward improving business ethics education. Journal of Business Ethics 117(4), 753–776.

Fournier, V., Grey, C., 2000. At the critical moment: conditions and prospects for critical management studies. Human Relations 53(1), 7–32.

French, J.J., Martin, M., 2013. The roof is on fire: the ethical minefield of the textile industry in Bangladesh. International Academy for Case Studies 20(1), 75–87.

Furman, F.K., 1990. Teaching business ethics: questioning the assumptions, seeking new directions. Journal of Business Ethics 9, 31–38.

Giacalone, R.A., Thompson, K.R., 2006. Business ethics and social responsibility education: shifting the worldview. Academy of Management Learning & Education 5(3), 266–277.

Giroux, H.A., November 2010. Public values, higher education, and the scourge of neoliberalism: politics at the limits of the social. Cultural Machine. www.culturemachine.net/index.php/cm/article/view/426/444

Gradín, C., 2012. Poverty among minorities in the United States: explaining the racial poverty gap for Blacks and Latinos. Applied Economics 44(29), 3793–3804.

Grey, C., 2004. Reinventing business schools: the contribution of critical management education. Academy of Management Learning and Education 3(2), 178–186.

Holland, K. (03.15.09). Is it time to retrain B-Schools. The New York Times.

Holvino, E., 2010. Intersections: the simultaneity of race, gender and class in organization studies. Gender, Work & Organization 17(3), 248–277.

Jackson, T., 2011. International Management Ethics: A Critical, Cross-Cultural Perspective. Cambridge University Press, New York.

Janssens, M., Steyaert, C., 2012. Towards an ethical research agenda for international HRM: the possibilities of a plural cosmopolitan framework. Journal of Business Ethics 111(1), 61–72.

Jones, B.D., 1999. Bounded rationality. Annual Review of Political Science 2(1), 297–321.

Jones Jr, R.G., Calafell, B.M., 2012. Contesting neoliberalism through critical pedagogy, intersectional reflexivity, and personal narrative: queer tales of academia. Journal of Homosexuality 59(7), 957–981.

Joy, S., Poonamallee, L., 2013. Cross-cultural teaching in globalized management classrooms: time to move from functionalist to postcolonial approaches? Academy of Management Learning & Education 12(3), 396–413.

Korn, M., 2012. Business schools short on diversity. Retrieved 05.31.2014 from: www.online.wsj.com/news/articles/SB10001424052702304830704577496901585090874

Lin, K.H., Tomaskovic-Devey, D., 2013. Financialization and US income inequality, 1970–2008. American Journal of Sociology 118(5), 1284–1329.

Manik, J., Yardley, J., 2012. Bangladesh finds gross negligence in factory fire. Retrieved 10.27.2013 from: www.nytimes.com/2012/12/18/world/asia/bangladesh-factory-fire-caused-by-gross-negligence.html

Mohanty, C.T., 2003. Feminism without borders: decolonizing theory, practicing solidarity. Duke University Press, Durham.

National Law Center on Homelessness & Poverty, 2013. Human right to housing report card 2013. Retrieved 05.31.2014 from: www.nlchp.org/reports

Nicholls, R., 2009. Research and indigenous participation: critical reflexive methods. International Journal of Social Research Methodology 12(2), 117–126.

Pfeffer, J., Fong, C.T., 2004. The business school 'business': some lessons from the US experience. Journal of Management Studies 41(8), 1501–1520.

Podolny, J., June 2009. The buck stops (and starts) at business school. Harvard Business Review, 62–67.

Prasad, A., Mills, A.J., 2010. Fertilizing the ground for social change: some promising ideas into critically approaching business ethics. Journal of Business Ethics 94, 223–225.

Prasad, P., Mills, A.J., Elmes, M., Prasad, A. (Eds.), 1997. Managing the Organizational Melting Pot: Dilemmas of Workplace Diversity. Sage Publications, Inc., Thousand Oaks, CA. doi: www.dx.doi.org/10.4135/9781452225807

Prieto-Carron, M., 2008. Women workers, industrialization, global supply chains and corporate codes of conduct. Journal of Business Ethics 83, 5–17.

Özkazanç-Pan, B., 2012. Postcolonial feminist research: challenges and complexities. Equality, diversity and inclusion. An International Journal 31(5/6), 573–591.

Rabouin, M., 1997. Lyin' T(*)gers, and "Cares," oh my: the case for feminist integration of business ethics. Journal of Business Ethics 16, 247–261.

Rubin, R.S., Dierdorff, E.C., 2009. How relevant is the MBA? Assessing the alignment of required curricula and required managerial competencies. Academy of Management Learning & Education 8(2), 208–224.

Schoemaker, P.J., 2008. The future challenges of business: rethinking management education and research. California Management Review 50(3), 119–140.

Simon, H.A., 1997/1947. Administrative Behavior, fourth ed. The Macmillan Company, New York.

Sims, R.R., 2004. Business ethics teaching: using conversational learning to build an effective classroom learning environment. Journal of Business Ethics 49, 201–211.

Stainback, K., Tomaskovic-Devey, D., 2012. Documenting desegregation: racial and gender segregation in private sector employment since the civil rights act. Russell Sage Foundation, New York.

Starkey, K., Tempest, K., 2006. The business school in ruins? In: Gagliardi, P., Czarniawska, B. (Eds.), Management Education and Humanities. Northampton, Edward Elgar, MA, pp. 101–112.

Thompson, J.J., 2010. The global moral compass for business leaders. Journal of Business Ethics 93, 15–32.

Tipton, F.B., 2008. "Thumbs-up is a rude gesture in Australia": the presentation of culture in international business textbooks. Critical Perspectives on International Business 4(1), 7–24.

Westwood, R.I., Jack, G., 2007. Manifesto for a post-colonial international business and management studies: a provocation. Critical Perspectives on International Business 3(3), 246–265.

22

The Eighth Summit
Women's ascent of organizations

Dianne Lynne Bevelander
Erasmus University, The Netherlands

Michael John Page
Bentley University, USA

Summiting the highest mountain on each of the seven continents is the pinnacle of achievement for many mountaineers. This chapter describes the development and successful implementation of an all-women MBA elective at the Rotterdam School of Management which involves participants attempting to summit Mount Kilimanjaro, one of the seven and the highest mountain in Africa. As the title suggests, the experiential course is designed to prepare young women for the challenges of ascending to the highest level of organizations. Using the mountain as a living metaphor, participants are invited to reflect upon their own aspirations and capabilities, to understand the importance of networks and relationships of trust, and to appreciate the importance of women supporting one another in their pursuit of challenging objectives. Participants report that the preparation, climb, and post-climb reflection made them more aware of their individual capabilities, resilience, and ability to build the mutually supporting networks needed to ascend their personal eighth summit—the organizations they wish to build and lead.

So, why even go through this ordeal? This whole expedition's purpose was about women empowering each other, and each of us growing beyond our boundaries. For me, I cracked some boundaries I actually didn't know existed—mainly about trusting others, asking for help, and giving support. What also cracked open were some of my own limiting self-beliefs about my own potential. It was incredible to reconnect so deeply with my strong body, especially in this new era in my life as a woman in her 30s. Beyond that, something has also been reinvigorated in me this year, some kind of "unlocking my mind", as one dear friend has said. I think I will have to continue unpacking those other lessons and insights for a long time afterwards.

(Maeve Quigley, 2013)

22.1 Introduction

Career challenges that women face in the corporate sector have been well documented in both the popular and academic literature. Women currently hold only 4.2% of Fortune 500 CEO positions, 16.9% of these companies' board seats and 14.6% of their executive officer positions (Catalyst Inc., 2013a, b). Furthermore, Ely, Ibarra and Kolb (2011) find that female graduates from leading business schools still lag behind their male counterparts in career progression. Gender bias within the corporate sector is often seen to explain these phenomena (Brass, 1984; Timberlake, 2005) with organizational research shifting from a focus on whether a dominant coalition is intentionally trying to stop women reaching leadership positions to what is called second-generation gender bias. When obstacles are not actually visible or explicit, bias can still be present. This, second-generation bias, may be due to structures and norms in the workplace, cultural beliefs regarding the role of women or because people interact with one another in a manner that favours men above women (Calás and Smircich, 2009; Ely and Meyerson, 2000; Kolb and McGinn, 2009; Sturm, 2001; Ely, Ibarra and Kolb, 2011).

Redressing gender imbalance in the corporate sector and in other organizational settings requires the involvement of educators generally and of business schools in particular. However, similar biases and imbalance of opportunity exist within business schools—19.7% of the advisory board members and 24.7% of the faculty across the Financial Times top 100 business schools (*Financial Times*, 2013), and 18% of the 480 deans responding to the AACSB Deans 2011–2012 Survey are female (AACSB International, 2013). From a secondary bias perspective, curricula broadly remain stereotypically male in numerous ways. Texts used in programs often contain an implied gender bias, very few business cases feature women as naturally dominant characters in executive positions, promotion committees are predominantly male, and there is a general paucity of female role models in business education (Mavin and Bryars, 1999; Meyerson and Kolb, 2000; Bevelander and Page, 2011). Furthermore, according to Ely et al. (2011), educational theories have not kept up with practice. Numerous programs adopt what Martin and Meyerson (1998: 312) refer to as an "add-women-and-stir" approach where the same leadership content is taught to men and women, or what Ely and Meyerson (2000: 5) refer to as a "fix-the-women" approach where women are taught male leadership skills (Ely et al., 2011: 475).

As Ely, Ibarra and Kolb (2011: 475) so clearly articulate: "While both approaches may impart some useful skills and tactics, neither adequately addresses the organizational realities women face nor is likely to foster in participants a sustained capacity for leadership". Consistent with this critique of historical approaches, and following extensive empirical analysis (Bevelander and Page, 2011), the Rotterdam School of Management added a new experiential elective to its portfolio of MBA program course offerings. The elective, that is only open to female students, neither "adds and stirs" or "fixes". Rather, it is specifically designed to address two of the key challenges women face progressing to the highest levels of organizations that have been identified in the literature—removing self-limiting personal perceptions, and expanding mutually supporting networks of trust among female peers (Bevelander and Page, 2011; Kelan and Jones, 2010; Mavin and Bryars, 1999; Meyerson and Kolb, 2000).

22.2 Motivation and design of the Kilimanjaro MBA Elective

Network development and networking exercises were explicitly introduced to the Rotterdam School of Management MBA curricula in 2006. As part of that initiative, MBA students were introduced to Stephenson's (2006) social network analysis methodology and invited to complete network surveys to assess the hierarchies of trust that existed among the student body. Based on response patterns observed across the classes over several years, Bevelander and Page (2011) found that female students experience a faster decline in the scale of their networks at higher levels of trust. More broadly, they find that female students tend to trust each other less in risky professional environments than do their male counterparts. These findings led to a series of modifications across all three formats of the MBA.[1] Further experiential elements were added and the network development exercises were embedded in the curricula with more attention being paid to expanding students' appreciation of the importance and consequences of the exercises for personal development and reflection. Central to these changes is a proactive process that focuses on empowering women through emphasizing the importance of reflecting on their own innate capabilities and of taking greater initiatives to help one another. These lessons are demonstrated and internalized through the leadership elective described and critiqued below—an elective that is open to female students across all the MBA programs and that is built around an effort to summit Mount Kilimanjaro.

---

1 The Rotterdam School of Management (RSM) offers three distinct MBA degrees: an international full-time MBA, an executive MBA, and a global consortium international executive OneMBA.

22.2.1 Elective purpose and conceptual design

The Kilimanjaro MBA Elective was specifically designed as the School's first women-only elective to support leadership, network capability, and trust development among women. Learning to mutually support one another has been found to be an important element for women's career progression in male-dominated organizations. *Networks of trust among* women help them build skills and create the individual and group knowledge necessary for success (Bevelander and Page, 2011; Bierema, 2005). The inclusion of men in the summit attempt was seen by the course designers as risking gender stereotyping because of the physical nature of the course. This could reduce the potential for female participants to truly register gender,[2] discover as much as possible about themselves and develop a deep appreciation of how to work with other women in high performance environments.

Kolb and Fry's (1975) effective learning framework informed the elective's conceptual design and it was operationalized using their four-step experiential learning cycle of experience, observation and reflection, generalization, and application in new situations. The learning cycle for the elective begins with the social network exercises that form part of the core curriculum of the Rotterdam School of Management MBA. This sequence of exercises sets a foundation for the elective by enhancing students' understanding of their personal preferences and innate biases when developing networks involving varying degrees of trust.[3] The exercises are reinforced through discussion and reflection with an experienced social networking theorist. This process served as a precursor to the intensive experiential activities leading up to and during the climb that form the core of the elective. Essays, videos and blog submissions required for the elective ensure that students observe and reflect on their own actions as well as those of their fellow climbers, both while preparing for the ascent and during the actual climb. Generalization occurs once the students return to The Netherlands and they are brought together to further personalize what they have learned. This third phase of Kolb and Fry's (1975) learning cycle brings the elective to a formal close. However, discussions held during the third phase are focused on ensuring students develop insight into their current behaviours as well as on formulating strategies and approaches for their future careers and social interactions—the application that constitutes the fourth phase of the cycle.

22.2.2 Design specifics

The elective employs a combination of story-telling, group discussion, coaching and the intensive experiences of training for and climbing Kilimanjaro to achieve the core learning outcomes—enhance self-awareness and a fuller appreciation of the importance

---

2 In this context, "register gender" refers to the requirement that gender enters participant's consciousness.
3 As an important part of the core curriculum, networking exercises provide students with personal insights that are of value for subsequent elective and advanced courses across the program. They are of particular relevance for the Kilimanjaro elective.

of networks of trust among women for career and life. Design specifics for the course included four stages: (1) the application process; (2) the pre-climb preparation and presentations; (3) the summit attempt; and (4) the post-climb debriefing and continued learning. As will be apparent from the detailed descriptions of the stages below, the full duration of the elective is somewhat in excess of six months and it therefore falls outside of the formal curricula sequencing of the MBA programs. This is accommodated by the fact that the week of the summit attempt occurs during a common break in the term structure of the programs.[4]

- *The application process*: Soliciting interest in the elective begins approximately six months prior to the summit attempt with an open briefing to all MBA students, both male and female, that describes the purpose of the women-only elective and that presents the motivation for and description of the climb up Kilimanjaro. Early stage guidance about the level of fitness required is also provided. Each student wishing to participate in the elective has to produce a three-minute application video wherein she makes the case for securing one of the 15 slots available. The video *elevator pitches* are reviewed by the lead faculty member, who is also the Associate Dean of MBA Programs,[5] by another female member of staff who is an experienced mountaineer, and by two graduates of the elective from prior years.[6] The 15 students who are deemed to have produced the best video motivation are selected for the course.

- *Pre-climb presentation and preparation*: Approximately one month after the applications are submitted and reviewed, the 15 selected students are brought together for an intensive session with respected journalist and author, Rebecca Stephens MBE, the first British woman to summit Everest and also one of very few women to have ascended all seven summits.[7] Students are asked to read Stephens' book entitled *The Seven Summits of Success,* coauthored by business guru Robert Heller (Heller and Stephens, 2005). During the session, Stephens provides an account of her ascent of Everest and the Seven Summits and motivates the students to reflect on various leadership and team building issues that have arisen in their lives. Reference material for the session, and more broadly for the elective, is made available on the School's Blackboard coursework platform. A Facebook site[8]—*The Kili Sisters*—is used to encourage ongoing dialogue among the group. Stephens ends the session speaking about the physical preparation that is required in the

---

4 All other elements of the program, including presentations, climb preparation, and reflection occur outside of the scheduled class hours.
5 And coauthor of this chapter.
6 When the elective was first launched, the reviews and selection were obviously completed without graduates.
7 Stephens achieved the goal of climbing the Messner list of seven continental summits on 24 November 1994 and the Bass list on 3 February 1996. She was the third and fourth woman to achieve these respective goals and the first and second British women to do so (www. en.wikipedia.org/wiki/Rebecca_Stephens_(climber) [accessed 12.18.13]).
8 https://www.facebook.com/RSMMBA/posts/361870550573779 (accessed 12.18.13).

months leading up to the flight to Tanzania and Mount Kilimanjaro. The Rotterdam School of Management climber—who is part of the application video reviewing team—works with individuals and the group over the months to support their preparation.

Following the session with Stephens, and prior to the summit attempt, students begin the formal storytelling part of the elective. Each student must write a pre-climb essay that answers three key questions: What are my intentions for the week's climb? How do I want to be during the climb? Who do I want to be at the end of the climb? In addition to the essay, the students write three 250-word blog postings over the months leading up to the summit attempt where they articulate and share their evolving thoughts—aspirations and fears—with one another.[9]

- *The summit attempt*: Standing on the highest point of Africa is a bold but realistic ambition. Although it is the highest mountain in Africa, and the tallest free-standing mountain in the world,[10] the slopes of Mount Kilimanjaro make it the world's highest *walkable mountain*. Towering 5,896 m (19,344 feet) over the hot, dry plains of the Masai steppe on the Kenya/Tanzania border, the summit remains snow-capped despite the mountain's proximity to the equator. Temperatures plummet below zero and the level of oxygen is less than half that at sea level; climbers are challenged as they traverse five climatic zones and confront potentially serious altitude difficulties. However, if they are steadfastly positive and support one another with the same intensity and concern they feel personally, the rewards are unparalleled—a sense of exhilaration and achievement combined with an overwhelming view from the highest point of Mount Kilimanjaro's crater rim across the vast expanse of Africa.

Although the routes followed have varied over the years, each of the expeditions begins at the arrival hotel in Tanzania with a Monday briefing by the guides who again explain what can be expected on the mountain. Following this, the expedition leader undertakes a comprehensive equipment check with each of the students and faculty participants.[11] The climb begins on a Tuesday at around midday, takes three-to-four hours, and covers around 2,600 m (8,530 feet). The following day sees the group ascend to 3,450 m (11,319 feet) and the second camp-site, *Second Cave*, where they spend the afternoon adjusting to the altitude and taking a short acclimatization walk up towards *Third Cave*. The evening is spent in the mess tent sharing experiences of the first two days of climbing. Thursday through to Saturday repeats the process daily as the team slowly ascends to *Kibo Camp* at an altitude of 4,700 m (15,420 feet). At this altitude, the team becomes

---

9 www.blog.rsm.nl/kilimanjaro (accessed 10.06.13).

10 www.ngureco.hubpages.com/hub/Worlds-Highest-Mountains-Worlds-Tallest-Mountain-and-Worlds-Largest-Mountain (accessed 12.18.13).

11 World Expeditions UK (www.worldexpeditions.co.uk) works with School management and with Rebecca Stephens who has accompanied the group on each ascent as one of two faculty advisors, to plan the itinerary and to arrange the local guides that accompany the team, support the climbers, serve as porters, set up the overnight camps, and ensure the safety of the 17 women.

truly cognizant of the challenge it is facing and what it might take to reach the summit. All suffer from the cold and are tired, some have headaches and nausea that are signs of altitude sickness, all appreciate that those wishing to continue and attempt to summit need to depart at midnight, and many are encouraged to eat copious amount of chocolate for energy and to take in lots of fluid. In spite of the School stressing throughout the elective that the essential lessons reside in the journey together and empowering one another rather than in just individually wanting to reach the summit, the excitement and desire to continue becomes palpable as midnight approaches. All desperately want to continue even while realizing that Sunday is the longest and most gruelling day of the climb.

The climb starts at midnight with a very slow torchlight walk on a switchback trail through loose volcanic scree to reach the 5,685 m (18,652 feet) crater rim at *Gillman's Point*. After a short rest, those who were still feeling strong enough begin the final leg to the summit, passing close to the spectacular glaciers and ice cliffs to reach *Uhuru Peak* at 5,896 m (19,344 feet). The descent includes a final overnight stop at the *Horombo Campsite* at 3,720 m (12,205 feet) before a Monday morning final descent to 1,830 m (6,004 feet) and a Land Rover ride back to the hotel for a long-overdue shower, an evening of celebration with a group that has genuinely become family, and a restful night in a real bed!

- *Post-climb debriefing and continued learning*: One month after the climb, the students again convene in a learning forum on campus. The key purposes of this are to continue the story-telling, debrief, and reflect upon how the elective has shaped their thinking, aspirations and sense of self. The learning forum begins with each student taking ten minutes to share her story. The group then provides feedback to one another on how individuals were perceived before, during, and subsequent to the summit attempt. The forum is coordinated by the lead faculty member in an environment that is designed to be supportive rather than judgemental. Students are also encouraged to share what actions they have taken with regard to their own leadership development since the climb, and reflect upon issues that might have arisen as a result. The storytelling element of the elective is further continued with the requirement that each student complete an essay and final 250-word blog reflecting upon her experiences and the lessons gleaned—many elect to engage through the blog platform and through *The Kili Sisters* Facebook site to a far greater extent.

22.3 The experience[12]

Using the mountain as an outside classroom and as a metaphor for business is proving to be inspirational on many levels for elective participants. The inclusion of Rebecca Stephens, a professional leadership and team coach, and the first British woman to

12 Images at the end of the chapter.

successfully conquer Mount Everest, further reinforces the core learning objectives of the program. She is committed to the elective as a fellow climber, as a role model, and because she believes that "the expedition is well-suited as a component of the MBA program because of the combination of three elements: the emotional storytelling element of several days' climbing in a different and beautiful landscape, far removed from the clutter of everyday life; the academic consideration of the expedition as an experience of leadership modeling; and the bonding and networking that inevitably takes place during such a challenging experience".

And so it has proved to be for the 45 unique women of different nationalities, ages, physical and mental abilities, and climbing experience that participated in the first three iterations of the Kilimanjaro Elective undertaken between 2011 and 2013. All of the students made it to the 4,700 m (15,420 feet) altitude *Kibo Hut* and many made it to *Gillman's Point*, a mere 211 m (686 feet) below the summit. Over a dozen made it all the way to the top to *Uhuru Peak* at 5,896 m (19,344 feet). As impressive as this feat is, those that could not summit because of altitude sickness came to appreciate that actually summiting was a minor aspect of the course. The real lessons and achievements were in the way they worked together, motivated and inspired one-another, and pushed themselves beyond what they previously had considered limits to their capabilities. Through the experience, each has come to appreciate that she is capable of pursuing anything she aims for in her professional and personal life. Each has reached a greater appreciation of how women can and must support one another in high performance environments.

Although students' motivations for participating in the Kilimanjaro Elective varied considerably, almost all viewed the course as a one-in-a-lifetime opportunity. Participants embraced the opportunity to test themselves and strive for a goal that would mean something for them as individuals but also signal something to family, friends and associates about who they were and who they want to become. Many also presented a cultural perspective related to education, challenge and career. In applying to participate in the inaugural class, an executive MBA student from Peru remarked that in her culture, women were not encouraged to pursue higher education and professional careers. Her grandfather even had told her "only ugly girls study". However, sentiments such as this had not stopped her from pursuing her MBA, holding a significant position at Nike, Inc., and continually wanting to prove to her family that it was possible to combine study, family and career. In spite of not being in any way athletic, as a wife and a mother with a nine-month old baby she saw the elective as an experience that only comes once in a lifetime, and as an opportunity to "change the perception I have of myself, of what can I do?" While clearly concerned about how her family would react to her leaving her baby in The Netherlands with its father during the week-long summit attempt, her desire for independence and excellence, and possibly her extended career with Nike, resulted in a video application that reflected a determination and "just do it" attitude that was inspiring.

Students are not selected on the basis of natural or practised athleticism and all quickly come to appreciate that the elective operates within a broader experiential learning framework. It includes the prior compulsory network development components of their programs and the reflective and further development processes they are be expected to complete before and after the climb. Importantly, it requires that they to prepare for the physical demands of the summit attempt by exercising, sometimes adjusting eating habits, and acquiring necessary and seemingly strange equipment in the months leading up to the flight to Tanzania. Preparation for the climb demonstrated the experiential nature of the elective in an early and visceral way and strengthened the notion of acting upon, rather than reading about, leadership demands that would be placed upon them throughout their careers. Training reminders as seemingly pedestrian as the *These Boots are Made for Walking* posted on the Blackboard course site reinforced this lesson when stating: "By now I would hope that all of you have bought your boots and are walking regularly in them to ensure they are fully broken in so that they become like a second skin on your feet. If not please buy them quickly and put them on at every opportunity, even to work or class and certainly around the house. Don't forget you will be wearing them for at least 8+ hours every day when you are on the mountain."

The time on Mount Kilimanjaro was designed to further support the students' efforts to work as a cohesive team, to support and look out for one another, and to reflect on self. The aim for each ascent is that bridges get built between individuals who may not relate well to one another in less challenging circumstances, and that relationships deepen as the result. Considerable time also exists for individuals to reflect on and be creative about how they want to lead, and be led, in the workplace. Every day includes an appointed time for discussion around the various aspects of leadership and teamwork. The students know they are required to document their individual learning and to pledge *action points* that they believe will enforce change and improved team performance when they continue their careers after the MBA. The extent to which these learning objectives are reached may be assessed best by reflecting upon the words of students.

One participant, Layla El Zein, gave a tribute to those teammates who were unable to reach the summit due to altitude sickness:

> Probably returning home without having been to the summit is not what you wish for when you set off on this trip. And for sure it is not the most pleasant option. But Kilimanjaro is only a mountain, isn't it? Let us not forget that it is a subject for us to learn about challenges, empowerment, support and leadership. It is not the goal as such; it is the road to the goal. The summit is the means to reach the goal, so the goal can be reached anywhere on the way to the summit. Which is more challenging, to conquer a mountain or to conquer your fears? Which is the hardest, to face a steep summit or to face unwanted difficulties that life throws on your path? In both cases you experience challenges, realize the importance of empowering each other and supporting one another, and learn about leadership. But in the latter case, you have to deal with negative feelings, disappointments and managing your expectations. It is a heavy package and very few are those who are able to conquer their own mind and win over their own heart. I must admit that inner pain is more painful than the physical one. And so I raise my glass in respect and admiration to the ladies who conquered it all, those who did not reach the summit, because they have made the most out of this trip; they have learned the most and reached the farthest in their self-realization journey. They have faced more challenges than all the rest. They won over the summit fever. It is always easier to move on than to turn back and that is why only those with enough determination, strength and wisdom make the right choice, the difficult one (El Zein, 2012a).

In reflecting on the lessons of achievement, teamwork and trust after returning to The Netherlands, Renate Speet (2013) blogged:

> For me the high of the trip was the feeling of sharing and connection with this amazing group of women as we made our way up. Of course I remember being sick, cold and tired, but these memories are fading already as I find them to be less important. . . . I haven't yet figured out how to bring these feelings back in my day-to-day work, but sitting to write this blog, made me realize that I definitely need to do so. I miss you girls! (Speet, 2013).

In her blog, Layla El Zein (2012b) reflected upon past disappointing and damaged relationships with female friends and associates over decades that had left an indelible impression and made her distrustful and risk-averse with women. She saw the elective and the climb in particular as an opportunity to reevaluate this life perspective by setting herself the goal of "socializing with everyone equally, sharing and showing my vulnerabilities, simply opening my heart up without restrictions". Somewhat to her surprise, she found that opening up to others during the climb proved easier than she could have imagined and it also represented a "turning point" thanks to the positive reaction she received from others. As she states in her blog, "I was so truly and genuinely touched by my friends' gratitude and thoughtfulness . . . Eventually, I will take this back home with me from the mountain. Uhuru was not only the highest point in Africa but the highest in my life so far."

22.4 Conclusion

With only three intakes it is perhaps too soon to draw definitive conclusions about this experiential elective. However, the early signs are extremely positive. Initial scepticism among some faculty members, students and corporations has been significant. Several naysayers have become converts, and companies increasingly ask Dianne Bevelander to speak to their leadership teams about her research and outcomes of the elective. Interestingly, these companies and others have started asking if some of their women executives can join the elective on a fee basis even if they are not registered for one of the School's MBA degrees. Beyond direct educational benefits for students, the course is also having a sustained positive impact for the business school more broadly. These benefits are described more fully below.

22.4.1 Core educational benefits

Independent of whether they reached the summit, participants on all three summit attempts repeatedly express the benefits of what they see as a transformative experience—an experiential elective that helped them reflect on who they are as individuals and as a group of women, and on what they need to do to fully realize their personal and professional aspirations.

In spite of their increasing global dispersion,[13] the 45 graduates of the elective and the faculty members who have been involved over the three years continue as an active and engaged community. This is evident through their ongoing Facebook dialogue as *The Kili Sisters* as well as through the bilateral and multi-lateral support they give one another with job searches, career development and coaching. Graduates talk about being less fearful of the future and of being more confident in making decisions, and most stress how the elective encouraged them to push beyond previous self-imposed limits. In their post-climb blogs, during the post-climb debriefing, and subsequently, many articulate how they pushed themselves, past fatigue, past fear and self-doubt, and how they came to appreciate how much they could accomplish as a team. One Asian participant who admitted to previously being petrified of public speaking gave an extended *Kilimanjaro* address at the School's MBA graduation to an audience of over 700. Another participant states how prior to the elective and summit attempt she had never really worked closely with other women or given much thought about how she might empower others. As stated by executive MBA student, Narcisa Tereza Radvanszky, during the 2013 debriefing session: "Indeed, I might have reached the Gilman peak alone with only the help of the guides, but it certainly would have taken me too much effort and pain. The encouragement I received from the other women, the inspiring attitude they showed me and the fact they communicated openly about their weaknesses, fears and pain made me realize that we were in the same situation and together I could enable others to step forward and look ahead."

Clear indicators exist to suggest that a women-only experiential course such as the Rotterdam School of Management's Kilimanjaro Elective offers significant benefits in empowering women by providing students with the opportunity to (1) deeply reflect on their innate capabilities; (2) take greater initiative in working with and supporting other women; and (3) very importantly, build mutually supporting networks of trust among one another.

22.4.2 Broader school benefits

The Rotterdam School of Management has received considerable international attention through the Kilimanjaro Elective. Articles have appeared in *The Wall Street Journal*, the *Financial Times*, and elsewhere that are significantly increasing support for the course and its impact, as well as increasing international awareness of the MBA programs among potential female applicants. Individuals previously somewhat negative or neutral about the idea of this type of experiential elective have become highly enthusiastic. The elective is increasingly bringing together female alumnae, business partners and students across the MBA programs into an

---

13 After completing their degrees, graduates often return home to pursue their careers to countries as diverse as Brazil, China, Mexico, Nigeria, South Africa, Switzerland and the United States, to name just a few.

expanding network of women who actively share in the desire to redress challenges that women face ascending organization ladders. Women's networking events have become a feature of the School's international calendar. An unexpected but exceedingly valuable benefit of the "hype" around a women-only elective that is so excitedly action-oriented is that male students across the portfolio of MBA programs are asking many more questions about gender-balanced leadership. They are also questioning some of their prior attitudes about individual potential and risk-taking, and about how dominant coalitions have the potential to self-reinforce even when this occurs at the cost of lost talent.

The virtuous cycle of pedagogical research to education impact to pedagogical research to education impact is also gaining momentum at the School. Although the elective grew out of research into how networks of trust develop among MBA students (Bevelander and Page, 2011), data gathered over the past three years offer interesting opportunities for further research oriented to confirming prior hypotheses and to generating new hypotheses about how to redress gender biases still so evident in organizational life.

Whether the Rotterdam School of Management's Women-only Kilimanjaro Elective entirely achieves its goals will only be fully discovered over the years and decades ahead. However, early indicators are that the course supports talented young women who better appreciate their individual potential and the supportive power of a network of women who trust one another. As exquisitely articulated in a blog post by student climber, Bonolo Sekhukhune (2013) entitled *In my Rucksack,* the signs are extremely encouraging.

> In my rucksack, I take all my mother's boundless understanding of a missing daughter this year.
>
> In my rucksack I take my father, whose memory reminds me of what it truly means to be great.
>
> In my rucksack, I take my sisters' broad shoulders that have carried me through this challenging and exciting time of my life with the four simple words "how can we help?"
>
> In my rucksack I take all the ups and the downs occasions in which I was not "present".
>
> In my rucksack, I take all my "girl" friends whose life journey's I am missing.
>
> In the rucksack, I take all my "boy" friends who have been a phone call away for this sometimes damsel in distress.
>
> In my rucksack I take my Misfits, who have made this year feel somewhat "normal".
>
> In my rucksack, I take the dreams and hopes of those who wish to be on the plane with me; and more importantly the ones who thought, "these things just don't happen to people like us".
>
> In my rucksack, I take the inspiration from the women I am about to meet who have already inspired me to no end.
>
> And lastly in my rucksack, I take me. The person I was, the person I am, and the person I chose to be.

Photo credit: © Ken Lin

Photo credit: © Ken Lin

Photo credit: © Lesley-Ann Calvert

Photo credit: © Rebecca Stephens

Photo credit: © Rebecca Stephens

Photo credit: © Rebecca Stephens

Photo credit: © Rebecca Stephens

Photo credit: © Rebecca Stephens

References

AACSB International, 2013. 2011–2012 Deans Survey, www.aacsb.edu/resources/administrator (accessed 10.15.13).

Bevelander, D.L., Page, M.J., 2011. Ms. Trust: gender, networks and trust—implications for management and education. Academy of Management Learning and Education 10(4), 623–642.

Bierema, L., 2005. Women's networks: a career development intervention or impediment? Human Resource Development International 8(2), 207–224.

Brass, D.J., 1984. Being in the right place: a structural analysis of individual influence in an organization. Administrative Science Quarterly 29, 518–539.

Calás, M.B., Smircich, L., 2009. Feminist perspectives on gender in organizational research: what is and is yet to be. In: Buchanan, D., Bryman, A. (Eds.), The Handbook of Organizational Research Models. Sage, London, pp. 246–269.

Catalyst Inc., 2013a. Women CEOs of the Fortune 1000, www.catalyst.org/knowledge/women-ceos-fortune-1000 (accessed 10.15.13).

Catalyst Inc., 2013b. US Women in Business, www.catalyst.org/knowledge/us-women-business-0 (accessed 10.15.13).

Ely, R.J., Ibarra, H., Kolb, D.M., 2011. Taking gender into account: theory and design for women's leadership development programs. Academy of Management Learning & Education 10(3), 474–493.

Ely, R.J., Meyerson, D.E., 2000. Theories of gender: a new approach to organizational analysis and change. Research in Organizational Behavior 30, 3–34.

El Zein, L., 2012a. www.blog.rsm.nl/kilimanjaro/2012/11/08/the-biggest-learning (accessed 10.19.13).

El Zein, L., 2012b. Post-climb reflective essay, unpublished.

Financial Times, 2013. Global MBA Rankings 2013, www.rankings.ft.com/businessschoolrank ings/global-mba-ranking-2013 (accessed 10.15.13).

Heller, R., Stephens, R., 2005. The Seven Summits of Success. Capstone Publishing, West Sussex, England.

Kelan, E.K., Jones, R.D., 2010. Gender and the MBA. Academy of Management Learning and Education 9(1), 26–43.

Kolb, D.A., Fry, R., 1975. Toward an applied theory of experiential learning. In: Cooper, C.L. (Ed.), Theories of Group Process. John Wiley, London, pp. 33–58.

Kolb, D.M., McGinn, K., 2009. From gender and negotiation to gendered negotiation. Negotiation and Conflict Management Research 2, 1–16.

Martin, J., Meyerson, D., 1998. Women and power: conformity, resistance, and disorganized coaction. In: Kramer, R., Neale, M. (Eds.), Power, Politics, and Influence. Sage, Newbury Park, CA, pp. 311–348.

Mavin, S., Bryars, P., 1999. Gender on the agenda of management education. Women in Management Review 14(3), 99–104.

Meyerson, D., Kolb, D.M., 2000. Moving out of the "Armchair": developing a framework to bridge the gap between feminist theory and practice. Organization 7(4), 553–571.

Quigley, M., 2013. Wake up! Never give up, www.blog.rsm.nl/kilimanjaro/2013/10/23/wake-never-give (accessed 10.15.13).

Sekhukhune, B., 2013. In my Rucksack, www.blog.rsm.nl/kilimanjaro/2012/10/22/in-my-ruck sack (accessed 10.14.13).

Speet, R., 2013. www.blog.rsm.nl/kilimanjaro/2013/10/23/coming (accessed 10.15.13).

Stephenson, K., 2006. The Quantum Theory of Trust: Power, Networks, and the Secret Life of Organizations, Financial Times. Prentice Hall, Harlow, England.

Sturm, S., 2001. Second generation employment discrimination: a structural approach. Columbia Law Review 100, 458–568.

Timberlake, S., 2005. Social capital and gender in the workplace. Journal of Management Development 24, 34–44.

Concluding comments
Going forward

Maureen A. Kilgour, Patricia M. Flynn and Kathryn Haynes

This book demonstrates that gender inequality in management education is pervasive and seemingly universal. Authors from a variety of countries, perspectives and educational backgrounds highlight gender inequality issues at institutional levels, classroom levels and within programs and curricula. While many challenges have been identified, many solutions also have been discussed. The positive outcomes of the interventions discussed in this book provide best practice examples that business schools and other management education institutions can adopt and adapt for their own programs and courses. While the chapters in this book establish that gender inequality occurs throughout management education, they also establish that there is no shortage of solutions, which is an encouraging and optimistic point of departure for the next steps.

The chapters in this book point to potential areas for intervention to advance towards the goal of gender equality in management education, with its promise of a larger positive impact on management and on public and private institutions in general. Three areas of intervention are identified—research, the practice of management education and the policies that frame management education. The following sections discuss examples of next steps in each of these areas.

1. Research

This book illustrates the depth and breadth of research on gender equality in management education that has been conducted and discussed over many decades. Yet significant gaps remain that need to be addressed in order to have a more complete understanding. Because of the highly contextual nature of the issue of gender equality, comparative research is very useful and can inform improvements to management education policy and practice. One particular area includes broadening the understanding of gender in management education by studying countries and regions under-represented or not discussed in this book. How does management education differ between regions that score higher and lower on the various gender equality measurement indices? What is the nature of management education in gender-segregated business schools and in countries where there are legal and/or social restrictions on women's participation in the paid labour market? Do management education institutions that have a religious orientation differ from those that do not, and how do women and men fare in these institutions?

Another important area of research concerns management education within institutions of higher learning, at both the organizational and curricular levels. What difference does it make on the issue of gender equality if a management education institution becomes accredited with an international accreditation body? Are differences observable between Principles for Responsible Management Education (PRME) signatories and those that have not signed on? What are the appropriate indicators for measuring progress on gender equality in management education? Among the business schools and other management education institutions that have made progress towards gender equality, what factors could be attributed to that progress? What are the barriers to gender equality in business schools? Are there case studies in addition to those in this book that can illustrate best practices and policies? What are the views of external stakeholders who have an influence or interest in management education institutions, on the importance of gender equality? Can they, do they and should they influence business schools on this issue? If so, how? Continued research in these areas would enhance our understanding of the factors that contribute to gender inequality in management education.

A third important avenue of research concerns men, masculinities and multiple levels of identity and gender equality in management education. Despite best efforts, it was difficult to identify researchers on men and gender equality who were able to participate in this book. This is unfortunate especially as there is some interesting scholarship on this issue. Sadly, there is a tendency for policy-makers, business school leaders and faculty members to view gender inequality in business schools as an issue pertaining only to women. In addition, women are often perceived to be a homogeneous group. Much research remains to be done on gender issues and men, as well as on the intersections of gender inequality with other forms of inequality, such as, for example, those arising out of disability, indigenous status, ethnic origin, gender identity and sexual orientation. Explorations of these multiple levels of identity in the context of management education would deepen our understanding of the issue of gender equality in general, and would allow for the development of policies, organizational cultures and practices that ensure that all members of the management education and business school communities are and feel valued and included.

The above-mentioned suggestions for further research are merely a few examples of what logically flows from the research and theoretical conceptualizations that have been discussed in this book. The development of knowledge on many related issues would no doubt serve to advance gender equality through furthering our understanding of the different manifestations of gender in management education, in addition to influencing practice and the development of policy.

2. Practice

The chapters in this book identify a range of issues that need to be addressed in order to move towards gender equality in management education. These issues concern the experiences of students and faculty members, and address gender from the classroom to the administration. Gender inequality has been discussed in terms of lack of gender parity vis-à-vis academic staff and administrators, and working conditions including difficult, sometimes hostile, workplace environments. On another level, gender inequality and positive interventions have been discussed in terms of the pedagogy, course requirements, integration of gender into a wide range of disciplines and experiences of students, which includes ensuring that they graduate with an awareness of gender as an important construct. Fortunately, these are not insurmountable goals.

The breadth and depth of the chapters included in this volume demonstrate that there are many existing programs and initiatives that can provide guidance on why it is important to integrate gender equality into management education and on how that can be accomplished. This book highlights the fact that case studies, textbooks and other curricular materials in business schools continue to focus, at times exclusively, on males. Fortunately, several chapters in the book provide examples of cases and courses that will help to fill the gaps in teaching materials by featuring female managers and leaders, portraying them as positive role models. Other chapters identify business school programs and policies that have bolstered organizational cultures that promote gender equality and that demonstrate to female as well as male students that there are many exciting and rewarding careers for women in business and in academia. Notwithstanding these examples of good practice, faculty members who want to incorporate gender into their courses and programs may have difficulty finding pedagogical materials to support that endeavour, and business schools have far to go in overcoming gender inequality within their own organizations and classrooms.

Resources are available to help faculty integrate gender into their courses and their research. The Aspen Institute, for example, has been a leader in providing an extensive array of teaching materials including those on gender issues through its caseplace.org library, which is targeted to business school faculty. The Gender Equality Principles Initiative, a public–private collaboration among the San Francisco Department on the Status of Women, the Calvert Group and Verité, also provides a database of case studies, best practices, reports and websites promoting gender equality. Professional associations, such as Atgender: The European Association for Gender Research and Documentation, CEMS' international faculty group on "Gender and Diversity Management", the Gender in Management Special Interest Group of the British Academy of Management, the Gender and Diversity in Organisations Division of the Academy of Management and The Committee for Women in Economics of the Economics Society of Australia, to name a few, provide professional networks, knowledge and research on gender and diversity, as well as advice and counsel on ways to overcome gender inequality.

To continue to promote the work of these organizations, the PRME Working Group on Gender Equality launched the PRME Global Repository in 2012. Many resources including a wide range of teaching materials, research outcomes and good practices on gender equality are identified and available on the Global Repository, which is hosted on the PRME website.[1] The Repository, developed by business school faculty throughout the world, encompasses 15 disciplines in which management students take courses; for example, in accounting, economics, entrepreneurship, finance, information technology and marketing. The PRME Gender Equality Repository includes, among other things, specific case studies, syllabi, texts and best practices that assess or otherwise address gender in various educational and workplace environments. The Repository also lists resources, including search engines, divisions/subgroups within professional academic associations and organizations such as those noted above that are designed to help faculty and administrators incorporate gender-related topics into management education curricula.

There is much more that can and should be done to help faculty integrate gender issues in their courses. Professional academic associations and various search engines can be the focal points for valuable guidance and resources for faculty members seeking to incorporate gender issues and discussion into their courses. There are, no doubt, faculty who already have excellent examples of how to accomplish that, but who have not posted their materials on websites or other databases. With the development of well-known and easily accessible sites for these materials, business school deans can assist in identifying these individuals and encouraging them to share their course syllabi and other curriculum materials.

Thus, diffusion of knowledge, course materials and best practices is an important element in working towards gender equality in management education. Human, financial and material resources are required in order to build on the significant amount of work done by faculty members and researchers, including those who have contributed to this book and other similar initiatives. Without those resources, it is difficult for continued progress to be made and significant diffusion to occur.

Development of the Global Repository of teaching and other resources is an important step in promoting and expediting the integration of gender issues in management education. The PRME Working Group's goal is to work with professional academic associations to expand the breadth and depth of materials they make available to their members on their websites. Moreover, the Repository allows the Working Group and others to pinpoint by discipline where major gaps exist in gender-related curriculum materials and best practices. The Working Group is available to work with business school deans and faculty to encourage individuals to commit to fill these gaps, possibly with funding from their institutions, or from foundations seeking to promote gender equality. The support, commitment and involvement of responsible management education leaders is a necessary element in the achievement of gender equality in management education. The next section discusses briefly some possible interventions in the realm of policies.

1   www.prmegenderequalityworkinggroup.unprme.wikispaces.net/Resource+Repository

3. Policies

Part I of this book addresses some of the broader themes that emerge concerning gender equality in management education. These chapters identify the current state of affairs and propose that more action and implementation is required in order to make significant progress on this issue. Kilgour (Chapter 1) argues that what is required at this stage, where the problem of gender inequality has been clearly identified and where many solutions have been proposed and validated, is action on the various commitments and initiatives that have been developed, such as the PRME. Flynn et al. (Chapter 2) underscore the importance of business schools' role in addressing the under-representation of women in the corporate and managerial worlds, and the need for business schools themselves to take more action on gender inequality within their own institutions. Haynes and Murray (Chapter 3) urge management education to ensure that gender equality is more fully addressed in programs and business school activities that are associated with the critical global issue of sustainability. In addition, they identify the lack of reporting on gender equality initiatives by business schools that participate in PRME. Verbos and Kennedy (Chapter 4) discuss the climate within which women work and study in business schools, and propose that significant progress on gender equality cannot be made unless a more psychologically safe environment is provided.

These four chapters provide much in the sense of a way forward from a policy perspective. Business schools and other management education institutions need to address "the elephant in the room", ensure gender is addressed in management education that focuses on sustainability, and provide a psychologically safe climate for students and faculty as a precursor to taking more proactive steps towards gender equality. Management education also needs to reflect on the seemingly glacial pace of progress on gender equality over the last four decades. While each institution should tackle these tasks individually, more attention on gender equality is needed within business school organizations and accreditation bodies. One such organization is PRME.

Over 600 business schools and other management education institutions have signed on to PRME, making a deliberate and explicit commitment to the Principles of PRME, which *de facto* include gender equality. These PRME signatories can and should be the leaders on the issue of gender equality in terms of their own institutions. The challenge for the PRME initiative is to make gender equality a more central and important part of its own work.

As a body situated within the UN Global Compact and part of the UN organization, PRME can legitimately take a leadership position in the area of gender equality. Gender equality is a fundamental goal of the UN. In addition to its status as a UN-supported initiative, it has a number of partner organizations that are highly influential bodies in the area of management education in most regions of the world:

- AACSB International (The Association to Advance Collegiate Schools of Business)
- Academy of Business in Society (ABIS)

- Association of African Business Schools (AABS)
- Association of Asia-Pacific Business Schools (AAPBS)
- Association of MBAs (AMBA)
- Central and East European Management Development Association (CEEMAN)
- European Foundation for Management Development (EFMD)
- Globally Responsible Leadership Initiative (GRLI)
- Graduate Management Admission Council (GMAC)
- Latin American Council of Management Schools (CLADEA)

PRME is in a strategic position to influence its partners, signatories, supporting organizations and other stakeholders. PRME must continue to reinforce the importance of gender in achieving its own mission and to work with other learned associations, global organizations and accreditation bodies to address the issues of gender equality in education and organizations. PRME is not the only organization that is in a position to effect change at the level of policy. The partner organizations of PRME can act independently on the issue of gender inequality, as can organizations such as funding agencies, faculty associations and unions, professional bodies and governments. As is the case with PRME, most if not all of these organizations already have mandates to address gender inequality. What is often lacking is the political will to move more quickly on that mandate.

In conclusion, this book highlights the breadth and depth of interest in gender inequality in management education, and calls attention to both the problems and the solutions. It builds on decades of scholarship and practice in this area. It also underscores widespread lack of progress and suggests that what is often missing is the will to make the necessary changes. As shown throughout these pages, positive interventions in the areas of research, practice and policies will help to move management education closer to the goal, and will reverberate through the business communities across the globe, ultimately contributing to the achievement of gender equality in society as a whole.

About the contributors

Susan M. Adams is a professor of management at Bentley University. She holds a PhD in management from Georgia Institute of Technology. She is a consultant and scholar who focuses on careers of women and prominent leaders, organizational change and gender equality. Her current studies concentrate on eliminating career barriers for women and increasing the number of women on corporate boards. Adams is a former chair of the Management Consulting and Careers Divisions of the Academy of Management.

Kara A. Arnold is an associate professor in organizational behaviour. She is committed to research and teaching focused on equality in the workplace and employee well-being. Her work has been published in the *Journal of Occupational Health Psychology, Journal of Applied Psychology* and *Equality, Diversity and Inclusion: An International Journal.*

Dawn M. Bazarko, DNP, MPH, RN, is the founder of UnitedHealth Group's Center for Nursing Advancement and Moment Health, a UnitedHealth Group business delivering mindfulness to organizations and care deliverers. She is an industry lead and adjunct professor at the University of St Thomas—Minnesota Executive Education in Nurse Leadership Program.

Regine Bendl is an associate professor at the Institute for Gender and Diversity in Organizations at the Vienna University of Economics and Business. She carries out research on gender and diversity management, subtexts and queer perspectives in organization theory. An author and editor of numerous books, her writings have been published in numerous journals. She is Convenor of the EGOS Standing Working Group of Gender and Diversity (2010–2016), has received a number of professional awards and is the president of the Austrian Society of Diversity (ASD).

Dianne Lynee Bevelander, MBA (Cape Town), PhD (Lulea), is a professor of management education at Rotterdam School of Management (RSM), Erasmus University in The Netherlands. Dianne is leading the drive for women empowerment at the RSM and increasingly within the broader Erasmus University. She relinquished her position as statutory director of the RSM b.v. and associate dean for MBA programs to establish the Erasmus Centre for Women and Organizations (ECWO) and serve as the inaugural executive director. Dianne is a member of the European Foundation for Management Development's EPAS board.

Diana Bilimoria, PhD, is a KeyBank professor and chair and professor of organizational behavior at the Weatherhead School of Management, Case Western Reserve University. She is a coauthor of *Women in STEM Careers: International Perspectives on Increasing Workforce Participation, Advancement and Leadership* (2014), *Gender Equity in Science and Engineering: Advancing Change in Higher Education* (2012), *Women on Corporate Boards of Directors: International Research and Practice* (2008) and *Handbook on Women in Business and Management* (2007). She has published extensively in leading journals and has contributed to several edited volumes. She has received several awards for her research, leadership and service.

Stacy Blake-Beard is a professor of management at the Simmons College School of Management, USA, and Senior Faculty Affiliate at the Center for Gender in Organizations at Simmons. She holds a BS in psychology from the University of Maryland at College Park and an MA and a PhD in organizational psychology from the University of Michigan. Her research focuses on mentoring relationships, with an emphasis on how they may be changing as a result of workforce diversity.

Kevin V. Cavanagh is a doctoral student at Case Western Reserve University. Kevin received his BS from Christopher Newport University in Newport News, Virginia, USA, and his MA in experimental psychology from The College of William & Mary in Williamsburg, Virginia, USA. Kevin's research interest is centred around the psychological construct of inspiration. In particular, his work looks to examine the ways in which individuals arrive at an inspirational state and how individuals transform their inspiration into goal-directed action.

Paola Cecchi-Dimeglio, Magistere-DJCE, LLM, PhD, is a researcher jointly appointed at Harvard Law School (Center on the Legal Profession [CLP] and Program On Negotiation (PON) and Harvard Kennedy School (Women and Public Policy Program [WAPPP]). She has been nominated expert-coordinator for several research projects on lawyers, Alternative Dispute Resolution and Gender funded by the EU and the UN.

Sandra Idrovo Carlier, PhD, is the professor of Managing People in Organizations at INALDE Business School—Universidad de La Sabana, in Colombia, where she is the research director and leads that same area. Her research interests and publications deal with harmonizing work and personal life, women in management and employee motivation. She has published in Colombian and international peer-reviewed journals on work–family balance and management education. She contributes often with analysis on organizational culture for Colombian media.

Rhonda L. Dever is an instructor within the JR Shaw School of Business at the Northern Alberta Institute of Technology, in Edmonton, Alberta, Canada, and a PhD student (Management) at Saint Mary's University in Nova Scotia, Canada. Her research interests include gender in organizations, organizational behaviour and management education.

Helga Eberherr is a senior researcher and lecturer at the Institute for Gender and Diversity in Organizations, WU Vienna. She studied sociology, political science and gender studies at the University of Vienna, and at the University Denis Diderot Paris. She holds a PhD in sociology from the University of Vienna, and was appointed a Marshall Plan Awardee for a visiting research fellowship at the University of California Berkeley. Her main areas of research are in the field of gendered organization and diversity studies, intersectionality, (re)production of inequalities, theory of social practices, ageing, methodology and triangulative research designs.

Krista Finstad-Milion is an associate professor at ICN Business School in France. She served as Director for the Executive MBA program for six years. Her research interests include women's networks, women's careers and innovative approaches to teaching sustainable development. She is ICN's female/male equality correspondent for the Conférences des Grandes Ecoles. She cocreated and is the president of EST'elles Executive, a leading women's network in Eastern France.

Patricia M. Flynn is a trustee professor of economics and management at Bentley University, USA, where she served as Dean of the McCallum Graduate School of Business for ten years. Flynn's research and teaching focus on corporate governance, women in business and technology-based economic development. She is the author of *Technology Life Cycles and Human Resources* and coauthor of *Turbulence in the American Workplace*, and *The Census of Women Directors and Executive Officers in MA Public Companies*, published annually since 2003.

Dale Foster is a passionate teacher whose research interests include the effectiveness of web advertising, the influence of communications technology on classroom structure and the impact of the internet on patient–physician relationships. Her work has been published in the *Journal of Advertising Research* and the *Journal of Information Systems Education*.

Mary Godwyn is an associate professor of sociology at Babson College and holds a BA in philosophy from Wellesley College and a PhD in sociology from Brandeis University. She applies social theory to issues of inequality in formal and informal organizations and studies entrepreneurship as a vehicle for the economic and political advancement of marginalized populations, especially women and minorities.

Julie Hall is the Deputy Provost Academic Development at the University of Roehampton and was originally a sociologist teaching in the areas of social justice and equality. Hall's research now focuses on pedagogic practices, the HE student experience and professional development. She is the vice-chair of SEDA (The Staff and Educational Development Association) and has contributed to nationally funded projects on assessment, gender and pedagogic relations, widening participation and Black and minority ethnic student attainment.

Edeltraud Hanappi-Egger has an educational background in computer science and is an experienced researcher and head of interdisciplinary teams. Since 2002 she has been full professor for Gender and Diversity in Organizations at WU Vienna. As an expert on organization studies and gender topics, Hanappi-Egger is in great demand as a reviewer for international conferences and journals and is also a member of national and international advisory boards and juries. She has published more than 350 articles, books and book chapters on gender and diversity, organization studies and diversity management.

Kathryn Haynes, PhD, is a fellow of the Institute of Chartered Accountants in England Wales and Deputy Director of Newcastle University Business School. Her research, which has been funded by grants from the Economic and Social Research Council (ESRC) in the United Kingdom, centres on issues of gender and social responsibility in relation to the professions; body and embodiment within organizations; identity; and sustainability. She is a cofacilitator of the PRME Working Group on Gender Equality.

Wendy Hein, PhD, is a lecturer in marketing at Birkbeck, University of London. Her research focuses on gender, marketing and consumer research, with a particular focus on men and masculinities. She is the coordinator of the marketing subject discipline of the PRME Working

Group on Gender Equality and involved in several gender equality research projects ranging from structural change to informing activist practices.

Anett Hermann holds a PhD in social and economic science and lectures at the Institute for Gender and Diversity in Organizations, WU Vienna. She has many years of professional experience in the field of gender and diversity management, working as a scientist, consultant and lecturer at universities, mainly in Germany and Austria. Her research work has won her several awards. Her particular fields of interest are teams (development of teams and teamworking), intercultural diversity management and the career paths of women. She has numerous publications to her name, and three years ago established her own consulting company.

Deanna M. Kennedy is an assistant professor in the School of Business at the University of Washington Bothell. She received her PhD in management science from the Isenberg School of Management, University of Massachusetts Amherst.

Maureen A. Kilgour, PhD, is an associate professor in the School of Business Administration, Université de Saint-Boniface (Winnipeg, Canada), teaching business and human rights, diversity and industrial relations. Her PhD (Warwick Business School, University of Warwick, UK) focused on the UN Global Compact, gender equality and global governance. She is a member of the UN Women's Empowerment Principles Leadership Group and cofounder and co-chair of the PRME Working Group on Gender Equality.

Thomas Köllen is an assistant professor in the Department of Management, Institute for Gender and Diversity in Organizations, WU Vienna. Köllen completed his studies in Business Administration in Jena, Germany, Turin, Italy, and Vienna, Austria. He was a DocTeam fellow of the Austrian Academy of Sciences (2006–2009) and a Visiting Scholar at Goethe University Frankfurt, Germany (2007) and Universidade Federal Fluminense (UFF) in Niteroi, Brazil (2012). Köllen's research focuses on issues related to bisexual and homosexual employees and entrepreneurs, nationalities and nationalisms in organizations, and business ethics.

Mari Kondo is a professor and director of the global business and management studies of the Graduate School of Business, Doshisha University in Kyoto, Japan. She teaches strategy, leadership, and business and society. She is involved in various activities related to mindfulness education and the UN global compact in Japan.

Gloria Kutscher is research and teaching assistant and PhD candidate in the Department of Management, Institute for Gender and Diversity in Organizations, WU Vienna. She completed her studies in Psychology with a specialization in Economic, Work and Organizational Psychology. She received the Dr Maria Schaumayer prize for her diploma thesis. Her research focuses on gender and diversity, especially on social class, inequality, and identity and consciousness in groups.

Michelle Ann Kweder is a consultant to mission-driven organizations in the non-profit and public sectors. She teaches leadership as adjunct faculty at Simmons College, Simmons School of Management. In addition, she is a doctoral candidate at the University of Massachusetts Boston where her research interests include the exclusion of issues of poverty and inequality from mainstream graduate management education.

Nan S. Langowitz is a professor of management and entrepreneurship at Babson College and earned her doctorate at Harvard Business School, an MBA from New York University and a BA from Cornell University. Her research examines entrepreneurial leadership, focusing especially on women, as well as the challenges and opportunities organizations and managers face developing and leveraging talent.

Heike Mensi-Klarbach studied Business Administration at WU Vienna and went on to obtain a PhD in 2009 on the business case for diversity. Currently she is Assistant Professor at the Institute for Gender and Diversity at the WU. In 2006 she was awarded a DocTeam fellowship from the Austrian Academy of Sciences. The main focus of her research is diversity in organizations, especially in top management teams. In addition, she lectures on selected topics within diversity management, business ethics and organizational behaviour. Her publications include a monograph, and several articles and book chapters.

Albert J. Mills, PhD, is the director of the Sobey PhD (Management) at Saint Mary's University in Nova Scotia, Canada. He is the author of 35 books and edited collections, including *Gendering Organizational Analysis* (Sage, 1991); *Gender, Identity and the Culture of Organizations* (Routledge, 2002); and *Sex, Strategy and the Strategy* (Palgrave, 2006). He is currently the cochair of the International Board of Critical Management Studies.

Lynda Moore is a professor at the Simmons College School of Management, USA, Faculty Affiliate at the Center for Gender in Organizations, and Fellow of the Leadership Trust Foundation, UK. Her scholarship and teaching focuses on women leaders, gender and diversity in management education and culturally competent leaders.

Christine Morin-Estèves is an associate professor and Project Leader in Sustainable Development and CSR at ICN Business School. Her current research interests include the question of moral and professional values in SMEs, the sustainable development reports of firms and gender equality. She is a member of the Conférence des Grandes Écoles. She cocreated the EST'elles Executive network and is a member of the board.

Alan Murray, PhD researches in the broad subject area of "responsible management", which encompasses issues of leadership in sustainability, circular economy, corporate responsibility and corporate citizenship; corporate social and sustainability reporting; and social and environmental accounting. He is the coauthor of the award-winning textbook *Corporate Responsibility* and is the founding chair of the regional PRME Chapter for the United Kingdom and Ireland.

Julia C. Nentwich is an associate professor in psychology at the University of St Gallen, Switzerland. She was in charge of developing the gender and diversity teaching program since 2004 and managed the program until the end of 2012. She is active in teaching gender and diversity issues to management students and has developed several interdisciplinary courses in this area.

Banu Özkazanç-Pan is an assistant professor of management at the College of Management, University of Massachusetts, Boston. She is currently the graduate program director for the Organizations and Social Change PhD program. Her research interests are in identity formation, diversity and inclusion in organizations, and gender equality. Currently, she's examining how technology incubators can become more inclusive of women and minorities as well as understand how social enterprise incubators impact the communities in which they are located.

Michael John Page, MBA (Cape Town), PhD (Cape Town), is the provost and vice president for Academic Affairs at Bentley University in the United States. He serves on the advisory boards of several international business schools and on the governing boards of the European Foundation for Management Development (EFMD), the Association to Advance Collegiate Schools of Business (AACSB International) and South Africa Partners.

Jo Peat is the head of Academic Professional Development in Higher Education and works in the Department of Academic Enhancement and the School of Education at the University of Roehampton. Peat was originally a modern linguist, teaching in a variety of schools in south-west London. Peat's research now focuses on pedagogic practices, the HE student experience, retention, and success in HE and professional development. Peat is a member of the SEDA Executive (The Staff and Educational Development Association) and has contributed to nationally funded projects on Black and minority ethnic students and attainment and gender and pedagogic relations.

Ujvala Rajadhyaksha is an associate professor in the Department of Business Administration and Economics at Saint Mary's College, Notre Dame, Indiana, USA. Previously she has held faculty positions at the Indian Institute of Management Calcutta and Indian Institute of Technology Bombay, India. Her research interests and training experience includes topics in the areas of gender in management, work and family issues and cross-cultural issues in management with a special regional focus on India and the South Asian context.

Teresa J. Rothausen, PhD, is Heckler Endowed chair professor and Ireland scholar at the Opus College of Business at the University of St Thomas, Minnesota. She teaches Leader Development and Organizational Behavior in the full-time MBA and researches job-related well-being and fulfilment, work–life, and gender and diversity in organizations.

Gudrun Sander is an associate professor of business administration with a special emphasis on Diversity Management at the University of St Gallen, Switzerland. She was involved in the early development of the gender and diversity teaching program as well as in teaching courses on diversity management as a leadership task.

Amy Klemm Verbos is an assistant professor of business law at the University of Wisconsin-Whitewater. She received her PhD in management science (Organizations and Strategic Management) from the University of Wisconsin-Milwaukee and a JD from the University of Wisconsin Law School.

Anna Wahl is a professor in Gender, Organization and Management at the Royal Institute of Technology (KTH), Stockholm, Sweden. Her current research interests are the gendering of management in different organizational contexts, work for change and the impact of gender equality in organizations.

Gloria Warmuth is a researcher and lecturer at the Institute for Gender and Diversity in Organizations, WU Vienna. She studied Business Administration at the Vienna University of Economics and Business and the Copenhagen Business School (CBS). In addition she holds a master's degree in mediation and conflict resolution. She recently obtained her PhD from the WU Vienna. The main focus of her research is on diversity-change in organizations, and gender and diversity in the SET (science, engineering and technology) field. She also lectures on diversity dimensions, intersectionality and strategic diversity management.